METROPOLITAN COLLEGE OF N~
LIBRARY, 12TH FLOOR
431 CANAL STREET
NEW YORK, NY 100:

# German Intellectuals and the Challenge of Democratic Renewal

This book examines how democracy was rethought in Germany in the wake of National Socialism, the Second World War, and the Holocaust. Focusing on a loose network of public intellectuals in the immediate postwar years, Sean Forner traces their attempts to reckon with the experience of Nazism and scour Germany's ambivalent political and cultural traditions for materials with which to build a better future. In doing so, he reveals, they formulated an internally variegated but distinctly participatory vision of democratic renewal – a paradoxical counter-elitism of intellectual elites. Although their projects ran aground on internal tensions and on the Cold War, their commitments fueled critique and dissent in the two postwar Germanys during the 1950s and thereafter. The book uncovers a conception of political participation that went beyond the limited possibilities of the Cold War era and influenced the political struggles of later decades in both East and West.

SEAN FORNER is Assistant Professor of History at Michigan State University.

# German Intellectuals and the Challenge of Democratic Renewal

*Culture and Politics after 1945*

Sean A. Forner
*Michigan State University*

CAMBRIDGE
UNIVERSITY PRESS

# CAMBRIDGE
## UNIVERSITY PRESS

University Printing House, Cambridge CB2 8BS, United Kingdom

Cambridge University Press is part of the University of Cambridge.

It furthers the University's mission by disseminating knowledge in the pursuit of education, learning and research at the highest international levels of excellence.

www.cambridge.org
Information on this title: www.cambridge.org/9781107049574

© Sean A. Forner 2014

This publication is in copyright. Subject to statutory exception and to the provisions of relevant collective licensing agreements, no reproduction of any part may take place without the written permission of Cambridge University Press.

First published 2014

Printed in the United Kingdom by Clays, St Ives plc

*A catalogue record for this publication is available from the British Library*

*Library of Congress Cataloguing in Publication data*
Forner, Sean A., 1973–
German intellectuals and the challenge of democratic renewal : culture and politics after 1945 / Sean A. Forner.
  pages  cm
Includes bibliographical references and index.
ISBN 978-1-107-04957-4 (hardback)
1. Democracy – Germany – History – 20th century.  2. Intellectuals – Political activity – Germany – History – 20th century.  3. Political culture – Germany – History – 20th century.  4. Political participation – Germany – History – 20th century.  5. Germany – Politics and government – 1945–1990.  6. Germany – Politics and government – 1990–  I. Title.
JN3971.A91F67    2014
320.94309′045 – dc23    2014012954

ISBN 978-1-107-04957-4 Hardback

Cambridge University Press has no responsibility for the persistence or accuracy of URLs for external or third-party internet websites referred to in this publication, and does not guarantee that any content on such websites is, or will remain, accurate or appropriate.

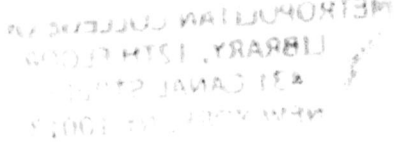

# Contents

|   |   |   |
|---|---|---|
| *Illustrations* | | *page* vi |
| *Acknowledgments* | | vii |
| *Abbreviations* | | x |
| | Introduction: democratic renewal and Germany's "zero hour" | 1 |
| 1 | Germans, occupiers, and the democratization project | 18 |
| 2 | Rethinking democracy: freedom, order, participation | 74 |
| 3 | Renewing culture: the "unpolitical German" between past and future | 114 |
| 4 | Subjects of politics: publicness, parties, elites | 149 |
| 5 | A parliament of spirit? Mobilizing the cultural nation | 192 |
| 6 | Into East Germany: intelligentsia and the Apparat | 238 |
| 7 | Into West Germany: nonconformists and the restoration | 279 |
| 8 | 1968, 1989, and the legacies of participation | 321 |
| *Select bibliography* | | 343 |
| *Index* | | 374 |

# Illustrations

**Map**

1 Germany and central Europe after 1945     *page* xii

**Figures**

| | | |
|---|---|---|
| 1.1 | Accepting the license for *Die Wandlung*, 1945 | 27 |
| 1.2 | Flyer advertising *Ost und West*, 1947 | 41 |
| 3.1 | Ernst and Christian Beutler amid Goethe House ruins, Frankfurt 1945 | 141 |
| 5.1 | Presidium at the First German Writers' Congress, Berlin 1947 | 213 |
| 5.2 | Centennial of the National Assembly in Frankfurt Paulskirche, 1948 | 227 |
| 6.1 | German writers' delegation, Leningrad 1948 | 246 |
| 6.2 | Wolfgang Harich on the cover of *Der Spiegel*, 1956 | 274 |
| 6.3 | Ernst Bloch and Hans Mayer, Tübingen 1963 | 277 |
| 7.1 | Eugen Kogon and coal miners at the Ruhr Festival, Recklinghausen 1950 | 301 |
| 7.2 | Erich Kästner and student at a vigil against atomic arms, Munich 1958 | 307 |

# Acknowledgments

The gestation period of this project has been long, and many people have, in many different ways, helped it see the light of day. It is a great pleasure to be able to thank them here.

My academic interests in Germany and in intellectual history were first stoked in sunny California, and I am grateful to numerous members of the German Studies Department and especially the History Department at Stanford University, to former teachers and former co-workers, for their inspiration and encouragement. Many thanks to Karen Kenkel and to Eric Oberle for mentorship above and beyond the call of duty, and to Megan McCarthy for her friendship.

At the University of Chicago, Michael Geyer guided the first incarnation of this project with a light hand and keen insight. What I have learned from him, overtly and otherwise, animates this book. Moishe Postone's critical acumen and personal generosity have meant much to me and to my work, and Bill Sewell's interventions have deeply imprinted my thinking. I am grateful for our conversations. Special thanks are also due all three of them as well as Jan Goldstein, Ron Suny, and Louis Post for advice and encouragement that helped me overcome some daunting hurdles late in the book-writing process. Some of the arguments below were first presented at Chicago's Modern European History and Social Theory Workshops, which remain my gold standard of collaborative intellectual community. Outside the seminar room, many comrades and coevals conspired to make the life of the mind also a whole lot of fun. Thanks to Cathleen Cahill, Andrew Oppenheimer, Paul Ross, Andrew Sandoval-Strausz, Tracy Steffes, and Amber Wilke, who formed the stable core.

During two longer research stays overseas, Wolfgang Hardtwig and Wolfgang Wippermann were both gracious hosts, generous with their time and their guidance. I was also fortunate to spend a productive year among stimulating colleagues at the University of Wisconsin-Milwaukee. Ellen Amster, Winson Chu, Doug Howland, Dan Sherman, and Lisa Silverman, especially, enriched my time there and since.

Michigan State University has proven a wonderful place to research and teach. I owe a debt of gratitude to all my colleagues there, who received me in such a warm and engaging way. Walter Hawthorne has been a consummately supportive chair, and Sayuri Shimizu and Susan Sleeper-Smith have generously given sage counsel. I was truly fortunate to find in Leslie Moch and Lewis Siegelbaum such model senior colleagues and even better friends. They are part of a remarkable group of transplanted Michiganders who sustain me, intellectually and otherwise – my heartfelt thanks to Denise Demetriou, Christina Kelly, Ed Murphy, Ani Sarkissian, Suman Seth, Mindy Smith, Mickey Stamm, Steve Stowe, and Naoko Wake. Up the road, I am grateful to Ron Suny, Geoff Eley, Kathleen Canning and Dena Goodman as well as, farther away, to Konrad, Jarausch and Eric Weitz. Their kind interest in my work and in my general well-being has been a boon to me.

This project has benefited greatly from the comments, challenges, suggestions, and assistance of fellow scholars. Among them were participants and commentators at many conferences, workshops, and colloquia, whom I thank collectively here. At various points, Arnd Bauerkämper, Benita Blessing, Bo-Mi Choi, Jaimey Fisher, Martin Geyer, Peter Gordon, Andrew Oppenheimer, and Devin Pendas provided helpful input. Alexander Gallus, Daniel Morat, Marcus Payk, and Stefan Vogt were engaging interlocutors and steady friends during sojourns in Germany, as was Moritz Föllmer on both sides of the Atlantic. For our ongoing discussions and countless references, I thank Dirk Moses and Till van Rahden. John Connelly, Konrad Jarausch, and Till van Rahden took precious time to read parts of the manuscript; Moritz Föllmer, Sayuri Shimizu, and Lewis Siegelbaum read it whole. All gave me valuable feedback. Two others read the entire manuscript with great care and expertise for the press. I am indebted to one anonymous and one no-longer-anonymous reader, Carl Caldwell; the book is much better for their comments. A final round of rethinking occurred during an invigorating postdoctoral year in Berlin. For conversations and camaraderie, I would like to thank Thomas Mergel and his entire brilliant team at the Humboldt University. It was my great pleasure to join them for a while.

Scholarship requires material support, and various agencies provided funding for both research and writing: the Jacob A. Javits Fellowship Program, the Alexander von Humboldt Foundation, the SSRC Berlin Program for Advanced German and European Studies, the University of Chicago's William Rainey Harper Fellowship, and MSU's Intramural Research Grant Program. Friendly and knowledgeable help from archival staffs has also been crucial, above all at the Archiv der sozialen

Demokratie, the Bundesarchiv's two houses, the Deutsches Literaturarchiv, the Staats- und Universitätsbibliothek Hamburg, the Stiftung Archiv der Akademie der Künste, and the Universitätsbibliothek Heidelberg. For access to restricted materials, I am indebted to Cornelia Ebeling, Ralph Giordano, Kurt Groenewold, Marianne Harich, Ingrid Kantorowicz, Alexius Kogon, Michael Kogon, and Curt Vinz, as I am to Stefan Moses for the use of his artwork. At MSU, prodigious efforts by German bibliographer Mary Black Junttonen and Denise Forro and her hardworking team at Interlibrary Services greatly facilitated the last phase of research. Staff members at the Bayerische Akademie der Schönen Künste, the Deutsche Fotothek, the Freies Deutsches Hochstift / Frankfurter Goethe-Museum, the Institut für Stadtgeschichte in Frankfurt a.M., and ITAR-TASS in Moscow helped with images and rights; an MSU HARP Production Grant defrayed the costs of permissions. I thank Eric Crahan, formerly of Cambridge University Press, for his initial interest and Michael Watson, my editor, for his advocacy and his patience. He, Amanda George, Sabine Koch, Tom O'Reilly, and Martin Thacker have shepherded me and my work through a complex process, capably and with unflappable good humor.

Yet scholarship does not live from its institutions alone. Thanks to my family for their love and support – to my mother Monika, who first taught me German and other, far more important things; to my brother Sven, whose good cheer and wonderful wit uplift me, and whose wisdom I admire; and to my father Ed, whose boundless enthusiasm buoyed me more than I knew. Klaus Lehmann, Renate Westermann, Jochen Tovote, and Martina Krauel have heartily re-embraced their nephew, and I thank them for that. I count myself lucky to know Jan Gilbert, Maya Gilbert, and Ami Gilbert-Forner. I am grateful to Jill and Terry Hanshew, who make winter visits to Minnesota much warmer.

Karrin Hanshew has read every word of what follows multiple times. She has lived with this project since its inception, pushing me to many fruitful insights and reconsiderations. Without our continuous dialogue, this book would be much poorer. Without her unflagging belief in me and her tireless support, it would not exist. For that and for much, much else, my deepest thanks go to her.

# Abbreviations

| | |
|---|---|
| APO | Extraparliamentary Opposition |
| CCF | Congress for Cultural Freedom |
| CDU | Christian-Democratic Union |
| DFB | German Freedom Library |
| DGB | German Federation of Unions |
| DVP | Democratic People's Party |
| ECSC | European Coal and Steel Community |
| EDC | European Defense Community |
| EUD | Europe Union Germany |
| FRG | Federal Republic of Germany |
| *FZ* | *Frankfurter Zeitung* |
| GDR | German Democratic Republic |
| GlavPURKKA | Main Political Administration of the Workers' and Peasants' Red Army |
| GVP | All-German People's Party |
| HICOG | Allied High Commission for Germany |
| ICD | Information Control Division |
| KdA | Fight Atomic Death |
| KfA | Campaign for Disarmament |
| KPD | Communist Party of Germany |
| MfS | Ministry of State Security |
| NSDAP | National Socialist German Workers' Party |
| NWDR | North-West German Radio |
| OMGUS | Office of Military Government for Germany, United States |
| PEN | Poets, Essayists, Novelists |
| PWD | Psychological Warfare Division |
| SAPD | Socialist Workers' Party of Germany |
| SDA | Protective Association of German Authors |
| SDS | Protective Association of German Writers (Chapter 5) |
| SDS | Socialist German Student League (Chapter 8) |

| | |
|---|---|
| SED | Socialist Unity Party of Germany |
| SFG | Socialist Supporters' Society |
| SPD | Social Democratic Party of Germany |
| SVAG | Soviet Military Administration in Germany |
| VVN | Union of Persecutees of the Nazi Regime |

Map 1 Germany and central Europe after 1945.

# Introduction: Democratic renewal and Germany's "zero hour"

"A wonderful Palm Sunday. The occupying powers were not yet there and the Nazis were already gone, and it was an especially beautiful spring day that will always remain in my memory."[1] This was how Walter Dirks, a journalist, independent-minded socialist, and devout Catholic, remembered his first day after National Socialism. That morning, the regime's local officials had fled Frankfurt, the US Army had taken control of nearby Darmstadt, and despite the surrounding destruction, the future seemed bright and open. This sense of rebirth became the shared point of departure for a diverse group of German intellectuals, opponents of Nazism who emerged from exile, incarceration, resistance, or – more often than not – from "inner emigration" during the spring and summer of 1945. The transition was both sobering and exhilarating. For sociology professor Alfred Weber, a "zero point" had been reached in humanity's development, a nadir that marked the German people with a special responsibility but also a special insight.[2] Axel Eggebrecht, a militantly unaffiliated leftist journalist in his mid forties, felt energized by the task at hand: "In May of 1945, I got ten years younger."[3] At that moment, jurist and literary critic Hans Mayer was making arrangements to return from Switzerland, having fled Germany as a Jew and a Communist in 1933. Decades later, and not without a melancholic note, he wrote, "We allowed ourselves much hope back then, when the war had ended and everything seemed possible."[4] Such men as these – and women too, though their roles and their voices were less prominent – experienced 1945 as

---

[1] *So alt wie das Jahrhundert: Walter Dirks – ein Journalist in drei Epochen* (television program, Hessischer Rundfunk, 1991); cited in Joachim Rotberg, *Zwischen Linkskatholizismus und bürgerlicher Sammlung: Die Anfänge der CDU in Frankfurt am Main 1945–1946* (Frankfurt a.M.: Knecht, 1999), 73.
[2] Alfred Weber, "Unsere Erfahrung und unsere Aufgabe," *Die Wandlung* 1, no. 1 (1945): 52.
[3] "Ein Rückblick auf die Zukunft: Hörspiel mit umgekehrtem Fernrohr," *Der Spiegel*, 15 March 1947, 19.
[4] Hans Mayer, *Ein Deutscher auf Widerruf: Erinnerungen* (Frankfurt a.M.: Suhrkamp, 1982), I:303.

their moment, one full of promise for a renewal of Germany by Germans, against National Socialism and independent of the Allied powers to whom they were indebted for the regime's defeat. Dirks would recall it as the time "when we rolled up our sleeves," when he and a host of likeminded compatriots set about the hard work of building a new Germany at the heart of a new Europe.[5] Not by accident do their statements carry an emotional charge. The extent of moral and material devastation as well as Germany's unprecedented crimes raised two questions with existential urgency: How exactly should the postwar order look? And what did it mean to address this rebuilding process as a German, that is, from the epicenter of the catastrophe?

In answering these questions, postwar Germans envisioned, desired, and repressed many things. This book explores a distinctive set of responses developed by engaged intellectuals in the years after 1945 that together amounted to a German rethinking of democracy. The first half of Europe's twentieth century has been called an "age of catastrophe," in which the continent was shaken by two total wars, genocide, economic collapse, and an ongoing civil war that pitted the forces of communism and fascism against each other and against an embattled liberal establishment.[6] Yet it was also an "age of democracy," for after the mobilization of nations through the First World War, the people's political demobilization was no longer possible, and subsequent regimes were compelled to claim legitimacy in democratic terms.[7] After the Second World War, in the wake of massive violence and upheaval, building a free, just, and stable new order stood at the top of Europeans' postwar agendas. But what about "democracy"? To contemporaries in 1945, the notion seemed attractive yet elusive or even dangerous, omnipresent yet strangely empty.[8] By that time, people across the continent had come to explain the century's calamities by the shortcomings of earlier answers to the questions of modern political order. This book contends that a novel approach to the problematic of popular self-government in a mass age

---

[5] Walter Dirks, "Als wir die Ärmel aufkrempelten – zum Beispiel in Frankfurt," *Neue Gesellschaft / Frankfurter Hefte* 32, no. 4 (1985): 316–18.

[6] Eric Hobsbawm, *Age of Extremes: The Short Twentieth Century, 1914–1991* (London: Michael Joseph, 1994); Mark Mazower, *Dark Continent: Europe's Twentieth Century* (New York: Knopf, 1998).

[7] Jan-Werner Müller, *Contesting Democracy: Political Ideas in Twentieth-Century Europe* (New Haven, Conn.: Yale University Press, 2011).

[8] Martin Conway and Volker Depkat, "Towards a European History of the Discourse of Democracy: Discussing Democracy in Western Europe 1945–60," in *Europeanization in the Twentieth Century: Historical Approaches*, ed. Conway and Kiran Klaus Patel (Basingstoke: Palgrave Macmillan, 2010), 134–44; Till van Rahden, "Clumsy Democrats: Moral Passions in the Federal Republic," *German History* 29, no. 3 (2011): 495–503.

appeared in an unlikely place: Germany itself, in the wake of Nazism, war, and Holocaust, defeated and occupied by American, British, French, and Soviet forces. It focuses on groups of public intellectuals and associated periodicals and organizations in the immediate postwar years. It then traces their trajectories over the foundation of two separate German states in 1949 and through the early years of both East and West German societies.

These groups, I argue, formulated a vision of democratic renewal that emphasized the intrinsic value of each person's participation in shaping the political and socio-economic life of all. This was simultaneously a general prescription for a well-constituted polity and a specific response to the Nazi past, conditioned by distinctly German issues and commitments. Drawn together by their antifascist convictions and their democratic hopes, these intellectuals' interactions generated a new social network that linked people from a range of previously disconnected social and political milieus across the four zones of occupied Germany. With Allied support, they established the journals, founded the associations, and convened the congresses that became the vehicles of their activism. Thereby, they helped rebuild a kind of "public sphere" under occupation, as the value of "publicness" became a topic of their discussions.[9] To register the substance of their ideas as well as the forms of their activity, I call them Germany's "engaged democrats."[10] Attempting to reckon with the causes and consequences of Nazism, they saw 1945 as a chance to break with the national past as well as an occasion to reflect on its ambivalent legacies. As they scoured German cultural and political traditions, they found rich democratic potentials embedded there, entangled in a catastrophe from which they could not simply be cut loose. Instead, the actors in question recovered and reconfigured select elements, forging these into a novel amalgam. The resulting positions on democratic renewal reveal important possibilities and limits of the political imagination in a watershed moment of German history.

Their proposed solutions to the perceived problem of mass democracy entailed recasting conventional views on the relationship between

---

[9] Classically, these terms are associated with Jürgen Habermas, *The Structural Transformation of the Public Sphere: An Inquiry into a Category of Bourgeois Society*, trans. Thomas Burger (Cambridge, Mass.: MIT Press, 1989). As I argue below, Habermas inherited concerns and orientations from these earlier figures.

[10] I borrow the term from Claudia Fröhlich and Michael Kohlstruck, who refer to those few Germans that urged an early reckoning with the Nazi past, like the intellectuals considered here. In my usage, it underscores their public interventions and participatory views as well. See Claudia Fröhlich and Michael Kohlstruck, introduction to *Engagierte Demokraten: Vergangenheitspolitik in kritischer Absicht*, ed. Fröhlich and Kohlstruck (Münster: Westfälisches Dampfboot, 1999), esp. 14–18.

elites and the populace. It is a commonplace of scholarship on modern Germany and Europe that privileged social strata had confronted the rise of mass politics since the late nineteenth century as "elites against democracy."[11] And after 1914, elitism in various guises permeated the political spectrum. Pressured from below, liberals and conservatives reconciled themselves to more meritocracy while still seeking to exclude "the masses." The parties of the left preached popular power, but their own ways of withholding trust in the people found expression in Social Democrats' state-centered paternalism as well as Communists' party-centered vanguardism.[12] On the populist right, the Nazi "people's community" – bound by racist nationalism and governed by acclamation – claimed to have realized a purer, leader-centered form of popular rule.[13] In contrast to these models, Germany's engaged democrats were prompted by the perceived rupture of 1945 to conceive a politics that neither transpired over the heads of the population nor sought to organize them from above but rested on popular participation from below. Rather than approach "the masses" as objects – of exclusion, organization, or paternalist concern – they imagined them as the self-civilizing subjects of a self-constituting public, that is, of "the people" as the sole ground of sovereign authority. Strikingly, this held true even for their fellow Germans, who would transform themselves from Nazi supporters to active citizens by participation: practicing self-rule in myriad forms would be the means as well as the end of their post-fascist self-education to democracy.

Intra-German discussions took place not in a vacuum but on the frontlines of a budding conflict among Germany's occupiers, the victors of the Grand Alliance. Directly following the war, the Allies tightly regulated print media and associations, though they put them largely in German hands. On a practical level, engaged democrats cooperated with the occupiers while maintaining that Germans' "reeducation" could be effected only by Germans themselves. On a programmatic level, they distanced their agenda from the rapidly polarizing positions of the incipient Cold War and sought to preserve a united, neutral Germany within a united,

---

[11] Walter Struve, *Elites against Democracy: Leadership Ideals in Bourgeois Political Thought in Germany, 1890–1933* (Princeton, N.J.: Princeton University Press, 1973).

[12] On the workers' movement's dual centralisms, see Geoff Eley, "Reviewing the Socialist Tradition," in *The Crisis of Socialism in Europe*, ed. Christiane Lemke and Gary Marks (Durham, N.C.: Duke University Press, 1992), 21–60.

[13] On the integrative authority of the *Volksgemeinschaft* and of Hitler's person, see Peter Fritzsche, *Germans into Nazis* (Cambridge, Mass.: Harvard University Press, 1998); Ian Kershaw, *The "Hitler Myth": Image and Reality in the Third Reich* (Oxford: Oxford University Press, 1987).

neutral Europe as an independent force.[14] The foundation of the Federal Republic of Germany (FRG) and the German Democratic Republic (GDR) in 1949 soon stymied these hopes and cleaved apart the spaces in which their network had arisen. On both sides of the divide – albeit under dissimilar conditions of liberal democracy and socialist dictatorship – engaged democrats' frustrated hopes fueled vocal dissent in the 1950s. This, in turn, transmitted impulses to protest mobilizations that would transform both Germanys from the 1960s to the 1980s.[15] In what follows, I trace the manifest and subterranean legacies of their vision, a German contribution to long-standing debates on the promises and perils of mass democracy. Domestically, they countered the still-powerful intellectuals of the radical right, whose decisionist, aristocratic political conceptions they vigorously opposed.[16] With their participatory, public orientations, they gave vital early stimuli to what Konrad Jarausch has called post-Nazi Germany's "recivilizing process."[17] In a broader frame, their vision represented one strand of an alternative postwar politics that, by contesting the terms of the global confrontation between welfare-capitalist liberal democracy and state-socialist "people's democracy," countered the Cold War era's bipolar fixities.

### The postwar conjuncture in Germany and Europe

This book stresses an initial sense of fluidity and hope that fostered creative impulses in the immediate postwar period and provoked forceful critiques as the Cold War system solidified. More conventionally, the history of political culture in Germany after 1945 is framed in terms of

---

[14] On German neutralisms, see Alexander Gallus, *Die Neutralisten: Verfechter eines vereinten Deutschlands zwischen Ost und West 1945–1990* (Düsseldorf: Droste, 2001). On the early movement for European federation, see Walter Lipgens, *A History of European Integration*, vol. I, *1945–1947*, trans. P. S. Falla and A. J. Ryder (Oxford: Clarendon, 1982); Vanessa Conze, *Das Europa der Deutschen: Ideen von Europa in Deutschland zwischen Reichstradition und Westorientierung (1920–1970)* (Munich: Oldenbourg, 2005), 291–321.

[15] Their story thus illuminates Germany's divided yet intertwined postwar history. See Christoph Kleßmann, "Verflechtung und Abgrenzung: Aspekte der geteilten und zusammengehörenden Nachkriegsgeschichte," *Aus Politik und Zeitgeschichte* B29/30 (1993): 30–41; Konrad H. Jarausch, "'Die Teile als Ganzes erkennen': Zur Integration der beiden deutschen Nachkriegsgeschichten," *Zeithistorische Forschungen* 1, no. 1 (2004): 10–30.

[16] Dirk van Laak, *Gespräche in der Sicherheit des Schweigens: Carl Schmitt in der politischen Geistesgeschichte der frühen Bundesrepublik* (Berlin: Akademie, 1993); Daniel Morat, *Von der Tat zur Gelassenheit: Konservatives Denken bei Martin Heidegger, Ernst Jünger und Friedrich Georg Jünger 1920–1960* (Göttingen: Wallstein, 2007).

[17] Jarausch, *After Hitler: Recivilizing Germans, 1945–1995*, trans. Brandon Hunziker (Oxford: Oxford University Press, 2006).

restoration and assimilation. The collapse of fascism led to great disorientation among Germans, the argument goes, while their occupiers proffered clear but divergent orientations; on that basis, reconstruction evolved in a two-fold process. On the one hand, Germans regained limited sovereignty and accommodated a bipolar world through "Sovietization" and "Americanization" or, more broadly, "Westernization."[18] On the other hand, political culture was shaped by "multiple restorations" of pre- and non-Nazi German traditions in both East and West.[19] As the best scholarship underscores, an interplay of assimilation and restoration indeed determined the dominant character of each postwar Germany. Geopolitical pressures provided the context in which certain traditions revived while others were sidelined; in the process, Germans and allies responded and adapted to each other in asymmetrical but bilateral interaction.[20] In this frame, the immediate postwar years appear as a mere prelude to polarization or a revival of the past. Alternately, they are treated in isolation as a peculiar period of dynamic yet disparate activity without lasting relevance.[21]

By contrast, this book foregrounds the significance of occupation-era developments as well as their legacies for subsequent conflicts in East and West Germany. To do so, it both contextualizes and takes seriously the conviction, prevalent among Germany's engaged democrats, that "restorations" were to be avoided and independent paths pursued at all costs. As Hans Mayer put it, he and like-minded compatriots imagined that something resembling "the synthesis of a democratically renewed

[18] Landmark statements include Jarausch and Hannes Siegrist, "Amerikanisierung und Sowjetisierung: Eine vergleichende Fragestellung zur deutsch-deutschen Nachkriegsgeschichte," in *Amerikanisierung und Sowjetisierung in Deutschland 1945–1970*, ed. Jarausch and Siegrist (Frankfurt a.M.: Campus, 1997), 11–46 and Anselm Doering-Manteuffel, *Wie westlich sind die Deutschen? Amerikanisierung und Westernisierung im 20. Jahrhundert* (Göttingen: Vandenhoeck & Ruprecht, 1999).
[19] Jeffrey Herf, *Divided Memory: The Nazi Past in the Two Germanys* (Cambridge, Mass.: Harvard University Press, 1997).
[20] On intellectuals and political culture, see Volker R. Berghahn, *America and the Intellectual Cold Wars in Europe: Shepard Stone between Philanthropy, Academy, and Diplomacy* (Princeton, N.J.: Princeton University Press, 2001); Peter C. Caldwell, *Dictatorship, State Planning, and Social Theory in the German Democratic Republic* (Cambridge: Cambridge University Press, 2003); Marcus M. Payk, *Der Geist der Demokratie: Intellektuelle Orientierungsversuche im Feuilleton der frühen Bundesrepublik: Karl Korn und Peter de Mendelssohn* (Munich: Oldenbourg, 2008); Nina Verheyen, *Diskussionslust: Zur Kulturgeschichte des "besseren Arguments" in Westdeutschland* (Göttingen: Vandenhoeck & Ruprecht, 2010).
[21] Along the latter lines, see Clare Flanagan, *A Study of German Political-Cultural Periodicals from the Years of Allied Occupation, 1945–1949* (Lewiston, N.Y.: Mellen, 2000); Michael Th. Greven, *Politisches Denken in Deutschland nach 1945: Erfahrung und Umgang mit der Kontingenz in der unmittelbaren Nachkriegszeit* (Opladen: Budrich, 2007). A welcome exception: Friedrich Kießling, *Die undeutschen Deutschen: Eine ideengeschichtliche Archäologie der alten Bundesrepublik 1945–1972* (Paderborn: Schöningh, 2012).

Soviet Union with a further development of Roosevelt's 'New Deal' thinking in the United States" could ground a distinct postwar order in Germany.[22] This possibility was rooted in the seemingly successful negotiation of a European settlement and, specifically, of common goals for four-power occupation of Germany at the Yalta and Potsdam conferences of 1945. It thus presumed continued effective – if not necessarily amicable – cooperation among the war's erstwhile allies.

Was such hope not an illusion? Historians of the Cold War remain divided on the Allies' intentions for Europe and for the world, a question in which Germany's fate looms large. For decades, debates dwelt on the question of responsibility for the superpower conflict, and the opening of some archives in the former Eastern bloc added new sources without settling old questions. Subsequent scholarship blends traditionalists' stress on Soviet expansionism, revisionists' stress on American economic imperialism and Soviet security concerns, and post-revisionists' emphasis on mutual misperceptions and escalatory reactions. While some assert that the orthodox view of Soviet aggression and Western defense had the basics right all along, others question such a strident conclusion.[23] Even the "revolutionary-imperial" drive of Soviet foreign policy confronted the imperative of security for the war-battered USSR. This required a buffer zone of influence to the west – and, in the long term, foresaw socialism across the globe – but much evidence suggests Stalin's initial approach was flexible, pragmatically averse to inter-Allied hostility and attentive to European agendas and responses. For its part, the USA – under Truman as well as Roosevelt – at first also privileged a cooperative spheres-of-interest settlement over zero-sum confrontation.[24] The antagonistic, polarized course soon taken was not set from the start.

The signal case of Germany highlights flux, not fixity, in relations between the Allies and within each camp. For neither the USSR nor the USA was policymaking monolithic. Even if the German Communist leadership eagerly pursued maximal control over a rump eastern state, there was no such consensus among their Soviet patrons. In Moscow as well as in Berlin, officials who sought their share of influence over a united, neutral, Soviet-friendly Germany contended with those who preferred to dominate an East German satellite. US elites were divided

---

[22] Mayer, *Ein Deutscher*, I:303.
[23] Compare John Lewis Gaddis, *We Now Know: Rethinking Cold War History* (Oxford: Oxford University Press, 1997) with Melvyn P. Leffler, "The Cold War: What Do 'We Now Know'?" *American Historical Review* 104, no. 2 (1999): 501–24.
[24] See the contributions by Leffler, Vladimir O. Pechatnov, and Norman M. Naimark to Leffler and Odd Arne Westad, eds. *The Cambridge History of the Cold War* (Cambridge: Cambridge University Press, 2010), I:67–73, 90–100, 175–83, 195–7.

between advocates of a West German solution and advocates of a pacified Germany under four-power stewardship. As tensions rose, American determination to harness West German industrial might for capitalism's reconstruction and Soviet reparations demands as well as political repression of non-Communists all contributed to division.[25] Crucially, to German actors on the ground, signals about the horizon of possible outcomes were decidedly mixed. Beneath the immediate postwar fluidity lay an ideological confrontation that made geopolitical rivalry likely, if not inevitable.[26] Yet the precise form this would take was murky in 1945. It was clear enough that two fundamentally different orders stood opposed in the international system, an opposition inscribed across the territory of occupied Germany. That this would entail the division of the country and the world as well as the blockage of all other paths was not a foregone conclusion.

Before occupation and superpower conflict, the end of the war brought liberation from National Socialism. The sense of renewal that infused engaged democrats' experience of 1945 resonates with a founding myth of both postwar Germanys: that this moment marked a "zero hour" (*Stunde Null*), clearing the ground of history and enabling a fresh start. This notion elides many-layered continuities across 1945, some of which were denied at the time, others embraced. Elite careers were little impacted. Despite denazification, all but the most tainted civil servants (including academics), jurists, military men, scientists, doctors, journalists, and businessmen successfully shored up or re-established their power, with some variation across fields and occupation zones.[27] Meanwhile, Germans of all social ranks experienced the years directly before and after war's end as uninterrupted "bad times" of dislocation and privation.[28] Memories of their own suffering – from air raids and mass

---

[25] Naimark, *The Russians in Germany: A History of the Soviet Zone of Occupation, 1945–1949* (Cambridge, Mass.: Harvard University Press, 1995); Carolyn Eisenberg, *Drawing the Line: The American Decision to Divide Germany, 1944–1949* (Cambridge: Cambridge University Press, 1996).

[26] For the Cold War as an ideological conflict between "liberty" and "justice" or competing claims to true "democracy," see Odd Arne Westad, *The Global Cold War: Third World Interventions and the Making of Our Times* (Cambridge: Cambridge University Press, 2005); Bernd Stöver, *Der Kalte Krieg 1947–1991: Geschichte eines radikalen Zeitalters* (Munich: Beck, 2007).

[27] West German elites are better researched than their Eastern counterparts. Compare, e.g., the synthetic Norbert Frei, ed. *Karrieren im Zwielicht: Hitlers Eliten nach 1945* (Frankfurt a.M.: Campus, 2001) with the article forum by Dolores Augustine, Heinrich Best and Axel Salheiser, Rüdiger Stutz, and Georg Wagner-Kyora, "Nazi Continuities in East Germany," *German Studies Review* 29, no. 3 (2006): 579–619.

[28] Ulrich Herbert, "Good Times, Bad Times: Memories of the Third Reich," in *Life in the Third Reich*, ed. Richard Bessel (Oxford: Oxford University Press, 1986), 97–110; Martin Broszat, Klaus-Dietmar Henke, and Hans Woller, eds. *Von Stalingrad zur*

rapes, as refugees from eastern territories, and as prisoners of war – overshadowed memories of complicity in Nazism.[29] Self-pity was exacerbated by resentment at indiscriminate charges of "collective guilt" leveled by a seemingly hostile world.[30] Dominant narratives of the recent past thus cast Germans predominantly as victims, implicitly or explicitly equating them with the victims of Germans – or simply passing in silence over the latter. The "zero hour" was a linchpin in this construction.

Just as it helped fashion usable individual and collective pasts, so the "zero hour" abetted the rehabilitation of both German states after 1949, domestically and internationally. Official memory in the GDR drew the starkest break of all, trading on leftists' resistance and persecution to disavow all continuities, claim an unequivocally anti-Nazi identity, and legitimate Communist rule. Although the early FRG acknowledged responsibility for crimes committed "in Germany's name," it coupled restitution payments and pro-Israel diplomacy with the reintegration of heavily compromised politicians and officials.[31] These self-representations merged seamlessly with broader Cold War orthodoxies, as state-sanctioned "antifascism" and anti-"totalitarianism" enabled each side to tar the other with the brush of Nazism and distance itself from that legacy.[32]

For all its ideological uses, the "zero hour" also names a deep rupture, the ethical and political as well as physical nadir wrought by unprecedented violence that many Germans clearly felt. Material hardship and avoidance of the past directed much attention to the present, but

*Währungsreform: Zur Sozialgeschichte des Umbruchs in Deutschland* (Munich: Oldenbourg, 1988).

[29] Elizabeth Heineman, "The Hour of the Woman: Memories of Germany's 'Crisis Years' and West German National Identity," *American Historical Review* 101, no. 2 (1996): 354–95; Robert G. Moeller, *War Stories: The Search for a Usable Past in the Federal Republic of Germany* (Berkeley: University of California Press, 2001); Frank Biess, *Homecomings: Returning POWs and the Legacies of Defeat in Postwar Germany* (Princeton, N.J.: Princeton University Press, 2006).

[30] Though partly imagined, these accusations were palpably felt. Norbert Frei, "Von deutscher Erfindungskraft; oder, Die Kollektivschuldthese in der Nachkriegszeit," *Rechtshistorisches Journal* 16 (1997): 621–34; Barbara Wolbring, "Nationales Stigma und persönliche Schuld: Die Debatte über Kollektivschuld in der Nachkriegszeit," *Historische Zeitschrift* 289, no. 2 (2009): 325–64.

[31] Herf, *Divided Memory*; Frei, *Adenauer's Germany and the Nazi Past: The Politics of Amnesty and Integration*, trans. Joel Golb (New York: Columbia University Press, 2002); Christoph Classen, *Faschismus und Antifaschismus: Die nationalsozialistische Vergangenheit im ostdeutschen Hörfunk (1945–1953)* (Cologne: Böhlau, 2004).

[32] Abbott Gleason, *Totalitarianism: The Inner History of the Cold War* (New York: Oxford University Press, 1995); Wolfgang Wippermann, *Faschismustheorien: Die Entwicklung der Diskussion von den Anfängen bis heute*, 7th edn. (Darmstadt: Wissenschaftliche Buchgesellschaft, 1997), 11–57; Anson Rabinbach, *Begriffe aus dem Kalten Krieg: Totalitarismus, Antifaschismus, Genozid* (Göttingen: Wallstein, 2009), 7–42.

openness and opportunity also sparked imaginings of the future.[33] To a few intellectuals, often German Jews in exile, the times were elegiac or austere; redemption seemed inaccessible after the civilizational caesura of Nazism and Holocaust.[34] On the ground in Germany, other intellectuals energized by their sense of radical "contingency" embraced the project of renewal.[35] The challenge, however, was how to move forward, and for educated elites, this involved assessing the nation's cultural heritage in the wake of discredit and defeat. What did it mean that the land of "poets and thinkers" had unleashed a politics of devastation? Scholars of German intellectual life have diagnosed two diverging responses in the wake of 1945: a minority attempt at a total break with the past versus a mainstream project to salvage its "good" elements from the "bad."[36] Alongside cool-headed arguments, deep-seated emotions associated with pollution and purity were also at stake. Operating at the nexus of cognition and affect, such bifurcated stances expressed an underlying psychological structure – a basic binary of disavowing versus defending Germanness – that shaped decades of polarized public wrangling over the meaning of the past.[37]

Neglected in these accounts is an inherently equivocal stance toward German traditions that was prominent in postwar discussions. On this view, the national cultural heritage was ambivalent *in itself*, simultaneously an indicator of Germans' disastrously apolitical past and a resource for their democratic future. For engaged democrats, notions of "culture" and "spirit" prevalent in German letters since the late eighteenth century implied a rich, specifically participatory way of thinking about freedom and agency; at the same time, they recognized, the very focus on things spiritual had fed a political quiescence – and a rearguard hostility to the disenchanted modern world – that paved the way for Nazism. After

---

[33] See, e.g., Kleßmann, "Stationen des öffentlichen und historiographischen Umgangs in Deutschland mit der Zäsur von 1945," in *Deutsche Umbrüche im 20. Jahrhundert*, ed. Dietrich Papenfuß and Wolfgang Schieder (Cologne: Böhlau, 2000), 460; Bessel, *Germany 1945: From War to Peace* (New York: HarperCollins, 2009).

[34] Rabinbach, *In the Shadow of Catastrophe: German Intellectuals between Apocalypse and Enlightenment* (Berkeley: University of California Press, 1997); Dan Diner, "'Rupture in Civilization': On the Genesis and Meaning of a Concept in Understanding," in *On Germans and Jews under the Nazi Regime*, ed. Moshe Zimmermann (Jerusalem: Hebrew University Press, 2006), 33–48.

[35] Greven, *Politisches Denken*, esp. 14–17.

[36] See, e.g., Stephen Brockmann, *German Literary Culture at the Zero Hour* (Rochester, N.Y.: Camden House, 2004); Jeffrey K. Olick, *In the House of the Hangman: The Agonies of German Defeat, 1943–1949* (Chicago: University of Chicago Press, 2005); Mark W. Clark, *Beyond Catastrophe: German Intellectuals and Cultural Renewal after World War II, 1945–1955* (Lanham, Md.: Lexington, 2006).

[37] A. Dirk Moses, *German Intellectuals and the Nazi Past* (Cambridge: Cambridge University Press, 2007).

1945, they sought neither to jettison nor to revive the cultural tradition but to extract the liberating potential at its heart and bring this to bear on the sphere of politics. In so doing, they both shared and complicated the influential diagnosis of the "unpolitical German," formulated around the same time by liberals in exile.[38] Working in this frame, scholars remain quick to align continuing concerns over the fate of "cultivation" in "mass society" with mandarin cultural conservatism and its anti-democratic proclivities.[39] Yet at the crucial post-fascist juncture, some voices within Germany charted a path to democratic politics precisely via a specific recourse to German culture. As I aim to show, the democratization of an elitist cultural patrimony was integral to a counter-elitist reimagining of politics by one segment of the educated elites themselves.

Conditions in postwar Germany – devastation, liberation, and Cold War conflict – obtained with variations all over Europe, and they generated a continent-wide political climate in which all sorts of political actors operated. This was the pre-Cold War "moment of antifascist unity," in which broad coalitions advanced a welter of reform and reconstruction agendas, in high politics and at a grassroots level. Typically, these were fronted by leftists who had played a leading role in resistance movements, but they incorporated forces from Christian Democrats through liberals to Communists.[40] Egalitarian values enjoyed broad currency, as resistance-era idealism and the social leveling apparently wrought by the war made plausible the notion of cross-class cooperation for the common good. These conditions proved favorable for corporatist cooperation and the welfare state in Western Europe as well as for communism's initial popular appeal in the East, where Stalinist dictatorships soon instrumentalized a language of "antifascism" they had not forged alone.[41] Not reflected in either of these state-centered orders, however, was the immediate postwar zeal for direct participation.[42] In 1945, this

---

[38] Classically, see Fritz Stern, "The Political Consequences of the Unpolitical German," *History* 3 (1960): 104–34; more recently, Wolf Lepenies, *The Seduction of Culture in German History* (Princeton, N.J.: Princeton University Press, 2006).

[39] See Fritz K. Ringer, *The Decline of the German Mandarins: The German Academic Community, 1890–1933* (Cambridge, Mass.: Harvard University Press, 1969) and, e.g., Axel Schildt, *Moderne Zeiten: Freizeit, Massenmedien und "Zeitgeist" in der Bundesrepublik der 50er Jahre* (Hamburg: Christians, 1995), 324–50.

[40] Eley, *Forging Democracy: The History of the Left in Europe, 1850–2000* (Oxford: Oxford University Press, 2002), 283–98. On corresponding intellectual agendas, see James D. Wilkinson, *The Intellectual Resistance in Europe* (Cambridge, Mass.: Harvard University Press, 1981).

[41] On Eastern Europe, see Bradley F. Abrams, "The Second World War and the East European Revolution," *East European Politics and Societies* 16, no. 3 (2002): 623–64; Rabinbach, *Begriffe*, 28–42.

[42] Eley, *Forging Democracy*, 296.

impulse was manifest in squatting and land seizures as well as in organs of small-scale self-government that sprang up spontaneously across Europe. These committees often blurred the bounds between workplace and civic authority, launching production, provisioning, and reconstruction efforts as well as local purges of Nazis and collaborators.[43] Thick on the ground in Germany, these were known as "antifascist committees" or simply *Antifas*.[44] In their own moment, they were effective if not uncontested vehicles of bottom-up authority; as autonomous and potentially unruly centers of German power, they were shut down as the occupiers consolidated control. A parallel stress on participation resonated among Germany's engaged democrats; it is the keynote to which their various programs and proposals resolve. In that respect, they constitute an intellectual corollary to the grassroots popular politics of the immediate postwar.

Their story also suggests other narratives of "democracy" in Germany after 1945 than the ones historians have tended to explore. Certainly, the second half of Germany's twentieth century – when viewed alongside the first – found a "remarkably happy ending," in Michael Geyer's words.[45] One strand of scholarship has thus focused on the Federal Republic's successful arrival in "the West," often celebrating its pluralist, parliamentary system as the definitive horizon of democracy itself.[46] To be sure, this development requires explanation, and intellectual historians have paid serious attention to a "second foundation" that followed on the FRG's first, institutional one. At stake has been how to understand the consolidation of its liberal democracy at the level of political culture, taking intellectual debates to both register and shape broader dispositions. Whether scholars emphasize the contribution of the republic's vigilant leftist critics or its liberalized conservative supporters – or propose, as A. Dirk

---

[43] On the complex politics of the latter, see István Deák, Jan T. Gross, and Tony Judt, eds. *The Politics of Retribution in Europe: World War II and its Aftermath* (Princeton, N.J.: Princeton University Press, 2000).

[44] See, classically, Lutz Niethammer, Ulrich Borsdorf, and Peter Brandt, eds. *Arbeiterinitiative 1945: Antifaschistische Ausschüsse und Reorganisation der Arbeiterbewegung in Deutschland* (Wuppertal: Hammer, 1976); more skeptically, Gareth Pritchard, *Niemandsland: A History of Unoccupied Germany, 1944–1945* (Cambridge: Cambridge University Press, 2012).

[45] Michael Geyer, "Germany; or, The Twentieth Century as History," *South Atlantic Quarterly* 96, no. 4 (1997): quote 664.

[46] See, e.g., Edgar Wolfrum, *Die geglückte Demokratie: Geschichte der Bundesrepublik Deutschland von ihren Anfängen bis zur Gegenwart* (Stuttgart: Klett-Cotta, 2006); Heinrich August Winkler, *Germany: The Long Road West*, trans. Alexander J. Sager, 2 vols. (Oxford: Oxford University Press, 2006–7). In intellectual history, see Matthew G. Specter, *Habermas: An Intellectual Biography* (Cambridge: Cambridge University Press, 2010).

Moses has, viewing political legitimacy as a "discursive achievement" that emerged from protracted debate between the two – this literature is centrally concerned with intellectuals' roles in forging the consensus that sustains today's Berlin Republic.[47] Germany's engaged democrats, too, are relevant to the paradoxical origins of the FRG's dominant political culture among those who initially questioned its legitimacy. My approach, however, sets their contributions in a different frame. I aim to reconstruct a conception of political participation that went beyond the limited possibilities of the Cold War era, one that emerged in eastern and western Germany after 1945 and remained relevant for democratic politics thereafter.

## Intellectual networks and political culture

This book begins by laying bare the connections among seemingly disparate discussions and endeavors over a broad political-cultural field. Its breadth indicates the initially centripetal force of antifascism in German public life, spurring cooperation across camps and milieus from 1945 to 1948. Our protagonists range from liberal political scientist Dolf Sternberger to Marxist theorist Ernst Bloch, from left-Catholic resister Eugen Kogon to Jewish re-émigré Alfred Kantorowicz, from septuagenarian Social Democratic sociologist Alfred Weber to precocious Communist philosopher Wolfgang Harich. All identified strongly with their rather varied anti-Nazi experiences, seeing themselves as antifascist elders responsible for shepherding Germany's nazified youth into a common future.[48] Moreover, they insistently linked cultural and political renewal, and they maintained that rebuilding was the Germans' task; it should proceed in cooperation with the occupiers but independent of their Cold War agendas. Not central to this investigation are those intellectuals who did not begin their public careers or return from exile until the 1950s as well as those who did not concern themselves with the culture-politics interface or initially seek a non-aligned Germany. This means that many

---

[47] See, centrally, Clemens Albrecht et al., *Die intellektuelle Gründung der Bundesrepublik: Eine Wirkungsgeschichte der Frankfurter Schule* (Frankfurt a.M.: Campus, 1999); Jens Hacke, *Philosophie der Bürgerlichkeit: Die liberalkonservative Begründung der Bundesrepublik* (Göttingen: Vandenhoeck & Ruprecht, 2006); Moses, *German Intellectuals*, quote 10, 50. For a selection of recent work, see Franz-Werner Kersting, Jürgen Reulecke, and Hans-Ulrich Thamer, eds. *Die zweite Gründung der Bundesrepublik: Generationswechsel und intellektuelle Worterbgreifungen 1955–1975* (Stuttgart: Steiner, 2010).

[48] On generational discourse, see Jaimey Fisher, *Disciplining Germany: Youth, Reeducation, and Reconstruction after the Second World War* (Detroit: Wayne State University Press, 2007).

14   German Intellectuals and Democratic Renewal

who were indisputably "engaged" or "democratic" are not treated as "engaged democrats" below.

The new social network that concerns us here was ideologically plural and loosely integrated, linking actors and institutions from Munich to Hamburg and Heidelberg to Berlin. It crossed the borders of occupation zones, the divide between returning exiles and those who had stayed in Germany, and the boundaries of traditionally insular socio-political milieus.[49] Yet it enjoyed this degree of coherence only early on; with the Cold War rupture, stark divergences emerged, even as earlier commitments continued to leave a mark. To chart these patterns of communication and association, I borrow from the sociology subfield of social network analysis. Its practitioners view society as composed of relational networks, "nodes" connected by interactive "ties" linking individuals and groups. These, in turn, can connect across "weak ties" between actors who participate in multiple groups and serve as "bridges" across them, weaving dense "clusters" into loose "networks of networks," such as the one that developed among the intellectuals addressed here.[50] Of course, the ties in question were grounded in a specific sort of social activity: diverse actors' pursuit of initially compatible political goals. In this sense, the network that linked Germany's engaged democrats represents not only a product but also the subject of their activities. The network model can tell us much about the form of interactions, especially among groups without firm boundaries, existing outside and between institutions. However, it tells us nothing about the content of these interactions.

To analyze the substance of intellectuals' discussions, I treat them as transactions on the field of political culture, as work done with and on the symbols and meanings by which Germans made sense of politics. That is, my approach blends intellectual-historical attention to how political concepts and languages develop and are deployed in context with cultural-historical concern for how they relate to – and operate as – broader patterns of collective representation.[51] From that perspective, asking what

---

[49] On the antagonism between "inner" and "outer" emigrations, see, e.g., Brockmann, *Literary Culture*, 90–114. For the classic analysis of distinct "social-moral milieus" that structured party politics, see M. Rainer Lepsius, "Parteiensystem und Sozialstruktur: Zum Problem der Demokratisierung der deutschen Gesellschaft," in *Wirtschaft, Geschichte und Wirtschaftsgeschichte*, ed. Wilhelm Abel (Stuttgart: Fischer, 1966), 371–93.

[50] See John Scott, introduction, Barry Wellman, "Structural Analysis: From Method and Metaphor to Theory and Substance," and Mark S. Granovetter, "The Strength of Weak Ties," in *Social Networks: Critical Concepts in Sociology*, ed. Scott (London: Routledge, 2002), I:1–21, 60–122.

[51] On the benefits and pitfalls, see, e.g., Müller, "European Intellectual History as Contemporary History," *Journal of Contemporary History* 46, no. 3 (2011): 574–90. On political-cultural history, see Wolfgang Hardtwig, introduction to *Politische Kulturgeschichte der*

enabled or provoked certain postwar Germans to rethink democracy in a participatory vein raises the question of how cultural change is possible at all. Current theories of culture tend to see its codes as structures of symbols that are not monolithic and tightly integrated but internally differentiated and destabilized in practice. One possibility for cultural change then appears in the transposability of ideas across the multiple contexts of meaning that coexist side-by-side.[52] In engaged democrats' case, their distinctive emphasis on participation emerged as they translated certain thought-figures from the narrowly "cultural" realm of classical German literature and philosophy into an explicitly political idiom.

This is thus a study in intellectuals and politics. Sociologist Pierre Bourdieu has defined intellectuals as those social actors who specialize in the "legitimate production, reproduction, and manipulation of symbolic goods," that is, in the interpretations and ascriptions of meaning by which legitimate authority of all sorts is claimed, challenged, and secured. He locates such operations on a relational "field" of "position-takings," where actors vie over both the stakes of the struggle and the authority to set its terms.[53] This analytic definition signals the relevance of intellectuals for political culture, and it suggests one key reason why studying them is worthwhile.[54] Of course, intellectuals have often been reprimanded for political activism by those who would preserve truth-seeking and truth-speaking from contamination by worldly interests and passions.[55] Such normative definitions of what qualifies as intellectual activity (and the ahistorical moral judgments they imply) help little in analyzing the

---

*Zwischenkriegszeit 1918–1939*, ed. Hardtwig (Göttingen: Vandenhoeck & Ruprecht, 2005), 7–22.

[52] For a lucid theoretical and empirical treatment building on Pierre Bourdieu, Anthony Giddens, Clifford Geertz, and Marshall Sahlins, see William H. Sewell, Jr., *Logics of History: Social Theory and Social Transformation* (Chicago: University of Chicago Press, 2005), esp. chaps. 4, 5, 8.

[53] Pierre Bourdieu, "Le marché des biens symboliques," *L'Année sociologique* 22 (1971): quote 118, incompletely rendered in Bourdieu, "The Market of Symbolic Goods," in *The Field of Cultural Production: Essays on Art and Literature*, ed. Randal Johnson (New York: Columbia University Press, 1993), 137. See also Bourdieu, "Intellectual Field and Creative Project," *Social Science Information* 8, no. 2 (1969): 89–119.

[54] For his later, more normative approach, see Bourdieu, "The Corporatism of the Universal: The Role of Intellectuals in the Modern World," *Telos* 81 (1989): 99–110. Generally, see David Swartz, *Culture and Power: The Sociology of Pierre Bourdieu* (Chicago: University of Chicago Press, 1997), esp. chaps. 9, 10.

[55] Reasonable, distanced, liberal political interventions, by contrast, define intellectual responsibility from this perspective. Classically, see Julien Benda, *The Treason of the Intellectuals*, trans. Richard Aldington (New York: Morrow, 1928). In the vein of Benda's 1927 polemic (but not his own later activist turn), see, e.g., Tony Judt, *Past Imperfect: French Intellectuals, 1944–1956* (Berkeley: University of California Press, 1992) and Mark Lilla, *The Reckless Mind: Intellectuals in Politics* (New York: New York Review of Books, 2001).

figures treated here. In their formative moment, the "zero hour," German intellectuals from a wide range of ideological backgrounds felt compelled to political engagement by both reasoned reflection and ethical commitment.[56] It seemed to them that the present was pregnant with possibility and nothing less than humanity's future was at stake.

The book that follows proceeds in three parts. The opening chapters lay its groundwork by uncovering the conceptual, rhetorical, and social interconnections among Germany's engaged democrats. Chapter 1 reconstructs the social network among them, situating its elements in the landscape of German and Allied groups planning for reconstruction. Occupiers and Germans alike considered rebuilding a public sphere crucial to democratization; this process was shaped by Allied policies but driven by trusted locals. Within this framework, Germany's engaged democrats established journals of cultural and political commentary and other bases of operations. Chapter 2 focuses on their participatory understanding of democracy. Conceptually, participation worked to reconcile of "freedom" and "order," a polarity they mapped onto the emergent Cold War. Practically, participation was the key to the self-transformation of the German masses into active citizens. This sense of democracy informed a range of concrete proposals that cohered into a loose agenda with broad appeal. In Chapter 3, I interrogate their tight intertwining of political with cultural renewal, relating this to the familiar figure of the "unpolitical German." In their distinctive relationship to the German high-cultural canon, engaged democrats reframed conventional intellectual investments to unconventional political ends.

Paradoxically, their commitment – however equivocal – to such traditions also carried elitist and nationalist residues at odds with their programmatic convictions. Such internal inconsistencies, together with Cold War dynamics, shaped their efforts to put theory into practice. Chapter 4 explores their modes of political activity – new parties, small discussion circles, broad-based initiatives, and their journalism itself – as attempts to recast conventional relationships among intellectuals, political elites, and the citizenry as a whole. As the deepening East–West divide overshadowed all German initiatives, however, such openings gave way to more traditional, elitist modes of intellectual politics. The following chapter

---

[56] Here, I invoke Max Weber's 1919 framing of the problem, which hinged on the disjuncture between the impassioned pursuit of principles and the measured consideration of consequences in politics. He endorsed a detached sense of proportion to mediate between an "ethics of conviction" and "ethics of responsibility." Max Weber, "The Profession and Vocation of Politics," in *Political Writings*, ed. Peter Lassman and Roland Speirs (Cambridge: Cambridge University Press, 1994), 352–69.

considers engaged democrats' affinities for cultural nationalism by addressing their cultural-political organizations and writers' congresses. Grounded in popular but vague appeals to the national cultural heritage, these organizations depended on intra-German alliances that became difficult to maintain in the face of polarization. In all spheres of their activity, the Cold War's mounting institutional and ideological pressures constrained the scope of practical possibilities.

The remaining three chapters trace engaged democrats' trajectories after the fracturing of their network and the foreclosure of their hopes by the foundation of two separate Germanys. This compelled a decision for one or the other state, and Chapters 6 and 7 explore the grounds for such reconciliations as well as for the disillusionment and dissent that followed. During the 1950s, engaged democrats in the GDR voiced an increasingly public critique of state-socialist dictatorship, belatedly articulating the anti-Stalinism entailed by their vision from the outset. After 1956, however, such dissent was crushed, and oppositional voices again moved underground. Meanwhile, engaged democrats in the FRG saw their demands for postwar renewal effaced by what they called the "restoration" of party-political structures, economic relations, and received horizons of political and social imagination. In the 1950s, these intellectuals helped sow seeds of protest that would reshape both Germanys in the decades to come. While their links to western activists of the 1960s are more direct, eastern activists of the 1980s also saw themselves in a dissident tradition stretching back to the 1950s. The concluding chapter demonstrates these connections for Germany and situates them as one eddy in an alternative political undercurrent that surfaced periodically within both European blocs. Common to immediate postwar reformers, 1950s dissenters, and the global eruptions of protest around 1968 and 1989 was a demand for greater participation than the two-sided Cold War order allowed. In the German case, this politics had one of its sources in the engaged democrats of the immediate postwar period.

# 1 Germans, occupiers, and the democratization project

As Nazism's total war drew to a close and Hitler's empire crumbled, destruction, chaos, and a flood of hopes and fears were loosed in Germany. The conflict left behind a "collapsed society" of dislocation, privation, and contrasting movement and stasis.[1] Especially in the ruined urban centers, basic necessities were hard to come by, and infrastructures of communication and supply were all but demolished. What was more, the shock and stigma of extreme violence cast a deep shadow over Germans' mental and emotional lives. Before them lay landscapes of rubble filled with bombing and combat casualties, refugees, foreign workers, other displaced people, and memories of the dead and missing. These places had earlier been emptied of Jewish co-inhabitants and others deemed undesirable; these now returned, unwelcome, in reports and images from concentration camps and killing centers and as Jewish refugees from the East. Such were the fruits of Nazism's "national revolution," made not only in Germans' name but also with their avid participation. A diffuse consciousness of the violence they had perpetrated mingled with acute awareness of the violence they had suffered.[2] And amid the debris, a diverse collection of actors confronted the question of what to do with Germany after the ravages it had wrought on Europe and on itself.

The dominant voices in this debate were those of the Grand Alliance, whose forces had defeated and liberated Germany and now exercised supreme authority. Each was influenced by views about Germany that

---

[1] Christoph Kleßmann, *Die doppelte Staatsgründung: Deutsche Geschichte 1945–1955*, 5th edn. (Göttingen: Vandenhoek & Ruprecht, 1991), 37–65.

[2] Michael Geyer, "The Stigma of Violence, Nationalism, and War in Twentieth-Century Germany," *German Studies Review* 15 (1992): 75–110; Richard Bessel, "The War to End All Wars: The Shock of Violence in 1945 and its Aftermath in Germany," in *No Man's Land of Violence: Extreme Wars in the 20th Century*, ed. Alf Lüdtke and Bernd Weisbrod (Göttingen: Wallstein, 2006), 69–99; Atina Grossmann, *Jews, Germans, and Allies: Close Encounters in Occupied Germany* (Princeton, N.J.: Princeton University Press, 2007). On "stigma," see A. Dirk Moses, *German Intellectuals and the Nazi Past* (Cambridge: Cambridge University Press, 2007), 24–31.

had been aired at home. If discussions in the USA varied widely, as calls for conciliation confronted those for a "hard" peace, British discussions were more consistently anti-German, fed by a longer-standing sense of rivalry and threat. Soviet images of Germans were most unforgiving, shaped by the brutality of their wartime experience, while French hostility was more ambiguous, given their complex relations of antagonism, defeat, occupation, and collaboration.[3] In all quarters, however, views of Germans as ultimately reformable – despite flaws of national character or national history – won out. These formed one basis for Allied policy, as proclaimed at the Potsdam Conference outside Berlin in August 1945. There, the "Big Three" statesmen – Joseph Stalin for the USSR, the USA's Harry Truman (after Franklin Delano Roosevelt's untimely death), and Britain's Winston Churchill (replaced midway by Clement Attlee, after Labour's electoral victory) – negotiated for two weeks. The resulting agreement, by which France's Provisional Government under Charles de Gaulle would also abide, stipulated general principles for the treatment of defeated Germany.[4]

Of these "three Ds" – demilitarization, denazification, and decartelization – the first two were paramount. All Wehrmacht and National Socialist German Workers' Party (NSDAP) institutions would be dismantled, leaders arrested, and personnel barred from positions of responsibility. Moreover, the doctrines and dispositions that had abetted their rise would be rooted out, so as "permanently to prevent the revival of German militarism and Nazism." On this ground, Germans could hope for the "eventual reconstruction of German political life on a democratic basis." Finally, the third principle suggested that "excessive concentration of economic power" in industrial cartels and trusts had also enabled aggression. On all fronts, the solution was "decentralization." For the economy, this was left unspecified, but in politics, it entailed rebuilding political parties and representative assemblies from the local level up. Although no central government was initially foreseen, the allies agreed to govern their zones uniformly and treat Germany as "a single economic unit" via five German-run administrations, or proto-ministries.[5]

---

[3] Michaela Hoenicke Moore, *Know Your Enemy: The American Debate on Nazism, 1933–1945* (Cambridge: Cambridge University Press, 2010); Jörg Später, *Vansittart: Britische Debatten über Deutsche und Nazis 1902–1945* (Göttingen: Wallstein, 2003); Silke Satjukow, *Besatzer: "Die Russen" in Deutschland 1945–1994* (Göttingen: Vandenhoeck & Ruprecht, 2008), 35–41; Dietmar Hüser, *Frankreichs "doppelte Deutschlandpolitik": Dynamik aus der Defensive 1944–1950* (Berlin: Duncker & Humblot, 1996), 48–64.

[4] Wolfgang Benz, *Potsdam 1945: Besatzungsherrschaft und Neuaufbau im Vier-Zonen-Deutschland*, 4th edn. (Munich: Deutscher Taschenbuch Verlag, 2005), 81–119.

[5] "Protocol of the Berlin (Potsdam) Conference, August 1, 1945," in *Documents on Germany, 1944–1959* (Washington, D.C.: U.S. Government Printing Office, 1959), 26–9.

The Potsdam Communiqué thus expressed a general understanding of the roots of Nazism and a "minimal consensus" about what was to be done. But several of the most fundamental and divisive provisions, such as those for Germany's unity and its democratization, were left vague, tabled for future negotiations.[6] Still, though all-German administrations never materialized, organs of four-power rule were established: an Allied Control Council, a Berlin Kommandatura, and a Council of Foreign Ministers to work out the details of a peace treaty. At the time, it seemed reasonable to conclude that the Potsdam consensus would underwrite whatever became of Germany.

These basic goals were shared by the allies' German interlocutors. Indeed, only those who embraced the consensus were seen as legitimate partners. Most prominently, these were the non-Nazi political parties and Christian churches, but Germany's engaged democrats also coalesced at this moment, outside established institutions. Some had been in exile, in hiding, or imprisoned; many had simply waited out the regime. Local groupings formed and came into contact with one another. While the logistics of coming together were laborious, this was a labor of conviction and commitment. Drawn together by antifascist experiences and democratic expectations, they formed a loosely integrated yet far-ranging social network, one that transcended old political camps and new occupation zones, as well as tensions between returning exiles, or "re-émigrés," and those who had remained in Nazi Germany, or "inner émigrés." Their disposition toward the occupying powers was determined by a basic agreement on the requisites of democratic renewal: eliminating Nazism and militarism, reconfiguring political and economic power, and preserving a united Germany. The Potsdam consensus thus enabled cooperation from both directions. Engaged democrats, however, sought to keep Germany a mediator, not a player, in East–West polarization and insisted – more strenuously than any Allies did – that Germans themselves be the agents of their own rehabilitation.

All sides concurred that reconstructing a space for public debate and dialogue was crucial to democratization. Gradually establishing an Allied-licensed, German-run press was central to occupiers' plans; for occupied Germans, whose political activities were sharply circumscribed, this opened attractive options. Under Allied auspices but with German initiative and involvement, the institutions of a public sphere were thus founded anew. An effervescence of intellectual activity ensued across

---

[6] Konrad H. Jarausch, *After Hitler: Recivilizing Germans, 1945–1995*, trans. Brandon Hunziker (Oxford: Oxford University Press, 2006), 16, 19–21, 130–1. Notably, the word "democratization" – like "denazification" – does not appear in the Potsdam protocol.

all zones, including in a raft of new "cultural-political" journals. These were so called because they self-consciously addressed both the cultural and the political realm as well as their interaction, in the politics of cultural affairs and, crucially, in the relevance of culture for politics.[7] Several of the most prominent such journals were established by engaged democrats, who also founded discussion clubs and civic organizations. These made up the institutional field on which their network emerged, a conglomeration of media- and assembly-based publics that sustained vibrant discussions on the pressing questions of postwar reconstruction. To grasp the on-the-ground interactions out of which these spaces arose, I take inspiration from the aforementioned approach of social network analysis. I use its terms qualitatively, to describe actors' mutual entanglements and inject micro-level concreteness into the abstractions of "the public sphere."[8] This chapter maps several relatively distinct groupings, locating the central figures on their common field, outlining the conditions of their activity, and reconstructing their networking. It highlights the connections among these intellectuals, which parallel the correspondences among the positions they took.

## A network of engaged democrats

The formative ties in engaged democrats' wider network were rooted in the "zero hour," in the wake of liberation. Obstacles to communication between zones or even localities – as well as to the centers of exile – were formidable. Still, old collaborations and friendships were re-established, while new ones were forged in pursuit of a new, post-fascist order. Central to these intellectuals' self-understanding were their prior stances of opposition and resistance to Nazism in the name of democracy. This antifascist background brought them together in 1945, around the urgent need to address a common past and possible future. In these aspects, they shared a diffuse generational identity. Most were born around 1900, a distinct minority of the generation of Great War-era youth: those whose

---

[7] See, centrally, Gerhard Hay, Hartmut Rambaldo, and Joachim W. Storck, eds. *"Als der Krieg zu Ende war": Literarisch-politische Publizistik 1945–1950* (Stuttgart: Klett, 1973); Ingrid Laurien, *Politisch-kulturelle Zeitschriften in den Westzonen 1945–1949: Ein Beitrag zur politischen Kultur der Nachkriegszeit* (Frankfurt a.M.: Lang, 1991); Jens Wehner, *Kulturpolitik und Volksfront: Ein Beitrag zur Geschichte der Sowjetischen Besatzungszone Deutschlands 1945–1949* (Frankfurt a.M.: Lang, 1992), 283–428; more recently, Clare Flanagan, *A Study of German Political-Cultural Periodicals from the Years of Allied Occupation, 1945–1949* (Lewiston: Mellen, 2000).

[8] On the historical study of public communication and its sites, see, e.g., Jörg Requate, "Öffentlichkeit und Medien als Gegenstände historischer Analyse," *Geschichte und Gesellschaft* 25, no. 1 (1999): 5–32.

careers were cut short or stagnated in the 1930s.[9] Yet they were joined by members of other cohorts too. The perception of a common formative context – despite a wide range of actual experiences and birth years – proved crucial.[10] It was the basis of the affinities that generated the nodes of their intellectual activity and the ties that linked them together.

For some, war's end meant quite literally a liberation. American troops entered Buchenwald concentration camp in April 1945, six years after journalist and political scientist Eugen Kogon (1903–1987). Orphaned and shaped by a conservative Catholic upbringing, he later moved to Vienna to study under Othmar Spann, whose anti-liberal, corporate state (*Ständestaat*) theory was embraced by Austria's clerical-authoritarian regimes in the 1930s. From pulpits in the right-Catholic press and the Christian unions, Kogon welcomed these developments. But the realities of "Austrofascism" and Nazism in power catalyzed a re-evaluation. Beginning in 1934, he coordinated support for anti-Nazi activities around Vienna, and he was arrested with Austria's annexation in 1938. Buchenwald completed his political transformation. There, he joined the camp resistance, where he befriended Werner Hilpert (1897–1957). In the last days of the war, they smuggled Kogon out to nearby Weimar, to contact both advancing Allied forces and camp officials; posing as a wrathful enemy officer, he sent a threatening letter to cow the latter into moderation.[11] When an intelligence team from the Psychological Warfare Division (PWD) arrived, Kogon's name stood atop their list of trustworthy inmates, and they appointed him head of a prisoners' committee to draft a report on life in the camp. He was subsequently commissioned to revise this "Buchenwald Report" into his book *Der SS-Staat*

---

[9] On those coevals who avidly served the regime, see Michael Wildt, *An Uncompromising Generation: The Nazi Leadership of the Reich Security Main Office*, trans. Tom Lampert (Madison: University of Wisconsin Press, 2009). Generally, see Ulrich Herbert, "Drei politische Generationen im 20. Jahrhundert," in *Generationalität und Lebensgeschichte im 20. Jahrhundert*, ed. Jürgen Reulecke (Munich: Oldenbourg, 2003), 95–114.

[10] Although their dates of birth cluster between 1899 and 1908, they span from 1868 (Alfred Weber) to 1923 (Wolfgang Harich). As the sociology of generations emphasizes, the binding force of shared historical experiences and the dispositional patterns that result are relatively independent of statistical birth cohorts. Classically, see Karl Mannheim, "The Problem of Generations," in *From Karl Mannheim*, 2nd edn., ed. Kurt H. Wolff (New Brunswick, N.J.: Transaction, 1993), 351–98.

[11] Gottfried Erb, "'Unsere Kraft reicht weiter als unser Unglück' (Ingeborg Bachmann): Eugen Kogon in der restaurativen Republik," in *Eigensinn und Bindung: Katholische deutsche Intellektuelle im 20. Jahrhundert*, ed. Hans-Rüdiger Schwab (Kevelaer: Butzon & Bercker, 2009), 363–5; Eugen Kogon, *Gesammelte Schriften*, vol. VI, *"Dieses merkwürdige, wichtige Leben": Begegnungen*, ed. Michael Kogon and Erb (Weinheim: Beltz Quadriga, 1997), 29–74; the letter is reprinted in Harry Stein, ed. *Konzentrationslager Buchenwald 1937–1945: Begleitband zur ständigen historischen Ausstellung* (Göttingen: Wallstein, 1999), 228.

(*The SS State*), published as an early contribution to "reeducation" efforts.[12]

While en route to PWD's central office in Paris, Kogon stopped over in bombed-out Frankfurt am Main, now the Western Allies' headquarters and abuzz with reconstruction.[13] There, he sought out Walter Dirks (1901–1991). Dirks had moved from the industrial Ruhr district to Hesse's largest city in the 1920s, where he studied at its new university, moved in leftist circles, and wrote antifascist commentaries in the press. After seven weeks in Nazi custody in 1933, he joined the *Frankfurter Zeitung (FZ)*, the great liberal daily that persisted, increasingly compromised, until it was shuttered in 1943. Dirks, like many of the staffers, was barred from further journalism but found other work for the war's final years. In 1945, he was called on to help with Frankfurt's post-Nazi transition in various capacities.[14] Kogon knew Dirks' 1920s journalism, and he and Hilpert had occasionally read the *FZ* in Buchenwald, too. Although they had occupied opposite poles of political Catholicism in the Weimar era, Kogon and Dirks found their views and plans fully compatible when they met in May 1945. The two soon began a life-long collaboration as Germany's pre-eminent left Catholics. Together with Hilpert and Dirks' associate Karl Heinrich Knappstein (1906–1989), they co-founded Frankfurt's Christian Democratic Union (CDU), at the short-lived left edge of what soon became the mainstream conservative party.[15] And together with another old friend of Dirks, Clemens Münster (1906–1998), they founded a cultural-political journal, the *Frankfurter Hefte (Frankfurt Journal)*.[16]

---

[12] Kogon, *Leben*, 74–7. Portions of the original report served as evidence at Nuremberg and other trials, and Kogon's book was widely distributed, across all four zones and Berlin. David A. Hackett, ed. *The Buchenwald Report* (Boulder, Colo.: Westview, 1995); Kogon, *Der SS-Staat: Das System der deutschen Konzentrationslager* (Frankfurt a.M.: Verlag der Frankfurter Hefte; Düsseldorf: Schwann; Munich: Alber, 1946).

[13] Rebecca Boehling, *A Question of Priorities: Democratic Reform and Economic Recovery in Postwar Germany: Frankfurt, Munich, and Stuttgart Under US Occupation, 1945–1949* (Providence, R.I.: Berghahn, 1996).

[14] Ulrich Bröckling, "Walter Dirks: Sozialist aus christlicher Verantwortung," in *Eigensinn und Bindung*, ed. Schwab, 323–30; Walter Dirks, *Der singende Stotterer: Autobiographische Texte* (Munich: Kösel, 1983), 11–24. On the *FZ*, see Günther Gillessen, *Auf verlorenem Posten: Die Frankfurter Zeitung im Dritten Reich* (Berlin: Siedler, 1986); Norbert Frei and Johannes Schmitz, *Journalismus im Dritten Reich* (Munich: Beck, 1989), 39–53.

[15] Kogon, *Leben*, 77–8; Dirks, *Stotterer*, 30–31; Joachim Rotberg, *Zwischen Linkskatholizismus und bürgerlicher Sammlung: Die Anfänge der CDU in Frankfurt am Main 1945–1946* (Frankfurt a.M.: Knecht, 1999). On the Weimar period, see Karl Prümm, *Walter Dirks und Eugen Kogon als katholische Publizisten der Weimarer Republik* (Heidelberg: Winter, 1984).

[16] The journal appeared monthly from April 1946 under American license, with a circulation of 50,000. Unusually, this rose amid the mid-1948 currency reform to 60,000

Their local network node had ties to one emerging in Heidelberg. In contrast to Frankfurt, this Badenese town cultivated a pre-industrial air; home to Germany's oldest university, it emerged nearly unscathed from the war. Dolf Sternberger (1907–1989), a native of Hesse, bridged the two locales. In the 1920s, he studied at Heidelberg with economist-turned-sociologist Alfred Weber (1868–1958) and psychologist-turned-philosopher Karl Jaspers (1883–1969).[17] Weber was a freethinking, political scholar who helped establish the left-liberal German Democratic Party (DDP) during the revolution of 1918 and endorsed – like his brother, Max Weber – an elitist "leadership democracy." He founded Heidelberg's Institute for Social and State Sciences (called InSoSta), where his speculative "cultural sociology" remained a one-man enterprise. At the Philosophy Seminar, Jaspers' new existentialism attracted droves of talented young students, including Hannah Arendt (1906–1975). There, she and Sternberger began a lasting friendship and parallel intellectual journeys from philosophy to political theory. As the university nazified, Jaspers and Weber took refuge in the ongoing weekly salons held by Max's widow Marianne Weber (1870–1954), a social scientist and women's movement leader. Her colleague Else Jaffé-von Richthofen (1874–1973) – Marianne's close friend, Max's sometime lover, and Alfred's long-term partner – also participated. In their circle, academic "inner émigrés" gathered in passive opposition, preserving a space for intellectual life and steering clear of politics.[18] Meanwhile,

but fell to 40,000 by January 1949 and 25,000 by January 1950. Laurien, *Zeitschriften*, 307–8; verso of covers to *Frankfurter Hefte* 3, no. 7 (1948), 4, no. 1 (1949), 5, no. 1 (1950). See Prümm, "Entwürfe einer zweiten Republik: Zukunftsprogramme in den 'Frankfurter Heften' 1946–1949," in *Deutschland nach Hitler: Zukunftspläne im Exil und aus der Besatzungszeit 1939–1949*, ed. Thomas Koebner, Gert Sautermeister, and Sigrid Schneider (Opladen: Westdeutscher, 1987), 330–43; Hans-Gerd Ewald, *Die gescheiterte Republik: Idee und Programm einer "Zweiten Republik" in den Frankfurter Heften 1946–1950* (Frankfurt a.M.: Lang, 1988); Flanagan, *Political-Cultural Periodicals*, 183–238; Michel Grunewald, "'Christliche Sozialisten' in den ersten Nachkriegsjahren: Die Frankfurter Hefte," in *Le milieu intellectuel catholique en Allemagne, sa presse et ses réseaux / Das katholische Intellektuellenmilieu in Deutschland, seine Presse und seine Netzwerke (1871–1963)*, ed. Grunewald and Uwe Puschner (Bern: Lang, 2006), 459–81.

[17] Claudia Kinkela, *Die Rehabilitierung des Bürgerlichen im Werk Dolf Sternbergers* (Würzburg: Königshausen & Neumann, 2001) 19–26; Dolf Sternberger, "Erinnerung an die Zwanziger Jahre in Heidelberg," in *Schriften*, vol. VIII, *Gang zwischen Meistern* (Frankfurt a.M.: Insel, 1987), 20–5, 28–9.

[18] Eberhard Demm, *Ein Liberaler in Kaiserreich und Republik: Der politische Weg Alfred Webers bis 1920* (Boppard a.R.: Boldt, 1990), 256–306; Demm, *Von der Weimarer Republik zur Bundesrepublik: Der politische Weg Alfred Webers 1920–1958* (Düsseldorf: Droste, 1999), 168–200, 223–34; Reinhard Blomert, *Intellektuelle im Aufbruch: Karl Mannheim, Alfred Weber, Norbert Elias und die Heidelberger Sozialwissenschaft der Zwischenkriegszeit* (Munich: Hanser, 1999), 177–82; Hans Saner, *Karl Jaspers in Selbstzeugnissen und Bilddokumenten* (Reinbek b.H.: Rowohlt, 1970), 37–45; Guenther Roth, *Max Webers deutsch-englische*

Sternberger had completed his studies in Frankfurt (with a thesis on Jaspers' friend Martin Heidegger) just as Nazism rose to power. In a subtle but significant response to the new regime, Sternberger stopped using his given name, Adolf, in favor of the shortened form, Dolf. Professionally, he began an editorial career at the *FZ*, one that ended in 1943, as it had for Dirks, in an occupational ban.[19]

In the early 1930s, he also made the acquaintance of neurologist-turned-psychoanalyst Alexander Mitscherlich (1908–1982). At the time, Mitscherlich consorted with "conservative revolutionaries" Ernst Jünger and Ernst Niekisch, and after Sternberger refused to associate with the group around Niekisch's journal *Widerstand*, citing ideological differences, they fell out of contact.[20] The journal's title had announced "resistance" first to the Weimar Republic, then to Nazism, and amid the ensuing persecutions, Mitscherlich spent a brief interlude in Switzerland and a few months in Gestapo custody. (Niekisch spent eight years in Nazi jails.) Thereafter, Mitscherlich joined Heidelberg University's neurology clinic. By the war's last years, he had distanced himself from Jünger and Niekisch and befriended Jaspers and Sternberger.[21] With Weber, they moved in Heidelberg's "inner émigré" circles, hoping for Germany's defeat.

When Allied victory came, Heidelberg was a hotbed of activity and another hub of American–German interaction.[22] One of the US military's first actions was to close the university, but at the urging of Emil Henk (1893–1969) – a Social Democratic Party (SPD) leader and

---

*Familiengeschichte 1800–1950* (Tübingen: Mohr Siebeck, 2001), 608–18. On the university and Nazism, see Steven P. Remy, *The Heidelberg Myth: The Nazification and Denazification of a German University* (Cambridge, Mass.: Harvard University Press, 2002).

[19] Kinkela, *Rehabilitierung*, 27–43. Sternberger's self-renaming dates to the weeks around the murderous intra-NSDAP purge of June 30, 1934, called the "Night of Long Knives"; compare Sternberger to Alexander Mitscherlich, 23 June 1934 and 22 July 1934, Deutsches Literaturarchiv (Marbach a.N., hereafter DLA) A:Sternberger/ 89.10.2309/1–2.

[20] Martin Dehli, *Leben als Konflikt: Zur Biographie Alexander Mitscherlichs* (Göttingen: Wallstein, 2007), 51–67. Niekisch's "national Bolshevism" – naively whitewashed by Mitscherlich – was a pastiche of racial-nationalist, decisionist-statist, and quasi-Leninist motifs; Louis Dupeux, *"Nationalbolschewismus" in Deutschland 1919–1933: Kommunistische Strategie und konservative Dynamik*, trans. Richard Kirchhoff (Munich: Beck, 1985), 216–54, 317–47, 409–18.

[21] Dehli, *Leben*, 67–78, 87–9, 108–11; Mitscherlich to Sternberger, 18 January 1944, DLA A:Sternberger/ 89.10.5960/19. As Dehli has shown, Mitscherlich's resistance and persecution were less extensive and more ambiguous than his own later accounts suggested.

[22] Friederike Reutter, *Heidelberg 1945–1949: Zur politischen Geschichte einer Stadt in der Nachkriegszeit* (Heidelberg: Guderjahn, 1994); Jürgen C. Heß, Hartmut Lehmann, and Volker Sellin, eds. *Heidelberg 1945* (Stuttgart: Steiner, 1996); Birgit Pape, *Kultureller Neubeginn in Heidelberg und Mannheim 1945–1949* (Heidelberg: Winter, 2000).

Alfred Weber's former student – they also convened a group to plan its reconstruction. This "Committee of Thirteen" included Henk, Jaspers, Weber, Mitscherlich, and others from Marianne Weber's circle and soon formed the School's de facto leadership.[23] After consulting Jaspers and Weber, officials also appointed Henk, Mitscherlich, and Sternberger to postwar Germany's first civilian government, in a short-lived southwestern province.[24] On its dissolution, press officers approached Sternberger to found a newspaper; he declined, proposing a journal instead. What emerged was *Die Wandlung* (*The Transformation*), the first such publication in the western zones and a flagship of the US licensing program (Figure 1.1). As co-editors, Sternberger enlisted Jaspers and Weber, and as publisher, Lambert Schneider (1900–1970).[25] Werner Krauss (1900–1976), a Romance scholar and German Communist Party (KPD) member, joined as fourth editor. After narrowly escaping execution for his involvement with resisters around Arvid Harnack and Harro Schulze-Boysen – the so-called Red Orchestra – Krauss had spent the war's last years in prison. Returning to his professorship at Marburg University, he met American officials who facilitated his contact with Sternberger.[26]

In 1945, when Dirks wrote Sternberger on *Die Wandlung*'s publication, the former *FZ* colleagues re-established contact. Thereafter, their respective journals remained in dialogue, though a planned regular article exchange never materialized. Additionally, Dirks and Kogon assisted

---

[23] Remy, *Heidelberg Myth*, 118–21. Jaffé-von Richthofen was involved but not inducted onto the all-male committee. Henk was the sole non-faculty member.

[24] This body operated only until July, when the "Middle Rhine-Saar" region was transferred from American to French control; Ulrich Springorum, *Entstehung und Aufbau der Verwaltung in Rheinland-Pfalz nach dem Zweiten Weltkrieg (1945–1947)* (Berlin: Duncker & Humblot, 1982), 61–6, 88.

[25] The journal appeared more-or-less monthly from November 1945. Its circulation was 30–35,000 until mid 1948, then 14,000 until it closed at the end of 1949. Monika Waldmüller, *Die Wandlung: Eine Monatsschrift* (Marbach a.N.: Deutsche Schillergesellschaft, 1988), 18–39, 139–68; Volker R. Berghahn, *America and the Intellectual Cold Wars in Europe: Shepard Stone between Philanthropy, Academy, and Diplomacy* (Princeton, N.J.: Princeton University Press, 2001), 35. See also Kinkela, *Rehabilitierung*, 127–44; Danièle Talata, "Die Wandlung: Pour un renouveau de l'Allemagne, revue politique et littéraire 1945-1949," *Allemagne d'aujourd'hui* 164 (2003): 145–60. Mitscherlich was busy with his own realized (*Psyche*) and unrealized (*VOX*) journal plans; Dehli, *Leben*, 135–7, 187–99.

[26] Waldmüller, *Wandlung*, 35–6; Karlheinz Barck, "Werner Krauss im Widerstand und vor dem Reichskriegsgericht," in *Die Rote Kapelle im Widerstand gegen Nationalsozialismus*, ed. Hans Coppi, Jürgen Danyel, and Johannes Tuchel (Berlin: Hentrich, 1994), 242–53. "Red Orchestra" was the Nazi name for a clandestine network of Communist cells across wartime western Europe supplying information to the USSR. Although the German group was loose, politically eclectic, and operationally independent of Moscow, the Nazi-supplied association stuck during the Cold War.

Figure 1.1 The first American journal license is presented, for *Die Wandlung*, on 23 October 1945. From left: Shepard Stone, Alfred Weber, Dolf Sternberger, Lambert Schneider, John Stanley. (*Source*: Deutsches Literaturarchiv, J:Verlag Lambert Schneider; courtesy of heidelberg-images.com)

initiatives of two Heidelberg-based groups: the Aktionsgruppe Heidelberg zur Demokratie und zum freien Sozialismus (Heidelberg Action Group for Democracy and Free Socialism) and the Deutsche Wählergesellschaft (German Voters' Society). A moving spirit in both these groups, Karl Geiler (1878–1953), was a friend and colleague of Weber's on the Heidelberg law faculty. After the war, however, he was called away to Wiesbaden and installed as postwar Hesse's first Prime Minister. The government he led through 1946 included Hilpert as Geiler's deputy and Knappstein as acting Minister of Reconstruction and Political Cleansing (later: Liberation), responsible for denazification.[27]

---

[27] Dirks to Sternberger, 29 December 1945, Archiv der sozialen Demokratie (Bonn, hereafter AdsD), NL Dirks 6A; Dirks to Sternberger, 13 December 1948, DLA A:Sternberger/Wandlung/ 74.10504/4; Walter Mühlhausen, *Hessen 1945–1950: Zur politischen Geschichte eines Landes in der Besatzungszeit* (Frankfurt a.M.: Insel, 1985), 45–9, 319. On these organizations, see Chapter 4.

In other corners of Germany, similar networking processes unfolded. As American troops liberated Buchenwald, the Red Army took control of Luckau, in Brandenburg, some 300 miles to the east. During the Nazi era, this town's penitentiary held both regular and political prisoners, such as jurist Wolfgang Abendroth (1906–1985), an anti-Stalinist Marxist active in the resistance group "New Beginning." Arrested in 1937, he spent four years in Luckau, was pressed into military service, and escaped to fight with Greek partisans. Captured by the British, he attended a reeducation seminar for select POWs near London. On his release, he was drawn not to the British but to the Soviet zone, where he held posts as a judge and law professor.[28] Novelist and playwright Günther Weisenborn (1902–1969) arrived in Luckau in 1942, after Abendroth's departure. Although Weisenborn was party-unaffiliated, his 1920s works carried a socialist and pacifist charge (like those of Bertolt Brecht, with whom he collaborated), and they were banned in 1933. Under Nazism, he published pseudonymously and worked as a dramaturge, until – like Krauss – he and his wife Joy (née Margarete Schnabel, 1914–2004) were arrested for their activities in the Harnack/Schulze-Boysen network. After the Soviets seized Luckau, Weisenborn was elected to the inmates' committee that ran the prison. And at war's end, his liberators appointed him district mayor. He spent several months organizing reconstruction and removing Nazis before returning to Berlin in August.[29]

He found the Reich's former capital devastated from the final, desperate struggle against the Red Army. In an evocative poem, Weisenborn described his "homecoming" to the empty space where his house once stood. Yet he also recalled postwar Berlin as an idyll of energy and commotion, where Germans and occupiers mixed: "In this peculiarly exciting city, this Pompeii of the north, we lived full of hopes, critical and unyielding."[30] Within months, he had helped refound the venerable Hebbel Theater. He also ran into graphic artist Herbert Sandberg (1908–1991), an old acquaintance and KPD activist who had spent ten years imprisoned, seven in Buchenwald. Sandberg had won American support for a satirical political journal of caricature and commentary, and Weisenborn joined as co-licensee of *Ulenspiegel*, modeled on

---

[28] Andreas Diers, *Arbeiterbewegung, Demokratie, Staat: Wolfgang Abendroth, Leben und Werk 1906–1948* (Hamburg: VSA, 2006), 222–39, 316–452.

[29] Manfred Demmer, *Spurensuche: Der antifaschistische Schriftsteller Günther Weisenborn* (Leverkusen: Kulturvereinigung Leverkusen, 2004), 15–29; Günther Weisenborn, *Der gespaltene Horizont: Niederschriften eines Außenseiters* (Munich: Desch, 1964), 21–47; Coppi, Danyel, and Tuchel, eds. *Kapelle, passim*.

[30] Weisenborn, "Heimkehr nach Berlin," *Die Weltbühne* 1, no. 5 (1946): 145; Weisenborn, *Horizont*, 33–9, quote 37.

*Simplicissimus*, the famous Wilhelmine and Weimar-era gadfly.[31] Their editor-in-chief was radical poet Karl Schnog (1897–1964), a friend of Sandberg and Kogon from Buchenwald, where his mordant verses had helped sustain the resisters. First Wolfgang Weyrauch (1904–1980), then Richard Drews (1902–1971) completed the team. In their offices, they held regular open meetings, inviting the city's writers and artists to join in discussions of politics, culture, and the challenges of rebuilding.[32]

Such encounters were typical for Berlin. The city embodied Germany's two faces in 1945: from a war-ravaged landscape sprouted myriad cultural-political initiatives. These began under Soviet occupation in May and continued after the Western allies took possession of their sectors in July. Before triggering the Cold War, the city's converging and cross-cutting forces stimulated great vitality.[33] Wolfgang Leonhard (b. 1921) arrived even before the fighting had stopped. He was returning from the USSR, where he and his mother Susanne Leonhard (née Köhler, 1895–1984) – who co-founded the KPD but left it in 1925 – had fled the Gestapo ten years before. In Moscow, Susanne fell victim to the Great Purges, landing in a labor camp while her son was groomed by the party. When he left for Berlin with an advance contingent under KPD leader Walter Ulbricht, Wolfgang was an ambivalent missionary. His mother's fate, Stalin's terror, and the non-aggression pact with Nazi Germany had fostered doubts about the Soviet system – "political bellyaches," he called them. Still, that Communists would lead Germany's "antifascist-democratic" transition seemed self-evident to him, and he was charged with contacting reliable Germans to assist in that effort.[34]

---

[31] *Ulenspiegel* appeared semimonthly from December 1945. Its circulation increased from 50,000 to 130,000 by 1948; that year, it switched to a Soviet license and closed in 1950. See Cora Sol Goldstein, *Capturing the German Eye: American Visual Propaganda in Occupied Germany* (Chicago: University of Chicago Press, 2009), 110–25; Weisenborn, *Horizont*, 56–61, 70–2; Herbert Sandberg, *Spiegel eines Lebens: Erinnerungen, Aufsätze, Notizen und Anekdoten* (Berlin: Aufbau, 1988), 59–80. The journal's title referred to a Belgian adaptation of a north-German folk story, transposed to the Low Countries' independence struggle against Spain. Its hero, their namesake, "battle[d] for the oppressed against all the world's tyrants"; Weisenborn, "Fehlt da nicht ein E?" *Ulenspiegel* 1, no. 5 (1946): 2.

[32] Eugen Kogon, afterword to Karl Schnog, *Jedem das Seine: Satirische Gedichte* (Berlin: Ulenspiegel, 1947), 94–5; Weisenborn, *Horizont*, 57; Sandberg, *Spiegel*, 60–1.

[33] Wolfgang Schivelbusch, *In a Cold Crater: Cultural and Intellectual Life in Berlin, 1945–1948*, trans. Kelly Barry (Berkeley: University of California Press, 1998).

[34] Wolfgang Leonhard, *Die Revolution entläßt ihre Kinder* (Cologne: Kiepenheuer & Witsch, 1955); Susanne Leonhard, *Gestohlenes Leben: Schicksal einer politischen Emigrantin in der Sowjetunion* (Frankfurt a.M.: Europäische Verlagsanstalt, 1956). On how the brutality of Nazi and Soviet terror shaped the KPD, see Eric D. Weitz, *Creating German Communism, 1890–1990: From Popular Protests to Socialist State* (Princeton, N.J.: Princeton University Press, 1997), 280–310.

Among those he found was the even younger Wolfgang Harich (1923–1995). Growing up under Nazism, Harich credited formal schooling in classical German philosophy and clandestine study of Marxist classics with inoculating him against the regime. From a refined household, he rubbed elbows with the wartime remnants of Weimar Berlin's cosmopolitan artistic elite, such as actors Victor and Michiko de Kowa and writer Erich Kästner. Drafted in 1942, Harich saw combat on the eastern front and deserted in 1944. Through the de Kowas, he joined an underground anti-Nazi organization to which Kästner also had connections. Red Army officers had noticed Harich sabotaging defenses during the battle for Berlin, and when Leonhard tracked him down, it was agreed he should work in cultural organizations or the press.[35]

This is just the path he took. First, Harich was personal secretary to actor and director Paul Wegener, a family friend who now presided over the Chamber of Art Makers. Together, they ran the Chamber as a cultural hub-cum-denazification agency, in which the 22-year-old saw himself as the 70-year-old's "political mentor."[36] Among Harich's other acquaintances were critic Friedrich Luft (1911–1990) and writer Erik Reger (1893–1954), whose 1931 novel *Union of the Firm Hand* (republished 1946) had sounded a warning about German industrialists' plans to use Nazism to scuttle the republic. Reger emerged as the leading figure at Berlin's American-licensed newspaper, *Der Tagesspiegel* (*The Daily Mirror*), but Harich was unable to parlay his connections into a staff position.[37] At the French-licensed *Kurier*, he wrote on politics and theater, and scathing send-ups of the culture scene. Calling himself Hipponax (after a Greek parodist), Harich claimed to recover an ancient art for the benefit of modern German artists, who took themselves too

---

[35] Siegfried Prokop, *Ich bin zu früh geboren: Auf den Spuren Wolfgang Harichs* (Berlin: Dietz, 1997), 9–19, 29–33; Wolfgang Harich, "Lebenslauf," [August 1945], Stiftung Archiv der Akademie der Künste Berlin (hereafter AdK) Reger-Archiv 311; Sven Hanuschek, *Keiner blickt dir hinter das Gesicht: Das Leben Erich Kästners* (Munich: Hanser, 1999), 237; Leonhard, *Revolution*, 352–5. On Gruppe Ernst, led by the enigmatic Alexander Vogel – KPD operative, Soviet spy, and Gestapo informant – see Schivelbusch, *Cold Crater*, 43–4; Lothar Berthold et al., eds. *Widerstand in Berlin gegen das NS-Regime 1933 bis 1945: Ein biographisches Lexikon* (Berlin: Trafo, 2004–5), III:40, VIII:105, X:27–8.

[36] Schivelbusch, *Cold Crater*, 39–55; Prokop, *Geboren*, 33–6; Brewster S. Chamberlin, *Kultur auf Trümmern: Berliner Berichte der amerikanischen Information Control Section, Juli-Dezember 1945* (Stuttgart: Deutsche Verlags-Anstalt, 1979), 42.

[37] Harich to Erik Reger, 23 August 1945, 5 September 1945, Reger to Harich, 5 September 1945, 12 September 1945, AdK Reger-Archiv 311. Harich was associated with a group around publisher Heinz Ullstein that ultimately lost the *Tagesspiegel* license to a group around Reger; Schivelbusch, *Cold Crater*, 135–63; Marcus M. Payk, *Der Geist der Demokratie: Intellektuelle Orientierungsversuche im Feuilleton der frühen Bundesrepublik: Karl Korn und Peter de Mendelssohn* (Munich: Oldenbourg, 2008), 90–6.

seriously.[38] Soon, he impressed friends and enemies alike as the *enfant terriblement intelligent* on the Berlin scene.[39] His editors distanced themselves from his "intemperate advance[s]," gladly printing them nonetheless. In the estimation of Rudolf Pechel (1882–1961) – conservative editor of the *Deutsche Rundschau (German View)*, who tussled publicly with Harich – his adversary's virtuoso parodies bespoke "pathological traits": Harich was "pure intellect on two legs, a sort of homunculus" whose overdeveloped critical faculties far outstripped his civility and self-control.[40] Yet he was more than an immature polemicist. Rightly regarded as an incisive critic and commentator at the time, Harich became one of the early GDR's most important philosophers.

As Berlin's premiere intellectual site, Wegener's Chamber was soon effectively absorbed by the Kulturbund zur demokratischen Erneuerung Deutschlands (Cultural League for the Democratic Renewal of Germany). This Soviet-licensed organization appeared in early summer 1945, the outcome of both advance planning in Moscow and spontaneous on-the-ground developments in Berlin. It became a key node in the engaged democrats' network. Despite – and because of – its role in Communist plans, it was a pluralist endeavor in its early years, seeking to gather all democratically minded, non- and anti-Nazi intellectuals. KPD figures – such as Johannes R. Becher (1891–1958), Heinz Willmann, and Alexander Abusch – held key positions, but so did non-Communist writers, artists, professors, politicians, and clergy. Harich and Weisenborn were among its founders, as were theater critic Herbert Ihering (1888–1977) and satirist and actor Horst Lommer (1904–1969).[41]

The Kulturbund founded its own publishing house, called Aufbau (Construction), which launched postwar Germany's first cultural-political journal in September 1945. While this namesake, *Aufbau*, was edited by KPD functionary Klaus Gysi, its fluid circle of "regular contributors" included Ihering and Weisenborn alongside economic historian

---

[38] Hipponax [Harich], "Nach berühmten Mustern," *Der Kurier*, 9 February 1946.
[39] I borrow the moniker from Schivelbusch, *Cold Crater*, 176.
[40] Editorial note to Harich, "Die Flucht nach innen," *Der Kurier*, 21 December 1945; Rudolf Pechel, "Von Himmler zu Harich," *Deutsche Rundschau* 69, no. 6 (1946): 176. On Pechel, see Claudia Kemper, "Rudolf Pechels intellektuelle Grundposition als Widerstand 'mit dem Rücken zur Wand,'" in *Rückblickend in die Zukunft: Politische Öffentlichkeit und intellektuelle Positionen in Deutschland um 1950 und um 1930*, ed. Alexander Gallus and Axel Schildt (Göttingen: Wallstein, 2011), 164–80.
[41] Gerd Dietrich, "Kulturbund," in *Die Parteien und Organisationen der DDR: Ein Handbuch*, ed. Gerd-Rüdiger Stephan, et al. (Berlin: Dietz, 2002), 530–6. On exile in the Soviet Union, see Jean-Michel Palmier, *Weimar in Exile: The Antifascist Emigration in Europe and America*, trans. David Fernbach (London: Verso, 2006), 171–84. On the Berlin Kulturbund and similar organizations, see Chapter 5.

32   German Intellectuals and Democratic Renewal

Jürgen Kuczynski (1904–1997) and jurist Peter Alfons Steiniger (1904–1980); CDU politician Ferdinand Friedensburg; writers and scholars such as Victor Klemperer, Theodor Plievier, and Ernst Wiechert; anti-Nazi resisters from Arnold Bauer (1910–?) of the Harnack/Schulze-Boysen group to Ernst Niekisch; and various icons of the exile left, including Hungarian philosopher Georg (György) Lukács, playwright Bertolt Brecht, and novelists Heinrich Mann and Anna Seghers.[42] Other Soviet-licensed journals followed, yet none gained *Aufbau*'s prominence and all-zone readership. A companion weekly newspaper soon followed, targeting a broader audience and titled simply *Sonntag (Sunday)*. From July 1946, its first editor-in-chief was Günter Brandt (1894–1968), a liberal jurist who joined the SPD in 1945 and entered the Socialist Unity Party (SED) in 1946, when it arose from the forced merger of SPD with KPD in the Soviet zone.[43]

Another Berlin journal laid claim to longer-term traditions than Kulturbund organs could. In 1945, Hans Leonard (1902–1966) joined the KPD and took an administrative post in the Soviet sector. During the war, he had befriended his neighbor Maud von Ossietzky, widow of Carl von Ossietzky, last editor of *Die Weltbühne (The World Stage)* – the fiercely independent, fearlessly muckraking platform of Weimar Germany's intellectual left. Although Maud von Ossietzky received several offers to revive the journal, she turned to Leonard for assistance. The latter had started a business career in publishing (interning briefly with Ossietzky's predecessor, Siegfried Jacobsohn) but was forced to quit the industry under Nazism, due to his part-Jewish heritage. Together, they held a British license (Maud was a UK citizen), until legal claims to the title arrived from exiles abroad – from Jacobsohn's heirs and from Hermann Budzislawski (1901–1978), who had led the journal's successor in Prague and Paris. The Soviets proved less concerned with such formalities. Armed with a new license, the *Weltbühne* went into production, with Ossietzky's widow as figurehead and Leonard as editor-in-chief.[44] In the preceding

---

[42] *Aufbau* appeared monthly under Soviet license. Its circulation rose from 20,000 to 100–150,000 by early 1946 and fell, after currency reform, to 10–12,000. Siegfried Scheibe, *Aufbau, Berlin 1945–1958: Bibliographie einer Zeitschrift* (Berlin: Aufbau, 1978), 35–6, 39–40. On the journal, see Wehner, *Kulturpolitik*, 304–19, 463–538; Flanagan, *Political-Cultural Periodicals*, 27–74. On its publisher, see Carsten Wurm, *Der frühe Aufbau-Verlag 1945–1961: Konzepte und Kontroversen* (Wiesbaden: Harrassowitz, 1996).

[43] Ursula Heukenkamp, "Geistige Auseinandersetzung: Das Konzept der demokratischen Erneuerung der Kultur im Spiegel der Zeitschrift 'Sonntag' (1946–1948)," *Weimarer Beiträge* 36, no. 4 (1990): 552–61; Wehner, *Kulturpolitik*, 319–32.

[44] Ursula Madrasch-Groschopp, *Die Weltbühne: Porträt einer Zeitschrift* (Berlin: Der Morgen, 1983), 398–411; Schivelbusch, *Cold Crater*, 171–5; Fritz Klein, "Die Neugründung der Weltbühne in der Sowjetischen Besatzungszone," in *Le milieu intellectuel de gauche*

months, none other than Wolfgang Harich had attempted to wrest control from Leonard, clearly disdainful of the ex-salesman. He failed and joined the journal's regular contributors alongside other new ones such as Brandt, Drews, and Lommer, as well as Weimar-era associates such as Schnog and stage actress Pauline Nardi (Margarete Karsch, née Clavier, 1893–1965).[45]

Other engaged democrats who hailed from the Weimar left-intellectual scene were drawn to the new *Weltbühne* and Kulturbund. Among them were Erich Kästner (1899–1974) and Axel Eggebrecht (1899–1991), friends who took circuitous routes to common ground. Both grew up in Saxony and served in the Great War, from which Kästner the draftee emerged with a pro-republican loathing for militarism and authority, while Eggebrecht the volunteer first gravitated to the nationalist right. His experience in the 1920 paramilitary putsch attempt by Wolfgang Kapp, however, provoked a political conversion. Within the year, he joined the new KPD and moved to Berlin, writing for party papers and working at Willi Münzenberg's film concern, a front organization, as well as at Wieland Herzfelde's Malik publishers, home of the far-left avant-garde. This, too, ended in disillusionment, and Eggebrecht left the party in 1925. A chance café encounter with Kurt Tucholsky led him to the *Weltbühne*, in whose eclectic milieu he met Kästner. Both stayed in Germany after 1933. Like tens of thousands on the left, Eggebrecht was taken into short-term "protective custody" after the Reichstag fire and briefly re-imprisoned later. Kästner was arrested and interrogated, and his socially critical poetry and prose won him a prominent place on the Nazis' "black list" of forbidden literature. (An exception was made for his well-loved children's novel *Emil and the Detectives*.)[46] Both men

---

en Allemagne, sa presse et ses réseaux / Das linke Intellektuellenmilieu in Deutschland, seine Presse und seine Netzwerke (1890–1960), ed. Grunewald and Hans Manfred Bock (Bern: Lang, 2002), 559–68. Die Weltbühne appeared semimonthly from June 1946. Its circulation grew quickly from 81,000 to 100–150,000; after April 1948, it appeared weekly in 80–100,000 copies, dropping to 20–25,000 after currency reform. Hans Leonard, "Auflagenentwicklung der Zeitschrift 'Die Weltbühne,'" 25 April 1951, Landesarchiv Berlin (herafter LAB) NL Madrasch-Groschopp, E Rep. 200–63, 55b. On the postwar journal, see also Wehner, Kulturpolitik, 376–405. On its predecessor, see István Deák, Weimar Germany's Left-Wing Intellectuals: A Political History of the Weltbühne and its Circle (Berkeley: University of California Press, 1968).

[45] Wehner, Kulturpolitik, 387; Madrasch-Groschopp, Weltbühne, 172, 195–6, 415. On Harich and Die Weltbühne, see Chapter 4.

[46] Thomas Berndt, Nur das Wort kann die Welt verändern: Der politische Journalist Axel Eggebrecht (Herzberg: Bautz, 1998), 33–75; Gallus, Heimat "Weltbühne": Eine Intellektuellengeschichte im 20. Jahrhundert (Göttingen: Wallstein, 2012), 157–74; Axel Eggebrecht, Der halbe Weg: Zwischenbilanz einer Epoche (Reinbek b.H.: Rowohlt, 1975), 247–8, 293–4; Hanuschek, Keiner blickt, 47–304; Klaus Doderer, Erich Kästner: Lebensphasen, politisches Engagement, literarisches Wirken (Weinheim: Juventa, 2002).

were forbidden to publish but eventually authored screenplays under Nazism.

After years of day jobs and night lives on Berlin's cultural scene, they each left the beleaguered capital by separate paths in early 1945. Kästner and his partner Luiselotte Enderle (1908–1991) headed into the Austrian Alps with a film crew pretending to shoot on location. Shortly after war's end, Kästner's old friend Peter de Mendelssohn (1908–1982), now an American information officer, tracked them down in their mountain hideaway. He enlisted Kästner for a newspaper launch in nearby Munich, and the couple settled in Bavaria's capital. Kästner marveled at the ruined city's infectious energy – "the *influenza vitalis* is going around... Vitality is contagious" – to which he contributed as feuilleton editor for the flagship US military government organ, *Die Neue Zeitung* (*The New Newspaper*), with Enderle assisting him. He also helped establish a youth magazine, *Pinguin*, and a cabaret, Die Schaubude (The Show Booth), which garnered rave reviews from the *Frankfurter Hefte*, among others. Kästner's section of the *Neue Zeitung* became a key venue for postwar intellectuals, including Bauer, Eggebrecht, Jaspers, Kogon, Mitscherlich, Sternberger, and Weisenborn.[47]

Eggebrecht fled Berlin in the opposite direction, to a lakeside retreat near the Danish border. Like Kästner, his name was on a list of anti-Nazi contacts, and British officers found him in June 1945. Eggebrecht declined their offer of a regional newspaper, in part because he was drawn to a new medium, radio: "It had been the last voice of the destroyed Hitler state; it must be the first voice of liberated Germans." So he relocated to Hamburg, where a large station had been seized by the British. At Radio Hamburg – soon Nordwestdeutscher Rundfunk (NWDR, Northwest German Radio) – he rose to prominence and played a central role in the station's development to a major venue and catalyst of intra-German dialogue. To the same end, he founded the *Nordwestdeutsche Hefte* (*Northwest German Journal*), which printed a selection of NWDR programs.[48]

---

[47] Hanuschek, *Keiner blickt*, 305–45; Erich Kästner, *Notabene 45: Ein Tagebuch* (Zurich: Atrium, 1961), 200; Hermann Wodak, "Die Schaubude," *Frankfurter Hefte* 1, no. 4 (1946): 88–9. Mendelssohn spent his exile in London and took British citizenship but moved from Anglo-American PWD to US Information Control in 1945; Payk, *Geist*, 81–6. On *Die Neue Zeitung*, see Jessica C. E. Gienow-Hecht, *Transmission Impossible: American Journalism as Cultural Diplomacy in Postwar Germany, 1945–1955* (Baton Rouge: Louisiana State University Press, 1999).

[48] Berndt, *Nur das Wort*, 77–97; Gallus, "*Weltbühne*," 174–83; Eggebrecht, *Weg*, quote 319; Hans-Ulrich Wagner, "Das Ringen um einen neuen Rundfunk: Der NWDR unter der Kontrolle der britischen Besatzungsmacht," in *Die Geschichte des Nordwestdeutschen Rundfunks*, ed. Peter von Rüden and Wagner (Hamburg: Hoffmann & Campe, 2005), 13–84. The *Nordwestdeutsche Hefte*, co-edited by Peter von Zahn (1913–2001), appeared monthly under British license in *c*. 100,000 copies. Anticipating a market shift he would later lead, their publisher Axel Springer transformed this cultural-political journal into

Like Dirks, he found the first issue of *Die Wandlung* inspiring, and he took up contact with Sternberger to trade materials and discuss common concerns.[49] Another of Eggebrecht's Hamburg associates was publisher Ernst Rowohlt (1887–1960), a friend from 1930s Berlin. Rowohlt was forced out of the industry in 1938, despite attempts to placate the Nazi rulers that included joining the NSDAP itself. He re-established his firm after 1945, acquiring licenses for all four zones and maintaining contact with an expanding network of friends and authors new and old, including Kästner and Weisenborn.[50] From their postwar locations, Eggebrecht, Rowohlt, and Kästner also helped connect the Berlin Kulturbund to similar organizations in the western zones.

Returned exiles were rare in the first years after 1945. This was the time of "first letters," when émigrés re-established contact with friends and acquaintances back home. Mixed emotions surfaced on both sides, encompassing hesitancy, enthusiasm, curiosity, solidarity, and not infrequently mistrust.[51] Many who left Germany had no intention of returning, and those who tried confronted a series of hurdles: a formal invitation by a German authority was required but issued at the relevant military government's discretion (in which the Americans, British, and French were less liberal than the Soviets). Under these conditions, only a fraction of the 500,000 German-speaking refugees returned. While 50–60 percent of 10,000 "political" (non-Jewish) émigrés – Communists, Social Democrats, unionists, and others mostly on the left – eventually reemigrated, no more than 25 percent of 2000 journalists and 12 percent of a similar number of academics did so. For the vast numbers of Jewish refugees who fled persecution also and above all on "racial" grounds, the rate of return was 4–5 percent.[52]

Although small in numbers, returnees made outsize contributions to reconstruction and renewal. In the engaged democrats' network, re-émigrés such as jurist and literary critic Hans Mayer (1907–2001) became crucial cross-cluster bridges. In the late Weimar Republic, Mayer

---

the illustrated magazine *Kristall* during 1948. Laurien, *Zeitschriften*, 310; Gudrun Kruip, *Das "Welt"-"Bild" des Axel Springer Verlags: Journalismus zwischen westlichen Werten und deutschen Denktraditionen* (Munich: Oldenbourg, 1999), 79–80.

[49] Only one side of their correspondence is preserved: Eggebrecht to Sternberger, 26 January 1946, 31 July 1946, DLA A:Sternberger/ Wandlung/ 74.10515/1–2.

[50] Eggebrecht, *Weg*, 296; David Oels, *Rowohlts Rotationsroutine: Markterfolge und Modernisierung eines Buchverlags vom Ende der Weimarer Republik bis in die fünfziger Jahre* (Essen: Klartext, 2013), 97–111, 164–94; Weisenborn, *Horizont*, 169–71.

[51] David Kettler, "'Erste Briefe' nach Deutschland: Zwischen Exil und Rückkehr," *Zeitschrift für Ideengeschichte* 2, no. 2 (2008): 80–108.

[52] Claus-Dieter Krohn, "Remigrants and Reconstruction," in *The United States and Germany in the Era of the Cold War, 1945–1990: A Handbook*, ed. Detlef Junker (Cambridge: Cambridge University Press, 2004), I:528–9; Marita Krauss, *Heimkehr in ein fremdes Land: Geschichte der Remigration nach 1945* (Munich: Beck, 2001), 9–10.

belonged to two of the small leftist formations – the Socialist Workers' Party (SAPD) and Communist Party-Opposition – struggling to forge a "united front" against fascism. Like many, he was doubly threatened as a Marxist and a Jew, and he emigrated to France in 1933. After brief affiliations with the exiled Institute for Social Research (the "Frankfurt School" around Max Horkheimer) and the Geneva Institute for International Studies (where his law mentor Hans Kelsen had landed), Mayer settled in Zurich. In its vibrant exile scene, he came to know actor and dancer Jo Mihaly (Elfriede Steckel, née Kuhr, 1902–1989), a KPD member who fled Germany with her Jewish husband, director Leonard Steckel, in 1933. Another associate was writer Stephan Hermlin (Rudolf Leder, 1915–1997), whose Communist activism got him expelled from high school in 1932 and whose Jewish heritage sent him into exile in 1936, through Palestine and Paris to Switzerland.[53]

By fall 1945, all three had relocated to Frankfurt with the American military's help. Mayer worked first at the German-American News Service (DANA) and then at Radio Frankfurt, where he was director of politics and news and Hermlin was editor for literature. Together, they produced a series on contemporary authors, and Mayer hosted a series of political reflections by Sternberger. At a radio directors' conference convened by American and British authorities near Hamburg, Mayer got on famously with Eggebrecht, whose journalism he remembered from the 1920s. Before long, he was contributing to Kästner's *Neue Zeitung* as well.[54] He also developed ties to the *Frankfurter Hefte*. In the local Kulturbund-style organization, Mayer met its co-founder Dirks. And with Kogon, he served as an officer of the Union of Persecutees of the Nazi Regime (Vereinigung der Verfolgten des Naziregimes, VVN), a cross-zonal organization for Nazism's political and "racial" targets.

[53] *Literarische Welt: Dokumente zum Leben und Werk von Hans Mayer* (Cologne: Historisches Archiv der Stadt Köln, 1985), 45–55; Ingrid Langer, Ulrike Ley, and Susanne Sander, *Alibi-Frauen? Hessische Politikerinnen*, Vol. I, *In den Vorparlamenten 1946 bis 1950* (Frankfurt a.M.: Helmer, 1994), 180–95; Karl Corino, *Aussen Marmor, innen Gips: Die Legenden des Stephan Hermlin* (Düsseldorf: ECON, 1996), 60–156. As Corino shows, accounts of Hermlin's imprisonment in Sachsenhausen and activities in the Spanish Civil War and French Résistance are rooted in his own untruths and embellishments. On exile in Switzerland, see Palmier, *Weimar*, 153–61.

[54] *Literarische Welt*, 55–60; Wagner, *"Der gute Wille, etwas Neues zu schaffen": Das Hörspielprogramm in Deutschland von 1945 bis 1949* (Potsdam: Verlag für Berlin-Brandenburg, 1997), 109, 128; Hans Mayer, *Ein Deutscher auf Widerruf: Erinnerungen* (Frankfurt a.M.: Suhrkamp, 1982), I:367–73, 398–9; Sternberger, *Dreizehn politische Radio-Reden 1946* (Heidelberg: Schneider, 1947); Stephan Hermlin and Hans Mayer, *Ansichten über einige neue Schriftsteller und Bücher* (Wiesbaden: Limes, 1947). At the radio conference, Mayer was also approached to help found a news magazine; had he accepted, he would have joined Rudolf Augstein at Hamburg's *Diese Woche*, predecessor of *Der Spiegel*.

Germans, occupiers, and the democratization project 37

There, a bond of "solidarity" developed between the two "comrades."[55] Their collaboration expanded, as the *Frankfurter Hefte* published Mayer's essays and Kogon and Mayer worked together (also with Sternberger) on radio programs.[56] By then, Mayer had transferred to the faculty at Frankfurt's Academy of Labor, an adult education college, before taking up a professorship at Leipzig University in fall 1948. (The latter was facilitated by his new friend Krauss, who had left Marburg – and *Die Wandlung* – for Leipzig the previous fall.) Mayer's relationship with the *Frankfurter Hefte* did not break off immediately, however. They still published his final report on a series of writers' congresses that attempted – optimistically but fruitlessly – to generate a forum for communication across the deepening East–West divide.[57]

Comparatively, transatlantic re-émigrés – from the USA, which absorbed one quarter of German-speaking refugees, or from Latin America – encountered more logistical difficulties, if they were not in the service of an occupying power. Such a case was the journalist and literary critic Alfred Kantorowicz (1899–1979). War's end found him and his wife Frieda (née Ebenhoech, 1905–1969) in New York City, where he directed foreign news at Columbia Broadcasting (CBS). When the first *Nordwestdeutsche Hefte* crossed his desk in June 1946, he learned that his old friend Eggebrecht had survived Nazism and was already at work. In an excited letter, Kantorowicz voiced hopes of homecoming: "For all our material well-being, we think of returning to Germany again. We are too bound up with developments over there." Eggebrecht reciprocated: "Excellent, we need you; for we are far too few."[58] During the waning Weimar era, they had all lived side by side in Berlin's "Artists' Colony" – called the "Red Block" – a housing development built by the actors' and writers' guilds and a stronghold of the cultural left. While Eggebrecht remained politically independent, Kantorowicz

---

[55] Mayer, *Ein Deutscher*, I:376–7; Boris Spernol, "Der Rote Winkel als 'Banner des Friedens': Friedenspolitik der VVN bis 1950," in *Friedensinitiativen in der Frühzeit des Kalten Krieges 1945–1955*, ed. Detlef Bald and Wolfram Wette (Essen: Klartext, 2010), 133–53; Kogon, *Leben*, 86; Mayer to Kogon, 21 December 1948, AdsD NL Kogon, EK Privat 1949 H-M, IIIc.
[56] Mayer, *Ein Deutscher*, I:355–9, 400–2; "Autorität, Freiheit und Furcht" (radio broadcast, Hessischer Rundfunk, 12 July 1948), Hörfunkarchiv des Hessischen Rundfunks (Frankfurt a.M.).
[57] *Literarische Welt*, 56, 60; Christine Wittrock, *Die Akademie der Arbeit in Frankfurt am Main und ihre Absolventen* (Frankfurt a.M.: dipa, 1991), 197; Waldmüller, *Wandlung*, 91–4; Mayer, *Ein Deutscher*, I:337, 373–5, 415. The writer Marie Luise Kaschnitz (1901–1974) succeeded Krauss at *Die Wandlung*.
[58] Alfred Kantorowicz to Eggebrecht, 4 June 1946, Eggebrecht to Kantorowicz, 9 August 1946, Staats- und Universitätsbibliothek Hamburg (hereafter SUBH) NL Kantorowicz NK: BI: E5–6; Kantorowicz, *Deutsches Tagebuch* (Munich: Kindler, 1959–61), I:126–9.

joined the KPD in 1931 and soon led the colony's party cell, which included Frieda, art historian Max Schroeder (1900–1958) and journalist Arthur Koestler (1905–1983). Becher, Mihaly, Steckel, Susanne and Wolfgang Leonhard, and Budzislawski (then of the SPD) lived there too, as did Kantorowicz's friends, poet Peter Huchel (1903–1981), philosopher Ernst Bloch (1885–1977), and Polish architect Karola Piotrkowska (later Karola Bloch, 1905–1994). Together, the unaffiliated Marxist Bloch and his KPD counterpart Lukács served as the colony's "spiritual advisors." Through these connections, Kantorowicz was also drawn to Ossietzky and the *Weltbühne* circle, as it battled authoritarianism, sectarianism, and the upsurging Nazi threat. Their combative journalism paralleled other actions by the colony's residents, from flyer campaigns to street theater to a "self-defense" militia that clashed ever more violently with Nazi paramilitaries, an activism they later recalled with pride.[59]

As the Nazis took power, Eggebrecht stayed behind and Kantorowicz and Schroeder fled to Paris. There, they met fellow exile Maximilian Scheer (Walter Schlieper, 1896–1978) and poet and playwright Rudolf Leonhard (1889–1953), who had emerged from the Great War a pacifist and revolutionary. Leonhard – Susanne's ex-husband and Wolfgang's father – had lived in Paris for years but wrote frequently for the Weimar *Weltbühne*, and Scheer published extensively in its exile incarnation. In Paris, they edited the short-lived antifascist journal *Die Aktion / l'Action* as unaffiliated leftists. (Leonhard passed through the Independent SPD, the KPD, and the Communist Workers' Party by 1922.) Together, Kantorowicz, Schroeder, Scheer, and Leonhard worked to build an anti-Nazi "popular front" among exiled German politicians and intellectuals – a Paris-centered project publicly led by Heinrich Mann, with behind-the-scenes support from the Comintern (Communist International).[60] In these efforts, Budzislawski's *Neue Weltbühne* played a vital role even before its relocation to Paris from Prague in 1938, just ahead of German troops.

---

[59] Wolfgang Gruner, *"Ein Schicksal, das ich mit sehr vielen anderen geteilt habe": Alfred Kantorowicz, sein Leben und seine Zeit von 1899 bis 1935* (Kassel: Kassel University Press, 2006), 180–248; Berndt, *Nur das Wort*, 67–9; Langer, Ley, and Sander, *Alibi-Frauen?*, 182; Kantorowicz, *Deutsches Tagebuch*, I:23–34, quote I:29, II:268–70; Eggebrecht, *Weg*, 252–71; Karola Bloch, *Aus meinem Leben* (Pfullingen: Neske, 1981), 68–72; Arthur Koestler, n.t., in *The God that Failed*, ed. R. H. S. Crossman (New York: Harper, 1949), 42–4. Other residents included Gustav Regler, Manès Sperber, Werner von Trott, and Erich Weinert; the broader circle included Brecht, Plievier, Tucholsky, and Friedrich Wolf. Kantorowicz had been engaged to Piotrkowska before he introduced her to Bloch in 1926. Gruner, *Schicksal*, 109–21.

[60] Gruner, *Schicksal*, 249–336; Bernd Jentzsch, *Rudolf Leonhard, "Gedichteträumer"* (Munich: Hanser, 1984), 13–37; Maximilian Scheer, *Ein unruhiges Leben: Autobiographie* (Berlin: Verlag der Nationen, 1975), 77, 175. On exile in France, see Palmier, *Weimar*, 184–218, 331–60. On the popular front, see Chapter 5.

Like many, Kantorowicz also volunteered in the International Brigades during the Spanish Civil War, his touchstone experience of antifascist struggle.[61]

The fall of Spain in 1939 and the fall of France in 1940 again reshaped the geography of exile. Initially interned in France as enemy aliens, Kantorowicz, Schroeder, Scheer, and Budzislawski secured passage to the United States, where all four rose to journalistic prominence. The latter two helped organize the Council for a Democratic Germany, an important émigré forum in which Kantorowicz, Bloch, Brecht, and Heinrich Mann were also involved.[62] Leonhard stayed in France, twice escaping from custody and joining the Résistance in Marseilles. In 1942, rumors circulated that he had been executed by the Gestapo. Obituaries appeared in Mexico City's exile press, and Kantorowicz gave a eulogy in New York. When news of Leonhard's survival reached his friends after the war, they cloaked their relief in jokes about resurrection and discussed their post-exile plans.[63] Meanwhile, Kantorowicz had given a list of presumably trustworthy antifascists who might (or might not) have survived inside Germany to his well-connected CBS colleague William L. Shirer, including the names Eggebrecht and Kästner.[64]

By mid 1946, Kantorowicz was making plans to return. He had already appeared in print, courtesy of Kästner's *Neue Zeitung*, but

---

[61] Dieter Schiller, *Der Traum von Hitlers Sturz: Studien zur deutschen Exilliteratur 1933–1945* (Frankfurt a.M.: Lang, 2010), 271–83; Josie McLellan, "The Politics of Communist Biography: Alfred Kantorowicz and the Spanish Civil War," *German History* 22, no. 4 (2004): 536–62.

[62] Gruner, "Alfred Kantorowicz – Wanderer zwischen Ost und West," in *Zwischen den Stühlen? Remigranten und Remigration in der deutschen Medienöffentlichkeit der Nachkriegszeit*, ed. Krohn and Schildt (Hamburg: Christians, 2002), 297–9; Wurm, *Aufbau-Verlag*, 75; Scheer, *Leben*, 142; Krauss, "Hans Habe, Ernst Friedlaender, Hermann Budzislawski: Drei Zonen, drei Städte, drei Schicksale," in *Zwischen*, ed. Krohn and Schildt, 252–4; Ursula Langkau-Alex and Thomas M. Ruprecht, eds. *Was soll aus Deutschland werden? Der Council for a Democratic Germany in New York 1944–1945* (Frankfurt a.M.: Campus, 1995), 160–2, 270–5. On exile in the United States, see Palmier, *Weimar*, 457–98.

[63] Jentzsch, *Leonhard*, 38–49; Scheer to Rudolf Leonhard, 17 September 1945, 31 July 1946, Kantorowicz to Leonhard, 17 August 1946, AdK Leonhard-Archiv 825/3, 818; Leonhard to Scheer, 4 July 1946, 6 August 1946, AdK Scheer-Archiv, Rudolf Leonhard (1945–53); Leonhard to Kantorowicz, 20 September 1946, SUBH NL Kantorowicz NK: BI: L6; Kantorowicz, *Deutsches Tagebuch*, I:132–4.

[64] Kantorowicz, "To Shirer," n.d., SUBH NL Kantorowicz NK Ostberlin: 137; Kantorowicz, *Deutsches Tagebuch*, I:108–10. The contents of this document suggest it was drawn up in 1944/5 for official use. Shirer, a former Berlin correspondent, took part in influential wartime study groups on occupation policy at the Council on Foreign Relations. He returned to Germany as a war correspondent and again to cover the Nuremberg Trial. See William L. Shirer, *End of a Berlin Diary* (New York: Knopf, 1947); Michael Wala, *Winning the Peace: Amerikanische Außenpolitik und der Council on Foreign Relations 1945–1950* (Stuttgart: Steiner, 1990), here 119, 288, 291.

he desired to be present in person. Once the State Department cleared them, he, Frieda, and Schroeder made the ocean voyage home in late 1946, in the first group to return from the USA on their own initiative. During an unanticipated delay in Bremen, Kantorowicz declined an American newspaper license and visited Eggebrecht in Hamburg. Through party contacts to the Berlin Kulturbund, he procured financial support and, in January 1947, an authorization to finish the journey.[65] In Berlin, Schroeder was made lead editor at Aufbau publishers, and Kantorowicz set about founding a cultural-political journal. To signal both independence and cooperation, he strove to set a "precedent" of four separate licenses and resolved "to live in the American sector and work in the Russian, or vice versa." His press contacts gave access to US authorities, and his old friend Weisenborn introduced him to their Soviet counterparts; top officials on each side responded favorably to his proposal.[66] Ultimately, he received no American license, and his journal *Ost und West* (*East and West*) – "the accent is on the 'and,'" he would often insist – appeared under Soviet sponsorship from July 1947.[67] Scheer was persuaded to reemigrate and become editor in chief; Budzislawski followed in late 1948, to a journalism professorship in Leipzig.[68] *Ost und West* aimed to open Germans' long-closed horizons and stimulate dialogue by exposure to international and German exile literature, Kantorowicz's emerging academic specialty (Figure 1.2). A less explicit, no less didactic agenda was to publicize the history of the antifascist struggle, via accounts of his friends' exemplary experiences.[69]

[65] Gruner, "Kantorowicz," 299–301; Kantorowicz, *Deutsches Tagebuch*, I:101, 213–73.
[66] Wurm, *Aufbau-Verlag*, 74; Kantorowicz to Walter Schlieper [Maximilian Scheer], 28 March 1947, AdK Scheer-Archiv, Materialsammlung Kantorowicz; Kantorowicz, *Deutsches Tagebuch*, I:277–87. Kantorowicz told all sides about his plans and reflected publicly on them in the journal's first issue: Kantorowicz to Sergei Tulpanov, [10 March 1947], Kantorowicz to Arthur Eggleston, 12 February 1947, SUB Hamburg, NL Kantorowicz NK: Ostberlin: 71; Kantorowicz, "Einführung," *Ost und West* 1, no. 1 (1947): 3, 6–8.
[67] *Ost und West* had a monthly circulation of 70–80,000, dropping to 30,000 in July 1948 and 8000 by its final issue in December 1949. See Barbara Baerns, *Ost und West: Eine Zeitschrift zwischen den Fronten: Zur politischen Funktion einer literarischen Zeitschrift in der Besatzungszeit 1945–1949* (Münster: Fahle, 1968), quote 169; Wehner, *Kulturpolitik*, 405–20; Flanagan, *Political-Cultural Periodicals*, 75–112. The denial of a US license – despite support from ICD Director General Robert McClure – was likely tied to a Hearst press campaign that painted Kantorowicz a Soviet spy and prompted a government investigation. Kantorowicz, *Deutsches Tagebuch*, I:299–311; Gienow-Hecht, *Transmission*, 111.
[68] Kantorowicz to Scheer, 28 March 1947, 14 May 1947, 24 June 1947, AdK Scheer-Archiv, Materialsammlung Kantorowicz; Leonhard to Scheer, 3 July 1947, AdK Scheer-Archiv, Rudolf Leonhard (1945–53); Krauss, "Hans Habe," 255.
[69] Kantorowicz, "Rudolf Leonhard," *Ost und West* 1, no. 2 (1947): 70–5; Kantorowicz, "Maximilian Scheer," *Ost und West* 1, no. 5 (1947): 51–3; Max Schroeder, "Heinrich Mann, der Deutsche," *Ost und West* 1, no. 1 (1947): 9–13; Kantorowicz, "Axel

Figure 1.2 A flyer advertises *Ost und West* in 1947. Touting the cross-border intellectual conversation the journal has hosted – including German, American, Russian, and French writers – it declares: "OST UND WEST opens the window to the world." (*Source*: Staats- und Universitätsbibliothek Hamburg, NK: C 15: 1)

Kantorowicz's energetic activity made him another crucial bridge among network nodes. With Krauss, he helped facilitate a university appointment for Bloch, enabling his and Karola's return from the USA (on the same ship as Wieland Herzfelde). Bloch and Herzfelde then joined Krauss, Mayer, and Budzislawski on the Leipzig faculty in 1949.[70] Kantorowicz also attended two meetings of the Imshausen Society (Gesellschaft Imshausen), which gathered at the Hessian family estate of another friend from the "Red Block," Werner von Trott zu Solz (1902–1965), to debate Germany's renewal. There, he met Dirks and Kogon. Kantorowicz returned to Berlin with not only "lasting impressions" but also "some memorable new acquaintances."[71] For another collaboration, a collection of biographical sketches on figures from all corners of the anti-Nazi opposition, he foresaw contributions by himself on Ossietzky, Kästner on Tucholsky, Weisenborn on Schulze-Boysen, Eggebrecht on Erich Mühsam (an anarchist murdered in Oranienburg concentration camp in 1934), and Werner von Trott on his brother Adam (a diplomat executed for his part in the 1944 attempt on Hitler's life). Harich, Leonhard, Scheer, Schnog, and Schroeder were also to contribute, alongside authors as diverse as Huchel, Niekisch, Seghers, and Wiechert.[72]

One culmination – also a beginning of the end – of engaged democrats' efforts was the First German Writers' Congress, held October 1947 in Berlin. Hundreds attended, from all four zones, attempting to constitute a kind of independent national representation for Germany. Conceived by Weisenborn, it was planned with Kantorowicz, Leonhard, Schroeder, and others; they invited Bauer, Bloch, Drews, Eggebrecht, Harich, Hermlin, Ihering, Jaspers, Kästner, Kogon, Lommer, Lukács, Mayer, Rowohlt, Scheer, Schnog, Steiniger, Sternberger, and many more, including Benno Reifenberg (1892–1970), editor of the Freiburg journal *Die Gegenwart* (*The Present*), and Walter Kolbenhoff (1908–1993), of Munich's *Der Ruf* (*The Call*). Although tensions boiled over between Soviet and American observers, many German participants

---

Eggebrecht fünfzig," *Ost und West* 3, no. 1 (1949): 81–2; Leonhard, "Lagerchronik in Versen," *Ost und West* 1, no. 2 (1947): 76–82; Scheer, "Rudolf Olden," *Ost und West* 1, no. 5 (1947): 4–5; Hermann Budzislawski, "Heimkehr," *Ost und West* 2, no. 10 (1948): 42–5; Wolfgang Weyrauch, "Günther Weisenborn: Memorial," *Ost und West* 2, no. 8 (1948): 88–9. After *Ulenspiegel*, Weyrauch joined *Ost und West* in October 1949; Kantorowicz, *Deutsches Tagebuch*, I:651.

[70] See, e.g., Kantorowicz to Paul Wandel, 11 March 1948, Krauss to Rocholl, 15 April 1948, Bundesarchiv (hereafter BArch) DR 3/B 14971/7, 83.

[71] Kantorowicz, *Deutsches Tagebuch*, I:400–3. On the Imshausen Society, see Wolfgang Schwiedrzik, *Träume der ersten Stunde: Die Gesellschaft Imshausen* (Berlin: Siedler, 1991) and Chapter 4.

[72] Kantorowicz, "Memorandum: Betr. antifaschistisches 'Heldenbuch,'" 23 February 1948, AdK Leonhard-Archiv 818. The project was never realized.

emphasized their commitment to counteract "East–West" polarization. In his report on the proceedings, Mayer approvingly cited Weisenborn, who had dubbed the congress "a first all-German parliament since the collapse... a parliament of writers."[73] The metaphor was an apt one for this postwar configuration as a whole, which coalesced around a sense of common mission.

### Allied-German cooperation and a mandate for renewal

The war's victors laid crucial ground for these activities and interconnections, implementing reeducation policies that called for German-run media and organizations. Indeed, the cultural politics of occupation set the institutional parameters within which all Germans operated. Although some resented this trusteeship, Germany's engaged democrats experienced it less as a constraint and more as a condition of their work. In their view, constructing the postwar polity had to be a cooperative enterprise between Germans and occupiers, in which the population at large also came to feel it had a stake.

Toward the end of the war, Allied authorities began planning for Germany's occupation. Yet these plans were not comprehensive or unified, and they were crosscut by competing agendas and interests, such that much of what became policy was the outcome of ad hoc negotiations and on-the-ground encounters.[74] Nonetheless, all built on the shared foundation of the Potsdam consensus. Culture, education, and the media were central to this agenda, as vital tools for turning Germans away from nationalism, militarism, and authoritarianism and toward democracy. Even if their understandings of the goal diverged, the victors all pursued the regulated reconstruction of the press and public life, with active

---

[73] Ursula Reinhold, Dieter Schlenstedt, and Horst Tanneberger, eds. *Erster deutscher Schriftstellerkongreß 4.–8. Oktober 1947: Protokoll und Dokumente* (Berlin: Aufbau, 1997), 14–27, 505–11. In the event, Bloch was still in exile; Lukács, Jaspers, and Sternberger were otherwise committed; and Kästner and Kogon were out of the country. Ibid., 489, 495; Sternberger to Peter de Mendelssohn, 5 September 1947, DLA A:Sternberger/Wandlung/ 74.10391; Mayer, "Macht und Ohnmacht des Wortes," *Frankfurter Hefte* 2, no. 12 (1947): 1179. On the congress, see Chapter 5.

[74] See, e.g., John Gimbel, *The American Occupation of Germany: Politics and the Military, 1945–1949* (Stanford, Calif.: Stanford University Press, 1968); Josef Foschepoth and Rolf Steininger, eds. *Die britische Deutschland- und Besatzungspolitik 1945–1949* (Paderborn: Schöningh, 1985); Norman M. Naimark, *The Russians in Germany: A History of the Soviet Zone of Occupation, 1945–1949* (Cambridge, Mass.: Harvard University Press, 1995); Edgar Wolfrum, Peter Fässler, and Reinhard Grohnert, *Krisenjahre und Aufbruchszeit: Alltag und Politik im französisch besetzten Baden 1945–1949* (Munich: Oldenbourg, 1996).

German involvement.[75] Wartime propaganda and postwar "information policy" was planned by two Allied groups, both with input from German exiles: first, in London and then Paris, by the Anglo-American Psychological Warfare Division (PWD), where the Free French were junior partners; and second, in Moscow, by ex-Comintern officers and the Seventh Section of the Red Army's Political Administration (GlavPURKKA). In late 1944, PWD laid out a formal, three-phase press plan. Initially, a "blackout" would mark the break between old and new systems of information control, that is, between Nazi propaganda and Allied reeducation efforts. On that would follow Allied-run German-language newspapers, after which a German-run press would gradually be established.[76]

During the war's final phase, these stages structured developments all across the collapsing Reich, albeit loosely and asynchronously. The British and French moved slower than the Americans, while the Soviets followed a faster course. PWD itself implemented no blackout, as press officers in the first subdued areas proved eager to begin work; one group skipped two stages, establishing postwar Germany's first German-led paper, the *Aachener Nachrichten (Aachen News)*, in January 1945. Hans Habe, an Austrian émigré of Hungarian-Jewish origins who returned to Europe as a US citizen and PWD press officer, followed official plans more closely. His team soon presided over a small empire of short-format, military-run "overt" newspapers. As the Red Army advanced, GlavPURKKA's Seventh Section established similar "news sheets," en route to the capital. Berlin's first postwar paper appeared on 3 May, one day after the city's capitulation, followed by the full-format *Tägliche Rundschau (Daily View)* on 15 May. This became the flagship publication for the Soviet zone, edited by Red Army officers but staffed and written primarily by Germans, featuring both re-émigrés such as Plievier and locals such as Harich, Lommer, and Weyrauch. Its success spurred similar western projects. In October, Habe launched *Die Neue Zeitung*, where editor-in-chief Hans Wallenberg and Stefan Heym (1913–2001) – both

---

[75] On cultural policy generally, see, e.g., Gabriele Clemens, ed. *Kulturpolitik im besetzten Deutschland 1945–1949* (Stuttgart: Steiner, 1994); Rebecca Boehling, "U.S. Cultural Policy and German Culture during the American Occupation," in *United States*, ed. Junker, I:388–93. On media, see, e.g., Harold Hurwitz, *Die Stunde Null der deutschen Presse: Die amerikanische Pressepolitik in Deutschland 1945–1949* (Cologne: Wissenschaft und Politik, 1972); Kurt Koszyk, *Pressepolitik für Deutsche 1945–1949* (Berlin: Colloquium, 1986); Peter Strunk, *Zensur und Zensoren: Medienkontrolle und Propagandapolitik unter sowjetischer Besatzungsherrschaft in Deutschland* (Berlin: Akademie, 1996); Arnulf Kutsch, "Rundfunk unter alliierter Besatzung," in *Mediengeschichte der Bundesrepublik Deutschland*, ed. Jürgen Wilke (Cologne: Böhlau, 1999), 59–90.

[76] Hurwitz, *Stunde Null*, 22–34, 45–51; Koszyk, *Pressepolitik*, 123–8, 261, 325–8, 386n23; Naimark, *Russians*, 16–18; Strunk, *Zensur*, 13–18.

German-Jewish exiles and naturalized Americans – oversaw a largely German staff, including Kästner. The analogous British paper appeared with Hamburg's *Die Welt* (*The World*) in April 1946, while the French added a bilingual edition to their Constance-based *Nouvelles de France* (*News from France*) in January 1947.[77]

These military-operated zonal papers were intended to serve as models for a licensed press. In practice, however, that third phase began before the second ended. In 1945, all four powers instituted licensing and censorship regimes with similar basic contours. Radio broadcasting remained directly in Allied hands, while German-run periodicals and publishers (like parties and other organizations) operated under license. In addition to vetting licensees, information officers screened all printed materials, from flyers to newspapers and journals to books. Overtly nationalist, militarist, or anti-democratic content was prohibited, and direct critique of Allied measures – whether by the Control Council or by a single power – was proscribed. Once full-fledged military governments were in place, oversight transferred to successor agencies: the Propaganda (later: Information) Administration of the Soviet Military Administration in Germany (SVAG); the Information Control Division (ICD) of the Office for Military Government for Germany, United States (OMGUS); and similar British and French offices.[78] Germany's internal borders were another obstacle. Printed matter passed them more easily than other goods (or people) did but was still hampered by infrastructural and bureaucratic hurdles. And whenever inter-Allied relations soured, materials licensed in one zone could be blocked at the border to another.[79]

Under these institutional auspices, a controlled yet vibrant immediate postwar public sphere developed. In June 1945, Soviets transferred the *Berliner Zeitung* to the German city administration and licensed the KPD organ. Its SPD, CDU, and liberal counterparts soon followed. In the American zone, the *Frankfurter Rundschau* (*Frankfurt View*) appeared in August, followed by Heidelberg's *Rhein-Neckar-Zeitung* and Berlin's

---

[77] Hurwitz, *Stunde Null*, 51–63, 79–91, 100–2; Koszyk, *Pressepolitik*, 24–35, 128–34, 204–16, 264–6, 329–30; Naimark, *Russians*, 18–19; Strunk, *Zensur*, 36–62; Gienow-Hecht, *Transmission*, 16–44; Daniel A. Gossel, *Die Hamburger Presse nach dem Zweiten Weltkrieg: Neuanfang unter britischer Besatzungsherrschaft* (Hamburg: Verlag Verein für Hamburgische Geschichte, 1993), 77–90; Stephan Schölzel, *Die Pressepolitik in der französischen Besatzungszone 1945–1949* (Mainz: Hase & Koehler, 1986), 180–2.

[78] Hurwitz, *Stunde Null*, 118–29, 328–9; Koszyk, *Pressepolitik*, 134–6, 269–70, 280–3; Naimark, *Russians*, 322–7, 338–41; Strunk, *Zensur*, 26–32, 65–6, 92–5.

[79] Hurwitz, *Stunde Null*, 325–33; Koszyk, *Pressepolitik*, 68, 194–8, 376n31; Heinz Sarkowski, "Die Anfänge des deutsch-deutschen Buchhandelsverkehrs (1945–1955)," in *Das Loch in der Mauer: Der innerdeutsche Literaturaustausch*, ed. Mark Lehmstedt and Siegfried Lokatis (Wiesbaden: Harrassowitz, 1997), 89–94; Werner Abelshauser, *Deutsche Wirtschaftsgeschichte seit 1945* (Munich: Beck, 2004), 84–6.

*Der Tagesspiegel* as well as Munich's *Süddeutsche Zeitung*. French-licensed papers also debuted in August, spreading to Berlin with *Der Kurier*. Although British licensing did not begin until 1946 – with the Hamburg weekly *Die Zeit* and Berlin's *Der Telegraf*, among others – they had earlier transferred two military newspapers to German control. By 1947, larger licensed papers cleared circulations of 2–300,000 in the zones and over 400,000 in Berlin, though these were small compared to 1 million or more for the military governments' flagships. Fewer than 200 newspapers but nearly 1,500 journals were licensed in all. Among these, cultural-political publications reached one third of the total, an unusually large proportion of such titles relative to professional or trade journals.[80]

While this rather illiberal public sphere shared formal elements across zones, there were crucial differences. In part, these mirrored differences in the occupiers' press traditions, especially regarding the role of parties and organizations. A party-centered press was foreign to American officials, who conferred licenses only on individuals. Moreover, they instituted a "panel" system, seeking multiple editors of varied political orientations per license. The model was applied to journals as well, and it was ICD who proposed that Krauss, a Communist, join the liberal and Social Democratic editors of *Die Wandlung*. This practice was scaled back relatively early on, however, and when the *Frankfurter Hefte* appeared in 1946, they had one licensee, Kogon, with only CDU-affiliated editors. The other western powers, more accustomed to political parties' media presence, implemented pluralism differently. The British also initially favored panels and licensed only individuals, but parties could nominate licensees, producing formally and informally aligned papers (such as *Der Telegraf*, close to the SPD). Similarly, the French first followed the US lead, then allowed a limited party press in 1947.[81]

Soviet policy stood at the other end of the spectrum. The same decree that permitted political parties and unions in June 1945 – three months earlier than in the western zones – also allowed a party press. Although unaffiliated individuals were soon also eligible for licenses, they were disadvantaged. For journals as well as newspapers, Soviet authorities favored applicants with links to parties or official organizations.[82] These distinctions are reflected in several of the journals mentioned above: *Aufbau*, the

---

[80] Koszyk, *Pressepolitik*, 25, 137, 330, 472–91; Frei, "Die Presse," in *Die Geschichte der Bundesrepublik Deutschland*, ed. Benz (Frankfurt a.M.: Fischer, 1989), IV:373–4, 379–80; Gienow-Hecht, *Transmission*, 79; Strunk, *Zensur*, 57–8; Gossel, *Hamburger Presse*, 82; Laurien, "Zeitschriftenlandschaft Nachkriegszeit: Zu Struktur und Funktion politisch-kultureller Zeitschriften 1945–1949," *Publizistik* 47, no. 1 (2002): 59.
[81] Hurwitz, *Stunde Null*, 40–4, 125–7, 138–43, 153–60; Waldmüller, *Wandlung*, 35; Ewald, *Republik*, 24; Koszyk, *Pressepolitik*, 139–40, 154–64, 265–7.
[82] Strunk, *Zensur*, 64–5, 85; Bettina Jütte, "Lizenzen und Listen: Grundlagen staatlicher Zeitschriftenpolitik in der SBZ," in *Zwischen "Mosaik" und "Einheit": Zeitschriften in*

Kulturbund organ, appeared as early as September 1945. *Die Weltbühne*, licensed the following year, was without formal organizational ties. But its start-up loan came from the KPD/SED, and its editor's closest counselors were party comrades and top functionaries: poet Erich Weinert was a veteran of the Moscow exile and higher-up at the Soviets' German-run licensing and censorship authority, the German Central Education Administration, while journalist Alexander Abusch, the *Weltbühne*'s de facto co-editor and in-house censor, led the Kulturbund's "ideological-cultural" department. In contrast, *Ost und West*, licensed just one year later, was Kantorowicz's private enterprise and the most consistently independent of the three.[83] Not accidentally, it was also the one that failed to survive the foundation of the GDR.

Differences among the censorship regimes were also soon manifest. Initially, all print media were subject to inspection before as well as after publication, in a system of "pre-censorship." Prior restraint was dropped in the US zone in September 1945 and soon phased out by the British as well. The stricter French followed in late 1946, as, officially, did the Soviets by spring 1947. Early on, censors focused on nationalist or militarist views as well as – more unevenly – on criticism of the occupiers, but even this limited mandate could justify invasive and arbitrary actions. Overall, Soviet censors had the heaviest (and most practiced) hand, and their editorial prescriptions preserved a high degree of de facto control even after prior restraint. Yet they too were concerned to avoid the impression of a univocal or merely propagandistic press.[84] More indirectly, SVAG shaped published opinion with paper allotments. While British and French authorities distributed paper among party organs in proportion to electoral support, Soviet authorities gave SED periodicals the lion's share of newsprint. These discrepancies grew more pronounced when elections approached.[85]

---

 der DDR, ed. Simone Barck, Martina Langermann, and Lokatis (Berlin: Links, 1999), 560–1.
[83] David Pike, *The Politics of Culture in Soviet-Occupied Germany, 1945–1949* (Stanford, Calif.: Stanford University Press, 1992), 97; Magdalena Heider, *Politik – Kultur – Kulturbund: Zur Gründungs- und Frühgeschichte des Kulturbundes zur demokratischen Erneuerung Deutschlands 1945–1954 in der SBZ/DDR* (Cologne: Wissenschaft und Politik, 1993), 56; Petra Kabus, "Hätte Tucholsky für die DDR-Weltbühne geschrieben? Zur Geschichte einer Zeitschrift zwischen humanistischer Tradition und Parteijournalismus," in *Die Weltbühne: Zur Tradition und Kontinuität demokratischer Publizistik*, ed. Stefanie Oswalt (St. Ingbert: Röhrig Universitätsverlag, 2003), 216, 220; Baerns, *Ost und West*, 80–1.
[84] Hurwitz, *Stunde Null*, 123–6; Koszyk, *Pressepolitik*, 136, 284–5, 293–6; Naimark, *Russians*, 399–400; Strunk, *Zensur*, 96–103, 107–13; Pike, "Censorship in Soviet-Occupied Germany," in *The Establishment of Communist Regimes in Eastern Europe, 1944–1949*, ed. Norman Naimark and Leonid Gibianskii (Boulder, Colo.: Westview, 1997), 217–42.
[85] Koszyk, *Pressepolitik*, 60, 136–7, 160, 270; Strunk, *Zensur*, 113–15.

In the postwar years, however, privileging Soviet and KPD/SED agendas coexisted with a kind of political pluralism. In fact, these aims coincided, for the international Communist strategy of the time was not one of revolutionary vanguardism and class struggle. Rather, it stood again under the sign of the 1930s "popular fronts," now revived as "national fronts." These de-emphasized an earlier internationalist, left-leaning antifascism, stressing local struggles and seeking even broader coalitions that reached into the conservative camp. Even if the intransigent German Communists were comparatively slow to adopt such pluralism and gradualism, these orientations guided them after the war.[86] The corollary theories of a "German road to socialism" and the German variant of a non-bourgeois but non-Soviet "people's democracy," formulated by Anton Ackermann and others, affirmed a non-revolutionary path as appropriate to postwar European conditions. Even if such positions were repudiated by 1948, amid the Cold War's closing of ranks, they set the tone in 1945.[87]

In an initial spirit of openness, then, all four Allies sought out Germans to help with reconstruction. Intelligence and information officers, including some German exiles, coordinated this process, guided by lists of non- and anti-Nazis compiled from trusted POWs' and émigrés' reports. The most comprehensive was PWD's master "white list," which included Dirks, Jaspers, Kästner, and Weber.[88] Just this sort of information also led the Allies to Eggebrecht and Kogon; other partners were found during occupation, as with Harich and Weisenborn. Under the military governments, this process continued, with émigrés as key mediators. Historian Golo Mann (son of Thomas), for instance, was the US control officer for Mayer and Hermlin at Radio Frankfurt, and novelist Alfred Döblin served as a French censor in Baden-Baden, where he also published the literary journal *Das Goldene Tor (The Golden Gate)*. Both were unsettled sojourners between their adopted lands and Germany.[89]

---

[86] Weitz, *German Communism*, 292–356; Naimark, *Russians*, 251–317; Anson Rabinbach, *Begriffe aus dem Kalten Krieg: Totalitarismus, Antifaschismus, Genozid* (Göttingen: Wallstein, 2009), 32–7.

[87] Anton Ackermann, "Gibt es einen besonderen deutschen Weg zum Sozialismus?" *Einheit* 1, no. 1 (1946): 22–32; Rudolf Appelt, "Ein neuer Typus der Demokratie: Die Volksdemokratien Ost- und Südosteuropas," *Einheit* 1, no. 6 (1946): 339–52; Appelt, "Volksdemokratie – ein Weg zum Sozialismus," *Einheit* 2, no. 3 (1947): 304–6; Ackermann, "Über den einzig möglichen Weg zum Sozialismus," *Neues Deutschland*, 24 September 1948.

[88] Hurwitz, *Stunde Null*, 29, 81; Koszyk, *Pressepolitik*, 26–7; Naimark, *Russians*, 11–13, 41–4, 252–3; Henric L. Wuermeling, *Die weiße Liste: Umbruch der politischen Kultur in Deutschland 1945* (Berlin: Ullstein, 1981), here 286–7, 292.

[89] Tilmann Lahme, *Golo Mann: Biographie* (Frankfurt a.M.: Fischer, 2009), 178–262; Alexandra Birkert, *Das Goldene Tor: Alfred Döblins Nachkriegszeitschrift* (Frankfurt a.M.: Buchhändler-Vereinigung, 1989).

For their part, engaged democrats perceived Allied and German roles as complementary. They too subscribed to the Potsdam consensus.[90] And they affirmed the occupation's legitimacy: political guardianship by the victors was justified by the evident political immaturity of the vanquished. This view was common among exiles, whose tenacious hopes for an internal uprising had been bitterly disappointed, but it was present also within Germany.[91] At the same time, engaged democrats asserted the Germans' right and responsibility to effect their own renewal. Introducing *Die Wandlung*'s first issue, Jaspers underscored "the dependence of our every action on the will of the occupying powers, who have freed us from the National Socialist yoke." All the more precious, then, was the opportunity a journal afforded: "We may speak publicly with one another. Let's see what we have to say!" Open discussion was key to "political self-education," even for political wards whose freedom was not yet self-made but authorized by their liberators. Eggebrecht took a similar position. The allies "won the war for us ... When it was still possible to stop Hitler, we did not do enough. Later, it was too late." Still, the occupied had a crucial role: "Now, finally, we can speak. I, in any case, want to speak – to like-minded people. And, more importantly, to the many that think the world is at an end. It's just now being born anew!"[92] The victors' rule provided the framework for Germans' circumscribed yet vital public activity. Both were integral to postwar renewal.

Audible in these comments is engaged democrats' zeal for the task at hand. They felt themselves the bearers of a mandate grounded in several sources of legitimacy. First, they had the occupiers' confidence. After several offers from American and Soviet authorities, Kantorowicz wrote to Scheer, who was still in exile: "There is an enormous field here, for us and our task; as difficult as it may be, it is rewarding ... My name still means something to many here, in all zones ... I am trusted. My words will have weight. I will not betray that trust." Given Europe's experience under Nazism, however, they emphatically distinguished cooperation with occupiers from collusion in tyranny. Speaking for his peers, Kogon described their relations with the Allies as "free collaborative work" in a spirit of "partnership" on the "common task" of renewing Germany and restoring its sovereignty. Theirs was no "collaboration in

---

[90] *Die Wandlung* even published the entire communiqué, to teach Germans the "legal foundation" of their "actual condition"; "Das Communiqué von Potsdam: Wortlaut der Erklärung der 'Großen Drei' auf der Potsdamer Konferenz," *Die Wandlung* 1, no. 1 (1945): 79–94; "Redaktionelle Anmerkungen," *Die Wandlung* I, no. 1 (1945): quote 96.
[91] See, e.g., Palmier, *Weimar*, 300–1, 406–8, 634–5.
[92] Jaspers, "Geleitwort," *Die Wandlung* 1, no. 1 (1945): 3–6; Jaspers, "Thesen über politische Freiheit," *Die Wandlung* 1, no. 5/6 (1946): 460; Eggebrecht, *Weg*, 320; also "Was wir wollen," *Nordwestdeutsche Hefte* 1, no. 1 (1946): verso of cover.

the despicable sense."[93] Not command and coercion but trust and shared goals shaped their interactions.

Second, engaged democrats sensed they had a receptive German audience, as their journals' high print runs seemed to suggest. Kogon and Dirks imagined a readership drawn from "all social strata, age groups, and 'orientations,'" engaging politically active citizens as well as those who were "curious and skeptical" or "simply hungry for reading." Soon after Scheer returned to Germany, he wrote Budzislawski: "Impressions: you rarely speak with someone who doesn't use twisted Nazi arguments. On the other hand, the new press and literature are greedily devoured."[94] Despite Nazism's lingering effects, these intellectuals felt themselves in dialogue with a broad cross-section of German society. Some caveats are in order here: The postwar economy, rationed and undersupplied, enjoyed artificial surpluses of disposable income; this inflated demand for non-essentials, including reading material. And while book production lagged, cultural-political journals filled the gap.[95] Moreover, the possibility that printed matter was used in unintended ways – as fuel, or toilet paper – was noted at the time. So the widespread impression that these journals reached a constituency beyond the educated middle class was partly illusion.[96] Still, levels of circulation and demand are striking. While the print runs of the *Frankfurter Hefte* and *Ost und West* were set at 50,000 and 70,000, respectively – quite high already, for such publications – each reported having more than 150,000 subscription requests in 1947, while favored Soviet-licensed journals such as *Aufbau* or *Die Weltbühne* in fact circulated that many copies.[97] These were, it seemed, favorable conditions for facilitating public dialogue and shaping political outcomes.

Finally, Germany's engaged democrats felt they bore a mandate grounded in their antifascist backgrounds. From their varied experiences

---

[93] Kantorowicz to Scheer, 28 March 1947, AdK Scheer-Archiv, Materialsammlung Kantorowicz; Kogon, "Zusammenarbeit mit Besatzungsmächten," *Frankfurter Hefte* 2, no. 11 (1947): 1101, 1098.
[94] "An unsere Leser!" *Frankfurter Hefte* 1, no. 1 (1946): 1–2; Scheer to Budzislawski, 22 October 1947, AdK Scheer-Archiv, H. Budzislawski; see also Scheer, "Erste Begegnungen in Deutschland," *Die Weltbühne* 2, no. 20 (1947): 870–3.
[95] Kleßmann, *Staatsgründung*, 48–50; Laurien, "Zeitschriftenlandschaft," 57–60.
[96] Schildt, "Kontinuität und Neuanfang im Zusammenbruch: Zu den politischen, sozialen und kulturellen Ausgangsbedingungen der Nachkriegszeit," in *Buch, Buchhandel und Rundfunk 1945–1949*, ed. Monika Estermann and Edgar Lersch (Wiesbaden: Harrassowitz, 1997), 23, 31; Lokatis, "Das Verlagswesen der Sowjetisch Besetzten Zone," in *Buch*, ed. Estermann and Lersch, 119.
[97] See footnotes above and Kogon, "Wir Publizisten," *Frankfurter Hefte* 2, no. 2 (1947): 198; Kantorowicz to Alexander Dymschitz, 30 July 1947, SUBH NL Kantorowicz NK: Ostberlin: 137.

Germans, occupiers, and the democratization project     51

under Nazism, each constructed narratives of persecution and resistance.[98] For former prisoners, this was relatively straightforward. Weisenborn, for instance, tirelessly publicized "the German resistance movement" in speeches, the press, and his literary work. He sought to counter both the widespread impression of Germans' passivity and the privileging of the 20 July 1944 attempt on Hitler's life by military and diplomatic elites. He had first-hand knowledge of a broader, longer-standing opposition based in socialist and communist milieus. This experience informed his well-received drama *The Illegals* as well as *Memorial*, an autobiographical novel that incorporated notes taken surreptitiously in prison.[99] He coordinated with Leonhard, who made similar efforts in France, and received materials from Krauss, who also wrote a resistance novel. Notably, Weisenborn's collaborations extended beyond leftist circles. He found a prominent ally in Ricarda Huch, an octogenarian novelist with national-liberal leanings. She too had begun to document the German opposition, and shortly before her death in late 1947, she bequeathed him some of her files. The fruit of his labors was the first comprehensive treatment of the anti-Nazi resistance, incorporating Gestapo reports and trial proceedings alongside recollections, diary excerpts, and letters from resisters.[100]

Some who barely escaped with their lives still had complicated biographies to process. Kogon, for example, greeted the authoritarian, clerical, pro-Fascist regime that superseded Austria's interwar republic with enthusiasm, and he briefly nurtured hopes that Germany's "Third Reich" might be shaped in this image. His resistance and imprisonment marked

[98] On the broader salience of "resistance" in postwar debates, see Karrin Hanshew, *Terror and Democracy in West Germany* (Cambridge: Cambridge University Press, 2012), 68–109.
[99] Weisenborn, "Rede über die deutsche Widerstandsbewegung," *Aufbau* 2, no. 6 (1946): 571–8; Weisenborn, "Es gab eine deutsche Widerstandsbewegung," *Die Neue Zeitung*, 9 December 1946; Weisenborn, "Es gab eine deutsche Widerstandsbewegung," *Aufbau* 3, no. 1 (1947): 87–90; Weisenborn, "Es gab einen deutschen Widerstand," *Frankfurter Hefte* 2, no. 6 (1947): 531–2; Weisenborn, *Die Illegalen: Drama aus der deutschen Widerstandsbewegung* (Berlin: Aufbau, 1946); Weisenborn, *Memorial* (Munich: Desch, 1948). See also Heukenkamp, "Das lautlose Deutschland: Widerstandsliteratur und ihre Rezeption," in *Unterm Notdach: Nachkriegsliteratur in Berlin 1945–1949*, ed. Heukenkamp (Berlin: Schmidt, 1996), 267–316.
[100] Leonhard to Weisenborn, 20 September 1946, 30 September 1946, 21 October 1946, DLA A:Weisenborn/ 87.20.272/2–4; Weisenborn to Leonhard, 29 August 1946, 3 October 1946, AdK Leonhard-Archiv 829; Krauss to Weisenborn, 7 October 1946, AdK Weisenborn-Archiv 948; Werner Krauss, *PLN: Die Passionen der halykonischen Seele: Roman* (Frankfurt a.M.: Klostermann, 1946); Weisenborn, ed. *Der lautlose Aufstand: Bericht über die Widerstandsbewegung des deutschen Volkes 1933–1945* (Hamburg: Rowohlt, 1953). Cf. Ricarda Huch, *In einem Gedenkbuch zu sammeln. . . . : Bilder deutscher Widerstandskämpfer*, ed. Wolfgang Schwiedrzik (Leipzig: Leipziger Universitätsverlag, 1997).

a reorientation in the 1930s, although in Kogon's own telling, this expressed continuity as well as change: the solidarism and pacifism of his worldview were gradually freed of their fixation on hierarchy and order. Clearly, however, it was in the Buchenwald resistance that a new outlook cohered. He later often recalled how Christians, socialists, and communists discussed not only their day-to-day struggle but also the future shape of Germany.[101] And this image of unified antifascist resistance grounded his postwar political vision. Solidarities across "confession and party membership," rooted in past "struggle and suffering," could inform a present "politics of conciliation, justice, and material security," a hope he invested above all in the VVN. Indeed, a number of his Buchenwald compatriots were prominent in the new organization, from Hilpert (CDU) to Hermann Brill (SPD) to Emil Carlebach (KPD).[102] Kogon's friend Schnog also lauded the VVN's potential as a "parliament of resistance fighters" that bridged "contradictions of zones and parties." Schnog placed the Buchenwald resistance at the center of his postwar writings; for him as for many others, the inmates' involvement in the camp's "self-liberation" gave it a special distinction.[103]

For émigrés, antifascism similarly provided orientation. Kantorowicz's first article on his return, entitled "My Place is in Germany," framed both exile and homecoming as one ongoing struggle against Nazism, fought on behalf of "the better, the humane, creative, peace-loving Germany." Returning home seemed to him a "self-evident" choice, and he knew he was not alone. When he described Scheer as a representative of "the non-Nazi Germany" overseas, who "knew from the time that he had to leave his fatherland that his place and his task would be at home, as soon as conditions again allowed," he clearly also described himself.[104] Such positions are especially striking in those who contributed to the minimal incidence of Jewish reemigration. For his part, Mayer – the title of whose memoirs, "German Pending Revocation," evokes his unsettled identity

---

[101] Prümm, *Walter Dirks*, 19–25, 111–18, 122–33; Kogon, *Leben*, 32–3, 37–9, 51–2, 91. As Prümm shows, Kogon's autobiographical writings soften his initial conservatism and locate the beginnings of a re-evaluation too early.
[102] Kogon, "Politik der Versöhnung," *Frankfurter Hefte* 3, no. 4 (1948): 317–24, quotes 321–2; Kogon, *Leben*, 86.
[103] Karl Schnog, "Viermal Dachau," *Die Weltbühne* 2, no. 15 (1947): 641–4, quotes 643–4; Schnog, "Männer aus Buchenwald," *Die Weltbühne* 1, no. 6 (1946): 176–8; Schnog, "Männer aus Buchenwald II," *Die Weltbühne* 2, no. 4 (1947): 151–3; Schnog, "Männer aus Buchenwald III," *Die Weltbühne* 2, no. 7 (1947): 296–7. On the camp's liberation, see Stein, *Konzentrationslager*, 227–37; on its instrumentalization in the GDR, see Manfred Overesch, *Buchenwald und die DDR oder die Suche nach Selbstlegitimation* (Göttingen: Vandenhoeck & Ruprecht, 1995).
[104] Kantorowicz, "Mein Platz ist in Deutschland," *Die Neue Zeitung*, 14 February 1947; Kantorowicz, "Maximilian Scheer," 53.

after 1933 – remembered heated debates in Switzerland, between exiles eager to return and most exiled Jews, whose total rejection of Germany he could not endorse.[105] Even after the Holocaust, Mayer continued to identify with an antifascist Germany that had persevered to rebuild after barbarism.

Most engaged democrats, however, had neither fled nor actively fought the regime. That this group experienced Nazism as onerous and oppressive is beyond doubt. A few also felt "racial" persecution personally and acutely. Steiniger, a *Weltbühne* author of part-Jewish heritage, was in a precarious position. Though his "mixed marriage" mitigated the effects of his "mixed-breed" status, he lost his civil service job in 1933 and his citizenship in 1935; to escape forced labor, he fled to a small Silesian town in 1944. After the war, he served briefly as its mayor and joined the KPD before returning to Berlin, where he joined the Humboldt University's new law faculty and the SED. The fates of non-Jews married to Jews, such as Jaspers and Sternberger, were reciprocally intertwined with those of their spouses – provisionally protected but insecure and endangered. As the husband of a "non-Aryan," Sternberger was dismissed from the *FZ* shortly before it closed in 1943. He and his spouse Ilse (née Rothschild) returned to Heidelberg, where they waited out the regime in seclusion. As a senior civil servant, Jaspers was forced from his university post in 1937. He and his wife Gertrud (née Mayer) made a suicide pact in the event of her deportation, keeping cyanide pills on their nightstand. Sternberger, too, carried one at all times.[106]

Some Heidelberg "inner émigrés" skirted the bounds of organized resistance. In the faculty's only overtly defiant act, Weber had a swastika flag removed from atop his building in March 1933, after publishing an open letter in protest. Shortly thereafter, he retired, and his institute was effectively dissolved.[107] Through Henk, he also had contact with Theodor Haubach and Carlo Mierendorff; all three were former

---

[105] Mayer, *Ein Deutscher*, I:296–8; Jack Zipes, "The Critical Embracement of Germany: Hans Mayer and Marcel Reich-Ranicki," in *Unlikely History: The Changing German-Jewish Symbiosis, 1945–2000*, ed. Leslie Morris and Zipes (New York: Palgrave, 2002), 183–201. See also Michael Brenner, *After the Holocaust: Rebuilding Jewish Lives in Postwar Germany*, trans. Barbara Harshav (Princeton, N.J.: Princeton University Press, 1997), 58–60.

[106] Gallus, *"Weltbühne,"* 279–89, 306; Kinkela, *Rehabilitierung*, 41–3; Saner, *Jaspers*, 44–7; Suzanne Kirkbright, *Karl Jaspers: A Biography: Navigations in Truth* (New Haven, Conn.: Yale University Press, 2004), 165–7, 177. See Marion A. Kaplan, *Between Dignity and Despair: Jewish Life in Nazi Germany* (Oxford: Oxford University Press, 1998), 74–93, 148–50, 190–1.

[107] Demm, *Weimarer Republik*, 223–31. Weber later asserted that he was forced into early retirement, but his biographer finds no evidence of pressure behind Weber's April 1933 sabbatical petition; he retired after his 65th birthday that July.

Heidelberg students and SPD members who later joined the Kreisau Circle, a diverse resistance forum and seedbed for the conservative-led 20 July 1944 plot. Haubach was among the roughly 200 people put to death after its failure.[108] Henk was also central to the Jaspers' plan to protect Gertrud; in the event of a deportation risk, she hid at his house. They had done so twice already when word came of a direct deportation order in April 1945. Only Heidelberg's timely occupation by American forces prevented a third, desperate attempt. Each time, Mitscherlich acted as courier, accompanying Gertrud to her hideaway. He felt at home in this "circle of anti-Nazis," though his earlier filiations on the right left him – like Kogon – with an ambivalent past.[109]

Non-exiles often crafted circuitous accounts of opposition that were crucial to their self-image yet limited in their degree of self-reflection. Eggebrecht, for instance, readily mentioned that he made a living writing screenplays – some twenty in all, with directors from Helmut Käutner, a nonconformist, to Veit Harlan, on whose party-commissioned, blatantly anti-Semitic *Jew Süß* Eggebrecht refused to work. But he insisted that film remained relatively free of Nazi agendas and referred to his own projects as "unpolitical films." He used this phrase in postwar letters and recollections, but first in a 1934 application for admission to the Reich Literature Chamber, which closed with the obligatory "Heil Hitler!" His request was granted.[110] Kästner wrote covertly, under an assumed name, but received official clearance for the screenplay to the popular 1943 comedy *Münchhausen*. He continued to frequent cafés and took up a daily tennis regimen, in which Eggebrecht was a regular partner. Both later justified their decision not to emigrate by their desire to record Nazism's reality and witness its downfall. Yet they evaded the question of what role the mass entertainment they produced played in supporting the regime.[111]

An even stronger claim to have resisted nazification was made by the *Frankfurter Zeitung*. Sternberger was a political editor, but he and

---

[108] Ibid., 240–1. On the resistance of the SPD's "Young Right," see Hans Mommsen, *Alternatives to Hitler: German Resistance under the Third Reich*, trans. Angus McGeoch (Princeton, N.J.: Princeton University Press, 2003), esp. 42–133, 218–26; Stefan Vogt, *Nationaler Sozialismus und Soziale Demokratie: Die sozialdemokratische Junge Rechte 1918–1945* (Bonn: Dietz, 2006), 356–454.

[109] Saner, *Jaspers*, 48; Kirkbright, *Jaspers*, 182–3; Dehli, *Leben*, 124–6.

[110] Berndt, *Nur das Wort*, 69, 73–9. See, e.g., Eggebrecht to Kantorowicz, 9 August 1946, SUBH NL Kantorowicz NK: BI: E6; Eggebrecht, *Weg*, 307. Eggebrecht even claimed oppositional tendencies for film: Eggebrecht, "Rückblicke ins Dritte Reich," *Nordwestdeutsche Hefte* 1, no. 1 (1946): 12–16.

[111] Hanuschek, *Keiner blickt*, 225, 294–7. For Kästner's never-finished novel of life under Nazism, see Kästner, *Das blaue Buch: Kriegstagebuch und Roman-Notizen*, ed. Ulrich Bülow and Silke Becker (Marbach a.N.: Deutsche Schillergesellschaft, 2006). On Nazi film, see, e.g., Eric Rentschler, *The Ministry of Illusion: Nazi Cinema and its Afterlife* (Cambridge, Mass.: Harvard University Press, 1996).

Reifenberg both wrote more for the feuilleton, where Dirks and Knappstein were editors. After the war, the paper was hailed – especially by its former staff – for having minimized compromises while preserving a bastion of covert critique. Sternberger later dubbed this "undercover writing," for which the model was his Christmas 1941 retelling of Aesop's fable of the wolf and the lamb that made thinly veiled reference to Nazi tyranny and the persecution of Europe's Jews. His courage earned him the censors' enduring scrutiny. And this was only the most pointed of many carefully crafted, overtly non-political but covertly oppositional glosses on language and culture he published.[112] Dirks, by contrast, underscored the ambivalences of such "writing between the lines." At the *FZ*, only the politics section's gradual assimilation to Nazi norms allowed the feuilleton to keep ideology off its pages – an apparent preserve of culture that, reciprocally, served as a feather in the regime's cap.[113] Before 1933, Dirks could point to his antifascist, pro-republican interventions, in the left-Catholic *Rhein-Mainische Volkszeitung* (alongside Knappstein) and the aptly named *Deutsche Republik* (where Sternberger, too, published).[114] After 1933, Dirks recalled committing everyday acts that contested the regime's aspirations to total control: greeting Jews on the street, risking anti-Nazi conversations, and planning for a post-Nazi future.[115] However, he also remembered the fear that had kept him from active opposition. To Dirks, this "sin of omission" left him "co-culpable" for Nazism's ability to hold onto power. Though Kogon often tried to persuade him otherwise, both remained aware of their divergent pasts. These occasionally made for tension, even after years of closest friendship and collaboration.[116]

Occupation authorities also viewed the *FZ* with ambivalence. If former staffers focused on its 1943 closing, American officials questioned its

---

[112] Gillessen, *Posten*, 191–8, 352–4; Sternberger, "Figuren der Fabel," *Frankfurter Zeitung*, 25 December 1941; Sternberger, *Figuren der Fabel* (Berlin: Suhrkamp, 1950), quote 211. See also Heidrun Ehrke-Rotermund and Erwin Rotermund, *Zwischenreiche und Gegenwelten: Texte und Vorstudien zur "Verdeckten Schreibweise" im "Dritten Reich"* (Munich: Fink, 1999), 194–222; William J. Dodd, *Jedes Wort wandelt die Welt: Dolf Sternbergers politische Sprachkritik* (Göttingen: Wallstein, 2007), 149–219.

[113] Dirks, *Stotterer*, 23–4, 30; Frei and Schmitz, *Journalismus*, 121–35.

[114] Dirks, *Stotterer*, 18, 21–2, 30; Prümm, *Walter Dirks*, 12, 25–31, 141–50; Dodd, *Jedes Wort*, 126–48; Prümm, "Antifaschistische Mission ohne Adressaten: Zeitkritik und Prognostik in der Wochenzeitschrift Deutsche Republik 1929–1933," in *Weimars Ende: Prognosen und Diagnosen in der deutschen Literatur und politischen Publizistik 1930–1933*, ed. Koebner (Frankfurt a.M.: Suhrkamp, 1982), 103–42.

[115] This kind of non-compliance came to be called *Resistenz*, as against the more overt or organized challenge of *Widerstand*; see, classically, Martin Broszat, "Resistenz und Widerstand: Zwischenbilanz eines Forschungsprojekts," in *Bayern in der NS-Zeit*, vol. IV, *Herrschaft und Gesellschaft im Konflikt*, ed. Broszat, Elke Fröhlich, and Anton Grossmann (Munich: Oldenbourg, 1981), 691–709.

[116] Dirks, *Stotterer*, 24–5, 30–1; Ferdinand Menne, "Dirks & Kogon: Eine Momentaufnahme," *Neue Gesellschaft / Frankfurter Hefte* 50 (2003): 76.

continued operation under dictatorship. Moreover, they were committed to licensing an entirely new press and showed little empathy for Nazi-era papers and journalists. These conditions precluded the *FZ*'s revival on terms Reifenberg could accept; he broke off discussions with PWD, feeling not only the paper's revered tradition but German honor itself at stake. At the same time, Allied officials sought out the paper's personnel in filling positions of responsibility. When PWD approached Sternberger with a newspaper project for Heidelberg, he first tried to bring Reifenberg on board before declining the offer. He shared his friend's aversion to newspaper work under any censor's oversight, though without Reifenberg's tinge of national resentment.[117] In his stead, Sternberger recommended liberal politician and *FZ* contributor Theodor Heuss, who eventually became one of the *Rhein-Neckar-Zeitung*'s licensees.[118] Reifenberg carried forth the *FZ* tradition in a new guise: with four colleagues who had all waited out the war near Freiburg, he founded the semimonthly, French-licensed journal *Die Gegenwart*, which debuted at Christmas 1945. In 1946, *FZ* editor and SPD politician Otto Suhr (1894–1957) founded *Das sozialistische Jahrhundert* (*The Socialist Century*), a Berlin-based political and economic journal to which Dirks, Kogon, and Weber also contributed.[119]

The central question faced by non-exiles in 1945 – whether and how their choices under the regime had compromised them – rarely brooked an easy answer. Many who faced work prohibitions, interrogation, or imprisonment also earned a living in some fashion. Even NSDAP membership did not necessarily preclude an anti-Nazi self-image. Lommer, for example, wrote well-received, passionately antifascist works after the war, in the *Weltbühne*, *Tägliche Rundschau*, and his satirical revue *The Thousand-Year Reich*. Only later was it revealed that he had joined the party in 1934.[120] Rowohlt did not deny joining the NSDAP in 1937 or

---

[117] Gillessen, *Posten*, 503–25; Waldmüller, *Wandlung*, 15–16; Pape, *Kultureller Neubeginn*, 102–8. On their stances toward the nation, compare Dagmar Bussiek, *Benno Reifenberg, 1892–1970: Eine Biographie* (Göttingen: Wallstein, 2011) with Michaela Hoenicke Moore, "Heimat und Fremde: Das Verhältnis zu Amerika im journalistischen Werk von Margret Boveri und Dolf Sternberger," in *Demokratiewunder: Transatlantische Mittler und die kulturelle Öffnung Westdeutschlands 1945–1970*, ed. Arnd Bauerkämper, Jarausch, and Payk (Göttingen: Vandenhoeck & Ruprecht, 2005), 218–50.

[118] The delay stemmed from American concerns over Heuss' vote for the 1933 "Enabling Law" and his journalistic career under Nazism, even without being aware of his work at Goebbels' weekly *Das Reich*. Hurwitz, *Stunde Null*, 134–5; Frei and Schmitz, *Journalismus*, 112.

[119] Gillessen, *Posten*, 512, 523; Bussiek, *Reifenberg*, 369–425; Hubertus Buchstein, *Politikwissenschaft und Demokratie: Wissenschaftskonzeption und Demokratietheorie sozialdemokratischer Nachkriegspolitologen in Berlin* (Baden-Baden: Nomos, 1992), 158–63.

[120] Wurm, *Aufbau-Verlag*, 40, 49.

Germans, occupiers, and the democratization project 57

serving in a Wehrmacht propaganda unit – responsible for anti-Semitic agitation in the Middle East – from 1941. Of course, he was quicker to mention his ejection from publishing in 1938 or his military discharge as "politically unreliable" in 1943. Moreover, he could point to Jewish editors and authors he protected. If his catalog was rightly known as leftist and liberal – many of its works were banned in 1933 – he also published conservatives such as his close friend, the anti-Nazi nationalist Ernst von Salomon, with whom Kantorowicz and Eggebrecht were acquainted as well.[121] Rowohlt's was an extreme case, but ambiguous pasts were an inescapable outcome of "inner emigration."

This helps explain the attraction of *Die Weltbühne* as a locus of identification. Politically independent yet implacably hostile to the regime – to all militarism and nationalism – it was shut down summarily in 1933 and never given the opportunity to compromise itself. In 1945, it attained iconic status, as an unsullied antifascist resource to which many laid claim.[122] Germany's engaged democrats did so, those who had written for its Weimar and exile incarnations as well as a host of new postwar authors and assorted admirers. The old guard contributed portraits of the Weimar-era editors: Ihering related memories of Jacobsohn, and Kästner lauded Tucholsky – as did new author Drews – for his razor-sharp barbs against the forces of reaction. Kantorowicz, Nardi, and Schnog honored Ossietzky's staunch anti-militarism and anti-Nazism, which landed him in prison before and after 1933. Eggebrecht likewise profiled his mentor as an all-too-rare German figure: not a "poet" but a "publicist," a "servant of the daily public word" who worked to hold the Republic to its best democratic ideals. The *Weltbühne* had been Ossietzky's "unshakable tribune," and "in his spirit we again begin anew."[123] These were key reference points for others too. Mayer confessed he "still stood in thrall of Tucholsky and his *Weltbühne*" when he met its author, Eggebrecht, in 1946. And Dirks recalled how he and his friends prized the journal's "combative spirit in the 1920s"; now, they made its program their own: "the cause of freedom *and* the cause of socialism." He praised the new

---

[121] Oels, *Rotationsroutine*, 7–10, 57–186; Gruner, *Schicksal*, 200, 321–2; Eggebrecht, *Weg*, 253–5.
[122] Gallus, *"Weltbühne,"* 62–79 and passim.
[123] Herbert Ihering, "Siegfried Jacobsohn," *Die Weltbühne* 1, no. 2 (1946): 35–7; Kästner, "Kurt Tucholsky, Carl v. Ossietzky, 'Weltbühne,'" *Die Weltbühne* 1, no. 1 (1946): 21–3; Drews, "Der, den wir schmerzlich vermissen," *Die Weltbühne* 2, no. 1 (1947): 16–18; Kantorowicz, "Begrabene Freiheit: Carl von Ossietzky auf dem Wege ins Gefängnis," *Die Weltbühne* 1, no. 10 (1946): 293–8; Pauline Nardi, "Seine letzte Rede," *Die Weltbühne* 3, no. 18 (1948): 457–8; Karl Schnog, "An Carl von Ossietzky," *Die Weltbühne* 3, no. 18 (1948): 456; Eggebrecht, "Carl von Ossietzky," *Die Weltbühne* 1, no. 4 (1946): 112–13, 116.

journal's first issues highly, except a piece by Weinert, whose doctrinaire polemics had "nothing to do with the tradition of the *Weltbühne*."[124] The latter stood for ideologically eclectic but supremely resolute anti-Nazism, carried by a broad antifascist coalition.

Over time, opinions diverged on the postwar journal's capacity to uphold this legacy, given its strong SED ties. By fall 1946, its editors faced attacks from – and launched attacks on – other Berlin papers, especially the *Telegraf* and *Tagesspiegel*. Their main adversary, a *Tagesspiegel* licensee named Walther Karsch (1906–1975, ex-husband of Pauline Nardi), had been an editor of the late Weimar *Weltbühne*. In 1945, he entered the KPD, made a failed bid to re-establish the journal, and left the KPD again. He soon accused the new journal of betraying its namesake and was branded a turncoat – "Chameleon Karsch" – in return. His friend and mentor Kurt Hiller (1885–1972), a central Weimar *Weltbühne* author, radical pacifist, and combative anti-Communist still in London exile, entered the fray. He summarily dismissed the new journal as a front; after only two issues, he asserted, it had already "veer[ed] into Russian territory."[125] Others reserved judgment for longer. Initially, Eggebrecht confided high hopes to Kantorowicz, imagining the new journal might become his primary venue. By 1947, he had reservations but still hoped to maintain ties, since "despite all the differences," it was "still something like a home."[126] This was not Eggebrecht's first disagreement with Hiller, whose unabashedly elitist calls for *Logokratie*, or rule by an intellectual aristocracy, he had long rejected. If Hiller projected a too-unified political program – his own – onto the Weimar-era *Weltbühne*, Eggebrecht idealized it as a model platform for eclectic yet committed critical intervention.[127] Not by accident was a cultural-political journal the strongest common denominator of the antifascist identities around which Germany's engaged democrats coalesced after 1945.

## Proclaiming unity, drawing distinctions

The intellectuals in question hoped to build the postwar polity on the broadest possible base. In that sense, their vision was plural and inclusive, aiming to transcend the political fragmentation that had helped Hitler to

---

[124] Mayer, *Ein Deutscher*, I:370; Dirks, "Die neue 'Weltbühne,'" *Frankfurter Hefte* 1, no. 6 (1946): 91.
[125] Schivelbusch, *Cold Crater*, 169–70, 174–5; Kurt Hiller to Kästner, 7 July 1946, DLA A:Kästner. On Hiller, see Gallus, *"Weltbühne,"* 80–156.
[126] Eggebrecht to Kantorowicz, 9 August 1946, SUBH NL Kantorowicz NK: BI: E6; Eggebrecht to Ralph Giordano, 7 February 1947, SUBH NL Eggebrecht NE: B128: 2, Bl. 7–9.
[127] Eggebrecht, *Weg*, 210; Gallus, *"Weltbühne,"* 64–71, 336–8.

power and mobilize wide swaths of post-fascist society for renewal. Only irredeemable Nazis were to be excluded. At the same time, they knew their views vied with others for influence on the postwar scene. This heady period of disorientation and reorientation saw myriad groups debating Germany's past and planning its future, and engaged democrats drew clear contrasts to the competition. Even as they advocated broad-based cooperation, they maintained the distinctness of their positions.

Their conviction that new kinds of coalitions were possible rested on a sense that sheer devastation had suspended the class-based conflicts of the capitalist era. As Kogon put it, "entrenched large-scale industrial-capitalist-agrarian class domination" had been reduced to "a rubble heap" in Germany, presenting an unprecedented opportunity "to build a liveable house in common." Given this shift, Sternberger underscored the need to rescue civic virtue from the crumbling social structures that had first nurtured it: "Why should burgher-ness (*Bürgerlichkeit*) not outlive the bourgeoisie (*das Bürgertum*)?" Others farther to the left were less sanguine about the dissolution of class society. But they concurred that renewal imperatives could and should override old antagonisms. Characteristically, Leonhard called for a "unity of all progressives and socialists, all those who truly desire and will a truly new Germany." Within this constellation, however, the "unity of both workers' parties" remained the "centerpiece of democratic unity." On such a foundation, Germany would build a "second republic" and never a "fourth *Reich*."[128] Postwar conditions seemed to enable the productive coalition-building that had eluded Germans in the past.

The decisive distinction was between forces of renewal and reaction, potential partners and unregenerate Nazis. Here, engaged democrats imagined themselves and their allies as members of one extended community, an "other Germany" that had challenged Nazism and its claims to represent the nation. The phrase had originated as the title of a 1920s pacifist journal, but it gained wider currency during the Nazi-era exile, reflected not least in the title of a 1940 manifesto by Erika and Klaus Mann, two more of Thomas' children. By disentangling Nazism and Germanness, they asserted an alternate national constituency, one that defended German culture abroad and hoped for self-liberation at home.[129] For many, this notion implied a series of oppositions: between exiles and "inner émigrés" or between a courageous antifascist minority

---

[128] Kogon, "Der Weg zu einem Sozialismus der Freiheit in Deutschland," *Frankfurter Hefte* 2, no. 9 (1947): 877; Sternberger, "Tagebuch: Bürgerlichkeit," *Die Wandlung* 3, no. 3 (1948): 199; Rudolf Leonhard, "Gedanken eines Heimgekehrten," *Die Weltbühne* 2, no. 16 (1947): 667–8.

[129] Helmut Donat and Karl Holl, eds. *Die Friedensbewegung: Organisierter Pazifismus in Deutschland, Österreich und in der Schweiz* (Düsseldorf: ECON, 1983), 26–9; Erika

and a majority who actively or passively supported the regime. Engaged democrats, by contrast, made the idea useful for a more conciliatory post-fascist politics.

Both exiles and non-exiles among them worked to mediate between these at times bitterly estranged camps. Kantorowicz's efforts to this end were especially persistent. Both groups, he insisted – "spiritually connected" though "physically separated" for years – had constituted "an other, non-Nazi Germany," and only together could they lay the foundations of renewal.[130] National Socialism, too, had made this connection, defaming and suppressing writers from both groups. This began with student-led book burnings in university towns across Germany on 10 May 1933, which consumed works by scores of authors deemed "un-German," from Marx, Heine, Freud, Heinrich Mann, Brecht, Kästner, and Seghers to Barbusse, Kollontai, and Sinclair. Marking this anniversary became a focus for Kantorowicz in exile; it was the topic of his first publication in postwar Germany, and he organized the first commemoration there.[131] With Drews, an "inner émigré," he produced an anthology titled *Banned and Burned*, which excerpted German works featured on the Nazis' ever-expanding "black lists." The focus was on contemporary writers, including Becher, Bloch, Brecht, Habe, Hermlin, Hiller, Kästner, Koestler, Kolbenhoff, Leonhard, all four Manns, Mayer, Ossietzky, Plievier, Schnog, Schroeder, Seghers, Tucholsky, and Weisenborn; also mentioned were Budzislawski, Eggebrecht, Ihering, Jaspers, Karsch, Kogon, Krauss, Lommer, Mitscherlich, Scheer, Steiniger, and many more.[132] Literati of various political persuasions, exiles and non-exiles, were presented without distinction, unified in persecution and opposition.

Also represented were the main antagonists of the "great controversy" of 1945: Frank Thieß, a well-known novelist, and the celebrated Thomas Mann, now a US citizen. Thieß had asserted that "those who stayed home" and endured Nazism in "inner emigration" could better understand Germany's predicament than those who merely observed the "German tragedy" from comfortable "balconies and parquet seats" abroad. Mann's scathing response described the painful "heart-asthma of exile,"

---

and Klaus Mann, *The Other Germany*, trans. Heinz Norden (New York: Modern Age, 1940). See, e.g., Palmier, *Weimar*, 124–8, 282–91.

[130] Kantorowicz, "Deutsche Schriftsteller im Exil," *Ost und West* 1, no. 4 (1947): 43, 47.
[131] Kantorowicz, "Erinnerung an den 10. Mai 1933," *Die Neue Zeitung*, 13 May 1946. On the 1947 ceremony, see Chapter 5. On the 1933 book burnings, see Werner Treß, *Wider den undeutschen Geist: Bücherverbrennung 1933* (Berlin: Parthas, 2003).
[132] Drews and Kantorowicz, eds. *Verboten und verbrannt: Deutsche Literatur 12 Jahre unterdrückt* (Berlin: Ullstein-Kindler, 1947).

and condemned the "stench of blood and disgrace" that clung to anything published in Germany under Nazism. He acknowledged his enduring ties, but he bluntly declined to return to Germany. Hostility toward exiles rose palpably in the wake of this high-profile dispute.[133] Engaged democrats were among the few in Germany who publicly advocated the recognition of both camps. As even liberal organs such as Reifenberg's *Gegenwart* challenged the legitimacy of exiles to speak for or about Germany, Sternberger called for more respect for Mann, as the fullest living fruit of the German literary tradition, while Kantorowicz lauded Mann's political essays as evidence of his deep co-suffering with the nation. Kästner, for his part, publicly chided Mann – not for having emigrated but for refusing to return. In a 1947 survey, Kästner was one of the very few who urged OMGUS to encourage Mann to reconsider.[134]

Questions of responsibility – of who counted as a Nazi and how far culpability extended – ignited fierce debate. Publicly, they provoked defensive reactions against supposed allegations of "collective guilt" and the Allies' "victors' justice." Private memories, meanwhile, trafficked still more in resentful rejections of guilt, exculpatory equivalences of suffering, or compensatory accounts of German heroism.[135] Troubled, Germany's engaged democrats attempted to nuance the debate. Kästner, for instance, agreed that "guilt" (*Schuld*) did not accrue to each German on account of Nazism. But a certain "debt" (*Schulden*) did, and he lamented that Germans were quick to feel accused of the former in order to divest themselves of the latter.[136] After Norwegian novelist Sigrid Undset pronounced the Germans collectively uneducable, Jaspers accepted her "indignation" while rejecting her attempt "summarily to

---

[133] The key interventions, published and republished widely in the German and foreign press, were soon collected as Thomas Mann, Frank Thieß, and Walter von Molo, *Ein Streitgespräch über die äußere und die innere Emigration* (Dortmund: Druckschriften Vertriebsdienst, 1946). See, e.g., Thomas Goll, *Die Deutschen und Thomas Mann: Die Rezeption des Dichters in Abhängigkeit von der politischen Kultur Deutschlands 1898–1955* (Baden-Baden: Nomos, 2000), 271–80; Stephen Brockmann, *German Literary Culture at the Zero Hour* (Rochester, N.Y.: Camden House, 2004), 93–106.

[134] "Briefe von draußen – Antworten von drinnen," *Die Gegenwart* 1, no. 1 (1945): 26; Sternberger, "Tagebuch: Thomas Mann und der Respekt," *Die Wandlung* 1, no. 6 (1946): 451–9; Kantorowicz, "Thomas Mann im Spiegel seiner politischen Essays," *Ost und West* 3, no. 8 (1949): 46–68; Kästner, "Betrachtungen eines Unpolitischen," *Die Neue Zeitung*, 14 January 1946; Jost Hermand and Wigand Lage, "*Wollt ihr Thomas Mann wiederhaben?*" *Deutschland und die Emigranten* (Hamburg: Europäische Verlagsanstalt, 1999), 141–2.

[135] See, e.g., Jeffrey K. Olick, *In the House of the Hangman: The Agonies of German Defeat, 1943–1949* (Chicago: University of Chicago Press, 2005); Harald Welzer, Sabine Moller, and Karoline Tschuggnall, *Opa war kein Nazi: Nationalsozialismus und Holocaust im Familiengedächtnis* (Frankfurt a.M.: Fischer, 2002).

[136] Kästner, "Der Schuld und die Schulden," *Die Neue Zeitung*, 3 December 1945.

judge... a people as a whole." Instead, he differentiated: each German citizen shared in "political" liability for the regime's actions, not automatically in "moral" guilt for its crimes. Crucial was that each examine the extent of their own complicity and acknowledge its relation to their present hardships. Germans' reeducation was indeed possible, he asserted, but only as a "self-education." These ideas were elaborated in Jaspers' 1946 *The Question of Guilt*, with its typology of criminal, political, moral, and "metaphysical guilt." The latter he grounded in a "solidarity between humans as humans that makes each co-responsible for all wrongs and injustices in the world, especially for crimes committed in their presence or with their knowledge." Self-reflection at this level was the key condition, he asserted, for a dialogue about past and present that was urgently needed for the future.[137] Engaged democrats rejected a uniform German guilt while exhorting fellow Germans to consider the degrees and modes of their personal responsibility.

Such questions had implications for denazification practice, one of the thorniest occupation policy issues. At the Nuremberg military tribunal, a handful of major Nazis stood criminal trial, as did twelve thousand more in other postwar courts.[138] Still, Germany was awash in minor Nazis, known as "little PGs" (or "party comrades"). NSDAP membership had grown from one million in 1933 to some 8.5 million, or one in five adults; legions more belonged to ancillary organizations. All told, two thirds of Germans were organized in and through the party.[139] Denazification was thus a mammoth undertaking. Differences in implementation arose across the zones, but basic procedures were common. Improvised arrests, internments, and dismissals were soon followed by regularized procedures involving questionnaires, screenings, and millions of quasi-judicial hearings before local, German-staffed boards (which often undermined the integrity of the process). The goal was to distinguish – largely by formal membership, office, and rank – between active and nominal Nazis, or the truly incriminated and mere "fellow travelers" (*Mitläufer*). While the latter were eligible for positions in public life, the former faced bans on

---

[137] Sigrid Undset, "Die Umerziehung der Deutschen," *Die Neue Zeitung*, 25 October 1945; Jaspers, "Antwort an Sigrid Undset," *Die Neue Zeitung*, 4 November 1945; Jaspers, *Die Schuldfrage: Ein Beitrag zur deutschen Frage* (Heidelberg: Schneider, 1946), quote 31. See above all Rabinbach, *In the Shadow of Catastrophe: German Intellectuals between Apocalypse and Enlightenment* (Berkeley: University of California Press, 1997), 129–65.

[138] See, e.g., Donald Bloxham, *Genocide on Trial: War Crimes Trials and the Formation of Holocaust History and Memory* (Oxford: Oxford University Press, 2001); Devin O. Pendas, "Retroactive Law and Proactive Justice: Debating Crimes against Humanity in Germany, 1945–1950," *Central European History* 43, no. 3 (2010): 428–63.

[139] See, e.g., Benz, introduction to *Wie wurde man Parteigenosse? Die NSDAP und ihre Mitglieder*, ed. Benz (Frankfurt a.M.: Fischer, 2009), 7–17.

all non-menial jobs (and other penalties, from fines and property losses to work camps). Though the intent was to discriminate, the practice felt punitive, and it was criticized for its wide sweep, slow outcomes, and too-schematic criteria, which were blind to degrees of conviction and the possibility of inner opposition.[140]

On denazification, engaged democrats also took a mediating stance. They sought to build "emergency bridges of understanding," as Eggebrecht put it, between the polarized views of zealous antifascists and bankrupt apologists. Including convinced Nazis and criminals as full postwar citizens was an ethical and political impossibility; renewal required a radical break with that past. But engaged democrats were conciliatory toward most Nazi followers, whom they considered redeemable. As Nardi pointed out, many a "naive PG" was far less culpable than nominally unaffiliated artists and writers who had propagated the Nazis' worldview and now claimed they were "passive resist[ers]." Kogon distinguished committing or abetting "crimes" from what he called "political error": the misguided ideas, poor judgment, opportunism, and weakness that also led many astray. "To err is human," he recited, doubtless with his own past in mind. And to errors accrued not "guilt" but a responsibility to "atone"; properly recognized, errors could trigger a learning process and prompt "making amends." As implemented, denazification muddied these distinctions, a fact that "incorrigible National Socialists" and their "entourage of chauvinists, nationalists, and militarists" misused to discredit the entire process.[141] Germany's engaged democrats did not support excluding nominal Nazis from the postwar polity, provided they committed unreservedly to a new, antifascist and democratic order.

Such commitments to an inclusive, yet bounded political unity were mirrored by their social network in practice. Engaged democrats' network was not tightly knit, nor did they constitute a singular political tendency or intellectual school; rather, the diversity of affiliations and influences is striking. But their views bore family resemblances, and their positions toward contemporary competitors paralleled one another. Accordingly, even as the linkages among them intertwined with those of other

---

[140] See, e.g., Clemens Vollnhals, introduction to *Entnazifizierung: Politische Säuberung und Rehabilitierung in den vier Besatzungszonen 1945–1949*, ed. Vollnhals (Munich: Deutscher Taschenbuch Verlag, 1991), 7–64; Armin Schuster, *Die Entnazifizierung in Hessen 1945–1954: Vergangenheitspolitik in der Nachkriegszeit* (Wiesbaden: Historische Kommission für Nassau, 1999); Timothy R. Vogt, *Denazification in Soviet-Occupied Germany: Brandenburg, 1945–1948* (Cambridge, Mass.: Harvard University Press, 2000).

[141] "'Entnazifizierung' – Notbrücken zum Verstehen," *Nordwestdeutsche Hefte* 1, no. 4 (1946): 12–14; Nardi, "Passiver Widerstand?" *Die Weltbühne* 2, no. 7 (1947): 294–6; Kogon, "Das Recht auf den politischen Irrtum," *Frankfurter Hefte* 2, no. 7 (1947): 649–52.

groupings, they simultaneously demarcated a distinct intellectual configuration.

One important axis of distinction was generational. These actors saw themselves as having come of age in time to escape Nazism's influence, unlike those whose formative years were molded by the regime. Thereby, they reproduced a common postwar frame, in which nazified "youth" appeared as the dangerous yet educable object of less tainted elders' intervention. They did so, however, against the grain of the apologetic memory politics it usually served.[142] Weber (b. 1868) spoke of the "guilt account" of older Germans, who failed to prevent Nazism, toward younger Germans, who bore its consequences. Kästner (b. 1899) decried older hypocrites who lamented young people's "false ideals" and lectured them with "pointed, wagging finger" as they swept their own past under the rug. And Harich (b. 1923) published a parody of the best-known such lament, Ernst Wiechert's "Speech to German Youth."[143] Yet even as they dismissed attempts to displace guilt onto the young, they deployed a generational lens. According to Kogon, his cohort of "forty- to fifty-year-olds" was the natural "mediator" between Germany's past and future. They would rebuild with the help of "young men and women between eighteen and thirty-five," who now emerged from the "fog" of Nazism as "illusion-free people with expectations" for a better world.[144]

The self-appointed spokesmen of this cohort were the writers around *Der Ruf*, journal of "the young generation" (as the subtitle had it). They too pressed for a democratic, socialist, neutral post-fascist Germany, albeit on the ground of different experiences. Co-editors Alfred Andersch (1914–1980) and Hans Werner Richter (1908–1993) had been drafted, sent into combat, and reeducated in American POW camps. Without being especially young, they identified with young ex-soldiers, misled by ideology and hardened by war, "separated from their elders by non-responsibility for Hitler [and] from their juniors by experiences of front and captivity, that is, by the 'committed' life." The *Ruf* circle espoused the

---

[142] Jaimey Fisher, *Disciplining Germany: Youth, Reeducation, and Reconstruction after the Second World War* (Detroit: Wayne State University Press, 2007).
[143] Alfred Weber, "Student und Politik," *Die Wandlung* 2, no. 3/4 (1947): 284–5; Kästner, "Die Jugend hat das Wort," *Die Weltbühne* 1, no. 6 (1946): 185; Hipponax [Harich], "500. Rede an die deutsche Jugend: Nach Ernst Wiechert," *Der Kurier*, 2 March 1946. *Der Ruf* reprinted Harich's piece in their first issue: "500. Rede an die deutsche Jugend: Eine Parodie, frei nach Ernst Wiechert," *Der Ruf* 1, no. 1 (1946): 12. On Wiechert, see Fisher, *Disciplining*, 156–71.
[144] Kogon, "Über die Situation," *Frankfurter Hefte* 2, no. 1 (1947): 37. The latter cohort corresponds roughly to what is called the "Hitler Youth," "skeptical," or "forty-fiver" generation; Moses, "The Forty-Fivers: A Generation between Fascism and Democracy," *German Politics and Society* 17, no. 1 (1999): 94–126.

radically self-grounding, individualized freedom of French existentialism, and they denied the authority of their elders' traditions. Vehemently, they rejected "collective guilt," advocated the German nation's interests, and questioned the occupation's legitimacy, setting them on a collision course with US officials.[145] Despite differences of experience and disposition, these postwar "youth" and Germany's engaged democrats each recognized in the other an ally. Before *Der Ruf*, Andersch worked under Kästner at *Die Neue Zeitung*, alongside Kolbenhoff, another ex-soldier. Andersch credited Kästner as a journalistic mentor, though they inhabited different intellectual worlds: "I spoke of Sartre, while he spoke of Lessing." After leaving *Der Ruf* and co-founding the literary forum Gruppe 47, Andersch joined the *Frankfurter Hefte*, where others of his colleagues also developed connections.[146] The two groups made common cause for a renewed Germany.

If generation was an important marker on this intellectual field, programmatic distinctions were more decisive. Neutrality versus alignment in the East–West conflict was a central issue around which distinct groupings emerged. Engaged democrats with close ties to Communism, for instance, were not among the KPD/SED's leading intellectual cadres. Figures such as Harich, Kantorowicz, Rudolf Leonhard, Mayer, and Schroeder did not hold prominent party and administrative posts, as did Abusch, Ackermann, Becher, or Weinert.[147] Socially, these circles intersected only minimally, and their members' itineraries before 1945 diverged as well. The former group spent the Nazi period in Germany, western Europe, and the USA. The latter returned mainly from

---

[145] [Alfred Andersch], "Das junge Europa formt sein Gesicht," *Der Ruf* 1, no. 1 (1946): quote 2. *Der Ruf* appeared semi-monthly from August 1946 in 20,000 to 70,000 copies. On the journal, see Jérôme Vaillant, *Der Ruf: Unabhängige Blätter der jungen Generation (1945–1949): Eine Zeitschrift zwischen Illusion und Anpassung* (Munich: Saur, 1978); Gallus, "'Der Ruf' – Stimme für ein neues Deutschland," *Aus Politik und Zeitgeschichte* 25 (2007): 32–8. On the ideological shaping of the Wehrmacht, see Omer Bartov, *Hitler's Army: Soldiers, Nazis, and War in the Third Reich* (Oxford: Oxford University Press, 1991).

[146] Gienow-Hecht, *Transmission*, 41–2; Stephan Reinhardt, *Alfred Andersch: Eine Biographie* (Zurich: Diogenes, 1990), 129–31, 149–51; Andersch, "Der Seesack: Aus einer Autobiographie," in *Das Alfred Andersch Lesebuch*, ed. Gerd Haffmans (Zurich: Diogenes, 1979), quote 98. Ex-*Ruf* authors reported on the youth's political mood and on the Gruppe 47's founding meeting: Andersch, "Das Unbehagen in der Politik: Eine Generation unter sich," *Frankfurter Hefte* 2, no. 9 (1947): 912–25; Friedrich Minssen, "Notizen von einem Treffen junger Schriftsteller," *Frankfurter Hefte* 3, no. 2 (1948): 110–11.

[147] Krauss, a partial exception, was elected to represent the Kulturbund in the Party Executive in February 1948, part of an effort to bind this supra-party organization tighter to the party; Dietrich, *Politik und Kultur in der Sowjetischen Besatzungszone Deutschlands 1945–1949* (Bern: Lang, 1993), 106–10.

the Moscow exile, hardened by years at the very center of Soviet power, or from Mexico, which had been relatively hospitable to Communists.[148] On the ground in Germany, the former group worked closely with Soviet officials and wrote not only for Kulturbund publications or *Die Weltbühne* but also for the party's *Deutsche Volkszeitung*, later *Neues Deutschland* (*New Germany*), and its theoretical journal *Einheit* (*Unity*), venues not sought out by more independent-minded peers.

Crucially, their views on the role of the party also diverged. Engaged democrats' call for broad-based cooperation was compatible with official Communist coalition building at the time. The latter strategy aimed to occupy not the top posts but the decisive ones with KPD/SED loyalists, leaving non-Communists in most formal leadership and many secondary roles. This maintained a veneer of pluralism while seizing the levers of effective power. Per Ulbricht's pithy, oft-cited directive: "It must look democratic, yet we must have everything firmly in hand."[149] In this frame, coalition politics figured as a means to co-opt "bourgeois" support during the party-managed transition from fascism to state socialism. This cynical approach found a clear-eyed critic in Harich: rather than a "forum for honest, contentious discussion," he asserted, it provided "a semblance of unity" over actual "despotism." In private, he was even more caustic: the KPD's proclaimed "united front" in fact "circumvented democracy" and branded any opposition "reactionary" under a "pretense of antifascism." Leonhard drew parallels to the 1930s. Just as concerted popular front action might have beaten fascism then, similar cooperation was required for post-fascist renewal now. Such "unanimity," however, must rest on "not a schematic, commanded unity but a manifold, living, organically effective unity."[150] Both Harich and Leonhard would join the KPD/SED in the coming months and years. Nonetheless, their initial position valued pluralist dialogue among all antifascist forces intrinsically, not merely tactically. At base, they did not share hardliners' convictions about the "leading role" of the party, or the discipline and unquestioning loyalty captured

---

[148] On Communists' exile geographies and their postwar legacies, see Jeffrey Herf, *Divided Memory: The Nazi Past in the Two Germanys* (Cambridge, Mass.: Harvard University Press, 1997), 13–105. On exile in Latin America, see Palmier, *Weimar*, 571–9.

[149] Ulbricht quoted in Wolfgang Leonhard, *Revolution*, 358. See, e.g., Peter Erler and Manfred Wilke, "'Nach Hitler kommen wir': Das Konzept der Moskauer KPD-Führung 1944/45 für Nachkriegsdeutschland," *Exilforschung* 15 (1997): 102–19; Frederike Sattler, "Bündnispolitik als politisch-organisatorisches Problem des zentralen Parteiapparates der KPD 1945/46," in *Anatomie der Parteizentrale: Die KPD/SED auf dem Weg zur Macht*, ed. Manfred Wilke (Berlin: Akademie, 1998), 119–212.

[150] Harich, "Parteikrise u. Einheitsfront," *Der Kurier*, 27 December 1945; Harich to Reger, 6 January 1946, AdK Reger-Archiv 311; Leonhard, "Gedanken," 668.

Germans, occupiers, and the democratization project 67

in their motto "the party is always right."[151] Official openness was thus a condition of some engaged democrats' affinities for Communism.[152] And their later reluctance to relinquish that principle in lockstep with party dictates fed their marginalization and opposition in the GDR.

To those engaged democrats who stood closer to the other side of the emergent divide, antifascist cooperation was no less important. Even the staunchest anti-Stalinists were not among those activists who, motivated by "consensus liberalism" and anti-Communism, sought to orient Germany firmly toward the "West."[153] Their most important venue was Berlin, hothouse of the proto-Cold War, where the *Tagesspiegel* under Reger, Karsch, and Edwin Redslob and the Berlin SPD around Suhr and Ernst Reuter worked toward this end, soon joined by others such as Pechel and Günther Birkenfeld. As they developed ties to a transatlantic network of American officials and émigré ex-Communists such as Koestler and Manès Sperber, these groups became the core constituency of the journal *Der Monat* (*The Month*, established 1948), and the Congress for Cultural Freedom (CCF, established 1950), key vehicles of the ideological struggle against the USSR. They also cultivated ties to Germany's engaged democrats, involving Jaspers, Weber, Mitscherlich, Sternberger, and Kogon at the CCF's foundation. Notably, however, some of the latter publicly disavowed the former group's militant Cold War partisanship.[154]

In the immediate postwar years, economist Wilhelm Röpke, writing from Swiss exile, provoked a series of telling disputes. Röpke later became a prominent *Monat* contributor and CCF member, and his work helped inspire the FRG's "social market economy."[155] As early as 1945, his

---

[151] Catherine Epstein, *The Last Revolutionaries: German Communists and Their Century* (Cambridge, Mass.: Harvard University Press, 2003), quote 12. As Epstein shows, these convictions held fast through all faction fights and dogma shifts for those party stalwarts who built and led the GDR.

[152] One can invert this logic and read the postwar embrace of pluralism as submission to the reigning orthodoxy; cf. Werner Müller, "Kommunistische Intellektuelle in der SBZ und in der frühen DDR," in *Kritik und Mandat: Intellektuelle in der deutschen Politik*, ed. Gangolf Hübinger and Thomas Hertfelder (Stuttgart: Deutsche Verlags-Anstalt, 2000), 239–65. On their later trajectories, which do not support such an assessment, see Chapter 6.

[153] See, e.g., Anselm Doering-Manteuffel, *Wie westlich sind die Deutschen? Amerikanisierung und Westernisierung im 20. Jahrhundert* (Göttingen: Vandenhoeck & Ruprecht, 1999), 75–102.

[154] Michael Hochgeschwender, *Freiheit in der Offensive? Der Kongress für kulturelle Freiheit und die Deutschen* (Munich: Oldenbourg, 1998); Berghahn, *America*. On *Der Monat* and the CCF, see Chapters 5 and 7.

[155] See, e.g., Josef Mooser, "Liberalismus und Gesellschaft nach 1945: Soziale Marktwirtschaft und Neoliberalismus am Beispiel von Wilhelm Röpke," in *Bürgertum nach*

interventions crystallized two central issues: the argument for a separate West Germany bound to the Western Allies as well as the robust defense of liberal ideals on which such arguments rested. Advocating the integration of Germany's western zones into an "Atlantic Community," Röpke posited a "complete divide of moral, political, social, and economic fundamentals" at the border to the Soviet zone, where "totalitarian Russia" ruled.[156] Harich took exception, disputing not only the identification of socialism with Nazism as "totalitarianism" but also the geopolitical project it underwrote: the division of Germany and consolidation of an anti-Soviet bloc. In 1948, as these positions gained traction, the *Frankfurter Hefte* juxtaposed Röpke's free-market Western alliance with Weber's plan for an independent, socialist yet democratic Europe. The former's "principle of freedom" – trumpeted as the heritage of the West, implacably opposed to Eastern "collectivism" – was no less or more than the "political freedom that liberalism secured for the bourgeoisie, at the expense of the broadest popular strata's economic and social freedom." In the present, they insisted, strictly "formal" freedom was anachronistic without a "material" complement. While Röpke's vision might appear more realistic, there was no choice but to embrace Weber's, which promised both greater justice and a more secure peace.[157]

Ideas about the "West" fed different, not necessarily congruent positions among postwar Germany's educated strata. At first, those who emphasized Atlantic affinities and Anglo-American leadership were in the minority. Rather, the tone was set by those who located Germany in continental Europe as a Christian "Occident" (*Abendland*). Such views had deep roots in Catholic mental geographies (with medieval Christendom as their reference) but also appealed to conservative Protestants. They were broadcast by a number of southern German journals, most stridently in Augsburg's *Neues Abendland* and more moderately in Baden-Baden's *Merkur*.[158] Although the *Abendland* notion, too, opposed

---

*1945*, ed. Manfred Hettling and Bernd Ulrich (Hamburg: Hamburger Edition, 2005), 134–63. Röpke was a leading neoliberal and a founding member of Friedrich Hayek's Mont Pèlerin Society in 1947.

[156] Wilhelm Röpke, *Die deutsche Frage*, 2nd edn. (Erlenbach-Zurich: Rentsch, 1945), 249–51; see also his pamphlet *Das Kulturideal des Liberalismus* (Frankfurt a.M.: Schulte-Bulmke, 1947).

[157] Harich, "Röpke, Pechel und der 'Totalitarismus,'" *Tägliche Rundschau*, 23 August 1946; "Deutschland, Europa und die Welt," *Frankfurter Hefte* 3, no. 5 (1948): 462–3.

[158] On *Merkur*, see, e.g., Bock, "Die fortgesetzte Modernisierung des Konservatismus: Merkur. Deutsche Zeitschrift für europäisches Denken 1947 bis 1957," in *Le discours européen dans les revues allemandes / Der Europadiskurs in den deutschen Zeitschriften (1945–1955)*, ed. Grunewald and Bock (Bern: Lang, 2001), 149–85; Friedrich Kießling, *Die undeutschen Deutschen: Eine ideengeschichtliche Archäologie der alten Bundesrepublik 1945–1972* (Paderborn: Schöningh, 2012).

Occidental "freedom" to Soviet "totalitarianism," it initially ran counter to Atlantic ties. For it demarcated Europe against both "West" and "East," rejecting the secularism and materialism each shared also with Nazism. Here, the USA figured as the apogee of liberal-industrial modernity, a "leveled," "cultureless," "mass society" threatening Europe's spiritual richness and organic order. Only the overriding threat of godless Bolshevism eventually sidelined this brand of resistance to a "Western" system and an Atlantic alliance.[159]

Germany's engaged democrats were among the earliest critics of these positions. Unsurprisingly, secular leftists and liberals had little patience with them, even as Jaspers and Sternberger reflected on Christian themes of duty and love, and Kantorowicz hoped for a "new, true humanism" grounded in Christian–Marxist dialogue.[160] But the staunchest opponents of *Abendland* thinking were its direct competitors, left Catholics Dirks and Kogon. They objected to its anti-modern, ostensibly apolitical piety, which hid a decidedly political agenda. Dirks analyzed the "romanticism" and "ressentiment" of its backward-looking "yearning for the intact Occident (the medieval *ordo* before the bourgeois-capitalist Fall)," by which a fraction of the bourgeoisie strove to evade forward-looking solutions to the crisis of their own era. For only socialism could recover and preserve the best of the "occidental heritage," in necessarily altered form. "The Occident will be socialist," Dirks insisted, "or it will not be. If Europe disintegrates into 'Occident' and 'socialism,' it will collapse into itself." From an avowedly Christian position, his circle countered Christian conservatism and advocated democratic socialism as the core of renewal.[161]

A fourth intellectual grouping agitated from a farther-right, behind-the-scenes standpoint. These were the protagonists of Germany's interwar conservative revolution, *personae non gratae* in the occupation-era public sphere. Their standard-bearers – who first welcomed, then

---

[159] See, e.g., Schildt, *Zwischen Abendland und Amerika: Studien zur westdeutschen Ideenlandschaft der 50er Jahre* (Munich: Oldenbourg, 1999), 21–82, 111–65; Brockmann, "Germany as Occident at the Zero Hour," *German Studies Review* 25, no. 3 (2002): 477–96; Vanessa Conze, *Das Europa der Deutschen: Ideen von Europa in Deutschland zwischen Reichstradition und Westorientierung (1920–1970)* (Munich: Oldenbourg, 2005), 27–206.

[160] Jürgen Kuczynski, "Ein neuer Held der deutschen Reaktion: Metternich," *Die Weltbühne* 3, no. 24 (1948): 702–5; Jaspers, "Geleitwort," 5–6; Sternberger, "Tagebuch: Reise in Deutschland – Sommer 1945," *Die Wandlung* 1, no. 3 (1946): 196; Kantorowicz, "Jeffersonbibel-Christentum-Marxismus," *Ost und West* 1, no. 6 (1947): verso of cover.

[161] Dirks, "Das Abendland und der Sozialismus," *Frankfurter Hefte* 1, no. 3 (1946): 75–6; see also Kogon, "Traum und Wirklichkeit des Abendlandes," *Frankfurter Hefte* 1, no. 4 (1946): 11–13.

distanced themselves from Nazism in the 1930s – were jurist Carl Schmitt, philosopher Martin Heidegger, and soldier-poet Ernst Jünger (with his brother, Friedrich Georg Jünger). After the previous war, their diverse writings had provided a thematic reservoir for Weimar's radical right. They lionized martial virtues of battle and brotherhood; valorized heroic, aristocratic individuals over inauthentic, mediocre masses; and rejected liberal pluralism and popular sovereignty in favor of an altogether different "democracy": an authoritarian state under a decisive leader with acclamatory support from a disciplined, powerful nation. Their affinities with Nazism ran less through chauvinism or racism – in which they were unremarkable – than through radical visions of hierarchy and order that blended archaic and ultramodern elements.[162] After their disillusionment with Nazism, these men withdrew into a kind of defensive posture; in place of an activism of the deed, they cultivated a passive quiescence. And this remained their stance after 1945. To the banalities and indignities of occupation and marginalization, silence seemed the only appropriate response. Integral to this strategy was their self-consciously private networking within expanding circles of friends and disciples. Secluded in various rural retreats, they remained a palpable presence.[163]

Of Germany's discredited right-intellectuals, Ernst Jünger was the celebrated case. His connections with military resistance circles could not neutralize his far-right reputation, and he was banned from publishing, just as Schmitt and Heidegger (party members, unlike Jünger) were barred from the university. Nonetheless, copies of Jünger's wartime manuscript *The Peace* circulated widely, sparking lively debate. This text folded Nazism, the Second World War, and oblique references to the destruction of the Jews into a narrative of technological civilization's descent into "nihilism" – Nietzschean code for the modern collapse of meaning and value. And it prescribed a surprising antidote: Europe's pacification and supranational unification under a Christian aegis, by a far-seeing elite. Yet Jünger's militarism and nationalism also seeped through: he cast Germany's "powerful reserves" of "spirit [and] nobility"

---

[162] See, e.g., Jeffrey Herf, *Reactionary Modernism: Technology, Culture, and Politics in Weimar and the Third Reich* (Cambridge: Cambridge University Press, 1984); Stefan Breuer, *Anatomie der konservativen Revolution* (Darmstadt: Wissenschaftliche Buchgesellschaft, 1993); Lutz Raphael, "Radikales Ordnungsdenken und die Organisation totalitärer Herrschaft: Weltanschauungseliten und Humanwissenschaftler im NS-Regime," *Geschichte und Gesellschaft* 27, no. 1 (2001): 5–40.

[163] See, above all, Dirk van Laak, *Gespräche in der Sicherheit des Schweigens: Carl Schmitt in der politischen Geistesgeschichte der frühen Bundesrepublik* (Berlin: Akademie, 1993); Daniel Morat, *Von der Tat zur Gelassenheit: Konservatives Denken bei Martin Heidegger, Ernst Jünger und Friedrich Georg Jünger 1920–1960* (Göttingen: Wallstein, 2007).

as a crucial resource for this new Europe, and he linked postwar renewal to the intensity of the war itself, which bred a "secret love" between noble adversaries.[164] Engaged democrats were skeptical of Jünger's seeming transformation. Harich assailed his vague metahistorical rumination, which "submerges German guilt in a mystical world guilt" and "willfully disregards the issue of making amends." Moreover, Jünger's arrogance, as a German, in issuing prescriptions to the world and his exaltation of the war experience betrayed old habits. Leading a discussion at the Kulturbund, Weisenborn maintained that neither Jünger's belated opposition to Nazism nor his recent "seeking refuge in the Church" could atone for his destructive influence. His was "a hopeless case."[165] On the radio, Eggebrecht likewise dismissed Jünger's bizarre new departure. Clearly, the writings of this "nihilistic, solitude-loving diabolist" could only have "disastrous effects on disoriented souls." Still, he should be allowed to publish, so he could be openly confronted. In this regard, Sternberger was most consistent: *Die Wandlung* refused to air the Jünger controversy as long as the accused could not defend himself in public.[166]

As their forceful stances suggest, Germany's engaged democrats considered these anti-democrats their antipodes on the postwar political-cultural field (despite – or because of – some of their own earlier entanglements on the right). They had lived through the same calamities yet drawn very different lessons, and they vied for postwar Germany's soul. For Kogon, Schmitt's "friend-foe theory" of politics had prepared the ground for Nazism, which also implemented Jünger's insight that "slavery can be intensified endlessly if given the appearance of freedom." According to Sternberger, Heidegger's preference for categories such as "anxiety" and "boredom" exposed him as a "nihilistic ontologist." Mayer aligned all three figures with a "poverty of the spirit" in recent European culture, in which ideologues of pessimism, actionism, and elitism cut themselves loose from any concern for historical progress toward human freedom. Weber too spoke of a wave of pop-Nietzschean "nihilism" that

---

[164] Ernst Jünger, *Der Friede: Ein Wort an die Jugend Europas und an die Jugend der Welt* ([Amsterdam]: Die Argonauten, n.d.), 42–4, 9. *Der Friede* was published privately in Amsterdam in 1946, in French and English translation in 1948, but not in Germany until 1949. Elliot Y. Neaman, *A Dubious Past: Ernst Jünger and the Politics of Literature after Nazism* (Berkeley: University of California Press, 1999), 122–38; Morat, *Von der Tat*, 270–99; Wuermeling, *Liste*, 17, 287.
[165] Harich, "Ernst Jünger und der Frieden," *Aufbau* 2, no. 6 (1946): 564–5; "Protokoll über die Sitzung der Arbeitskommission 'Literatur' am 8. Mai 1946," 15 May 1946, BArch DY 27/224, 5. Weisenborn argued against Niekisch and another Weimar-era rightist, Karl Korn; Payk, *Geist*, 196–201.
[166] "Debatte über Ernst Jünger," *Nordwestdeutsche Hefte* 1, no. 7 (1946): 14; Waldmüller, *Wandlung*, 49.

crested in Nazism and was now to be overcome.[167] What they meant was that Germany's right-intellectuals had amplified the pernicious groundlessness they purported to diagnose. Now, they offered a vision of politics diametrically opposed to what was urgently needed, one of states over citizens, decision over dialogue, enmity over amity, and authority over self-rule. Even in their chastened mood, they represented a past with which postwar Germans had to break at all costs.

If various distinctions separated Germany's engaged democrats from other groupings, in what sense did they hang together? Their network bears comparison to a social movement, though it certainly did not constitute one: their social identities and political affiliations were too varied, their networks too far flung to sustain a sense of "common purpose" and "solidarity" in "collective challenge" to authority. (Moreover, they sought to form a new order rather than contest an existing one.) Still, the literature on social movements illuminates engaged democrats' situation by highlighting informal social networks as a ground of collective political action.[168] Like social movement actors, the intellectuals in question had a political stake in their networking; the form of their relations was determined also by their content, in a reciprocally conditioning process.

These postwar Germans came together around their sense of shared antifascist experiences and compatible democratic aims. The Potsdam consensus seemed to enable practical cooperation on common priorities with the Allies; indeed, they viewed the occupation above all as a framework for German activity and initiative, toward a belated self-liberation from National Socialism. For generations of self-proclaimed antifascists in both successor states, resistance became, in Michael Geyer's words, an "ongoing project" of dissent-as-renovation. This project's moment of birth – after its gestation in exile and opposition – was the immediate

---

[167] Kogon, "Das deutsche Volk und der Nationalsozialismus," *Frankfurter Hefte* 1, no. 2 (1946): 65, 69; Sternberger, "Gibt es eine nihilistische Literatur?" *Die Wandlung* 3, no. 6 (1948): 544; Mayer, *Karl Marx und das Elend des Geistes: Studien zur neuen deutschen Ideologie* (Meisenheim a.G.: Hain, 1948), 93–107; Weber, "Unsere Erfahrung und unsere Aufgabe," *Die Wandlung* 1, no. 1 (1945): 52; see also Weber, *Abschied von der bisherigen Geschichte: Überwindung des Nihilismus?* (Hamburg: Claassen & Goverts, 1946), 170–217, 222.

[168] Sidney G. Tarrow, *Power in Movement: Social Movements and Contentious Politics*, 3rd edn. (Cambridge: Cambridge University Press, 2011), quote 9. See Tarrow's chapter on "Networks and Organizations" and, classically, Mario Diani, "The Concept of Social Movement," *Sociological Review* 40, no. 1 (1992): 1–25.

postwar.[169] Engaged democrats' projects were among its earliest manifestations, and their anti-Nazi self-conception infused their activities to the core. Even at far-removed nodes of their network, actors unaware of the links between them worked within an initially shared horizon of democratic expectations. Acting under the oversight but with the trust of the Allies, buoyed by the seeming interest of the broader population, they sought to shape Germany's renewal.

[169] Geyer, "Resistance as Ongoing Project: Visions of Order, Obligations to Strangers, and Struggles for Civil Society, 1933–1990," in *Resistance against the Third Reich, 1933–1990*, ed. Geyer and John W. Boyer (Chicago: University of Chicago Press, 1994), 325–50.

## 2 Rethinking democracy: freedom, order, participation

The content and connotations of the term "democracy" – who should count as the "people" and how to construe their "rule" – have varied and shifted over time and place. Well into the nineteenth century, the notion's dominant valences remained negative, associated with the leveling and dangerous rule of the rabble. And elites' reservations only intensified as the logic of liberal demands for constitutional government and expanded suffrage threatened to empower the masses as well. At the same time, positive senses of democracy that affirmed the direct exercise of popular power, both within formal political institutions and in the workplace or in the streets, were upheld by socialists and anarchists. The tendency to identify democracy exclusively with its liberal variant – above all, with representative government and parliamentary politics – is of more recent vintage, cemented by liberalism's eventual victory over its ideological competitors in the twentieth century.[1] But during the unsettled mid 1940s, all this was in flux. The circumscribed, managed liberalism of postwar Western Europe was not yet consolidated, nor was effective one-party rule in the East, while leader-centered, acclamatory fascism had been officially discredited (even if its legacies were far from overcome). Conversely, the broad-based, inchoate antifascism of the popular front and the more militant, class-centered Soviet model still exerted powerful appeal. Amid this constellation, the meaning of democracy was vigorously contested.[2] Even postwar Germany's barren

---

[1] Raymond Williams, "Democracy," in *Keywords: A Vocabulary of Culture and Society*, rev. edn. (New York: Oxford University Press, 1985), 93–8. See also Werner Conze et al., "Demokratie," in *Geschichtliche Grundbegriffe: Historisches Lexikon zur politisch-sozialen Sprache in Deutschland*, ed. Otto Brunner, Conze, and Reinhart Koselleck (Stuttgart: Klett, 1972), I:821–99; Oliver Hidalgo, "Conceptual History and Politics: Is the Concept of Democracy Essentially Contested?" *Contributions to the History of Concepts* 4, no. 2 (2008): 176–201.

[2] See, e.g., Martin Conway, "Democracy in Postwar Western Europe: The Triumph of a Political Model," *European History Quarterly* 32, no. 1 (2002): 59–84; Tom Buchanan, "Anti-Fascism and Democracy in the 1930s," *European History Quarterly* 32, no. 1

landscape proved fertile ground for debate on its most basic elements and conditions.[3]

For their part, Germany's engaged democrats saw in the openness of the immediate postwar moment an opportunity to rethink the question of popular self-government anew, from the roots up. In their politics, however, they were a motley lot. Some had been politicized in the 1920s or earlier, others only after the rupture of 1945, and they drew inspiration from sources as varied as parliamentarism, council republics, union syndicalism, municipal self-management, and Christian social gospel. Broadly speaking, their orientations ran from liberal to Leninist, though those labels, too, were loosened in the immediate postwar years. Not a few liberals re-examined their core opposition of state power to individual freedom, while orthodox Communists revised old truths about the vanguard party and "bourgeois" liberties. Still, Germany's engaged democrats never aimed to develop a common platform of proposed institutions; indeed, some were quite vague on institutional details. Rather, they developed a common mode of thinking and talking about "democracy," one that emphasized the spontaneous, creative participation of people giving form to the structures that govern all spheres of social life. Such a sense of democracy linked a wide array of concrete political and economic proposals, whose stress on popular power raised the general issue of "'the masses'" fitness for self-rule as well as the specific concern that the populace in question had until quite recently supported Nazism – and tenaciously so. This did not deter Germany's engaged democrats. They viewed participatory institutions both as the core of an ideal polity and as a historical necessity for Germany: the only means by which its citizens, stunted by twelve years of fascism and by authoritarian traditions of longer standing, could raise themselves to political maturity.

How precisely did they construe their roles in this process? As specialists for words and ideas, they were sensitized to distortions of language and thought wrought by National Socialism. These concerns spawned a new genre of writing, critical lexica devoted to excavating the ways everyday linguistic usage registered the persistence of Nazi ideology in German minds. The most prominent exemplar was by Victor Klemperer, a literature professor of Jewish heritage who survived by dint of his marriage to an "Aryan." His analysis of the *lingua tertii imperii* or

---

(2002): 39–57; David Priestland, "Soviet Democracy, 1917–91," *European History Quarterly* 32, no. 1 (2002): 111–30; Jan-Werner Müller, *Contesting Democracy: Political Ideas in Twentieth-Century Europe* (New Haven, Conn.: Yale University Press, 2011), 125–70.

[3] See, e.g., Jörg Kilian, "'Demokratie' als Merkwort der Nachkriegszeit: Linguistische Begriffsgeschichte im Zeichen der kognitiven Semantik," in *Herausforderungen der Begriffsgeschichte*, ed. Carsten Dutt (Heidelberg: Winter, 2003), 105–31.

"language of the Third Reich" was published in 1947 by Aufbau.[4] Several cultural-political journals ran series of articles with the same intent, by Dolf Sternberger, Gerhard Storz, and Wilhelm Süskind in *Die Wandlung*; by Axel Eggebrecht in the *Nordwestdeutsche Hefte*; and by Horst Lommer in *Die Weltbühne*.[5] Sternberger was eloquent on their goals: "Language is the gift of humanity alone... Each word it speaks transforms the world in which it moves, transforms its self and its place in that world." In that sense, "the corruption of language" represented the "corruption of humanity" itself. As their experience of Nazism had shown, the "antihuman also has its vocabulary... It is, unfortunately, not an unfamiliar language." By compiling its dictionary, however, Sternberger and his colleagues hoped precisely "to make that language foreign to us."[6] In their view, the word had a privileged role to play in redeeming the world.

If Nazism had deformed central terms and concepts, the welter of competing perspectives under four-power occupation also served to cloud crucial issues. Accordingly, German intellectuals took it as their first task to elucidate the most elementary socio-political ideas, setting them back on firm ground. To contemporaries, this program went by the name "clarification of concepts," and they pursued it with missionary zeal.[7] Postwar intellectuals frequently reflected on the dramatic openness and pervasive instability of the semantic climate in which they operated. Günther Weisenborn, addressing the 1947 writers' congress, vividly described the problem:

Never have more thought systems, slogan fronts, and concept swarms fought their language battles than today, and all have left behind the ruined concepts,

---

[4] Victor Klemperer, *LTI: Notizbuch eines Philologen* (Berlin: Aufbau, 1947); Klemperer, "Die deutsche Wurzel," *Aufbau* 3, no. 3 (1947): 201–8. On Klemperer, see Steven E. Aschheim, *Scholem, Arendt, Klemperer: Intimate Chronicles in Turbulent Times* (Bloomington: Indiana University Press, 2001), 70–98.

[5] The entries were collected as Dolf Sternberger, Gerhard Storz, and Wilhelm E. Süskind, *Aus dem Wörterbuch des Unmenschen* (Hamburg: Claassen, 1957). See also Axel Eggebrecht, "Braundeutsch," *Nordwestdeutsche Hefte* 1, no. 6 (1946): 59–60; Eggebrecht, "'Garant' und 'Vorhaben' (Braundeutsch II)," *Nordwestdeutsche Hefte* 1, no. 7 (1946): 58–60; Eggebrecht, "Ein drittes Kapitel 'Braundeutsch,'" *Nordwestdeutsche Hefte* 2, no. 2 (1947): 63–4; Horst Lommer, "Aus dem Vokabelheft der Nazis I," *Die Weltbühne* 2, no. 11 (1947): 484–7; Lommer, "Aus dem Vokabelheft der Nazis II," *Die Weltbühne* 2, no. 14 (1947): 602–4; Lommer, "Aus dem Vokabelheft der Nazis III," *Die Weltbühne* 2, no. 19 (1947): 848–50; Lommer, "Aus dem Vokabelheft der Nazis IV," *Die Weltbühne* 3, no. 3/4 (1948): 89–91.

[6] Sternberger, "Aus dem Wörterbuch des Unmenschen I," *Die Wandlung* 1, no. 1 (1945): 75. See William J. Dodd, *Jedes Wort wandelt die Welt: Dolf Sternbergers politische Sprachkritik* (Göttingen: Wallstein, 2007), 220–64.

[7] This was the title, for instance, of an essay volume to which Arnold Bauer, Axel Eggebrecht, Dolf Sternberger, and Ernst Niekisch contributed; Herbert Burgmüller, ed. *Zur Klärung der Begriffe: Beiträge zur Neuordnung der Werte* (Munich: Weismann, 1947).

slogan remnants, and crippled or bloated terms that haunt the dialogues of our day... The time has come for writers to intervene and subdue our unsettled language, [for] only in so far as there are words is the world made accessible.[8]

By late 1947, Cold War fault-lines were clearly drawn. As early as 1945, however, Herbert Ihering had similarly urged vigilance, not only toward "National Socialist falsifications and fogginess" but also toward newly encroaching "obfuscations and misunderstandings." Lest their most vital ideas become mere "slogans," a "clarification of concepts" was indispensable.[9] Such comments conveyed the conviction that this task was a crucial condition of socio-political renewal. Germans needed a clear, concrete language in which to understand their past, grasp the present, and conceive a future. With that in mind, Germany's engaged democrats set about formulating an agenda that would repair Nazism's damage while charting a resolutely independent course, between the polarized solutions offered by "West" and "East," as they understood them.

## Freedom and order

As a point of departure, the intellectuals in question often seized on the national cultural patrimony represented by the likes of Goethe, Schiller, Kant, and Hegel – even if their assessment of this bequest was deeply ambivalent. References to such towering icons were ubiquitous in the postwar public sphere. But the specific insistence with which Germany's engaged democrats intertwined discussions of culture and politics had to do – sometimes explicitly, often implicitly – with a style of thought embedded in the cultural canon, one invoked by the key categories *Kultur* (culture), *Geist* (spirit), and *Bildung* (self-formation, self-cultivation, or self-education). These referenced the possibility of a human subjectivity that was self-determining and self-developing, shaping itself and its world simultaneously through creative, autonomous activity.[10] It was, as we shall see, a crucial image informing engaged democrats' sense of the self-constituting freedom at stake in participation. Anthropologist

---

[8] Günther Weisenborn, "Tod und Hoffnung," *Ost und West* 1, no. 4 (1947): 30–1.
[9] Herbert Ihering, "Lessing und Paul Wegener," *Aufbau* 1, no. 2 (1945): 148.
[10] On the history of this conceptual cluster, see Raymond Geuss, "Kultur, Bildung, Geist," in *Morality, Culture, and History: Essays on German Philosophy* (Cambridge: Cambridge University Press, 1999), 29–50; Koselleck, "On the Anthropological and Semantic Structure of Bildung," in *The Practice of Conceptual History: Timing History, Spacing Concepts*, trans. Todd Samuel Presner (Stanford, Calif.: Stanford University Press, 2002), 170–207; also Andrew Sartori, "The Resonance of 'Culture': Framing a Problem in Global Concept-History," *Comparative Studies in Society & History* 47, no. 4 (2005): 676–99.

Dominic Boyer has referred to *Kultur, Geist,* and *Bildung* as the "key tropes of intellectual selfhood" among Germany's educated elites, which took shape around the turn of the nineteenth century but remained operative through the twentieth. Together, these tropes anchored a mode of understanding the relationship between the human self and the social world that emphasized the dialectical tension – and potential resolution – between internal, subjective freedom and external, formal rules.[11]

In this light, it is significant that discussions of Germany's postwar reconstruction often foregrounded the relationship between the terms "freedom" and "order." These structured a number of programs drafted in the resistance underground or in exile networks that sought to balance freedom and order or uphold one against excesses of the other.[12] Moreover, after 1945 this binary opposition acquired geopolitical referents. It mapped out the alternatives seemingly proffered by Germany's occupiers: individualized freedom and representative institutions in the West versus collectivized order and a centralized party-state in the East. Germany's engaged democrats considered each of these poles insufficient in itself or, at best, inadequate to German conditions. As Eugen Kogon put it in the *Frankfurter Hefte*, each side promoted a different image of "true democracy." It was up to the German people to decide "if they are drawn toward the world of the West or the world of the East, or whether they will develop a distinct form of economic existence and political life between individualism and collectivism." He passionately advocated the latter course.[13] Writing in *Die Weltbühne*, Wolfgang Harich rejected local opportunists that assimilated to one or the other global camp; instead, he declared it Germans' "patriotic duty" to achieve a "west-eastern synthesis."[14] Germany's engaged democrats helped shape the discourse of freedom and order, with emphasis on participation as a mediating third term that would overcome the tension between the first two, realizing freedom in the spontaneous, collaborative ordering of social life. This theme was an ideologically promiscuous one, as can be seen in the immediate postwar writings of three exemplary figures: liberal Dolf Sternberger, left Catholic Walter Dirks, and Marxist Ernst Bloch.

---

[11] Dominic Boyer, *Spirit and System: Media, Intellectuals, and the Dialectic in Modern German Culture* (Chicago: University of Chicago Press, 2005), 55–60, quote 55.

[12] See, e.g., Gerhard Ringshausen and Rüdiger von Voss, eds. *Die Ordnung des Staates und die Freiheit des Menschen: Deutschlandpläne im Widerstand und Exil* (Bonn: Bouvier, 2000); Wolfgang Benz, "Konzeptionen für die Nachkriegsdemokratie: Pläne und Überlegungen im Widerstand, im Exil und in der Besatzungszeit," in *Deutschland nach Hitler: Zukunftspläne im Exil und aus der Besatzungszeit 1939–1949*, ed. Thomas Koebner, Gert Sautermeister, and Sigrid Schneider (Opladen: Westdeutscher, 1987), 201–13.

[13] Eugen Kogon, "Demokratie und Föderalismus," *Frankfurter Hefte* 1, no. 6 (1946): 68.

[14] Wolfgang Harich, "Ewiger Irrtum," *Die Weltbühne* 1, no. 3 (1946): 70.

As a bookish student in the 1920s, Dolf Sternberger delved into literature and sociology but was gripped by his encounter with philosophy – specifically the "existence philosophy" of his Heidelberg teacher Karl Jaspers, who with Martin Heidegger represented a school then insurgent against the seemingly tired formalisms of neo-Kantianism. As Sternberger understood, Jaspers' focus on "existential communication" signaled, at base, a "philosophy of intimacy" concerned with the space that authentic dialogue could open between two individuals. In that form, this emphatically "privatistic" principle had no direct bearing on "publicity," yet Sternberger would later credit Jaspers' ethical ideal for teaching him a formative political lesson: it was precisely the *res intima* among individuals that the *res publica* was called to protect. Politicized by the experience of National Socialism – as was his mentor – Sternberger reoriented his career to journalism and eventually to the "science of politics," for which he received Germany's first postwar teaching appointment at Heidelberg in 1947.[15] Sternberger's retrospective is colored by his further development, as a scholar and public intellectual, into one of West Germany's most prominent liberal voices. Today, he is remembered as a champion of *Bürgerlichkeit* (literally "burgher-ness") and "constitutional patriotism" and as an old-guard adversary of 1960s student radicals.[16] After 1945, however, even this most classically liberal of Germany's engaged democrats considered individual liberty insufficient as a first principle.

In an essay entitled "The Rule of Freedom" in *Die Wandlung* in 1946, Sternberger rendered the issue thus. The liberalism of the English, American, and French revolutionary traditions assumed a "sharp conflict of freedom and law as of individual and society." It failed to recognize that the negative freedom to do whatever was not prohibited by the state's laws was "incomplete" and dangerously close to *Willkür* (arbitrariness or despotism), that is, to a false freedom all too familiar from Nazism.[17] Post-Nazi German politics needed the will to deny rights to adherents

---

[15] Sternberger, "Erinnerung an die Zwanziger Jahre in Heidelberg," in *Schriften*, vol. VIII, *Gang zwischen Meistern* (Frankfurt a.M.: Insel, 1987), 21–3, 29–32. These themes, central to Jaspers' *Philosophy* (1932) but sounded already in his *Psychology of Worldviews* (1919), were a red thread of his life and thought; Suzanne Kirkbright, *Karl Jaspers: A Biography: Navigations in Truth* (New Haven, Conn.: Yale University Press, 2004).

[16] See, e.g., Claudia Kinkela, *Die Rehabilitierung des Bürgerlichen im Werk Dolf Sternbergers* (Würzburg: Königshausen & Neumann, 2001); Greven, "Betrachtungen über das Bürgerliche: Dolf Sternberger und die Metamorphosen des Bürgers nach 1945," *Vorgänge* 44, no. 2 (2005): 21–32.

[17] Sternberger, "Herrschaft der Freiheit," *Die Wandlung* 1, no. 7 (1946): 556–8. For the classic distinction between negative and positive freedom, see Isaiah Berlin, "Two Concepts of Liberty," in *Four Essays on Liberty* (Oxford: Oxford University Press, 1969), 118–72.

of such anarchic, destructive freedom.[18] More than that, it needed some way to mediate the tension of freedom and law to achieve a "general freedom... better, deeper, [and] stronger" than liberalism's "individual freedom." Defining politics broadly – as the "ordering... of the collective life of people and groups within a polity" – Sternberger saw the solution in a "democratic ethos" of "sociable decency" that would permeate all citizens' relations. Although such conduct could not be "commanded," it could be "taught" in schools; above all, it had to be "practiced" in political institutions designed to enshrine and promote it. To clarify this indistinct notion, Sternberger likened its effects in an ideal parliament to its role in an ideal marriage; parties to both enjoyed a "freedom... bound by a spirit (*Geist*) of loyalty" that gave their interactions the character of a "reciprocal self-formation (*Bildung*) in free play." Once such ethical comportments conditioned institutionalized politics, and vice versa, freedom would "rule" the polity, which would "itself *create* freedom" in turn. Properly constituted order thus generated positive freedom, transforming liberalism's "passivity into activity" and its "formal democracy into substantive democracy."[19] Here lay the germ of what he soon began to call *Bürgerlichkeit*, a code of civic virtue and civil conduct that was not necessarily bound to the fading "bourgeois" era.[20] In 1946, however, Sternberger spoke in terms of "democratic" forms that transcended the opposition of freedom and order.

If Sternberger came to political engagement in the postwar period, Walter Dirks' activism was rooted in the Weimar era. It began within the *Quickborn* – a Catholic youth league that partook of the broader youth movement's pathos of group emancipation and spiritual renewal – and it evolved into journalistic calls for a broad and vigorous antifascist coalition as Germany's first republic eroded.[21] Dirks' dual intellectual foundations were also laid in the Weimar period, the first by an early,

---

[18] On debates over such a "militant democracy," see Karrin Hanshew, *Terror and Democracy in West Germany* (Cambridge: Cambridge University Press, 2012), 27–67.
[19] Sternberger, "Herrschaft der Freiheit," 558–9, 567–71 (emphasis in original). See also Michaela Hoenicke Moore, "Heimat und Fremde: Das Verhältnis zu Amerika im journalistischen Werk von Margret Boveri und Dolf Sternberger," in *Demokratiewunder: Transatlantische Mittler und die kulturelle Öffnung Westdeutschlands 1945–1970*, ed. Arnd Bauerkämper, Konrad H. Jarausch, and Marcus M. Payk (Göttingen: Vandenhoeck & Ruprecht, 2005), 236–43.
[20] Sternberger, "Tagebuch: Bürgerlichkeit," *Die Wandlung* 3, no. 3 (1948): 199–200. Sternberger's inspiration was an 1899 declaration by classical historian and liberal politician Theodor Mommsen: "I have always been an *animal politicum* and wished to be a burgher"; Theodor Mommsen, "Ich wünschte ein Bürger zu sein," *Die Wandlung* 3, no. 1 (1948): 69.
[21] Walter Dirks, *Der singende Stotterer: Autobiographische Texte* (Munich: Kösel, 1983), 15–17, 21–2. On youth movements, see Mark Roseman, ed. *Generations in Conflict:*

European strand of liberation theology.[22] In the 1920s, reformist Catholic thinkers who questioned the Church's hostility to the secular labor movement began to advocate a non-Marxist "ethical socialism" and solidarity with Social Democracy. The most important such lay theologians, Ernst Michel and Theodor Steinbüchel, were mentors to the *Rhein-Mainische Volkszeitung* circle and to Dirks directly, as was their ordained patron, Romano Guardini.[23] Dirks' second formative encounter was with recent innovations in heterodox Marxism. Above all, the work of German-Hungarian theorist Georg Lukács stimulated interest in Hegelian questions of subjectivity, alienation, and historical praxis that were soon reinforced by the recovery of Marx's early writings.[24] For Dirks, it was Lukács who broke open the objectivistic orthodoxies of official Social Democracy and Communism (despite his own capitulations to the latter) and exposed their blind spot: "the personal dimension, the freedom and love of the concrete individual human being."[25] Among Dirks' interlocutors was Theodor W. Adorno, then also a Frankfurt University student and later – along with his associates at Max Horkheimer's Institute for Social Research – a key thinker of "Western Marxism." Adorno and Dirks discussed philosophy and social theory as well as their common passion for music, where the former taught the latter to appreciate the modernism of composer Arnold Schönberg and his school.[26] Dirks' roots in pre-Nazi left-Catholic and socialist thought were intertwined sources on which he would draw in imagining post-fascist democratic renewal.

The couplet of freedom and order figured in several of Dirks' postwar essays. He, too, began by exposing a "capricious" freedom that

*Youth Revolt and Generation Formation in Germany, 1770–1968* (Cambridge: Cambridge University Press, 1995).

[22] Gerd-Rainer Horn, *Western European Liberation Theology: The First Wave, 1924–1959* (Oxford: Oxford University Press, 2008).

[23] Dirks, *Stotterer*, 17–18; Joachim Rotberg, *Zwischen Linkskatholizismus und bürgerlicher Sammlung: Die Anfänge der CDU in Frankfurt am Main 1945–1946* (Frankfurt a.M.: Knecht, 1999), 51–62; Andreas Lienkamp, "Socialism Out of Christian Responsibility: The German Experiment of Left Catholicism, 1945–1949," in *Left Catholicism 1943–1955: Catholics and Society in Western Europe at the Point of Liberation*, ed. Gerd-Rainer Horn and Emmanuel Gerard (Leuven: Leuven University Press, 2001), 196–227.

[24] On Lukács and his impact, see Martin Jay, *Marxism and Totality: The Adventures of a Concept from Lukács to Habermas* (Berkeley: University of California Press, 1984), 81–127 and *passim*.

[25] Dirks, *Stotterer*, 19, 199–200; Ulrich Bröckling, *Katholische Intellektuelle in der Weimarer Republik: Zeitkritik und Gesellschaftstheorie* (Munich: Fink, 1993), 112–21. Dirks was completing a dissertation under Steinbüchel on "historicity" in Lukács' *History and Class Consciousness* (1923) that was cut short in 1933. After the war, Dirks sought to republish this text but was rebuffed by Lukács, who had long since recanted his early work. Georg Lukács to Dirks, 25 September 1947, Archiv der sozialen Demokratie (Bonn, hereafter AdsD), NL Dirks 17B.

[26] Dirks, *Stotterer*, 19.

"does not check itself" as a kind of unfreedom that "leads... directly into constraint, namely into dependence on instincts, interests, and accidents." Such a one-sided perspective remained blind to the "hidden secret" that true freedom must "develop" its limits "out of itself" and "impose them on itself." In that sense, "actual freedom realizes itself in being bound... The freest person is one who says yes from the heart to the essence of all these bonds. As paradoxical as it sounds, responsible obedience to which one freely assents is the purest form of freedom." This Dirks called a "democratic truth." His colleague Kogon similarly rejected a view of freedom "as unconditional, absolute, and sovereign," speaking of it instead "as the fruit of not constraining but rather stabilizing bonds." Such was the freedom of a "well-ordered democracy."[27] The *Frankfurter Hefte*'s editors treated freedom, order, and democracy in a language of mystery, revelation, and willing submission that suggested its religious provenance.

Dirks thus cautioned against conflating the Christian perspective with a conservative one. In fact, he questioned the utility of received labels like "conservative" or "right" and "progressive" or "left." Fundamentally, these terms distinguished a "pathos of order" that sought to preserve what existed from a "pathos of freedom" that pushed to transform it (a binary he, like Sternberger, aligned with that of "law and freedom"). The task of their historical moment, however, was to move beyond this opposition, and not in the realm of theory alone; "each person must work it out positively within their own life."[28] In particular, Dirks highlighted the role that the Christian principle of charity could play in motivating democratic engagement, if it were redirected toward the worldly realm. *Caritas* would then appear "in the new form of a political love of one's neighbor," founded on the recognition that their "distress... is grounded in the disorder of human institutions." For all those "entangled" in these institutions – whether "co-beneficiaries" or "co-sufferers," they were "co-carriers" of a shared situation – this realization would generate a sense of "co-responsibility" with "agonizing sharpness" that could spark a will to social transformation. So modified, charity taught that "the social order need not be accepted as a God-given fate, a kind of second nature, but must be seen as a historical order among people that can be changed" by free, collective action.[29] This position built on yet far exceeded Catholic social doctrine. For the latter, class society remained a providential order;

---

[27] Dirks, "Die Freiheit der Presse," *Frankfurter Hefte* 2, no. 1 (1947): 13; Kogon, "Demokratie und Föderalismus," 75.
[28] Dirks, "Rechts und Links," *Frankfurter Hefte* 1, no. 6 (1946): 24, 28.
[29] Ibid., 35. Presumably, the resonance with Lukács' notion of society as a reified "second nature" – one that appears beyond the control of those whose activities constitute it –

a solidaristic ethic and more equitable distribution of resources would suffice to defuse antagonisms and renew harmony.[30] Dirks, by contrast, called for citizens' political self-mobilization with transformative intent.

The most prominent treatment of the problem of "freedom and order" from a Marxist perspective was in a book of that title by Ernst Bloch. Like his friend and counterpart Lukács, he had been an influence and inspiration for legions of young interwar intellectuals, including Dirks and Sternberger.[31] The broad appeal of his work had to do with its eclectic, encyclopedic range and its messianic impulses. For Bloch, Marxism alone was too coldly economistic to grasp the full range of human experience and potential liberation; it required completion by other, especially religious, modes of thought.[32] This was the crux of his long-standing disagreement with Lukács, who disparaged as irrationalism Bloch's continuing allegiance to a romanticism they had shared in their youth.[33] Politically, each was plagued by their ambivalent, even tortured relationship with Communist orthodoxy. Unlike Lukács, Bloch never joined the party and was not drawn to Moscow, passing his exile in obscurity in the northeastern United States. At the same time, his forward-looking philosophy of "anticipatory consciousness," or what he called the "not-yet," reconciled itself all too easily with present unfreedom in return for a promised utopia always on the horizon. This political deficit was clearly expressed in Bloch's unwavering solidarity with the Soviet Union, which culminated in his public defense of Stalin's purges and show trials in

---

echoes themes of Dirks' lost dissertation. See Georg Lukács, *Geschichte und Klassenbewußtsein: Studien über marxistische Dialektik*, in *Werke*, vol. II, *Frühschriften* (Neuwied: Luchterhand, 1968), 161–518.

[30] The Church's response to industrial modernity is recorded in the papal encyclica *Rerum Novarum* (1891) and *Quadragesimo Anno* (1931); Horn, *Liberation Theology*, 34–5, 55–9.

[31] Sternberger and Bloch were friends from Weimar-era Frankfurt; contact seems to have lapsed during Bloch's exile and resumed by 1960. Dirks did not know Bloch personally but always felt a "clandestine closeness" to his work. Sternberger, *Gang zwischen Meistern*, 458–9; Ernst Bloch to Sternberger, 9 November 1934, 8 June 1960, Deutsches Literaturarchiv (Marbach a.N., hereafter DLA) A:Sternberger/ 89.10.3618/1–2; Dirks to Bloch, 15 October 1960, AdsD NL Dirks 122.

[32] On Bloch, see Jay, *Marxism*, 174–95; Anson Rabinbach, *In the Shadow of Catastrophe: German Intellectuals between Apocalypse and Enlightenment* (Berkeley: University of California Press, 1997), 27–65.

[33] The contrast of their approaches is instructive: rather than supplement Marx, Lukács subsumed insights from others – Hegel, Max Weber, Luxemburg and Lenin – in a Marxian frame. See Moishe Postone, "Lukács and the Dialectical Critique of Capitalism," in *New Dialectics and Political Economy*, ed. Robert Albritton and John Simoulidis (Basingstoke: Palgrave Macmillan, 2003), 78–100; Andrew Feenberg, "Post-Utopian Marxism: Lukács and the Dilemmas of Organization," in *Confronting Mass Democracy and Industrial Technology: Political and Social Theory from Nietzsche to Habermas*, ed. John P. McCormick (Durham: Duke University Press, 2002), 45–69.

the 1930s.[34] This stance was rooted not only in his original enthusiasm for the Russian Revolution but also (as with many "fellow travelers" of Communism) in his single-minded commitment to the antifascism of the popular front moment. While Bloch's politics inclined toward orthodoxy, his thought remained persistently anti-dogmatic. And although it was philosophical in content, it was rife with political implications.

Bloch's book *Freedom and Order* (1946), composed in exile and published before his return, marked a key station between his early *Spirit of Utopia* (1918) and his magnum opus, *The Principle of Hope* (1954–9), of which it became the longest chapter.[35] Together, these texts chart Bloch's lifelong project to scour the actual past for moments of possibility that expressed the human species' yearning for a better world. *Freedom and Order*, as its subtitle indicated, presented a "survey of social utopias." It uncovered anticipatory traces of utopian consciousness in a dizzying array of manifestations, ranging from Stoic philosophy, medieval theology, and the modern novel to Owenite communities, the early women's movement, and Zionism. On Bloch's account, utopian visions had oscillated historically between two prescriptive poles, exemplified in two early modern classics: the "freedom-pathos" of Thomas More's *Utopia* and the "order-pathos" of Tommaso Campanella's *City of the Sun*. It was Karl Marx's achievement to dialectically unify and overcome these two strands for the modern era.[36] In Marx's vision, Bloch asserted:

> Freedom has become positively identical to order. Not a fixed order, much less one imposed from outside or above... The order that arises out of unalienated subject-objectification is rather itself – as the fruit of freedom – what has yet to be discovered: order is the *actual realm in the realm of freedom*... Utopia-become-concrete provides the key to this, to unalienated order in the best of all possible societies.[37]

For Bloch, Marx's core insight was to recognize the social world as a product of humanity's own potentially free activity, even as he analyzed

---

[34] On Bloch's politics, see, e.g., Jan Robert Bloch, "How Can We Understand the Bends in the Upright Gait?" *New German Critique* 45 (1988): 9–39; Trantje Franz, "Philosophie als revolutionäre Praxis: Zur Apologie und Kritik des Sowjetsozialismus," in *Ernst Bloch*, ed. Heinz Ludwig Arnold (Munich: Text + Kritik, 1985), 239–73.

[35] *Freiheit und Ordnung* first appeared in 1946 with Aurora in New York (led by Wieland Herzfelde and co-founded by Bloch), and the rights were acquired the following year by Aufbau, who would later publish *The Principle of Hope*. Ernst Bloch, *Freiheit und Ordnung: Abriß der Sozial-Utopien* (Berlin: Aufbau, 1947); Bloch, *Das Prinzip Hoffnung* (Berlin: Aufbau, 1955), II:32–194. See Carsten Wurm, *Der frühe Aufbau-Verlag 1945–1961: Konzepte und Kontroversen* (Wiesbaden: Harrassowitz, 1996), 76–81.

[36] Bloch, *Freiheit und Ordnung*, 91. The proximity of Bloch's formulations to Dirks', published before Bloch's text crossed the Atlantic, is striking.

[37] Ibid., 213–14.

the unfree conditions under which it appeared to them as an externally imposed order. Bloch spun out the implications:

> Humanity everywhere still lives in prehistory, indeed everything still stands before the creation of the world as a just one. True genesis... begins only when society and being become radical, that is, grasp themselves by the root. The root of history, however, is the laboring human; once he grasps himself and what's his, without alienation, grounded in real democracy, there emerges in the world a place where no one yet has been: home.[38]

Invoking this language at the close of his book, Bloch presented Marxian theory as the fullest expression of a human striving for utopia sedimented across millennia of cultural history. It envisioned a reconciliation of humanity with itself and its surroundings, conscious of its freedom as reflected in an order of its own making. This condition Bloch associated with fully achieved democracy.

Bloch thus rendered engaged democrats' discourse of participation in his distinctive idiom. Its Marxian roots are unmistakable. Yet just as Sternberger and Dirks kept a distance from conventional liberal and Christian views of freedom, Bloch maintained some distance to Marxist orthodoxy on that question. The latter was enshrined in Friedrich Engels' dictum "freedom is the insight into necessity," a bowdlerized gloss of Hegel that would long haunt official Marxism. In Engels' account, objective "laws" governed both nature and society, and the essence of subjective freedom was action in accord with those laws, properly understood.[39] Here, grasping freedom involved subordinating it to necessity, a perspective that infused Social Democracy's mechanistic faith in progress as well as Bolshevism's voluntaristic view of the party as necessity's executor. Bloch cited Engels with approval, then made a substantively different claim: "At work essentially in freedom is the counter-move of a subjective factor against that necessity to which humans are bound without their will... Freedom only becomes freedom in its utopian or essential sense by mediating itself concretely with the forces of necessity."[40] The contrast of Bloch's and Engels' formulations is significant.[41] It rests on very different appropriations of Hegel, whose dialectics both Engels

---

[38] Ibid., 214. Bloch would later use this passage to conclude his three-volume work; Bloch, *Das Prinzip Hoffnung* (Berlin: Aufbau, 1959), III:489.
[39] Friedrich Engels, *Herrn Eugen Dührings Umwälzung der Wissenschaft*, in Karl Marx and Engels, *Werke* (Berlin: Dietz, 1962), XX:106–7. On the legacies of Engels' scientism, see: Paul Thomas, *Marxism and Scientific Socialism: From Engels to Althusser* (London: Routledge, 2008).
[40] Bloch, *Freiheit und Ordnung*, 85–6.
[41] On this issue, see also Peter C. Caldwell, *Dictatorship, State Planning, and Social Theory in the German Democratic Republic* (Cambridge: Cambridge University Press, 2003), 97–140. Caldwell, however, treats *Principle of Hope* integrally, as a text of Bloch's

and Bloch extended to nature. But where Engels proclaimed a science of objective natural laws governing all material reality, Bloch projected subjectivity onto a humanized nature.[42] What Bloch considered Hegel's core insight was the unrelenting emphasis on becoming, on the "living movement" of a "self" he called spirit (*Geist*), a "subject that dialectically interpenetrates itself with the object" and vice versa, constituting itself in endless process.[43] For this sort of subject, discerning and accommodating objective laws – as externally imposed order – could hardly count as freedom.

Bloch's *Freedom and Order* enjoyed a speedy, enthusiastic reception among engaged democrats. In his journal, Alfred Kantorowicz excerpted Bloch's ambivalent portrait of the fin-de-siècle youth movement: though grounded in a utopian rejection of "instrumentally rational" civilization, middle-class youth's emotional, back-to-nature escapism ultimately helped support the society they despised.[44] Hans Mayer reviewed the book, also in *Ost und West*. Referring to Bloch, Mayer told his readers: "whoever travels this path with him, the path of transformative praxis, will no longer perceive freedom and order as opposites." He called the book's publication in Germany, Bloch's first since 1933, a "true intellectual event" and expressed his hope that the author would soon return.[45] It is clear, however, that this text was a symptom – not the cause – of these two terms' prominence in postwar German discussions. Engaged democrats' contributions, though they proceeded from a variety of ideological positions, shared a distinctive form: the diametric opposition of freedom and order was not presented as static; rather, democracy appeared as the dynamic realization of each side in the other.

### Self-government as self-education

Such reflections on the tension of social order and social freedom sound rather abstract, but they had concrete consequences for thinking about politics. For the proposed resolution – participation – pointed toward an

---

mid-1950s "revisionism," without addressing its partial pre-publication in the mid 1940s.

[42] Jay, *Marxism*, 184–7.

[43] Bloch, *Subjekt-Objekt: Erläuterungen zu Hegel* (Berlin: Aufbau, 1951), 10. This text was drafted in exile, complete by 1947, and first published two years later, in Spanish translation in Mexico.

[44] Bloch, "Programm der Jugendbewegung," *Ost und West* 1, no. 3 (1947): 83–6; cf. Bloch, *Freiheit und Ordnung*, 161–6.

[45] Hans Mayer, "Ernst Bloch: 'Freiheit und Ordnung,'" *Ost und West* 2, no. 3 (1948): 89–90. Mayer helped reintroduce Germans to Lukács as well, on the occasion of Aufbau's multi-volume publication of his exile writings; Mayer, "Georg Lukács," *Ost und West* 2, no. 12 (1948): 88–93.

approach to mass democracy that revised the basic elitisms of modern politics. Coming to trust the people was not easy, since conventional doubts about "the masses'" political maturity were only exacerbated by the popular support Nazism had enjoyed. Germany's engaged democrats saw just one solution to this conundrum: Germans required a democratic "reeducation," it was true, but this could succeed only as a *self*-education. Manifold popular participation figured as both means and goal in this process; only by practicing self-government could the people effectively learn to govern themselves. In that spirit, the intellectuals in question sought to uncover the many forms of heteronomy in contemporary mass societies, and they advocated an assortment of institutional arrangements to deepen democratic principles in politics and expand them to economy and society.

A parallelism of political and economic proposals characterized their positions. On the economic side, they partook of the short-lived but widespread anti-capitalist mood of the mid 1940s. The conviction that untrammeled capitalism had shown itself indifferent to human well-being and prone to systemic, disastrous crises was fueled by the experience of the 1920s and '30s, when hyperinflation and depression gave way to fascism and war. The pressures of material privation, the war-wrought flux in property relations, and the example of wartime state intervention also encouraged a search for peacetime alternatives. Socialization, planning, steering, corporatism, and "economic democracy" were watchwords across political camps. For many advocates, these measures responded pragmatically to postwar scarcity and the danger of social unrest by institutionalizing redistribution and interest-group negotiation.[46] Engaged democrats' proposals, however, were justified in other terms. They sought not to keep social peace in lean times or to balance competing interests but to empower people as spontaneous subjects, not instrumentalized objects of economic processes. In this regard, they reflected a basic postwar trend to construe the economy in political terms, as a realm open to conscious control, not an autonomous system of anonymous forces.

One of the most comprehensive programs came from Alexander Mitscherlich and Alfred Weber. On encountering each other in the

---

[46] Diethelm Prowe, "Economic Democracy in Post-World War II Germany: Corporatist Crisis Response, 1945–1948," *Journal of Modern History* 57, no. 3 (1985): 451–82; Prowe, "Socialism as Crisis Response: Socialization and the Escape from Poverty and Power in Post-World War II Germany," *German Studies Review* 15, no. 1 (1992): 65–85; Prowe, "Ordnungsmacht and Mitbestimmung: The Postwar Labor Unions and the Politics of Reconstruction," in *Between Reform and Revolution: German Socialism and Communism, 1840–1990*, ed. David E. Barclay and Eric D. Weitz (New York: Berghahn, 1998), 397–420.

war's immediate wake, they found their views were compatible and soon co-authored a pamphlet entitled *Free Socialism* – part historical sociology, part policy platform. While contrasting emphases appeared in the authors' contributions, they had a common point of departure: at the middle of the twentieth century, civilization confronted "the question: totalitarian bureaucracy or socially saturated freedom," to which they offered "the answer: free socialism." This socialism was a form of humanism. It was at base not an economic project but a "spiritual task" designed to produce "the human being who will be the equal of this situation and this danger."[47]

Mitscherlich grounded the problem in the uncontrolled dynamism of modern technology. In the guise of capitalist industrialization, as Marx had recognized, it dissolved the old corporate order into the class society of the nineteenth century. Out of the ensuing social conflicts had emerged the mass society, monopolistic economy, and monolithic state of the twentieth century, a new form of domination Marx had not foreseen. As technology's runaway "self-realization" first released productive forces and then revealed its destructive potentials, no one was spared. Workers were absorbed by "the apparatus" while owners and managers were reduced to "functionaries" of enterprise and the state "grew into a Moloch," under monopoly capitalism as well as state socialism. Finally, the accumulation of advanced weapons by imperialist states endangered naked physical existence, as the atomic bomb had shown. To Mitscherlich, these phenomena were all of one piece. They amounted to "the victory of technology over humanity," as the latter came to serve the former's ends, not vice versa. Moreover, this condition of "powerlessness" was all too easily exploited by "nihilistic dictators," whom Mitscherlich likened to "buffoons."[48] Anticipating his later social psychology, he suggested that the overdevelopment of rational capacities and blockage of non-rational ones by "technicization" eventually provoked a backlash, unleashing a "destructive drive" that disposed people to violence and subordination.[49]

Weber framed the core issue as one of bureaucracy, to similar effect. This concern drew on ideas he had developed decades earlier, in dialogue with his brother Max.[50] After 1945, it became the crux of his thought. According to Weber, tendencies toward an all-engulfing "totalitarian

---

[47] Alexander Mitscherlich and Alfred Weber, preface to *Freier Sozialismus* (Heidelberg: Schneider, 1946), 5–6.
[48] Mitscherlich, "Entwicklungsgrundlagen eines freien Sozialismus," in *Freier Sozialismus*, 11, 20–1, 23, 27.
[49] Mitscherlich, *Endlose Diktatur?* (Heidelberg: Schneider, 1947), 20, 24.
[50] Eberhard Demm, *Ein Liberaler in Kaiserreich und Republik: Der politische Weg Alfred Webers bis 1920* (Boppard a.R.: Boldt, 1990), 107–20; Reinhard Blomert, *Intellektuelle*

bureaucratism" worldwide posed a grave threat to "free spontaneity and self-formation."[51] Since the nineteenth century, bureaucracy's stultifying structures had expanded outward from the state's civil service and standing army to colonize all corners of social life, spreading functional specialization and rational routinization.[52] This sealed the fate of deep dispositions toward freedom that, in Weber's vitalist philosophy of history, had lain dormant in the Germans since they subjugated themselves first to princes and then to modern states and firms, habituating themselves to "lifeless obedience." Bureaucratization reproduced the same pattern everywhere: the control of "leader-cliques" over the "great masses," precluding any "upswell of living forces" from below. Elites as well as masses, however, became mere cogs in a vast machine, easily pressed into service by "fascist-Nazi totalitarization."[53] Weber feared an irreversible atrophy of those capacities for freedom that he believed had animated humans to make their own history since antiquity, struggling against natural and social constraints. This would amount to the passing of what he called the "third human type" – the successor to pre-historical humanity – and the advent of a "fourth human type" that "relinquishes the self-ordering and self-formation of its existence and... surrenders itself as a functionary, by actively becoming part of the functioning."[54] Weber's diagnosis, like Mitscherlich's, trafficked in well-worn tropes of cultural critique that decried "massification" and "technology" and exalted the "cultivation" of "personality." Yet assimilating their perspectives to a nostalgic, elitist anti-modernism would miss the mark.[55] Although the proximities are relevant, closer examination suggests important distinctions.

Their proposals stressed not the containment or uplift of masses by elites but rather the masses' agency in effecting their own self-development. The crucial condition was a break with statist and centralizing approaches that impeded participation. Politically, Mitscherlich

*im Aufbruch: Karl Mannheim, Alfred Weber, Norbert Elias und die Heidelberger Sozialwissenschaft der Zwischenkriegszeit* (Munich: Hanser, 1999), 61–70. This theme links Alfred Weber's 1910 article "Der Beamte" (an inspiration to Franz Kafka, among others) with his *Ideen zur Staats- und Kultursoziologie* (1927) and *Kulturgeschichte als Kultursoziologie* (1935).

[51] Weber, "Freier Sozialismus: Ein Aktionsprogramm," in *Freier Sozialismus*, 64.
[52] Weber, "Bürokratie und Freiheit," *Die Wandlung* 1, no. 12 (1946): 1037–41; Weber, "Das Ende des modernen Staates," *Die Wandlung* 2, no. 6 (1947): 467–8.
[53] Weber, "Freier Sozialismus," 42, 64.
[54] Weber, "Der vierte Mensch oder der Zusammenbruch der geschichtlichen Kultur," *Die Wandlung* 3, no. 4 (1948): 295.
[55] Cf. Martin Dehli, *Leben als Konflikt: Zur Biographie Alexander Mitscherlichs* (Göttingen: Wallstein, 2007), 140–3; Tobias Freimüller, *Alexander Mitscherlich: Gesellschaftsdiagnosen und Psychoanalyse nach Hitler* (Göttingen: Wallstein, 2007), 81–3. More nuanced is Eberhard Demm, *Von der Weimarer Republik zur Bundesrepublik: Der politische Weg Alfred Webers 1920–1958* (Düsseldorf: Droste, 1999), 254, 268. On engaged democrats' relationship to this mandarin ideology, see Chapter 3.

and Weber endorsed parliamentarism as the only feasible framework for "mass democracy." While Weber saw parties as inescapable vehicles for the formation of popular political will, he insisted that the "selection" of "elites" – representatives and officers – be driven by a continual, self-renewing process "from below."[56] He also countenanced keeping a tenured senior civil service, partly as a check on the parties' power. Mindful of the deference bureaucrats had shown their state patrons, he set strict conditions: their ranks would be drastically reduced – mainly to the higher judiciary – and they would be "bound to the democratic principle," charged with a "duty to resist" abuses of state power. As the vital institutional context, however, Weber emphasized "local and regional self-management," the development throughout the polity and at all levels of "free, democratic forms of life based on self-responsibility and self-formation." Mitscherlich spoke of the "intensification of local political life," building upward from the municipality to the region. In the first instance, "social freedom" was realized "in life within a surveyable group," a group that each member "co-embodies," whose directives they each "co-issue to themselves."[57]

In the economy, they likewise emphasized decentralization, to "break... the influence of capital" without simply exchanging capitalist for state-socialist bureaucracies. Their plan rested on three pillars. First, a sweeping socialization would not abolish but reorganize private property, wherever possible, into collectively owned units under regulated competition. Their forms ranged from public-law corporations in heavy industry and banking to cooperatives in manufacturing and agriculture; in certain specialized instances, Weber also favored public foundations. Nationalization would be strictly limited to transit and communications.[58] Second, workers' rights and roles would be dramatically expanded. New laws would treat hours, wages, union rights, and profit-sharing. Crucially, decision making within firms would be restructured to ensure maximal "codetermination" by employees alongside employers, through works councils in the shop and production boards at the firm level. These measures would be enforced by "economic senates" within the judiciary (which would also direct public enterprise and provide public credit). Third, the fragmented nature of labor itself would

---

[56] Weber, "Freier Sozialismus," 64, 67. The language of "elite selection" is imported from the "leadership democracy" Weber advocated – as his brother Max had – in the Weimar period. After 1945, however, Weber revised his "oligarchical" and "inegalitarian" restrictions on the scope and nature of "the masses'" participation. On *Führerdemokratie*, see Demm, *Ein Liberaler*, 294–306.

[57] Weber, "Freier Sozialismus," 42, 62, 71; Weber, "Bürokratie und Freiheit," 1048; Mitscherlich, "Entwicklungsgrundlagen," 28, 33.

[58] Weber, "Freier Sozialismus," 74–5. See also Weber, *Sozialisierung zugleich als Friedenssicherung* (Heidelberg: Schneider, 1947).

be recast. For Weber, giving workers equal decision-making authority would in effect "transform production," even at non-socialized firms. Mitscherlich envisioned a re-skilling and de-division of labor to counter its "atomization," once "cooperative-like" enterprises reintegrated the assembly line and managerial office, while workers themselves circulated across agricultural, craft, and industrial sectors.[59] Animated by the young Marx's critique of alienation and echoing solutions proposed by "utopian" socialists, Mitscherlich and Weber reworked ideas from the dawn of industrialization.[60] In the age of proletarians and managers, they sought to return to workers a measure of artisanal and entrepreneurial control – over the process as well as the products of their labor.

In its affinity for the local and small-scale, this may appear a neoromantic vision. Indeed, it was derided as "petty-bourgeois socialism" by contemporaries further to the left.[61] It was, however, an explicitly forward- not backward-looking program. Mitscherlich readily conceded "there is no going back from the industrial-technical-rationalized form of life," and Weber asserted the need for "large-scale organization" in the modern era. Into the apparatus, however, he proposed to inject self-governing organs as "living counterforces" to the fullest possible extent.[62] Such institutions were not themselves the "goals" but rather the "means" of their project; the popular participation they entailed cultivated the kind of human being Weber and Mitscherlich affirmed – the free "personality." Practicing free socialism would revive dormant dispositions to freedom, countering the people's habituation to "authoritarian" order through their own "independent democratic activity." This, in turn, enabled their "self-liberation" from external control and internal egoism, as they "order[ed] people's freedoms among one another" in a process of collective "education."[63] The German people were to be its subjects as well as its objects, in a reeducation by which the masses transformed themselves into self-developing personalities on the neohumanist ideal.[64]

---

[59] Weber, "Freier Sozialismus," 76, 80–2; Mitscherlich, "Entwicklungsgrundlagen," 29, 31–2.
[60] Iring Fetscher, "Alexander Mitscherlich: Zur Pathologie der bundesdeutschen Gesellschaft," *Psyche* 37, no. 4 (1983): 301; see also Demm, *Weimarer Republik*, 254.
[61] Fritz Behrens, "'Freier' Sozialismus oder sozialistische Freiheit? Eine Kritik des kleinbürgerlichen Sozialismus aus Heidelberg," *Einheit* 2, no. 4 (1947): 389–98. This charge – echoing Marx and Engels' critique of Sismondi – was leveled in the SED's theoretical organ, by a prominent party economist but no mere party hack; Caldwell, *Dictatorship, State Planning*, 14–56.
[62] Mitscherlich, "Entwicklungsgrundlagen," 24; Weber, "Freier Sozialismus," 66.
[63] Weber, "Freier Sozialismus," 39, 63, 87; Mitscherlich, "Entwicklungsgrundlagen," 13, 32.
[64] Eberhard Demm notes (then dismisses) Weber's shift in emphasis from "elite selection" to "mass education" after 1945, treating the latter as a matter of tutelage rather than participatory *self*-education; Demm, "Alfred Webers 'Freier Sozialismus,'" in *Heidelberg*

Weber's and Mitscherlich's embrace of parliamentarism, shared across their circle, was also qualified. Mass party politics had turned bureaucratic and sclerotic, these Heidelbergers asserted. Their proposed remedy joined a postwar debate on electoral systems, where they campaigned for direct, majority voting (first-past-the-post in single-member districts) over indirect, proportional representation. Tellingly, they referred to these as "person elections" versus "list elections."[65] Sternberger made their case in an essay for *Die Wandlung*. Playing on the dual meaning of *Wahl* as both "choice" and "vote," he asserted that choosing and revising choices as "I form and transform myself" is a fundamental human freedom, one violated when the terms of our existence "are simply assigned" to us from outside. In politics, identified as *the* quintessentially human activity, the election process should engage voters and candidates as "persons," not "objectified ... ballots" and "seats" brought into proportion by political parties. Majority elections made citizens active "subject[s]," freely deliberating and delegating deputies to higher-level assemblies. Parties remained "living and flexible" means to that end, emerging, dissolving, and reforming in the process. Not so proportional representation, which made parties into "actual subject[s]" that campaigned as preformed entities with preselected candidate lists and left citizens to "ossify into vote-masses and party-blocs." The outcome was a "scale reproduction of quantities of votes" that froze political life into a composite of party affiliations, favoring "status habit" and perceived "class interest" over reflective judgment.[66]

At base, proportionality misrecognized the nature of popular sovereignty. For this point, Sternberger drew on Rousseau. He aligned proportional voting's concern that "no voice be lost" with the "will of all," which simply aggregated the "private interest" of each individual. In contrast, majority voting allowed a "general will" that intended "the common good" to emerge. Revising Rousseau, however, he cautioned that the "general will" was never a "given" but rather a question "posed," always in the process of "becoming." By "the *formation* (*Bildung*) of the majority," the constitution of the opposition, and their ongoing interaction, the majority principle could "bring forth the whole in an unending process";

---

*1945*, ed. Jürgen C. Heß, Hartmut Lehmann, and Volker Sellin (Stuttgart: Steiner, 1996), 331; Demm, *Weimarer Republik*, 290–1. Less attuned still to such revisions is Morten Reitmayer, *Elite: Sozialgeschichte einer politisch-gesellschaftlichen Idee in der frühen Bundesrepublik* (Munich: Oldenbourg, 2009), 229–35.

[65] See, e.g., Weber, "Listen oder Personen?" *Rhein-Neckar-Zeitung*, 12 June 1946. On their campaign in the context of these debates, see Chapter 4.

[66] Sternberger, "Über die Wahl, das Wählen und das Wahlverfahren," *Die Wandlung* 1, no. 10/11 (1946): 923, 928–32, 942.

as participants' capacities "form themselves," the population "forms the political people."[67] Proportional representation, he asserted, "blows apart" the people into ideology- and interest-based parties, producing unstable coalitions, legislative deadlock, and a creeping dissatisfaction with parliamentarism that Nazism had mobilized against democracy itself. Moreover, the "anonymity" of party-list voting first sapped citizens' interest and eventually provoked a "shriek for ... the strong man," as the Weimar Republic's implosion had shown.[68] In its reversal of subjects and objects, ends and means, proportionality distorted a qualitative, dynamic process involving persons into a quantitative, static procedure involving parties.

Worse, it perpetuated the people's immaturity. By most accounts, proportional representation was linked historically to democratization. It had helped enable parties representing working people to displace parties of aristocratic and bourgeois notables, and it was enshrined in constitutions across continental Europe, including Weimar Germany, leaving only Britain majoritarian.[69] Sternberger inverted these claims: proportionality and mass parties in fact impeded democracy by curtailing citizens' direct participation. Majority voting maximized that participation and served as "an educational institution (*Bildungsinstitut*)" in the process.[70] To those who asserted that Germans were not yet ready for politics unmediated by parties, he responded, "how are they ever to become independent if you don't give them the chance?" All arguments for "benevolent guardianship" overlooked the fact that "you cannot learn to swim on dry land."[71] Sternberger's position touted a British electoral model and affirmed French republicanism, but it was justified in terms that resonated with classical German thought and the *Bildung* ideal. Steeped in high culture, this argument for radical democracy looked to deliberative bodies as both vehicles and schools of popular sovereignty.

---

[67] Ibid., 926–7, 932–5 (emphasis in original). Sternberger saw the majority principle as the best possible approximation of unanimity, a "truly human substitute for unity" and a bulwark against totality. He saw the potential for a "totalitarian degeneration of the polity and the general will" latent already in Rousseau, anticipating later critics from J. L. Talmon to François Furet.

[68] Ibid., 935, 939.

[69] Carles Boix, "The Emergence of Parties and Party Systems," in *The Oxford Handbook of Comparative Politics*, ed. Boix and Susan C. Stokes (Oxford: Oxford University Press, 2007), 511–20; Eckhard Jesse, *Wahlrecht zwischen Kontinuität und Reform: Eine Analyse der Wahlsystemdiskussion und der Wahlrechtsänderungen in der Bundesrepublik Deutschland, 1949–1983* (Düsseldorf: Droste, 1985), 51–6.

[70] Sternberger to Werner Krauss, 7 January 1946, DLA A:Sternberger/ Wandlung/ 74.10309/1.

[71] Sternberger, "Tagebuch: Zu hundertfünfzig Briefen," *Die Wandlung* 1, no. 12 (1946): 1028.

The Heidelbergers' allies at the *Frankfurter Hefte* also presented a comprehensive renewal program. Dirks called it Germany's "Second Republic," underscoring the opportunity to redeem Weimar's failure.[72] That this new order would be "democratic" was "self-evident," he asserted. The term "republic" emphasized a crucial additional ingredient, those "civic virtues" of "manly responsibility for public things" that focused on "ties and duties" as much as "freedoms and rights."[73] And yet, this was not civic republicanism of a classical stripe. An "epochal shift" was required to expand self-government's scope and realize the "economic democracy" Germany's first republic had failed to implement. While all citizens had a "vital interest" in such a democratic socialism, non-workers did not feel this interest directly; farmers and the propertied class could recognize it only in "mediated" fashion, through "social reflection on the whole." For that, Christian convictions could provide the impetus, motivating what Dirks and his circle called "socialism from Christian responsibility." If Weimar's coalition of Social Democracy, middle-class liberalism, and political Catholicism had collapsed – clearing the way for fascism's coalition of monopoly capitalists, aristocratic-military elites, and a desperate petite bourgeoisie – postwar conditions were ripe for a productive coalition of "workers and Christians." Dirks intended this cooperation to extend far beyond official politics into the everyday. The new Germany's "spirit" should reside not in institutions but in the "people who carry them," not in political parties but in "republicans" themselves, and not in socialized enterprises but in the "socialist human being."[74]

Squarely at the center of their imagined polity, then, stood the concrete person. There, left-Catholic "personalism" converged with engaged democrats' distinctive concern for spontaneous subjectivity.[75] And yet, the fact that the people in question were products both of mass society and of Germany's disastrous past gave these intellectuals pause. In its political

---

[72] Dirks, "Die Zweite Republik: Zum Ziel und zum Weg der deutschen Demokratie," *Frankfurter Hefte* 1, no. 1 (1946): 12–24. Dirks had outlined the conception as early as 1932; Karl Prümm, "Entwürfe einer zweiten Republik: Zukunftsprogramme in den 'Frankfurter Heften' 1946–1949," in *Deutschland nach Hitler*, ed. Koebner, Sautermeister, and Schneider, 332–3.

[73] Dirks, "Demokratie und Republik," *Frankfurter Hefte* 1, no. 3 (1946): 90.

[74] Dirks, "Die Zweite Republik," 17–19, 22–23.

[75] On Jacques Maritain's "integral humanism," Emmanuel Mounier's "personalism," and their influence on Dirks and Kogon, see Horn, *Liberation Theology*, 89–103; Kogon, "Jacques Maritain – Frankreichs Botschafter beim Vatikan," *Frankfurter Hefte* 1, no. 3 (1946): 77–8; Dirks, "Emmanuel Mounier," *Frankfurter Hefte* 4, no. 11 (1949): 960–3. On the broader context, see Thomas Keller, *Deutsch-französische Dritte-Weg-Diskurse: Personalistische Intellektuellendebatten der Zwischenkriegszeit* (Munich: Fink, 2001).

maturity, Dirks cautioned, the German population offered a mixed picture: fully-fledged "humans" one could simply "bring to action," "fools" whose influence they must "neutralize," and "slaves" one must "carefully guide" – albeit temporarily. The new democracy aimed "eventually to return both fools and slaves to human reflectiveness and freedom." And that was possible in no other way than through their participation in its institutions. Political parties, for instance, could play a vital role. Those that remained trapped in narrow interests and received worldviews were obstacles, to be sure (as were those that overlooked the limits of their authority over bodies of more "original validity," namely family and Church). Those Dirks called "true parties," however, each evolved on the basis of their partial perspective a "design for the future" that also reflected on the social whole. By taking part in this process, citizens learned to articulate and then overcome their particular perspective, traveling the path "to political maturity."[76]

Restructuring the state itself along federalist lines, these Frankfurters argued, served the same ends. To counter the Prussian centralization that had engulfed the German lands since the 1860s, they looked to a different German tradition rooted in the west and south.[77] Such views resonated with apologetic affirmations of a good Catholic Germany against malignant "Prussianism," and they drew on an organicist, localist language with romantic, conservative tendencies. It would be hasty to conclude, however, that these left Catholics yearned for pre-modern order or blood-and-soil community.[78] Rather, ideas of conservative provenance were deployed and adapted within a participatory-democratic frame. Federalism, Kogon explained, departed from Western individualism and Eastern collectivism alike in conceiving the state as not a "mechanism" (for protecting property or centralizing power) but an "organism," a "subdivided order" of self-governing units, each with its own "original authority" and "competencies." Such an order realized democracy as the "living political solidarity of all citizens" in all social arenas, a principle that extended from family to factory, church to party, and city to state to supranational system. Above all, by placing "the personality of every single person in the center of ordered arenas of self-management, surveyable at each level,"

[76] Dirks, "Partei und Staat," *Frankfurter Hefte* 1, no. 9 (1946): 822, 827, 830–1.
[77] Kogon, "Berliner Zentralismus oder Frankfurter Bundesregierung?" *Frankfurter Hefte* 1, no. 1 (1946): 5–7; Dirks, "Ein Deutscher Bund," *Frankfurter Hefte* 1, no. 6 (1946): 1.
[78] Cf. Peter Heil, "Föderalismus als Weltanschauung: Zur Geschichte eines gesellschaftlichen Ordnungsmodells zwischen Weimar und Bonn," *Geschichte im Westen* 9, no. 2 (1994): 174; Undine Ruge, "Regionen als organische Gemeinschaften: Der integralföderalistische Diskurs in Deutschland nach 1945," in *Das Erbe der Provinz: Heimatkultur und Geschichtspolitik nach 1945*, ed. Habbo Knoch (Göttingen: Wallstein, 2001), 82–3, 86.

federalism ensured citizens' "immediate civic participation in their most proximate public life."[79] Dirks insisted that, though unitary structures might be more efficient, federalism represented the "form of German self-government... that will allow us most effectively to learn democratic life by 'practice.'"[80] It was federalism's affinity for participation that made it relevant to Germany's renewal.

Implemented in the economy, this principle resulted in what Kogon dubbed a "socialism of freedom."[81] Like Mitscherlich's and Weber's, it was non-economistic. Kogon defined socialism as "cooperatively free living," while Dirks pointed to its underlying mutualism: as the word's Latin root – *socius* or "comrade" – suggested, socialism sought to reconcile "individual" and "community."[82] Its implementation must proceed "from below," to generate "ordered areas of fitting freedom" at all levels, reunify the functions of "capital and labor," and enable people's control over their economic lives. Concretely, they called for broad socialization with a limited state sector and private ownership in small enterprise. Between these poles – expressly in mining, heavy industry, large-scale agriculture, and banking – they proposed "cooperative firms" collectively owned by their stakeholders, including employees, suppliers, consumers, and even government agencies, depending on the nature of the enterprise. Planning would be similarly "decentralized," effected by indirect "steering" mechanisms (e.g., investment, wage, and price controls) rather than direct "command" (e.g., production quotas and rationing), and through a pyramidal structure of agencies, from local chambers for every industry to a central office responsible only for what was beyond lower levels' capacities. Where the Heidelberg program reserved a few crucial functions for the judiciary, the Frankfurters implemented code-termination structures at all levels. They also emphasized councils in the workplace itself and insisted on parity-composition boards for private firms. All socialized enterprises, meanwhile, would be run by "control committees" to which employees' shareholder majorities would elect the majority of delegates, while workers received parity representation in all planning organs, from the locality to the peak "economic chamber."[83]

---

[79] Kogon, "Demokratie und Föderalismus," 74, 76.
[80] Dirks, "Ein Deutscher Bund," 3.
[81] A basic sketch was presented by Karl Heinrich Knappstein, "Die Stunde der Sozialreform," *Frankfurter Hefte* 1, no. 3 (1946): 1–3; it was elaborated in detail by Kogon, "Der Weg zu einem Sozialismus der Freiheit in Deutschland," *Frankfurter Hefte* 2, no. 9 (1947): 877–96.
[82] Kogon, "Sozialismus der Freiheit," 878; Dirks, "Das Wort Sozialismus," *Frankfurter Hefte* 1, no. 7 (1946): 630, 632.
[83] Kogon, "Sozialismus der Freiheit," 882, 885, 887, 891–3.

Thoroughgoing codetermination, coupled with socialization and planning measures, became a hallmark of the Frankfurt program. In Karl Heinrich Knappstein's words, it constituted a degree of "actual participation" that would transform workers from "objects or even raw materials of the economy" into its "responsible co-carriers." Kogon identified it with the moment of "real, material freedom" in their socialism that "permit[ted] the free personality its necessary unfolding," in contrast to "state socialism," which imposed "bureaucratic guardianship in all life's arenas." To those who feared workers did not yet possess sufficient self-restraint or breadth of vision for robust codetermination, Dirks responded with a familiar metaphor: only the act of exercising responsible control "would require them to jump in the water and... learn to swim."[84] Full democratic participation in an expanded polity that encompassed the economy alongside formal politics would allow working people to develop the whole range of their faculties, in a self-educative process.

By advocating codetermination and socialization, these intellectuals took up long-standing demands of the labor movement. Indeed, they echoed discussions of "economic democracy" in unions and socialist parties at the time, which in turn drew on precedents from the Weimar era and earlier.[85] What is striking is that these proposals had such purchase among educated elites after 1945. Germany's engaged democrats deployed the notion of codetermination, in particular, in an expansive register that resonated broadly across postwar journals. An *Aufbau* author touted workers' "right to codetermination" as crucial to any "truly democratic polity," in which "laboring people... can take their fate, their future, in their own, good, democratic hands." Another in the *Nordwestdeutsche Hefte* saw "codetermination not only in politics but also in the economy" as the foundation of a "new form of democracy independent of the parties."[86] That such a structure might operate not alongside but instead of a parliament – in a system of councils, the direct-democratic, workplace-based alternative that had emerged during the revolution of 1918/19 and, incipiently, in summer 1945 – was not seriously discussed. All four Allies and the newly licensed German parties concurred that the new system would be parliamentary.[87] Yet the councils' promise

---

[84] Knappstein, "Stunde der Sozialreform," 3; Kogon, "Sozialismus der Freiheit," 879; Dirks, "Zuschriften und Antworten," *Frankfurter Hefte* 1, no. 9 (1946): 882.
[85] See, e.g., Christoph Kleßmann, *Die doppelte Staatsgründung: Deutsche Geschichte 1945–1955*, 5th edn. (Göttingen: Vandenhoek & Ruprecht, 1991), 121–35.
[86] Rolf Helm, "Freie Kollektivität?" *Aufbau* 2, no. 8 (1946): 838–9; Erich Vollbrecht in Wilhelm Heitmüller and Vollbrecht, "Für und wider Wirtschafts-Demokratie," *Nordwestdeutsche Hefte* 1, no. 5 (1946): 8–9.
[87] See, e.g., Geoff Eley, *Forging Democracy: The History of the Left in Europe, 1850–2000* (Oxford: Oxford University Press, 2002), 160–9, 297.

of unmediated popular participation infused some engaged democrats' thinking nonetheless. In an internal memo circulated among NWDR's German staff, Axel Eggebrecht put the point explicitly: While councils represented "a protosocialist emergent form" of democracy, parliaments were "a late-capitalist residual form," their parties mired in "vocabulary" and "ideology" of the past. In principle, the choice was clear. And in practice, as they should not hesitate to underscore to their radio audience, "to decide for no party is no disgrace!"[88]

The bounds of the possible were set not by Germans but by their occupiers, however, and key aspects of engaged democrats' discussions also figured in Allied policy debates. Codetermination and socialization enjoyed some support from British authorities, whose new Labour government was nationalizing basic industries and building the postwar welfare state at home. In the British-occupied Ruhr district, this enabled some lasting gains: legislation passed there in 1947 codified works councils' competencies and implemented board-level parity codetermination in the coal, iron, and steel industries. Developments in the western zones, however, were increasingly consolidated under US leadership, and continuing initiatives to socialize heavy industry and expand codetermination ran aground on American opposition.[89] On federalism and majority elections, the western Allies were more receptive. Federalism was in fact central to American plans (the British preferred centralization, the French a loose confederation), and the western Allies' constitutional prescriptions ultimately mandated a federal structure for the FRG. American advisers, however, favored this primarily as a means to secure the representation of German states' interests at the federal level and to limit the concentration of central power (the key French goal as well).[90] As we have seen, engaged democrats privileged federalism above all as a means to invigorate local participation. Similarly, their model for majority over proportional representation was Anglo-American.[91] They valued the stability to which it led, but their discussions hinged on other issues, not

---

[88] Eggebrecht, "Zu den zehn politischen Hauptfragen," 3 May 1946, Bundesarchiv N 1524/975.

[89] Kleßmann, *Staatsgründung*, 110–13, 133–4; Carolyn Eisenberg, "The Limits of Democracy: U.S. Policy and the Rights of German Labor, 1945–49," in *America and the Shaping of German Society, 1945–1955*, ed. Michael Ermarth (Providence, R.I.: Berg, 1993), 60–81; James C. Van Hook, "From Socialization to Co-Determination: The USA, Britain, Germany, and Public Ownership in the Ruhr, 1945–51," *Historical Journal* 45, no. 1 (2002): 153–78.

[90] Erich J. Hahn, "US Policy on a West German Constitution, 1947–1949," in *American Policy and the Reconstruction of West Germany, 1945–1955*, ed. Jeffry M. Diefendorf, Axel Frohn, and Hermann-Josef Rupieper (Cambridge: Cambridge University Press, 1993), 21–44.

[91] See, e.g., Walter G. Becker, "Das englische Wahlsystem," *Die Wandlung* 2, no. 3/4 (1947): 319–33.

effective outcomes so much as citizens' self-development. Even where they overlapped most with those of the allies, then, engaged democrats' positions referenced their own understanding of democracy, one defined less in terms of interest, representation, and stable government and more in terms of the intrinsic value of participation for the reciprocal formation of person and polity.

Such participation hinged on decentralization in the widest sense, and on this score, the approach taken in the eastern zone diverged significantly. The hallmark of institutional structures there was early and thorough centralization, part of a Soviet-style transformation effected as much out of habit as by design.[92] The groundwork was laid during the first two years of occupation. In constitutional debates, Soviets and their KPD/SED clients showed themselves hostile to federalism, pushing a unitary, centralized state. Authorities encouraged a debate on fundamentals, but it was channeled through the parties, with the SED playing an ever more dominant role. Not long thereafter, a series of central administrations modeled on all-German government ministries were built, as was an economic commission that served as a proto-state. Among its functions was to manage the zone's larger firms, seized by Soviet occupiers and confirmed as "the people's own property" by referendum in Saxony.[93] If socialization was very much on the agenda, codetermination was another matter: the workers' control initiatives that flourished during liberation were endorsed rhetorically but soon sidelined in practice, as works councils were absorbed by rigidly centralized labor unions.[94] Policymakers in the Soviet zone regarded unpredictable, grassroots councils as superfluous – or threatening – to a well-planned economy.

Nonetheless, German intellectuals there too floated proposals that resonated with the participatory tenor of the time, and powerful critiques of lock-step centralization came from inside the socialist camp. Harich, for instance, took aim at this trend while making no bones about his Marxist convictions and communist leanings.[95] On the example of the theater workers' union, whose local Berlin group posed as an all-German

---

[92] Norman M. Naimark, *The Russians in Germany: A History of the Soviet Zone of Occupation, 1945–1949* (Cambridge, Mass.: Harvard University Press, 1995), 467. On countervailing tendencies and possible alternate paths, see also Eric D. Weitz, *Creating German Communism, 1890–1990: From Popular Protests to Socialist State* (Princeton, N.J.: Princeton University Press, 1997), 353–6.
[93] Kleßmann, *Staatsgründung*, 72–4, 82–3; Naimark, *Russians*, 52–55.
[94] Kleßmann, *Staatsgründung*, 272–4; Siegfried Suckut, *Die Betriebsrätebewegung in der sowjetisch besetzten Zone Deutschlands 1945–1948* (Frankfurt a.M.: Haag + Herchen, 1982), esp. 492–528. For supportive rhetoric, see, e.g., Alfred Kämmer, "Die Praxis der Betriebsräte," *Einheit* 2, no. 2 (1947): 221–2.
[95] On the résumé he circulated in August 1945, for instance: Harich, "Lebenslauf," n.d., Stiftung Archiv der Akademie der Künste Berlin (hereafter AdK) Reger-Archiv 311.

agency, he diagnosed a general tendency to establish ostensibly representative organizations by bureaucratic fiat. He discerned the same pattern in the Soviet zone's parties, whose hastily constituted "*Reich* leaderships" and "central committees" amounted to "nothing better than despotism (*Willkür*)" if they were not "authorized by the trust of their constituents." Such developments violated the cardinal principle that political activity "should develop itself 'from below,' out of the regionally bounded germs of political life" rather than suffer "organizational forms clapped down on political life from above." These concerns were still clearer in his correspondence, where he railed against the squandered opportunity to jettison "authoritarian and centralist" traditions in favor of "federalist tendencies" that might "build an organically subdivided new Germany."[96] Harich would soon reconsider, becoming a firm believer in the Communist Party's vanguard role before evolving into a GDR dissident. His initial views, however, combined resolute criticism of Germans' authoritarian proclivities with the clear sense that the best remedy lay not with party or state leaders but in the people's self-organization.

Wolfgang Leonhard, the young functionary who first contacted Harich, provides another example. The "political bellyaches" he brought back from Moscow only worsened in Germany, where he witnessed Ulbricht's dictatorial style and the KPD's dissolution of the *Antifa* committees firsthand. As Leonhard later understood, centralizing power was second nature for hardliners, who reflexively suppressed just those spontaneous democratic energies that inspired him.[97] At the time, he voiced his concerns not directly, as a critique of Soviet-zonal developments, but indirectly, by affirming conditions elsewhere. In a piece for *Die Weltbühne*, he lauded the USSR's putatively governing organs, the popularly elected *soviets* or "councils." On the one hand, he cautioned that a system built on non-partisan deliberation was suited to a classless society, which Germany was not yet. On the other, he highlighted the soviets' "federative" structure and the direct election of delegates at each level, which ensured that "personality" not party affiliation was the decisive criterion. By these virtues, he asserted, the councils embodied "real popular rule."[98] While Leonhard certainly perpetuated illusions regarding the power of the USSR's soviets relative to its party and state apparatus, the

---

[96] Harich, "Eine gefährliche Personalunion," *Der Kurier*, 17 December 1945; Harich, "Parteikrise u. Einheitsfront," *Der Kurier*, 27 December 1945; Harich to Erik Reger, 6 January 1946, AdK Reger-Archiv 311.
[97] Wolfgang Leonhard, *Die Revolution entläßt ihre Kinder* (Cologne: Kiepenheuer & Witsch, 1955), 381–9.
[98] Leonhard, "Wie wird in der Sowjetunion gewählt?" *Die Weltbühne* 2, no. 2 (1947): 53–4, 56.

participatory terms of his endorsement also implied a critique of state socialist reality.

This position informed a budding interest in Yugoslavia, where he visited in 1947. His published reports introduced his German audience to the heroic narrative of how, alone among Europeans, Josip Broz Tito's multinational Partisans had liberated themselves from Axis occupation and tackled reconstruction in a groundswell of popular activism. This was a highly sanitized account, but it shows Leonhard's enthusiasm for the dedication he clearly perceived among the population at large. He praised the local "people's committees" that emerged during the resistance – through free, equal, direct elections – and soon formed the bedrock of the "federal people's republic," which subsumed parties under a popular front as a "united political force." Yugoslavia was forging its own postwar path, as he hoped Germany would. He applauded its refusal to "bind itself one-sidedly," cultivating relations with the Soviet Union and Eastern Europe alongside Western powers.[99] Leonhard remained in Berlin, serving as an instructor at the new Party College for SED cadres, whose first cohort included Harich. But he felt himself drawn to Belgrade, where – after Yugoslavia's 1948 ejection from the Cominform – a new socialist society declared its independence. Making his own break with Stalinism, Leonhard fled there in 1949. The SED vilified him as a "Trotskyite-Titoist" and launched a new round of interrogations and ideological policing.[100] Safely beyond their grasp, Leonhard witnessed the birth of Yugoslavia's experiment in decentralized authority and worker self-management, which would capture the imaginations of democratic socialists across the globe in the 1950s.[101]

And yet, the language of participation was not the exclusive domain of future dissidents and defectors. It was also mobilized by socialist intellectuals who contributed to the non-dogmatic openness of the postwar years but never broke with the later GDR. Jurist Peter Alfons Steiniger, for instance, developed a Communist approach to participatory institutions

---

[99] Leonhard, "Reise nach Belgrad," *Die Weltbühne* 2, no. 17 (1947): 722–3; Leonhard, "Ein Land hatte Geburtstag," *Die Weltbühne* 2, no. 24 (1947): 1055.

[100] Leonhard, "Im Fadenkreuz der SED: Meine Flucht von der Parteihochschule 'Karl Marx' im März 1949 und die Aktivitäten der Zentralen Parteikontroll-Kommission," *Vierteljahrshefte für Zeitgeschichte* 46, no. 2 (1998): 283–310. On the context, see Leonid Gibianskii, "The Soviet–Yugoslav Split and the Cominform," in *The Establishment of Communist Regimes in Eastern Europe, 1944–1949*, ed. Norman Naimark and Gibianskii (Boulder, Colo.: Westview, 1997), 291–312.

[101] For an overview, see John R. Lampe, *Yugoslavia as History: Twice There Was a Country*, 2nd edn. (Cambridge: Cambridge University Press, 2000), 255–64. The classic analysis is A. Ross Johnson, *The Transformation of Communist Ideology: The Yugoslav Case, 1945–1953* (Cambridge, Mass.: MIT Press, 1972).

from within the SED.[102] Like many leftists, he maintained that material destruction had not eliminated class tensions in German society, and he defended mass parties and proportional representation as the best means for their expression. Still, he agreed these institutions were in need of reform, and he published a program to do so in *Aufbau*. Steiniger presented his "democratic bloc system" as an updated parliamentarism, with both legislature and government constituted in proportion to votes cast. The latter, a "permanent bloc" of all parties, formed an "obligatory" coalition for the electoral period's duration. Using liberal constitutional theorist Hans Kelsen and his far-right antipode Carl Schmitt as foils, Steiniger rejected liberalism's competiton of government and opposition along with fascism's imposition of unity and vilification of dissent. He envisioned the bloc as a "centripetal" rather than "centrifugal" system, one that addressed the fractious instability of multiparty systems. In that respect, he claimed, it offered a truer, fuller form of popular sovereignty. Just as citizens themselves had no choice but to continue living and working together, even in the face of sharp disagreements, so their representatives would have no choice but to reach consensus. Against Schmitt's view of politics as the struggle with the enemy, Steiniger defined good government as an "alliance of friend and foe in mutual effort."[103]

Although he defended mass parties, Steiniger also lamented their bureaucratic character and the candidate lists that delivered mandates to pre-selected appointees, not elected delegates. He proposed a constitutional requirement that parties (restructured as corporations of public law, not private associations) be governed internally by the same principle as the rest of the polity: by the proportional votes of their constituents. Primary elections among the membership, not administrative decrees, would determine candidates and leadership, enlivening parties from the grassroots up. He sought to address the problem diagnosed by the *Wandlung* circle, without prematurely sidelining parties. Where the Heidelbergers upheld elections as a participatory training ground, Steiniger viewed parties themselves, if democratized internally, as the "preschool[s] of activist citizens."[104] The difficulty was that Steiniger's

---

[102] See also Berndt Musiolek, "Peter Alfons Steiniger: Zwischen Illusion und Wirklichkeit," in *Rechtsgeschichtswissenschaft in Deutschland 1945 bis 1952*, ed. Horst Schröder and Dieter Simon (Frankfurt a.M.: Klostermann, 2001), 253–73; Alexander Gallus, *Heimat "Weltbühne": Eine Intellektuellengeschichte im 20. Jahrhundert* (Göttingen: Wallstein, 2012), 291–302, who addresses Steiniger's Weimar-era variations on "bloc politics" as well.

[103] Alfons Steiniger, "Demokratisches Blocksystem," *Aufbau* 2, no. 11 (1946): 1083, 1086, 1088. On the Weimar-era debate, see David Dyzenhaus, *Legality and Legitimacy: Carl Schmitt, Hans Kelsen, and Hermann Heller in Weimar* (Oxford: Clarendon, 1997).

[104] Steiniger, "Demokratisches Blocksystem," 1088; also Steiniger, "Aktion Heidelberg," *Aufbau* 3, no. 2 (1947): 102–10.

own party, the SED, was busily dismantling all mechanisms of intra-party democracy. And the centerpiece of his proposal corresponded to the nominal coalition practices of the Soviet zone. In effect, he provided a prominent justification for the "bloc of antifascist-democratic parties," a seemingly pluralist veil behind which the SED extended its control.[105] Assimilated to official conceptions uninterested in intra-party democracy and only tactically committed to coalitions, Steiniger's "bloc system" became an intermediary stage toward one-party rule, as it was taking shape in "people's democracies" across Eastern Europe.[106] And as the gap between principle and reality widened, he never left the Soviet zone.

## Reeducation as self-education

For all their distinctions, the proposals outlined above shared an emphasis on direct participation in political and economic self-government as the key to democratic self-education, a path that was simultaneously the goal. They addressed the general citizenry of a new, post-fascist German polity. Notably, a similar thrust characterized engaged democrats' approaches to two specific populations: Germany's young people and its former National Socialists. Here, they ventured onto two fields of occupation policy the allies took especially seriously. First and most immediate was denazification, in which military governments removed millions from their positions in order to exclude convinced Nazis from public life. Second was reeducation, a longer-term, deeper-seated process to wean the German people as a whole off those habits and dispositions that had enabled Nazism. Schools and universities were its central vehicles, and the much-observed German youth its primary target.[107]

In that sense, the transformation of formal education was integral to both Allied and indigenous democratization plans. A thorough purge seemed indispensable, of both nazified instructors and authoritarian or

---

[105] Andreas Malycha, "Die Transformation des Parteiensystems in der SBZ 1945–1949," in *Die Parteien und Organisationen der DDR: Ein Handbuch*, ed. Gerd-Rüdiger Stephan, et al. (Berlin: Dietz, 2002), 21–45; Musiolek, "Steiniger," 257, 264; Heike Amos, *Die Entstehung der Verfassung in der Sowjetischen Besatzungszone/DDR 1946–1949: Darstellung und Dokumentation* (Münster: LIT, 2006), 218–19.

[106] For the official SED treatment, compare Rudolf Appelt, "Wesen und Ziele der Blockpolitik," *Einheit* 2, no. 9 (1947): 825–36. On the context, see Norman Naimark, "The Sovietization of Eastern Europe, 1944–1953," in *The Cambridge History of the Cold War*, ed. Melvyn P. Leffler and Odd Arne Westad (Cambridge: Cambridge University Press, 2010), I:175–97.

[107] See Kleßmann, *Staatsgründung*, 92–8 and, e.g., Manfred Heinemann, ed. *Umerziehung und Wiederaufbau: Die Bildungspolitik der Besatzungsmächte in Deutschland und Österreich* (Stuttgart: Klett-Cotta, 1981); Heinemann, ed. *Zwischen Restauration und Innovation: Bildungsreformen in Ost und West nach 1945* (Cologne: Böhlau, 1999).

militarist curricula. The basic structure of the system, too, was at issue. Many hoped to dismantle the traditional arrangement in which, after four years of common primary education, ten-year-olds were separated into one of three secondary tracks: a rudimentary, largely vocational training for the vast majority; more thorough preparation for business and technical careers for a second group; and immersion in classical letters at the neohumanist Gymnasia for a privileged minority. Only the third track led to university study and, thereafter, the liberal professions or higher civil service. Access to the post-secondary level was thus a key concern, to break the class monopoly on higher education. Actual outcomes varied widely. Reformers' long-pursued goals – a public, secular, coeducational, eight-year "unity school" for all plus an influx of non-elite students to universities – were realized only in the eastern zone, with strong and soon coercive Soviet backing. For all the nonpartisan idealism infusing this "antifascist-democratic" transformation, the system soon disadvantaged middle-class students and "bourgeois" educators, serving a doctrinaire Marxism-Leninism and SED rule.[108] Similar structural initiatives in the western zones largely faltered, and universities kept their narrow social base and politically tainted faculties well into the postwar period. At the same time, a slow reform process was at work in curriculum, pedagogy, and student government, especially in the schools.[109]

In this debate, Germany's engaged democrats landed unambiguously on the side of neither transformation nor conservation. They sought to eliminate class stratification, yet many felt a strong allegiance to the forms of elite education they themselves had enjoyed – even if, as we shall see, they took an equivocal stance toward traditional *Bildung*. Most stopped short of plans to abolish tracking or the gymnasium completely, advocating measures such as the internally "differentiated unity school," longer common schooling, or greater mobility across traditional tracks instead. All agreed, however, that access to university should be merit-based and fee-free, and many endorsed preferential policies for

---

[108] John Connelly, *Captive University: The Sovietization of East German, Czech, and Polish Higher Education, 1945–1956* (Chapel Hill: University of North Carolina Press, 2000); Benita Blessing, *The Antifascist Classroom: Denazification in Soviet-Occupied Germany, 1945–1949* (New York: Palgrave Macmillan, 2006).

[109] James F. Tent, *Mission on the Rhine: Reeducation and Denazification in American-Occupied Germany* (Chicago: University of Chicago Press, 1982); Steven P. Remy, *The Heidelberg Myth: The Nazification and Denazification of a German University* (Cambridge, Mass.: Harvard University Press, 2002); Brian M. Puaca, *Learning Democracy: Education Reform in West Germany, 1945–1965* (New York: Berghahn, 2009). West Berlin – at its new Free University and in its schools – was the center of reform outside the East.

underprivileged youth.[110] Their journals prominently featured key reformers' plans.[111]

Questions of pedagogy drew more sustained attention. Clemens Münster, in the *Frankfurter Hefte*, called for new educational content – pre-eminently, on the causes and consequences of Nazism. He also addressed innovative forms, favoring "discussion circles" based on open and active debate over traditional lectures. Quoting émigré sociologist Karl Mannheim, Münster underscored how vital it was that students learned to engage their peers not merely with "passive toleration" but with that "fundamental curiosity that seeks to grasp each person... in their otherness."[112] Writing in *Aufbau*, Roland Schacht rejected a view of *Bildung* as the unquestioned absorption of fixed knowledge. It was instead a collaborative adventure in which the material "must be worked up personally" by the students, while the teacher "binds themselves to [the students]... and shares all the efforts and dangers with them." The crucial point, Dirks asserted, was that, at all levels – school, university, or adult education – "the one to be educated is not the object of the educator; rather, they face them as a subject: the work of education is a form of encounter." Indeed, "all *Bildung* is self-*Bildung*," and teachers provided learners less with education than "assistance in education."[113] Such positions converged with those of veteran reformers, whose proposals acquired new urgency in the postwar moment. For one, Werner Bloch, a learning process driven by students' questions and guided but not led by instructors expressed a distinctively modern project: to "free oneself from received authorities." Practicing the independent, public use of reason – Kant's definition of enlightenment – was the signal condition for education, as well as for any future democracy.[114]

---

[110] See, e.g., Weber, "Freier Sozialismus," 88–90; Dirks, "Wer soll studieren dürfen?" *Frankfurter Hefte* 2, no. 5 (1947): 435–7. Notably, even the Soviet zone's *Einheitsschule* retained some differentiated curricula until 1948; Blessing, *Antifascist Classroom*, 42.

[111] Erwin Stein, "Die neue Schule: Pläne zur hessischen Schulreform," *Frankfurter Hefte* 2, no. 10 (1947): 1016–28; Günther Rönnebeck, "Was wird aus der deutschen Schule?" *Nordwestdeutsche Hefte* 2, no. 1/2 (1947): 36–9.

[112] Clemens Münster, "Die Universität 1946," *Frankfurter Hefte* 1, no. 1 (1946): 8. The German-Hungarian Mannheim, a childhood friend of Lukács and former student of Alfred Weber, was now professor of education at the University of London. Münster cited Karl Mannheim, "Die Rolle der Universitäten: Aus einer deutschen Sendung des Londoner Rundfunks," *Neue Auslese* 1, no. 4 (1945/46): 49–53.

[113] Roland Schacht, "Bildung und Volkshochschule," *Aufbau* 2, no. 4 (1946): 427; Dirks, "Bildungsarbeit heute: Sinn und Grenzen der Volksbildung," *Frankfurter Hefte* 2, no. 9 (1947): 901, 904.

[114] Werner Bloch, "Die überhörten Gänsefüßchen," *Die Weltbühne* 1, no. 4 (1946): 122, 124; also Heinrich Deiters, "Wandlungen im Selbstbewußtsein des Lehrers," *Aufbau* 2, no. 8 (1946): 794; Paul Oestreich, "Die Aufgaben der deutschen Lehrer," *Ost und West* 1, no. 3 (1947): 89–90. All three were SPD school reformers in the 1920s and took up

The intellectuals in question also applied such principles beyond the classroom, in the broader life of the institution. Weber and the Heidelberg group, for instance, strenuously advocated rotating "pupil self-management" organs that shared in school administration, so that "*each* [pupil] be given the opportunity to lead." These extended the goal of student-centered pedagogy: to confront the learner with situations that demanded "free self-responsibility" and "the courage to self-assertion," culminating in "self-managing communal action." Only such self-developing experience could prepare Germans to meet the challenges of "modern mass democracy."[115] Here, the parallel between the general population's self-education to democracy and students' self-education to maturity were made explicit. In both, learning happened only if carried out by the learner, as an active participant in the process.

Engaged democrats' most prominent role in education reform debates came with the *Wandlung* circle's involvement in the reopening of Heidelberg University. Jaspers and Weber, above all, aimed to recover the basic framework of the university's old constitution, both internally – as an institution self-governed largely by its small circle of full faculty – and externally – as a state-financed entity nonetheless independent of state authority. This was, in many respects, the classic stance of Germany's mandarin professoriate, who had coped with the seeming despiritualization wrought by industrial modernity by casting the university as a citadel of cultivation and spiritual freedom. There, humanistic scholars resisted incursions by a utilitarian world, from the admission of working-class youth to the rise of the natural sciences.[116] This ideal revived after 1945, partly in response to the university's subjugation by the Nazi state. Yet it also abetted the rehabilitation of politically compromised professors by their colleagues, a fact not lost on German and Allied reformers. (Victor Klemperer, returning to Leipzig University, questioned whether German faculties were ready for such a "beautiful

---

posts in Berlin schools in 1945 (Deiters and Oestreich, but not Bloch, joined the SED); Gert Geißler, "Exil und Schulreform: Zur Geschichte der Schulreformpläne der KPD Herbst 1944 bis Januar 1946," in *Zwischen Restauration*, ed. Heinemann, 96–8. For the background, see Marjorie Lamberti, *The Politics of Education: Teachers and School Reform in Weimar Germay* (New York: Berghahn, 2002).

[115] Weber, "Freier Sozialismus," 90; Weber, "Gedanken zur Volksschulbildung," [May 1947], Universitätsbibliothek Heidelberg, NL Weber, Box 3, Aktionsgruppe Nov. 49 und April 50, 2, 9. The Aktionsgruppe Heidelberg submitted the latter document to Württemberg-Badenese and American authorities; Lambert Schneider to Sternberger, 5 May 1947, Deutsches Literaturarchiv (Marbach a.N.) A:Sternberger/ Aktionsgruppe/ 89.10.8130; Demm, *Weimarer Republik*, 290.

[116] The classic account is Fritz K. Ringer, *The Decline of the German Mandarins: The German Academic Community, 1890–1933* (Cambridge, Mass.: Harvard University Press, 1969).

democratic right" as self-management.[117]) In Heidelberg, even Jaspers and Weber – far more supportive of a thorough purge than most – worked to preserve the university's self-governing status, while Jaspers responded defensively to accusations that denazification was failing. Both also advocated retaining the gymnasium diploma as an application requirement, opposing efforts to dramatically expand access. Their resistance to structural reform is generally taken – not without reason – as a failure to uphold their democratic principles within their own institutional sphere.[118]

What is often overlooked is that their positions had also to do with a vision of the university as a specific kind of self-governing, self-educating community. In various postwar writings, Jaspers promulgated his "idea of the university" – one rooted in the Prussian reforms of Wilhelm von Humboldt – as the site of "the becoming-apparent of truth through the communal labor of researchers who are teachers as well." This conceived the university as an entity whose nature simultaneously entailed and suspended a series of status distinctions. Neither the "researching lecturer" nor the "learning student" was the equal of the full professor, an asymmetry intrinsic to the educational enterprise. Nonetheless, they were to be treated as such, within bounds, as "mature . . . citizens of the university" (hence the exacting admissions requirements). What knit the community of teachers and learners together was all members' active participation in the basic mission of research, as an ongoing dialogue from which truth emerged.[119] For Jaspers, then, the university remained an "order of the aristocracy of the spirit," but he was adamant that it should "manage itself in democratic forms" that expressly included a role for junior faculty as well as students, albeit a circumscribed, consultative one.[120] Self-government was intrinsically related to the university's

---

[117] Klemperer, "Unsere Leser Schreiben," *Aufbau* 2, no. 4 (1946): 439.

[118] See Remy, *Heidelberg Myth*, 116–76. For typical assessments, see ibid., 122, 170; Demm, *Weimarer Republik*, 325, 339; Christian Jansen, "Mehr pragmatisch denn liberal: Politische Initiativen und Argumentationsmuster von Walter Jellinek, Gustav Radbruch und Willy Hellpach im Kontext der Wiedereröffnung der Universität Heidelberg," in *Heidelberg 1945*, ed. Heß, Lehmann, and Sellin, 179–80.

[119] Karl Jaspers, "Volk und Universität," *Die Wandlung* 2, no. 1 (1947): 54–5. This expands on themes from Jaspers' address at the August 1945 reopening, elaborated in a 1946 rewriting of his 1923 book; cf. Jaspers, "Erneuerung der Universität," *Die Wandlung* 1, no. 1 (1945): 68; Jaspers, *Die Idee der Universität* (Berlin: Springer, 1946), 9.

[120] Cited in Renato De Rosa, "Politische Akzente im Leben eines Philosophen: Karl Jaspers in Heidelberg 1901–1946," in Jaspers, *Erneuerung der Universität: Reden und Schriften 1945–46*, ed. De Rosa (Heidelberg: Schneider, 1986), 376. The 1945 constitution, which Jaspers took the lead in drafting, in fact provided for such limited representation; Hermann Weisert, *Die Verfassung der Universität Heidelberg: Überblick 1386–1952* (Heidelberg: Winter, 1974), 141–4; cf. Remy, *Heidelberg Myth*, 120. For a rare reading of Jaspers attuned to both aristocratic-elitist and democratic moments, see Jaimey Fisher,

mission, which demanded that the pursuit of truth operate according to its own laws, free of "ends imposed from the outside." This applied not only to scholarship but to hiring, firing, and admissions decisions. Jaspers acknowledged that the university was not yet fully cleansed of Nazism's influence but insisted it was "capable and willing to reform of its own accord." It retained a core of "unimpeachable men" ready to set in motion an "uninterrupted self-education" from within.[121] The university's specific autonomy crystallized a combination of self-government and self-education that translated engaged democrats' thinking on democratic renewal to a hierarchical context. In an editorial comment, *Die Wandlung* put the point explicitly: the "principle of self-management" made the university "exemplary for the life of free bodies within a democratic polity and for the possibility of such freedom at all."[122]

The relationship of politics per se to the academy, however, remained controversial. In light of student radicalization during Weimar's crisis years, followed by the overt politicization of the Nazi university, there was surely cause for concern. Jaspers drew the clearest line, affirming that politics could be an object of detached study while warning that it threatened to derail the disinterested pursuit of truth. In contrast, Weber – like most engaged democrats – saw the study of political conditions as bound up with the formation of judgments about them. In large part, these positions reprised an older debate around Max Weber's distinction of values from facts in scholarship and his thoughts on the possibility of objective, "value-free" enquiry.[123] After 1945, however, even sober Jaspers asserted that the life of the academy had political relevance: in its different métier, the "humane state" shared the university's commitments to "solidarity" and "freedom" as a collaborative, self-corrective process. The state generated "with power simultaneously the self-limitation of power" and thereby realized law and justice in the world, just as the university did with truth. In that sense, the state could find in the university "the well-spring of its citizens' education."[124] The two had parallel and complementary roles to play.

*Disciplining Germany: Youth, Reeducation, and Reconstruction after the Second World War* (Detroit: Wayne State University Press, 2007), 131–55.

[121] Jaspers, "Volk und Universität," 55, 59–60.
[122] "Redaktionelle Anmerkungen," *Die Wandlung* 2, no. 8 (1947): 747.
[123] Jaspers, "Volk und Universität," 56–7; Weber, "Student und Politik," *Die Wandlung* 2, no. 3/4 (1947): 290–4. In the 1920s, Alfred Weber already urged his students to question this distinction; Demm, *Weimarer Republik*, 91–2, 106. On the debates, see Joshua Derman, *Max Weber in Politics and Social Thought: From Charisma to Canonization* (Cambridge: Cambridge University Press, 2012), 46–79.
[124] Jaspers, "Erneuerung der Universität," 74. Arnold Bauer underscored this political valence in a review of Jaspers' book: "Über die demokratische Geistesbildung," *Die Neue Zeitung*, 30 August 1946.

Of course, the relationship between the university and politics – of knowledge and power more generally – marked a major fault line between liberals and their critics. In Berlin, the advancing Marxist-Leninist politicization of the Humboldt University – a complex of curricular, admissions, and staffing changes, effected administratively but also by coercion, expulsions, and arrests – precipitated the foundation of the Free University in the American sector in 1948.[125] By the time Ernst Bloch arrived at Leipzig University in 1949, he was full of invective for the putatively apolitical scholars of "the West," blind as they were to the embeddedness of all thought in the material, social forces of human history. This was a central insight of Marxism, which any true science rejected at its peril. From that perspective, he partially affirmed Jaspers' "idea of the university" as a communal project of intellectual labor toward truth, though he cautioned that bourgeois truth succumbed to "wishy-washiness" by refusing to connect the life of the mind to that of "the people in struggle." With that proviso, he endorsed Jaspers' vision of the university as an ideal community, whose truth-seeking labor was, in the sense of Marxism's unified "theory-praxis," itself a form of emancipatory activity. And he agreed its realization required a sustained encounter with the humanist tradition, with the likes of Plato and Aeschylus, Augustine and Dante, Descartes and Shakespeare, Hegel and Goethe. Yet his was a politically ambivalent vision. On the one hand, Bloch called for an open, non-deterministic search for truth; on the other, he painted Lenin and Stalin as its heroes and Soviet-style central planning as its instantiation.[126]

Engaged democrats' positions on denazification paralleled their approach to educational reform. Eliminating Nazism's influence demanded a similarly self-activated process. Kogon hailed the potential for denazification to become a "revolutionary self-liberation" and make up for the anti-Nazi uprising that never took place. This would require the German public to take active part: as members of civilian courts, as honest witnesses, and by identifying with the process and its goals. In fact, however, most were quickly alienated by denazification's shortcomings; the average German, Kogon alleged, "feels like an object, not the subject of liberation, and experiences it precisely as its opposite."[127] Behind this disaffection lay the seemingly indiscriminate, bureaucratic, too often corrupt nature of proceedings that were also uneven across

---

[125] Connelly, *Captive University*, 119–25. See also James F. Tent, *The Free University of Berlin: A Political History* (Bloomington: Indiana University Press, 1988); Siegward Lönnendonker, *Freie Universität Berlin: Gründung einer politischen Universität* (Berlin: Duncker & Humblot, 1988).

[126] Bloch, "Universität, Marxismus, Philosophie," *Ost und West* 3, no. 11 (1949): 67, 74, 76. Bloch quoted Jaspers directly in this, his fall 1949 inaugural address.

[127] Kogon, "Die allmähliche Revolution," *Frankfurter Hefte* 1, no. 7 (1946): 670.

zones. Worse, many "bigger fish" were let off the hook as the political will behind denazification petered out. While engaged democrats shared this sense of injustice, their critique emphasized the process' excessively "formal" character. On one side, the Allies' procedures were too focused on external markers of party and organizational membership; on the other, implicated Germans vouched unreflectively and cynically for each others' alleged anti-Nazism. Such maneuvers impeded two urgent tasks: not only the exclusion of Nazism's true activists and beneficiaries from influence but also the relentless self-examination that would reform pro-Nazi views and build antifascist commitments. These were matters of internal "conviction" that required "inner purification" and were ill served by schematized, ritualized procedures in which Germans felt no direct investment.[128]

To remedy this participatory deficit, it was not enough to transfer denazification to German hands, as was done in all zones between late 1945 and early 1947. So Knappstein argued, taking stock of his work as acting minister and "driving force" for denazification in Hesse.[129] He insisted that, although formalistic Allied directives could effect a "mechanical purge," they "remained stuck in the external and the negative," even when implemented by German officials. A "true self-purification" required the German people to "seize hold of the task and make it, of their own accord, into a test of their democratic consciousness." Unfortunately, the too-broad denazification program undermined this very goal, spreading anti-occupation and ultimately anti-democratic resentment while generating a "false solidarity" between the hordes of "hangers-on" and the "real Nazis," who hid all the better in a sea of millions. Under such conditions, Knappstein feared a burgeoning "renazification." These considerations lay behind engaged democrats' conciliatory plea that nominal Nazis be not excluded from society but put back to work in and for the new Germany. As Kogon put it, "to win them over" would entail giving them a strictly "supervised chance" at re-integration and eventual citizenship, for "only real democracy is positive liberation."[130] Imposing denazification from without was initially

---

[128] Ibid., 669–70; Kogon, "Das Recht auf den politischen Irrtum," *Frankfurter Hefte* 2, no. 7 (1947): 645–9. See also Paul Ronge, "Das Problem der 'Anderen,'" *Aufbau* 3, no. 8 (1947): 122–3; Walther von Hollander, "Ein Jahr Entnazifizierung," *Nordwestdeutsche Hefte* 2, no. 2 (1947): 37. Ronge and Hollander served on denazification panels in the Soviet and British zones. The German affidavits were known as *Persilscheine*, or "whitewash certificates," after a leading laundry detergent.

[129] Armin Schuster, *Die Entnazifizierung in Hessen 1945–1954: Vergangenheitspolitik in der Nachkriegszeit* (Wiesbaden: Historische Kommission für Nassau, 1999), quote 417.

[130] Knappstein, "Die versäumte Revolution: Wird das Experiment der 'Denazifizierung' gelingen?" *Die Wandlung* 2, no. 7/8 (1947): 663, 674–5, 672; Kogon, "Das Recht auf den politischen Irrtum," 641, 655.

necessary, good for neutralizing the minority of Nazi activists. A lasting break with the Nazi past, however, had to be executed from within, through the cooperation of the vast majority of Germans in building their own democratic future.

In mid 1949, Mitscherlich responded to a request by the *Frankfurter Hefte* to assess the preceding years' denazification efforts. Psychically, he declared, it would have been "easier to deal with the National Socialist past" had the regime been swept away by "a true political revolution, not just an administrative movement on paper." Because of the bureaucratic character of these procedures, the affective energies ordinary Germans had invested in the regime "have not neutralized and freed themselves for new bonds." Effective psychosocial denazification required enabling ex-Nazis to work through their loss by forging attachments to the new polity through active involvement. As Mitscherlich explained, "a new form of life... can be won only with the participation of *all*. If there are still Nazis among us – which only hypocrites would deny – then also through their cooperation." While this solution courted obvious dangers, the new Germany had no choice but to embrace it: "*We must... give former Nazis the opportunity to participate in political fair play.*"[131] Overcoming the legacy of Nazism required not only moral confrontation but also political self-education, and time was running out. In years to come, Mitscherlich would lament that postwar West Germans had failed at just this task.

In 1945, by contrast, engaged democrats were strikingly optimistic that the renewal they envisioned could redeem the German catastrophe and forge an ideal polity in the process. While their inspirations and institutional proposals were diverse, they shared a common approach to the question of democracy, one that evinced both potentials and limitations of the postwar political imagination. In one important limitation, although their prescriptions applied equally to men and women without formal exclusions, their thinking was still cast in gendered terms. Its addressees were the generic citizens of the republic – adult and implicitly male – who inhabited the public spaces of civic activism, political decision-making, and productive work. Long-standing assumptions that construed this sphere as separate from the private spaces of home and family and exempted the latter from critical scrutiny remained effectively unquestioned for these intellectuals, as for so many contemporaries.[132]

---

[131] Printed in Karl Wilhelm Böttcher, "Menschen unter falschem Namen," *Frankfurter Hefte* 4, no. 6 (1949): 509 (emphasis and "fair play" – an opaquely affirmative reference to Anglo-American democracy – in original).

[132] For two classic critiques, see Jean Bethke Elshtain, *Public Man, Private Woman: Women in Social and Political Thought* (Princeton, N.J.: Princeton University Press, 1981); Carole Pateman, *The Sexual Contract* (Stanford, Calif.: Stanford University Press, 1988).

Thus, they offered few resources for a democratization of relations in those spheres, as a restorative gender regime arose not only in West Germany but also – more belatedly, partially, and contestedly – in the East.[133] In the FRG, a critical questioning of the roles of fathers and husbands relative to mothers and wives began only in the late 1950s. When it did, however, it built on the sustained reconsideration of generic authority initiated by engaged democrats in the postwar years.[134]

If gendered inequities and private hierarchies marked a blind spot of their thinking, their romance with "the people" as a unitary, expressive subject reflected a different historical legacy. After the divisive traumas of total war and revolution, interwar political discourse was suffused with an emphatic rhetoric of the *Volk* as a unified, harmonious, egalitarian entity and made its well-being and self-realization the central principle of politics. This language could tend in dictatorial as well as democratic, exclusionary as well as inclusionary directions, as was clear when Hitler and the NSDAP succeeded in mobilizing such expectations more persuasively than any other party of the embattled Weimar Republic.[135] Yet to construe widespread "synthesis-thinking" and idealization of "all-embracing community" during the immediate postwar years as primarily a residue of National Socialism would be one-sided.[136] Certainly, Germany's engaged democrats believed that a singular common interest and a common good existed, different in kind from the outcomes of competition and compromise among organized interest groups. If their political thought was anti-pluralist in this strict sense, however, it was not anti-plural, for they emphasized dialogue and cooperation among diverse constituents as the process by which "the people" and its will were constituted. They construed this not as a paradox but – implicitly or explicitly – as a dialectical position.

This expresses the forward-looking potential of their political thought: its stress, in a surprisingly popular vein, on citizens' unmediated, spontaneous involvement in the institutions of political and economic

---

[133] See, e.g., Robert G. Moeller, *Protecting Motherhood: Women and the Family in the Politics of Postwar West Germany* (Berkeley: University of California Press, 1993); Donna Harsch, *Revenge of the Domestic: Women, the Family, and Communism in the German Democratic Republic* (Princeton, N.J.: Princeton University Press, 2007).

[134] Till van Rahden, "Fatherhood, Rechristianization, and the Quest for Democracy in Postwar West Germany," in *Raising Citizens in the "Century of the Child": The United States and German Central Europe in Comparative Perspective*, ed. Dirk Schumann (New York: Berghahn, 2010), 141–64.

[135] See, e.g., Thomas Mergel, "Dictatorship and Democracy, 1918–1939," in *The Oxford Handbook of Modern German History*, ed. Helmut Walser Smith (Oxford: Oxford University Press, 2011), 423–52.

[136] C.f. Prowe, "Demokratisierung in Deutschland nach 1945: Die Ansätze des Schlüsseljahres 1947," in *Deutsche Umbrüche im 20. Jahrhundert*, ed. Dietrich Papenfuß and Wolfgang Schieder (Cologne: Böhlau, 2000), here 453–4.

self-rule. Self-government in this emphatic sense was not only an end to be realized but a pedagogical means to its own realization. Despite elites' traditional disdain and postwar Germans' specific and intense worry for the general population's political maturity, engaged democrats insisted that the latter could be cultivated only through the process of politics itself. By conceiving participation as the realization of political freedom through the collective self-imposition of order, they echoed a figure of thought informed by the cultural tropes of *Geist*, *Kultur*, and *Bildung*, one centrally concerned with the interactive, reciprocal development of self and world.

# 3 Renewing culture: the "unpolitical German" between past and future

Contrary to popular wisdom, the early postwar period saw not only silence and avoidance with regard to the German past. This image of the late 1940s and '50s was crafted largely during the 1960s, and it bears the imprint of that era's generational conflicts. The truth to such charges was that early memories of the Nazi period were highly selective and shaped by complex psychological mechanisms: taboo and trauma, resentment and repression, apology and avoidance. But there was no shortage of debate over the past's meaning, especially in the first years after 1945. Germany's engaged democrats shaped all aspects of this conversation, taking positions on the causes of National Socialism, the nature of its crimes, and the degrees and kinds of ordinary Germans' responsibility. A related question in which they and other educated elites were heavily invested concerned the status of Germany's proud high-cultural traditions after Nazism.

At stake was a native humanism they located in the flowering of German arts and letters in the late eighteenth and early nineteenth centuries. That era saw extraordinary achievements in philosophy, literature, music, and even natural science, by such luminaries as Goethe and Schiller, Mozart and Beethoven, Lessing and Herder, Kant and Hegel. Over time, those self-consciously cosmopolitan figures came to represent an explicitly national cultural heritage (*Kulturerbe*), a central reference point for the products of Germany's humanist gymnasia and universities. These were the nineteenth-century social strata later known as the *Bildungsbürgertum*, a twentieth-century neologism.[1] This group's need for orientation after 1945 was manifest in the invocations of Germany's iconic cultural figures, excerpts from their compositions, and general affirmations of their "humanity" that abounded during the immediate postwar years. Above all, it was in cultural-political journals that the

---

[1] Ulrich Engelhardt, *Bildungsbürgertum: Begriffs- und Dogmengeschichte eines Etiketts* (Stuttgart: Klett-Cotta, 1986). See also Reinhart Koselleck, ed. *Bildungsbürgertum im 19. Jahrhundert, Teil 2: Bildungsgüter und Bildungswissen* (Stuttgart: Klett-Cotta, 1990).

educated middle classes negotiated a collective self-understanding in the wake of Nazism.[2] Germany's engaged democrats were thus far from alone in hearkening back to this national patrimony. Given the intervening catastrophe, however, they insisted any appropriation of such traditions required a critical reformulation rather than a return. This was what they meant by their programmatic insistence on "renewal" and what set them apart from their interlocutors.

The question of the bearing of cultural traditions on political outcomes in modern Germany is a vexed one, historically and historiographically. According to one venerable thesis, modern Germany's "educated bourgeoisie" identified with cultural ideals to the detriment of its political formation. Fixated on the realm of ideas and disposed to inwardness, it deferred to real-world authority, stunting the rise of an indigenous liberalism and paving the road to National Socialism. As a diagnosis, this has a long and transnational lineage. Outlined at various earlier points, its classic formulations came from German émigrés fleeing Nazism, especially liberal historians who settled in the United States. These scholars bequeathed to us an influential figure, the "unpolitical German," who haunts academic and popular conceptions up to the present day.

This critical, outsider discourse around "culture" emphatically inverted the moral signs of its predecessor. Before 1945, middle-class Germans celebrated the profundity of their "spirit," a virtue that anchored their senses of self and collective belonging. Their simultaneously nationalist and elitist commitments fueled hostile cultural critiques of an allegedly soulless, mechanized, too-politicized liberal modernity abroad as well as anxious social distancing from the unwashed laboring "masses" at home. Correspondingly, culture was valorized as educated mandarins' sphere of pre-eminence, one they cordoned off from the profane world of material goods, interests, and transactions. This basic stance was common to reform-minded liberals as well as staunchly antimodern conservatives, and it fed widespread ambivalence toward Germany's first republic.[3] During Weimar's final years, long-standing fears of mass society and mass politics climaxed in an infectious alarmism among those who claimed cultivation (*Bildung*) as their distinctive property

---

[2] Axel Schildt, "Kontinuität und Neuanfang im Zusammenbruch: Zu den politischen, sozialen und kulturellen Ausgangsbedingungen der Nachkriegszeit," in *Buch, Buchhandel und Rundfunk 1945–1949*, ed. Monika Estermann and Edgar Lersch (Wiesbaden: Harrassowitz, 1997), 22–32.

[3] See, e.g., Fritz K. Ringer, *The Decline of the German Mandarins: The German Academic Community, 1890–1933* (Cambridge, Mass.: Harvard University Press, 1969); Aleida Assmann, *Arbeit am nationalen Gedächtnis: Eine kurze Geschichte der deutschen Bildungsidee* (Frankfurt a.M.: Campus, 1993).

(*Besitz*). The grave threat such worldly upheavals posed to the putatively decisive, cultural foundations of existence was proclaimed in works like Karl Jaspers' *The Spiritual Situation of the Age* and literary scholar E. R. Curtius' *German Spirit in Danger*.[4] In many respects, these authors' perspectives – existentialist on the one hand, classicist on the other – diverged dramatically, but their common culturalist commitments left them, like most of their peers, prone to interpret the Republic's economic and political collapse as epiphenomenal of a deeper cultural crisis, clouding their eye for all-too real threats as well as for practical solutions.[5]

After 1945, claims to superior German culturedness stood on shaky ground. Yet for many, especially established older figures, the nation's disgrace only invigorated the compensatory function of culture. They sought refuge in its lofty achievements, maintaining the defensive, aloof posture of the *Kultur* tradition toward politics in new form. In numbers and clout, they far outweighed a group of disillusioned younger writers, who pronounced those same traditions irredeemable and insisted on a clean break. A focus on "unpolitical Germans" and their adversaries, however, has rendered other modes of recourse to *Kultur* less visible. What has escaped notice is a third position in the debate, one articulated by intellectuals whose experiences of Weimar's collapse and Nazi rule provoked an equivocal reassessment. For engaged democrats, national cultural traditions were key factors in what had gone awry in German history as well as key resources for overcoming their own pernicious legacies. The intellectuals in question developed their surprisingly popular politics in part via affirmative recourse to a decidedly elitist cultural heritage.

In the two-sidedness of their position, Germany's engaged democrats both concurred with and dissented from their aforementioned émigré contemporaries in the USA. The "unpolitical German" diagnosis is familiar today as one element in the once-dominant *Sonderweg* thesis on German exceptionalism, which explained the triumph of National Socialism by Germany's "special path" of delayed and incomplete modernization.[6] Yet the familiarity obscures a longer, more layered genealogy.

---

[4] Karl Jaspers, *Die geistige Situation der Zeit* (Berlin: de Gruyter, 1931); Ernst Robert Curtius, *Deutscher Geist in Gefahr* (Stuttgart: Deutsche Verlags-Anstalt, 1932).

[5] Frank Trommler, "Verfall Weimars oder Verfall der Kultur? Zum Krisengefühl der Intelligenz um 1930," in *Weimars Ende: Prognosen und Diagnosen in der deutschen Literatur und politischen Publizistik 1930–1933*, ed. Thomas Koebner (Frankfurt a.M.: Suhrkamp, 1982), 34–53. Weimar's crisis-talk constituted, however, not a uniformly declinist "cultural pessimism" but a variegated field on which apocalyptic warnings were yoked to projections of the future in myriad ways; Rüdiger Graf, *Die Zukunft der Weimarer Republik: Krisen und Zukunftsaneignungen in Deutschland 1918–1933* (Munich: Oldenbourg, 2008).

[6] See, e.g., George Steinmetz, "German Exceptionalism and the Origins of Nazism: The Career of a Concept," in *Stalinism and Nazism: Dictatorships in Comparison*, ed. Ian Kershaw and Moshe Lewin (Cambridge: Cambridge University Press, 1997), 251–84.

The notion of an otherworldly German culturedness had been deployed with political intent in a range of times and places: by Napoleon's opponent Germaine de Staël in the 1810s, by radical German exiles of the 1830s and 40s such as Heinrich Heine and Moses Hess, and by domestic critics of the Bismarckian Empire's philistine cultural pretentions.[7] During the Great War, American commentators John Dewey and George Santayana blamed Germany's pernicious politics on its vaunted philosophizing, in texts they republished during the Second World War. Indeed, it was Nazism that gave the "unpolitical German" its lasting lease on life, above all among German émigrés. In California, Thomas Mann developed his incisive, ambivalent critique of German "inwardness."[8] Pioneering reflections came from sociologists and philosophers Helmuth Plessner in the Netherlands and Norbert Elias in Britain as well. In New York, Herbert Marcuse exposed culture's "affirmative" function: by projecting an idealized realm of fulfillment and freedom, bourgeois society had long reconciled people to an impoverished and unfree material reality (while preserving the longing for a better one).[9]

For the "unpolitical German's" later scholarly career, the work of émigré historians and social scientists in the USA from the 1940s onward was of paramount importance. One especially formative set of relationships was forged at the Research and Analysis branch of the wartime Office of Strategic Services. This political platypus (and unlikely predecessor to the CIA) brought together American experts and "enemy alien" refugee scholars, predominantly liberals and leftists, to generate intelligence reports and historically grounded political analyses for the US military's use. Hajo Holborn directed its Central European Section. There, exiled Marxists from the Frankfurt Institute for Social Research, Marcuse and Franz Neumann, worked alongside exiled liberal historians such as Holborn and Felix Gilbert, as well as a number of their students. Underlying the reports and memoranda they produced was an emerging consensus that Nazism marked the culmination of Germany's authoritarian, irrationalist deviation from the liberal, rationalist path of

---

[7] Warren Breckman, "Diagnosing the 'German Misery': Radicalism and the Problem of National Character, 1830–1848," in *Between Reform and Revolution: German Socialism and Communism from 1840 to 1990*, ed. David E. Barclay and Eric D. Weitz (New York: Berghahn, 1998), 33–62; Günther Blaicher, "Die Deutschen als 'das Volk der Dichter und Denker': Entstehung, Kontexte und Funktionen eines nationalen Stereotyps," *Historische Zeitschrift* 287, no. 2 (2008): 319–40.

[8] Wolf Lepenies, *The Seduction of Culture in German History* (Princeton, N.J.: Princeton University Press, 2006), 11–12, 62–3, 140–2.

[9] Helmuth Plessner, *Das Schicksal deutschen Geistes im Ausgang seiner bürgerlichen Epoche* (Zurich: Niehans, 1935); Norbert Elias, *Über den Prozess der Zivilisation: Soziogenetische und psychogenetische Untersuchungen* (Basel: Haus zum Falken, 1939), I:1–43; Herbert Marcuse, "Über den affirmativen Charakter der Kultur," *Zeitschrift für Sozialforschung* 6, no. 1 (1937): 54–94.

its western neighbors. Despite their political differences, most OSS intellectuals drew a shared moral from the story: Germany's wrong turn away from the West and into catastrophe was to be rectified.[10]

It was within this early *Sonderweg* framework that the "unpolitical German" took final form, infused the scholarship of America's leading Europeanists, and was re-imported to Germany, where it informed the critical historiography of later decades.[11] As Holborn put it in a famous 1952 essay, the key historical problem to grasp was "Germany's original separation from western Europe and America." He addressed the role in this process of what he broadly termed "German idealism," exposing the national cult of *Kultur* as both a rearguard strategy of social distinction and a secularized Protestantism, aspects whose interplay led the middle classes to idealize the authoritarian state so many of them served.[12] A few years later, his younger friend and fellow exile Fritz Stern elaborated on Holborn's arguments. He condemned the "political consequences" of the German bourgeoisie's self-consciously "unpolitical" stance, rooted in a "vulgar idealism" that cloaked political servility, social arrogance, and private self-satisfaction in the mantle of allegedly higher values. Furthermore, this *Kultur*-religion fed fatefully into a reactionary, anti-modern folk-nationalist ideology on the right that eventually made common cause with Nazism.[13] The underlying argument recurs to the present day. Just as Stern denounced Germans' "worship of culture" and "depreciation of politics" some fifty years ago, eminent sociologist Wolf Lepenies more recently lamented their tendency to "overrat[e] culture at the expense of

---

[10] Barry M. Katz, *Foreign Intelligence: Research and Analysis in the Office of Strategic Services, 1942–1945* (Cambridge, Mass.: Harvard University Press, 1989), esp. 44, 74, 187; Tim B. Müller, *Krieger und Gelehrte: Herbert Marcuse und die Denksysteme im Kalten Krieg* (Hamburg: Hamburger Edition, 2010), 31–185. Among the young American historians who cut their teeth at OSS were Gordon Craig, Franklin Ford, H. Stuart Hughes, Leonard Krieger, and Carl Schorske.

[11] Bernd Faulenbach, "Der 'deutsche Weg' aus der Sicht des Exils: Zum Urteil emigrierter Historiker," *Exilforschung* 3 (1985): 11–30.

[12] Hajo Holborn, "Der deutsche Idealismus in sozialgeschichtlicher Beleuchtung," *Historische Zeitschrift* 174 (1952): 359–84. On Holborn, see Otto P. Pflanze, "The Americanization of Hajo Holborn," in *An Interrupted Past: German-Speaking Refugee Historians in the United States after 1933*, ed. Hartmut Lehmann and James J. Sheehan (Cambridge: Cambridge University Press, 1991), 170–9.

[13] Fritz Stern, "The Political Consequences of the Unpolitical German," *History* 3 (1960): 104–34; Stern, *The Politics of Cultural Despair: A Study in the Rise of the Germanic Ideology* (Berkeley: University of California Press, 1961). Though Stern was too young for OSS, he moved in its circle after the war and was influenced by Neumann, Krieger, and Holborn himself, Stern's informal mentor; Stern, *Five Germanys I Have Known* (New York: Farrar, Straus and Giroux, 2006), 191–3, 204–6, 257. On Stern, see Gangolf Hübinger, "Fritz Stern zwischen Europa und Amerika: Eine Fallstudie zum Geschichts-Intellektuellen," in *Intellektuelle im Exil*, ed. Peter Burschel, Alexander Gallus, and Markus Völkel (Göttingen: Wallstein, 2011), 219–40.

politics." In his mordant phrase, it was the "seduction of culture" that lured the Germans down an apolitical – or, more precisely, illiberal – path, for over two centuries.[14]

After 1945, these liberal German exiles and Germany's engaged democrats shared a diagnosis, but they disagreed about the remedy. Both conceived the "unpolitical German" as a foil for the new postwar Germans they hoped to foster. By and large, however, the exiles formulated this as a question of leaving behind the overestimation of culture and returning to Western political norms from which Germans had deviated. This position was entirely compatible with the "consensus liberalism" that brought not only liberals in the strict sense but also wide swaths of the non- and anti-Communist left on both sides of the Atlantic into the ideological orbit of the Cold War's Western alliance.[15] And their subsequent influence has overshadowed engaged democrats' contrasting position, which advocated an independent German solution that insistently entwined notions of cultural and political renewal.

## "Culture" between obedience and autonomy

Given the intensity of educated Germans' investments as a class in the national cultural patrimony, it is unsurprising that postwar intellectuals felt compelled to evaluate its status and political relevance. The challenge posed by Nazism to their self-image as representatives of a "cultured" and "cultural nation" (*Kulturnation*) prompted urgent reassessments of the high-cultural canon and the rhetorics of "culture" and "spirit." In the first postwar years, however, intellectuals on the ground in Germany did not share the same space of debate with peers an ocean away. And it was on occupied Germany's unsettled political-cultural field that engaged democrats had to contend. There, three stances are discernible: while an escapist embrace of cultural tradition characterized the majority response and a vocal minority opted for distancing rejection, engaged democrats claimed a likewise minoritarian space between and apart from the other two.

For the mainstream, the cultural heritage served as a sanctuary of Germany's timeless achievements and highest values, from which it had

---

[14] Stern, "Political Consequences," 106; Lepenies, *Seduction*, 5, 8.
[15] Richard H. Pells, *The Liberal Mind in a Conservative Age: American Intellectuals in the 1940s and 1950s* (New York: Harper & Row, 1985); Michael Hochgeschwender, *Freiheit in der Offensive? Der Kongress für kulturelle Freiheit und die Deutschen* (Munich: Oldenbourg, 1998). Müller's provocative account extends this association to Marcuse (and Neumann), better known as a critic of "one-dimensional" Cold War mentalities; Müller, *Krieger*.

strayed but to which it could now return. Such a perspective was voiced by the doyen of German historians, Friedrich Meinecke (doctoral supervisor to Holborn and Gilbert), whose early work had lauded modern Germany's fusion of "culture" (*Kultur*) and "power" (*Macht*) under the aegis of the state. Not so his 1946 analysis of *The German Catastrophe*. After recounting modern Germany's decline into power politics and spiritual nihilism, he closed with a now famous "wish image": that Germans would gather – on Sundays, ideally in chapels – to form "Goethe congregations" around public recitals of classical German music and readings of the likes of Goethe, Schiller, and Hölderlin. These solemn occasions were crucial, since "whoever immerses themselves wholly" in these "most German" of writings would "sense, amid the destruction, something indestructible, a German *character indelebilis*."[16] Meinecke invoked the invisible grace of the Christian sacraments to suggest that German culture impressed upon the German soul a sanctifying mark of permanent distinction unsullied by the trials of the profane world. A similarly influential and reassuring formulation came from Frank Thieß, strident spokesman of the "inner emigration," who urged a "homecoming to Goethe." After all, the "depth and humanity" of the poet's "spirit," preserved in Germans' stalwart hearts, was all that had prevented their "total poisoning and self-destruction" under Nazism. By renewing their commitment to Goethe – that "star of German worldwide prestige, shining brighter than ever" – as their true "leader" (*Führer*), Germans could atone for their sins and find the "path to freedom."[17] Such assertions, typical for the time, reveal the ease with which idealizing high culture as a refuge from past horrors and present difficulties could underwrite an apolitical and apologetic escapism.

Confronting this salvage project were small pockets of intellectuals who demanded a purifying, total break with what was, in their view, an utterly compromised cultural tradition. Their most prominent representatives were younger writers affiliated with *Der Ruf*, who later established the

---

[16] Friedrich Meinecke, *Die deutsche Katastrophe: Betrachtungen und Erinnerungen* (Wiesbaden: Brockhaus, 1946), 173–6. See also Jeffrey K. Olick, *In the House of the Hangman: The Agonies of German Defeat, 1943–1949* (Chicago: University of Chicago Press, 2005), 161–74; Mark W. Clark, *Beyond Catastrophe: German Intellectuals and Cultural Renewal after World War II, 1945–1955* (Lanham, Md.: Lexington, 2006), 33–9; Jaimey Fisher, *Disciplining Germany: Youth, Reeducation, and Reconstruction after the Second World War* (Detroit: Wayne State University Press, 2007), 92–107; Michael Th. Greven, *Politisches Denken in Deutschland nach 1945: Erfahrung und Umgang mit der Kontingenz in der unmittelbaren Nachkriegszeit* (Opladen: Budrich, 2007), 49–61.

[17] Frank Thieß, "Heimkehr zu Goethe," *Nordwestdeutsche Hefte* 1, no. 1 (1946): 29–32. See also Stephen Brockmann, *German Literary Culture at the Zero Hour* (Rochester, N.Y.: Camden House, 2004), 105–6.

literary forum Gruppe 47. In the words of their spokesman Hans Werner Richter, the German youth stood on a "landscape of ruins," surrounded by "a pile of moral, spiritual, and ethical rubble." In that light, "every possibility of reconnecting to the past," the past of their elders, seemed foreclosed, "a paradox." Rather, "spiritual rebirth" was required, through an "absolute and radical starting over."[18] A pathos of militancy clung to their words, and they spoke forcefully for the German nation; later critics interpreted these as deep imprints of Nazi-era socialization on these members of the front generation. Subsequent revelations about their compromises under the Third Reich have stirred further controversy. Nonetheless, they continue to stand as the starting point for a more critical postwar political culture: out of their yearning for a cleansing rupture grew a literature that thematized, albeit selectively, the past others sought to forget. This group of writers – which expanded from Richter and Alfred Andersch to include Heinrich Böll, Günter Grass, and many more of their literary generation – are widely credited as the political conscience of early West German society and the vanguard of a left-leaning intelligentsia.[19]

In the postwar years, engaged democrats took a more equivocal stance toward the national cultural heritage. They neither celebrated nor condemned this bequest but attempted a searching examination of its at once positive and negative potentials. For them, this endeavor was indispensable for understanding Germany's disastrous past as well as its route to a redeemed future. In his address at the reopening of Heidelberg University, Jaspers cautioned that Germany's "new beginning... cannot simply take up conditions from before 1933. Too much has happened; the catastrophe is too thoroughgoing... We have to distance ourselves from a past that is around us and within us." And yet, he insisted that "we want to live not out of rejecting the bad but out of affirming the good, out of the depths of the true past that carries us" – a past embodied in "Kant and

---

[18] [Hans Werner Richter], "Warum schweigt die junge Generation?" *Der Ruf* 1, no. 2 (1946): 2. See also Brockmann, *Literary Culture*, 186–95.
[19] Compare Urs Widmer, *1945 oder die "Neue Sprache"* (Düsseldorf: Schwann, 1966) and Justus Fetscher, Eberhard Lämmert, and Jürgen Schutte, eds. *Die Gruppe 47 in der Geschichte der Bundesrepublik* (Würzburg: Königshausen & Neumann, 1991) with Rob Burns and Wilfried van der Will, *Protest and Democracy in West Germany: Extra-Parliamentary Opposition and the Democratic Agenda* (New York: St. Martin's, 1988), 17–71 and Ingrid Gilcher-Holtey, "'Askese schreiben, schreib: Askese': Zur Rolle der Gruppe 47 in der politischen Kultur der Nachkriegszeit," *Internationales Archiv für Sozialgeschichte der Deutschen Literatur* 25, no. 2 (2000): 134–67. For a sense of the most recent controversies – around Andersch's wartime divorce of his Jewish wife and Grass' Waffen-SS membership – see the theme issue "Gruppe 47," *Aus Politik und Zeitgeschichte* B25 (2007).

Goethe and Lessing."[20] Tradition could and should serve as a resource for renewal, albeit an inherently ambivalent one.

Engaged democrats did affirm and seek to reconnect with the German cultural heritage, especially its fruits from the half-century around 1800. Behind the recourse they had to that tradition lay a specific affinity between the sort of freedom it implied – signaled by such notions as *Kultur*, *Geist*, and *Bildung* – and their participatory understanding of democracy. At the heart of both stood the active human subject, developing itself as it interactively shaped the world.[21] This idealist keynote was first sounded by Immanuel Kant. His call to Enlightenment urged humanity's self-liberation from its "self-incurred immaturity" into the independent use of its critical faculties, and his Copernican revolution in philosophy put the spontaneous, autonomous subject – governed only by laws it itself supplies – at the center of both the cognitive and the moral universe. And yet Kant opened new grounds for dissatisfaction, since he left worldly objects unknowable in themselves and rendered ethics a formalist exercise in maxim-making. Subsequent idealists such as J. G. Fichte and Friedrich Schelling sought to build on Kant but reconnect thought and being, is and ought, in some more "absolute" medium. Their successor G. W. F. Hegel reconceived the self-determining subject as a collective, social and historical one he called "spirit," which realized itself in coming to recognize its world as, in some sense, a creation of its own self-moving activity, and thus know itself as an "identical subject-object." Whatever else that might mean – and debates have simmered ever since – it is clear that, for Hegel, spirit's self-formation in the world was nothing other than the drama of human history, a process that tended ineluctably (albeit in non-linear fashion) toward freedom.

Nor was the trope of autonomous, self-developing selfhood confined to the rarefied realm of idealist philosophy per se. It was central to the writings of J. W. von Goethe and Friedrich Schiller as well as to the political and educational theories of Wilhelm von Humboldt. Schiller was best known for his historical plays, but his *Letters on the Aesthetic Education of Man* posited the sphere of art and its distinctive "play drive" as that realm of experience wherein humans could learn to reconcile their

---

[20] Jaspers, "Erneuerung der Universität," *Die Wandlung* 1, no. 1 (1945): 67–8.
[21] More recent accounts of idealism, classicism, romanticism, and neohumanism have underscored such themes. The literature is vast; for the summary presented here, see Terry Pinkard, *German Philosophy 1760–1860: The Legacy of Idealism* (Cambridge: Cambridge University Press, 2002), supplemented by Frederick C. Beiser, *Enlightenment, Revolution, and Romanticism: The Genesis of Modern German Political Thought, 1790–1800* (Cambridge, Mass.: Harvard University Press, 1992); Robert J. Richards, *The Romantic Conception of Life: Science and Philosophy in the Age of Goethe* (Chicago: University of Chicago Press, 2002).

sensuous and rational faculties and thus glimpse practical freedom in the material world. While Goethe's wildly popular *Passions of Young Werther* portrayed a sentimental genius' tragic quest, his first *Wilhelm Meister* novel became the exemplary instance of a new genre, the *Bildungsroman*, which narrated its hero's life-course as his self-formation through youthful journeys and worldly experiences into a complete human being. Just such a cultivation of the self, the full development of its potentialities and powers, constituted Humboldt's *Bildungsideal*. That vision then guided him as Prussian education minister, when he instituted the reforms on which Germany's humanist gymnasia and universities were built.

These writers had in common not only thematic resonances but also a geographic location and political moment. With the exception of Kant, who was nonetheless present via his student J. G. Herder and his own towering influence, their paths all crossed in that age's remarkable cultural hothouse: the neighboring towns of Weimar, a ducal seat, and Jena, home to a major university. Moreover, the energies of Europe's revolutionary age helped galvanize their radical thought. The nature of their own political involvement ranged from Fichte's Jacobin activism to Goethe's courtly service to Kant's entirely academic pursuits. Their political commitments varied too, from Schiller's radical republicanism to Humboldt's constitutional reformism to Hegel's much-debated trajectory – from early wonderment at the French Revolution through dismay at the Terror to, in many accounts, apologies for the repressive Prussian state. These differences notwithstanding, all responded in some fashion to the era's radicalism, contradictions, and aftermath. Their political attitudes were in any case not identical with those of their later epigones in the *Bildungsbürgertum*, carriers of what Fritz Stern would deride as the "vulgar idealism" that bred the "unpolitical German."

After 1945, it was the original focus on autonomous, self-developing subjectivity in these literary and philosophical traditions that engaged democrats attempted to make useful for Germany's renewal. To be sure, the interface of culture with politics was often left implicit. It could be heard in Eugen Kogon's recommendation that readers return to Herder, "a German classic" who could teach the present much about "humanity," though not in order to gloss over the "barbarism" barely past. It echoed in Dolf Sternberger's assertion that, for Goethe, *Kultur* referred not to hallowed texts or eternal values but rather to a practical activity, "the cultivation of human existence." It resonated in Axel Eggebrecht's comment that Schiller always "approached the world with the manly intent of a formative will," although his "boyish defiance" at the world's deficiencies also provoked retreat into the "non-commitment" of sheer aestheticism.[22] In *Aufbau*, Fichte was lauded for proclaiming the "absolute freedom of the self-magnificent human ego" in the French Revolution's wake, despite the solipsistically "one-sided" character of his self- and world-positing *Ich*. And in *Die Wandlung*, Humboldt was praised for the self-unfolding "autonomous personality" at the core of his ideal of *Bildung*, even if his focus on the "higher, ethical domain" of the "world of ideas" betrayed an aristocratic distance to the "world of reality."[23]

On occasion, the specifically political potentials embedded in the cultural tradition were drawn out explicitly. Ernst Bloch linked Fichte's philosophical "pathos of active reason" to his blueprint for a well-ordered social utopia, a "rational state" that pointed toward a "harmony of educated, ethically mature individuals" in perfect freedom. Georg Lukács stressed the "developmental doctrine" anticipated by Goethe but realized in Hegel's *Geist*, a subject whose restless self-movement constituted the collective self-development of the species. In this "humanistically unified world history," the progress of "reason" was actualized (among other manifestations) in ever-evolving forms of law and the state. This set Hegel, Lukács argued, in implacable opposition to Nazism. While the latter saw history as a struggle among distinct races for dominance and survival, humanity as a whole was the subject of Hegel's history. Nations, like social institutions, were fated to arise, be superseded, and fade away. Moreover, Nazism ruled by dictatorial terror, openly despising civil rights and liberal freedoms, whereas a Hegelian view foresaw the preservation of bourgeois accomplishments in future, ever higher forms of free self-rule that reconciled individuals' limited "subjectivity" in new institutional "objectivity" they themselves created.[24] Doubtless, Lukács had a Marxian socialism in mind, and many engaged democrats indeed presented Marx's thought as a consummate humanism. For Walter Dirks, it was Marx's achievement to work from "within the richness of bourgeois culture" but to dethrone "the idea" from its center in favor of the "concrete human being" as the "productive... subject of its own life." This latter was capable of redeeming humanity's dehumanization in a remaking of the existing order. Hans Mayer referred in a similar vein to the burning "flame of [Marx's] humanism," which had ignited his

---

[22] Eugen Kogon, "Förderung der Humanität," *Frankfurter Hefte* 2, no. 1 (1947): 108–9; Dolf Sternberger, "Tagebuch: Das Frankfurter Goethehaus – Im dunkelsten Deutschland," *Die Wandlung* 2, no. 3/4 (1947): 200; Axel Eggebrecht, *Weltliteratur: Ein Überblick* (Hamburg: Springer, 1948), 175–6, 178.

[23] Wolf Franck, "Fichte als Schriftsteller," *Aufbau* 2, no. 1 (1946): 53; Otto Regenbogen, "Preußen am Scheidewege: Aus Wilhelm von Humboldts politischer Korrespondenz," *Die Wandlung* 1, no. 3 (1946): 232, 241–2.

[24] Ernst Bloch, *Freiheit und Ordnung: Abriß der Sozial-Utopien* (Berlin: Aufbau, 1947), 112, 118; Georg Lukács, "Die Nazis und Hegel," *Aufbau* 2, no. 3 (1946): 281–2, 288.

Renewing culture: the "unpolitical German" 125

commitment to "liberate humanity as a whole."[25] Such readings of Marx drew explicitly on his early writings of the 1840s, when – in dialogue with friends such as Heine and Hess – he had effected his own appropriation of idealism, in the service of his vision of an emancipated, post-capitalist society.[26]

The kernel of democratic possibility was latent within idealism from the start, however, long before its materialist inversion by Marx. Recall Alfred Weber's account, in which the nineteenth-century hypertrophy of bureaucratic institutions had sealed the demise of true freedom, "in the sense of *actively* radiant freedom, the free spontaneity of individual and group action."[27] Germany presented an extreme case, where the "life-less obedience" perfected and inculcated by Prussian military service had bred an "order-loving animal." A potential antidote, however, lay in enlightenment-era *Kultur*: poets and philosophers in Germany and elsewhere had recognized the unique capacity for "continual self-formation through freedom," by which humans created the conditions of their own existence and thus their own history. Herein, according to Weber, lay the true content of Kant's injunction that humanity develop itself "from immaturity, that is, from the disuse of freedom, to maturity, that is, to its self-controlled use." Recovering this eighteenth-century insight could provide the key to "mass self-government" in the mid twentieth.[28] Just this sort of freedom – to participate self-consciously in shaping the structures that govern one's own agency – Weber considered the core of democratic renewal. Implicit in these intellectuals' turn to the classical canon was a reappropriation of the idealist legacy for the practical, political world.

What troubled them, however, was the yawning gap between the liberating potentials of the cultural heritage and the actual course of modern German history. The latter, as engaged democrats conceived it, hinged on a pernicious, supine relationship to authority with both socially general and class-specific aspects. In the Reformation era, the German people

---

[25] Walter Dirks, "Marxismus in christlicher Sicht," *Frankfurter Hefte* 2, no. 2 (1947): 127–8, 130; Hans Mayer, *Karl Marx und das Elend des Geistes: Studien zur neuen deutschen Ideologie* (Meisenheim a.G.: Hain, 1948), 5, 97.
[26] John Edward Toews, *Hegelianism: The Path Toward Dialectical Humanism, 1805–1841* (Cambridge: Cambridge University Press, 1980); Warren Breckman, *Marx, the Young Hegelians, and the Origins of Radical Social Theory: Dethroning the Self* (Cambridge: Cambridge University Press, 1999).
[27] Alfred Weber, "Bürokratie und Freiheit," *Die Wandlung* 1, no. 12 (1946): 1033; emphasis in original.
[28] Weber, "Unsere Erfahrung und unsere Aufgabe," *Die Wandlung* 1, no. 1 (1945): 58–9, 61. This was the abridged final chapter of his soon-to-be-published *Abschied von der bisherigen Geschichte: Überwindung des Nihilismus?* (Hamburg: Claassen & Goverts, 1946), 230–1, 234.

had stood at the leading edge of human emancipation, when a questioning of religious authority catalyzed the questioning of all established authority, and radical clergy stood shoulder-to-shoulder with rural folk (and not a few city-dwellers) against lords and princes. Yet after the ruthless suppression of this Peasants' War – Germans' last true uprising and first failed revolution – freedom there went into decline.[29] In framing this narrative, engaged democrats deployed contrasting national histories, with the revolutionary French in the vanguard role and the Germans prostrate before an absolutism they never truly cast off. This was evident throughout the German lands, they argued, but especially in authoritarian Prussia, whose perfection of centralized, bureaucratic militarism made possible its rise among European powers.[30] It was Prussia that rejected the all-German constitutional monarchy proposed by Frankfurt's National Assembly during the failed 1848 revolution, effectively quashing the liberal project of national unity "from below." And it was Prussia that co-opted the defeated opposition through its "revolution from above" in 1871, establishing by conquest and fiat a unified Germany that only inherited Prussia's pathologies.[31] Postwar commentators were unanimous about the outcome: a "lifeless obedience" (*Kadavergehorsam*) and "spirit of subjugation" (*Untertanengeist*) took root among the German people, who became not autonomous, freedom-loving citizens but pliable subjects, habituated to passivity yet disciplined for military adventure at the state's orders.[32] Engaged democrats were intensely preoccupied

---

[29] Affirmation of the "revolution of 1525" has also been mobilized more recently against the canard of a timeless German authoritarianism; Peter Blickle, *Obedient Germans? A Rebuttal*, trans. Thomas A. Brady, Jr. (Charlottesville: University Press of Virginia, 1997).

[30] Here, they continued an older left-liberal, socialist, and anarchist critique associating "militarism" and Prussian authoritarian statism; Nicholas Stargardt, *The German Idea of Militarism: Radical and Socialist Critics, 1866–1914* (Cambridge: Cambridge University Press, 1994); Wolfram Wette, ed. *Schule der Gewalt: Militarismus in Deutschland 1871–1945* (Berlin: Aufbau, 2005).

[31] For the above, see Wolfgang Harich, "Die Verhinderung Großdeutschlands," *Der Kurier*, 19 December 1945; Alfred Kantorowicz, "Das deutsche Schicksalsjahr 48," *Ost und West* 2, no. 1 (1948): 5–6; Kogon, "Das Dritte Reich und die preußisch-deutsche Geschichte," *Frankfurter Hefte* 1, no. 3 (1946): 44–57; Kogon, "Die deutsche Revolution: Gedanken zum zweiten Jahrestag des 20. Juli 1944," *Frankfurter Hefte* 1, no. 4 (1946): 17; Rudolf Leonhard, "Schwarz, Rot und Gold," *Die Weltbühne* 3, no. 24 (1948): 684–5; Mayer, *Karl Marx*, 36–47; Sternberger, "Begriff des Vaterlands," *Die Wandlung* 2, no. 6 (1947): 505–8; Weber, "Freier Sozialismus: Ein Aktionsprogramm," in Alexander Mitscherlich and Weber, *Freier Sozialismus* (Heidelberg: Schneider, 1946), 41–2; Willy Huhn, "'Militaristischer Sozialismus': Ein Beitrag zur Enthüllung der nationalsozialistischen Ideologie," *Aufbau* 2, no. 4 (1946): 368–81; Jürgen Kuczynski, "Betrachtungen zur deutschen Geschichtsschreibung," *Aufbau* 2, no. 7 (1946): 745–6; Heinrich Mann, "Die Französische Revolution und Deutschland," *Aufbau* 1, no. 3 (1945): 205–10.

[32] Additionally, see Eggebrecht, "Heldentum," *Nordwestdeutsche Hefte* 1, no. 2 (1946): 14; Harich, "'Die überragende Persönlichkeit,'" *Die Weltbühne* 2, no. 21 (1947): 923;

with diagnosing this German malady – as a matter of national history, not national character – whose catastrophic effects extended across the incomplete revolution of 1918/19 and culminated in National Socialism. In its general contours, this diagnosis was widely shared.[33] Engaged democrats' abiding concern, however, was with the consequential split between "spirit" and "power" that afflicted the intellectual class and distorted its most cherished institutions. Unlike firebrand Reformation clerics or radical Jacobin orators, modern Germany's educated elites had lost touch with the people's struggle for liberty. Rather than exercise their free self-development in the political world, they confined the realization of their freedom to intellectual life; their vibrant cultural heritage was thus symptomatic of an otherworldly inwardness that led all too easily into worldly quietism. As Kogon lamented, Germany's greatest theoreticians of freedom, "heroes of German *Geist*... remained philistines in political practice." Other outcomes were still open in the early nineteenth century, but the warnings of isolated critics like Heine went unheeded. The split of spirit from power was cemented after 1848, when members of Frankfurt's "professors' parliament" brought their ineffectual demands to the crown. Martin Luther was frequently cited as an early offender, for severing the spiritual and worldly realms and invoking scripture to counsel obedience in the latter, helping to crush the rebellions his theology helped inspire. Traces of this obedient orientation were detected far and wide, in Kant's formalist conception of duty, in Hegel's deification of the state, and in the aestheticized purity of Schiller's "beautiful soul."[34]

Humboldt's old ideal of *Bildung* was complicit too. In practice, Dirks asserted, its institutions had not produced self-actualizing, well-rounded

---

Frank Joseph [Alexander Mitscherlich], "Kadaver-Deutschland," *Rhein-Neckar-Zeitung*, 12 January 1946; Ernst Ferger [Ernst Friedlaender], "Gehorsam," *Nordwestdeutsche Hefte* 1, no. 5 (1946): 32; Paul Hofmann, "Mitverantwortung," *Aufbau* 1, no. 1 (1945): 18; Bernhard Kellermann, "Gewogen und zu leicht befunden," *Aufbau* 1, no. 2 (1945): 92; Rudolf Kurtz, "Das tragische Volk der Deutschen," *Aufbau* 1, no. 2 (1945): 124–5; Paul Oestreich, "Die Aufgaben der deutschen Lehrer," *Ost und West* 1, no. 3 (1947): 89; Karl Schnog, "1848," *Die Weltbühne* 3, no. 11/12 (1948): 241; Paul von Schoenaich, "Kadavergehorsam," *Die Weltbühne* 3, no. 43 (1948): 1364.

[33] See, e.g., Barbro Eberan, *Luther? Friedrich "der Grosse"? Wagner? Nietzsche? Wer war an Hitler schuld? Die Debatte um die Schuldfrage 1945–1949*, 2nd edn. (Munich: Minerva, 1985); Jean Solchany, *Comprendre le nazisme dans l'Allemagne des années zéro 1945–1949* (Paris: Presses universitaires de France, 1997).

[34] Kogon, "Die deutsche Revolution," 17–26, quote 19; Mayer, *Karl Marx*, 47–54; Weber, "Freier Sozialismus," 42–3; Günter Brandt, "Vom unpolitischen Menschen," *Sonntag*, 7 July 1946; Friedlaender, "Gehorsam," 32; Hofmann, "Mitverantwortung," 18; Kuczynski, "Betrachtungen zur deutschen Geschichtsschreibung," 744; Kurtz, "Das tragische Volk," 124–6; Karl Gerhard Steck, "'Jedermann sei Untertan der Obrigkeit': Zur christlichen Lehre vom Staat," *Die Wandlung* 1, no. 4 (1946): 305; Gert H. Theunissen, "Der deutsche Intellektuelle und die Politik," *Die Weltbühne* 1, no. 2 (1946): 41–4.

human beings. Rather, they had reproduced the educated bourgeoisie as a privileged caste, offering students a "fixed stock of predominantly literary knowledge" plus grooming in the "manners . . . of the upper crust." *Bildung* needed an update for a new, "democratic" era. Education should translate learners' "lively participation in a collectively formed spiritual heritage" into "the readiness and capacity for politics, that is, for action that reaches into and determines the future." Instead of an apolitical "personality ideal," an *Aufbau* author chimed in, it should cultivate a "political knowledge . . . the science of people's living together in bounded communities" constituted by their own "collective labor."[35] So reframed, the *Bildung* ideal would teach postwar Germans that politics was a realm of people's collective making, not a realm of fixed and frozen givens.

It was incumbent upon German intellectuals to remedy these shortcomings, but the erosion of public life under Nazism had left their condition more precarious than ever. Lukács observed that German intellectuals' long-standing habituation to "pure interiority," lack of "civic courage," and "servility . . . toward political authority" had only worsened under dictatorship, leaving them even more "helpless . . . when political decisions are required." Although Wolfgang Harich conceded he could not begrudge his fellow intellectuals their "flight into interiority" under the "duress and horror" of the Third Reich, the post-fascist present brooked no such "flight from reality." Rather, it demanded the properly "spiritual instinct" of a "watchful openness" turned "not inward but outward," resolutely "toward the world." As Dirks and Kogon insisted, just this kind of engagement was urgently needed to draft "the vision of a goal," to "determine the direction" of Germany's renewal: "It must not be that the German intelligentsia . . . yet again forfeit the realization" of its ideas. "In the past, the riches of the spirit isolated them idealistically; today, the radicality of the beginning must not render us powerless." Alfred Kantorowicz echoed this call. The hour had finally come to reconcile "spiritual and political power," to overcome the "German misery" under which "our poets and thinkers . . . cut themselves off from the social and political life of our people."[36] As we shall see, these publicists construed their own activities – especially their critical, political

[35] Dirks, "Bildungsarbeit heute: Sinn und Grenzen der Volksbildung," *Frankfurter Hefte* 2, no. 9 (1947): 898–901; Alfons Kauffeldt, "Zurück zum deutschen Bildungsideal," *Aufbau* 2, no. 1 (1946), 34.
[36] Lukács, "'Das innere Licht ist die trübste Beleuchtungsart'," *Aufbau* 1, no. 1 (1945): 52–3; Harich, "Die Flucht nach innen," *Der Kurier*, 21 December 1945; "Ob man ein Programm machen darf?" *Frankfurter Hefte* 1, no. 1 (1946): 11; "Suchende Jugend: Briefwechsel zwischen der Studentin Käte Fuchs und Alfred Kantorowicz," *Ost und West* 2, no. 2 (1948): 89.

journalism – as both antipode and antidote to the disengaged culturalism of the "unpolitical German." Such comments went beyond commonplace yearnings for political influence to offer a specific solution to Germany's postwar predicament.

## German continuities and the German catastrophe

In the immediate shadow of National Socialism, the intellectuals in question grappled with the relationship between Germany's recent past and the broader sweep of its history. In the process, they made their own contributions to framing the postwar master narrative about modern Germany's flawed "special path." Fully fledged, the exceptionalism thesis plotted the divergence of romantic mentalities and authoritarian institutions in the German lands from the liberal-constitutional, enlightened course charted by such states as Britain and France, a deviation that crystallized in moments when German history "failed to turn" (in British historian A. J. P. Taylor's revealing phrase of 1945). The botched bourgeois revolution of 1848 loomed large, as the conclusive defeat of a native middle-class liberalism that left the state's dominance in the political sphere uncontested. As its critics observed, this narrative rested on some dubious assumptions. It not only elided a range of distinctly bourgeois institutions and practices that did develop in German-speaking central Europe, but it also relied on a factually inaccurate and ideologically freighted foil: an idealized "Western" history set as a universal norm of "modernization."[37] Engaged democrats did not aim to return Germany to a path of Western-style liberal democracy from which it had strayed. But they shared the assessment of insufficiently revolutionary and atavistically authoritarian continuities in Germany's past.

This view of the German proclivities out of which National Socialism grew suffused the whole range of their writings. Two different journals' series on the nazification of language, for instance, chose the same word, *Ausrichtung* – the "orientation" toward a pre-given end, or "carrying out" of a directive – as the focus of their first installment. In *Die Wandlung*, Sternberger highlighted its long-standing use as the military

---

[37] For the foundational critique, see David Blackbourn and Geoff Eley, *The Peculiarities of German History: Bourgeois Society and Politics in Nineteenth-Century Germany* (Oxford: Oxford University Press, 1984). It revised the *Sonderweg* literature by nuancing the German historical record as well as exposing the counter-construct of progressive, linear liberalization long since discredited by historians of Britain and France. On that ground, debate has continued. For a recent stock-taking, see James J. Sheehan, "Paradigm Lost? The 'Sonderweg' Revisited," in *Transnationale Geschichte: Themen, Tendenzen und Theorien*, ed. Gunilla Budde, Sebastian Conrad, and Oliver Janz (Göttingen: Vandenhoeck & Ruprecht, 2006), 150–60.

command to stand at attention. As an imperative, however, it could call forth either the addressee's compliance or their non-compliance, preserving some scope for reflexive, self-directed action. Tellingly, Sternberger asserted, Nazi-era language built on this usage but supplanted the direct command *richtet Euch!* by the imperious, impersonal infinitive *ausrichten!* and eventually sapped the word of every "last bit of tension and life" by favoring the nominalization *Ausrichtung*, in which all action "petrified."[38] In *Die Weltbühne*, Horst Lommer similarly underscored the militarist associations of this "barracks-yard concept." Not for nothing was it a favorite Nazi term, since it verbally prefigured their plan to transform Germany into "one great barracks" and compel all Germans, civilians and soldiers alike, to "snap into formation" at their leader's command.[39] A related diagnosis informed some of Erich Kästner's cabaret work from the period, such as the ironically titled "On the State's Beneficent Influence on the Individual." Its verses told a story of the ever-expanding modern state and its decidedly non-salutary effects. Kästner, too, dated the historical split between an all-embracing "state apparatus" and the citizen as a powerless but "contented automaton" to the Imperial period and saw it culminate in Nazism. The end result of the state's grand ambitions, however, was only destruction and self-destruction, as was surely evident to his audience from their devastated surroundings.

Now, that was the total state –
isn't what it got us great![40]

Delivered on a sparse stage set only with rubble, this concluding couplet presented Kästner's final assessment in wry, stark terms.

A similar image of National Socialism appears in engaged democrats' less literary reflections as well. Alongside the broad historical treatments just discussed, there were the more focused ones referenced in Chapter 2, such as Sternberger's on the pathologies of mass-party politics or Dirks' on the societal coalitions that carried the Weimar and Nazi regimes. Some strove to address more directly the distinctiveness of National Socialist rule itself. Weber, for instance, explained Nazism's striking success at popular mobilization by its ability to build

[38] Sternberger, "Aus dem Wörterbuch des Unmenschen I," *Die Wandlung* 1, no. 1 (1945): 76–7.
[39] Horst Lommer, "Aus dem Vokabelheft der Nazis I," *Die Weltbühne* 2, no. 11 (1947): 487.
[40] Erich Kästner, "Vom wohltätigen Einfluß des Staates auf das Individuum," *Die Weltbühne* 1, no. 11 (1946): 330–1. "Das war der totale Staat – / und nun hab'n wir den Salat!" In a similar vein: Kästner, "Die Schildbürger," *Die Weltbühne* 2, no. 21 (1947): 908–14.

a "terror-regime" on the foundation of long-standing German tendencies, availing itself of the "most modern" means of mass organization and mass suggestion while channeling individuals' "most primitive instincts" and tapping into previously dormant "collective, suprapersonal... dark, demonic forces."[41] Here, concrete socio-historical analysis merged with the more abstract, vitalist speculation of Weber's cultural sociology.

The most fully developed early account of Nazism came from Kogon, framed in terms of his circle's core concerns with authority and democracy. For him, Nazism's appeal was grounded in Germans' authoritarian character traits as well as in the political exhaustion, economic insecurity, and national resentment that the contingencies of Germans' recent historical experience had produced. Describing the regime's rule, he played on the name of its leisure and tourism agency to distinguish two pillars of popular compliance: "strength through joy," or the promise of material well-being, and "strength through fear," or the threat of arbitrary terror. Politically, Nazism peddled the "uniformed collective" of its "national community" as a higher form of "true democracy," but it was in reality ruled by a "new aristocracy." Accomplished facts were periodically put before the people for acclamation, and they were rewarded for dutiful work by a degree of creature comfort. Yet the polity was fashioned as a racial hierarchy, based on a "materialism of the blood" that decreed the "eradication of Jewry" as well as the breeding of SS elites to exacting biological standards, as a "racial master stratum." The latter formed a state-within-a-state, at once the center of the regime's power and the means of its reproduction.[42] By 1948, Kogon developed a typology of "terror as a system of rule" that associated – without equating – Nazism and Bolshevism through a set of common conditions and methods. Both had been encouraged by recurrent socio-economic upheavals, which prompted individuals to seek out the seeming security of mass movements. As tyrannies in the age of popular sovereignty, moreover, each required an ideology of broad-based legitimacy, which the "fascist-totalitarian" variant found in a myth of plebiscitary consensus and the "Bolshevik-totalitarian" variant in a claim to vanguard representation. Both seized power by force, ruled by fear and limitless violence,

---

[41] Weber, "Unsere Erfahrung," 53–5.
[42] Kogon, "Das deutsche Volk und der Nationalsozialismus," *Frankfurter Hefte* 1, no. 2 (1946): 63, 65–7; Kogon, "Deutschland im Schatten von Gestern," *Frankfurter Hefte* 2, no. 8 (1947): 788–99. The latter became the new first chapter of his *SS-Staat*: Kogon, *Der SS-Staat: Das System der deutschen Konzentrationslager*, 2nd edn. (Berlin: Druckhaus Tempelhof, 1947), 20–34.

and evinced a contradictory mix of rational regimentation and arbitrary brutality.[43]

Writing in US exile, Hannah Arendt – the German-Jewish political theorist whose work has powerfully influenced subsequent understandings of Nazism – echoed such themes in her own first approaches to the topic. These were published by her friends Jaspers and Sternberger in *Die Wandlung*. In her analysis, the expansion of Nazism's criminal activities and knowledge about them outward from a core of "terror-formations" such as the SS gradually entangled ever more "average German[s]" in an expanding web of active and passive collusion. In this sense, "total mobilization" tended toward "total complicity," forestalling awareness of personal responsibility and generating a widespread solidarity with the regime. Moreover, Nazism had made use of a population already buffeted by interwar economic crises into a sense of extreme insecurity that had fateful moral consequences. Ordinary "jobholders and . . . family men," when they feared for their "naked existence," all too easily restricted their moral sense to private life, blind to their public role as "functionar[ies]" of the "annihilation machine." Although she insisted the modern "mass man" was a transnational type, his advent had been well prepared in Germany by the underdevelopment of "the classical virtues of public life."[44] This left Germans particularly susceptible to terror's innovative techniques, she argued, but terror as a system could only be perfected at society's margins, in the camp system. Merging reports from Buchenwald and Auschwitz with images of the Soviet GULag, Arendt presented the camps as sites of "total domination" – factories for the systematic eradication of human spontaneity and the systematic production of human corpses. Their ultimate goal was to render humans themselves "superfluous" to their own existence. Rumors of the unimaginable reality inside the camps' walls fostered the "indeterminate fear" that kept society outside in line. Although her views on anti-Semitism as the ideological "amalgamator" of "totalitarianism" in its German variant were still being worked out, Arendt here introduced central elements of her 1951 classic, *The Origins of Totalitarianism*.[45]

---

[43] Kogon, "Der Terror als Herrschaftssystem," *Frankfurter Hefte* 3, no. 11 (1948): 985–1001. Again, this essay was prepended to his book: Kogon, *Der SS-Staat: Das System der deutschen Konzentrationslager*, 3rd edn. (Frankfurt a.M.: Verlag der Frankfurter Hefte, 1949), 1–19.

[44] Hannah Arendt, "Organisierte Schuld," *Die Wandlung* 1, no. 4 (1946): 334, 341–2, first published in English translation as Arendt, "Organized Guilt and Universal Responsibility," *Jewish Frontier* 12, no. 1 (1945): 19–23.

[45] Arendt, "Konzentrationsläger [sic]," *Die Wandlung* 3, no. 4 (1948): 328–9. This piece became the first edition's crucial final chapter; Arendt, *The Origins of Totalitarianism* (New York: Harcourt Brace, 1951), 414–28. See Margaret Canovan, *Hannah Arendt: A*

These thoughts both paralleled and pointed beyond engaged democrats' reflections on National Socialism. From their writings, a rather two-dimensional picture emerged. Some contributed to the widespread demonization that ascribed Nazism to atavistic, ultimately incomprehensible forces, but many also tried to specify its social and political conditions and effects. At their best, they anticipated later work by integrating psychological and sociological perspectives and querying the relationship between generally modern and specifically German factors. Their emphasis on authoritarian continuities, however, cast National Socialism first and foremost as the culmination of a militarist-bureaucratic state tradition, a framework ill-suited to grasp either the centrality of the Holocaust to the Nazi project or the specificity of Jewish persecution. In the events' immediate wake, their focus was more on the seeming incongruities of German cultivation and German barbarism. In this vein, they were among the first to comment on the paradoxical proximity of classical Weimar to the Nazi camp at Buchenwald, overlooking the city. In Kogon's words, a typically Prusso-German "connection of brutality and romanticism" expressed itself in this nearness of "Weimar's Goethe temples" to the "sadistic goings-on at ... Buchenwald."[46] Engaged democrats sought to grapple with this tension analytically, not evade it or simply decry it, like so many of their contemporaries. The frame of their approach, however, left them better equipped to understand a concentration camp such as Buchenwald than a death factory such as Auschwitz or the killing fields farther east. Even the most forthright early German attempts to confront Nazi crimes did so in a universalizing, abstract mode that elided the specifics of genocide and its predominantly Jewish victims. The framings of Allied reeducation programs and war crimes trials often encouraged this process.[47]

Their positions were nonetheless unusual in the early postwar period, simply for their emphasis on the extent of German atrocities and the breadth of German complicity. They construed a large part of their mission to be bringing the crimes committed by the regime and by their countrymen out of obscurity and silence and into the light of public discussion. While Jaspers' *Schuldfrage* of 1946 profoundly shaped the debate on German guilt and responsibility, Kogon's *SS-Staat*, published

---

*Reinterpretation of Her Political Thought* (Cambridge: Cambridge University Press, 1992), 17–62.

[46] Kogon, "Das Dritte Reich," 54.

[47] Y. Michal Bodemann, "Eclipse of Memory: German Representations of Auschwitz in the Early Postwar Period," *New German Critique* 75 (1998): 57–89; Donald Bloxham, "The Genocidal Past in Western Germany and the Experience of Occupation, 1945–6," *European History Quarterly* 34, no. 3 (2004): 305–35.

that same year, attempted the first comprehensive analysis of the camps as an integral system central to the regime. The book rose instantly to authoritative status on both sides of the Atlantic, hailed as indispensable by experts in Germany as well as by influential exiles such as Max Horkheimer and Arendt herself, who drew on it extensively in her own work.[48] Their interventions were not confined to the scholarly realm, however. Eggebrecht delivered a series of sober but searing radio reports from the trial of the Bergen-Belsen camp staff by a British military court in the fall of 1945. It was the first such proceeding in the western zones. Though received defensively by German listeners, these reports secured Eggebrecht a position of journalistic prominence for the occupation period and after. Kästner was among the few German correspondents present at the International Military Tribunal in Nuremberg in 1945–6. In his trademark, lightly ironizing and demystifying tone, he reported on war crimes and sketched war criminals for a largely skeptical public.[49] Finally, Mitscherlich co-authored two documentary exposés of Nazi-era medical experiments based on material revealed at one of Nuremberg's successor trials, the Doctors' Trial of 1946–7. He had been sent there to observe as a representative of the German Medical Association, but the uncompromising and widely read reports that resulted stymied his professional career for years to come.[50]

At the same time, engaged democrats were all too aware that legal reckoning with officials and their policies represented only the beginning. Ordinary Germans, collectively and individually, needed to call themselves to account before their own personal tribunals. On his return from exile, Kantorowicz urged that "all Germans" – even those who had proven most "immune" to Nazism – seize the opportunity for an "inner rehabilitation" and so reap "the moral benefit of defeat."[51] Similarly,

[48] Clark, *Beyond Catastrophe*, 64–7; Joachim Perels, "Eugen Kogon – Zeuge des Leidens im SS-Staat und Anwalt gesellschaftlicher Humanität," in *Engagierte Demokraten: Vergangenheitspolitik in kritischer Absicht*, ed. Claudia Fröhlich and Michael Kohlstruck (Münster: Westfälisches Dampfboot, 1999), 31–4.

[49] John Cramer, *Belsen Trial 1945: Der Lüneburger Prozess gegen Wachpersonal der Konzentrationslager Auschwitz und Bergen-Belsen* (Göttingen: Wallstein, 2012), 317–19; Franz Josef Görtz and Hans Sarkowicz, *Erich Kästner: Eine Biographie* (Munich: Piper, 1998), 261–3.

[50] Tobias Freimüller, *Alexander Mitscherlich: Gesellschaftsdiagnosen und Psychoanalyse nach Hitler* (Göttingen: Wallstein, 2007), 97–133. The medical reports were published as Mitscherlich and Fred Mielke, *Das Diktat der Menschenverachtung: Eine Dokumentation* (Heidelberg: Schneider, 1947); Mitscherlich and Mielke, *Wissenschaft ohne Menschlichkeit: Medizinische und eugenische Irrwege unter Diktatur, Bürokratie und Krieg* (Heidelberg: Schneider, 1949).

[51] Kantorowicz, "Vom moralischen Gewinn der Niederlage," in *Vom moralischen Gewinn der Niederlage: Artikel und Ansprachen* (Berlin: Aufbau, 1949), 341–3. In this January

Dirks called each of his peers, from staunch antifascists to the irresolute majority, to an "unrelenting" self-examination. Public dialogue was crucial to the process, but the individual conscience was necessarily the final judge. Nonetheless, a "collective liability" for Nazism did exist, and although "collective guilt" was an ethically nonsensical notion, it was useful shorthand for the "self-knowledge" that specific groups and the population at large needed to attain. Unfortunately, most Germans seemed to disagree. Dirks detected a mounting "inner resistance" to any introspection whatsoever, one that manifested itself in private resentment as well as public hypocrisy.[52]

Indeed, the intellectuals in question were among the earliest to remark on Germans' readiness to dwell on their own suffering, to equate it with the suffering inflicted on others, or to avoid discussion of German crimes altogether. Karl Schnog, for one, rebuked readers who responded to his reports of concentration camp life by emphasizing their own hardships, after the motto: "Victim of fascism? – so are we all!"[53] Most engaged democrats approached the issue with greater sympathy. Mitscherlich, for instance, conceded that feeling the world's "hate-saturated ostracization" was likely to provoke "self-righteousness" and that material "misery" was hardly conducive to spiritual "reflection." And yet, he maintained that every German should be able to transcend this narrow perspective, recognize their part in "the guilt of an era," and properly parse cause and effect: "what we endure today has its root in our own actions."[54] Kogon wryly noted that, having abetted the "mass murder" of millions, ordinary Germans "now loudly demand justice – for ourselves!" Yet he also charged Allied "reeducation" policies and the "reproach of collective guilt" with contributing to Germans' defensiveness. Specifically, he mentioned the early Allied photos of "piles of naked corpses" from liberated camps, thrust before Germans who had been desensitized to such carnage by the sight of their own loved ones' "charred remains" in bombed-out cities. Soon, due to others' "awful shouting [and] their own blindness, they wanted to hear nothing more about introspection." Sounding a

---

1947 radio broadcast, Kantorowicz reported conversations overheard on his first train trip back home: much resentful talk about the hardships of occupation but also a heartening debate in which Germans criticizing Nazism got the better of vocal pro-Nazis; Kantorowicz, *Deutsches Tagebuch* (Munich: Kindler, 1959), I:225–6.

[52] [Dirks], "Der Weg zur Freiheit: Ein Beitrag zur deutschen Selbsterkenntnis," *Frankfurter Hefte* 1, no. 4 (1946): 52, 59.

[53] Schnog, "Sachsenhausen 1940: Ein notwendiges Nachwort," *Die Weltbühne* 2, no. 22 (1947): 960–2.

[54] Mitscherlich, "Die schwersten Stunden: Überschlag eines Jahres," *Die Fähre* 1 (1946): 132, 134.

recurrent theme, he insisted that externally mandated self-examination could only backfire. Although the German people desperately needed "reflection, reflection, and again reflection," all attempts to prescribe it were "not only unpedagogical but also undemocratic"; small wonder, then, that the Allies' "shock therapy" of 1945 "led less to insight than to hardening."[55] These interventions were carefully calibrated, rejecting collective guilt while attempting to spur ordinary Germans to confront their own complicity.

Finally, engaged democrats also registered the fate of Europe's Jews and the contours of what has come to be called the Holocaust. While Kogon made anti-Semitism central to his analysis of Nazism, most referred obliquely to this element of collective experience. Herbert Ihering, for instance, decried the effects of an atavistic "racial doctrine" and prescribed the tolerant, "humane spirit" of G. E. Lessing's *Nathan the Wise* – a favorite of the postwar stage – as antidote.[56] Some authors probed anti-Jewish animus more directly, locating its roots in the formalization of race science; in the dark, irrationalist side of romantic sensibilities; or in social and psychic insecurities afflicting the middle classes. These phenomena were not uniquely German, they acknowledged.[57] Still, Eggebrecht was not alone in lamenting that Germany never had its equivalent of France's Dreyfus Affair, in which the trumped-up prosecution of a Jewish army officer in the 1890s spurred a confrontation with anti-Semitism and re-energized ideals of republicanism and justice.[58] Many authors also addressed the mass killing of Jews, although this was rarely their central theme. One exception was Pauline Nardi, who named the bare facts of the crime: "six million people were tormented to death... We know they were hungry, we know they were beaten, hunted with dogs, infected with diseases, subjected to experiments... beaten, shot, gassed. The bodies were burned." From these atrocities, she attempted to draw concrete conclusions. Remarkably, a subset of "Jews who escaped the 'Death Mills'"

---

[55] Kogon, "Der Kampf um Gerechtigkeit," *Frankfurter Hefte* 2, no. 4 (1947): 373; Kogon, "Gericht und Gewissen," *Frankfurter Hefte* 1, no. 1 (1946): 26, 28–9; Kogon, "Über die Situation," *Frankfurter Hefte* 2, no. 1 (1947): 32. Kogon's position is often cited without appreciation of its full logic; cf. Olick, *In the House of the Hangman*, 184–6. On US "atrocity propaganda," see Cora Sol Goldstein, *Capturing the German Eye: American Visual Propaganda in Occupied Germany* (Chicago: University of Chicago Press, 2009), 21–39.

[56] Herbert Ihering, "Lessing und Paul Wegener," *Aufbau* 1, no. 2 (1945): 147.

[57] See, e.g., Arnold Bauer, "Der Einbruch des Antisemitismus im deutschen Denken," *Aufbau* 2, no. 2 (1946): 152–64; Victor Klemperer, "Die deutsche Wurzel," *Aufbau* 3, no. 3 (1947): 201–8.

[58] Eggebrecht, "Die Affäre, die uns leider fehlte," *Die Weltbühne* 1, no. 2 (1946): 37–41.

Renewing culture: the "unpolitical German" 137

seemed inclined to stay in Germany, and Nardi emphasized material restitution and legal safeguards against recrudescent anti-Semitism as moral imperatives.[59] Dirks and Kogon made similar arguments and were later active in Frankfurt's Society for Christian–Jewish Cooperation, alongside Sternberger.[60] Efforts at reconciliation, of course, had as much to do with the rehabilitation of non-Jewish Germans as with justice for Jewish survivors.

Sternberger helped publicize one of the earliest important documents of the persecution of Europe's Jews, an SS report on the Warsaw ghetto uprising of 1943. This handmade commemorative album, titled "The Jewish Quarter of Warsaw Is No More!" and known after 1945 as the "Stroop Report" (after SS Brigadier General Jürgen Stroop, who led the German forces), served as evidence at the Nuremberg Trial and remains a key source today. It saw its first publication in *Die Wandlung*. In photographs and the attached report, it detailed the systematic leveling of the Warsaw ghetto by SS, police, and military units to destroy poorly armed bands of resisters, after which the remaining 56,000 Jewish inhabitants were deported.[61] Sternberger described the report's bewildering psychic effect, feeling compelled to understand while lacking the tools to do so. Neither avoidance nor comparing one's own suffering nor "indignation" and "great pathos" seemed adequate responses. For him, reading this account of how fellow Germans "'exterminated'... Jews (that is, humans and not beetles or mosquitoes)" – in street fighting or later, by gassing – brought home a "solidarity of human guilt" in which he felt implicated as a concrete individual being, not in the name of "humanity" – which he judged an "abstract excuse." The report imparted a "duty to know," the pursuit of which could itself be a kind of "penance" and eventually a hope for "grace." Above all, Sternberger insisted that Germans had to confront these deeds, for there was "no freedom without... knowledge" and "no future without a past." He was not heartened by readers' letters, some of which were performatively "indignant about

---

[59] Pauline Nardi, "Ignorabimus," *Die Weltbühne* 1, no. 9 (1946): 272–3; Nardi, "Die Wartenden," *Die Weltbühne* 2, no. 3 (1947): 101–4. On the ICD documentary film she referenced, see Goldstein, *Capturing*, 51–7.
[60] Kogon, "Christen und Juden," *Frankfurter Hefte* 1, no. 6 (1946): 6–8; Dirks, "Noch einmal: Christen und Juden," *Frankfurter Hefte* 1, no. 7 (1946): 583–4; Josef Foschepoth, *Im Schatten der Vergangenheit: Die Anfänge der Gesellschaft für Christlich-Jüdische Zusammenarbeit* (Göttingen: Vandenhoeck & Ruprecht, 1993), 99–108.
[61] "Die Vernichtung des Warschauer Ghettos im April und Mai 1943," *Die Wandlung* 2, no. 6 (1947): 524–53. Sternberger obtained a photocopy from US authorities, reproducing the report without its extensive photographic material. Neither was readily available until the facsimile edition: Jürgen Stroop, *Es gibt keinen jüdischen Wohnbezirk in Warschau mehr!* (Neuwied: Luchterhand, 1960).

the contents of the document" and others defensively "indignant about the fact of its publication." Neither seemed to grasp the central question he had hoped to raise: how might German people have a future after such a past?[62] For that, it seemed the minimal condition was each person's critical introspection regarding their own responsibility. These intellectuals had begun to despair of that possibility.

## Reconstructing Goethe

Engaged democrats' two-sided stances on the question of German guilt and the question of German cultural tradition paralleled each other. One insisted on a reckoning with past complicities while drawing distinctions of degree and kind, while the other highlighted ambivalent legacies that were an actual burden as well as a potential boon. Both made manifest a more general conviction about the temporality of 1945: inevitably, it blended continuity and rupture. Occasionally, they put this point in general terms. The editors of the *Frankfurter Hefte*, with reference to the title of their Heidelberg counterpart, stressed a "precious chance for 'transformation' (*Wandlung*)" while also insisting "there is no *tabula rasa*... no wholly new beginning." Such an illusion denied humans' "historical nature," always "extended between the origins and the goal." Post-Nazi Germans had first to face "the hour of judgment that we hold over ourselves." But their next, urgent task was to combine critical examination of their "rich heritage" with the courageous "projection of a genuine future" and pursue the latter's realization.[63] Mitscherlich concurred. Germans' "renewal" was possible neither by "mere reconnection to a better past," nor by "comforting separation" from an unsettling one. Rather, "constructive plans" were needed, whose very possibility hinged on the "tension-energy" of humans' existence "between times."[64] On principle, they and their colleagues rejected a totally new beginning as well as an unproblematic return to an earlier state. Postwar Germans' fate – one that illuminated a general human condition – was to live suspended between past and future.

The national cultural heritage remained the crucial site for their navigation of these issues. And if the likes of Kant or Schiller were ubiquitous in the postwar public sphere, first among them all was Goethe.[65]

---

[62] Sternberger, "Tagebuch: Zwischen Vergangenheit und Zukunft," *Die Wandlung* 2, no. 6 (1947): 456–9, 461; Sternberger, "Tagebuch: Ein Brief an den Herausgeber – Friede?" *Die Wandlung* 2, no. 9 (1947): 751.
[63] "Ob man ein Programm machen darf?" 11.
[64] [Mitscherlich], "Kadaver-Deutschland."
[65] On postwar Goethe discussions, see Karl Robert Mandelkow, *Goethe in Deutschland: Rezeptionsgeschichte eines Klassikers* (Munich: Beck, 1989), II:135–52; Brockmann, *Literary Culture*, 106–41.

Renewing culture: the "unpolitical German" 139

Positions on this iconic figure stood in for positions on the tradition as a whole, and here too, Germany's engaged democrats registered characteristic reservations. Most prominently, Karl Jaspers did so on accepting the city of Frankfurt's coveted Goethe Prize for 1947. He seized the chance to grapple with the crucial question head-on: although Goethe was a remarkable, "exemplary" German, he could be no "model to imitate" for Germany's future. This was not primarily because Goethe and his corpus were flawed, though that was also the case. Rather, it was because after the "catastrophe," even Germany's "most valid traditions" were in need of "re-examination and new appropriation." An unbridgeable "abyss" now separated Goethe's world from theirs, it was true, but the long-standing "Goethe cult" had not been salutary even in its own time. For there was "only one step" from the "seriousness" of Goethean self-development to "egocentric isolation from the world," from the "liberating" treatment of experience in verse to "aesthetic non-commitment," from "depth" to "fuzziness" of thought. These were traps that Goethe himself had not always avoided and to which the post-Goethe *Bildung* ideal had most disastrously succumbed. In this spirit, Jaspers called for a "revolution in Goethe appropriation."[66]

During a Goethe bicentennial shot through with no shortage of controversy, Jaspers' lecture was republished. His measured iconoclasm earned bitter recrimination from his sometime ally in cultural critique, E. R. Curtius. By then, Jaspers had left Germany in disappointment for Basel, a demerit his opponent did not fail to highlight. Above all, however, the philologist objected to the philosopher's plea for a critical relationship to Goethe, that greatest of national icons. Styling himself a new *praeceptor germaniae* – so Curtius alleged – Jaspers had delivered "a rebuke both subaltern and arrogant" that sullied "the reputation of German *Geist*," just as he had earlier hectored the German people about their "collective guilt." This striking – though not uncommon – misrepresentation is symptomatic of the bluntness of Curtius' position. Polemically, he boiled the issues down to a choice of "Goethe or Jaspers" and left his own allegiance in no doubt.[67] In the years since the chaos of the collapsing Weimar Republic, their two paths had diverged.

Engaged democrats' most notable interventions on this theme, however, came amid an earlier dispute over the fate of Goethe's childhood home in Frankfurt. That debate brought their prescription of a critical

---

[66] Jaspers, "Unsere Zukunft und Goethe," *Die Wandlung* 2, no. 7/8 (1947): 561, 574–6.
[67] Curtius, "Goethe oder Jaspers?" *Die Zeit*, 28 April 1949 (first published: *Die Tat*, 2 April 1949); Jaspers, *Unsere Zukunft und Goethe* (Bremen: Storm, 1949). See also Mandelkow, *Goethe*, II:140–3; Brockmann, *Literary Culture*, 127–9; Clark, *Beyond Catastrophe*, 73–4.

relationship to the past into vivid relief.[68] Built in the sixteenth century, the house was immortalized in the eighteenth, as the setting of Goethe's autobiographical *Poetry and Truth*. The history of the site itself embodies the cultural contradictions that so preoccupied our protagonists after 1945. It was acquired in the 1860s by the Freies Deutsches Hochstift für Wissenschaften, Künste und allgemeine Bildung (Free German Foundation for the Sciences, Arts, and General Education), an organization established by veterans of the 1848 revolution to carry forth their liberal-democratic political ideals under Goethe's cultural banner. Soon, however, it acquired a conservative bent as the custodian of imperial Germany's Goethe cult, as its headquarters became a shrine for pilgrimage and secularized worship.[69] So it remained across 1918 and 1933, until the so-called Goethe House was reduced to rubble – along with most of Frankfurt's city center – by Allied bombs. After the war, its fate became a celebrated public cause. The controversy over whether and how to reconstruct the building lay at the intersection of two key arenas of renewal debate: architects' and planners' discussions of the built environment and writers' discussions of the literary and philosophical canon.

The lead was taken by Ernst Beutler, a devoted Goethe scholar who also directed the Hochstift and its Goethe Museum (Figure 3.1). He mobilized a network of locally and nationally prominent figures in support of rebuilding the house in perfect replica, fully faithful to the destroyed original. (At war's outbreak, he had stored its contents off-site and meticulously documented both interior and exterior.) In the vein of Thieß or Meinecke, Beutler put Goethe at the center of a *Kulturreligion* endowed with redemptive power. Speaking in August 1945, he decried Germans' fall away from the poet's ideals of cosmopolitanism and culture into power, commerce, and chauvinism, away from the clear light of reason into the romance of will. Nonetheless, amid the ruins of Germany's lost empire, he insisted, "we remain Germans," who could find "in each word of Goethe, even his bitterest, a healing power." In fact, Goethe's sense for "the transformability of all things," for "the holy meaning of suffering," for the "power of reconciliation, of faith in life and faith in God" now held new meaning for them. Even a hostile world loved this "noblest blossom of pure humanity . . . once born of our

---

[68] For full accounts on which I draw here, see Bettina Meier, *Goethe in Trümmern: Zur Rezeption eines Klassikers in der Nachkriegszeit* (Wiesbaden: Deutscher Universitäts-Verlag, 1989), 16–85; Joachim Seng, *Goethe-Enthusiasmus und Bürgersinn: Das Freie Deutsche Hochstift – Frankfurter Goethe-Museum 1881–1960* (Göttingen: Wallstein, 2009), 498–544.

[69] Seng, *Goethe-Enthusiasmus*, 11, 164–72.

Figure 3.1 Ernst Beutler and his son Christian linger among the ruins of Goethe's childhood home in Frankfurt on 28 August 1945, the 196th anniversary of the poet's birthday. (*Source*: Freies Deutsches Hochstift / Frankfurter Goethe-Museum)

people," and through him, Germans could again learn to love themselves.[70] Ably interweaving repentance and redemption, he pleaded to rebuild the sacred site of Goethe's youth. The national petition drive he organized brought overwhelmingly supportive responses, above all from literati and professors including Curtius, Hermann Hesse, and Benno Reifenberg. Armed with such testimonials, Beutler first won over the Hochstift's board and then persuaded city leaders. In a nearly unanimous vote, the latter endorsed his plan in April 1947.

This activism had also galvanized a counter-movement, for which Dirks and Sternberger – former colleagues at the *Frankfurter Zeitung* – joined forces as public spokesmen. Sternberger, on receiving Beutler's petition, expressed great unease. To him, the plan reflected a desire to reclaim Goethe as "a salvaged good, a comforting possession," in the face of the "definitive, final, irrevocable" destruction of his childhood home. It implied that whatever it sought to recover had been shattered not as

---

[70] Ernst Beutler, *Besinnung: Ansprache zur Feier von Goethes Geburtstag* (Wiesbaden: Dieterich, 1946), 30–1.

a result of Germans' own actions but by Germany's enemies during the war. It thus elided an intimate link between the building's destruction and the city's moral and physical self-destruction under Nazism. Sternberger had himself witnessed Frankfurt's true ruin, not by Allied bombs in March 1944 but by the *Kristallnacht* pogrom in November 1938, the "Night of Broken Glass" that raged all across Germany. To this event, as he put it, all that followed was an "epilogue." He described the burning synagogues, the wanton violence, and the roundups of Jews, to which ordinary Frankfurters turned a blind eye: "Granted, that is over. But it did happen and cannot be wiped away." The ethical and political imperative to confront the history of this entwined, dual destruction made any easy recovery of the cityscape or of Goethe – one that returned to a status quo ante – untenable. Rather, it demanded of Germans that they "renew this precious memory... '*Erwirb es, um es zu besitzen!*' (Make it yours to possess it!)."[71] On the authority of Goethe's own words, Sternberger advocated a critical reappropriation of tradition under the changed circumstances of the present.

Dirks objected on similar grounds. The understandable yet dangerous impulse "faithfully to rebuild" the Goethe House occluded the "bitter logic" it embodied: the concurrence in Goethe's person of the spirit of "measure and humanity" with the fateful self-alienation of the "people of poets and thinkers" from the realities of "economics and power." In that regard, the building "was not destroyed 'by accident'"; rather, it was "devastated in a historical event that has very much to do with its essence." In the classical cultural tradition's distance to the practical world lay the link of the house to the circumstances of its destruction, that is, of the Goethean heritage to Nazism and to the war it set in motion. Recourse to Goethe in 1945 thus demanded a "*critical* relationship," one that "makes distinctions," saying both "yes" and "no" to him

---

[71] Sternberger, "Frankfurter Goethehaus," 192, 194–5. Notably, Sternberger took this robustly modernist credo from Goethe's most ambivalent protagonist Faust (*Faust* I, line 683). I diverge a bit from the standard translation, given here in context:

| | |
|---|---|
| Was du ererbt von deinen Vätern hast, | It's from our fathers, what we inherit, |
| Erwirb es, um es zu besitzen. | To make it ours truly, we've got to earn it. |
| Was man nicht nützt, ist eine schwere Last, | What's never used weighs like lead; |
| Nur was der Augenblick erschafft, das kann er nützen. | What's useful responds to a living need. |

Johann Wolfgang von Goethe, *Faust I & II*, trans. Stuart Atkins (Cambridge, Mass.: Suhrkamp/Insel, 1984), 20.

and precluding a simple "reconstruction" of his house. The "telling word 'reconstruction'" itself, Dirks argued, signaled the threat of a broader and deeper "restoration" – a concept he would make famous as a diagnosis of the 1950s. In 1947, it was still a forward-looking warning: naively reconstructing the Goethe House would squander the opportunity for renewal and amount to a "failure before the future," which required instead that Germans "take leave of what is irretrievably past."[72] This would cater to powerful psychic needs in the present – as he wrote, on a prescient note, to the mayor – but would beg objections later, when "the most honest and uncompromising of our grandchildren will want to despise us for our weakness."[73] Faced with a widespread desire to whitewash a past complicit in catastrophe, Dirks implored, "you must resist the beginnings."[74] It is not difficult to imagine that, for both writer and audience, this language evoked Germans' lack of resistance to Nazism, exhorting a more vigorous response to the challenges of its legacy.

Opposition to Beutler's plans was organized by local representatives of the re-established German Werkbund. This association of artists, artisans, and intellectuals, rooted in the *fin de siècle* arts and crafts movement, was by the late 1920s a pillar of modernism in design, architecture, and planning. Unlike the closely related Bauhaus school, however, many of its leading lights were not driven into exile, and a refoundation occurred soon after 1945. Its members were thus key players in postwar debates over how to rebuild, advocating for modernism and new construction against traditionalism and preservation.[75] In Hesse, the central figure was honorary chair Otto Bartning, an architect whose publishing outlet – before the foundation of the key postwar trade journals – was the *Frankfurter Hefte*, no doubt facilitated by his fellow Werkbund member Dirks.[76] It was Bartning who made a Goethe House proposal that both

---

[72] Dirks, "Mut zum Abschied: Zur Wiederherstellung des Frankfurter Goethehauses," *Frankfurter Hefte* 2, no. 8 (1947): 820, 825–8 (emphasis in original). On the "restoration" critique, see Chapter 7.

[73] Dirks to Walter Kolb, 18 April 1947, quoted in Meier, "Goethe in Trümmern: Der Streit um den Wiederaufbau des Goethehauses in Frankfurt," in *Erinnerung ist unsere Aufgabe: Über Literatur, Moral und Politik 1945–1990*, ed. Jochen Vogt (Opladen: Westdeutscher, 1991), 36.

[74] Dirks, "Mut zum Abschied," 819. This classical reference (to Ovid's *principiis obsta*, taken up by Seneca) is just the sort of erudite gesture favored by *Bildungsbürger* – an unintended irony here; cf. Hubertus Kudla, ed. *Lexikon der lateinischen Zitate: 3500 Originale mit Übersetzungen und Belegstellen*, 2nd edn. (Munich: Beck, 2001), 20.

[75] See Werner Durth and Niels Gutschow, *Träume in Trümmern: Planung zum Wiederaufbau zerstörter Städte im Westen Deutschlands 1940–1950*, 2 vols. (Braunschweig: Vieweg, 1988); Jeffry M. Diefendorf, *In the Wake of War: The Reconstruction of German Cities after World War II* (Oxford: Oxford University Press, 1993).

[76] Otto Bartning, "Ketzerische Gedanken am Rande der Trümmerhaufen," *Frankfurter Hefte* 1, no. 1 (1946): 63–72; Bartning, "Erneuerung aus dem Ursprung," *Frankfurter*

Sternberger and Dirks endorsed. He called for a new structure that would reflect the proportions and position of the destroyed original but forego all attempts to replicate it in style or material. Its remaining physical traces – the foundation and identifiable bits of rubble – were, however, to be integrated into the new building.[77] This concept materialized the critical reappropriation of tradition so central to engaged democrats' postwar vision.

Formidable forces were thus arrayed against Beutler's restorative plans. The Hessian Werkbund had conducted a national petition drive as well, targeting architects and planners; the responses they received were uniformly against a reconstruction in replica. Bartning's appeal to municipal leaders, however, failed to sway them, just as Beutler had overridden Dirks on the Hochstift's board (on which the latter also sat). Even after the city council sided with Beutler – over the abstention of Mayor Walter Kolb and the objection of the councilor responsible for construction, Werkbund member Eugen Blanck – the opponents continued their agitation. Dirks attempted to win over their former colleague Reifenberg, while Sternberger supplied copies of his article and other critical public responses to the Hochstift's board, from which Dirks resigned in protest.[78] Despite these prodigious efforts, they were unable to derail reconstruction. It began in July 1947; in 1951, Theodor Heuss, now West Germany's first president, gave the address at the unveiling. By then, the Goethe House controversy had long simmered down, for it had drawn its energy less from questions of material restoration and reconstruction and more from those of postwar Germans' relationship to their national past.[79]

As such, it was a particularly illuminating setting for engaged democrats to fashion their equivocal position on a field of alternatives. With advocates of rupture, they shared a fervent desire to begin anew, but not the need to discount German traditions wholesale, as irredeemably contaminated. With advocates of continuity, they shared an impulse to reclaim elements of the national past, but not the need to declare any of

---

    *Hefte* 1, no. 6 (1946): 37–41; "Verzeichnis der Mitglieder des Werkbundes (Hessen) Stand 15.11.46," Archiv der sozialen Demokratie (Bonn, hereafter AdsD), NL Dirks 353.

[77] "Ruine, Rekonstruktion oder Neubau? Antworten auf die Frage des Frankfurter Goethehauses," *Die Wandlung* 2, no. 3/4 (1947): 271–4; Sternberger, "Frankfurter Goethehaus," 201n; Dirks, "Mut zum Abschied," 825n. Jaspers, in contrast, had responded affirmatively to Beutler's earlier survey, albeit with an ambivalence – "this site may be neither a relic nor a place of worship" – foreign to Beutler's approach; Jaspers, "Unsere Zukunft," 577; cf. Seng, *Goethe-Enthusiasmus*, 523.

[78] Dirks to Benno Reifenberg, 23 April 1947, AdsD NL Dirks 19A; Dirks to Beutler, 24 April 1947, AdsD NL Dirks 353; Sternberger to Dirks, 13 June 1947, Deutsches Literaturarchiv (Marbach a.N.) A:Sternberger/ Wandlung/ 74.10079/1.

[79] See also Meier, *Goethe*, 13–14.

them pure and unstained. On this latter point, they also parted ways with some other skeptics, who sensed in a rekindled enthusiasm for German culture the desire to escape from recent German politics yet reproduced basic assumptions of the views they rejected. Returning from US exile to witness the Goethe bicentennial in 1949, literary historian Richard Alewyn, a former student of both Curtius and Jaspers at Heidelberg, exemplified such a stance. In his widely circulated lecture "Goethe as Alibi?" he chastised Germans for ostentatiously celebrating the poet at every turn, "as though nothing had happened, or as though something could thereby be undone." Not so, he proclaimed: "Between us and Weimar lies Buchenwald. We just cannot get around that... There is only Goethe *and* Hitler, humanity *and* bestiality."[80] Alewyn took a courageous and insightful stand, one often cited as an exceptional early call for a more honest confrontation with Germany's dual past of culture and catastrophe.[81] Still, Alewyn shared with the apologists he criticized the notion that Goethe represented a "good" side of German history – one inextricably intertwined with the "bad" but not itself internally fraught and ambiguous. It was just this notion that Germany's engaged democrats rejected.

Attending closely to engaged democrats' positions on *Kultur* complicates conventional accounts of the relationships among culture, politics, and democracy in Germany. Doubtless, the immediate postwar years saw a reinvigoration of educated elites' fixation on culture. But the lingering force of the "unpolitical German" paradigm has desensitized us to the different uses made of these same resources by different actors on the political-cultural field. Accordingly, a number of scholars have suggested that all who invoked culture – even to lament the historical split between "spirit" and "power" – did so in a basically "moral" and "unpolitical" register.[82] This was indeed the majority position, but it had prominent critics at the time, and not only among the still-marginal writers of Gruppe 47 or the far-away émigrés who framed the *Sonderweg* thesis in hopes of returning Germany to the Western fold. Like those dissenters, engaged democrats asserted the complicity of cultural tradition in Germany's political catastrophe, but they also identified within that

---

[80] Richard Alewyn, "Goethe als Alibi?" *Hamburger Akademische Rundschau* 3, no. 8–10 (1949): 685–7.
[81] See, e.g., Mandelkow, *Goethe*, II: 221; Meier, *Goethe*, 17–18; Brockmann, *Literary Culture*, 131–2.
[82] Georg Bollenbeck, *Bildung und Kultur: Glanz und Elend eines deutschen Deutungsmusters* (Frankfurt a.M.: Insel, 1994), 302; Anson Rabinbach, "Restoring the German Spirit: Humanism and Guilt in Post-War Germany," in *German Ideologies since 1945: Studies in the Political Thought and Culture of the Bonn Republic*, ed. Jan-Werner Müller (New York: Palgrave Macmillan, 2003), 29.

tradition an emancipatory spark. Implicitly and explicitly, they held that recovering the forms of freedom embedded in the cultural semantics of *Geist*, *Kultur*, and *Bildung* and bringing them to bear on a political plane constituted one crucial basis for democratic renewal in a homegrown, German mode. They took up these schemas from one arena and transposed them to solve similarly shaped problems in another, and this transposition informed and enabled their reconceptualization of politics in a popular, participatory vein.[83]

In this light, interpreting their recourse to *Kultur* as evidence of a revived apolitical or even anti-democratic culturalism – a persistence of the "unpolitical German" – falls wide of the mark. In fact, engaged democrats found in the bourgeois cultural ideal an image of freedom they considered both fatefully incomplete and hopefully recuperable. Breaking with both the rearguard cultural pessimism of the fading Weimar Republic and the blinkered cultural optimism of the postwar mainstream, they no longer played a realm of spirit off against the profane world. Instead, they turned to the German cultural heritage with explicitly political intent. This marked a novel departure within the political imaginary of the German *Bildungsbürgertum*, one accomplished by engaged democrats' rearticulation of the dominant relationship between two of its most resonant rhetorics: those of "culture," on the one hand, and "power" – the domain of the state and politics, masses and democracy – on the other. Rather than affirm the former's essential distinction from and priority over the latter, they brought the two together and altered both in the process. In this fashion, the turn to humanism, the classical canon, and the cultural heritage after 1945 acquired an overlooked radical-democratic variant.

At the same time, discussions over cultural renewal were also an attempt to navigate the vicissitudes of Germany's recent history in fascism, war, and genocide. In the immediate aftermath, this past was often addressed obliquely, refracted into myriad questions that bore only indirectly on it. In this sense, engaged democrats' critique and rehabilitation of the national cultural heritage represented a kind of early memory-work. A. Dirk Moses has usefully analyzed West German intellectuals' agonized debates over the meaning of the past in terms of an underlying binary framework that mapped arguments about German politics onto deep-seated emotions around German identity. Those who felt their Germanness iredeemably tainted by Nazism became "redemptive

---

[83] Here and below, I draw on the above-mentioned framework for understanding cultural and social change in William H. Sewell, Jr., *Logics of History: Social Theory and Social Transformation* (Chicago: University of Chicago Press, 2005), esp. chaps. 4, 5, 8.

republicans," calling for a cathartic break with the past and a radical refoundation of the polity. Those who sought to defend a viable German identity attempted to dissociate the collectivity from its stigma and became "integrative republicans," endorsing the FRG's political institutions and its reliance on personnel from the prior regime. Moses' focus is on the generation of "forty-fivers," those born in the 1920s and early 1930s for whom 1945 marked a traumatic rupture in their adolescent socialization. As the main carriers of postwar public culture, they are credited with initiating a sustained interrogation of the German cultural heritage and critical dialogue over the Nazi past.[84] Germany's engaged democrats, members of somewhat older cohorts, illuminate the need for other categories to grasp the contours of immediate postwar debates. Vociferous proponents of redemptive democratic renewal, they nonetheless advocated the integration of wayward but still educable elements in the population as well as flawed but still promising aspects of national traditions. As Germans who came of age before Nazism, they felt they had access to recoverable resources from the past, and as intellectuals, they considered it their mission to chart a path to the future for the people at large.[85]

For all its critical ambivalence, these intellectuals' devotion to a nineteenth-century cultural canon transmitted two vestiges of mandarin tradition, generating tensions the following chapters will explore. First, the key terms of the cultural heritage had come into widespread use as the lexicon of cultural nationalism, and despite their critique of chauvinist excesses, a kind of national sentiment clearly informed their positions. Second, the *Bildung* ideal was bound up historically with the arrogance and anxiety of educated elites vis-à-vis "the masses," legacies that sat uneasily with engaged democrats' counter-elitist convictions. They were aware of these problematics. Eggebrecht posed the key question: "can the *Geist* be popular?" For him, there was no doubt that the answer had to be affirmative, adequate to the world now rising from the ruins of the bourgeois epoch, when "spirit" had been jealously guarded, exclusive property. Notably, this end could not be served simply by commodifying classical culture as mass culture – Eggebrecht derided such

---

[84] A. Dirk Moses, *German Intellectuals and the Nazi Past* (Cambridge: Cambridge University Press, 2007). On "forty-fiver" journalists, see also Christina von Hodenberg, *Konsens und Krise: Eine Geschichte der westdeutschen Medienöffentlichkeit 1945–1973* (Göttingen: Wallstein, 2006).

[85] Moses notes that members of West Germany's older "founder generation" could be "redemptive republicans" without being "Non-German Germans." They escaped the structural logic by which political languages were indexed to psychological types for younger cohorts. Moses, *German Intellectuals*, 45, 109.

"blasphemy" as the popular "Mozart Balls" confections and "Schiller Curls" pastries. Rather, he suggested, the cultural tradition's noble vision of self-determining self-cultivation might be actualized on a new social foundation, one that was truly of the people.[86] Engaged democrats considered themselves the privileged bearers of that tradition. At their most consistent, however, they insisted that they could not lead the German nation down the path to renewal; it could be trod only by the people themselves, severally and together, through their direct participation in processes of self-rule and self-education.

[86] Eggebrecht, "Kann der Geist populär sein?" *Nordwestdeutsche Hefte* 2, no. 8 (1947): 55–8.

# 4 Subjects of politics: publicness, parties, elites

After war's end, as Germany's engaged democrats re-examined democracy's conceptual underpinnings, they also cast about for ways actively to promote their vision's realization. How did the contents of these actors' ideas relate to the forms of their activities?[1] And what external constraints did the latter encounter? Their modes of political intervention evolved out of their political thinking on the one hand and the horizon of their possible activity on the other, which was increasingly determined by the Cold War conflict. Moreover, practical political activity of any sort begged questions about the warrant and scope for Germans' political agency: did Germany itself or the German people still constitute a legitimate subject of politics? If so, then in what sense? And who could rightly claim to represent the nation?

The latter questions related to a vigorous legal debate on the status of German sovereignty after hostilities. At one pole were those who, in light of Germany's total defeat and unconditional surrender, insisted that not only sovereign control but the state itself had been lost; Germany had ceased to exist as a legal subject, and its lands were now a "condominium" ruled by the war's victors. Others argued that German sovereignty persisted in a suspended condition while the occupiers exercised "supreme authority" (as Allied agreements had it) over German territory.[2] Even

---

[1] Methodologically, I attempt to consider the formulation of ideas and other types of social action together, on the same analytic plane. For a different approach to the same issue, see Daniel Wickberg, "Intellectual History vs the Social History of Intellectuals," *Rethinking History* 5, no. 3 (2001): 383–95.

[2] Michael Stolleis, "Besatzungsherrschaft und Wiederaufbau deutscher Staatlichkeit 1945–1949," in *Handbuch des Staatsrechts der Bundesrepublik Deutschland*, vol. I, *Historische Grundlagen*, ed. Josef Isensee and Paul Kirchhof (Heidelberg: Müller Juristischer Verlag, 2003), 283–7. In American exile, Hans Kelsen took the former position. Most German jurists, including Wolfgang Abendroth and Peter Alfons Steiniger, argued the latter; Andreas Diers, *Arbeiterbewegung, Demokratie, Staat: Wolfgang Abendroth, Leben und Werk 1906–1948* (Hamburg: VSA, 2006), 458–64; Berndt Musiolek, "Peter Alfons Steiniger: Zwischen Illusion und Wirklichkeit," in *Rechtsgeschichtswissenschaft in Deutschland 1945 bis 1952*, ed. Horst Schröder and Dieter Simon (Frankfurt a.M.: Klostermann, 2001), 265–6.

if few engaged democrats contributed directly to the debate, their positions hinged on the latter reasoning. They recognized the suspension of effective statehood as a legitimate consequence of the Nazi regime's criminality and Germans' acquiescence to it. The logic of their commitments, however, gave primacy to the fact of popular sovereignty over its institutional embodiments. With the discredited actors and frameworks of politics-as-usual neutralized, engaged democrats turned to the people as the first site and principle of sovereign authority. The avenues of political intervention with which they experimented were shaped by this conviction.

Impinging on their ability to imagine alternatives were the received elitisms of modern politics. On the one hand, a nineteenth-century tradition viewed politics as the preserve of loosely organized local notables with independent means, inhabiting a realm above and apart from the masses.[3] Intellectuals were drawn from similar strata, and their sociability took similar forms, privileging informal circles and face-to-face communication. They felt bound, however, by a "double membership": committed to the sphere of culture, they mingled freely in politics while also cultivating a self-image as critical outsiders to power.[4] Some commented and advised on public matters; others held themselves apart. Either stance reproduced and affirmed the distinction of a political – or unpolitical – elite from the general populace. On the other hand, the clash of these norms and forms with those of mass politics defined the transition to the twentieth century. The rise of mass politics and mass parties – in Germany, those of the workers' movement, political Catholicism, and, increasingly, radical nationalism – brought with it another, differently elitist role: that of the party-affiliated intellectual.[5] Alongside the attendant, no less dramatic shift from a liberal to a mass media, these developments shaped the range of possible

---

[3] On *Honoratiorenpolitik*, see, classically, Max Weber, "The Profession and Vocation of Politics," in *Political Writings*, ed. Peter Lassman and Roland Speirs (Cambridge: Cambridge University Press, 1994), 318–52; also David Blackbourn and Geoff Eley, *The Peculiarities of German History: Bourgeois Society and Politics in Nineteenth-Century Germany* (Oxford: Oxford University Press, 1984), 224–5, 251–76.
[4] Wolfgang Eßbach, "Intellektuellengruppen in der bürgerlichen Kultur," in *Kreise – Gruppen – Bünde: Zur Soziologie moderner Intellektuellenassoziation*, ed. Richard Faber and Christine Holste (Würzburg: Königshausen & Neumann, 2000), 23–33. This self-image is reproduced in many theories of "the intellectual," from Max Weber and Julien Benda to M. Rainer Lepsius and the later Pierre Bourdieu.
[5] This development is registered in Antonio Gramsci's theorization of intellectuals' inevitable political role, the third major interwar treatment alongside Weber and Benda; Antonio Gramsci, *Selections from the Prison Notebooks*, trans. and ed. Quintin Hoare and Geoffrey Nowell Smith (New York: International, 1971), 5–23.

Subjects of politics: publicness, parties, elites 151

modes of intellectual activity throughout the early twentieth century and beyond.[6]

After 1945, Germany's engaged democrats ventured a different approach. Their experiences and convictions drew them to a politics that did not attempt to exclude or direct the masses but sought to enable and maximize their participation. Despite their class backgrounds, they were suspicious of the gulf separating conventional forms of intellectual politics from the population at large. Also, they were convinced that the fragmentation of political culture along party lines – defined narrowly by interest and rigidly by ideology – had helped derail potential defenses against National Socialism. A few engaged democrats were involved in early initiatives for new parties that hoped to shake off this legacy. The party system that soon emerged under Allied oversight, however, seemed to them a revival of pre-1933 conditions – modified by the absence of the radical right – and they rapidly grew disillusioned with formal politics. Instead, they tended to favor political discussion and advocacy groups outside the party framework. These became the vehicles of a project that pursued publicness (*Öffentlichkeit*) as a political good, not primarily in terms of educating or influencing public opinion but in terms of constituting a political public in the first place, as an autonomous organ of authority. In a polarizing, restorative political climate that left ever less room for independent positions and programs, however, these attempts did not directly influence outcomes. In the end, journalism itself remained these actors' dominant and most effective mode of political activity.

This chapter charts the diverse forms of political mobilization that engaged democrats pursued – from parties through public associations to closed discussion circles – and examines the shifting conceptions of the relationship between intellectuals and politics as well as between elites and the broader populace that these forms evinced. At first, the heady openness of the postwar moment fostered grassroots innovations toward popular empowerment; in response to Cold War polarization and Germany's incipient partition, however, they reverted to more conventional modes of intervention. While the narrowing horizon of political possibilities was thus one crucial factor in their political activities, these were fraught with internal tensions from the outset, the same tensions between participatory aspirations and elitist residues that characterized their vision as a whole.

---

[6] See, e.g., Gangolf Hübinger, "Die politischen Rollen europäischer Intellektueller im 20. Jahrhundert," in *Kritik und Mandat: Intellektuelle in der deutschen Politik*, ed. Hübinger and Thomas Hertfelder (Stuttgart: Deutsche Verlags-Anstalt, 2000), 30–44.

152   German Intellectuals and Democratic Renewal

**From anti-restorative parties to a new press**

Analyzing the shortcomings of the first German republic and avoiding their repetition became a fixation for postwar Germans, who exhibited a "Weimar syndrome" or "Weimar complex" after 1945.[7] Engaged democrats were no exception, and political parties figured prominently in their diagnosis of interwar failures. As we have seen, these intellectuals did not oppose a parliamentary system, yet they also held that mass parties had generated a fractiousness and rigidity that impeded democratic processes and outcomes. While liberals on one end and Communists on the other envisioned very different solutions to this problem, both thought changes were needed. Politics should entail cooperation among active citizens, not confrontations among bureaucratic institutions. In part, they echoed interwar critics on the right and left who, frustrated with the seemingly interminable and ineffectual squabbling of "formal" democracy, sought a politics above or beyond parliaments and parties. Such anti-liberal dispositions had contributed to the appeal of the KPD's class vanguardism and the NSDAP's racial nationalism, with each affirming – to opposite ends – action and commitment over negotiation and compromise.[8] After 1945, however, Germany's engaged democrats feared the reverse problem: not too much discussion but too little. Mass parties tended to pre-structure the field of debate in ways that stifled popular participation and stymied the collaborative pursuit of the common good, core elements of their publicness ideal.

Nonetheless, some of their number joined, planned, or even founded political parties in the immediate postwar moment. Crucially, these were conceived in non-conventional terms, to remedy historical deficiencies. Two rifts had inhibited the kind of pluralist political unity they urgently advocated in 1945: within the labor movement and between Christian and secular progressives. Concretely, bridging these divides implied a unified socialist party and an ecumenical Christian party advancing robust secular reforms, and engaged democrats were not alone in attempting to usher in such developments. While active cooperation and even organizational union between Social Democrats and Communists initially had strong rank-and-file support, old antagonisms quickly

---

[7] A. Dirk Moses, *German Intellectuals and the Nazi Past* (Cambridge: Cambridge University Press, 2007), 48–9; Sebastian Ullrich, *Der Weimar-Komplex: Das Scheitern der ersten deutschen Demokratie und die politische Kultur der frühen Bundesrepublik 1945–1959* (Göttingen: Wallstein, 2009), 16–18.

[8] Kurt Sontheimer, *Antidemokratisches Denken in der Weimarer Republik: Die politischen Ideen des deutschen Nationalismus zwischen 1918 und 1933* (Munich: Nymphenburger Verlagshandlung, 1962); Riccardo Bavaj, *Von links gegen Weimar: Linkes antiparlamentarisches Denken in der Weimarer Republik* (Bonn: Dietz, 2005).

resurfaced. And these were sealed by the actual development of the SED, as not a united socialist front but a front for Communist hegemony.[9] Likewise, many local Christian Democratic parties, rooted in both Catholic and Protestant milieus, appeared in 1945, and prominent groups in Berlin, Cologne, and Frankfurt had a strong leftward bent. Yet this "Christian socialist" tendency was soon marginalized and decisively repudiated by 1949, as the new CDU found its distinctive profile in the broad, cross-confessional appeal of conservative values and anti-socialist politics.[10] Before such paths were set, however, engaged democrats saw potential in these two new party-political configurations.

For independent-minded communists, party membership had long been a fraught issue. To join demonstrated dedication, but it also imposed discomforting strictures. As we have seen, a commitment to "antifascist-democratic" pluralism, rather than the party's "leading role," distinguished engaged democrats close to the KPD/SED from the party's core cadres. In intra-party relations, they similarly opposed a "democratic centralism" that effectively proscribed internal dissent. Here, the case of Wolfgang Harich is instructive. It is often reported that he joined the KPD immediately in 1945, moving into the SED as a matter of course.[11] In fact, Harich's option for the party capped a long process rooted in shifting circumstances and agonized deliberation; it appears likely that he was never a KPD member, first joining the SED shortly after its April 1946 foundation. He attributed this "change of heart," one reached in "inner anguish," to an encroaching danger: Early Cold War tensions – fanned by the likes of Wilhelm Röpke and his own ex-mentor Erik Reger – were abetting Germans' political regression. Encouraged by anti-"totalitarianism," nationalist resentments and Nazi-era anti-Bolshevism were reviving, feeding revenge fantasies of a new war on the side of the West against the USSR. Faced with these alarming developments, Harich came to view the SED's strong hand as the only bulwark against

---

[9] Norman M. Naimark, *The Russians in Germany: A History of the Soviet Zone of Occupation, 1945–1949* (Cambridge, Mass.: Harvard University Press, 1995), 271–98; Andreas Malycha, *Die SED: Geschichte ihrer Stalinisierung 1946–1953* (Paderborn: Schöningh, 2000), 52–277.

[10] Rudolf Uertz, *Christentum und Sozialismus in der frühen CDU: Grundlagen und Wirkungen der christlich-sozialen Ideen in der Union 1945–1949* (Stuttgart: Deutsche Verlags-Anstalt, 1981); Frank Bösch, *Die Adenauer-CDU: Gründung, Aufstieg und Krise einer Erfolgspartei 1945–1969* (Stuttgart: Deutsche Verlags-Anstalt, 2001), 21–83.

[11] E.g., in the standard reference Helmut Müller-Enbergs et al., eds. *Wer war wer in der DDR? Ein Lexikon ostdeutscher Biographien*, 5th edn. (Berlin: Links, 2010), 487. A possible source of this error is the party book issued him after 1990, in which the refounded KPD dated Harich's membership to 1945; Siegfried Prokop, *Ich bin zu früh geboren: Auf den Spuren Wolfgang Harichs* (Berlin: Dietz, 1997), 173.

renazification and remilitarization, until a firm socialist foundation could eliminate the possibility of a fascist resurgence.[12]

Reaching this conclusion did not dispel Harich's reservations about the party. From the beginning, he was critical of Communists' cynical invocations of pluralism and cooperation. He viewed the KPD–SPD merger in the Soviet zone in similar terms, as an imposed "absorption politics" that only "stiffened" old "fronts" within the workers' movement and impeded genuine reconciliation. Even as a party member, and despite his rejection of "totalitarianism" per se, Harich worried about affinities between SED and Nazi methods, confessing unease at his own irrepressible, visceral associations between past performances of "unity... under the disciplined direction of the right" and present ones "under the (not quite so disciplined) direction of the left." But some such discipline was now necessary. In light of the evident dangers, more permissive approaches – including those of the "Heidelberg Jaspers circle" addressed below – amounted to "idealistic illusions."[13] For Harich, mounting mistrust of the potentially renazified German masses pushed him away from his early bottom-up politics and toward a more conventional vanguardism.

Reconciled to the party, Harich moved to counter its anticipated dogmatism. During the run-up to the SED's foundation, he approached *Die Weltbühne*'s editor, Hans Leonard, with a proposal.[14] Any hope for socialist unity, so crucial to their new democracy, was being undermined by both "overzeal[ous]" KPD and "hesitant" SPD members. This paralleled a larger difficulty: Germany's hope of mediating the Allies' divergent understandings of "democracy" was being undermined by the myopic "nationalism" of German politicians, who attempted to play the occupiers against each other. Harich argued that the *Weltbühne*, at the epicenter of both conflicts in Berlin, should take up this dual project of "synthesis." Resolutely independent of all occupiers and parties, it could become a platform for open and intense intra-German dialogue, leveling relentless critique, debating a pluralist socialism, and upholding the journal's best traditions. As Harich told one potential contributor, he envisioned a "left-radical united front of the proletariat" that would reconcile

---

[12] Wolfgang Harich to Erik Reger, 17 September 1946, AdK Reger-Archiv 311. There, he dates his entry into the SED to May 1946. Later, he recalled joining the KPD in February 1946; cf. Harich, *Ahnenpass: Versuch einer Autobiographie*, ed. Thomas Grimm (Berlin: Schwarzkopf & Schwarzkopf, 1999), 156.

[13] Harich to Paul Rilla, 16 April 1946, AdK Rilla-Archiv 386; Harich to Reger, 17 September 1946.

[14] See also Wolfgang Schivelbusch, *In a Cold Crater: Cultural and Intellectual Life in Berlin, 1945–1948*, trans. Kelly Barry (Berkeley: University of California Press, 1998), 177–80.

the "revolutionary verve" of the Marxist-Leninist tradition with "the fair, free spirit of the Western democracies." The *Weltbühne* would be its organ, taking to task Communists for "intra-party dictatorship" and Social Democrats for a corrosive "politics of division."[15] As the independent gadfly of a unified left, it would challenge the SED in the name of real democracy, pluralism, dialogue, and critique.

Over the following months, Harich doggedly pursued his plan. When Leonard refused to step aside, he went directly to Soviet authorities. At their suggestion, he drew up a formal proposal for a *Weltbühne* under his direction, with Leonard and Erich Weinert as well as Axel Eggebrecht and even Karl Korn on the editorial board. The wide-ranging list of potential authors included Anton Ackermann, Johannes Becher, Günther Birkenfeld, Herbert Ihering, Erich Kästner, Wolfgang Leonhard, Theodor Plievier, Karl Schnog, and Günther Weisenborn. He also took a page from *Ulenspiegel*'s operations: the *Weltbühne* would be shaped by monthly open-door sessions involving all editors, contributors, and interested members of Berlin's wider intellectual public – writers, actors, artists, even occupation officials.[16] Although Harich's Soviet contacts responded favorably at first, Leonard's SED allies intervened to keep him at the helm. Harich came on board as a frequent contributor. The *Weltbühne* did host an initially spirited exchange between SED and SPD perspectives (to which Rudolf Leonhard also contributed); however, it did not continue past 1947, and Social Democrats were blamed for its breakdown.[17] Harich's own contribution – a critique of both sides that grounded the necessity of unity theoretically and historically but spared no criticism of the "dictatorial" methods by which it was effected – remained unpublished.[18] Far removed from the SED's corridors of power, Harich had little hope of reforming it from within.

---

[15] Harich to Hans Leonard, 7 April 1946, Landesarchiv Berlin (herafter LAB) NL Madrasch-Groschopp, E Rep. 200–63, 67d; Harich to Rilla, 16 April 1946.

[16] "'Die Weltbühne': Exposé und Programm," [July 1946], LAB NL Madrasch-Groschopp, E Rep. 200–63, 55b.

[17] It began September 1946, restarted the following fall, but devolved into discussion of the virtues of the "bloc system" by 1948. Josef Grunner and Alexander Abusch, "Für Entgiftung des politischen Kampfes," *Die Weltbühne* 1, no. 6 (1946): 161–70; Rudolf Leonhard, "Gedanken eines Heimgekehrten," *Die Weltbühne* 2, no. 16 (1947): 665; Josef Grunner, "'Der Feind steht rechts!'" *Die Weltbühne* 2, no. 17 (1947): 713–16; Wilhelm Meißner, "Es geht um Deutschland!" *Die Weltbühne* 2, no. 18 (1947): 761–5; Leonhard, "Noch einmal zur Einheit," *Die Weltbühne* 2, no. 21 (1947): 905–7; Ingo von Koerber, "Um eine Diskussion zur deutschen Einheit," *Die Weltbühne* 3, no. 3/4 (1948): 49–52. The main SPD contributor, Josef Grunner, was a politics editor at *Der Telegraf*; Susanne Grebner, *Der Telegraf: Entstehung einer SPD-nahen Lizenzzeitung in Berlin 1946–1950* (Münster: LIT, 2002), 141.

[18] Harich, "Um die Einheit des Proletariats," n.d., LAB NL Madrasch-Groschopp, E Rep. 200–63, 67d.

Yet he mobilized what resources he could to transform the *Weltbühne* into a platform for the party's constructive and public critique, still seeking a political unity not orchestrated from without but constituted from within.

Engaged democrats in Frankfurt also made forays into party-political innovation. In spring 1945, as US forces occupied the area, they drew heavily on *Frankfurter Zeitung* staff for the local administration: Walter Dirks worked at the Hessian labor office, serving also with Karl Heinrich Knappstein on Frankfurt's advisory citizens' council.[19] To that body, in late May 1945, Dirks presented his proposal for a new "Socialist Unity Party" (SEP) that would absorb SPD and KPD and realize the "properly understood heritage" of both. Although this plan was immediately opposed by local party leaders, it is noteworthy for both anticipating and diverging from Dirks' later approach. His proposed party would pursue not only the "immediate interests of the workers" but also the "general interests" of the entire "people." Socialization would proceed along two vectors: from the "state center" toward the "collectively planned economy" and from the "working person" toward the "democratization of the economy." In a markedly elitist register, however, Dirks named "leading the masses" the party's central task, for reasons that betrayed a certain pessimism. After Nazism and war, Germans were "demoralized, exhausted, [and] filled with resentment," and under these conditions, they "must first be regenerated, healed, educated, and led to full democracy."[20]

His next party-political venture retained that plan's pluralism and non-centralizing socialism while breaking with its elitism. Together with Eugen Kogon and Werner Hilpert, Dirks and Knappstein helped found Frankfurt's Christian Democratic Party (CDP) in fall 1945, whose program they also drafted.[21] It disavowed the Prusso-German "idea of force" for the "idea of right," defined as "respect toward one's co-citizen." It grounded these notions in a "Christian image of humanity" while

---

[19] Rebecca Boehling, *A Question of Priorities: Democratic Reform and Economic Recovery in Postwar Germany: Frankfurt, Munich, and Stuttgart Under US Occupation, 1945–1949* (Providence, R.I.: Berghahn, 1996), 83–5, 178–80; Ulrich Borsdorf and Lutz Niethammer, eds. *Zwischen Befreiung und Besatzung: Analysen des US-Geheimdienstes über Positionen und Strukturen deutscher Politik 1945* (Wuppertal: Hammer, 1976), 95–6; Wilhelm Hollbach to Walter Dirks, 16 June 1945, Kurt Blaum to Dirks, 1 September 1945, Archiv der sozialen Demokratie (Bonn, hereafter AdsD), NL Dirks 354.

[20] N.t., 29 May 1945, AdsD NL Dirks 358; published as Dirks, "Vorschlag zu einer Sozialistischen Einheitspartei," in *Christen für den Sozialismus*, vol. II, *Dokumente (1945–1959)*, ed. Dirks, Klaus Schmidt, and Martin Stankowski (Stuttgart: Kohlhammer, 1975), 42–4; see also Dirks, "Als wir die Ärmel aufkrempelten – zum Beispiel in Frankfurt," *Neue Gesellschaft / Frankfurter Hefte* 32, no. 4 (1985): 316–18.

[21] Joachim Rotberg, *Zwischen Linkskatholizismus und bürgerlicher Sammlung: Die Anfänge der CDU in Frankfurt am Main 1945–1946* (Frankfurt a.M.: Knecht, 1999).

asserting their accord with secular humanist ideals. Unremarkably, it affirmed constitutionalism and political democracy, and unsurprisingly, it invoked the family's inviolability and externality to politics, where the wife's "co-responsibility for public affairs" was mediated through her spouse. Unique among Christian manifestos, however, was its robust call for a democratic socialism of cooperatives in agriculture and manufacture, planning and social ownership in industry, and fully implemented "economic democracy" to realize the "equal participation of workers in the management of the economy." Notably absent was a vanguard or paternalist role for the party. As Dirks later explained, the SEP proposal focused on a "new leading political force," while the CDP conception emphasized a "foundational pact among democrats."[22] Yet this proved a fleeting moment of party history. The anti-socialist constituency fast gained ground in all affiliates of what became the CDU (except in Bavaria, where it was called the Christian Social Union, or CSU), and Knappstein, Dirks, and Kogon withdrew from active involvement in spring 1946. Hilpert tenaciously held the Hessian party chairmanship and various ministerial posts until electoral defeats forced him to step down in 1952.[23] Dirks and Kogon, for their part, shifted their energy to the *Frankfurter Hefte*.

Others saw Social Democracy as the most promising party force but hoped for a new program in the postwar era. Alfred Weber, for instance, joined the SPD in fall 1945. This affiliation was atypical among his associates; Alexander Mitscherlich sympathized with but did not join the SPD, while Dolf Sternberger remained independent on principle.[24] Weber's move also departed from his liberal roots. Convinced that parties had a crucial role to play, he sought to work through the one that best represented his views. And as he told an old acquaintance, "I have become a Social Democrat because I feel myself a socialist."[25] He also sought to break the SPD out of its statist, centralist traditions, frustrated that even party reformers "equate[d] socialism with the planned

[22] "Frankfurter Leitsätze," in Rotberg, *Linkskatholizismus*, 223, 225, 227, 231; Dirks, "Zwiespältige Erfahrungen," in *Weihnachten 1945: Ein Buch der Erinnerungen*, ed. Claus Hinrich Casdorff (Munich: Deutscher Taschenbuch Verlag, 1984), 88–9.
[23] Rotberg, *Linkskatholizismus*, 219–20.
[24] Eberhard Demm, *Von der Weimarer Republik zur Bundesrepublik: Der politische Weg Alfred Webers 1920–1958* (Düsseldorf: Droste, 1999), 315; Timo Hoyer, *Im Getümmel der Welt: Alexander Mitscherlich, ein Porträt* (Göttingen: Vandenhoeck & Ruprecht, 2008), 18–19; Claudia Kinkela, *Die Rehabilitierung des Bürgerlichen im Werk Dolf Sternbergers* (Würzburg: Königshausen & Neumann, 2001), 111–12.
[25] Alfred Weber to Gustav Wyneken, 7 September 1946, in *Alfred Weber-Gesamtausgabe*, vol. X, *Ausgewählter Briefwechsel*, ed. Eberhard Demm and Hartmut Soell (Marburg: Metropolis, 2003), I:312. Weber's biographer downplays this shift, asserting a lifelong continuity of social-reformist liberalism; Demm, *Weimarer Republik*, 436–7.

economy." This mistaken notion was one he and Mitscherlich sought to counter in their *Free Socialism*.[26] As a policy platform, it had been written for the SPD, and they pushed to have it published in time for consideration at the May 1946 convention in Hanover. That meeting came in the wake of the forced merger in the Soviet zone, and it served to consolidate a trizonal "Western" SPD under Kurt Schumacher's stridently anti-Communist leadership. Yet even at that juncture, Weber urged the SPD to form a "socialist unity party." His caveat was that its dedication to "freedom" and "real democracy" must remain absolute. Any "dictatorial tendencies" lurking behind a veneer of "false unity" would turn the new party from a "powerful counterforce" into the shepherd of "totalitarianism."[27]

Around the same time, remarkably, other engaged democrats also echoed Weber. Dirks endorsed a united socialist front, underscoring that the historic promise of such a coalition could be realized only if the SPD became "less doctrinaire-Marxist and more lively-socialist" and the KPD "foreswore dictatorship once and for all."[28] Eggebrecht, in an internal NWDR memo, presented a "socialist unity party" as a historical necessity. A Marxism updated for the mid-twentieth century could provide its programmatic basis, above all by re-examining the role of private initiative. Marx had also argued that a socialist transition was possible only through dictatorship, while Eggebrecht kept open the possibility of a democratic path, to which Germany's postwar economic structures and conditions seemed especially amenable. Echoing Harich, however, he conceded that, if it were not possible otherwise, "which would be terrible for us survivors," then better a "second dictatorship" than "no socialism at all. For without it, the 'democratic world' lurches inevitably toward new imperialist dictatorships."[29] His prognosis for parliamentary politics on a pure capitalist basis was dire, which gave a unified socialist party its

---

[26] Weber to Gert von Eynern, 12 December 1946, Universitätsbibliothek Heidelberg (hereafter UBH) NL Weber, Box 3, Aktionsgruppe.

[27] Demm, *Weimarer Republik*, 318; Tobias Freimüller, *Alexander Mitscherlich: Gesellschaftsdiagnosen und Psychoanalyse nach Hitler* (Göttingen: Wallstein, 2007), 81; Kurt Klotzbach, *Der Weg zur Staatspartei: Programmatik, praktische Politik und Organisation der deutschen Sozialdemokratie 1945–1965* (Berlin: Dietz, 1982), 78–81; Alfred Weber, "Freier Sozialismus: Ein Aktionsprogramm," in Alexander Mitscherlich and Weber, *Freier Sozialismus* (Heidelberg: Schneider, 1946), 68.

[28] Dirks, "Die Zweite Republik: Zum Ziel und zum Weg der deutschen Demokratie," *Frankfurter Hefte* 1, no. 1 (1946): 22.

[29] Axel Eggebrecht, "Zu den zehn politischen Hauptfragen," 3 March 1946, Bundesarchiv (hereafter BArch) N 1524/975. On Eggebrecht's consideration of "dictatorship," cf. Thomas Berndt, *Nur das Wort kann die Welt verändern: Der politische Journalist Axel Eggebrecht* (Herzberg: Bautz, 1998), 93–4; Alexander Gallus, *Heimat "Weltbühne": Eine Intellektuellengeschichte im 20. Jahrhundert* (Göttingen: Wallstein, 2012), 178–9.

urgency. Even as this unity was being realized in the distorted form of the SED, these intellectuals thus continued to work toward a productive reconciliation of the two socialist traditions.

Although they considered the renewal of party politics crucial, Germany's engaged democrats did not view this as their primary arena. As Erich Kästner put it, "the Archimedean point for writers like us is to be found... not in party affairs at all." Rather, they pursued public commentary and engaged journalism, where they could grapple with another pernicious German legacy: the insufficient development of public opinion as a political force. As Hans Mayer affirmed, this was just what had been lacking after 1848, when "public opinion," that "conscious freedom of the citizen over against the state," went into its long decline. And Eggebrecht pointed out that true "public opinion," which "forms (*bildet*) itself in critique and debate, in the free words of free citizens," was just what Nazism had so concertedly attacked. More than just suppressing open discussion, the Nazis had substituted for it a publicity "made artificially, fabricated and steered" by Goebbels' propaganda machine.[30] Engaged democrats' media activities sought to undo this damage.

Their efforts hit on a deep tension in the occupation project. Many praised the Anglo-American press, in particular, as models of keen observation and relentless reporting, in contrast to a German press historically hobbled by state censorship.[31] Former exiles Alfred Kantorowicz and Maximilian Scheer knew American conditions first hand, and Kogon and Sternberger were invited on the first US study tour for German journalists in fall 1948.[32] At the same time, many German (and Allied) observers perceived a contradiction between the goal of a free press and the persistence of licensing and censorship. Accordingly, the transfer of media regulation to German hands was often discussed, most avidly in the US zone, where debate peaked in mid 1948, as OMGUS

---

[30] Erich Kästner to Kurt Hiller, 8 October 1946, Deutsches Literaturarchiv (Marbach a.N., hereafter DLA) A:Kästner; Hans Mayer, *Karl Marx und das Elend des Geistes: Studien zur neuen deutschen Ideologie* (Meisenheim a.G.: Hain, 1948), 46; Eggebrecht, "Rückblicke ins Dritte Reich," *Nordwestdeutsche Hefte* 1, no. 1 (1946): 8.

[31] See, e.g., Eugen Kogon, "Öffentliche Meinung als Kontrollinstanz," *Frankfurter Hefte* 1, no. 5 (1946): 10–11; Dirks, "Die Freiheit der Presse," *Frankfurter Hefte* 2, no. 1 (1947): 12; Alfred Kantorowicz, "William L. Shirer," *Ost und West* 1, no. 3 (1947): 29–30; Maximilian Scheer, "Howard K. Smith," *Ost und West* 1, no. 4 (1947): 4–5.

[32] "Seminar for German Publishers and Editors: Tentative Daily Program," n.d., AdsD NL Kogon, Reden (bis 1963), Reden 8.48–4.49; Kogon, *Gesammelte Schriften*, vol. VI, *"Dieses merkwürdige, wichtige Leben": Begegnungen*, ed. Michael Kogon and Gottfried Erb (Weinheim: Beltz Quadriga, 1997), 112–13; Dolf Sternberger, *Gefühl der Fremde* (Wiesbaden: Insel, 1958), 81–108. On study tours, see Hermann-Josef Rupieper, *Die Wurzeln der westdeutschen Nachkriegsdemokratie: Der amerikanische Beitrag 1945–1952* (Opladen: Westdeutscher, 1993), 390–420.

directed state governments to draft appropriate legislation. By then, emphatically anti-Nazi journalists arguing for rapid devolution of control found themselves with strange bedfellows: groups of so-called former publishers who had operated under Nazism and had thus been ineligible for licenses.[33] Kogon parsed this issue in terms of engaged democrats' conception of democracy. While licensing had initially been necessary, it only made sense as a temporary measure. He likened it to a "playpen": "you develop yourself inside it, then you climb over its rails. So it is with the emergence of democracy in general: the German people are not permanently a class of disabled schoolchildren in need of remedial instruction."[34] One could learn democracy only by practical experience; this principle held for journalistic practice as well.

Conversely, it also applied to journalists' mission of helping form public opinion. Engaged democrats fought a conviction enshrined in long-standing German traditions and in Allied licensing regulations: the "*idée fixe*," as Sternberger called it, "that the press exists to educate people." Paradoxically, journalists had to "assume from day one that they deal with mature readers," or those readers "will never become mature." Kogon put the point bluntly: "The journalist is no schoolmaster and the reader no idiot"; they should aim at "a conversation among equals."[35] Such statements construed the audience as active interlocutors, not passive receivers of information. Accordingly, these intellectuals proposed a positive "freedom of information" as well as a negative "freedom of the press." The former obliged all government agencies to furnish the press with information on demand, recognizing not only the press' right to inform the public but also the public's right to inform itself from all possible sources. As Sternberger remarked, "no instruction is worth anything that one doesn't get for one*self*." A press free in both senses was vitally necessary "so that the people can participate, can contribute ... so that – simply put – sovereignty can derive from the people."[36] Only out of the encounter between published commentary and the active interest and insight of the population at large could democratic public opinion emerge.

[33] Harold Hurwitz, *Die Stunde Null der deutschen Presse: Die amerikanische Pressepolitik in Deutschland 1945–1949* (Cologne: Wissenschaft und Politik, 1972), 173–95; Kurt Koszyk, *Pressepolitik für Deutsche 1945–1949* (Berlin: Colloquium, 1986), 116–22, 255–8, 314–16.
[34] Kogon, "Vom Elend unserer Presse," *Frankfurter Hefte* 3, no. 7 (1948): 616–17. Tellingly, Kogon's Austrian term for "playpen" (*Gehschule*) translates literally as "walking school."
[35] Sternberger, "Demokratie der Furcht oder Demokratie der Courage?" *Die Wandlung* 4, no. 1 (1949): 14; Kogon, "Vom Elend unserer Presse," 623.
[36] Sternberger, "Das Kernstück der Pressefreiheit," *Die Wandlung* 3, no. 8 (1948): 734–6; Sternberger, "Demokratie der Furcht," 14 (emphasis in original).

Germany's engaged democrats thus viewed journalists in a dialogical, not didactic relationship with the broader public, in news reportage as well as cultural-political commentary. They demonstrated a commensurate discomfort with self-aggrandizing images of the intellectual. With Dirks and Kogon, they still identified a privileged role for "political publicists" – "we argue, we reason, we enlighten" – but insisted that "writer" and "reader" were "participants" in the same critical process. As a journalist, Kogon advised, one should "intervene critically and farsightedly" in the larger dialogue while recognizing "oneself as an effective component within public opinion, which one helps as a whole ... to find its voice." Kantorowicz described responding to readers' letters as the experience of "a host, sitting among his guests, taking part in the conversation. That the conversation is happening in his house gives him no priority as a discussion partner."[37] This undermined the dominant stance of media elites toward the public, questioning high-handed German traditions that saw the press as disseminating enlightened opinion and managing consensus.[38] These were views they revised without entirely dismantling, in an equivocal counter-elitism of elites.

They explored several vehicles for a critical dialogue with their readership. Letters-to-the-editor columns represented an Allied-prescribed change in the licensed press that was durably embraced.[39] Additionally, some editors engaged their readership as a whole via surveys on their journals' overall content as well as on specific questions. The *Frankfurter Hefte* were delighted that so many responses to their 1947 survey expressed a desire for "a closer connection with us and to each other" and especially that hundreds of "reading circles" had formed to discuss each new journal issue (and share scarce copies). They took this as a sign of successful "engagement" between writers and readers from both sides. Of course, they hoped to spark dialogue on a broad social basis, and this aspiration went largely unfulfilled. Survey returns for both the *Frankfurter Hefte* and *Die Wandlung* confirmed that most readers were educated professionals, but a handful of craftsmen, workers, and farmers

---

[37] "In eigener Sache," *Frankfurter Hefte* 2, no. 12 (1947): 1184; Dirks and Kogon, "Die Rolle der Publizisten," *Frankfurter Hefte* 2, no. 12 (1947): 1187–8; Kogon, "Vom Elend unserer Presse," 619; "Suchende Jugend: Briefwechsel zwischen der Studentin Käte Fuchs und Alfred Kantorowicz," *Ost und West* 2, no. 2 (1948): 87.

[38] See Christina von Hodenberg, *Konsens und Krise: Eine Geschichte der westdeutschen Medienöffentlichkeit 1945–1973* (Göttingen: Wallstein, 2006), 139–41; 133–9, 195–204, 280–2. For Hodenberg, even the likes of Dirks, Kogon, and Eggebrecht remained beholden, no longer to conformist "consensus journalism" but still to the tutelary self-conceptions of "opinion journalism."

[39] Hurwitz, *Stunde Null*, 277–8.

did also respond.[40] Even on this narrower ground, it was in their view of the media as a venue for the co-constitution of a public by authors and audience together that engaged democrats' conception of publicness was most clearly articulated and most practically viable.

### Forming a public

If published commentary was their main avenue of engagement, it was not the only one. Finding novel ways to translate participation into social practice acquired urgency as new prospects for Germans' own involvement in their political reconstruction appeared on the horizon. One hotbed of such mobilization was Heidelberg, whose professors and literati were renowned for a vibrant, socially exclusive intellectual culture, exemplified in the early twentieth century by the Stefan George circle's secretive, anti-modern aesthetes as well as by the reform-minded cosmopolitans of Max and Marianne Weber's salon. Indeed, the latter persisted across 1945 to become the seedbed of activities examined below.[41] This sort of local, face-to-face intellectual sociability flourished across Germany amid the collapse.[42] Distinctively, however, these Heidelbergers made it their explicit project to build outward from such enclaves into an extra-institutional space of political participation. In late 1946, they founded the Aktionsgruppe Heidelberg zur Demokratie und zum freien Sozialismus (Heidelberg Action Group for Democracy and Free Socialism) and the Deutsche Wählergesellschaft (German Voters' Society).[43] Both emerged from the campaign against proportional representation,

---

[40] Two thirds of 2,700 responders to the *Frankfurter Hefte*'s survey were university educated, while only 3.4 percent were manual laborers. Workers submitted some 3 percent of 2,000 responses to *Die Wandlung*, in a more focused poll discussed below. Women constituted 11 percent of respondents in the former but nearly one quarter in the latter. "An unsere Leser!" *Frankfurter Hefte* 2, no. 4 (1947): 321; "In eigener Sache," quote 1184; Valentin Siebrecht, "Selbstbildnis der Leser: Zahlen und Tatsachen aus der Umfrage der Frankfurter Hefte," *Frankfurter Hefte* 2, no. 12 (1947): 1264, 1266; "Redaktionelle Anmerkungen," *Die Wandlung* 2, no. 2 (1947): 184.

[41] Hubert Treiber and Karol Sauerland, eds. *Heidelberg im Schnittpunkt intellektueller Kreise: Zur Topographie der geistigen Geselligkeit eines Weltdorfes 1850–1950* (Opladen: Westdeutscher, 1995); Guenther Roth, *Max Webers deutsch-englische Familiengeschichte 1800–1950* (Tübingen: Mohr Siebeck, 2001), 572–619; Robert E. Norton, *Secret Germany: Stefan George and his Circle* (Ithaca: Cornell University Press, 2002).

[42] Dirk van Laak, *Gespräche in der Sicherheit des Schweigens: Carl Schmitt in der politischen Geistesgeschichte der frühen Bundesrepublik* (Berlin: Akademie, 1993), 42–52, 63–9. On the longer-term context, see Moritz Föllmer, introduction to *Sehnsucht nach Nähe: Interpersonale Kommunikation in Deutschland seit dem 19. Jahrhundert*, ed. Föllmer (Stuttgart: Steiner, 2004), 9–44.

[43] On the Aktionsgruppe, see Demm, *Weimarer Republik*, chap. 5 *passim*; Birgit Pape, *Kultureller Neubeginn in Heidelberg und Mannheim 1945–1949* (Heidelberg: Winter,

and just as that campaign has been seen as a plea for old-style liberal politics, so these organizations have been dismissed as "notables' associations" seeking to influence the public from on high.[44] Such assertions correspond to the groups' social basis, but they ignore their attempts to grapple with elitist legacies and find modes of intervention more consistent with the popular politics they professed. Closer scrutiny reveals that these organizations signaled an innovative – albeit short-lived – stance on publicness.

Their postwar activism was deeply rooted in Heidelberg's convivial academic milieu, galvanized by the political developments of the postwar. The seedbed was Marianne Weber's salon, from which several of the central figures hailed: Sternberger, Alfred Weber, Karl Geiler, journalism professor Hans von Eckardt, and sociology lecturer Marie Baum. Publisher Lambert Schneider was a Weber family friend, and Alfred's nephew Konrad Mommsen, who worked at OMGUS, became their contact in Berlin.[45] Weber and Geiler first met Mitscherlich in yet another early discussion circle, where they talked politics with jurist Hans Huber and Heidelberg's first postwar mayor Ernst Walz, who both also joined the Aktionsgruppe.[46] Elections began in the American zone – first to municipal, then state assemblies and constitutional conventions – in early 1946, all conducted by proportional representation.[47] In response, the Heidelberg group mounted a press campaign. In their journal, in newspapers, and on the radio, they broadcast their critique of "list elections" and pushed "person elections" as the superior vehicle of direct

---

2000), 313–22; Gallus, *Die Neutralisten: Verfechter eines vereinten Deutschlands zwischen Ost und West 1945–1990* (Düsseldorf: Droste, 2001), 138–46; Katharina Hausmann, *"Die Chance, Bürger zu werden": Deutsche Politik unter amerikanischer Besatzung: Die "Heidelberger Aktionsgruppe" 1946–47* (Heidelberg: Regionalkultur, 2006). On the Wählergesellschaft, see Erhard H. M. Lange, *Wahlrecht und Innenpolitik: Entstehungsgeschichte und Analyse der Wahlgesetzgebung und Wahlrechtsdiskussion im westlichen Nachkriegsdeutschland 1945–1956* (Meisenheim a.G.: Hain, 1975), 307–17.

[44] Demm, *Weimarer Republik*, 315; Lange, *Wahlrecht*, 308, 310.

[45] Sternberger, "Aktionsgruppe Radio Stuttgart Interview am 27. Februar 1948," n.d., DLA A:Sternberger/ Aktionsgruppe Heidelberg/ 89.10.8112; Lambert Schneider, *Rechenschaft über vierzig Jahre Verlagsarbeit 1925–1965* (Heidelberg: Schneider, 1965), 87. Sternberger also mentioned Carlo Schmid, a nationally prominent politician (SPD). Schmid was their guest and interlocutor but not a core member.

[46] Friederike Reutter, *Heidelberg 1945–1949: Zur politischen Geschichte einer Stadt in der Nachkriegszeit* (Heidelberg: Guderjahn, 1994), 203–4; Martin Dehli, *Leben als Konflikt: Zur Biographie Alexander Mitscherlichs* (Göttingen: Wallstein, 2007), 136. One or more meetings occurred between May and June 1945; they ran afoul of the initial prohibition on political activities and were quickly shut down.

[47] Wolfgang Benz, *Auftrag Demokratie: Die Gründungsgeschichte der Bundesrepublik und die Entstehung der DDR 1945–1949* (Berlin: Metropol, 2009), 119–21; Lange, *Wahlrecht*, 32–68.

participation and democratic self-education.[48] When the draft constitutions themselves threatened to carve proportionality into the legal bedrock of postwar Germany, their agitation intensified.

The vigorous debate they joined ran along older fault lines. As we have seen, the workers' parties generally saw proportional representation as their achievement, whereas majority voting had favored established elites. Although this conviction was little shaken after 1945, some socialists showed interest in reforming proportionality's impersonal character. If Peter Alfons Steiniger developed the most important KPD/SED position, the key SPD voice belonged to Hermann Brill. He too called for assembling party lists – i.e., nominating candidates – by primaries rather than by bureaucratic fiat (alongside other measures for intra-party democratization).[49] Similar views informed the dissent of *Die Wandlung*'s Communist co-editor, Werner Krauss. He objected to his colleagues' excessive personalization of politics: citizens chose representatives in their "supra-personal" capacity, as carriers of "ideas in which the force of future action slumbers." Parties were the institutional embodiment of such ideas, and their proportional share in power was indispensable to political legitimacy. Still, he acknowledged a need for reform, suggesting that they encourage readers to "enliven" the parties through their own active "participation."[50] Like other critics, Krauss held that social reality had not yet rendered modern parties irrelevant, even as he recognized the need to develop new forms of engagement within them.[51] Strikingly, reformers from different camps shared an impulse to dissolve parties' bureaucratic character via participation.

Convinced, for their part, that proportional representation was beyond repair, the Heidelberg group redoubled their activism. They aimed to prevent proportionality's ratification in the state constitutions, preferably via separate referenda on the relevant articles. First, they circulated an appeal distilling their arguments that called for public support and exhorted others to seize the initiative. Second, they distributed a flyer

---

[48] See, e.g., Alfred Weber, "Listen oder Personen?" *Rhein-Neckar-Zeitung*, 12 June 1946; Sternberger, "Herrschaft der Freiheit," *Die Wandlung* 1, no. 7 (1946): 570–1; Sternberger, *Dreizehn politische Radio-Reden 1946* (Heidelberg: Schneider, 1947), 49–70. For their arguments, see Chapter 2.

[49] Hermann L. Brill, "Für das Verhältniswahlrecht," *Das sozialistische Jahrhundert* 1, no. 5/6 (1947): 65–7. Brill did not also endorse institutionalizing a "bloc system," as Steiniger did.

[50] Werner Krauss to Sternberger, 24 October 1946, DLA A:Sternberger/ Wandlung/ 74.10661/31. For the public reply, see Sternberger, "Tagebuch: Zu hundertfünfzig Briefen," *Die Wandlung* 1, no. 12 (1946): 1026–8.

[51] Krauss to Sternberger, 23 December 1946, DLA A:Sternberger/ Wandlung/ 74.10661/36. This disagreement preceded – though it did not cause – Krauss' withdrawal from the editorial panel; Monika Waldmüller, *Die Wandlung: Eine Monatsschrift* (Marbach a.N.: Deutsche Schillergesellschaft, 1988), 91–4.

and response card in *Die Wandlung* that polled readers' views on the electoral system and whether it should be put to a separate popular vote.[52] Their initiative sparked a larger movement. Locally, a petition at Heidelberg University was signed by more than 800 students – over one in five – in just a few days.[53] In the press, Berlin's *Der Tagesspiegel* began to canvass its own readers, publicized and reprinted the Heidelbergers' appeal, and serialized Sternberger's treatise on electoral methods.[54] Regional papers such as the *Stuttgarter Zeitung* and the *Frankfurter Neue Presse* joined the cause, as did *Der Ruf*. And Sternberger, at least, considered the petition drive a great success. Of nearly 2,000 responses by March 1947, all but 73 rejected proportionality for majority elections. The surveys by *Der Tagesspiegel* and another daily, Würzburg's *Main-Post*, added over 1,600 more signatures.[55]

Ultimately, however, the states declined to submit the electoral system to a separate referendum, prompting an eleventh-hour tactical shift. Now calling itself the Aktionsgruppe, the Heidelberg group held a debate "For and against the Constitution," two nights before the Württemberg-Baden referendum. Weber urged voters to reject the constitution itself in order to force a revision of its electoral provisions. Responses came from a local SPD leader and liberal jurist Walter Jellinek, but most of the 1,200-strong audience was behind Weber.[56] Although this mobilization failed to block ratification, US authorities held it responsible for the disproportionately high no-votes in Heidelberg. These were cast predominantly in more affluent districts, home to the professoriate and higher civil servants.[57] It seems the campaign's appeal remained markedly

---

[52] "Aufruf gegen das Verhältniswahlrecht," reply card, and cover letter, 9 November 1946, UBH NL Weber, Box 3, Aktionsgruppe; "An die wahlberechtigten Leser der Wandlung in der amerikanisch besetzten Zone Deutschlands," *Die Wandlung* 1, enclosure to no. 10/11 (1946).

[53] "Drei Meinungen über: Personen- oder Listenwahl?" *Rhein-Neckar-Zeitung*, 19 November 1946. Enrollment was just under 4,000 at the time.

[54] "Für Erneuerung des Wahlrechtes," *Der Tagesspiegel*, 9 November 1946; Sternberger, "Das Wesen der Wahl," *Der Tagesspiegel*, 12 December 1946; Sternberger, "'Landkarte' und 'Landschaft'," *Der Tagesspiegel*, 13 December 1946; Sternberger, "Die innere Friedensordnung," *Der Tagesspiegel*, 14 December 1946; "Aufruf gegen das Verhältniswahlrecht," *Der Tagesspiegel*, 15 December 1946.

[55] "Redaktionelle Anmerkungen," *Die Wandlung* 2, no. 2 (1947): 184; Jérôme Vaillant, *Der Ruf: Unabhängige Blätter der jungen Generation (1945–1949): Eine Zeitschrift zwischen Illusion und Anpassung* (Munich: Saur, 1978), 96–7.

[56] Stuttgart State Ministry to Weber, 19 November 1946, UBH NL Weber, Box 3, Aktionsgruppe; "Aktionsgruppe gegen die Verfassung," *Rhein-Neckar-Zeitung*, 26 November 1946; Emil M. Stranz, "Subject: Intelligence Report No: 370/ Weekly Political Intelligence Report" 26 November 1946, Hauptstaatsarchiv Stuttgart (hereafter HStAS) J384 OMGUS microfiche, RG 260 12/8–1/6.

[57] 28 percent and 27 percent opposed the constitution in Heidelberg and nearby Mannheim, as against 16 percent and 18 percent in Stuttgart and Karlsruhe; Reutter, *Heidelberg*, 255–7.

bourgeois, as contemporary critics suggested. The group soon departed from its narrow focus on the perils of proportional representation, but that campaign's public character shaped its foundations.

In its further development, the Aktionsgruppe embodied an attempt to initiate a broad-based extraparliamentary movement for Germany's democratic renewal. From the start, they were at pains to insist they were "not set against the parties," but the allegation was not without merit. Although the group's vision did not exclude parties, it privileged a realm of popular self-organization outside re-established institutions. Sternberger called its core a "loose grouping" of Heidelbergers who refused "to leave public affairs to appointed party leaders and officials." Rather, they "endeavor[ed] to be citizens," gathering to discuss the pressing questions of the day and promulgate possible solutions. Those who disparaged such extra-institutional activity succumbed to an authoritarian identification of "political action" with either "commanding or obeying."[58] Against such habits, the Aktionsgruppe pursued their avowed goal: to "contribut[e] to the formation of a genuine public opinion in Germany," that is, to the constitution of a "political public sphere."[59] At times, these pronouncements had a conventional feel, in which the public was an external entity to be informed or influenced by their deliberations.[60] More often, the public figured as a body still in formation, of which the Aktionsgruppe's dialogues represented an exemplary instance.[61] In the latter usage, these terms evoked both a kind of political space – independent of formal politics yet eminently political – and a kind of political entity – constituted by private citizens coming together to deliberate matters of public concern.

They thus hoped to build their movement on the broadest possible social base. Eckardt told hundreds assembled at an inaugural rally that the Aktionsgruppe did not mean to repeat the arrogance of press organs and parties that, while representing "only part of public opinion," considered themselves "privileged to know better." In contrast, their group

---

[58] "Aktionsgruppe Heidelberg," *Der Tagesspiegel*, 13 December 1946; Sternberger, "Aktionsgruppe Radio Stuttgart Interview."

[59] See, e.g., Lambert Schneider in Ernst Mugdan, ed. *Die Neutralität Deutschlands und der Friede: Beiträge zur Bildung einer öffentlichen Meinung in Deutschland* (Heidelberg: Schneider, 1947), 7; Weber to Schwamberger, 28 December 1946, UBH NL Weber, Box 3, Aktionsgruppe. See also Hausmann, *"Die Chance"*, 34–5.

[60] See, e.g., preface to Mugdan, ed. *Neutralität*, 5; introduction to Mugdan, ed. *Unteilbarkeit des Friedens und Unteilbarkeit Deutschlands: Eine Diskussion* (Heidelberg: Schneider, 1947), 5; introduction to Mugdan, ed. *Zur völkerrechtlichen Lage Deutschlands – Ruhrfrage und Friedenssicherung – Zur künftigen deutschen Gesamtverfassung* (Heidelberg: Schneider, 1948), 5.

[61] See, e.g., Weber and Schneider in Mugdan, ed. *Neutralität*, 32, 76; Sternberger, Hans von Eckardt, and Ernst Walz in Mugdan, ed. *Unteilbarkeit*, 8, 20–1, 57.

Subjects of politics: publicness, parties, elites 167

hoped to become a "private people's parliament," one that would dialogue with "all citizens" and thus transcend the "false... dissonance between the masses and the intelligentsia."[62] In practice, however, their initiative remained confined to the latter. Its founders lamented but soon reconciled themselves to this fact. To critics who noted the absence of workers from their discussions, Weber replied that they could hope at best for "workers' *representatives*, since unfortunately workers themselves were generally unavailable" for such meetings. This was an "undeniable shortcoming." Given that workers already had unions to transmit their views in the public arena, however, it was not unjustified that he and his collaborators "see ourselves in the first instance as an *intellectual* group," albeit one that included labor leaders.[63]

High politics gave the Aktionsgruppe its impetus, but their intent was to establish an alternative to just such official channels. From spring 1947, OMGUS began soliciting input from parties and unions on the shape of a future constitutional order and the terms of an eventual peace. This set off a flurry of activity among Germans, who gathered in venues such as the American zone's Council of States or the new German Office of Peace Questions to draft proposals. The Aktionsgruppe, however, objected that only a much broader spectrum of voices could constitute "the public opinion of our country" in full. Chief among the excluded were those "who have not bound themselves party-politically" – church and university representatives, publicists, and other "independent personalities." The group announced their intent to initiate such a discussion in what became a series of conferences.[64] While party membership was no grounds for exclusion, and various politicians were invited, the clear implication was that they were welcome despite – not because of – the posts they held.[65] Enclosed with the announcement were a set of "minimal conditions for German unity," cast in terms that contrasted the "democratic" rule of organs in "immediate contact with the people's

---

[62] Eckardt cited (in translation) in Stranz, "Subject: Intelligence Report No: 382/ The Heidelberg Action Group," 17 December 1946, HStAS J384 OMGUS microfiche, RG 260 12/8–1/6.
[63] Weber to Rudolf Agricola, 10 May 1947, UBH NL Weber, Box 3, Aktionsgruppe Tagung v. 10. und 11. April 1947 (emphasis in original). Although Fritz Tarnow, co-secretary of the Bizone's Union Council, was always invited, he attended only one session. Prominent union adviser Ludwig Preller was a regular participant.
[64] Benz, *Auftrag Demokratie*, 160–1, 354; Eckardt, "Aufforderung zur Teilnahme an einer Aussprache über die Neutralität Deutschlands und den Frieden," 20 March 1947, UBH NL Weber, Box 3, Aktionsgruppe Tagung v. 10. und 11. April 1947.
[65] Fritz Eberhard (SPD), head of the German Office of Peace Questions, declined their invitation, voicing dismay at the "mistrust" it expressed toward party officials; Eberhard to Aktionsgruppe, 9 April 1947, UBH NL Weber, Box 3, Aktionsgruppe Tagung v. 10. und 11. April 1947.

will" to the "authoritarian" rule of a "bureaucratic apparatus."[66] Such language, redolent of engaged democrats' participatory convictions, suffused the subsequent discussions.

The conversation evolved during 1947, in tandem with a deepening geopolitical rift. Internationally, the Council of Foreign Ministers turned with mounting acrimony to unresolved issues concerning Germany. Domestically, an attempted conference of Prime Ministers in Munich failed to constitute an all-German representative body. With their politicians manifestly unable to address "questions absolutely decisive for our existence," the Aktionsgruppe felt duty-bound "as Germans" to do so, to "give voice" to their "common spirit" and constitute themselves as a political "subject" rather than a mere "object" of Allied policy. Accordingly, they did not orient themselves to the occupiers' authority. Rather than seek audience and influence with the Allies, their goal was "to help form a German public opinion."[67] To that end, the Aktionsgruppe convened three two-day meetings in April, June, and October that each drew 100 to 150 participants, most but not all from the American zone. These included journalists, academics, and other professionals, with a smattering of politicians, officials, and military government representatives. Publicists were a key constituency: journal editors from *Frankfurter Hefte*, *Die Gegenwart*, *Der Ruf*, *Aufbau*, and *Sonntag*; newspaper editors from *Der Tagesspiegel*, the *Rhein-Neckar-Zeitung*, the *Stuttgarter Zeitung*, *Der Kurier*, *Der Telegraf*, *Die Neue Zeitung*, and *Die Zeit*; and Hans Mayer were invited. Although many did not attend – interzonal travel still required special authorization – all four zones and Berlin were represented at the meetings.[68] The events received extensive and favorable coverage in newspapers across the western zones and Berlin and as far away as New York City.[69] The discussions incorporated social dimensions

---

[66] "Mindestforderungen zur deutschen Einheit," n.d., UBH NL Weber, Box 3, Aktionsgruppe Tagung v. 10. und 11. April 1947. These were drafted by Weber and signed by a team of self-proclaimed "left-oriented German democrats": Baum, Eckardt, Huber, Schneider, Walz, and Weber, plus theologian Martin Dibelius, physician Ernst Engelking, and jurists Walter Jellinek and Gustav Radbruch.

[67] Christoph Kleßmann, *Die doppelte Staatsgründung: Deutsche Geschichte 1945–1955*, 5th edn. (Göttingen: Vandenhoek & Ruprecht, 1991), 185–7; Weber in Mugdan, ed. *Neutralität*, 62; Sternberger in Mugdan, ed. *Unteilbarkeit*, 8.

[68] Sternberger, "Aktionsgruppe Radio Stuttgart Interview"; Mugdan, ed. *Neutralität*, 107–9; Mugdan, ed. *Unteilbarkeit*, 121–23; "Liste der Einzuladenden zur Tagung am 26./27. Juni 1947," n.d., UBH NL Weber, Box 3, Aktionsgruppe Tagung v. 10. und 11. April 1947; Ursula Martens to Helene Krauß, 4 October 1947, DLA A:Sternberger/ Aktionsgruppe/ 89.10.8118/4. No attendance list exists for the third meeting.

[69] See, e.g., "Für Reform der Entnazifizierung," *Rhein-Neckar-Zeitung*, 12 April 1947; "Heidelberger Aussprache zum Friedensproblem," *Der Tagesspiegel*, 13 April 1947; "Aussprache über die Friedensfrage," *Die Neue Zeitung*, 14 April 1947; Delbert Clark,

into what had been a narrow political agenda. Together, the resolutions they debated, passed, and publicized – usually drafted in advance by Weber and other core members – articulated a comprehensive program for peace and democratic renewal.[70]

The opening frame, however, was the question of Germany's position within the international system and its bipolar tensions. The hope that participants would take a strong stand for "neutrality," announced in the invitations, was not uncontroversial. Reger and his *Tagesspiegel* colleagues, for instance, rejected such a position as their own advocacy of an orientation to the West intensified.[71] And clearly, a declaration of neutrality begged crucial legal and ethical questions. The organizers acknowledged that Germany was in no position to make demands or enter into contractual relationships as a state. Nonetheless, the German people had a right and an obligation publicly to assert their will to neutrality and so shape later sovereign action.[72] Concerns were also voiced over whether neutrality strayed too close to Germans' fateful political passivity. As Eckardt, Schneider, and Weber made clear, however, they intended neutrality as an emphatically "active program." It entailed the rejection of "power politics" and a position of "nonpartisanship" between the occupying powers, but it also rested positively on a notion of "humanity," and it envisioned a special German task. According to their first resolution, neutrality entailed "the will to equalize the given ideal and practical tension between East and West... by means of internal German democratic politics."[73] It passed unanimously, endorsing engaged democrats' contention that what was at stake in the construction of an independent German democracy was Germany's constitution as a geopolitical mediator.

The second meeting elaborated this point, with a shift of emphasis from "neutrality" to "unity." Intervening months had brought important international developments: US Secretary of State Marshall announced

---

"Heidelberg Forum Urges Democracy," *New York Times*, 6 July 1947; "Ist Deutschland noch Staat?" *Die Welt*, 18 October 1947.
[70] For a detailed summary, see also Hausmann, *"Die Chance"*, 52–110.
[71] Eckardt, "Aufforderung zur Teilnahme," Reger to Weber, 8 April 1947, UBH NL Weber, Box 3, Aktionsgruppe Tagung v. 10. und 11. April 1947; Weber to Reger, 6 August 1947, UBH NL Weber, Box 3, Aktionsgruppe; Reger to Weber, 4 September 1947, UBH NL Weber, Box 3, Aktionsgruppe, Oktober-Tagung. Although he was consistently invited, Reger did not attend.
[72] Eckardt in Mugdan, ed. *Neutralität*, 14, 18. A later resolution formalized their position: a German state still existed, with effective sovereignty suspended. This was clear in international law and implicit in Allied practice: since occupation had been justified as an intervention to transform Germany, it presumed rather than precluded Germany's continued existence. Mugdan, ed. *Zur völkerrechtlichen Lage*, 51.
[73] Walter Hüsken, Eckardt, Schneider, and Weber in Mugdan, ed. *Neutralität*, 18–27, 34.

plans for economic aid to Europe, and former President Hoover proposed a "separate peace" with Germany's western zones, vaulting that term into public discussion. When the Aktionsgruppe convened, a minority including Eckardt and Mommsen was reluctant to oppose such a solution, on the grounds that it would spur recovery and take a step toward peace. The rest of the core group rejected it as a step toward irrevocable division. Their reasoning was threefold. Economically, Weber asserted that any investment to restructure western Germany as one element in an integrated western European economy would preclude reunification, since that would undermine the earlier investment's profitability. Politically, since global tensions mapped onto those threatening Germany, a separate peace would help consolidate larger blocs and intensify superpower confrontation. Sternberger cautioned that a "pax americana" confronting a "pax sovietica" would mean "no peace at all," an observation Baum endorsed. Mitscherlich clarified that their plea for German unity expressed commitments not to nationalism but to a "truly supranational solution" of global tensions. Finally, a separate peace would undo German democracy's role as East–West mediator. After all, Sternberger recalled, democracy was threatened in the West too, by bureaucratic "partytocracy." A separate peace, Weber and others asserted, would undermine the blending of political with economic democracy in Germany. Still, consensus remained elusive. A revised resolution that prefaced its call for an "undivided, peaceful Germany" with conciliatory reference to "well-meaning ideas of a separate peace" passed with only a slim majority. Opposing views were aired, as organizers had wished; even if they presented draft resolutions as discussion starters, they did not aim "to force a unified opinion."[74]

Other positions typical of Germany's engaged democrats also proved controversial in this larger forum, notably regarding the National Socialist past. On denazification per se there was little debate. Knappstein, the invited expert, applauded denazification's devolution to German control yet pressed for a reform of its schematism and scope. He highlighted the difficulties of prosecuting throngs of minor party members, which delayed justice for the truly guilty and created a "dangerous solidarity" between "little" and "big Nazis." While the latter should be excluded from all influence, a streamlined procedure for the former would foster reeducation rather than resentment. The resolution, which emphasized self-denazification and reintegration, passed unanimously – of course,

---

[74] Benz, *Auftrag Demokratie*, 267–8; Eckardt, Konrad Mommsen, Weber, Sternberger, Marie Baum, Mitscherlich, Preller, and Schneider in Mugdan, ed. *Unteilbarkeit*, 7, 11–18, 23–55, 61–2.

it was compatible not only with Knappstein's logic but also with more exculpatory agendas. These came to the fore as the discussion turned to the question of guilt. Weber, Sternberger, and Schneider advocated a public declaration of all Germans' collective entanglement in Nazism's crimes, as the necessary precondition for any further assertions or claims. Weber urged a confession of "guilt" that went beyond legal issues to acknowledge the widespread absence of "disobedience" or even "passive resistance (*Resistenz*)" in the face of "atrocity."[75] These proposals provoked objections. Some raised ostensibly tactical concerns over the effects of such admissions on diplomatic negotiations. Others pursued common apologetic maneuvers, emphasizing the victors' co-responsibility for the war, asserting Soviet atrocities as precedent for Nazism's, or equating the suffering of Germans and Jews. The revised resolution skirted the "moral" language of "guilt," calling Germans "internally obligated" to take "legal responsibility" for the war and the "illegal actions and inhumanities" perpetrated by "Hitlerdom" on "conquered peoples" and "persecuted races."[76] It passed unanimously.

Related disagreements arose over Germany's new eastern border, set at the Oder-Neiße line. Discourses of overpopulation and resource scarcity that had long fed expansionist claims to "living space" were still operative on all sides.[77] Weber and Sternberger, however, insisted that German crimes in the East were the vital context for any discussion of territorial losses and population "expulsion," which figured so prominently in postwar narratives of German victimhood. As Weber detailed, "we ourselves" precipitated the territorial shifts by inviting the Soviet Union into eastern Poland in 1939, losses which now sought compensation farther west; "we ourselves" killed almost one fifth of Poles, displaced and resettled countless others, and "murdered millions of Jews from all European lands." To reinforce the latter point – and to make the "shadow" of the events "more palpable" – Sternberger read extensively from the SS report on the Warsaw ghetto liquidation. The determined connection of German crimes to German loss met with both support and vocal opposition, including from Marianne Weber. She suggested a first-hand account of Germans' expulsion be read, in order to "balance" that from the Warsaw

---

[75] Karl Heinrich Knappstein, Weber, Eckardt, Sternberger, and Schneider in Mugdan, ed. *Neutralität*, 43–50, 60–8, 74–6.
[76] Geiler, Otto Vogel, Walter Roemer, and Knappstein in Mugdan, ed. *Neutralität*, 49, 64, 66, 72–3, 83. Even the relatively vigilant made spurious equivalences; Knappstein, for instance, likened proposals to mark former Nazis' identification cards to the practice of forcing Jews to wear the yellow star.
[77] See, e.g., Vejas Gabriel Liulevicius, *The German Myth of the East: 1800 to the Present* (Oxford: Oxford University Press, 2009).

ghetto. Her fellow participants rejected this formulation. In its final form, the resolution made mention of the expulsions only to reject their use to relativize German crimes, of which it gave a detailed account. After extensive discussion, it also rendered the murder of "Jews" as the murder of "people."[78] Their public statement thus distinguished German victims from the victims of Germans, but it did so without naming the specific position of Jews among the latter.

With this framework in place, the third conference turned to Germany's domestic institutions. The so-called Ruhr question provided their entrée. For the Ruhr district was not only the site of struggles over socialization and codetermination. Its coal mines and heavy industry – part of the French-Belgian-German industrial heartland – also stood for the threat of German war production, the promise of reparations, and the possibility of (west) European integration and recovery. Its future was a nodal point of Allied debates.[79] Aktionsgruppe members agreed on the need for internationalization while diverging on its terms. Weber, supported by Mitscherlich and several others, viewed Soviet claims to co-control as legitimate and as the only path to lasting peace; another group supported Mommsen's counterproposal for an international agency that both excluded the Soviets and owned Ruhr industry directly. Weber couched his opposition in nationalist terms that decried German "workers in foreign employ"; his goal, however, was for local control to enable a "thoroughly revolutionary" restructuring on the lines of his and Mitscherlich's "free socialism." As he explained, the latter foresaw ownership through public corporations or foundations; most crucially, it socialized "from below." It entailed strong rights of worker codetermination, while Mommsen's "authoritarian" plan arrogated all decisions to distant international owners. And for peacekeeping purposes, grassroots control and public ownership of heavy industry were the best guarantee against its misuse for war production.[80]

For these sorts of economic proposals, Weber could count on sympathy from prominent SPD reformers in attendance. One was Harald

---

[78] Weber, Sternberger, Marianne Weber, Kyra Stromberg, and Gustav von Hartmann in Mugdan, ed. *Unteilbarkeit*, 74–9, 86–9, 93, 98–9; Mugdan, ed. *Zur völkerrechtlichen Lage*, 125–7. The resolution was revised again for the third meeting, where it passed unanimously.

[79] Kleßmann, *Staatsgründung*, 103–6, 110–13, 209–10; John Gillingham, *Coal, Steel, and the Rebirth of Europe, 1945–1955: The Germans and French from Ruhr Conflict to Economic Community* (Cambridge: Cambridge University Press, 1991), 97–177.

[80] Weber, Mommsen, Ferdinand Friedensburg, Karl Geiler, and Mitscherlich in Mugdan, ed. *Zur völkerrechtlichen Lage*, 52–69, 77–8. Mommsen's and Weber's talks were published, revised and expanded, as "Ruhrgebiet und Friedenssicherung: Eine Diskussion," *Die Wandlung* 2, no. 9 (1947): 768–91.

Koch, the economics minister responsible for implementing the Hessian constitution's socialization provisions. He outlined his conception of *Sozialgemeinschaften* (social communities): non-state but non-private bodies composed of labor, government, and other public representatives that would be installed at multiple levels of organization, to administer firms as well as to steer the economy.[81] Carlo Schmid, a Württemberg-Hohenzollern minister, endorsed this attempt to steer clear of both private and "state capitalism," voicing reservations about the "syndicalist" tendencies of Weber's proposals. He agreed, however, that letting non-statist socialism take root in Germany, at the core of a future integrated Europe, could transform Europe from a passive space to an active East–West mediator, what they called a "third partner" or "third potency" in the configuration. Here, the Aktionsgruppe forged links to prominent party intellectuals amid the vibrant yet ultimately ineffectual discussions of socialization in the western zones. Their participatory emphasis, however, was attenuated in the final resolution, where concessions to Mommsen's counterproposal displaced references to organs of worker control. It passed with minimal opposition and some abstentions.[82]

Participatory impulses also figured in discussions of a future all-German constitution. For that point, Ferdinand Friedensburg (CDU) – visiting from Berlin – set the terms.[83] He underscored that the constitution's main aim must be to effect "real democratic renewal" by establishing institutions that fostered an "immediate relationship" between the people and the government, promoting the former's "political maturation." Federalism was well suited to that end, not as "separatism" but as a balance to the centralizing "unitarism" that a large-scale polity and economy also required. Crucially, federalism called for "self-management in small units" and thus provided the "seedbed of democracy," defined as

---

[81] Mugdan, ed. *Zur völkerrechtlichen Lage*, 81–2. Koch and Weber differed on important details but shared a general thrust, and Koch's proposal was a key contribution to postwar socialization debates. After its ratification by separate referendum, the socialization article of the Hessian constitution was suspended by OMGUS in 1947 and ultimately undone by non-implementation in 1950. Harald Koch, *Rechtsform der Sozialisierung: Unter besonderer Berücksichtigung der Sozialisierung in Hessen* (Hamburg: Gesetz und Recht, 1947); Diethelm Prowe, "Socialism as Crisis Response: Socialization and the Escape from Poverty and Power in Post-World War II Germany," *German Studies Review* 15, no. 1 (1992): esp. 70–1; Walter Mühlhausen, *Hessen 1945–1950: Zur politischen Geschichte eines Landes in der Besatzungszeit* (Frankfurt a.M.: Insel, 1985), 409–62.

[82] Mugdan, ed. *Zur völkerrechtlichen Lage*, 70–5, 79–80, 82–3, 131–2. See also Karl [Carlo] Schmid, "Das deutsch-französische Verhältnis und der dritte Partner," *Die Wandlung* 2, no. 9 (1947): 792–805; Weber, "Europa – das dritte Element," *Das sozialistische Jahrhundert* 2 (1948): 62–5.

[83] Weber and Friedensburg had confirmed their basic agreement in advance; Weber to Friedensburg, 16 August 1947, Friedensburg to Weber, 28 August 1947, UBH NL Weber, Box 3, Aktionsgruppe, Oktober-Tagung.

"the lively participation of the population in the destiny of the whole." For Sternberger, federalism entailed building "decentralization" as a core principle into every level of the social and political order (through majority voting, for instance). Such a foundation, Weber emphasized, would allow the realization of "democracy" and forestall tendencies toward its opposite, "bureaucracy." Consensus easily emerged around federalism in that sense, and a minimally revised resolution passed almost unanimously.[84]

The Aktionsgruppe continued to couple debate on key issues with reflection on their further role in the formation of a German public. In keeping with its extra-institutional thrust, the group did without firm structures or formal membership, bringing a shifting circle of people together in common discussion instead. This they hoped would set a vital and readily replicable example, one that would work as "leavening," by "stimulation," or even "infection." Similar groups, they imagined, might spring forth on their own initiative across Germany, each working independently yet sharing a commitment to become "genuine organ[s] of public opinion" and help constitute Germans' "spiritual unity." As likely nuclei of such activities, they mentioned their close contacts at the *Frankfurter Hefte* and *Die Gegenwart* as well as the editors of *Aufbau*, *Das sozialistische Jahrhundert*, *Der Tagesspiegel*, and even *Einheit* in Berlin, alongside other clusters of acquaintances and allies from Freiburg to Leipzig, a list that included union officials and SPD and CDU politicians. They explicitly hoped to attract SED members, although they questioned whether the party would allow their involvement. Such self-constituting civic forums were indispensable to renewal. As Sternberger put it, "if this space of free but responsible discussion is not held open, the state is of no use, even if it is called democratic. This is no luxury, but life-breath, a life necessity: public spirit, *Bürgerlichkeit* – in the political sense of the word."[85] As such statements reflect, their concern was to constitute, not exert influence over, a democratic public conceived on grassroots lines.[86]

Meanwhile, the momentum of their initial mobilization had led to a separate association devoted to overturning proportionality, the Deutsche Wählergesellschaft. The call for its formation, enclosed with a spring 1947 issue of *Die Wandlung*, envisioned an association of citizens from all parties and zones who shared a commitment to "study, discuss, and

[84] Mugdan, ed. *Zur völkerrechtlichen Lage*, 87–96, 101, 108–9, 115–16, 122–4.
[85] Sternberger, "Aktionsgruppe Radio Stuttgart Interview"; Schneider, "Besprechung der Mitglieder der Aktionsgruppe am 8. Oktober 1947," 9 October 1947, DLA A:Sternberger/ Aktionsgruppe Heidelberg/ 89.10.8133.
[86] Of previous commentators, Pape has best recognized this impulse; Pape, *Kultureller Neubeginn*, 315, 321.

realize" the majority electoral system. Its personnel indicate a strong overlap with the Aktionsgruppe: Sternberger was chair, vice-chairs Emil Walk and Gustav von Hartmann were both active in the Aktionsgruppe, and Mommsen sat on its executive board. The advisory board included Baum, Geiler, Schneider, Weber, and politicians of national stature such as Heinrich von Brentano (CDU) and Hermann Lüdemann (SPD).[87] As Sternberger underscored at the founding conference in September, the Wählergesellschaft's primary concern was the relation of electoral procedure to democracy: proportional representation meant rule by parties, while majority elections enabled rule by the people.[88] This view also shaped the means they used, such as their spring 1948 petition campaign for a popular referendum in Hesse, whose constitution, unlike those of other states, allowed for such an action.[89] There, they noted with approval, "the people need not exercise their sovereignty only through elected representatives" but could also do so "immediately," even to amend the constitution over the parties' resistance. While Hesse ultimately did not pass implementation legislation for referenda during the occupation period, the possibility of an appeal to direct popular power remained a central Wählergesellschaft emphasis.[90]

Organizationally, Heidelberg's dual mobilizations took different paths. Sternberger emphasized this fact: the Aktionsgruppe was an informal discussion forum, while the Wählergesellschaft was an officially registered association, a legal entity with statutes, governing board, and formal structure.[91] Nonetheless, the Wählergesellschaft mirrored the other group's grassroots approach in its own fashion. It quickly launched a drive to establish constituent local associations, on which would devolve dues collection as well as the bulk of the initiative for activities. Only weeks after the parent organization's foundation, work had already begun in nine local branches totaling 1,400 members.[92] Procedures were

---

[87] "Aufruf zur Bildung der Deutschen Wählergesellschaft," *Die Wandlung* 2, enclosure to no. 3/4 (1947); "Daten über die Entwicklung der Wählergesellschaft," [1954], DLA A:Sternberger/ Wählergesellschaft/ 89.10.10939; "Zusammensetzung des Beirats der Deutschen Wählergesellschaft," [1947], DLA A:Sternberger/ Wählergesellschaft/ 89.10.10945.

[88] Published as Sternberger, "Macht und Ohnmacht des Wählers," in *Die grosse Wahlreform: Zeugnisse einer Bemühung* (Cologne: Westdeutscher, 1964), 60–70.

[89] On this campaign, see "Arbeitsausschuß für Personen- und Mehrheitswahl in Hessen," [April 1948], "Die Macht dem Wähler! Aufruf an die Wähler!" [April 1948], DLA A:Sternberger/ Wählergesellschaft/ 89.10.10759.

[90] Erich Bindert and Christian-Claus Baer, "Vom Volksbegehren zum Wahlgesetz," [1950], DLA A:Sternberger/ Wählergesellschaft/ 89.10.10734; "Daten über die Entwicklung der Wählergesellschaft."

[91] Sternberger, "Aktionsgruppe Radio Stuttgart Interview."

[92] Hartmann, "Vorstandssitzung vom 26.9.47," 27 September 1947, DLA A:Sternberger/ Wählergesellschaft/ 89.10.10945; Hartmann, "Rundschreiben über Bildung und Arbeit

subsequently set for the collaboration of local associations in regional ones to coordinate state-level actions, such as the referendum petition in Hesse, but the board insisted that local associations remained the organization's "cornerstones."[93] This pyramidal structure manifested an underlying popular impulse, building local nodes of activity into a German public outside mainstream political institutions whose legitimacy they questioned.

These deeper affinities are unsurprising, given that the same circles of engaged democrats stood behind both groups. In their ideas about democracy and in their modes of mobilization, they conceived political and social order from the bottom up, grounded in widespread local self-organization. In this aspect, their vision bore just as strong an affinity for radical-democratic traditions as for liberal-notable ones. In fact, this was a conscious filiation. Not for nothing did Sternberger liken their interest in a democracy beyond parties – indeed, in a "democracy without parties" – to "the original soviet council conception," before it devolved into "single-party dictatorship."[94] In this mode, their concern was less to influence public opinion from above than to begin building a postwar German public in the first place, from below. Theirs was a vision of civil society, but in a decidedly grassroots and active, self-governing rather than self-regulating vein. It bore the hallmark of a peculiarly popular, public politics from the immediate postwar moment.

### Elitist retrenchments in the Cold War

Such was their stance in the 1946–7 conjuncture, soon transformed by Cold War confrontation. First, ideological polarization rendered the kinds of independent and neutralist positions around which they mobilized far less tenable, at least in public. Second, concrete moves were made that heralded the foundation of two separate German states. As a result, an even more urgent tone entered engaged democrats' discussions, while their efforts to open spaces for intra-German public deliberation gave way to attempts at direct influence on Allied and German officials.

---

örtlicher Vereinigungen," 7 October 1947, DLA A:Sternberger/ Wählergesellschaft/ 89.10.10922; "Vorstandssitzung der Deutschen Wählergesellschaft am 3.11.1947 in Heidelberg," n.d., DLA A:Sternberger/ Wählergesellschaft/ 89.10.10945. That "local associations" would be the primary venues of activity was announced already in the founding call; "Aufruf zur Bildung der Deutschen Wählergesellschaft."

[93] Emil Walk, "Über die Bildung und die Tätigkeit von Landesgemeinschaften," 19 March 1948, DLA A:Sternberger/ Wählergesellschaft/ 89.10.10944.

[94] Sternberger, "Skizze des langfristigen Studienprogramms," 2 October 1947, DLA A:Sternberger/ Wählergesellschaft/ 89.10.10759.

These interrelated dynamics encouraged a return to the more conventional intellectual politics of small, closed discussion circles and personal lobbying, marking a reversion from a more popular to a more elitist orientation.

This is not to suggest that discussion circles were strictly a function of Cold War polarization. Rather, private or quasi-public conversations remained a widespread mode of intellectual sociability after 1945, also as the germs of other activities. While engaged democrats, for their part, soon sought to transcend the bounds of a dialogue among elites, such efforts also coexisted with smaller-scale, more exclusive projects. As discussions began over Hesse's constitution, for instance, the group around the *Frankfurter Hefte* called together a number of "political friends" – fellow CDP founders, local journalists, and officials – that came to be called the Oberursel Circle, after the Frankfurt suburb where they convened during the second half of 1946. Their intent was to "trade perspectives and experiences" but also "to prepare or exert certain influences on politics and the press." Given the circle's makeup, this seemed a reasonable goal; Hilpert, after all, was deputy chair of the preparatory committee for the constitutional assembly. In Kogon's estimation, they effectively drafted what became the most radical articles of the Hessian constitution, the "duty to resist" – which established citizens' obligation to act against unconstitutional exercises of state power – as well as a whole roster of socio-economic provisions on land reform, labor rights, and socialization.[95] Despite the intermingling of more and less public forms of mobilization, however, a trajectory from the former to the latter was common among engaged democrats.

The transition to overt superpower confrontation between 1947 and 1948 had far-reaching consequences within Germany, and its ripple effects shaped the further development of the Aktionsgruppe. As inter-Allied and intra-German cooperation broke down, steps were taken toward a separate West German state, and officials in the Soviet zone launched a propaganda offensive for national "unity" that culminated in the German People's Congress for Unity and a Just Peace, a "movement" involving delegates from all parties and zones but orchestrated by the SED. Many Germans in both eastern and western zones,

---

[95] Kogon, "Betr.: Donnerstag-Zusammenkünfte in Oberursel," 18 May 1946, AdsD NL Dirks 356; Kogon, *Leben*, 87–8; Mühlhausen, *Hessen*, 232–3; Helmut Berding, ed. *Die Entstehung der hessischen Verfassung von 1946: Eine Dokumentation* (Wiesbaden: Historische Kommission für Nassau, 1996). Besides Dirks, Hilpert, Knappstein, Kogon, and Münster, the circle included Josef Arndgen and Valentin Siebrecht (Hessian officials who also wrote for the *Frankfurter Hefte*) and Hugo Stenzel and Marcel Schulte (of the *Frankfurter Neue Presse*).

however, independently raised concerns over the absence of any "national representation" to advocate forcefully Germans' own desire for unity. The efforts of Jakob Kaiser – co-chair of the CDU in Berlin and the Soviet zone until he was deposed for opposing the People's Congress – were only one high-profile project among many.[96] In this context, the Aktionsgruppe promulgated a manifesto for "unity" together with several prominent figures from "the East." The initiative proved highly controversial, and it generated such fallout that the Heidelbergers backed away from the limelight they had previously sought.

At the periphery of the Aktionsgruppe's October conference, Geiler, Weber, and Friedensburg decided to convene a small, suitably representative circle to discuss and draft a declaration of unity in advance of the Council of Foreign Ministers' upcoming meeting in London.[97] Of twenty invitees, twelve gathered in Berlin's Wannsee suburb on 9 November: seven men from Berlin, three from the American zone, and two from the Soviet zone, spanning all party-political camps. They included Johannes R. Becher and Brandenburg's Prime Minister (both SED), Paul Löbe (of the Berlin SPD), Saxony-Anhalt's Prime Minister (of the liberal LDPD), one CDU member from Frankfurt, and two of Friedensburg's CDU Berlin colleagues. Their manifesto presented the demand of "the German people" for its lost "unity," recognizing the latter as a crucial condition of peace "for itself, for Europe, [and] for the world." They cited Allied promises of unity as well as Germans' rights to unity, and they proposed concrete steps to achieve it: dissolving zonal borders, drafting a uniform occupation statute, and building all-German "central administrations," as had been agreed at Potsdam.[98] This "Call to German Unity" was addressed to the Allied Control Council and all four military governors. It was circulated to hundreds of politicians, academics, and journalists for support and widely publicized.[99] The Americans – initially skeptical – gave the manifesto a warm if officious response, and

---

[96] Kleßmann, *Staatsgründung*, 185–208; Gallus, *Neutralisten*, 57–61. On the consequences of this dynamic for cultural organizations, see Chapter 5.
[97] Geiler in Mugdan, ed. *Zur völkerrechtlichen Lage*, 41–2; Weber and Geiler, "Zu den 'Hintergründen der Friedensburgaktion' und der 'Rolle des Botschafters Nadolny'," n.d., UBH NL Weber, Box 3, Aufruf Berlin 10.XI.47. See also Demm, *Weimarer Republik*, 396–7; Gerhard Keiderling, *Um Deutschlands Einheit: Ferdinand Friedensburg und der Kalte Krieg in Berlin 1945–1952* (Cologne: Böhlau, 2009), 202–7; Friedensburg, *Es ging um Deutschlands Einheit: Rückschau eines Berliners auf die Jahre nach 1945* (Berlin: Haude & Spener, 1971), 176–94.
[98] The original is deposited as: "Aufruf," n.d., BArch N 1114/36, 10.
[99] "Liste der zur Unterschrift unter den Aufruf zur deutschen Einheit Aufgeforderten," n.d., UBH NL Weber, Box 3, Aufruf Berlin 10.XI.47; "Einheit Deutschlands: Ein Aufruf für London," *Rhein-Neckar-Zeitung*, 29 November 1947.

Subjects of politics: publicness, parties, elites 179

it elicited a courteous reply from the French.[100] Still, this independent German appeal had little hope of success. When the 2,225-member People's Congress dispatched a delegation from Berlin to London, they were not even granted entry visas, much less an audience with the ministers.

As a suture joining East and West, Berlin had seemed a logical venue in which to draft a declaration of German unity. It was also the center of the emergent ideological storm, whose pull they could not escape, as the aftermath revealed. The organizing role played by Friedensburg – a founding Kulturbund officer who was a key Soviet zone official before becoming a deputy mayor of greater Berlin – seemed to put the initiative firmly in the "Eastern" orbit. Backroom pressure from the CDU ensued, while SPD opposition was even more forceful.[101] The party's Hanover executive publicly condemned the "Friedensburg action" as an SED-inspired maneuver designed to strengthen the Soviet hand in London.[102] The SPD had no leverage over Weber, but it took punitive action against Löbe, arguably its most respected elder statesman, ejecting him from the foreign policy committee he chaired.[103] For a final layer of intrigue, it was suggested that the event's real organizer was Rudolf Nadolny, former ambassador to Moscow, acting at Soviet behest.[104] Geiler and Weber countered with a series of rebuttals, insisting that the initiative for the plan had come from them, that Friedensburg had been responsible only for logistics, and that Nadolny – a distant acquaintance of Weber's – had been completely uninvolved.[105] The controversy was damaging,

---

[100] The Office of Military Government, Berlin Sector (OMGBS) authorized the meeting only reluctantly; "Vermerk," 1 November 1947, "Aktenvermerk," 5 November 1947, BArch N 1114/34, 320–1. For the official responses, see GMZFO to Friedensburg, 13 December 1947, OMGUS/CAD to Friedensburg, 27 December 1947, UBH NL Weber, Box 3, Aktionsgruppe Februar 48.

[101] Geiler to Weber, 19 November 1947, Friedensburg to Weber, 21 November 1947, UBH NL Weber, Box 3, Aufruf Berlin 10.XI.47. Intra-party pressures may well have played a role in the absences of Hans Ehard (CSU), Hermann Lüdemann (SPD), and Schmid; all three had been invited. Friedensburg to Ehard, Lüdemann, and Schmid, 25 October 1947, BArch N 1114/26, 59.

[102] "Vom Vorstand der Sozialdemokratischen Partei Deutschlands wird mitgeteilt," 3 November 1947, UBH NL Weber, Box 3, Aufruf Berlin 10.XI.47; Friedensburg, *Deutschlands Einheit*, 180–1.

[103] Fritz Heine to Weber, 3 November 1947, UBH NL Weber, Box 3, Aufruf Berlin 10.XI.47; Friedensburg, *Deutschlands Einheit*, 193. Löbe then distanced himself from the initiative, though he insisted he had come away looking better than his dogmatic party leadership; Paul Löbe to Weber, 11 December 1947, UBH NL Weber, Box 3, Aktionsgruppe Februar 48.

[104] "Die Rolle Botschafter Nadolnys: Hintergründe der Friedensburg-Aktion," *Die Welt*, 6 December 1947. On Nadolny, see Gallus, *Neutralisten*, 146–8.

[105] "Aufruf für London vorbereitet," *Der Telegraf*, 11 November 1947; "Zu den 'Hintergründen der Friedensburgaktion' und der 'Rolle des Botschafters Nadolny'," *Telegraf*, 13 December 1947; "Noch einmal: 'Freidensburg-Aktion'," *Die Welt*,

however. Friedrich von Prittwitz und Gaffron, a former ambassador to the USA based in Bavaria who had undertaken a parallel effort, asserted that any such project launched in Berlin clearly begged "misinterpretations" that were well-nigh "unavoidable." In the event, "an operation by many became, for the public, an Operation Friedensburg," and the ensuing "fuss and bother spoiled everything" for similar undertakings elsewhere.[106]

The organizers emerged chastened, which had significant consequences for the Aktionsgruppe's subsequent relationship to publicity. The group remained committed to constructive activity, albeit only via a "closed gathering" in Heidelberg, "not as a continuation of the Berlin conference." Even the question of "whether it would be correct to approach the public" with future resolutions would have to be considered case by case; for the time being, it seemed prudent to keep "everything absolutely confidential." A small-group discussion was scheduled for February 1948 under Aktionsgruppe auspices, and politicians from the eastern zone and Berlin including Kaiser and Löbe were among the invited. As Weber reassured Löbe, this conversation would be "closed" and "inconspicuous," held "without notifying or attracting the press." They had learned from the Berlin effort's mistakes: "too much uninhibitedness vis-à-vis the public."[107] These words announced a significant shift. The Aktionsgruppe's early view of itself as an integral element of a German public-in-formation gave way to a view of the public as something external, which they might choose to approach as they saw fit and as conditions required. And they would think twice about doing even that.

The February meeting continued what was now a defensive and losing battle against Germany's division. As in the past, organizers invited a mix of journalists, academics, and politicians, but with heavier emphasis on the latter and without inviting SED members. Given the recent controversy, Weber took the extraordinary step of urging Friedensburg not to accept his invitation because his participation might lead others to

---

16 December 1947. Weber and Geiler downplayed Friedensburg's role in their zeal to salvage the initiative. Initial conversations had indeed taken place between Geiler and Friedensburg; Geiler to Weber, 2 September 1947, UBH NL Weber, Box 3, Aktionsgruppe, Oktober-Tagung.

[106] Friedrich von Prittwitz to Weber, 26 November 1947, UBH NL Weber, Box 3, Aufruf Berlin 10.XI.47. Prittwitz had attempted to join forces with the Heidelbergers before the Berlin meeting; Heinrich von Brentano to Sternberger, 18 October 1947, Sternberger to Weber, 24 October 1947, DLA A:Sternberger/ Aktionsgruppe/ 89.10.8112.

[107] Weber to Friedensburg, 10 January 1948, UBH NL Weber, Box 3, Aktionsgruppe Februar 48; Weber to Löbe, 17 January 1948, AdsD NL Löbe 30.

decline. Ultimately, Friedensburg came.[108] This seems to have kept some Berliners away, while others encountered transportation and scheduling difficulties. Neither Löbe nor Kaiser attended.[109] On the agenda were options for currency reform, widely recognized as necessary to economic recovery, and the question of what proactive steps could be taken "in the interest of German unity." On the latter point, proposed measures included replicating the Anglo-American Bizone's administrative organs in Berlin, to strengthen the capital as one of the few remaining "brackets of cohesion" for all of Germany, as well as immediate and direct elections to an all-German constitutional assembly.[110] The adopted resolution, however, only advocated in very general terms retaining a single currency and passing a uniform occupation statute – one that clearly delineated rights and duties of occupiers and occupied and specifically guaranteed "general human rights of personal freedom and legal security" to the German population, in the Aktionsgruppe's first oblique expression of concern over conditions in the Soviet zone.[111] The fruit of their labors was publicized neither to Germans nor occupiers, and the meeting faded into obscurity.

In 1948, these Heidelbergers convened no large, public meetings, nor did they pursue plans to let similar groups bloom all across Germany. Instead, they held closed, small-group discussions. In place of press campaigns and petitions, they emphasized personal lobbying of politicians. Moreover, they pulled back from their comprehensive renewal agenda to address specific aspects of what they hoped would be temporary West German institutions. In this, they responded to a cascade

---

[108] "Einstweilige Liste der Eingeladenen," n.d., Weber to Friedensburg, 4 February 1948, Friedensburg to Weber, 12 February 1948, UBH NL Weber, Box 3, Aktionsgruppe Februar 48.
[109] Friedensburg's presence likely deterred Otto Suhr, Louise Schroeder, and Arno Scholz of the Berlin SPD. In an editorial, the pro-SPD *Telegraf* denounced Friedensburg's egotism. Regrets came on short notice from their colleagues Gert von Eynern, who denied any connection to Friedensburg, and Löbe, who cited the mounting disruptions of train travel from Berlin westward. Kaiser sent a regretful letter and a colleague in his stead. "Der reisende Bürgermeister," *Der Telegraf*, 27 February 1948; Gert von Eynern to Weber, 27 February 1948, Löbe to Weber, 12 February 1948, Jakob Kaiser to Weber, 25 February 1948, UBH NL Weber, Box 3, Aktionsgruppe Februar 48.
[110] "Tagesordnung für die Aussprache am 28. und 29. Februar 1948," n.d., UBH NL Weber, Box 3, Aktionsgruppe Februar 48; Mommsen, "Verlegung westlicher Verwaltungsorgane nach Berlin?" n.d., DLA A:Sternberger/ Aktionsgruppe/ 89.10.8132; Geiler, "Ein Vorschlag für eine deutsche Aktion zur Erlangung der deutschen Einheit," n.d., "Erklärung," n.d., UBH NL Weber, Box 3, Aktionsgruppe Februar 48.
[111] "I. Besatzungsrecht / II. Wirtschaftliche Einheit" (printed flyer), n.d., UBH NL Weber, Box 3, Aktionsgruppe Februar 48. Anti-Communism became one key postwar use of "human rights" language; Lora Wildenthal, *The Language of Human Rights in West Germany* (Philadelphia: University of Pennsylvania Press, 2013), esp. 10–11.

of events that began when the three Western Allies set the framework for a separate West German state in February 1948 and ended with the promulgation of a constitution, the so-called Basic Law, in May 1949.[112] Trying to shape this outcome on their own terms, the Aktionsgruppe and Wählergesellschaft urged that the delegates entrusted with drafting the provisional "statute" (as opposed to "constitution") not be selected by what they derisively termed "super-proportionality": proportional appointment by state assemblies that were themselves elected proportionally.[113] Such a crucial moment demanded a direct general election instead, lest the "democratic hopes of the people" be violated. Their declaration went to the western Prime Ministers – who were charged with convening the assembly – as well as to parliamentary and party leaders, military governors, and the press.[114] It was, however, disregarded. Each state sent party-appointed, proportionally distributed delegates, the aggregate of which split the 65-seat Parliamentary Council largely between CDU/CSU and SPD (27 each), with five liberals and two each from the Catholic Center, Deutsche Partei, and rump KPD. This body convened in Bonn in September 1948 to draft the de facto constitution of the new FRG.[115]

The Aktionsgruppe and Wählergesellschaft attempted to influence two key aspects of those deliberations, mainly via direct contact with delegates. For its part, the Wählergesellschaft mobilized to enshrine majority elections as the law of the land. In a July resolution, they urged that the Basic Law and companion Electoral Law be submitted to popular referenda for ratification, restating their claim that majority elections would ensure that representatives act as the "delegates" of constituents and thereby foster "a true democracy that derives from the people."[116] They also provided the Parliamentary Council with draft legislation, provoking a counterproposal from Jellinek – a proponent of modified

---

[112] Benz, *Auftrag Demokratie*, 325–419; Michael Feldkamp, *Der Parlamentarische Rat 1948–1949: Die Entstehung des Grundgesetzes* (Göttingen: Vandenhoeck & Ruprecht, 1998).

[113] See, e.g., Hartmann to Sternberger, 31 May 1948, DLA A:Sternberger/ Wählergesellschaft/ 89.10.10780.

[114] An initial telegram was followed by a more formal statement issued jointly by the Aktionsgruppe and the Wählergesellschaft. "Telegramm an die Konferenz der Ministerpräsidenten in Frankfurt," [14 June 1948], DLA A:Sternberger/ Aktionsgruppe/ 89.10.8119/3; "An die Ministerpräsidenten der Westzonen etc.," 5 July 1948, DLA A:Sternberger/ Aktionsgruppe/ 89.10.8111; list of recipients, n.d., Schneider to all Landtagspräsidenten, 6 July 1948, Sternberger to Bruno Dörpinghaus, Ernst Mayer, and Erich Ollenhauer, 6 July 1948, DLA A:Sternberger/ Wählergesellschaft/ 89.10.10941.

[115] Feldkamp, *Der Parlamentarische Rat*, 36–7.

[116] Text of the "Homburger Resolution": n.t., 17 July 1948, DLA A:Sternberger/ Wählergesellschaft/ 89.10.10941.

proportional representation – that elicited a rebuttal in turn. In October, the Wählergesellschaft parlayed a personal connection to the Committee on Electoral Law into an audience at one of its sessions. A small delegation including Walk, Hartmann, and Mommsen presented their positions. (Sternberger was on study tour in the USA.)[117] They followed up with another mailing and "New Year's Greeting" to the entire Parliamentary Council. Therein, they contrasted the "truly democratic mandate" of direct election to the anonymity of mandates conferred by proportionality and "party bureaucracies." Rejecting the claim that "the German people are not yet mature enough for a strong democracy," they asked instead whether politicians felt secure enough to succeed without "the crutch of an officious party list."[118] Rather than fear majority elections, democratic elites should embrace the direct popular mandate these conferred.

Despite their efforts, the tide of opinion was shifting in the opposite direction. The SPD had always been the standard-bearer for proportional representation, while most of the CDU backed the majority system. A potential consensus emerged, however, around a compromise that blended direct and indirect voting while retaining proportionality in the assembly's overall composition (Jellinek's core innovation).[119] For the Wählergesellschaft, this merely grafted a personalizing veneer onto a flawed system, and they again raised their "primordially democratic demand" for a referendum on majority versus proportionality. The campaign culminated in a rally at Frankfurt's Paulskirche, under the polemical banner, "Is a Democratic Germany Being Born in Bonn?"[120] They pursued the referendum itself, however, not by popular petition but by enlisting the CDU to introduce it as a motion. Even referenda, which

---

[117] Wählergesellschaft Political Bureau to Executive Committee members, 1 September 1948, DLA A:Sternberger/ Wählergesellschaft/ 89.10.10944; Walter Jellinek, "An den Parlamentarischen Rat," 14 September 1948, "Stellungnahme der Deutschen Wählergesellschaft zum Schreiben des Herrn Prof. Jellinek an den Parlamentarischen Rat," 6 October 1948, A:Sternberger/Wählergesellschaft/ 89.10.10919; Harald Rosenbach, ed. *Der Parlamentarische Rat 1948–1949: Akten und Protokolle*, vol. VI, *Ausschuss für Wahlrechtsfragen* (Boppard a.R.: Boldt, 1994), 246–74.

[118] Mommsen and Walk to the members of the Parliamentary Council, 23 October 1948, "Warum Mehrheitswahl für das Deutsche Parlament?" 23 October 1948, DLA A:Sternberger/ Wählergesellschaft/ 89.10.10759; "Offener Neujahrsgruß der Deutschen Wählergesellschaft an die Mitglieder des Parlamentarischen Rates," 27 December 1948, DLA A:Sternberger/ Wählergesellschaft/ 89.10.10944.

[119] Feldkamp, *Der Parlamentarische Rat*, 84–93; Lange, *Wahlrecht*, 317, 329–408, 768.

[120] See the printed resolution, press release, and published speeches: "Resolution," 4 February 1949, n.t., 23 February 1949, DLA A:Sternberger/Wählergesellschaft/ 89.10.10919; Karl Geiler et al., *Das Wählen und das Regieren: Das Problem der parlamentarischen Demokratie* (Darmstadt: Deutsche Wählergesellschaft, 1949).

they once touted as key vehicles for the extra-institutional expression of popular will, were now sidelined in favor of direct contact with decision makers. Brentano, a Parliamentary Council member, played a key role in this effort.[121] It too failed, and the aforementioned compromise became the basis of West German electoral law.[122] The Wählergesellschaft's other demand, that the Basic Law itself be submitted to referendum, fared no better. After the constitution's ratification by the state assemblies, Brentano wrote Sternberger of his regret that he had been unable to secure sufficient support on either issue.[123] But it was the shift in the form of their interventions that most troubled Sternberger's colleague Hartmann. Initially, they had sought to "work in the broader public," a foundational commitment manifest in their dedication to locally based activities, petitions, and the like, while recently, they had focused on "winning over leading party personalities." This only reproduced the "politics behind closed doors" that had been the target of their critique, he charged.[124]

While the Wählergesellschaft focused on electoral issues, the Aktionsgruppe turned to provisions regarding the media. In October 1948, they were approached by a circle of "former publishers" around Walther Jänecke to convene a discussion on press freedom. The Aktionsgruppe agreed, seeing an opportunity to reprise their interventions from the press legislation debates in a new context, with an eye to the occupation statute and forthcoming Basic Law. They invited some 100 guests – primarily publishers, editors, and journalists – to a meeting in late November. Sternberger set the overall framework with his conception of a positive "freedom of information" as the "centerpiece of press freedom."[125] He was followed by Jänecke, whose calls for an end to licensing and censorship and a return to "clear responsibility" and "transparent ownership

---

[121] Brentano to Sternberger, 2 January 1949, 8 February 1949, 23 April 1949, Sternberger to Brentano, 27 January 1949, 21 April 1949, DLA A:Sternberger/ Wählergesellschaft/ 89.10.10958.

[122] This novel procedure is known to political science as the "mixed member proportional" electoral system; David M. Farrell, *Electoral Systems: A Comparative Introduction* (Basingstoke: Palgrave, 2001), 97–120.

[123] Brentano to Sternberger, 22 May 1949, DLA A: Sternberger/Wählergesellschaft/ 89.10.10958.

[124] Hartmann, "Notiz für den Vorstand," 25 October 1948, DLA A:Sternberger/ Wählergesellschaft/ 89.10.10944.

[125] Weber to Klabunde, 22 October 1948, Weber to Schmid, 23 October 1948, 14 November 1948, Schneider, "Die Zukunft der deutschen Presse," n.d., UBH NL Weber, Box 3, Aktionsgruppe 26.XI.48 Pressefragen; "Leitsätze für ein Pressegesetz: Denkschrift der Aktionsgruppe Heidelberg," *Die Wandlung* 4, enclosure to no. 4 (1949), 1–2. The group's invitations now used a new letterhead identifying it simply as the Aktionsgruppe Heidelberg, without expressing commitments to "democracy and free socialism."

relations" were both conventional and clearly self-serving.[126] Wary of being identified with the interests of Jänecke and his group, the organizers balanced his contribution with another by Erich Klabunde, journalist and chair of the Hamburg SPD. Klabunde outlined a proposal to retain limited licensing and collectivize newspapers as non-profit enterprises in order to eliminate the distorting effects of "capitalist influences" on the press.[127] While the meeting as a whole did not pursue Klabunde's socialist restructuring, neither did it endorse Jänecke's liberal deregulation.

In keeping with Sternberger's framing, they put the issue differently: as a question of the public dialogue they considered crucial to democracy. A small commission – Knappstein, Kogon, Sternberger, and Ernst Walz – drafted a proposed constitutional article, which received other participants' unanimous support. It asserted a "right to information" for the press and a reciprocal "duty to inform" for authorities, because only access to information as "continuous and as extensive as possible enables the citizen to form (*bilden*) an opinion for themselves." They argued that these positive rights and duties were, in principle, no less a matter of constitutional law than was a negative freedom of expression.[128] Again, their proposal was heard by dint of a personal connection: ex-publisher Lambert Lensing (CDU), present at the Aktionsgruppe-sponsored meeting, also sat on the relevant Parliamentary Council committee, and he facilitated contact with its chairperson. And again, their suggestion was rejected, on the grounds that a freedom of information was too specialized for the constitutional catalog of basic rights and was best addressed in a future press law.[129] Although this was the Aktionsgruppe's last formal submission to the Parliamentary Council, personal connections between members persisted, leading to a final small-group discussion in July 1949. On the agenda were general reflections on the constitutional

---

[126] Compare the statement circulated by Jänecke's group: Arbeitsgemeinschaft für Pressefragen, "Pressefreiheit und Demokratie," n.d., UBH NL Weber, Box 3, Aktionsgruppe 26.XI.48 Pressefragen. In the western zones, unlicensed publishers had retained ownership but not control of their facilities. These were used to print licensed media, for which owners received leasing fees deposited into locked accounts. Koszyk, *Pressepolitik*, 74–116, 130–1, 135.

[127] Klabunde to Weber, 28 October 1948, Weber to Klabunde, 14 November 1948, UBH NL Weber, Box 3, Aktionsgruppe 26.XI.48 Pressefragen.

[128] "Vorschlag der Heidelberger Aktionsgruppe für einen Verfassungsartikel über das Informationsrecht," n.d., UBH NL Weber, Box 3, Aktionsgruppe 26.XI.48 Pressefragen.

[129] Sternberger to Hermann von Mangoldt, 27 November 1948, Mangoldt to Sternberger, 6 December 1948, UBH NL Weber, Box 3, Aktionsgruppe 26.XI.48 Pressefragen; Eberhard Pikart and Wolfram Werner, eds. *Der Parlamentarische Rat 1948–1949: Akten und Protokolle*, vol. V, *Ausschuss für Grundsatzfragen* (Boppard a.R.: Boldt, 1993), 766–8.

deliberations, delivered by leading lights from the two largest parties, Brentano and Schmid.[130]

As these Heidelberg-based activities highlight, a persistent tension between elitist and popular moments characterized engaged democrats' practical interventions. Under pressure, they readily reverted to the former mode. Still, their principled commitment to publicness led to misgiving about such accommodations, which are clearest in contrast with Germany's right-intellectuals. In the same period, figures such as Carl Schmitt, Martin Heidegger, and Ernst and Friedrich Georg Jünger preferred to dialogue "in the security of silence." Ensconced amid devotees and disciples, they convened "esoteric communication circles" at their provincial retreats that served a double strategy of self-preservation and self-assertion. There, they cultivated both aristocratic ideas and a resolutely private style, forming a counter-public disdainful of publicness in principle.[131] And it was precisely this divergence that made engaged democrats uneasy when their paths crossed.

In the autumn of 1945, the Margrave of Baden held a gathering at his estate in Salem, near Lake Constance. Before this "small circle," Friedrich Georg Jünger read aloud Ernst Jünger's illicit manuscript *The Peace*, approaching the event itself as an initial step toward implementing the project his brother's pamphlet proposed: "to gather and unify European elites." Mitscherlich, their old acquaintance, was among the guests. As another guest later recalled: "I can only say he exploded. The distinctive Jüngerian manner, which did not conceive the new order from the perspective of human emancipation but rather intended for an elite to ordain it from above, outraged Mitscherlich"; it was an affront to his "passionately democratic" character.[132] Indeed, in their subsequent correspondence, Mitscherlich took Ernst Jünger to task precisely for his inability to recognize the emancipatory potential in Europe's traditions of popular politics, protest, and revolt, in the French Revolution, socialism, and the left as a whole. "It's not as though humane existence begins in some aristocratic elites," he chided his erstwhile father figure. This

---

[130] See the invitation: Schneider, n.t., n.d., UBH NL Weber, Box 3, Aktionsgruppe Nov. 49 und April 50; Brentano, "Schlechte Voraussetzungen – erträgliche Lösungen," *Die Wandlung* 4, no. 7 (1949): 646–52; Schmid, "Rückblick auf die Verhandlungen," *Die Wandlung* 4, no. 7 (1949): 652–69.

[131] Laak, *Gespräche*, here 33, 127; Daniel Morat, *Von der Tat zur Gelassenheit: Konservatives Denken bei Martin Heidegger, Ernst Jünger und Friedrich Georg Jünger 1920–1960* (Göttingen: Wallstein, 2007), 314–60, quote 350.

[132] Friedrich Georg Jünger to Ernst Jünger, 6 October 1945, quoted in Morat, *Von der Tat*, 333; see also ibid., 351–2; Hellmut Becker, "Freiheit, Sozialismus, Psychoanalyse: Anmerkungen zu Begegnungen mit Alexander Mitscherlich von einem Nichtanalysierten," *Merkur* 32 (1978): 923–4.

was the climax of Mitscherlich's long turn away from Jünger (and Ernst Niekisch), one that had emotional as well as reflective components.[133] For by 1945, his radicalism had broken decisively with Jünger's. According to the latter, the problem with Nazism in power had been not a deficit but a surfeit of democracy: "the *demos* is its own tyrant," as his wartime epigram had it.[134] Meanwhile, Mitscherlich's antifascism had come to express itself in the opposite impulse, radicalizing the democratic principle Jünger scorned. It is unlikely that the affinity between the content and the form of the 1945 reading of *The Peace* were lost on Mitscherlich, who attended no further such gatherings. Instead, he helped build the Aktionsgruppe from its face-to-face foundation into a self-consciously public endeavor.

A related dynamic played out in Dirks' relationship to similarly exclusive gatherings that he himself had a hand in organizing. In late 1946, he helped Frankfurt's new mayor Walter Kolb (SPD) approach a number of public figures with an invitation to convene in private, for "round table" discussions "at a certain fruitful remove" from the "wrangling" of everyday politics. Working with Dirks was his recent acquaintance Werner von Trott, personal assistant to Prime Minister Geiler. Among the invited were Kogon and Knappstein as well as Hilpert and Wilhelm Knothe, chairs of the Hessian CDU and SPD. The group's aim was to address concrete aspects of socio-political order under a rubric that echoed Dirks' political conception: how the "young German democracy" might successfully unite the "true conservatives and true revolutionaries, the radical Christians and radical socialists," so as to form a robust coalition of progressive forces, not a tepid *juste milieu*. In such a circle, Dirks underscored, they would "not come together 'officially'... as party representatives, but rather privately... and in common concern for the general good."[135] Here, their self-conception resonated with that of the Aktionsgruppe, which saw itself – in the first instance – as a grouping of private people gathered to consider matters of public concern, beyond the fronts of party politics. Unlike the Aktionsgruppe, however, this was a fundamentally inward- not outward-looking configuration.

---

[133] Mitscherlich to Ernst Jünger, 21 May 1946, quoted in Dehli, *Leben*, 79; see ibid., 72–80.

[134] Ernst Jünger, *Blätter und Steine*, 2nd edn. (Hamburg: Hanseatische Verlagsanstalt, 1941), 221. On Jünger's interpretation of Nazism and its influence on his brother and Heidegger, see Morat, *Von der Tat*, 205–45.

[135] Dirks to Werner von Trott, 28 October 1946, handwritten list of invitees, n.d., "Gespräch am 12. November 1946 im Hause des Herrn Oberbürgermeister Kolb," n.d., Dirks to Werner Hilpert, 13 December 1946, AdsD NL Dirks 353.

188  German Intellectuals and Democratic Renewal

It is unclear how long these discussions continued, but they were a prelude to those of the Imshausen Society. That enterprise, of which Werner von Trott was the driving force, developed in a direction quite contrary to the Aktionsgruppe's orientation.[136] Together with Wilhelm Kütemeyer, a Heidelberg doctor with ties to *Die Wandlung*, as well as Dirks and Kogon, Werner von Trott and his brother Heinrich invited small, fluid groups of writers, civil servants, politicians, and clergy to the family estate at Imshausen in northern Hesse. The three meetings in August 1947, December 1947, and May 1948 grew in size from fewer than twenty to nearly fifty participants, all drawn from the organizers' extensive personal connections. Through their brother Adam von Trott, executed in 1944, the brothers had connections to the conservative resistance and the Kreisau Circle; Werner von Trott and Kütemeyer also had links to the Harnack/Schulze-Boysen network as well as to "national revolutionary" circles. Dirks and Kogon drew on their left-Catholic friends and their contacts in press, politics, and the Church. These constituencies were all well represented among the guests, who included Knappstein and Kantorowicz (Werner von Trott's old friend) as well as Alfred Andersch and Erich Kuby of *Der Ruf*. Werner Krauss, Hans Mayer, Benno Reifenberg, and Carlo Schmid were among those who were invited but did not attend. This was true of the Jünger brothers as well; Niekisch, in contrast, played a visible part. Prominent German politicians and officials attended, and OMGUS sent representatives from Berlin.[137] The organizers' aim was to bring together leading personalities from all political camps to debate the German situation and counteract East–West polarization, for the sake of the nation's future.

The idea was fundamentally Werner von Trott's, and his inspiration was the anti-Nazi resistance, which gave the Imshausen Society a conspiratorial imprint. Trott was convinced that "democracy was not rooted in the natural will of the [German] people," who had been "made immature" by centuries of authoritarian rule; rather, its possibility resided only "in that absurdly small minority who actively resisted Hitler." The "decisive question" was how to gather this "democratic elite" and ensure their recognition by the occupiers as postwar Germany's natural leaders, the true "bearers of the state."[138] His views shaped both substance and

---

[136] See Wolfgang Schwiedrzik, *Träume der ersten Stunde: Die Gesellschaft Imshausen* (Berlin: Siedler, 1991). Dirks and von Trott had discussed possibilities for a "political institute" at Imshausen since mid 1946, a project likely related to their activities with Kolb; cf. ibid., 25–6.
[137] Ibid., 17–20, 26–30, 74–6, 109–11, 144, 153–7.
[138] Werner von Trott zu Solz, "Protokoll über die erste Zusammenkunft der Gesellschaft Imshausen vom 19. bis 21. August 1947," in *Der Untergang des Vaterlandes: Dokumente*

style of the Imshausen project. Trott saw no paradox in the quest for a "democratic elite," but it seems Dirks did. In his presentation on "socialization as self-management," Dirks argued within the Imshausen idiom for the importance of a "socialist elite" with expertise in state planning. Yet he quickly insisted that this stratum "may not glorify its function" or arrogate "absolute power" to itself. Planning was only one aspect of a "pluralist" socialization that had to be completed "in the structure of production itself, as collectivization in many forms," with "the assumption of graded levels of responsibility" by all actors. People could realize their responsibility and the "concrete freedom" it entailed "only by practicing it, by 'being thrown in the water.'" Activity at a whole range of "practice sites" for such responsible freedom – at work and in other arenas of a cooperatively reorganized social life – would make a "broad elite" of the entire laboring population.[139] Expanding the initial notion of an elite beyond recognition, Dirks transformed an elitist into a counter-elitist position.[140] Although the question of the masses' maturity represented the signal problem of the age, Dirks located its solution in institutions for the masses' practical, participatory self-development, not in the tutelage of self-appointed superiors.

Questions of elitism notwithstanding, it was the far more overt tensions of the Cold War on which the Imshausen project ran aground. The latent antagonism between "East" and "West" was vividly manifest at the third gathering in May 1948. There, heated debates between partisans of each side drew Kantorowicz and Kogon into polemical exchanges, behind which their visions of Germany's mediating path receded. The spark was Niekisch's pleas for Germany's "East-orientation," to which Kantorowicz lent measured support and which Kogon vigorously opposed. The polarized atmosphere was only exacerbated by an American officer's interjection that Germans and Europeans would do well to avoid "illusions" about the possibility of a third way between socialism and capitalism. The meeting ended in a failure to generate either potential solutions or even

---

*und Aufsätze* (Olten: Walter, 1965), 19. Trott spoke of "the resistance" in this role as early as April 1945, to local military officials; Schwiedrzik, *Träume*, 21. As we have seen, Kogon's identification with the resistance was not coupled with von Trott's contempt for non-resisters, while Dirks was more circumspect altogether about his activities under Nazism.

[139] Dirks' address, "Sozialisierung als Selbstverwaltung," is preserved only in a summary of the proceedings compiled by Trott; "Zweite Tagung der Gesellschaft Imshausen vom 5.–8. Dezember 1947" (printed pamphlet), n.d., AdsD NL Dirks 360, 17–19.

[140] Schwiedrzik reads Dirks as endorsing Trott's elitism. But as he informs us, Dirks was coached by Trott regarding how to "frame" his talk in line with "the conference's total concept"; cf. Schwiedrzik, *Träume*, 89–90.

serious dialogue across ideological fronts. For his part, Kogon vowed never to return to Imshausen.[141]

Dirks distanced himself from the project as well, but for other reasons. As he later recalled, he found the strong emphasis on elite cultivation "a rather dangerous notion," citing it as "one of the reasons . . . why I eventually withdrew."[142] After the third meeting, an attempt was made to rally a small, dedicated cadre to redouble their own efforts and seek influence via personal contact with politicians. Dirks remained conspicuously absent, despite entreaties from the brothers Trott and Kütemeyer.[143] Although no direct record of the ensuing conversations remains, a response drafted by Dirks suggests his view of the basic issue. Over time, his commitment to the *Frankfurter Hefte* as his primary focus had come into conflict with the Trotts' view of the Imshausen Society as a "conspiratorial community" that demanded adherents' undivided loyalty. Not only did his co-organizers remain uninterested in his journalistic pursuits – so Dirks alleged – but they had always exhibited a "palpable disdain" for activities they deemed "confined to the political foreground." This revealing language juxtaposed two conflicting modes of intellectual intervention, one that privileged closed discussions and behind-the-scenes influence versus one that sought to engage and help constitute a more expansive public realm. Shortly thereafter, Dirks stepped down from the Imshausen Society's board, citing "differences of opinion on the path to be taken" and confirming his intent to pursue "another way to realize our common tasks."[144] In his ambivalent politics, the public moment again won out.

Engaged democrats' political interventions were thus shaped by the ways tensions internal to their democratic thinking played themselves out in practice and on the rapidly shifting terrain of the emerging Cold War. Under these dual influences, their activities developed along a general trajectory. Initially, they experimented with forms of intervention that corresponded to their participatory, counter-elitist views and moved deliberately outside mainstream institutions. These projects rested on a distinctive model of publicness, one that sought not to influence a public from outside or above, but to contribute to building one from below.

---

[141] Ibid., 163–74.
[142] "Gespräch mit Walter Dirks," in Schwiedrzik, *Träume*, 226–7. Schwiedrzik discounts this as post facto rationalization, referring instead to the long-discarded vanguardism of Dirks' May 1945 SEP proposal to assimilate Dirks' position to Trott's; cf. ibid., 35–8, 42, 89–90.
[143] Ibid., 176–7; Trott and Kütemeyer to Dirks, 18 August 1948, AdsD NL Dirks 360.
[144] Dirks to Heinrich von Trott, 1 September 1948 (unsent), Dirks to Werner von Trott, 14 September 1948, AdsD NL Dirks 360.

Moreover, this public's role was not conceived as a check on established power; rather, constitutive groupings of the public were seen as organs of political authority in their own right. By implication, they were the kernels of a spontaneously self-organizing and self-governing polity. Under Cold War pressures, engaged democrats often retreated to more conventional patterns, despite their own misgivings. Either way, their direct influence on immediate outcomes proved negligible, though the deliberative and participatory thrust of their theory and early practice had other afterlives.

Strikingly, the tension between elitist and popular moments in these mobilizations resolved itself consistently in the direction of a particular kind of journalistic engagement. The intellectuals addressed here repeatedly confirmed journalism as their primary sphere, recasting its relationship to the public as a dialogical rather than tutelary one. This pattern was common to eastern and western Germany, but conditions for non-journalistic undertakings varied significantly across the deepening divide. Given the powerfully centralizing course of developments in the eastern zone, even in the first postwar years, the scope and impetus for independent, local political initiatives was much more limited. There, engaged democrats' energies flowed more exclusively into organizations with a primarily cultural bent, the focus of the next chapter.

# 5 A parliament of spirit? Mobilizing the cultural nation

If Germany's engaged democrats tended away from politics per se, they embraced more informal modes of public intervention. In their writerly activities they also mobilized in ways that went beyond producing texts. Reviving an institutional tradition they had kept alive in exile, a number of them helped establish writers' associations after the war, a project that had as much to do with the intersections of culture and politics as with mutual aid and professional organization. A second, more important venue was a series of new cultural groups, associations that were broader in both basis and mandate and bound up with distinctively postwar dynamics. Eventually, these two strands converged in a series of high-profile writers' congresses. These relatively distinct organizational activities all circled around one of engaged democrats' core concerns: the relevance of German culture and its correlate – the unity of the German cultural nation – for political renewal.

A strong affinity can be traced between intellectuals and the modern nation. In Europe, and then across Europe's global empires, the expansion of print media and literacy provided an infrastructure for the emergence and diffusion of nationalism, as the sense of belonging to a linguistically, culturally, or ethnically bounded, politically sovereign collectivity across actual differences and distances. Given the imaginary dimension of this process, it is unsurprising that intellectuals – as specialists for symbolic goods, language, and ideas – have played a pivotal role in the "articulation of the nation." In return, the modern figure of the intellectual has been shaped by this relationship to the nation, whose voice or conscience intellectuals often claim and are taken to represent.[1] The term "intellectual" itself was coined in 1898 – in both acclaim and opprobrium – during France's Dreyfus Affair, when the notion of speaking

---

[1] See, e.g., Ernest Gellner, *Nations and Nationalism* (Ithaca: Cornell University Press, 1983); Benedict Anderson, *Imagined Communities: Reflections on the Origin and Spread of Nationalism* (London: Verso, 1983); Ronald Grigor Suny and Michael D. Kennedy, eds. *Intellectuals and the Articulation of the Nation* (Ann Arbor: University of Michigan Press, 1999).

moral truth to political power established itself as a legitimate expression of nationhood on a field of contending claims.[2]

German-speaking Europe is no exception, where educated elites were preoccupied with defining the parameters of Germanness throughout the modern era. In the standard narrative, nineteenth-century German writers and their public forged a national identity around intertwined notions of language, *Kultur*, and the *Bildung* ideal they themselves embodied. Its force was sustained precisely by the tension between the cultural unity it asserted and the political multiplicity of extant German lands. National unification in 1871 appeared to dissolve this tension, as the new "state-based nation" reduced the "cultural nation's" salience. And in later decades, the self-consciously unpolitical stance of the educated bourgeoisie happily accommodated the politics of several expansionist regimes. This came to a halt with the defeat of 1945, which ended both Germany's far-flung empire and its effective statehood, thus revitalizing the older, compensatory cultural identity. After a brief yet widespread renaissance, the latter was again displaced, this time by the non- and post-national identifications that emerged in both postwar Germanys.[3] In this telling, the first years after the Second World War figure predominantly as a return to the cultural nationalism of the past. What that obscures, however, are the distinct strands within this development and the multiple, not always compatible valences of both "culture" and "nation" during this period. The convergences and divergences among them are crucial to understanding the politics of culture under occupation.

Germany's engaged democrats, for example, mobilized organizationally behind a distinctive understanding of "culture." They did not operate with narrow, static notions of culture as a realm distinct from the world or a stock of timeless goods and values. Rather, they took an expansive view of culture as process, paradigmatic of free human activity as such and thus also relevant to society and politics. This activist conception derived from their interpretation of the national cultural heritage, in which the tropes of *Kultur*, *Bildung*, and *Geist* signaled the possibility of a simultaneously self- and world-shaping form of freedom. As elements

---

[2] Christophe Charle, *Naissance des "intellectuels" 1880–1900* (Paris: Minuit, 1990). On the German reception, see Dietz Bering, *Die Intellektuellen: Geschichte eines Schimpfwortes* (Stuttgart: Klett-Cotta, 1978).

[3] Bernhard Giesen, *Intellectuals and the German Nation: Collective Identity in an Axial Age*, trans. Nicholas Levis and Amos Weisz (Cambridge: Cambridge University Press, 1998); also John Breuilly, "Nation and Nationalism in Modern German History," *Historical Journal* 33, no. 3 (1990): 659–75. On *Kulturnation* and *Staatsnation*, see M. Rainer Lepsius, "Nation und Nationalismus in Deutschland," in *Nationalismus in der Welt von heute*, ed. Heinrich A. Winkler (Göttingen: Vandenhoeck & Ruprecht, 1982), 12–27.

of a specifically German patrimony, these ideas took on a national tint. Indeed, engaged democrats' attachments to the cultural nation seemed to give them pause, and they coupled affirmations of German tradition and calls for German unity with professions of anti-nationalism and cosmopolitanism. Paradoxically, their recourse to the nation was predicated on a break with the national past that sought to recover its liberating political potentials from a disastrous political history.

This ambivalence was reflected in their projects, for which a novel type of organization – the so-called *Kulturbund*, or Cultural League – was the distinctive vehicle. They conceived this new form of intellectual association as neither an exclusive club nor a disciplined vanguard but rather a platform for the broadest possible social strata. In practice, these pursuits brought engaged democrats together with others who likewise affirmed the "cultural nation" but did so less equivocally. Such coalitions would have been unstable under the best circumstances; under Cold War pressures, they proved impossible to sustain. If, for engaged democrats, "culture" implied a duality of "unity" and "freedom," ideological polarization soon recast the meanings of these two key terms and drove a wedge between them. From late 1947, official voices in the Soviet zone staked out the ground of "unity" in response to the West's moves toward a separate peace, while the West highlighted the "freedom" that distinguished it from Bolshevism. Each side regarded the other's rhetoric with suspicion. Little room remained for attempts to sustain both moments, dooming the alliances engaged democrats had forged. Conversely, the possibility that they might be instrumentalized by one or the other side in the confrontation was also raised. The independent German path they sought between East and West soon foundered on the mutually reinforcing effects of internal tensions and external pressures.

These postwar intellectuals were not the first to explore organizational couplings of culture and politics. The socialist labor movement had long attempted to bring culture to the masses, and Social Democracy's temporary triumph after the Great War further invigorated its "worker culture" programs. Adopting a typically middle-class paternalism, these aimed primarily to ennoble the proletariat through access to high cultural goods.[4] The revolution of 1918/19 itself had called forth more radical movements, as expressionist artists and writers launched themselves into a politics of "activism." They were inspired by Heinrich Mann's 1911 manifesto "Spirit and Deed," a passionate but

---

[4] On the 1920s, see W. L. Guttsman, *Workers' Culture in Weimar Germany: Between Tradition and Commitment* (Oxford: Berg, 1990); Helmut Gruber, *Red Vienna: Experiment in Working-Class Culture, 1919–1934* (New York: Oxford University Press, 1991).

inconsistent plea for an intellectual aristocracy that would birth an egalitarian society. Amid short-lived council movements in cities such as Berlin and Munich, writers charted this voluntaristic course.[5] And in the unsettled Weimar Republic, this avant-gardism refracted in various directions, from Kurt Hiller's "logocratic" leftists within the *Weltbühne* milieu to the young conservatives around Hans Zehrer's *Die Tat*.[6]

In the later 1920s, writers' groups and associations emerged that more closely resembled their postwar counterparts in form. Pluralist organizations such as the liberal Protective Association of German Writers (Schutzverband Deutscher Schriftsteller, or SDS) and the left-leaning Gruppe 1925 rallied against censorship and for free expression. Meanwhile, ancillary party organizations such as the League of Proletarian-Revolutionary Writers and the Battle League for German Culture propagated a radical politicization of culture in opposed directions, at the behest of the KPD and NSDAP, respectively.[7] Most of the educated middle class opted out of such mobilizations (although the Battle League boasted a sizeable membership even before 1933), influenced by deep-seated dispositions that still opposed culture to politics and society. But they shared with their activist peers the pretention that a special connection to "culture" legitimated them to lead, educate, or despise the population at large. This conventional conception of culture and its endemic elitism became the objects of some concerted wrangling by Germany's engaged democrats after 1945.

## Kulturbund, Berlin and elsewhere

Across occupied Germany, intellectuals broadly construed – writers, artists, students, teachers, clergy, professors, journalists, politicians, and some trade unionists – came together around the conviction that the renewal of German culture was a key element and possibly the lynchpin of democratic renewal itself. In the resulting burst of organizational activity,

---

[5] Heinrich Mann, "Geist und Tat," *Pan* 1, no. 5 (1911): 137–43. See, e.g., Britta Scheideler, "Kunst als Politik – Politik als Kunst: 'Literatenpolitik' in der Revolution 1918/19," in *Kritik und Mandat: Intellektuelle in der deutschen Politik*, ed. Gangolf Hübinger and Thomas Hertfelder (Stuttgart: Deutsche Verlags-Anstalt, 2000), 117–37.

[6] See, e.g., Alexandra Gerstner, *Neuer Adel: Aristokratische Elitekonzeptionen zwischen Jahrhundertwende und Nationalsozialismus* (Darmstadt: Wissenschaftliche Buchgesellschaft, 2008), 257–77, 421–63; Gangolf Hübinger, "Die Tat und der Tat-Kreis: Politische Entwürfe und intellektuelle Konstellationen," in *Le milieu intellectuel conservateur en Allemagne, sa presse et ses réseaux / Das konservative Intellektuellenmilieu in Deutschland, seine Presse und seine Netzwerke (1890–1960)*, ed. Michel Grunewald and Uwe Puschner (Bern: Lang, 2003), 407–26.

[7] Jost Hermand, *Die deutschen Dichterbünde: Von den Meistersingern bis zum PEN-Club* (Cologne: Böhlau, 1998), 209–31.

these firmly held yet fruitfully vague notions allowed for consensus across diverse constituencies. Groups sprouted in dozens of cities and towns, often taking as their inspiration the first and most prominent among them, Berlin's Kulturbund zur demokratischen Erneuerung Deutschlands (Cultural League for the Democratic Renewal of Germany).

The Berlin Kulturbund formed with much fanfare in the summer of 1945, months before similar groups elsewhere. It was fueled not only by enterprising Berliners but also by strong support from the Soviets, the city's sole occupying power at the time. The group's roots reached back into the Moscow exile. There, plans for cultural policy were laid by Johannes R. Becher and others, in German–Soviet discussions involving intellectuals and party leaders. By autumn 1944, they had in mind a cultural organization, modeled on ones that had sprung up among exiles in London and Mexico City. Through a publishing house, periodicals, and a full range of programming, it would mobilize Germany's educated strata in support of the German people's cultural-political reorientation. Strategically, it would eschew vanguardism for a broad, inclusive membership, but – as Becher stressed to his Moscow audience – on all decisive issues, it would orient itself toward the KPD and their Soviet patrons.[8] Shortly after his Initiative Group touched down in Germany, Walter Ulbricht wired to request that Becher be sent to join them. Back in Moscow, Wilhelm Pieck had drafted detailed plans for the organization by early June.[9]

Clearly, this Kulturbund must be seen as an integral element of plans for a Soviet and KPD-led "antifascist-democratic transformation." When Becher arrived in Berlin, however, he found compatible initiatives already underway. What became the Kulturbund emerged at the intersection of spontaneous local activity and pre-formed outside agendas.[10] Becher worked closely with fellow Moscow exiles Heinz Willmann and Fritz Erpenbeck, the Ulbricht Group's press officer. They operated out of a

---

[8] Participants included writers Fritz Erpenbeck, Theodor Plievier, Erich Weinert, and Friedrich Wolf alongside functionaries and party leaders Ulbricht, Pieck, Anton Ackermann, and Heinz Willmann; Jens Wehner, *Kulturpolitik und Volksfront: Ein Beitrag zur Geschichte der Sowjetischen Besatzungszone Deutschlands 1945–1949* (Frankfurt a.M.: Lang, 1992), 46–67.

[9] Magdalena Heider, *Politik – Kultur – Kulturbund: Zur Gründungs- und Frühgeschichte des Kulturbundes zur demokratischen Erneuerung Deutschlands 1945–1954 in der SBZ/DDR* (Cologne: Wissenschaft und Politik, 1993), 33; David Pike, *The Politics of Culture in Soviet-Occupied Germany, 1945–1949* (Stanford, Calif.: Stanford University Press, 1992), 81–2.

[10] On the founding, see Heider, *Kulturbund*, 33–40; Wolfgang Schivelbusch, *In a Cold Crater: Cultural and Intellectual Life in Berlin, 1945–1948*, trans. Kelly Barry (Berkeley: University of California Press, 1998), 72–7. Schivelbusch is especially attuned to the confluence of endogenous and exogenous factors.

grand villa in Dahlem, a southwestern district preferred by the wealthy and cultivated. As of 4 July, this neighborhood lay in the American sector, but on 26 June, Becher met an eclectic mix of non- and anti-Nazis he had been wooing there. Present were local KPD members including Herbert Sandberg, publisher Klaus Gysi, and chemist (and later GDR dissident) Robert Havemann; affiliates of the Chamber of Art Makers including Paul Wegener, Wolfgang Harich, and Herbert Ihering; politicians Ferdinand Friedensburg (CDU) and Gustav Dahrendorf (SPD); academics such as philosopher Eduard Spranger and art historian Edwin Redslob; and an assortment of others, from pastor Otto Dilschneider to novelist Bernhard Kellermann. Those assembled drafted a manifesto and charged Becher with procuring the new organization's license. This proved no difficulty, since – according to the date it carried – Soviet authorities had prepared it in advance.[11]

Thus was the Kulturbund constituted Berlin-wide under Soviet sponsorship. Its debut rally was held on 3 July, on the eve of the western allies' entry into the former capital. Before a studio audience of 1,500 at Radio Berlin (in the western Charlottenburg district), Becher, Harich, Kellermann, Wegener, and others broadcast the group's intentions: their "movement for spiritual renewal" would be built on a solidly "antifascist" as well as "democratic unity," preserving a "diversity of ideological and political convictions." Only on such a foundation could the German people "withstand the trials brought on us by our own guilt" and "again take our place in the community of nations as a free, truly democratic people."[12] In August, a founding conference convened. A somewhat larger group including Horst Lommer and Günther Weisenborn – just returned from the provinces – named Harich, Ihering, and Friedensburg to a presiding council of some thirty men and one woman, sculptor Renée Sintenis. They also elected Becher president over his own protestations. Anton Ackermann, KPD propaganda and culture secretary, called this "no victory, but a defeat." The party had favored a non-Communist figurehead, with Becher as vice president and Willmann as secretary wielding actual control over day-to-day affairs.[13] Thwarted machinations aside, the Kulturbund thrived. Its publishing house and

---

[11] As Schivelbusch points out, advance planning explains this discrepancy more plausibly than a dating error; Schivelbusch, *Cold Crater*, 74.

[12] "Programm (der Gründungsversammlung)," n.d., Bundesarchiv (hereafter BArch) DY 27/2751; preface to *Manifest und Ansprachen: Gehalten bei der Gründungskundgebung des Kulturbundes zur demokratischen Erneuerung Deutschlands am 4. Juli 1945* (Berlin: Aufbau, 1945), 3. Archival documents make clear that the rally took place on 3 July, not 4 July as printed on the pamphlet.

[13] "Protokoll der Gründungskonferenz des Kulturbundes zur demokratischen Erneuerung Deutschlands am 8. August 1945," n.d., BArch DY 27/907, 1; Günther Weisenborn,

198    German Intellectuals and Democratic Renewal

journal were established by September, while it expanded quickly within Berlin and inspired affiliates across the Soviet zone; Theodor Plievier co-founded the Kulturbund in Thuringia, while Victor Klemperer did so in Saxony. In aggregate, the organization swelled to 10,000 members by the end of the year, 45,000 by mid 1946, and 114,000 by late 1947. They came primarily from all corners of the cultural professions, but not exclusively so: in Berlin, one quarter were civil servants or officials, 11 percent engineers, and 7 percent workers.[14]

Historians debate the extent of the Kulturbund's integration into the nascent Cold War. For some, it was never more than a Communist front, its "ceaseless assertions of nonpartisanship" mere "deception"; for others, it attempted a "popular-front-against-Stalinism" that subordinated partisanship to pluralism, rather than vice versa.[15] While the latter case is more difficult to make for Becher (still more for his deputy Alexander Abusch), it does capture the commitments of engaged democrats. To be sure, the Kulturbund project and personnel showed strong continuities to 1930s initiatives partly driven by the Comintern's purely tactical coalition building. Nonetheless, to dismiss the organization's diversity is to disregard its characteristic "openness" through 1947, the period of its "interzonal, supra-party, and plural orientation."[16] This early pluralism enabled the involvement of many of the Kulturbund's own later critics – West-oriented intellectuals such as Redslob, Günther Birkenfeld, and Rudolf Pechel – alongside unaffiliated leftists such as Ihering and Weisenborn and later GDR dissidents such as Harich and Alfred Kantorowicz.[17]

Its founding documents expressed clear affinities for engaged democrats' positions, tightly linking political renewal to cultural tradition while embracing cosmopolitanism and disavowing elitism. The Kulturbund's goal was the "new birth of German spirit under the sign of a militantly democratic worldview"; it entailed the "integration of other peoples' spiritual achievements" and "rediscovery... of our people's free humanist, truly national traditions."[18] *Aufbau*'s first issue expressed this

*Der gespaltene Horizont: Niederschriften eines Außenseiters* (Munich: Desch, 1964), 45–6; Heider, *Kulturbund*, 38–9.

[14] Heider, *Kulturbund*, 48, 51, 206–7; Schivelbusch, *Cold Crater*, 80.
[15] Pike, *Politics of Culture*, 82; Schivelbusch, *Cold Crater*, 104.
[16] Gerd Dietrich, "Kulturbund," in *Die Parteien und Organisationen der DDR: Ein Handbuch*, ed. Gerd-Rüdiger Stephan, et al. (Berlin: Dietz, 2002), 535. On the initial "radical-democratic" and "pluralistic" Kulturbund concept – associated too unreservedly with Becher – see Dietrich, *Politik und Kultur in der Sowjetischen Besatzungszone Deutschlands 1945–1949* (Bern: Lang, 1993), 24–36, 95–110. The case for continuity is presented in Wehner, *Kulturpolitik*.
[17] Schivelbusch, *Cold Crater*, 73, 100–2, 160; Heider, *Kulturbund*, 34, 39, 57, 80, 83.
[18] "Leitsätze des Kulturbundes zur demokratischen Erneuerung Deutschlands," *Aufbau* 1, enclosure to no. 1 (1945).

agenda, coupling essays on Russian literary criticism and the English novel with an excerpt by French poet Paul Valéry on "the politics of spirit." Becher, in his lead essay, associated "democracy" not only with political discussion and participation but also with a "life outlook" – approaching one's neighbor as a fellow human being, not an "essenceless thing" – taught, among others, by the "German classicism, German humanism" of Goethe or Humboldt.[19] A bard of German unity, Becher did not shrink from a romantic national imagery that engaged democrats rejected.[20] Yet he likewise was convinced that the nation's cultural past contained valuable resources for its political future. And for all its educated-bourgeois orientation, the Kulturbund was quick to deny aspirations to tutelage over the masses. After fascism, Germans desperately needed an "education to truth and freedom," but "today more than ever, the teacher is also a learner." At the same time, the group saw itself as "nothing less... than a spiritual and cultural parliament of our land," in Kellermann's words.[21] This last metaphor recurred frequently in Kulturbund-associated discussions, asserting a privileged representativity that lingered alongside its counter-elitism.

Official Kulturbund pronouncements often operated with an indeterminate notion of "culture," but when they elaborated on that term, its valences were processual and expansive. At the reopening of Berlin University (soon renamed after the brothers Humboldt), its new rector and Kulturbund officer Johannes Stroux titled his address "On the Essence of Culture." A classical philologist, he pointed to the concept's roots in the Latin *colere* and Greek *paideia*. These showed "culture" to be no "sum of objective contents" but the "activity" of cultivation: *Kultur* was "the *Bildung* of *Geist*," spirit's active self-formation. Out of this classical "theory of culture" had developed a "theory of labor" as the reciprocal shaping of both self and world: "Nature transforms itself through cultivating ennoblement, and the human being transforms itself by developing its spiritual capacities," in two-sided, "continual interaction." There, Stroux concluded, the received oppositions of culture and civilization as well as of mental and manual labor were overcome. The contrast to official KPD

---

[19] Alfred Kurella, "Dobroljubow als Kritiker," *Aufbau* 1, no. 1 (1945): 35–41; Walter F. Schirmer, "James Joyce und der englische Roman," *Aufbau* 1, no. 1 (1945): 41–6; Paul Valéry, "Die Politik des Geistes," *Aufbau* 1, no. 1 (1945): 32–5; Johannes R. Becher, "Deutsches Bekenntnis," *Aufbau* 1, no. 1 (1945): 9–10.

[20] E.g., in the poem "Homecoming," which cast Germany as his "daybreak" and "eventide," "sunshine" and "starlight"; Becher, "Heimkehr," *Aufbau* 1, no. 2 (1945): 172–4. On his nationalism, see Ursula Heukenkamp, "Becher fuhr nicht nach Wrocław," in *Schriftsteller als Intellektuelle: Politik und Literatur im Kalten Krieg*, ed. Sven Hanuschek, Therese Hörnigk, and Christiane Malende (Tübingen: Niemeyer, 2000), 173–96.

[21] "Zum Geleit," *Aufbau* 1, no. 1 (1945): 1; *Manifest und Ansprachen*, 10.

rhetoric is instructive. For Ackermann, culture also took "dual form," in the sense that it included both "material [and] spiritual goods." As two types of "culture makers," then, "the worker and the intellectual belong together!" Here, culture as dynamic process disappeared entirely behind culture as static product. When Ihering wrote of the Kulturbund's conviction that "spirit may not isolate itself" but must bring "culture and politics into close interaction" in the world, the affinity was clearly to Stroux over Ackermann.[22]

On that ground, engaged democrats took vital part in the Kulturbund's discussions. Beyond the pages of *Aufbau* and *Sonntag*, these occurred face-to-face in the Club of Culture Makers. Programs were regularly held in its stately rooms, and, on occasion, unrationed meals were served – a conspicuous privilege amid widespread privation.[23] There, Klemperer presented his analysis of Nazi language, Friedensburg addressed Berlin's economic situation, Dilschneider outlined a renewed Christian humanism, and Harich participated in a panel discussion on anti-Semitism.[24] The clubhouse also hosted guests from far afield, such as British economist William Beveridge or Rudolf Leonhard, visiting from Paris. The latter presented his call for a "politics of spirit" that culminated in a "vigorous defense of democratic forces in Germany," the topic of a book he had just published in France. When Kantorowicz's return from exile coincided with a visit by Ernst Rowohlt from Hamburg, Weisenborn presided over a joint reception welcoming his two friends.[25]

Kulturbund groups in the Soviet zone were soon integrated into a centralized structure headquartered in Berlin.[26] Not so the smaller cultural associations that sprang up in the western zones; as a rule, they were founded on local initiative but stood in contact with the Berlin organization. These relationships have been generally overlooked,

---

[22] Johannes Stroux, "Vom Wesen der Kultur," *Aufbau* 2, no. 2 (1946): 111–16; Anton Ackermann, "Unsere kulturpolitische Sendung," in *Um die Erneuerung der deutschen Kultur: Erste Zentrale Kulturtagung der Kommunistischen Partei Deutschlands* (Berlin: Neuer Weg, 1946), 36–7; Herbert Ihering, "Zwischen heute und morgen," *Sonntag*, 18 May 1947.

[23] Jägerstrasse 2–3 had housed exclusive, conservative men's clubs until Soviet forces seized the house. On the material perks that flowed to intellectuals via the Kulturbund, see Schivelbusch, *Cold Crater*, 81–2.

[24] See "Die Sprache des 'Dritten Reiches,'" *Der Tagesspiegel*, 14 May 1946; K. H., "Humanismus oder Humanität?" *Der Tagesspiegel*, 3 April 1947; "Über den Antisemitismus," *Der Telegraf*, 29 April 1947 and BArch DY 27/267 for other announcements and invitations.

[25] "Lord Beveridge im Kulturbund," *Neues Deutschland*, 4 February 1947; "Verteidigung der Demokratie," *Berlin am Mittag*, 2 September 1947; Rudolf Leonhard, *Plaidoyer pour la démocratie allemande* (Paris: Raisons d'être, 1947); Gustav Leuteritz, "Ernst Rowohlt über seine Rotationsromane," *Tägliche Rundschau*, 12 March 1947.

[26] Heider, *Kulturbund*, 40–55.

underestimated, or reduced to a question of party-Communist manipulation.[27] Indisputably, the latter was a concern for some Allied officials and anti-Communist politicians, especially within the SPD. The organizers themselves, however, cultivated cross-zonal relationships from both sides, and to many in the west, taking the successful organization as model and interlocutor seemed self-evident. On the one hand, local KPD members were often involved in these foundations, and their comrades in Berlin monitored developments closely. On the other hand, the Kulturbund model spread as much by virtue of *Aufbau*'s high quality – postwar Germany's first cultural-political journal reached the western zones in small numbers but found large resonance – as on the basis of coordinated KPD/SED efforts.[28] Conduits of direct communication also stretched in both directions.

A closer look reveals how these dynamics intertwined. While the Deutscher Kulturbund Stuttgart, for instance, was founded on local KPD initiative, Theodor Heuss (DVP), culture minister of Württemberg-Baden, and Carlo Schmid (SPD), his counterpart in Württemberg-Hohenzollern, were prominently involved. No great friends of Communism, they nonetheless sought out collaboration with Berlin. Heuss addressed a rally there in spring 1946, and in return, Becher spoke in Stuttgart and Tübingen. On the same trip, Becher and Gysi also visited a Munich Kulturliga, a Lake Constance Kulturkreis (where they made contact with the Freiburg circle around *Die Gegenwart*), and a Kulturbund Heidelberg.[29] In Hamburg, the Berlin Kulturbund disclaimed the early, narrowly partisan efforts of a KPD city councilor and cultivated ties to independent intellectuals such as Axel Eggebrecht instead. By 1947, things had taken a more pluralist turn, and Rowohlt – on the

---

[27] Cf. ibid., 54–5; Wehner, *Kulturpolitik*, 263–5; Eberhard Demm, *Von der Weimarer Republik zur Bundesrepublik: Der politische Weg Alfred Webers 1920–1958* (Düsseldorf: Droste, 1999), 316; Carola Spies, "Der Kulturbund zur Demokratischen Erneuerung Deutschlands: Seine Anfänge in Westdeutschland aufgezeigt anhand der Entwicklung in Düsseldorf," in *Öffentlichkeit der Moderne, die Moderne in der Öffentlichkeit: Das Rheinland 1945–1955*, ed. Dieter Breuer and Gertrude Cepl-Kaufmann (Essen: Klartext, 2000), 69–84. Given western Allies' policies against licensing supra-zonal parties and associations, formal ties to the Soviet zone's Kulturbund were impossible in any case.

[28] On the journal's reception in Hamburg, Heidelberg, Frankfurt, Munich, Stuttgart, and elsewhere, see Willmann to Major Davidenko, 4 January 1946, BArch DY 27/291; "Protokoll: Präsidialratssitzung des Kulturbundes am 24. Juni 1946," n.d., BArch DY 27/908, 129.

[29] Willi Bohn, "Bericht über den deutschen Kulturbund, Stuttgart," n.d., BArch DY 27/291; "Unser Schicksal und unsere Aufgabe," *Der Tagesspiegel*, 19 March 1946; Wolfgang Harich, "Mittler zwischen Ost und West," *Der Kurier*, 20 March 1946; Jens-Fietje Dwars, *Abgrund des Widerspruchs: Das Leben des Johannes R. Becher* (Berlin: Aufbau, 1998), 534, 561; "Protokoll: Präsidialratssitzung des Kulturbundes am 24. Juni 1946," 126–8.

aforementioned Berlin visit – spoke with his colleagues there about the new Kulturbund Hamburg. Not long thereafter, Erich Kästner made a similar visit representing Munich's Kulturliga.[30] Organizations named "Kulturbund" appeared in Göttingen, Karlsruhe, and Ludwigshafen as well. One year after the war, there were about thirty western groups with 6,500 members, over half in the British zone (which also saw the most significant working-class membership).[31] This was due in no small part to the activists at Kulturbund Düsseldorf, which modeled itself most directly on Berlin and maintained close ties. It soon formed the basis of an organization for all North Rhine-Westphalia, which absorbed a number of nearby groups and became a Cold War bridgehead in the West.[32]

Parallel associations emerged early on from the cultural-political ferment of Frankfurt and Heidelberg. In Frankfurt, the plural composition and program of the Freie Deutsche Kulturgesellschaft (Free German Cultural Society), founded December 1945, also mirrored those in Berlin. The group's manifesto linked the "renewal of German cultural life" to the possibility of "democratic freedom" after Nazism, calling for the "unification of all spiritual forces" in a "new humanism"; this was a "national duty" no less imperative than "material reconstruction." Among its signatories were Walter Dirks, Else Epstein, and Werner Hilpert (CDU), Leo Bauer and Jo Mihaly (KPD), municipal culture councilor Eberhard Beckmann (SPD), Baron Otto von Recum, and Ernst Beutler, Dirks' opponent in the Goethe House controversy. Beckmann was elected chair and Bauer, Beutler, Dirks, Mihaly, and Recum to the board.[33] The wider circle included leftist writers Hans Mayer, Stephan Hermlin (KPD), and Walter Pollatschek (KPD); Protestant pastor Otto Fricke; left-Catholic newspaperman Wilhelm Karl Gerst; and

---

[30] "Bestrebungen zur Gründung von Kulturbundorganisationen im Westen Deutschlands," n.d., BArch DY 27/291; "Protokoll der Sitzung der Kommission Literatur am 14. März 1947," 21 March 1947, "Protokoll der Sitzung der Kommission 'Literatur' am 2. Apr 1947," 15 April 1947, BArch DY 27/224, 9–10, 14. The Hamburg official in question was Franz Heitgres, well-respected Senator for Restitution and Refugee Aid as well as head of Hamburg's VVN chapter; Boris Spernol, "Der Rote Winkel als 'Banner des Friedens': Friedenspolitik der Vereinigung der Verfolgten des Naziregimes bis 1950," in *Friedensinitiativen in der Frühzeit des Kalten Krieges 1945–1955*, ed. Detlef Bald and Wolfram Wette (Essen: Klartext, 2010), 137.

[31] Heider, *Kulturbund*, 54–5; Karl-Heinz Schulmeister, *Auf dem Wege zu einer neuen Kultur: Der Kulturbund in den Jahren 1945–1949* (Berlin: Dietz, 1977), 70. The figures are from the GDR Kulturbund's house historian and could not be corroborated elsewhere.

[32] Spies, "Der Kulturbund." In these respects, the Düsseldorf organization was exceptional; to take it as typical, as Spies does, is a mistake.

[33] "Aufruf der Freien Deutschen Kulturgesellschaft," *Frankfurter Rundschau*, 7 December 1945; Jo Mihaly to Walter Dirks, 30 December 1945, Archiv der sozialen Demokratie (Bonn, hereafter AdsD) NL Dirks 353; "Freie Deutsche Kulturgesellschaft Frankfurt a. M.," *Frankfurter Rundschau*, 1 February 1946.

A parliament of spirit? Mobilizing the cultural nation 203

conservative jurist Walter Hallstein – law professor, CDU politician, and later architect of the FRG's non-recognition doctrine toward the GDR.[34]

The prehistory of the Frankfurt organization began in wartime Zurich. There, Mihaly played the central role, leading a cultural organization of German exiles that had ties to the KPD-inspired, broadly antifascist Free Germany movement. Mayer and Hermlin edited the feuilleton of its journal *Über die Grenzen* (*Over the Borders*), the first of many collaborations.[35] A delegation of its members returned to Frankfurt in early summer 1945, where Bauer facilitated the return of other émigrés, including Mayer and Mihaly. Working closely with Beckmann, he established the Kulturgesellschaft's initial base of contacts, a task Mihaly completed on her arrival. It was through Bauer that the group had strong yet ambivalent ties to Berlin. Ulbricht likened the Hessian KPD under his leadership to an internal opposition, and this incomplete subordination would haunt Bauer later.[36] At a mid-1947 meeting of western cultural associations with Kulturbund officials in Berlin, Bauer spoke for the Frankfurt group. He welcomed the potential for collaboration, but he cautioned against too-close affiliation, a position echoed by others present. As a first step, he suggested Berlin more frequently send independent-minded intellectuals westward – Stroux and Ihering were mentioned, among others – to counteract accusations that all Kulturbund organizations were little more than Communist fronts.[37]

Only the Heidelbergers were not represented at this meeting. At its foundation, the Heidelberger Kulturbund zur demokratischen Erneuerung Deutschlands modeled itself enthusiastically on Berlin, as their name suggested. The initiative emerged from discussions around

---

[34] Kurt Krispien, "Protokoll der ersten, ordentlichen Mitgliederversammlung der Freien Deutschen Kulturgesellschaft am 13. Mai 1947," 14 May 1947, AdsD NL Dirks 353; Hans Mayer, *Ein Deutscher auf Widerruf: Erinnerungen* (Frankfurt a.M.: Suhrkamp, 1982), I:376–7.

[35] Ingrid Langer, Ulrike Ley, and Susanne Sander, *Alibi-Frauen? Hessische Politikerinnen*, Vol. I, *In den Vorparlamenten 1946 bis 1950* (Frankfurt a.M.: Helmer, 1994), 192–4; Werner Mittenzwei, *Exil in der Schweiz*, 2nd edn. (Frankfurt a.M.: Röderberg, 1981), 328–76; Mayer, *Ein Deutscher*, I:296–9. On the Moscow model for Free Germany, see Bodo Scheurig, *Verräter oder Patrioten: Das Nationalkomitee "Freies Deutschland" und der Bund Deutscher Offiziere in der Sowjetunion 1943–1945*, 2nd edn. (Berlin: Propyläen, 1993).

[36] Leo Bauer, "Kommunistische Partei Frankfurt Abteilung Kultur und Volksbildung / Bericht über die bisherige Tätigkeit," 8 October 1945, BArch DY 27/1404; Langer, Ley, and Sander, *Alibi-Frauen?*, 195–9; Walter Mühlhausen, *Hessen 1945–1950: Zur politischen Geschichte eines Landes in der Besatzungszeit* (Frankfurt a.M.: Insel, 1985), 103–5; Peter Brandt et al., *Karrieren eines Außenseiters: Leo Bauer zwischen Kommunismus und Sozialdemokratie 1912 bis 1972* (Berlin: Dietz, 1983), 123–65. On Bauer's fate in the GDR, see Chapter 6.

[37] "Protokoll der Besprechung mit Vertretern der Kulturorganisationen aus West- und Süddeutschland am 22. Mai 1947 im Klubhaus," 30 May 1947, BArch DY 27/291.

Mayor Ernst Walz in fall 1945, involving Dolf Sternberger and Lambert Schneider, among others. While city officials had in mind a coordinating agency for cultural programming, stakeholders from art historian Gustav Hartlaub (DVP) to union leaders Franz Ringer (SPD) and Max Bock (KPD) pushed successfully for a more ambitious mandate. The organization's founding statement praised *Aufbau*, quoted Becher at length, and foresaw "close contact" to the Berlin Kulturbund, touting their "constructive work" toward a shared goal: the "formation (*Bildung*) of true German humanity."[38]

Although intensive contact with the divided capital was proclaimed, it was never realized. As early as 1946, they took pains to clarify that they represented no "local group or the like" of the larger Kulturbund. Drawing an implicit contrast, they insisted that "in our work... we pursue no party-political goals" but rather the "principle of a total tolerance." After visiting Heidelberg, Gysi reported with satisfaction that his assurances of the Berlin Kulturbund's supra-party, plural profile had cleared up incipient misunderstandings: "Here, too, closer collaboration will be possible in the future."[39] His optimism notwithstanding, their erstwhile offspring pointedly renamed themselves the Heidelberger Bund für demokratische Kultur (Heidelberg League for Democratic Culture) in spring 1947. This time, Willmann was sent as an envoy, only to be rebuffed. An affiliation with the Berlin Kulturbund, his hosts explained, would raise the specter of SED influence, while coordinating with the larger organization would involve a layer of bureaucracy they preferred to avoid.[40] Whether a visit from a critic, playwright, or poet like Ihering or Weisenborn or even Becher himself might have revitalized ties is unclear; diplomatic missions by officious functionaries, in any event, did not. Even so, the Heidelberg group thrived. Its membership spanned clergy, politicians, labor leaders, academics, and journalists. Figures from the *Wandlung* circle were especially active. Sternberger presented his thoughts on the "Rule of Freedom" for their first public event. An early panel discussion featured Alexander Mitscherlich and Alfred Weber on Marx's

---

[38] Birgit Pape, *Kultureller Neubeginn in Heidelberg und Mannheim 1945–1949* (Heidelberg: Winter, 2000), 78–80; "Kulturbund zur demokratischen Erneuerung," *Rhein-Neckar-Zeitung*, 15 December 1945.

[39] Gustav Hartlaub, "Freie Lehrstätte für die geistig Aufgeschlossenen: Zur Gründung des Heidelberger Kulturbundes," *Rhein-Neckar-Zeitung*, 4 May 1946; "Protokoll: Präsidialratssitzung des Kulturbundes am 24. Juni 1946," 128.

[40] Luitgard Nipp-Stolzenburg, "Eine 'Freie Lehrstätte für die geistig Aufgeschlossenen': 50 Jahre Volkshochschule Heidelberg," in *"Volksbildung nötiger denn je...": 50 Jahre Volkshochschule Heidelberg* (Heidelberg: Winter, 1996), 76; Emil Stranz, "Subject: Intelligence Report No: 463/ Weekly Intelligence Report," 3 July 1947, Hauptstaatsarchiv Stuttgart J384 Mikrofiche-Sammlung OMGUS, RG 260 OMGWB 12/7–3/14.

contemporary relevance and the possible contours of a new socialism. And under Kulturbund auspices, Sternberger helped establish Heidelberg's adult education college (*Volkshochschule*).[41]

The task of articulating the group's basic principles fell to Hartlaub and Sternberger, who together with Ringer formed its founding board. Their two programmatic statements gave exemplary expression to two divergent stances on *Kultur*. Hartlaub juxtaposed "the bankruptcy of the illusory values" foisted by Nazism upon the Germans to "all that is true, good, and beautiful." A compass for "the real and the right" remained buried within them, which the new Kulturbund would help "uncover again."[42] Here, culture stood as a fixed repository of eternal values from which Germans had been led away and to which they could simply return. In Sternberger's formulations, culture figured quite differently, as a process with expansive referends, one that had directly to do with democracy and renewal. "Culture means cultivating," he asserted, the opposite of the "savaging" (*Verwilderung*) they had witnessed under Nazism. As such, culture pertained to social life as a whole:

Culture consists not only of theater and concerts. It begins with eating and dwelling, with feeling, thinking, speaking and comportment, and it realizes itself in the ordering of collective life among the people. It comprises the production and distribution of goods as much as ethics and works of the spirit.

Moreover, this process was relevant to democracy. "Democracy means rule by the people," which seemed "at first a purely political concept." A truly "democratic life," however, required the "cultivation" of "certain shared material [and] spiritual bases":

Free codetermination by all individuals demands not only equal rights but unending effort toward a human, dignified existence for all individuals in their elementary needs... Furthermore, it demands a general and communal formation (*Bildung*) of intellect, disposition, speech, and comportment.

Finally, this project could succeed only by means of a renewal, neither reverting to the old nor insisting on radical novelty:

Renewal lies between preservation and upheaval, thus between a conservative and revolutionary position, in the good middle. Renewal is our task, an unending task as difficult as it is inviting. We do not know whether it will succeed. But if renewal succeeds, it will lay the foundations of a new tradition.[43]

---

[41] Nipp-Stolzenburg, "Eine 'Freie Lehrstätte,'" 71–2, 75–6, 182; "Herrschaft der Freiheit," *Rhein-Neckar-Zeitung*, 7 May 1946; "Mit oder ohne Marx," *Rhein-Neckar-Zeitung*, 20 July 1946.
[42] Hartlaub, "Freie Lehrstätte."
[43] Dolf Sternberger, "Grundsätze," *Rhein-Neckar-Zeitung*, 4 May 1946.

The group's mandate was ambitious: to enable the collective reforging of tradition and the free ordering of a new, democratic community in all social spheres. This process Sternberger called *Kultur*.

The proximity of his formulations to those by Stroux in *Aufbau* is striking. One represented the Berlin Kulturbund and the other the western counterpart that kept them at greatest distance. Both bore the expansive and processual hallmark of engaged democrats' concept of culture, which correlated to the self-developing and world-transforming freedom that underlay their vision of participatory politics.

### The Writers' Congress as national assembly

Envisioned as broad-based, cross-class forums, Kulturbund groups were an immediate postwar phenomenon *sui generis*. More tied to conventional, exclusive modes of intellectual organization was another platform, writers' congresses. The gatherings that launched the cultural Cold War have been best remembered: the World Peace Movement conferences in Wrocław in August 1948 and in Paris, in Prague, and at New York's Waldorf-Astoria in 1949; the Congress for Cultural Freedom's ripostes in West Berlin in 1950 and Paris in 1952.[44] Analogous events were also held before the bipolar order consolidated. Europe-wide, the inaugural 1946 meeting of the Rencontres internationales in Geneva heard such luminaries as Julien Benda, Karl Jaspers, and Georg Lukács reflect on the state of "The European Spirit."[45] In Germany, several congresses were also held in late 1947 and early 1948. These were invested with great hopes but shot through with increasing tensions, and only the first of them was considered – even by its supporters – to have been at all productive.[46] In leading the charge for the First German Writers' Congress of October 1947, engaged democrats intended to open a national forum for deliberation of all issues associated with postwar renewal. Convening a cultural congress was an eminently political endeavor.

Congress organizers programmatically asserted the "unity" of representatives of German *Geist* across old divisions of region, confession, and party (their class composition, by contrast, was not discussed directly)

---

[44] See, e.g., David Caute, *The Fellow-Travellers: A Postscript to the Enlightenment* (New York: Macmillan, 1973), 289–93; Frances Stonor Saunders, *The Cultural Cold War: The CIA and the World of Arts and Letters* (New York: New Press, 2000), 45–56, 73–84, 113–28.

[45] See the published proceedings: *L'Esprit européen* (Neuchâtel: Baconnière, 1947).

[46] See, e.g., Michael Hochgeschwender, *Freiheit in der Offensive? Der Kongress für kulturelle Freiheit und die Deutschen* (Munich: Oldenbourg, 1998), 139–45; Anne Hartmann and Wolfram Eggeling, *Sowjetische Präsenz im kulturellen Leben der SBZ und frühen DDR 1945–1953* (Berlin: Akademie, 1998), 35–62; Stephen Brockmann, *German Literary Culture at the Zero Hour* (Rochester, N.Y.: Camden House, 2004), 151–7.

as well as across newer fronts separating "inner émigrés" from exiles and the four occupation zones from each other. Their commitment to such unity is easily misread. First, viewed solely through the Cold War lens, such a Berlin-based, Soviet-supported initiative allows for only two roles: party-Communist orchestrators or fellow-traveling dupes.[47] Second, invocations of national cultural heritage can seen uncomplicated expressions of nationalism seeking to restore a legitimate post-Nazi Germanness. Both dynamics played their part in the congress, but engaged democrats' investments had a different center of gravity (and, whatever their roles, they were savvy actors in the drama, attuned to the agendas in play). As we have seen, their idea of "culture" evoked both German unity and world-shaping freedom. As the keepers of a politically essential cultural patrimony – here, the residually elitist moment of their politics shone through – they felt a duty and a right to help shape the postwar order. The congress was intended as a venue within which to constitute German intellectuals as an independent force for renewal.

This model of writers' politics was grounded in memories of antifascist activism by writers' organizations in the 1930s, as bastions of the "other Germany." The defining moment was the Berlin SDS chapter's mobilization of 1933. By then, it counted as something of a left opposition within the statutorily politically neutral national association. Days after Hitler was named Chancellor, the Berliners publicly urged their colleagues to relinquish their "unpolitical" stance and revolt against the "threatening fascistization of the spirit." At one meeting, Carl von Ossietzky reportedly proclaimed: "I belong to no party. I have battled on all sides; more with the right, but also with the left. Today, however, we should know that to our left stand only allies. The flag to which I pledge is ... the banner of the united antifascist movement."[48] Like many, the *Weltbühne* editor was soon imprisoned; unlike most, he was never released. He received the Nobel Peace Prize for 1935 and died of tuberculosis in 1938. Ossietzky's credo became a rallying cry for subsequent efforts at antifascist unity. Kantorowicz often invoked it as a solemn "bequest" after 1945: "We have yet to realize it today. We will realize it – we or those who come after us."[49]

---

[47] Cf., e.g., Michael Rohrwasser, "Vom Exil zum 'Kongreß für kulturelle Freiheit': Anmerkungen zur Faszinationsgeschichte des Stalinismus," in *Schriftsteller*, ed. Hanuschek, Hörnigk, and Malende, 137–58.

[48] Hermand, *Dichterbünde*, 217–21, 235–6, quote 236; Carl von Ossietzky, *Sämtliche Schriften*, ed. Bärbel Boldt, et al., vol. VII, *Briefe und Lebensdokumente* (Reinbek b.H.: Rowohlt, 1994), 1042–3.

[49] Gerhard Kraiker and Elke Suhr, *Carl von Ossietzky* (Reinbek b.H.: Rowohlt, 1994), 98–127; Alfred Kantorowicz, "Carl von Ossietzky's Vermächtnis," *Die Weltbühne* 2,

Engaged democrats were among those who felt themselves heirs to this legacy, and they struggled to preserve it. Leonhard and Kantorowicz were instrumental in founding the Paris SDS in 1933. It was to be an ongoing vehicle of antifascist "unity," "a sort of popular front" that would gather forces for the fight against Nazism. Leonhard served as chair, under honorary president Heinrich Mann and alongside Max Schroeder, Maximilian Scheer, and others, including liberal philosopher Ludwig Marcuse and art historian Paul Westheim, Communist authors Gustav Regler and Anna Seghers, and literary apparatchik Alfred Kurella. The Paris SDS worked to aid exiles, held lectures and readings, and publicized Nazism's attacks on culture; its first event was a rally to support Ossietzky. Prompted by the book burnings, they founded a German Freedom Library (Deutsche Freiheitsbibliothek, or DFB), conceived by Kantorowicz and directed by Schroeder. At once a repository for suppressed literature, a resource center on the Third Reich, and a publisher for exiles, it was also a celebrated international cause backed by figures from Gaston Gallimard to H. G. Wells. Heinrich Mann, Lion Feuchtwanger, André Gide, and Romain Rolland formed its all-star Franco-German presidium.[50]

The broader context of these independent initiatives was the popular front movement, which transformed 1930s Paris into Europe's "capital of antifascism."[51] There, German exiles mingled with like-minded activists from France and elsewhere. As bitterly estranged Social Democrats and Communists sought common ground, also with liberals, and intellectuals debated, the Comintern provided crucial infrastructure behind the scenes. Media magnate Willi Münzenberg was the central figure. His 1933 publication on the Reichstag fire (to which Kantorowicz, Regler, and Schroeder contributed) established a powerful imagery of the struggle, pitting deviant Nazis against virtuous Communists who fought for the whole nation's interests. Soon, Münzenberg's World Committee for the Victims of German Fascism supported the DFB as well.[52] Becher played the key role among the literati, from his position on the SDS

---

no. 9 (1947): 375; Kantorowicz, "Begrabene Freiheit: Carl von Ossietzky auf dem Wege ins Gefängnis," *Die Weltbühne* 1, no. 10 (1946): 298.

[50] Hermand, *Dichterbünde*, 253–5; Ursula Langkau-Alex, *Deutsche Volksfront 1932–1939: Zwischen Berlin, Paris, Prag und Moskau* (Berlin: Akademie, 2004), I:100–13, quote 106; Dieter Schiller, *Der Traum von Hitlers Sturz: Studien zur deutschen Exilliteratur 1933–1945* (Frankfurt a.M.: Lang, 2010), 85–125.

[51] Anson Rabinbach, "Paris, Capital of Anti-Fascism," in *The Modernist Imagination: Intellectual History and Critical Theory*, ed. Warren Breckman et al. (New York: Berghahn, 2009), 183–209.

[52] *Braunbuch über Reichstagsbrand und Hitler-Terror* (Basel: Universum-Bücherei, 1933); Rabinbach, "Staging Antifascism: The Brown Book of the Reichstag Fire and

board. Such was the backdrop to German participation in the highprofile International Writers' Congress for the Defense of Culture of June 1935. Renowned writers and fellow travelers Ilya Ehrenburg and André Malraux led the planning, assisted by Becher (assisted, in turn, by Kantorowicz and Regler). They attracted a celebrity cast including Louis Aragon, Isaac Babel, Henri Barbusse, Julien Benda, Bertolt Brecht, E. M. Forster, Aldous Huxley, Robert Musil, and Boris Pasternak, alongside Heinrich Mann, Feuchtwanger, and Gide – 230 intellectuals from thirty-eight nations, all told. Before audiences of up to 3,000, they presented a diverse yet unified front.[53] Comintern networks were vital in shaping this and other initiatives. But antifascism had its own logic in 1930s Europe, irreducible to the pro-Communism with which it intertwined.

The congress marked the apex of antifascist solidarity in France, a heady atmosphere for Germany's postwar engaged democrats. Bloch and Leonhard joined the German Popular Front Committee, avidly supported by SDS and DFB. Although a united front among the German parties never emerged – despite the inspiring French example – cultural alliances thrived for a time. Moreover, many were galvanized by the era's other great cause, the Spanish Civil War. Yet the disputes that soon fractured antifascism Europe-wide – over intra-left clashes in Spain and purges and show trials in the USSR – splintered the German exile community as well. A few disillusioned "renegades" left the KPD, including Münzenberg and Arthur Koestler; more would follow after the German–Soviet non-aggression pact, including Regler. Nor was the Paris SDS spared, as a rival anti-Communist foundation, the Free Press and Literature League, attracted more centrist members. Still, it remained active until September 1939, when French authorities banned it as a "Soviet agency" and interned its members as enemy aliens.[54] Under the sign of Nazi–Soviet accommodation and Hitler's expanding empire, the years that followed were dark ones for Europe's antifascists.

In the final throes of the war, Germany's engaged democrats were at the forefront of efforts to revive this tradition of writers' self-organization.

---

Hitler Terror," *New German Critique* 35, no. 1 (2008): 97–126; Langkau-Alex, *Deutsche Volksfront*, I:111; Schiller, *Traum*, 109.

[53] Langkau-Alex, *Deutsche Volksfront*, I:107–16; Rabinbach, "Paris," 196–209; Wolfgang Gruner, *"Ein Schicksal, das ich mit sehr vielen anderen geteilt habe": Alfred Kantorowicz, sein Leben und seine Zeit von 1899 bis 1935* (Kassel: Kassel University Press, 2006), 326–35; Sandra Teroni and Wolfgang Klein, eds. *Pour la défense de la culture: Les textes du Congrès international des écrivains, Paris, juin 1935* (Dijon: Éditions universitaires de Dijon, 2005). Other German speakers included Bloch, Kantorowicz, Leonhard, Klaus Mann, Ludwig Marcuse, Regler, Seghers, and Weinert.

[54] Hermand, *Dichterbünde*, 254–5; Langkau-Alex, *Deutsche Volksfront*, III:283; Schiller, *Traum*, 91, 100, 116–19, 143–57.

The first stirrings came from neutral Switzerland, where a new group bore the name SDS, to make explicit their debts and their lineage.[55] As Jo Mihaly explained, they aimed to represent writers' interests but also to help rebuild a liberated Germany, in homage to their precedessors. At the founding meeting in May 1945, playwright Georg Kaiser was elected president, Mihaly chair, and Mayer and Hermlin to the board. With earlier conflicts fresh in mind, some prospective members pressed her on the Swiss SDS's political affiliation. Her response was unequivocal: the Swiss SDS embraced Communists, Social Democrats, unionists, liberals, conservatives, Christians, as well as "pure – that is, party-unaffiliated – lyricists." All had come together "to forge a *united front of spirit*, for the protection of a new German literature" but also "for the protection of freedom and peace."[56] Both goals seemed self-evidently fitting for writers' postwar agendas.

By late 1945, many of its founders had gained passage into Germany, and the Swiss SDS wound down. Shortly before his reemigration, Mayer established contact with a similar organization emerging in Berlin, the Protective Association of German Authors (SDA). Its secretary Werner Schendell explained that, despite the revised, more inclusive name, they still claimed the mantle of the SDS, whose last Berlin secretary he had been. "It will take us a long time to rebuild to the level of 1933," the non-émigré acknowledged; "once our banned [authors] return and are *working* alongside us," that process could begin.[57] The SDA grew out of discussions at the Chamber of Art Makers. Operating under Soviet license, its co-chairs were Pechel, Redslob, Weisenborn, and Roland Schacht, and its board included Becher, Birkenfeld, Walther Karsch, Kellermann, Lommer, Friedrich Luft, Reger, and Friedrich Wolf. Kantorowicz joined on his return, and Leonhard did during his visit in 1947.[58] As their intertwined roots and personnel suggest, the SDA and Kulturbund pursued a common cultural-political project in distinct organizational modes.

The Berlin SDA was only one of many such groups appearing across Germany. Eggebrecht joined a Northwest SDA in Hamburg; Beckmann, Pollatschek and Marie Luise Kaschnitz headed a Frankfurt SDS; Kästner co-founded a Munich SDS. In keeping with Soviet-zone centralism, all

---

[55] See, e.g., Mittenzwei, *Exil*, 371–6; Mayer, *Ein Deutscher*, I:325.
[56] Mihaly to Karl Wilczynski, 15 May 1945, Deutsche Nationalbibliothek, Deutsches Exilarchiv 1933–1945 (Frankfurt a.M.) NL Karl Wilcynski EB 87/100; Mihaly quoted in Mittenzwei, *Exil*, 374–5 (emphasis in original).
[57] Werner Schendell to Mayer, 3 December 1945, Stiftung Archiv Akademie der Künste Berlin (hereafter AdK) Archiv Schriftstellerverband 206/1/47.
[58] Schendell, "Der neue Schutzverband," *Der Autor* 1, no. 1 (1947): 6–10; Ulrike Buergel-Goodwin, "Die Reorganisation der westdeutschen Schriftstellerverbände 1945–1952," *Archiv für die Geschichte des Buchwesens* 18 (1977): cols. 377–88.

A parliament of spirit? Mobilizing the cultural nation             211

writers' organizations there were branches of the SDA. In the western zones, no fewer than ten separate writers' associations had sprouted by 1947. Like their Kulturbund counterparts, they confronted the question of their relations with Berlin. For its part, the Berlin-based SDA cultivated ties with peer organizations and key exiles such as Mayer in Zurich and Leonhard in Paris, but it took care "to avoid the impression" of attempting to play "headquarters" for all.[59] Their caution proved well founded. Although Hamburg and Frankfurt were receptive to a planned all-German umbrella organization, this project faltered on stiff Bavarian resistance (as well as Allied disinclination). In promoting material interests, organizing legal aid, and the like, these organizations rebuilt the old SDS's professional mission, and several temporarily fulfilled the longstanding hope of formal unionization.[60] Alongside such practical aims, they also took up their predecessors' larger political goals.

The latter aspect was central for the engaged democrats involved, and it inspired the First German Writers' Congress, held on 4–8 October 1947.[61] In the new SDA journal, Weisenborn drove home the stakes: for decades, two camps had stood opposed in German letters, "the criers of international humanity, of free *Geist*" versus "the chauvinists and warmongers" (such as Ernst Jünger) who had abetted Germany's "barbaric" turn. The task was to consolidate the now dispersed former camp, the "other Germany" that had fought and fled Hitler, into a "broader front" against "residual fascism, militarism, and reaction."[62] This was the congress' mission. Weisenborn had first proposed the event in 1945, and the Berlin SDA and Kulturbund Literature Commission, both under his chairmanship, began planning in fall 1946. Kantorowicz, Leonhard, Schroeder, and Wolfgang Weyrauch as well as Becher, Birkenfeld, Elisabeth Langgässer, Luft, Redslob, Reger, Schacht, Schendell, and Wolf took part.[63] On a smaller scale, the first "Day of the Free Book" – 10 May 1947, on Berlin's Opera Square, site of the most famous Nazi

---

[59] Buergel-Goodwin, "Reorganisation," cols. 391–3, 407–10, 483–4, 499–500; "Protokoll über die Vorstandssitzung des Schutzverbandes Deutscher Autoren am 14. Dezember 1945," 16 December 1945, AdK Archiv Schriftstellerverband 206/1/51.
[60] Buergel-Goodwin, "Reorganisation," cols. 417–32, 458–9. The Berlin, Frankfurt, and Munich groups were each organized in zonal union confederations, overcoming the divide between the "free professions" and organized labor; these affiliations were each dissolved in 1950.
[61] See also Ursula Reinhold and Dieter Schlenstedt, "Vorgeschichte, Umfeld, Nachgeschichte des Ersten Deutschen Schriftstellerkongresses," in *Erster deutscher Schriftstellerkongreß 4.–8. Oktober 1947: Protokoll und Dokumente*, ed. Reinhold, Schlenstedt, and Horst Tanneberger (Berlin: Aufbau, 1997), 13–76.
[62] Weisenborn, "An die deutschen Dichter im Ausland: Aus eine Gedächtnisrede für Ernst Toller," *Der Autor* 1, no. 1 (1947): 4–5.
[63] Reinhold and Schlenstedt, "Vorgeschichte," 14–24.

book-burning – provided a trial run. Jointly sponsored by Kulturbund and SDA, it was organized by Kantorowicz, continuing his exile commemorations in France and the USA. With evident satisfaction, he described a scene of unity: SED functionaries such as Becher, anti-Communists such as Birkenfeld, and fence-sitters such as his friend Weisenborn shared the podium, while putatively "Eastern" figures such as Seghers, Wolf, Ludwig Renn, and Kantorowicz himself mingled with putatively "Western" ones such as Langgässer, Kästner (in from Munich), and Alfred Döblin (from Baden-Baden).[64] Representing exiles and non-exiles from various corners of the land, each had seen their work suppressed under Nazism.

Of course, the Writers' Congress was a larger, more complicated undertaking. Preparations were beset by a host of difficulties, from objections to its all-German orientation to grumblings about the Berlin Kulturbund – which withdrew as co-sponsor at Weisenborn's urging – to a proposal to limit the agenda to "professional-economic" topics and bracket "political-ideological" ones. Moreover, questions about accommodation and travel remained unresolved after months of postponements. When another delay loomed, Weisenborn and Kantorowicz insisted on the need to hold firm. Given mounting East–West tensions, they urged, "the execution of such an event may well be jeopardized" in the future. Their pleas prevailed, with Becher's support.[65] When the congress convened, most of its 280 participants came from outside Berlin, representing all zones as well as several exile ports of call. Demonstratively, the American sector's Hebbel Theater was chosen for the opening ceremony, while subsequent sessions were held at the Soviet sector's Deutsches Theater.[66] Still – as was not lost on observers – the Soviets played primary host, providing meals, lodging, and a lavish reception at their headquarters, with the western Allies in a secondary role.[67] Given its scale and public

[64] [Kantorowicz], "Vorschläge für die Organisierung von Feierlichkeiten und Manifestationen am Jahrestage der Bücherverbrennungen," [April 1947], AdK Becher-Archiv 6502; Kantorowicz, *Der Tag des Freien Buches: Zum Gedenken an die Bücherverbrennungen vom 10. Mai 1933* (Berlin: Deutsche Verwaltung für Volksbildung, 1947); Kantorowicz, *Deutsches Tagebuch* (Munich: Kindler, 1959), I:327–30; Weisenborn, *Horizont*, 61–3. Opera Square was renamed Bebel Square later that year.

[65] "Protokoll über die Vorstandssitzung des Schutzverbandes Deutscher Autoren in der Gewerkschaft für Kunst und Schrifttum F.D.G.B. am 15. November 1946," n.d., "Protokoll über die Vorstandssitzung des Schutzverbandes Deutscher Autoren in der Gewerkschaft für Kunst und Schrifttum F.D.G.B. am 27. November 1946," n.d., "Protokoll über die Vorstandssitzung des SDA am 11. August 1947," n.d., "Protokoll der Zusammenkunft der Vorstandsmitglieder am 27.8.," [1947], AdK Archiv Schriftstellerverband 206/1/140, 146, 206/2/104–5, 118–19.

[66] Weisenborn later highlighted this attempted bipartisanship; Weisenborn, *Horizont*, 64.

[67] "Protokoll der Vorstandssitzung am 8. September 1947," n.d., "Protokoll der Vorstandssitzung am 15. September 1947," 19 September 1947, AdK Archiv Schriftstellerverband 206/2/130–1, 139.

A parliament of spirit? Mobilizing the cultural nation 213

Figure 5.1 Presidium members listen during the First German Writers' Congress in Berlin, 5 October 1947. Those seated include, from left: Günther Birkenfeld (not visible), Rudolf Leonhard, Günther Weisenborn, Ricarda Huch, Hertha von Gebhardt, Alfred Kantorowicz, and Elisabeth Langgässer. (*Source*: SLUB Dresden / Deutsche Fotothek / Abraham Pisarek)

resonance, the congress was regarded by both supporters and detractors as the most significant cultural-political happening of the postwar years.

As such, it afforded engaged democrats a prominent platform, and they worked to frame the undertaking in their terms (Figure 5.1). In his opening remarks, Weisenborn lamented that Germans had been "repeatedly disappointed" by their "so-called politicians," who were tearing the nation apart rather than pulling it together. In response, he declared the assembled writers a "parliament of spirit," one that would bridge this distance to "our people." He enjoined his colleagues, as "representatives of German spirit," to recast its legacy of strictly "inner freedom" and never revert to the "dangerous cult of false inwardness that negates or despises the ugly world outside." In the process, the "great spirit of this old and beautiful people" would overcome its "isolation" and absorb "leavening from the spirit of all countries of the globe."[68] His appeal

---

[68] Günther Weisenborn, "Von Tod und Hoffnung der Dichter," *Der Autor* 1, no. 8 (1947): 7–8. Here and below, published versions occasionally diverge from the transcript; cf. Ursula Reinhold, Dieter Schlenstedt, and Horst Tanneberger, eds. *Erster deutscher*

correlated *Geist* to a national yet cosmopolitan unity as well as a this-worldly freedom, countering the quietism and the chauvinism they associated with the "unpolitical German." In this vein, a draft of the congress manifesto pledged participants, as "heirs to the German humanist tradition," to "work tirelessly and resolutely for the freedom and unity of German *Geist*."[69] But the conference was built on alliances among groups that interpreted and weighed these goals differently.

Crucially, engaged democrats opposed views of culture as a self-sufficient, enclosed sphere. This theme was prominent in Mayer's address, "The Writer and Society." For writers to "striv[e] only... to create in spiritual freedom," he argued, was insufficient; they must "identify what our society's questions are and help generate what the great old Immanuel Kant called the conditions of possibility of actual freedom." Their role in moving from a one-sidedly spiritual freedom to a fuller, social freedom hinged on "overcoming the tension... in German literature between the poet and the writer." In the era of Goethe and Lessing, "great stylists" had also been "undaunted writers" attentive to "the problems of their time." Since the failed 1848 revolution, Germany had produced mainly "poets" who "prided themselves on being as unpolitical, as... immediately, intuitively creative as possible."[70] And in the extreme, such culturalism had ultimately enabled barbarism. To illustrate the point, Mayer cited the habit of Hans Frank – the Nazi Governor-General of occupied Poland sentenced to death at Nuremberg – to spend his evenings serenely at the piano, playing Chopin and Bach. Postwar intellectuals were called to "overcome this terrible split," manifest so grotesquely in Frank, by achieving "a unified humaneness in private and public life."[71] Nazism and its crimes gave long-standing questions of spirit and power a new urgency after 1945.

Mayer's comments won applause from some conferees, but calls for "proximity to the times" (*Zeitnähe*) in literature had detractors as well. Albin Stuebs, an editor at Radio Hamburg, protested that such views

---

*Schriftstellerkongreß 4.–8. Oktober 1947: Protokoll und Dokumente* (Berlin: Aufbau, 1997), 107–9.

[69] "Manifest des ersten deutschen Schriftsteller-Kongresses," n.d., Staats- und Universitätsbibliothek Hamburg (hereafter SUBH) NL Kantorowicz NK Ostberlin: 65. The final version substituted a pledge "to work for peace, in our country and in the world"; "Manifest des Ersten Deutschen Schriftstellerkongresses," *Der Autor* 1, no. 8 (1947): 3.

[70] Reinhold, Schlenstedt, and Tanneberger, eds. *Schriftstellerkongreß*, 211–12. As we have seen, this basic argument was common coin among engaged democrats. Mayer referenced Lukács' influential version of 1939, soon republished as Georg Lukács, "Schriftsteller und Kritiker," in *Essays über Realismus* (Berlin: Aufbau, 1948), 216–65.

[71] Reinhold, Schlenstedt, and Tanneberger, eds. *Schriftstellerkongreß*, 416. See Martyn Housden, *Hans Frank: Lebensraum and the Holocaust* (Basingstoke: Palgrave Macmillan, 2003).

conjured a straw man: the aesthete who "sits locked away from the world or writes for eternity" no longer existed, while the danger of reducing literature to "propaganda" was quite present. Birkenfeld likewise urged that they "guard against... too strongly politicizing the literary word." And Wilhelm Süskind, of Munich's *Süddeutsche Zeitung*, raised similar concerns. Even as he disavowed "the purity of language in the sense of *l'art pour l'art*," he cautioned against misusing language to manipulate rather than as a "means to truth and an instrument of freedom."[72] There was, as yet, no great divide, but an incipient fault line between those who saw culture's freedom realized in, and those who saw it threatened by, an orientation to the world.

Just as differences emerged regarding "freedom," so too with "unity." Congress organizers explicitly intended to assert German unity in the face of the increasingly potent East–West conflict. In a widely lauded address, Becher urged opposition to any force that would "experiment with the division of Germany, so perilous for world peace." Working for peace in their moment meant "striving for an independent German position that expresses itself in the national unity of Germany."[73] Engaged democrats similarly pushed to preserve national unity but took pains to distinguish this from apologetic celebration of Germanness. For Kantorowicz, the progressive core of nationhood – "*Geist* and *Kultur*" – had survived Nazism embodied in all who either "went into the catacombs in Germany or sought refuge outside Germany." By bringing these groups together, the congress validated its initiators' "conviction that Germany's spiritual unity will be preserved." He was quick to protest, however, that this "has nothing in common with nationalism." It merely recognized the "self-evident" fact that "to erect divisive barriers all across Germany" would be "to regress, in the age of the airplane, to before the era of the postal carriage."[74] Tacking awkwardly between idealist culture and modernization theory, these justifications bespoke a post-Nazi discomfort with the nation.

Not all conferees felt the need for provisos and qualifications. Among them was the doyenne of German letters, Ricarda Huch. One of a handful of women in the Prussian Academy of Arts in 1933, she had refused to sign a loyalty oath to the Nazi regime and resigned alongside Döblin, the brothers Mann, and others. As honorary president of the 1947 congress,

---

[72] Reinhold, Schlenstedt, and Tanneberger, eds. *Schriftstellerkongreß*, 171, 267–8, 338–40.
[73] Becher, "Vom Willen zum Frieden," *Aufbau* 3, no. 11 (1947): 326; Reinhold, Schlenstedt, and Tanneberger, eds. *Schriftstellerkongreß*, 363.
[74] Kantorowicz, "Deutsche Schriftsteller im Exil," *Ost und West* 1, no. 4 (1947): 42; Reinhold, Schlenstedt, and Tanneberger, eds. *Schriftstellerkongreß*, 142; Kantorowicz, "Gruß an den 1. Deutschen Schriftsteller-Kongreß," *Ost und West* 1, no. 3 (1947): 93.

Huch focused her address squarely on the issue of nationalism. In her estimation, the Germans' problem had been not an excess but a deficit of "national sentiment." The nation's belated development had left them with a too-weak sense of nationhood that provoked a too-strong surge after unification. Postwar Germans now had to find the kind of balanced collective feeling that was "natural and self-evident" in the life of any nation, the "self-love" out of which "love for the other" could grow. Although she had often "despaired" of her fellow Germans during the Nazi years, she also witnessed "heroism and high virtue." And since war's end, the nation had endured "immeasurable misery." Surely, she asserted, "the wickedness is thereby equalized."[75] Even prominent anti-Nazis washed out the specificities of perpetration and victimhood in apologetic accounts of parallel sufferings.

Nor did the congress forge unity on other fundamental issues, its primary objective. Various discussions exposed moments of manifest disunity and important differences of emphasis. The session on the "outer" and "inner" emigrations, for instance, proved divisive. Kantorowicz's conciliatory affirmation of both groups contrasted starkly with Langgässer's critical reflections on the dangers and compromises entailed by writing under the Third Reich. Harich's polemical attack on so-called inner émigrés, meanwhile, was truly controversial. As a youth in Nazi Germany, he charged, non-exiles' aestheticized "flight into interiority" had offered him little defense against the regime: "If I had been left to depend on this literature alone, I might well have become a strapping SS-man."[76] Overtly politicized disputes also erupted around the binary of "objectivity" versus "partisanship" as well as around the terms "humanity," "violence," and "truth."[77]

The most explosive encounter, however, did not involve Germans directly. On day two of the congress, Soviet playwright Vsevolod Vishnevsky cracked the veneer of inter-Allied cooperation. His short but pointed speech injected into German cultural-political debate the "two camps" rhetoric recently promulgated by Andrei Zhdanov, Stalin's chief ideologue and lieutenant for cultural affairs, at the inauguration of the Cominform (the Comintern's postwar successor). Vishnevsky urged his audience to join the camp fighting for "world peace," "world democracy," and a "united Germany" against the "militarism" of an American

---

[75] Ricarda Huch, n.t., *Der Autor* 1, no. 8 (1947): 1–2; cf. Reinhold, Schlenstedt, and Tanneberger, eds. *Schriftstellerkongreß*, 102–3.
[76] Elisabeth Langgässer, "Schriftsteller unter der Hitler-Diktatur," *Ost und West* 1, no. 4 (1947): 36–41; Kantorowicz, "Deutsche Schriftsteller im Exil," 42–51; Reinhold, Schlenstedt, and Tanneberger, eds. *Schriftstellerkongreß*, 136–47, 159.
[77] See Reinhold and Schlenstedt, "Vorgeschichte," 47.

A parliament of spirit? Mobilizing the cultural nation 217

and British-led "world reaction"; the USSR would stand "shoulder to shoulder" with any who opposed this new menace.[78] The Soviet delegation, rounded out by Boris Gorbatov and Valentin Kataev, had been sent at the request of Sergei Tulpanov, SVAG's head of Information Administration. Among Soviet policymakers, Tulpanov (like Zhdanov) belonged to the faction that pushed, together with the SED leadership, for the division of Germany and the Sovietization of the east.[79] Vishnevsky's intervention was designed to provoke, and it succeeded.

A reply came the next morning. In an impromptu session, Melvin Lasky – a US Army historian during the war and now Berlin correspondent for *The New Leader* and *Partisan Review* – delivered a riposte he had composed overnight. His theme was "cultural freedom," in the sense of the "unrestricted freedom of opinion... critique, [and] opposition" without which, Lasky asserted, American political and cultural life was "unthinkable." Its existential foe was "totalitarianism," and the writers' responsibility was to make the fight for this freedom their own. This framing clearly echoed the Truman Doctrine, the Western counterpart to Zhdanov's two camps. Lasky proceeded to mount a passionate critique of censorship and repression in the USSR, proclaiming solidarity with Soviet writers and artists – poet Anna Akhmatova, filmmaker Sergei Eisenstein, satirist Mikhail Zoshchenko, and countless others subjected to tyranny's whims.[80] That afternoon, Kataev gave the no less inflammatory Soviet response, addressing "the so-called writer Lasky": "It is a great pleasure finally to meet a live warmonger face to face."[81] With this, the opening salvos of the cultural Cold War were exchanged in Berlin, between an unknown, twenty-seven-year-old journalist from New York and three towering figures of Soviet literature.

Some portray Lasky's intervention as a courageous stand for cultural freedom, a consummately intellectual act of speaking truth to power under hostile circumstances. Others see an underlying cynicism, given the USA's coordinated anti-Communist offensive abroad and ongoing hearings by the House Un-American Activities Committee at

---

[78] Reinhold, Schlenstedt, and Tanneberger, eds. *Schriftstellerkongreß*, 245–7. On Zhdanov's "two camps," see Wilfried Loth, *The Division of the World, 1941–1955* (New York: St. Martin's, 1988), 159–64.
[79] Norman M. Naimark, *The Russians in Germany: A History of the Soviet Zone of Occupation, 1945–1949* (Cambridge, Mass.: Harvard University Press, 1995), 318–52, 412; Hartmann and Eggeling, *Sowjetische Präsenz*, 39–40, 53–8.
[80] Hochgeschwender, *Freiheit*, 141–2; Reinhold, Schlenstedt, and Tanneberger, eds. *Schriftstellerkongreß*, 295–7, 300–1. On the Truman Doctrine, see Loth, *Division*, 139–42. On Lasky's milieu, see Alan M. Wald, *The New York Intellectuals: The Rise and Decline of the Anti-Stalinist Left from the 1930s to the 1980s* (Chapel Hill: University of North Carolina Press, 1987).
[81] Reinhold, Schlenstedt, and Tanneberger, eds. *Schriftstellerkongreß*, 336.

home.[82] For present purposes, the crucial point is that, for Lasky as for Birkenfeld – who had engineered Lasky's appearance – the sphere to which cultural freedom pertained was narrowly construed. Lasky did not share Birkenfeld's reservations about the politicization of art; on the contrary, he vigorously asserted political effect as an aesthetic criterion.[83] But both rendered "cultural freedom" as a negative freedom with circumscribed ambit. This differed qualitatively from engaged democrats' expansive and positive conception of cultural freedom as the cultivation of self and world, a model of human freedom in general.

Although the conference did not break into open conflict, this eruption of East–West tensions shaped assessments of the whole event. Generally, those friendly to communism dismissed or were scandalized by Lasky's intervention, while those lining up on the opposite side of the divide were heartened. And although the intra-German tensions that did emerge were not straightforwardly partisan, their political valences mapped onto the global divide.[84] Accordingly, many reports emphasized the disunity or even bifurcation of German conferees. Pechel called East-West boundaries "lines of foreign powers' interests forced upon the Germans." These had dropped an "'iron curtain' straight through the hall" that regrettably encouraged "sentimental vagueness, personal ambition, [and] party-political demagoguery" from the native "publicistic zealots" who dominated the congress.[85] Arnold Bauer wrote of "two kinds of language," a split between those who embraced and those who rejected "loud watchwords and slogans," which correlated only roughly to the "political opposition of 'East' and 'West.'" For him, organizers' "all-too-loud call for unity" only highlighted such fractures. Birkenfeld regretted that "only isolated German–Western voices rose up against the impressively well-tuned German–Eastern orchestra." Above all, this basic imbalance underscored the "necessity... that Germans of Eastern and Western thought-styles remain in dialogue."[86] The metaphors of

---

[82] See, e.g., Pike, *Politics of Culture*, 473 and Jost Hermand, *Kultur im Wiederaufbau: Die Bundesrepublik Deutschland 1945–1965* (Munich: Nymphenberger, 1986), 145–6, respectively. Such positions recapitulate those staked out at the time.

[83] See also Giles Scott-Smith, "'A Radical Democratic Political Offensive': Melvin J. Lasky, Der Monat, and the Congress for Cultural Freedom," *Journal of Contemporary History* 35, no. 2 (2000): 266–8; Brockmann, *Literary Culture*, 153–4.

[84] Hochgeschwender, *Freiheit*, 142–3.

[85] [Rudolf Pechel], "Ein Spiegelbild Deutschlands," *Deutsche Rundschau* 70, no. 11 (1947): 135. This connected the definitive Cold-War metaphor back to its original theater context; Patrick Wright, *Iron Curtain: From Stage to Cold War* (Oxford: Oxford University Press, 2007).

[86] Arnold Bauer, "Zweierlei Sprache: Zum ersten deutschen Schriftstellerkongreß in Berlin," *Die Neue Zeitung*, 10 October 1947; Günther Birkenfeld, "Flucht aus der Gegenwart," *Horizont* 2, no. 24 (1947): 3; also Birkenfeld in Reinhold, Schlenstedt, and Tanneberger, eds. *Schriftstellerkongreß*, 418.

two languages and of orchestrated unity established themselves in critical commentary.

A striking number of responses, however, distanced German concerns and dynamics from those of their occupiers. Gunter Groll, from Munich, insisted on proceeding "as if" East-West synthesis, world peace, and the German unity that both demanded continued to be possible: "spirit" need not "play along in the quarrels of the victorious powers." Germans spoke not yet "two languages, but two dialects, one western and one eastern... the unity of our culture still exists and must be preserved." Süskind concurred, observing that writers from Germany's south and west had come "without commission," while others had received "a few too many marching orders." Nonetheless, he was full of praise and thanks. The conference had evoked for him Goethe's one-stanza poem "Hope," which captured "the hope of the transformable, the hope of activity that can bring about transformation." In that possibility, Süskind asserted, "our hope as writers" merged with "our hope as human beings."[87] Here, he echoed the vision of culture – as both a shared national heritage and a transformative freedom – that provided one of the conference's underpinnings.

Germany's engaged democrats too emphasized unity over disunity. Closing the congress, Weisenborn acknowledged that it had been "charged with an inner tension." Nonetheless, reprising his opening remarks, he affirmed its significance as "the first German parliament, the parliament of spirit." Introducing a special issue of *Ost und West* that printed several congress talks, Kantorowicz emphasized that strides had been made toward "our goal [of] spiritual understanding among Germans."[88] Reports by Harich, Ihering, and Leonhard all recognized the tensions yet underscored the commonalities that had also been evident. This shared ground demanded that they "remain in dialogue!" – as Harich's title had it – in order to address the crucial tasks of the moment.[89] Mayer cited with approval both Weisenborn's designation of the congress as "a first all-German parliament... a parliament of writers"

---

[87] Gunter Groll, "Münchener Epilog zum 1. Deutschen Schriftstellerkongreß: Wir gehören zusammen," *Ost und West* 1, no. 5 (1947): 89–90; Wilhelm E. Süskind, "Wort des Dankes," *Ost und West* 1, no. 4 (1947): 59, 61; also Süskind in Reinhold, Schlenstedt, and Tanneberger, eds. *Schriftstellerkongreß*, 437–9.

[88] Reinhold, Schlenstedt, and Tanneberger, eds. *Schriftstellerkongreß*, 439; [Kantorowicz], "Zu unseren Beiträgen," *Ost und West* 1, no. 4 (1947): verso of cover. The issue contained contributions from Huch, Weisenborn, Langgässer, Kantorowicz, Eggebrecht, and Süskind.

[89] Wolfgang Harich, "Im Gespräch bleiben!" *Die Weltbühne* 2, no. 20 (1947): 886–92; Ihering, "Friedenskongreß des Geistes," *Sonntag*, 19 October 1947; Rudolf Leonhard, "Der erste deutsche Schriftstellerkongreß," *Wissen und Tat* 2, no. 18/19 (1947): 39–42.

and Langgässer's assertion that participants belonged to "one spiritual community." Moreover, he cautioned naysayers against mistaking a "discussion of fundamentals" for a "chaos of opinions." Conflicts had emerged between Allied guests, and, yes, crucial issues remained unresolved. Even so, "a dialogue between German writers took place. There are forces that may not have wanted this. The dialogue has opened and should now continue.... No one should see this as a failure."[90] Their comments juxtaposed manifest conflict between occupiers with potential unity among Germans.

The intellectuals in question also voiced more ambiguous assessments, however. In his memoir, Mayer emphasized the divisive effects of the confrontation between Lasky and the Soviets. Kantorowicz likewise sounded a disillusioned note over SED influence in his diary.[91] This underscores a key point: they sought not to proclaim a false unity in the face of real divisions but to posit unity as a goal toward which to strive. Among the contributions Kantorowicz selected for publication were Eggebrecht's impromptu closing remarks. These were cautionary in tone, lamenting the intra-German conflicts that dogged their discussions. He pointed to the irony that, in Hamburg, he often felt himself an embattled "outpost of the great, unified army of active German *Geist*," for which he was branded a tool of the East. Yet to his unpleasant surprise, he felt similarly at sea during the Berlin proceedings, confronted by misunderstanding, suspicion, and partisanship. He urged his colleagues, in future encounters, to "let such words as friendship, unity of language, struggle for freedom, critique, [and] tolerance take on a much higher degree of reality and form." At the same time, he invited them to reflect on moments when the aspirational unity had come into view. The future held "difficult struggles" that required a "living, evolved – not merely an arranged or even orchestrated unity." At the conference, Mayer had endorsed Eggebrecht's thoughts. Quoting Hegel, he insisted: "The truth is the whole! If we think through this sentence ... in the sense of a conflict that unites, that forgets not for a moment that we form one spiritual community," then the congress' purpose would be well served.[92] Germany's engaged democrats rejected the notion that unity could be declared by fiat. Rather, it could only be constituted by the collaborative, creative activity of its constituents.

---

[90] Mayer, "Macht und Ohnmacht des Wortes," *Frankfurter Hefte* 2, no. 12 (1947): 1179–81.
[91] Rohrwasser cites the relevant passages, rather selectively, as evidence of duplicity, blindness, or both; "Vom Exil," 144–6.
[92] Axel Eggebrecht, "Kritik und Verbindlichkeit," *Ost und West* 1, no. 4 (1947): 53–5, 58; cf. Reinhold, Schlenstedt, and Tanneberger, eds. *Schriftstellerkongreß*, 410–14; ibid., 416.

## The polarization of culture in the Cold War

If the First German Writers' Congress marked the zenith of such efforts, its successors charted their decline. This was bound up with a polarization of public discourse driven by inter-Allied dynamics but shaped by many Germans' willing involvement. Above all, it entailed the fission of engaged democrats' two-sided notion of culture into its component parts. For a growing rift soon separated "unity" from "freedom," a local German variant of the "peace" versus "freedom" dichotomy that structured the cultural Cold War globally.[93] Opposing terms were appropriated by opposing camps, and the tone-setting declarations by Truman and Zhdanov, refracted in the Vishnevsky–Lasky clash, soon resonated in intra-German debates. As the full weight of polarization set in, positions that straddled both sides were left homeless and suspect on the new ideological landscape.

The semantic confrontation paralleled developments in diplomacy. There, acrimony mounted over 1947, with the formation of the Bizone, the Truman Doctrine and Marshall Plan, the Cominform, and stalled foreign ministers' conferences in Moscow and London. First Soviet, then British and American information officers suspended concern for inter-Allied harmony and shifted toward an overtly antagonistic line. US officials publicly proclaimed "Operation Talk Back" in late October: Soviet disinformation, they insisted, demanded a propaganda counteroffensive explaining the merits of liberal democracy and the dangers of totalitarianism. The ensuing battles were fought first and foremost by newspapers and broadcasting under direct military control. But in the four-power hotspot Berlin, the licensed *Telegraf* and *Tagesspiegel* had struck an anti-Communist course even earlier, galvanized by the forced merger of SPD and KPD in 1946. *Die Neue Zeitung* was similarly disposed. Gradually, their critiques of SED measures expanded to Soviet policy. In response, SVAG blocked and confiscated all three papers at decisive moments, seeking to ensure a monopoly for the *Tägliche Rundschau*, the SED's *Neues Deutschland*, and the nominally independent *Berliner Zeitung*. These actions provoked reactions in kind.[94] Personnel turnover also accompanied the policy shift as conciliatory control officers and

---

[93] Anselm Doering-Manteuffel, "Im Kampf um 'Frieden' und 'Freiheit': Über den Zusammenhang von Ideologie und Sozialkultur im Ost-West Konflikt," in *Koordinaten deutscher Geschichte in der Epoche des Ost-West-Konflikts*, ed. Hans Günter Hockerts (Munich: Oldenbourg, 2004), 29–47. From the Soviet perspective, German "unity" correlated to world "peace" because it was capitalism's imperialist dynamic that threatened both goals.

[94] Harold Hurwitz, *Die Stunde Null der deutschen Presse: Die amerikanische Pressepolitik in Deutschland 1945–1949* (Cologne: Wissenschaft und Politik, 1972), 333–49;

editorial staff – American New Dealers and German leftists – were replaced with hard-line anti-Communists. Among those whose contracts went unrenewed were Hermlin and Mayer at Radio Frankfurt as well as Eggebrecht's friend Heinz Norden at the Munich illustrated *Heute* and his sister Ruth Norden at American sector radio in Berlin. When *Neue Zeitung* editor Hans Wallenberg resigned in protest against prescriptive controls (not anti-Communism), Kästner and several others followed suit.[95]

These tensions set the tone for institutional changes among German-run journals and organizations as well. In April 1947, ICD withdrew its license from Alfred Andersch and Hans Werner Richter for *Der Ruf*. Officially, the charges were nationalism and militarism. Also, their outspoken advocacy of democratic socialism in an independent, unified Germany and Europe was increasingly at odds with the direction of US policy (though they were no partisans of the USSR).[96] The following year, a similar process began for *Ulenspiegel*, also a thorn in ICD's side. As with *Der Ruf*, official displeasure first led to a cut in paper allotment; rather than bend to pressure, Weisenborn and Herbert Sandberg returned their license. Soon, Sandberg was running *Ulenspiegel* as sole Soviet licensee, in the Soviet sector.[97] Meanwhile, *Die Weltbühne* published partisan exposés by leftist journalists purged in the western zones: Hans-Günther Cwojdrak, ejected from Radio Hamburg, and Emil Carlebach, whose *Frankfurter Rundschau* license was revoked.[98] In this period, resolutely

---

Peter Strunk, *Zensur und Zensoren: Medienkontrolle und Propagandapolitik unter sowjetischer Besatzungsherrschaft in Deutschland* (Berlin: Akademie, 1996), 52–60; Jessica C. E. Gienow-Hecht, *Transmission Impossible: American Journalism as Cultural Diplomacy in Postwar Germany, 1945–1955* (Baton Rouge: Louisiana State University Press, 1999), 95–109, 121–34; Susanne Grebner, *Der Telegraf: Entstehung einer SPD-nahen Lizenzzeitung in Berlin 1946–1950* (Münster: LIT, 2002), 167–94.

[95] Hans-Ulrich Wagner, *"Der gute Wille, etwas Neues zu schaffen": Das Hörspielprogramm in Deutschland von 1945 bis 1949* (Potsdam: Verlag für Berlin-Brandenburg, 1997), 108–9; Heinz Norden to Eggebrecht, 6 October 1947, SUBH NL Eggebrecht NE: B302; Schivelbusch, *Cold Crater*, 114–22; Gienow-Hecht, *Transmission*, 113; Christina von Hodenberg, *Konsens und Krise: Eine Geschichte der westdeutschen Medienöffentlichkeit, 1945–1973* (Göttingen: Wallstein, 2006), 121–5. As Hodenberg shows, not only anti-Communism but also efforts by Nazi-era media elites to reclaim the positions they lost in 1945 shaped these personnel changes.

[96] Jérôme Vaillant, *Der Ruf: Unabhängige Blätter der jungen Generation (1945–1949): Eine Zeitschrift zwischen Illusion und Anpassung* (Munich: Saur, 1978), 14–16, 82–4, 106–50. The journal continued under Erich Kuby, soon followed by the unabashedly pro-Western Walter von Cube.

[97] Cora Sol Goldstein, *Capturing the German Eye: American Visual Propaganda in Occupied Germany* (Chicago: University of Chicago Press, 2009), 116–21; Herbert Sandberg and Weisenborn to Brune Buttles (Information Services, OMGBS), 10 May 1948, AdK Weisenborn-Archiv 1344/2. Goldstein's assertion that Weisenborn first left the project, then Sandberg returned the US license is incorrect.

[98] Emil N. Carlebach, "Offener Brief an General Clay," *Die Weltbühne* 2, no. 23 (1947): 985–6; Hans-Günther Cwojdrak, "Demokratie und Maulkorb," *Die Weltbühne* 2,

A parliament of spirit? Mobilizing the cultural nation 223

independent authors such as Eggebrecht and Kästner began to fade from *Die Weltbühne*'s pages as anti-Western and pro-Soviet voices gained prominence, and the journal quietly lost a sizeable portion of its initial readership.[99]

The most celebrated case, however, was the Berlin Kulturbund. On the last day of the First German Writers' Congress, news reached participants that a Kulturbund ban was imminent. Indeed, its activities were soon prohibited in the American and British sectors, based on a reinterpretation of licensing regulations.[100] To its still broad constituency, however, this was tantamount to a ban, and it was vociferously opposed by figures from Becher to Birkenfeld. A protest rally again packed the great hall at Radio Berlin, where the founding rally had been. Writing in *Aufbau, Sonntag,* and *Die Weltbühne,* Abusch, Becher, Ihering, and Leonhard lodged public objections; as president, Becher sent an open letter to UNESCO and the international PEN Club. In fact, political controversy had already begun to siphon support from the Berlin Kulturbund, with local membership dropping from early 1947, even as overall membership figures rose.[101] Nor did the Kulturbund have only western detractors. Tulpanov and SED leaders had long been dissatisfied with its too "bourgeois," insufficiently partisan character under Becher, and they repeatedly floated plans for binding it more tightly to the party. By late 1947, they also appreciated that a ban by Western authorities had its propagandistic uses.[102]

1948 was the watershed to open Cold War. After the Allied Control Council broke down, the Berlin crisis erupted in June: currency reform in the west was met with not only a new eastern currency but also the Soviet blockade of Berlin's western sectors, provoking an Anglo-American airlift of basic supplies. While the spring saw a round of reciprocal bans by

---

no. 19 (1947): 1046–8; Hurwitz, *Stunde Null,* 314–21; Peter von Rüden and Wagner, eds. *Die Geschichte des Nordwestdeutschen Rundfunks* (Hamburg: Hoffmann & Campe, 2005), 50–1.

[99] Schivelbusch, *Cold Crater,* 181. It is, however, easy to overstate this case; cf. Wehner, *Kulturpolitik,* 389. Though Eggebrecht was too busy for original contributions after 1946, he continued to identify with the new journal into 1947. Kästner's new poems and chansons ran intermittently through mid 1948, but he broke off contact thereafter. Eggebrecht to Ralph Giordano, 7 February 1947, SUBH NL Eggebrecht NE: B128: 2, Bl. 7–9; "Aktennotiz," 22 February 1949, Landesarchiv Berlin NL Madrasch-Groschopp, E Rep. 200–67e.

[100] Reinhold, Schlenstedt, and Tanneberger, eds. *Schriftstellerkongreß,* 417. See Schivelbusch, *Cold Crater,* 97–101.

[101] *Freiheit dem Kulturbund: Die Kundgebung in den Sälen des Berliner Funkhauses am 26. Nov. 1947* (Berlin: Aufbau, 1947); Alexander Abusch, "Das Exempel Kulturbund," *Die Weltbühne* 2, no. 22 (1947): 945–8; Becher, "Offener Brief an die UNESCO und an den internationalen PEN-Club," *Aufbau* 3, no. 12 (1947): 373–4; Ihering, "Der mißverstandene Kulturbund," *Sonntag,* 23 November 1947; Leonhard, "Kulturspalter," *Die Weltbühne* 2, no. 23 (1947): 1003–5; Heider, *Kulturbund,* 206.

[102] Naimark, *Russians,* 402–5; Schivelbusch, *Cold Crater,* 99–101.

SVAG and OMGUS on each other's licensed publications, overt cultural polarization set in during the blockade. This was manifest in several institutional counter-foundations: In June, refugee students from the Humboldt University and their supporters convened a committee to establish a US-sponsored "Free University." In July, Kulturbund defectors around Birkenfeld, Karsch, and Redslob formed a "Free Kulturbund" in Berlin's western sectors, soon renamed the "League for Intellectual Freedom."[103] This central trope of the cultural Cold War – "freedom" of thought and expression – was gaining currency. Vitally important was the foundation of *Der Monat*, a journal conceived by Lasky to mobilize German intellectuals in defense of the "Atlantic community's" shared liberal values. Published by OMGUS, it appeared with much fanfare in October 1948 and – fueled by star-studded, international contributors and generous subsidies – it immediately under- and outsold its competitors.[104] The path, however, had been well cleared. Materially, the currency reforms restructured consumption (available goods as well as buyers' preferences), eliminated artificial surpluses of disposable income, and conclusively split the nationwide market in two. Very few cultural-political journals survived. The Soviet blockade, meanwhile, proved a failed gambit politically, and in the battle for hearts, minds, and stomachs it was a disaster. As the airlift also demonstrated, the western occupiers did not expect their charges to live by bread alone. Together with much-needed food, American transports airlifted stacks of *Der Monat* into the beleaguered, divided city.[105]

Feeling the pressure – and Soviet encouragement – the SED likewise stepped up its cultural activism in 1948. A heavier hand was evident at its First Culture Conference in May, where national "unity" propaganda was officially formulated as cultural policy. The key resolution proclaimed: "We pledge ourselves to an all-German democratic cultural program, indebted to all progressive spiritual tendencies... Cultural unity must be protected." At the same time, it juxtaposed an "insurmountable crisis

---

[103] Hurwitz, *Stunde Null*, 338; James F. Tent, *The Free University of Berlin: A Political History* (Bloomington: Indiana University Press, 1988), 125–35; Wehner, *Kulturpolitik*, 796–800.

[104] Hochgeschwender, *Freiheit*, 149–60; Scott-Smith, "'A Radical Democratic Political Offensive,'" 268–73. Sternberger was acutely aware of *Der Monat*'s competition and the enviable financing that enabled its low price. Fearing for *Die Wandlung*'s survival, he even chastised Jaspers for contributing to *Der Monat*; Sternberger to Jaspers, 23 February 1949, 2 March 1949, Deutsches Literaturarchiv (Marbach a.N., hereafter DLA) A:Sternberger/ Wandlung/ 74.10263/3–4.

[105] Ingrid Laurien, "Zeitschriftenlandschaft Nachkriegszeit: Zu Struktur und Funktion politisch-kultureller Zeitschriften 1945–1949," *Publizistik* 47, no. 1 (2002): 77–8; Saunders, *Cultural Cold War*, 30. See also Paul Steege, *Black Market, Cold War: Everyday Life in Berlin, 1946–1949* (Cambridge: Cambridge University Press, 2007).

of bourgeois thought" to the "spiritual strength of Marxism," which it asserted – in an especially vulgar materialism – had been "prove[n]" by the Red Army's victories.[106] Alongside such partisan pronouncements, echoes of pluralism rang hollow. Meanwhile, SED co-chair Otto Grotewohl revised the leadership's geopolitical line. At a June 1948 meeting, he consigned visions of a "bridge between East and West" officially to the dustbin of the past. Only one "orientation" was possible: "firmly and unequivocally toward the East." At the same meeting, the SED resolved to transform itself into a hard-line, Bolshevik-style "party of the new type." Soon, Ackermann recanted his theory of a distinctive, reformist "German road to socialism."[107] Notions of Germany mediating between East and West and of the SED mediating between Communism and Social Democracy were now anathema; official "unity" lost its veneer of pluralism and took on a partisan cast.

As champions of both "freedom" and "unity," engaged democrats were highly sensitized to the Cold War's rhetorical tremors, even far away from their epicenter in Berlin. The "Call to German Unity" issued by Weber and Karl Geiler with Friedensburg, Becher, and others had run afoul of the new fault line. When Sternberger withheld his signature, it split the Heidelberg group. The resolution sought "unity" on the basis of "democracy and freedom," which he called a "formula ... so overused" that it required further specification: "legally secured democracy and personal freedom." Otherwise, he thought it might strengthen the hand of a "'Russo-German' unity demand" against the West, and in private, he admitted he would sooner see a "West German emergency solution" than sacrifice freedom for unity. In public – quoting Becher from the Berlin Writers' Congress – Sternberger nonetheless continued to emphasize that "a divided Germany is a peaceless Germany," a symptom of "world unpeace" and a portent of grave danger.[108] Dirks too reflected on the relationship of "freedom" to "that which, on the other side of the Elbe, they now call 'unity,'" concluding that he could not accept one without the other. Moving into a different register, he advocated a third principle: "Subdivision mediates ... It is the basic law of every political order

---

[106] "Entschließung zur Kulturpolitik," in *Protokoll der Verhandlungen des Ersten Kulturtages der Sozialistischen Einheitspartei Deutschlands 5. bis 7. Mai 1948* (Berlin: Dietz, 1948), 265–6; Dietrich, *Politik und Kultur*, 122–7.

[107] Dirk Spilker, *The East German Leadership and the Division of Germany: Patriotism and Propaganda, 1945–1953* (Oxford: Oxford University Press, 2006), 145, 162–9, quote 167.

[108] Sternberger to Weber, 21 November 1947, DLA A:Sternberger/ Aktionsgruppe Heidelberg/ 89.10.8112; Sternberger, "Tagebuch: Ein Brief an den Herausgeber – Friede?" *Die Wandlung* 2, no. 9 (1947): 756; cf. Becher, "Vom Willen zum Frieden," 326; Reinhold, Schlenstedt, and Tanneberger, eds. *Schriftstellerkongreß*, 363.

that remains human, simultaneously the law of freedom and unity."[109] Here, Dirks conjoined engaged democrats' socio-political and cultural discourses, locating true freedom in decentralized forms of unity.

Against this backdrop, two further writers' gatherings were held in Frankfurt, in which these intellectuals and their program played an ever more marginal role. In January, a coordinating committee of writers' organizations established at the Berlin congress met; the Frankfurt SDS hosted delegates from Hamburg, Munich, and other western locales, while the Berlin representatives did not receive travel authorization in time. At a closing rally, Eggebrecht and Pollatschek spoke. The latter emphasized that German writers' "most pressing concern" was "the unity of spiritual life across Germany's entire area... Cosmopolitanism and nation are the stars by which we chart our ship's course."[110] At the second gathering, such pledges of cultural-national unity were barely heard, despite the context: the centennial of the National Assembly in Frankfurt's Paulskirche (Figure 5.2). The imposing church had burned out during the war and was rebuilt just in time for the festivities, which began on 18 May and included a three-day writers' congress.[111] As a crucial juncture in the histories of authority, freedom, the nation, and the "unpolitical German," 1848 was a moment engaged democrats – like many others – were eager to revisit. In greetings sent to the Frankfurt gathering, Leonhard underscored that "it was the revolution that made clear Germany's tasks: unity and democracy. These tasks still stand before us today." He hoped Frankfurt would pick up where – in his mind – Berlin had left off: with a debate on how best to further these goals through "what our French friends call *littérature engagée*."[112] This did not come to pass. A different view of literature held sway in Frankfurt, with the goal of unity present largely as an absence and the goal of democracy circumscribed. In one historian's estimation, that meeting marked the consolidation of a "liberal-democratic and antitotalitarian concept of freedom" that would undergird West Germany's intellectual Cold War.[113]

---

[109] Dirks, "Einheit und Freiheit," *Frankfurter Hefte* 3, no. 3 (1948): 193, 196.

[110] Buergel-Goodwin, "Reorganisation," 422–4; "Generalversammlung des Schutzverbandes Deutscher Autoren am 17. April 1948," n.d., AdK Archiv Schriftstellerverband 206/3/48; Walther Pollatschek, n.t., *Ost und West* 2, no. 2 (1948): 94–5.

[111] Peter Reichel, *Schwarz, Rot, Gold: Kleine Geschichte deutscher Nationalsymbole nach 1945* (Munich: Beck, 2005), 111–12; Waltraud Wende-Hohenberger, preface to *Der Frankfurter Schriftstellerkongreß im Jahr 1948*, ed. Wende-Hohenberger (Frankfurt a.M.: Lang, 1989), i–li.

[112] Leonhard, "An den deutschen Schriftstellerkongreß in der Paulskirche in Frankfurt, Mai 1948," 18 May 1948, AdK Leonhard-Archiv 806; also Leonhard, "Schwarz, Rot und Gold," *Die Weltbühne* 3, no. 24 (1948): 685.

[113] Hochgeschwender, *Freiheit*, 145.

Figure 5.2 The centennial celebration of the National Assembly in the reconstructed Paulskirche in Frankfurt on 18 May 1948. As the procession gathers outside, official guests mingle with onlookers and other city-dwellers. (*Source*: ullstein bild - dpa)

228    German Intellectuals and Democratic Renewal

The Frankfurt congress broke with its Berlin predecessor in intended and unintended ways. It was not initiated by the local writers' association; rather, the city charged nearby Bollwerk publishers with organization. The title was simply "German Writers' Congress," without the modifier "Second," acknowledging no filiation with the "First." At the same time, the lead planner, Karl Ludwig Schmidt of Bollwerk, clearly had its predecessor in mind, as a positive model and a negative foil. He repeatedly underscored that "writers of *all zones*" would be invited, and he contacted the Berlin SDA for help. However, the Congress' focus was to remain purely literary, to avoid drawing out "deep ideological and political differences." Many of those involved in organizing the 1947 event – including Becher, Kantorowicz, Leonhard, Schendell, Weyrauch, and Weisenborn – were contacted during planning. Eggebrecht, Kästner, Kogon, and Mayer were also consulted.[114] But of them all, only Mayer attended. And in the end, the event passed entirely without participants from Berlin or the Soviet zone. After initially accepting, Becher withdrew in early May, citing US officials' refusal to renew his interzonal travel pass. Kantorowicz, Weisenborn, and Weyrauch cancelled last-minute by telegram, within days of each other.[115]

The reasons for the absences were varied and, in part, murky. Kogon was busy presiding over another portion of the Paulskirche program, a meeting of European federalists. Others may have been deterred because the writers' associations – the coordinating committee as well as the Berlin, Frankfurt, Hamburg, and Munich groups – withheld their endorsement in protest that a publishing house had control.[116] Still other absences were bound up with decidedly political conflicts that, Schmidt's protestations notwithstanding, shaped the event. In Pollatschek's view – speaking for the local SDS and KPD – the congress was convened not

---

[114] Karl Ludwig Schmidt to Kantorowicz, 18 February 1948, 16 March 1948, SUBH NL Kantorowicz NK: Ostberlin: 65 (emphasis in original); Schmidt to Kogon, 9 March 1948, AdsD NL Kogon, Reden 45–7.48; Schmidt to Leonhard, 17 March 1948 and 15 April 1948, AdK Leonhard-Archiv 831.

[115] Schmidt, "Zur Frage der Nichtbeteiligung deutscher Schriftsteller aus der Ostzone am Frankfurter Schriftsteller-Kongreß," n.d., Historisches Archiv der Stadt Köln NL Mayer 1333 Box 51/1. This privately circulated pamphlet exhaustively documents Schmidt's communications. It makes plain his efforts to include "Eastern" writers, and it is corrobarated by archival holdings elsewhere, e.g., "Protokoll über die Vorstandssitzung am 13. Mai 1948," 14 May 1948, AdK Archiv Schriftstellerverband 206/3/115; Kantorowicz to Schmidt, telegram 15 May 1948, SUBH NL Kantorowicz NK: Ostberlin: 65.

[116] "Weltfest des Geistes in der Paulskirche," *Die Neue Zeitung*, 20 May 1948; Helmut Peitsch, "Ein Brennpunkt der Nachkriegsliteratur: Der deutsche Schriftstellerkongreß in Frankfurt am Main 1948," in *Heiss und kalt: Die Jahre 1945–69* (Berlin: Elefanten, 1986), 177. On Kogon's pro-Europe activism, see Chapter 7.

only by "a not at all competent authority," but by an "SPD party publisher" to boot. In a circular to friends, he speculated that Bollwerk and the SPD-led city administration, allied in anti-Communism, might be conspiring to raise Frankfurt's profile as the potential capital of a future West German state.[117] In this polarizing atmosphere, the SED hastily convened a competing May 18th celebration in Berlin, with a keynote address by Becher. As internal documents show, the party did indeed forbid its members to attend the Paulskirche events and resolved to prevail upon Kantorowicz, Weisenborn, and Mayer (who had by then accepted his Leipzig post) to pull out as well.[118]

Gauging the party's influence on the outcome is another matter. There is little reason to doubt Weyrauch's intentions. Unlike the others, he had no KPD/SED ties. When a family emergency kept him in Berlin, he sent his prepared remarks to Frankfurt, where they were read by Arnold Bauer. Weisenborn, in contrast, found his plane reservation suddenly cancelled, and he suspected SED meddling. Anticipating the fallout, his telegram sent an unambiguous message: "[I] stress that I never subscribe to the slogan of any party... We German writers must travel the German path, reject every either-or, battling today's hysteria." Only Kantorowicz was unspecific about the "unforeseen difficulties" behind his absence. His diary, however, confirms that pressure by the party kept him away. Having narrowly escaped the closure of *Ost und West*, whose orientation was now explicitly at odds with the SED program, he presents his nonappearance as an unavoidable concession to the reigning authorities.[119]

The event did attract major figures from the western zones, however. Presiding were Langgässer, Mayer, and Richter, with well-known writers Kasimir Edschmid, Rudolf Hagelstange, and Rudolf Alexander Schröder, the assembly's honorary president. Theodor Plievier – who returned from Soviet exile to Weimar in 1945, then moved to Munich in October 1947 – also spoke, alongside several less prominent authors and two SPD politicians. In part, Plievier's talk echoed Weisenborn's telegram. It was a hymn to freedom in many guises – from social justice

---

[117] Walther Pollatschek, "Schriftstellertreffen in Frankfurt a.M.," *Wissen und Tat* 3, no. 6 (1948): 26; Pollatschek, "Hintergründe 'eines deutschen Schriftsteller-Kongresses,'" n.d., SUBH NL Kantorowicz NK: Ostberlin 65.

[118] "Protokoll Nr. 70 (II) der Sitzung des Zentralsekretariats am 3.5.48," n.d., "Protokoll Nr. 73 (II) der Sitzung des Zentralsekretariats am 10.5.48," n.d., BArch DY 30/IV 2/2.1 194, 2, 197, 1. The main SED-sponsored events – above all, the Second People's Congress on 18 March – had commemorated barricade battles with a stronger "worker" component earlier in 1848, not the "professors' parliament" in May; Steege, *Black Market*, 147–51, 168.

[119] Schmidt, "Zur Frage der Nichtbeteiligung," 13–14; Kantorowicz, *Deutsches Tagebuch*, I:456.

to property rights – with clear references to unfreedom in both state-socialist and liberal, capitalist systems. But it was also a call to work against Germany's division. While writers might lack geopolitical influence, he asserted, they could refuse to endorse any one occupying power and "sit between all chairs" rather than "take a comfortable seat." Plievier expressly cautioned against equating the choice (e.g., his) to "leave the East" with a decision "to commit oneself to the West."[120] His remarks emboldened Hagelstange to stir controversy nonetheless. Asserting that "outside forces" had prevented the Berlin delegation's participation, he proposed – repeatedly – a resolution of sympathy with the Soviet zone's oppressed writers. As moderators, Mayer and Edschmid countered that this was speculative and constituted unwarranted criticism of an occupying power. In Mayer's words, they thwarted the "Lasky method[s]" of "an anti-Eastern faction" that stood "in constant contact with American headquarters." The eventual resolution simply expressed solidarity with absent colleagues, whether in the East or exile. A second resolution demanded the unfettered circulation of printed matter and of writers across zonal borders.[121]

Substantively, discussion revolved around the appropriate relation of writing to politics. As Leonhard had hoped, the issue was now addressed via the French discussion of "committed" versus "pure literature" ignited by philosopher Jean-Paul Sartre. In the intervening months, his play *The Flies* had been performed in Germany, with Sartre and Simone de Beauvoir in attendance at the Berlin premiere. The events had spurred Germans' awareness of existentialism and the Sartrean terminology, which framed debate at the Frankfurt congress.[122] Against Leonhard's hopes, however, the partisans of "pure literature" prevailed, defending the normative autonomy of the cultural realm. Schröder, for instance, a lay Protestant preacher, identified the "secret of eternity" as the writer's essential concern. In its timelessness, all true art sought "to illuminate [the] good, true, and beautiful" within its object, without which the latter "had no reality at all." Catholic novelist and pedagogue Leo Weismantel inveighed against the intrusion of "unqualified functionaries" into

---

[120] Theodor Plievier, *Einige Bemerkungen über die Bedeutung der Freiheit* (Nuremberg: Nest, 1948), 14.
[121] "Dann ist alles Gequatsche: Leere Stühle – hochexplosiv," *Der Spiegel*, 29 May 1948, 26; Mayer, *Ein Deutscher*, I:397; Wende-Hohenberger, *Frankfurter Schriftstellerkongreß*, 89.
[122] See Brockmann, *Literary Culture*, 146–7, 227–9; Weisenborn, *Horizont*, 135–7; Félix Lusset, "Sartre in Berlin (Januar 1948): Zur Arbeit der französischen Kulturmission in Berlin," in *Französische Kulturpolitik in Deutschland 1945–1949: Berichte und Dokumente*, ed. Jérôme Vaillant (Constance: Universitätsverlag Konstanz, 1984), 107–19. The lively post-performance debate with Sartre in Berlin was moderated by Weisenborn.

aesthetics. He called for a "German cultural parliament" in which the "culture-making estates" would champion "the primacy of spiritual culture," with its truths of "inner morality" and "divinity," over worldly politics. Most conferees were not as extreme in severing art from the world, and notes of dissent were also heard. Walter Kolbenhoff, for instance, issued a passionate if rather blunt call for a realism that thematized social ills. As long as children starve, he demanded, "who dares appeal to eternal values?"[123] Such interventions only set off the majority position.

Several participants in this debate addressed the specificity of cultural freedom. Here too, Hagelstange took the most emphatic position. Just as he insisted on a distinct "spiritual realm of art" in which "things reveal their value ... by the criterion of their harmony with themselves," he asserted that "the status and essence of writing demand that it enjoy ... full and unrestrained freedom." The meaning of this was "self-evident" to all true authors: "to be allowed to read and write, hear and say ... what appears to us – in the unabated will to truth – to be right." His unabashedly "purist" position, however, also resonated with others who made more concessions to "commitment." Süskind, for example, acknowledged that societal changes had transformed the writer's role. In "our 'feuilletonistic' age," he – like many others – was increasingly "a writer with less of a *literary* and more of a *publicistic* accent." A stark divide between literature and social life was no longer possible, and in itself, this was nothing to lament. And yet, writers should take care not to "enter into" but only to "approach" politics, to remain a *"floating* authority." In that regard, he drew an explicit contrast to the Berlin conference. There, he had heard "much about writers' ideological, political, and antifascist duties" but little about their "occupational-moral duty," which bound them to "truth and freedom" alone, above "their people" or "humanity."[124] For Süskind, as for Hagelstange, writers were free in so far as they spoke truths in perfect freedom from interference. And both advocated, albeit to differing degrees, defensive barriers between the aesthetic and socio-political realms.

Overall, the congress tended toward this basic, two-pronged consensus. It informed but did not exhaust a confrontation between Mayer and

---

[123] Rudolf Alexander Schröder, "Aufgaben der Dichtung in der Zeit," in *Literatur und Politik: Sieben Vorträge zur heutigen Situation in Deutschland*, ed. Heinrich Bechtoldt (Constance: Asmus, 1948), 52, 56; Leo Weismantel, "Ein deutsches Kulturparlament," in *Leo Weismantel: Leben und Werk: Ein Buch des Dankes zu des Dichters 60. Geburtstag* (Berlin: Nauck, 1948), 224–5; Wende-Hohenberger, *Frankfurter Schriftstellerkongreß*, 45.

[124] Rudolf Hagelstange, "Die unveräußerlichen geistigen Grundlagen der Dichtung," in *Literatur und Politik*, ed. Bechtoldt, 95–6; Süskind, "Wandlung des Schriftstellers," in *Literatur und Politik*, ed. Bechtoldt, 127–9, 135–7 (emphases in original).

Kurt Marek, a Rowohlt editor who had been present yet silent in Berlin.[125] In Frankfurt, Marek made a prominent contribution. He rejected what he called a "literature of the general line" – i.e., socialist realism – which represented given "facts" according to a political scheme, distorting "reality" and celebrating "the cadre's supremacy over against the individual." (He quoted Goethe on the true poet's "free spirit" and "impartial view" to buttress his point.) However, he advocated neither naturalist realism nor social disengagement. Rather, Marek praised literature that grappled with the essence of the present era's "upheaval" – in which not the "individual" but the "collective," not "qualities" but "affiliations" dominated – yet still projected "a share of individual freedom" against the reality it revealed. In addition to fiction by Franz Kafka and the contemporary novelist Hermann Kasack, Marek lauded non-fiction works: José Ortega y Gasset's *Revolt of the Masses* (1930), Ernst Jünger's *The Worker* (1932), James Burnham's *Managerial Revolution* (1941), Arthur Koestler's "The Yogi and the Commissar" (1945), and Hans Zehrer's *Man in This World* (1948).[126] Marek's remarks put elitist cultural critique, ex-Communists' pessimistic liberalism, conservative technocratic fantasies, and existentialist Kafka appropriations into play around a common theme: the modern confrontation of individual and institution.

The post-talk discussion focused primarily on politicization in literature, but Mayer decided to confront Marek on the full ground of his argument. He rewrote his own talk overnight and retitled it "The Writer and the Crisis of Humanity," taking Marek's depiction of the modern condition as his point of departure.[127] On Mayer's somewhat tendentious reading, Jünger, Koestler, Burnham, Sartre, and Albert Camus had all effectively resigned themselves to "the reality of our mechanized, alienated, and thus dehumanized world." Rather than ask after "the causes of this development or the possibilities of its overcoming," they hypostatized an abstract, decisionist individual freedom in response. How could, Mayer asked, either the vertiginously absurd world of the

---

[125] Reinhold, Schlenstedt, and Tanneberger, eds. *Schriftstellerkongreß*, 509. A journalist by trade, Marek, like Hagelstange (and Rowohlt and Peter von Zahn), worked in a Wehrmacht propaganda company during the war. In 1949, as C. W. Ceram, he wrote *Götter, Gräber und Gelehrte*, West Germany's first bestseller. Peitsch, "Brennpunkt," 181; Ralf Schnell, *Geschichte der deutschsprachigen Literatur seit 1945*, 2nd edn. (Stuttgart: Metzler, 2003), 21.

[126] Kurt W. Marek, "Der Schriftsteller und die Wirklichkeit," in *Literatur und Politik*, ed. Bechtoldt, 65–6, 69–71.

[127] Wende-Hohenberger, ed. *Frankfurter Schriftstellerkongreß*, 51. Mayer's planned topic had been "The German and the European Novel Today"; "Deutscher Schriftsteller-Kongreß, Paulskirche Jahrhundertfeier," n.d., SUBH NL Kantorowicz NK: Ostberlin 65.

existentialists or the seamlessly administered world of the management theorists account for the basic insights of humanism? Both had in common a "static pessimism" that missed the "fundamental historical realization" that "humanity has transformed itself profoundly" over time, a self-"transformability" that revealed its self-"educability." Moreover, the interaction of "societal forms and forms of life" with the "thoughts and dreams of poets and interpreters" was crucial to the latter process; for that reason, writers had a key social and historical role to play.[128] Where Marek criticized a bureaucratically politicized literature from the standpoint of an individual freedom that despaired of its own efficacy, Mayer rejected the abstract opposition of modern self and modern world for a view of subjectivity as self- and world-shaping. And on that basis, he called for a committed literature with political – that is, socially transformative – intent.

As these exchanges make plain, the goal of unity projected by the Berlin congress appeared fractured beyond repair in Frankfurt. One commentator expressed a widely shared view when he noted that "basic contrasts" in the literary discussion manifested a "veiled political background." In Mayer's estimation, if the Berlin congress had been marked by intra-Allied tensions and German dialogue, the Frankfurt one featured lopsided debates among Germans themselves that moved within an increasingly reified "East-West" framework. Disillusioned, he concluded that all-German initiatives with "independent" aims – those that sought to operate outside the competition between the parties and the powers – had a "right to exist" only "if they are capable of a common direction, not merely a common debate."[129] His words recalled engaged democrats' project of renewal and cultural-national unity; by mid 1948, even some of its staunchest advocates doubted its continued viability.

Yet even the worst conditions did not forestall one more initiative. In the superheated atmosphere of the Berlin blockade, Birkenfeld, Pechel, and Weisenborn took action against the suddenly palpable possibility of a relapse into armed conflict. Like the first writers' congress, this idea was hatched by the Berlin SDA board and involved Kulturbund-style coalition building. In early July, conversations were held among "spiritual representatives of all political tendencies," on the basis of which the three colleagues – a West-oriented liberal, an old-guard conservative, and a Communist-friendly radical – joined forces to draft a "Berlin

---

[128] Mayer, "Der Schriftsteller und die Krise der Humanität," in *Literatur und Politik*, ed. Bechtoldt, 84–6, 89.
[129] Gustav René Hocke, "Zwischen Geist und Macht," *Die Neue Zeitung*, 23 May 1948; Mayer, "Vom ersten zum zweiten deutschen Schriftstellerkongreß," *Frankfurter Hefte* 3, no. 8 (1948): 693–4.

Manifesto." On behalf of the "German people," they issued an "appeal of desperation" to the "world powers," to halt their strident brinksmanship. It did not deny the rifts among the Allies or the Germans: "We, the undersigned, do not deceive ourselves about the dominant contradictions. Our views of the path to a happier future are, in part, radically opposed." Still, it built on common ground: As "Germans living in Berlin [who] daily feel the white heat of the conflict," and "as people who feel bound to the spirit of humanity, we declare war the most disgraceful of means." This statement circulated to some ninety cultural figures, from SED members such as Becher and Wolf and non-party communists such as Kantorowicz and Paul Rilla through left-liberals such as Ihering and Kellermann to anti-Communists such as Karsch and Redslob and apolitical or unaffiliated types such as Langgässer and Stroux.[130]

The initiative, however, was stillborn. Before signatures could be collected and the manifesto published in Berlin's newspapers, the plan was pre-emptively attacked by Susanne Kerckhoff of the SED (Harich's older half-sister). As an SDA board member, she had been privy to the discussions, and as a feuilleton editor at the *Berliner Zeitung*, she had a prominent podium. Although she did not name the plan explicitly, she derided the very notion of a manifesto by a few "well-known Berlin publicists" who eschewed "party viewpoints"; this was an ineffectual, self-important response to serious crisis. Why not join the parties in a potentially effective, mass-based initiative instead, such as the referendum on unity and peace spearheaded by the SED-orchestrated People's Congress? Pechel responded in defense of the group, insisting on intellectuals' "obligation" not only to "raise their voices when deadly dangers approach" but to do so "outside political parties." This Kerckhoff again rejected as elitist and illusory.[131] Hers was an explicitly partisan, dogmatic intervention, and it made clear the inhospitable climate confronting attempts at pluralism. In its wake, Birkenfeld, Karsch, and Redslob founded their explicitly anti-Communist Free Kulturbund. Pechel decided not to join, for fear it would only exacerbate the polarization he and Weisenborn had hoped to counteract. But he also withdrew from the Kulturbund. Similar dynamics eventually split the SDA itself, with a counter-foundation by Karsch

---

[130] Birkenfeld, Pechel, and Weisenborn, "Berliner Manifest" (with cover letter and list of recipients), 12 July 1948, BArch N 1160/I/25a. See also Malende, "Zur Vorgeschichte eines öffentlichen Briefwechsels zwischen Johannes R. Becher und Rodolf Pechel im Dezember 1950," in *Schriftsteller*, ed. Hanuschek, Hörnigk, and Malende, 210–13.

[131] Susanne Kerckhoff, "Der lodernde Strohhalm: Die Intellektuellen und die politische Lage," *Berliner Zeitung*, 13 July 1948; Pechel and Kerckhoff, "Die allzu bloßgelegten Adern," *Berliner Zeitung*, 18 July 1948; Heukenkamp, ed. *Unterm Notdach: Nachkriegsliteratur in Berlin 1945–1949* (Berlin: Schmidt, 1996), 542.

A parliament of spirit? Mobilizing the cultural nation 235

and others in September 1949, at the very moment that two separate German states were being established.[132]

The parallel yet phase-delayed trajectory of the German PEN club provides a coda to this story.[133] A German branch of the international Poets, Essayists, Novelists organization had existed until 1933, when its dissolution was followed by the foundation of a group in exile. Becher – a member of the latter – helped coordinate the efforts of writers in Berlin, Hamburg, and Munich to re-establish a section in Germany after 1945. Among those working with him from the start were Weisenborn, Kästner, and Eggebrecht. Becher and Kästner attended the international PEN conference in Zurich in 1947, where Thomas Mann also pleaded their cause. Connections were further strengthened at the Berlin Writers' Congress, which Hermon Ould, head of PEN international, attended as a distinguished guest. These efforts bore fruit at the next year's PEN gathering in Copenhagen, which received a German delegation from all zones and Berlin and sanctioned a twenty-member German PEN club. Remarkably, it was constituted with all-German scope in November 1948. Among the founders were Becher, Birkenfeld, Eggebrecht, Kästner, Langgässer, Plievier, Seghers, Sternberger, Weisenborn, and Wolf. Scores more were co-opted in just the first year, from Bloch, Brecht, and Lukács to Kantorowicz, Leonhard, and Mayer to Döblin, Kellermann, and Kogon to Hagelstange, Pechel, and Weismantel.[134]

But even this avowedly non-partisan organization succumbed to the inescapable polarization. Birkenfeld, Pechel, and Plievier filed a complaint in November 1950, charging that Becher had maligned his PEN colleagues with a public attack on the West Berlin "Congress for Cultural Freedom" conference. It was no longer possible to work with him and others from the GDR, who represented a "system of cultural unfreedom."[135] In October 1951, the organization split, nominally over

---

[132] Pechel to Birkenfeld, 26 July 1948, Pechel to Becher, 26 July 1948, BArch N 1160/II/1; Buergel-Goodwin, "Reorganisation," cols. 383–6.
[133] On the below, see Malende, "Die 'Wiedererrichtung' und Trennung des P.E.N.-Zentrums Deutschland 1946/48 bis 1951/53," *Zeitschrift für Germanistik* 5 n.s., no. 1 (1995): 82–95; Dorothée Bores, *Das ostdeutsche P.E.N.-Zentrum 1951–1998: Ein Werkzeug der Diktatur?* (Berlin: de Gruyter, 2010), 50–155.
[134] See, e.g., SDA Berlin to Weisenborn, 14 May 1946, AdK Weisenborn-Archiv 1346/3; Becher to Eggebrecht, 8 February 1947, Kästner to Becher, 4 February 1947, AdK Becher-Archiv 954, 10135; Becher to Kästner, 25 February 1947, DLA A:Kästner/ 98.3; Bores, *Das ostdeutsche P.E.N.*, 74–5, 1031–59.
[135] Pechel, Plievier, Birkenfeld to German PEN Center, 20 November 1950, DLA A:Kästner/ PEN; see also Hochgeschwender, *Freiheit*, 335–45. For Becher's remarks, see Becher, "Die gleiche Sprache," *Aufbau* 6, no. 8 (1950): 697–703. Birkenfeld, who spearheaded the counterattack, had also sought support from Sternberger and Kogon. The former rebuffed him politely yet firmly, while the latter concurred in principle but

this faction's opposition to Becher's repeated re-election as president. Strikingly, it was the keywords of the cultural Cold War – "freedom" versus "peace" or "unity" – over which the German PEN derailed. These controversies were amplified by external agencies on both sides, as the FRG's new Ministry of All-German Questions and the GDR Kulturbund, now integrated into the state apparatus, each intervened. At the same time, the tensions had internal roots, in postwar intellectual discussions as well as in the PEN charter, which similarly committed its members to both "freedom" and "peace." With the terms of debate also cast as weapons in a high-stakes rhetorical battle reinforced by geopolitics, a consensus on their meaning and relative valuation was effectively impossible.[136]

The German PEN's division marked only the final, belated throes of a project that had long since failed: the attempt to constitute a cultural-national unity with progressive political intent among postwar German intellectuals. It was a project that engaged democrats pursued out of deep yet ambivalent convictions. These were informed by a specific, dual notion of "culture" that had particularly German valences. Expansive and activist, it implied both self- and world-transforming "freedom" and national "unity." One after another, however, the platforms they built to actualize such notions – broad-based cultural organizations, more narrowly professional associations, and writers' conferences – failed to generate the unity they sought, cracking under a complex mix of internal and external pressures. Motivated by their critical analysis of the "unpolitical German," engaged democrats refused to assign conventional cultural pursuits to a distinct sphere with a privileged sort of freedom. Yet just this position became ever more prominent among their partners in various initiatives, seeming to confirm their fears that this German propensity might make a comeback after the war.

Dirks' old acquaintance Theodor W. Adorno suggested as much when, during his initial return from exile in 1949/50, his first essay in

---

did not sign on. Birkenfeld to Hermann Kesten, Kogon, and Sternberger, 13 November 1950, Sternberger to Birkenfeld, 29 November 1950, DLA A:Sternberger/ PEN/ 89.10.9846/2, 89.10.9833; Kogon to Birkenfeld, 4 December 1950, AdsD NL Kogon, Kongress f. Kulturelle Freiheit.

[136] Hanuschek, *Geschichte des bundesdeutschen PEN-Zentrums von 1951–1990* (Tübingen: Niemeyer, 2004), 9–43; Bores, *Das ostdeutsche P.E.N.*, 78–155. For rival brochures that framed the conflict in terms of a "decision" for "freedom" or "peace," see Bundesministerium für Gesamtdeutsche Fragen, *Die Freiheit fordert klare Entscheidungen: Johannes R. Becher und der Pen-Club* (Bonn, 1951); Kulturbund zur demokratischen Erneuerung Deutschlands, *Standort des deutschen Geistes; oder, Friede fordert Entscheidung: Johannes R. Becher und der Pen-Club, eine Antwort* (Berlin, 1951).

postwar West Germany appeared – not accidentally, in the *Frankfurter Hefte*. Teaching at Frankfurt University, he was struck by what he ironically termed a "resurrection of culture" among post-Nazi Germans. Skeptically, he analyzed the compensatory and repressive functions it seemed to serve, as a compensation for or flight from politics. Such psychosocial dynamics did not bode well for public life.[137] Ironically, engaged democrats would also rally behind "cultural freedom" in a narrow sense in the first years after 1949. For some in the FRG, it warranted a temporary partisanship for the West in the opening, hot moments of Cold War conflict. For those in the GDR, their own intellectual endeavors were the site at which they most directly experienced the repressive nature of the regime, which gave basic freedoms of expression a new currency and salience.

[137] Theodor W. Adorno, "Auferstehung der Kultur in Deutschland?" *Frankfurter Hefte* 5, no. 5 (1950): 469–77. On the strategy he developed in response, see Alfons Söllner, "'Political culturalism?' Adorno's 'Entrance' in the Cultural Concert of West-German Postwar History," in *Exile, Science, and Bildung: The Contested Legacies of German Emigré Intellectuals*, ed. David Kettler and Gerhard Lauer (New York: Palgrave Macmillan, 2005), 185–200.

## 6 Into East Germany: intelligentsia and the Apparat

Partition was effectively accomplished before the actual foundation of the Federal Republic of Germany (FRG) and the German Democratic Republic (GDR) in September and October of 1949. From mid 1948, as the Berlin blockade dragged on and the airlift held firm, the SED was given free rein to Sovietize the eastern zone in earnest, and German politicians in the other three zones completed the infrastructures of a separate West German state. Meanwhile, the de facto economic division effected by separate currency reforms – along with the increased availability of consumer goods in the West – caused the demand for cultural-political journals to contract. This left them in dire financial straits and undermined engaged democrats' sense of a public calling. *Ost und West* and *Die Wandlung* both lasted until December 1949, but their closings were each long-term effects of currency reform. It seemed a decisive shift had taken place, at least in the West. As Hans Mayer put it: "... then came the currency reform, and people had other concerns."[1] If the postwar debates on renewal had ended all too often in acrimony, they now seemed to be petering out into irrelevance.

For engaged democrats, the foundation of two separate states marked the end of their hopes for democratic renewal independent of both East and West, and it compelled a decision, for want of a better option, in favor of the one or the other Germany. The ties that linked their network frayed and sometimes broke under the stresses of ideological consolidation and political division. Still, some relationships were maintained and some conversations carried forth, even under inhospitable conditions. In early 1950, Axel Eggebrecht – now writing from the FRG to the capital of the GDR – commiserated with his old friend Alfred Kantorowicz over the division of Germany and the world. The final "estrangement" of the blocs consigned all who, since 1945, had "positioned themselves

---

[1] Alfred Kantorowicz, "Abschied," *Ost und West* 3, no. 12 (1949): 77; Dolf Sternberger, "Versuch zu einem Fazit," *Die Wandlung* 4, no. 8 (1949): 699; Hans Mayer, *Ein Deutscher auf Widerruf: Erinnerungen* (Frankfurt a.M.: Suhrkamp, 1982), I:378, 401, 402.

consciously and openly between the two great powers" to an impotent "isolation." Under the sign of this polarization, he lamented, "what a wicked sorcerer's dance is being staged around the word, around the concept of democracy!"[2] He was referring specifically to the GDR, but – as we will see – he diagnosed a similar dissembling in the West as well. His comments register both the frustration and the persistence of engaged democrats' hopes into the postwar era.

As an alternative vision and an unrealized opportunity, their immediate postwar project provided the basis for trenchant critiques of the Cold War order on both sides. During the 1950s, as a rule, these intellectuals traveled parallel trajectories from hope through disillusionment to dissent, becoming vocal opponents within each new German state. They were branded "revisionists" in the GDR and, with less vitriol, "nonconformists" in the FRG.[3] This shift of political affect also mapped onto a shift in political function: Before a clear order took shape, they aimed to play a constitutive role. With the consolidation of the postwar regimes, their interventions became contestative, tending toward critiques of specific aspects of the established order and away from general programs. While this reflected the overall climate of closure, it also related to a self-consciously practical moment in their thought, what Walter Dirks called "productive utopia" and Ernst Bloch "concrete utopia." Rather than abstractly oppose idealized blueprints to actual reality, this perspective sought to lay bare the germs of a liberated future contained within the present.[4] By 1949, the horizon of immanent possibilities had contracted severely.

For all the commonalities among engaged democrats, crucial differences shaped their interventions in the two Germanys. First, those intellectuals who opted for the East initially gave the new state their steadfast, if not unqualified, support. To them, the FRG seemed a restoration of capitalism as familiar as it was dangerous, while the GDR, however flawed, was the first experiment in socialism on German territory. As such, it had drawn the right conclusions from National Socialism. This identification with East Germany's own claims to legitimacy – its ideal projection of socialism as antifascism, not the distorted reality – was

---

[2] Axel Eggebrecht to Kantorowicz, 8 February 1950, Staats- und Universitätsbibliothek Hamburg (hereafter SUBH) NL Kantorowicz NK: BI: E8.
[3] See, e.g., Hans Joachim von Kondratowitz, "Nonkonformismus," and Helga Grebing, "Revisionismus," in *Handbuch zur deutsch-deutschen Wirklichkeit: Bundesrepublik Deutschland / Deutsche Demokratische Republik im Kulturvergleich*, ed. Wolfgang R. Langenbucher, Ralf Rytlewski, and Bernd Weyergraf (Stuttgart: Metzler, 1988), 536–7, 612–14.
[4] Walter Dirks, "Die zweite Republik: Zum Ziel und zum Weg der deutschen Demokratie," *Frankfurter Hefte* 1, no. 1 (1946): 15–16; Ernst Bloch, *Freiheit und Ordnung: Abriß der Sozial-Utopien* (Berlin: Aufbau, 1947), 208–14.

key to intellectuals' durable loyalty and the authority they accorded the party.[5] Second, engaged democrats faced more limited possibilities for critique in the East, where dissent was stifled from the start by repression as well as self-censorship. In the GDR, basic conditions for public life in the liberal sense did not obtain, since the party-state's aspiration to permeate and to organize all spaces between it and society was too powerful. But aspirations to total control were realized incompletely, and the attempt promoted and provoked other, non-liberal types of publicity. Socialism's official public sphere, for all its regimentation, was not univocal, and challenges to orthodoxy were on occasion mounted there. Moreover, unofficial counter-publics proliferated, though they remained generally isolated from one another. Informal clusters of discussion – among co-workers, colleagues, friends, and neighbors, both within formal institutions and outside them – sought to compensate for the shortcomings of official publicity by refusing or resisting its parameters. For this alternate, paradoxically private sort of publicity, the so-called intelligentsia provided an important constituency.[6] Within both kinds of spaces, approximations of the dialogues engaged democrats had earlier conducted were possible, in altered form or on a smaller scale.

In the GDR, as in other state socialist societies, the intelligentsia – technicians, scientists, professors, schoolteachers, journalists, writers, and other cultural functionaries – presented a problem. The regime needed but mistrusted the old intelligentsia. So it barred many white-collar workers from their posts and sought to co-opt the rest through a system of privileges until a new intelligentsia could be generated.[7] The party-state distinguished among intellectuals by function and political reliability. Nearest the center of power stood the party cadres, veteran Communists often from worker backgrounds who set the tone for the official public sphere and policed adherence to orthodoxy (itself a moving target).

---

[5] John C. Torpey, *Intellectuals, Socialism, and Dissent: The East German Opposition and its Legacy* (Minneapolis: University of Minnesota Press, 1995); Eberhart Schulz, *Zwischen Identifikation und Opposition: Künstler und Wissenschaftler der DDR und ihre Organisationen von 1949 bis 1962* (Cologne: PapyRossa, 1995); Jeffrey Herf, *Divided Memory: The Nazi Past in the Two Germanys* (Cambridge, Mass.: Harvard University Press, 1997), 13–39, 162–200.

[6] David Bathrick, *The Powers of Speech: The Politics of Culture in the GDR* (Lincoln: University of Nebraska Press, 1995), 31–50; Detlef Pollack, "Die konstitutive Widersprüchlichkeit der DDR oder War die DDR-Gesellschaft homogen?" *Geschichte und Gesellschaft* 24, no. 1 (1998): 110–31.

[7] On higher education, see Ralph Jessen, *Akademische Elite und kommunistische Diktatur: Die ostdeutsche Hochschullehrerschaft in der Ulbricht-Ära* (Göttingen: Vandenhoeck & Ruprecht, 1999); John Connelly, *Captive University: The Sovietization of East German, Czech, and Polish Higher Education, 1945–1956* (Chapel Hill: University of North Carolina Press, 2000).

Further out stood a motley collection of bourgeois Marxists, usually educated comrades of more recent vintage who were ideologically drawn to socialism and the party. Their non-dogmatic orientation chafed against the SED's strictures yet never precipitated a break with the GDR, and they remained committed to both, albeit in "loyal subversion."[8] Relative to this latter group, engaged democrats inside and outside the party were likewise dedicated to socialism and antifascism but often more suspect to authority. If anything, they found themselves in still less secure positions.

Engaged democrats did eventually break with the regime, moving from more private to more public opposition and from narrowly cultural to socio-political critique, which also addressed the lack of publicness itself. In the early GDR, they sought out pockets of institutional space where they could pursue their intellectual activities relatively unmolested. Even these retreats, however, did not protect them from a Stalinized bureaucracy geared to impose order from above. The private critique of cultural policy that they formulated in response served as the seedbed of more public opposition in the crisis years following Stalin's death in 1953. Encouraged by the seeming promise of destalinization, engaged democrats brought grievances and proposals into the open. In 1956, a comprehensive opposition platform emerged, calling for the total overhaul of the cultural, political, and economic institutions of the GDR. To the reformers' misfortune, its leaders proved adept at negotiating the crisis and reconsolidated their power on no less repressive terms. For those critics not swept up in the purges and show trials of 1957, isolation and persecution drove them to emigrate. What was disparagingly called *Republikflucht* or "flight from the republic" had long functioned as a pressure-release valve for dissent. As their disillusionment came to overshadow their loyalty, the GDR's engaged democrats made use of it as well.

### Freezing over: unmixing and accommodation

The division of Germany saw an ambiguous mix of disappointments and attempted alignments with their respective regimes among engaged democrats. Both moments must be kept in view to understand their positions, especially in the GDR. If the aftermath of Hitler's empire had seen a geographic "disentanglement of populations" that left wide swaths

---

[8] Werner Müller, "Kommunistische Intellektuelle in der SBZ und in der frühen DDR," in *Kritik und Mandat: Intellektuelle in der deutschen Politik*, ed. Gangolf Hübinger and Thomas Hertfelder (Stuttgart: Deutsche Verlags-Anstalt, 2000), 239–65; Axel Fair-Schulz, *Loyal Subversion: East Germany and its Bildungsbürgerlich Marxist Intellectuals* (Berlin: Trafo, 2009).

of Europe ethnically more homogeneous, so the setting-in of Cold War occasioned an unmixing of political cultures.[9] The latter re-ordering of multiplicity was a watershed in the lives of many politically active Europeans, especially in a dividing Germany. On the one hand, it is vital not to misconstrue the decision to live in one or the other Germany as an unqualified endorsement. On the other hand, it was no accident that people settled where they did. As polarization intensified, some of those who felt stronger affinities for the other side relocated. Alternately, reshuffling could take place without physical displacement, or entirely outside of Germany (in exile), or entirely inside one locale (politically polyglot Berlin). The taking of sides was not fully determined by geography; it was embedded in the novel geopolitical field of a global Cold War, where ideological affiliation correlated with but was not ultimately bound to physical location.

Jurists Peter Alfons Steiniger and Wolfgang Abendroth provide an illuminating contrast. In 1949, Steiniger's full-length treatise on the "democratic bloc" appeared, aspects of which were enshrined in the new GDR constitution he helped draft.[10] There, his proposals had been shorn of all pluralist, participatory inflection. Their practical demise had already been sealed, as bloc committees – the organs of cross-party collaboration – convened less and less frequently at all levels, all over the Soviet zone. At the GDR's foundation, they were absorbed by first the SED-led National Front and then the People's Chamber. The latter was a rubber-stamp parliament elected by multiparty "unity lists" that institutionalized the SED's "leading role" in a permanent, legally codified majority over the "bloc parties" and non-party "mass organizations." Steiniger's defeat in theory followed in 1950, when his work was prominently censured as "bourgeois formalism" by the more doctrinaire jurist Karl Polak.[11] Abendroth, in contrast, had earlier grown disenchanted with the gap between

---

[9] Winston Churchill's 1944 phrase referred as precedent to what Lord Curzon had called the "unmixing of peoples" in the Balkans after 1918. Jessica Reinisch, introduction to *The Disentanglement of Populations: Migration, Expulsion and Displacement in Post-War Europe, 1944–9*, ed. Reinisch and Elizabeth White (Basingstoke: Palgrave Macmillan, 2011), quote xviii.

[10] Alfons Steiniger, *Das Blocksystem: Beitrag zu einer demokratischen Verfassungslehre* (Berlin: Akademie, 1949); Heike Amos, *Die Entstehung der Verfassung in der Sowjetischen Besatzungszone/DDR 1946–1949: Darstellung und Dokumentation* (Münster: LIT, 2006), 219–20, 240, 273–83.

[11] Berndt Musiolek, "Peter Alfons Steiniger: Zwischen Illusion und Wirklichkeit: Das Blocksystem als Verfassungsprinzip," in *Rechtsgeschichtswissenschaft in Deutschland 1945 bis 1952*, ed. Horst Schröder and Dieter Simon (Frankfurt a.M.: Klostermann, 2001), 264–7; Kurt Schneider and Detlef Nakath, "Demokratischer Block, Nationale Front und die Rolle und Funktion der Blockparteien," in *Die Parteien und Organisationen der DDR: Ein Handbuch*, ed. Gerd-Rüdiger Stephan, et al. (Berlin: Dietz, 2002), 78–102.

legal norms and political practice in the Soviet zone, a "contradiction between the democratic theory of the proposed constitution . . . and the undemocratic exclusion of free political discussion" that continued to grow. He went west in late 1948, where he became a prominent political scientist, judge, and SPD intellectual.[12] Steiniger, meanwhile, resigned himself to this discrepancy, remained in Berlin, and undertook several rounds of self-criticism, recanting earlier positions and confessing political shortcomings. After submitting to the new orthodoxy, he enjoyed a long career at the Humboldt University, heading several legal institutes and serving as Dean of its law faculty.[13]

The fault lines of a dividing world refracted political, collegial, and even the most personal relations, such as those among Rudolf, Susanne, and Wolfgang Leonhard. In the USSR, Susanne's five-year sentence had morphed into ten at an Arctic labor camp and two more in Siberia, but she returned to Germany in 1948, after Wolfgang prevailed on SED co-chair and future GDR president Wilhelm Pieck to intervene. She took up residence near her son in Berlin's Soviet sector, alienated irretrievably from the party though not from the cause of socialism. Shortly after his March 1949 defection to Yugoslavia, she fled to the American zone, where she was first detained by the Counter Intelligence Corps. In this period, she re-established contact with Rudolf, who was living in post-occupation Paris. An amicable, even intimate correspondence developed between them, but it was shot through with political disagreements. She urged him to read the new canonical texts of ex-Communism – by Manès Sperber and Arthur Koestler, her long-ago neighbors in Weimar Berlin – while also insisting that her break with the East was not a vote for the West. In return, he regaled her with his conviction that the world's two emerging camps brooked no spaces between.[14]

This was the same argument Wolfgang faced when he explained to his father his flight to Belgrade. Certainly, Rudolf conceded, thinking leftists should have "concerns" about the Soviet camp; the challenge was to remain loyal despite all misgivings. By the inexorable logic of the world's

---

[12] Wolfgang Abendroth to Marie Torhorst, Education Minister of Thuringia, 29 December 1948, quoted in Andreas Diers, *Arbeiterbewegung, Demokratie, Staat: Wolfgang Abendroth, Leben und Werk 1906–1948* (Hamburg: VSA, 2006), 479; see ibid., 474–80.
[13] Musiolek, "Steiniger," 267–8; Alexander Gallus, *Heimat "Weltbühne": Eine Intellektuellengeschichte im 20. Jahrhundert* (Göttingen: Wallstein, 2012), 302, 306–26.
[14] Susanne Leonhard, *Gestohlenes Leben: Schicksal einer politischen Emigrantin in der Sowjetunion*, 3rd edn. (Stuttgart: Steingrüben, 1959), 593–629, 739–40; Wolfgang Leonhard, *Die Revolution entläßt ihre Kinder* (Cologne: Kiepenheuer & Witsch, 1955), 518–22; Susanne to Rudolf Leonhard, 10 October 1949, 25 December 1949, 15 February 1950, Stiftung Archiv der Akademie der Künste Berlin (hereafter AdK), Leonhard-Archiv 819/1.

"two fronts" – "future" versus "past," "revolution" versus "reaction," "peace" versus "war" – "partisanship" was unavoidable, and a breach of solidarity meant material support for the other side. Wolfgang disputed this understanding of solidarity: it was precisely the cause of "peace, democracy, and socialism" that required "open discussion" of what was "negative" and "dangerous" in their own ranks – above all, regarding the USSR and the asymmetrical relations within its sphere. He was witnessing the realization of a truer socialism in Yugoslavia, which alone among the "people's democracies" was rejecting Soviet hegemony both domestically and internationally.[15] Indeed, his enthusiasm was fired by the Yugoslav Communist Party's roll-back of its own control through decentralization and worker self-management initiatives that were just beginning. Still, he also felt the urge to return to Germany, and – after Rudolf moved to the GDR – Wolfgang joined Susanne in the FRG in November 1950. There, he was active in the short-lived, Titoist Independent Workers' Party (UAPD). Wolfgang later studied in England and taught for decades in the USA, as one of the West's foremost Eastern bloc authorities. His hopes for a reformed Communism free of Stalinist residues never died, and in the 1970s, he became an optimistic observer of "Eurocommunism" in Western parliamentary systems.[16]

Within Germany too, decisions to relocate across the developing divide were reached under myriad conditions. Werner Krauss felt ill at ease at Marburg University, dismayed at the successful resistance to US-led denazification. Expecting a more consistent antifascism at Leipzig, he took up his professorship there in fall 1947.[17] Mayer proved more reluctant, even after his and Stephan Hermlin's ouster at Radio Frankfurt, where polarization had made it difficult "to steer an independent German course." He sympathized with Jo Mihaly's "inner fatigue," which had helped drive her back to Zurich as early as mid 1946. The hopes of 1945 were evaporating, but he still saw potential good in teaching at the Academy of Labor and working with the VVN. As yet, he had no trouble publishing. Hermlin, encouraged by Günther Weisenborn, was already planning his relocation. Like others who left broadcasting in the western

[15] Rudolf to Wolfgang Leonhard, 17 September 1949, 24 March 1950, SUBH NL Kantorowicz NK: BI: L24,1–2; Wolfgang to Rudolf Leonhard, 24 November 1948, 8 April 1950, AdK Leonhard-Archiv 819/1; See also Wolfgang Leonhard, *Meine Geschichte der DDR* (Berlin: Rowohlt, 2007), 122–6.
[16] Wolfgang Leonhard, *Meine Geschichte*, 112–22, 126–9, 157–9; Helmut Müller-Enbergs et al., eds. *Wer war wer in der DDR? Ein Lexikon ostdeutscher Biographien*, 5th edn. (Berlin: Links, 2010), I:789; Wolfgang Leonhard, *Eurokommunismus: Herausforderung für Ost und West* (Munich: Bertelsmann, 1978).
[17] Peter Jehle, preface and appendix to Werner Krauss, *Briefe 1922 bis 1976*, ed. Jehle (Frankfurt a.M.: Klostermann, 2002), 10, 958.

Into East Germany: intelligentsia and the Apparat    245

zones, he was offered a post at Soviet-controlled Radio Berlin, which stood out for its still relatively open programming.[18] Mayer lasted several more months before accepting his own call to Leipzig University in October 1948. The price, he later asserted, was having to master the local "slave language" (*Sklavensprache*) – an idiom of dissemblance and camouflage, one that expressed dominant agendas overtly and hidden ones covertly. This self-evaluation captures the tensions between his vision of a German Democratic Republic and that of the SED leadership; it also obscures the hope and resolve he felt, projecting backward a self-conscious dissidence that took years to develop.[19]

Berlin remained a special case. Long before a physical wall divided the former capital, Cold War geography grafted itself onto the cityscape, in vehicle checkpoints and infrastructure shifts navigated by Berliners who circulated among the sectors.[20] Kantorowicz, who had so demonstratively insisted on living his East–West synthesis on a day-to-day basis – residing in the American sector while working on the Soviet side – accommodated the spatial reorganization. In May 1949, he grudgingly moved to the outskirts of the city, just inside what would soon be the GDR. Herbert Ihering, by contrast, was unperturbed. From his West Berlin home, he remained a Kulturbund officer, a member of *Aufbau*'s editorial board, and dramaturge at East Berlin's flagship stage, the Deutsches Theater, well into the 1950s.[21] Weisenborn, after a series of disappointments, opted to leave the city. As tensions gave way to blockade in mid 1948, he faced the original *Ulenspiegel*'s demise, his blocked trip to the Frankfurt Writers' Congress, and attacks on the Berlin Manifesto. In the following months, he began scouting destinations in the West and stepped down from his chairs at the SDA and Kulturbund. "One day, I had had enough of everything," he later recalled. After the "tricky tensions" of "harshest

---

[18] Mayer to Jo Mihaly, 26 February 1947, Deutsche Nationalbibliothek, Deutsches Exilarchiv 1933–1945 (Frankfurt a.M.) EB autogr. 582; Wolfgang Schivelbusch, *In a Cold Crater: Cultural and Intellectual Life in Berlin, 1945–1948*, trans. Kelly Barry (Berkeley: University of California Press, 1998), 125–6.

[19] Mayer, *Ein Deutscher*, I:415–19, quote 415; Mayer, *Ein Deutscher*, II:9–10; Franziska Meyer, "The Literary Critic Hans Mayer: From West to East, from East to West," in *German Writers and the Cold War, 1945–1961*, ed. Rhys W. Williams, Stephen Parker, and Colin Riordan (Manchester: Manchester University Press, 1992), here 186. On GDR intellectuals' use of "Sklavensprache" (following Lenin's coinage), see Mayer, *Der Turm von Babel: Erinnerung an eine Deutsche Demokratische Republik* (Frankfurt a.M.: Suhrkamp, 1991), 261.

[20] Paul Steege, *Black Market, Cold War: Everyday Life in Berlin, 1946–1949* (Cambridge: Cambridge University Press, 2007), 250–71.

[21] Kantorowicz, *Deutsches Tagebuch* (Munich: Kindler, 1959), I:287, 617; Karin Herbst-Meßlinger, "Der Kritiker als Intellektueller," in *Herbert Ihering: Filmkritiker* (Munich: Text + Kritik, 2011), 57–65; Siegfried Scheibe, *Aufbau, Berlin 1945–1958: Bibliographie einer Zeitschrift* (Berlin: Aufbau, 1978), 539.

Figure 6.1 A delegation of German "culture makers" visiting the USSR poses on St. Isaac's Square in Leningrad, April 1948. From left: Ellen Kellermann, Günther Weisenborn, Jürgen Kuczynski, Bernhard Kellermann, Wolfgang Harich, Anna Seghers, Stephan Hermlin, Wolfgang Langhoff, Michael Tschesno-Hell, Eduard Claudius, their Soviet handler Mikhail Apletin, and Heinrich Ehmsen. (*Source*: ITAR-TASS Photo Agency)

Berlin," Günther and Joy "finally wanted calm." By early 1949, the family lived in a village near Lake Constance, with "fields and forests and peace all around." There they remained – while he made frequent trips back to Berlin, to Cologne, or to Hamburg – until 1951, when he took up the dramaturgy post at the Kammerspiele Theater.[22]

Others who had earlier resisted it now embraced the climate of partisanship. If Harich made an early first step with his choice for the SED, he was in the vanguard by mid 1948. He and Weisenborn were recently returned from the first official German writers' tour of the Soviet Union (Figure 6.1). Weisenborn, whom their hosts considered the delegation's

---

[22] Günther Weisenborn to Werner Schendell at SDA Board, 25 October 1948, AdK Weisenborn-Archiv 1346/3; Magdalena Heider, *Politik – Kultur – Kulturbund: Zur Gründungs- und Frühgeschichte des Kulturbundes zur demokratischen Erneuerung Deutschlands 1945–1954 in der SBZ/DDR* (Cologne: Wissenschaft und Politik, 1993), 57n141; Weisenborn, *Der gespaltene Horizont: Niederschriften eines Außenseiters* (Munich: Desch, 1964), quote 181; Eggebrecht to Sternberger, 20 January 1949, Deutsches Literaturarchiv (Marbach a.N., hereafter DLA) A:Sternberger/ Wandlung/ 74.10515/6; Manfred Demmer, *Spurensuche: Der antifaschistische Schriftsteller Günther Weisenborn* (Leverkusen: Kulturvereinigung Leverkusen, 2004), 40–5.

least reliable member, had been alone in raising questions about cultural repression – on the example of Mikhail Zoshchenko's ejection from the Writers' Union – during the visit.[23] Back in Germany, Harich tackled this issue head-on, refuting the charge that the USSR had eliminated cultural freedom like its "totalitarian" cousin Nazism. In a series for *Die Weltbühne*, he explained that Western critics overlooked the intimate bond that connected "the Soviet intellectual" to "broad popular masses," who were themselves "active, critical formers" not "passive consumers" of culture. Zoshchenko's fate had not been imposed from on high. Rather, it carried out "a democratic judgment of the people," the outcome of extensive "public criticism and self-criticism." These had shown that Zoshchenko's satires, critically edgy in the 1920s, had not "grow[n]" along with society; fixated on humans' "incorrigible weaknesses," they disregarded the "socialist humanist" perspective of transformability and perfectibility.[24] Harich's argument mixed echoes of engaged democrats' initial vision with dogmatic "socialist realist" justifications, as they were given in Moscow. A young SED member whose star was rising, he spoke from a position of relative security. Some of those whose loyalties to the emerging GDR were more suspect undertook even more ingratiating accommodations.

The final phase of occupation brought mounting difficulties for Kantorowicz. Although *Ost und West* did not close until the end of 1949, tensions with the SED arose earlier. In April 1948, Kantorowicz learned from a Soviet officer of the party leadership's plan to terminate his journal. At that point, SVAG's intercession ensured its preservation; as the licensing authority and occupying power, the Soviets retained control. Under their cover, Kantorowicz defended his journal to the SED with evidence of its prominence as a "gathering place for thousands of intellectuals, non-party affiliated but open to free and progressive ideas, from all zones of Germany." He even dared to reprimand the powerful: "one does not dispose such resolutions over the heads of the affected." Such secretive and bureaucratic procedures contravened "publicly proclaimed principles of socialist politics" as well as "simple considerations of human decency." As Kantorowicz also pointed out, his endeavors were

---

[23] Anne Hartmann and Wolfram Eggeling, *Sowjetische Präsenz im kulturellen Leben der SBZ und frühen DDR 1945–1953* (Berlin: Akademie, 1998), 277–8, 287–8; Weisenborn, *Horizont*, 91–132. On the longer-term context, see Michael David-Fox, *Showcasing the Great Experiment: Cultural Diplomacy and Western Visitors to the Soviet Union, 1921–1941* (Oxford: Oxford University Press, 2011).

[24] Wolfgang Harich, "Gleichschaltung?" *Die Weltbühne* 3, no. 21 (1948): 582–5; Harich, "Gleichschaltung?" *Die Weltbühne* 3, no. 22 (1948): 618–19; Harich, "Gleichschaltung?" *Die Weltbühne* 3, no. 23 (1948): 666–7.

in keeping with the party's renewed emphasis on "unity."[25] He was oblivious to shifts occurring beneath the rhetoric, registered in Otto Grotewohl's rejection of all East–West "bridge" positions just weeks later. By mid 1948, the language that Kantorowicz had publicly made his own since war's end was being stigmatized at the highest levels.

The reprieve thus proved temporary. In March 1949, Kantorowicz appealed directly to President Pieck, whom he and others considered a potential ally. Acknowledging long-circulating rumors – now "impossible to ignore" – that he was viewed "in leading party circles" with "aversion and mistrust," he requested an opportunity to respond to whatever might be their grounds for dissatisfaction.[26] Clearly, *Ost und West* faced difficult times once the SED's power was secured in a rump East Germany. At the same time, the journal was ever less welcome elsewhere. US authorities had confiscated 4,500 copies – well over half, by then – of the first 1949 issue, when they crossed a strip of American sector between the printer and bindery.[27] By the GDR's founding, Kantorowicz's journal faced critical financial difficulties. He circulated a plea to various state and party authorities, proposing possible solutions: ideally, indirect support through obligatory library subscriptions or, alternately, direct subsidies or affiliation with some state agency.[28] He was willing – in the worst case – to trade his vaunted institutional independence for the survival of his journal.

The new regime, however, was only too happy to let the incongruous enterprise fold. The denial of Kantorowicz's request came from Stefan Heymann, of the SED's Culture and Education Department (and once Kogon's collaborator on the Buchenwald report). He cited practical considerations, but with a clear ideological subtext: Given the demands of economic rebuilding, the party preferred to concentrate available resources on the Kulturbund organ *Aufbau*. Moreover, "the question of the relationship between East and West Germany" had changed. While *Ost und West* had initially been welcome, new conditions called for other means. Soon thereafter, Heymann made officials' disfavor public with a frontal, post-mortem attack in *Sonntag*. He peppered his article with insinuations that Kantorowicz had never fully embraced Communism

---

[25] Kantorowicz, *Deutsches Tagebuch*, I:452–5, 458–61; Kantorowicz to Behling at SED Zentralsekretariat, 14 May 1948, AdK Scheer-Archiv, Ost und West. While there is no trace of proceedings against *Ost und West* in the Central Secretariat archive, Kantorowicz's letter suggests his account is no fabrication.

[26] Kantorowicz to Wilhelm Pieck, 23 March 1949, SUBH NL Kantorowicz NK: BI: P1.

[27] Barbara Baerns, *Ost und West: Eine Zeitschrift zwischen den Fronten: Zur politischen Funktion einer literarischen Zeitschrift in der Besatzungszeit 1945–1949* (Münster: Fahle, 1968), 83–5, 169.

[28] Kantorowicz, form letter, 21 October 1949, AdK Scheer-Archiv, Ost und West.

and maintained close ties to US intelligence. Heymann reserved his worst invective, however, for Kantorowicz's obstinate refusal to draw clear distinctions between the camps of "progress" and "reaction." If this had been merely "questionable" in 1947, it was "absolutely impossible... under the conditions of our struggle today."[29] The concept of mediation so central to *Ost und West* had long been passé in party circles; with the foundation of the East German state, it was a dangerous error.

Kantorowicz was unsettled, but he did not follow this denunciatory rebuke with a round of self-criticism, as a savvy functionary might have. Like his friend Rudolf Leonhard, he was not yet a party member and felt more anxiety than enthusiasm about the new socialist state. Far away in Paris, Leonhard had waited in vain since mid 1948 for final notification regarding his relocation to Berlin. He had taken seriously ill and passed his own sixtieth birthday without much official recognition. He now worried that Kantorowicz shared his fate, lamenting that neither of them was entrusted with the responsibility their "talent, personality, and accomplishments would merit." Regardless, Leonhard insisted, "I won't let myself be excluded, not from my work, not from taking part in events, and not from the positions that make taking part possible."[30] Kantorowicz responded in sympathy, quoting a passage of his Spanish Civil War diary that seemed pertinent: "We can count on nothing but ourselves. On ourselves, a handful of the despised, or those that will be despised tomorrow... A few will perhaps survive. It will be their task to sow the seeds of the consciousness of freedom anew."[31] They felt isolated and insecure, as well as skeptical at the course developments were taking. Still, each held out a margin of hope for the future.

They responded with exaggerated loyalty. Both Kantorowicz and Leonhard penned laudatory essays in honor of Stalin's seventieth birthday, in December 1949, two months after the founding of the East German satellite. Neither had expressed allegiance to Communism in such a classically blinkered fashion before, and their essays are striking for their illusions and their cynicism. But they are noteworthy as well for melding hymns of praise to the Soviet dictator with lip service to engaged democrats' postwar ideals. Kantorowicz extolled Stalin's

---

[29] Stefan Heymann to Kantorowicz, 1 November 1949, SUBH NL Kantorowicz NK: Ostberlin: 92; Heymann, "Ein schlechter Abgesang," *Sonntag*, 5 February 1950. See also Baerns, *Ost und West*, 85–90.

[30] Paul Merker to Rudolf Leonhard, 18 June 1948, AdK Leonhard-Archiv 820; Leonhard to Kantorowicz, 21 November 1949, 9 January 1950, SUBH NL Kantorowicz NK: BI: L15, L16; Bernd Jentzsch, *Rudolf Leonhard, "Gedichteträumer"* (Munich: Hanser, 1984), 51–2.

[31] Kantorowicz to Leonhard, 15 December 1949, AdK NL Leonhard 818; cf. Kantorowicz, *Spanisches Tagebuch* (Berlin: Aufbau, 1948), 359–60.

"leading role" in building a multinational socialist state cohesive enough to withstand "trial by fire" in war and occupation. Stalin's injunction to allow "national cultures the opportunity to develop and unfold themselves, to show their potential powers," as well as his critique of nations that reduced others' "right to self-determination" to a mere "right to cultural autonomy" while exercising "political power" over them were prominently cited. Kantorowicz then turned to decry the rump FRG's "half-colonial dependency" on "Western imperialists." This was blind to brutal realities of Stalinist nationalities and population policy in the 1930s and 40s.[32] Also left unsaid – though perhaps not unintended – was how Stalin's stated positions recalled the now repudiated project of "national roads to socialism." It was this approach that had opened the space for *Ost und West*, which closed when the proto-GDR oriented itself explicitly toward the Soviet model. Even as Kantorowicz sought to ingratiate himself with the new regime, his earlier commitments made for continued tension with the official agenda.

In his essay, Leonhard more fully embraced conventions of fealty and adulation, and he did so in a more poetic register. He did not shrink from lyrical descriptions of Stalin's face, creased from smiling and contemplation, or of the musical quality of Stalin's philosophical compositions. Regarding the "Stalin cult," he asked rhetorically whether the Soviet leader, in his "greatness," did not "simply deserve" such devotion. The essay's crux, however, was Leonhard's confession that "certainly, I am a Stalinist... but only because I hold convictions that this man most strongly represents... defends, and realizes." As Lenin's successor, Stalin had "realized the kingdom" in which labor was a socialist "blessing" rather than a biblical "curse." Its transformation from "a work of sweat and tears" to the "fortunate affair" and "personal concern" of each and all was "the greatest achievement for the personality, the greatest humanist work ever effected."[33] Here, Leonhard reprised the image of creative subjectivity so central to engaged democrats' immediate postwar vision, and not only in its Marxist variant. Attempting to find a place in the postwar order, the two friends embraced Stalin himself – but only after coding him an ally in their struggle for a participatory-democratic, independent postwar Germany.

Indicating his capitulation to the new realities, Kantorowicz applied in 1950 for the SED party membership he had declined with self-assurance

---

[32] Kantorowicz, "Stalin als Lehrmeister der nationalen Selbstbestimmung," *Ost und West* 3, no. 12 (1949): 3–9. For a pointed account, see Norman M. Naimark, *Stalin's Genocides* (Princeton, N.J.: Princeton University Press, 2010), 80–98.

[33] Leonhard, "Gedanken eines Stalinisten," *Die Weltbühne* 5, no. 29 (1950): 897–8.

in 1947. Leonhard followed suit in 1952.[34] While their requests were granted, their feeling of exclusion remained, and they failed to recover any sense of their earlier political mandate. Leonhard passed away in 1953, but he would have been cheered by the memorial volume to which Mayer, Scheer, Schroeder, Weisenborn, and other comrades from better times contributed.[35]

### Thawing out? Between repression and reform

The first years of the GDR were ones of consolidation and instability, as a new order was built under SED leadership and Soviet guidance. Across east-central Europe, the hallmarks of this transformation were similar: Communist parties secured a monopoly on political power, enforced ideological conformity, reshaped education, and reconstructed work and production (and, less concertedly, reproduction), displacing old social hierarchies and forging new ones in the process. There was some variation across the "people's democracies," and the GDR's path to Stalinized state socialism was paved by German Communism's own hardened traditions of intransigence and discipline.[36] Everywhere in the Soviet bloc, radical change also brought frictions, and simmering tensions boiled over in the years after Stalin's death in 1953, initially and spectacularly in East Germany; thereafter, ameliorative measures suggested a renewed openness. It was in this context of repression and potential reform that engaged democrats attempted to shape their lives and the developing regime.

Political repression was central to the SED's consolidation of power in the GDR. Under occupation, various German agencies had served as auxiliaries to Soviet secret police, monitoring German officials and other suspicious elements, from youth groups to clergy to politicians, who were subjected to harassment, internment, or worse. In 1950, these agencies fed into a new self-standing Ministry of State Security (MfS, called "Stasi") charged with policing the population at large. Deviations within the SED itself were the concern of the Central Party Control Commission and its state and local affiliates, which were active from early 1949. These agencies worked together – and in close contact with Soviet security organs – in operations that ranged from observation and

---

[34] Baerns, *Ost und West*, 59; Kantorowicz, *Deutsches Tagebuch*, I:298; Leonhard to Zentralkomitee SED, 25 August 1952, AdK Leonhard-Archiv 806.
[35] Maximilian Scheer, ed. *Freunde über Rudolf Leonhard* (Berlin: Verlag der Nation, 1958).
[36] Christoph Kleßmann, *Die doppelte Staatsgründung: Deutsche Geschichte 1945–1955*, 5th edn. (Göttingen: Vandenhoek & Ruprecht, 1991), 261–91; Eric D. Weitz, *Creating German Communism, 1890–1990: From Popular Protests to Socialist State* (Princeton, N.J.: Princeton University Press, 1997), esp. 357–86.

intimidation to judicial and extra-judicial interrogation, imprisonment, kidnapping and torture.[37] From its inception, then, the GDR developed what Hannah Arendt soon identified as the signal characteristics of "totalitarian" rule, implementing an apparatus of "terror" to reshape society and human activity in accord with its "ideology."[38]

In this early phase, repression was focused and overt, targeting real and imagined opponents of the regime, above all within the party's own ranks. In a first wave, former members of the SPD and fringe leftist groups were purged for such offenses as "social democratism," "Trotskyism," or "Titoism." Actual conspiratorial activities were rare; one case was a group around council communist Alfred Weiland, to which Pauline Nardi had ties.[39] A broader purge began in 1950, bound up with the so-called Field Affair. It unfolded amid the paranoia of the erupting Cold War and a mania to eliminate all independent stirrings within the Soviet camp. Its pretext was victims' contact with Noel Field, an American Communist who had been central to wartime refugee aid networks in Axis-dominated Europe, with bases in France and Switzerland. (The affair led to show trials around László Rajk in Hungary and Rudolf Slánský in Czechoslovakia; a planned trial in the GDR never came to pass.) As Ulbricht's "Muscovites" consolidated power in East Germany, former "West-émigrés" were accused of espionage, sabotage, "cosmopolitanism," and "Zionism" – as elsewhere, Jews were overrepresented among the victims. One of them was Leo Bauer, purged from the SED in 1950 and arrested and tried in 1952; his death sentence was commuted to 25 years' forced labor in Siberia. Although the top defendant, Politburo member Paul Merker, was not Jewish, he had worked assiduously for restitution to Jewish victims in the East and for good relations with Israel.[40]

---

[37] See, e.g., Jens Gieseke, *Mielke-Konzern: Die Geschichte der Stasi 1945–1990* (Stuttgart: Deutsche Verlags-Anstalt, 2001), 21–68; Thomas Klein, *"Für die Einheit und Reinheit der Partei": Die innerparteilichen Kontrollorgane der SED in der Ära Ulbricht* (Cologne: Böhlau, 2002), 17–267.

[38] After writing her 1951 classic in the shadow of Nazism, Arendt reflected further on Marxism and Stalinism, producing the "Ideology and Terror" essay she appended to the 1958 edition; Hannah Arendt, *The Origins of Totalitarianism*, 2nd edn. (Cleveland: World, 1958), 460–79; Margaret Canovan, *Hannah Arendt: A Reinterpretation of Her Political Thought* (Cambridge: Cambridge University Press, 1992), 63–4, 86–94. As an object of intellectual history, the "totalitarianism" thesis remains interesting; as a frame for historical analysis, its value is questionable. See, e.g., Anson Rabinbach, *Begriffe aus dem Kalten Krieg: Totalitarismus, Antifaschismus, Genozid* (Göttingen: Wallstein, 2009), 7–27; Michael Geyer and Sheila Fitzpatrick, eds. *Beyond Totalitarianism: Stalinism and Nazism Compared* (Cambridge: Cambridge University Press, 2009).

[39] Michael Kubina, *Von Utopie, Widerstand und Kaltem Krieg: Das unzeitgemässe Leben des Berliner Rätekommunisten Alfred Weiland* (Münster: LIT, 2001), 149–298, here 274.

[40] Herf, *Divided Memory*, 106–61; Wolfgang Kießling, *Partner im "Narrenparadies": Der Freundeskreis um Noel Field und Paul Merker* (Berlin: Dietz, 1994). Bauer was released

The purges, with their arbitrary brutality and anti-Semitic subtext, were noted with alarm by critical communists. For Mihaly, observing from Zurich, they precipitated a final break with the party. Mayer wrote a statement in support of Bauer, his and Mihaly's friend from the Swiss emigration who had coordinated his return to US-occupied Germany in 1945. To his dismay, this was used as further evidence of collaboration with "American agents." He was troubled by the return of old scripts featuring Jews as conspirators and scapegoats; it appeared "the Jew will burn" yet again. Kantorowicz too was acquainted with several defendants, whom he considered doctrinaire apparatchiks incapable of the disloyalty to which they confessed. But he registered particular shock at a snippet of news from Czechoslovakia. A son had publicly endorsed the death penalty for his father, one of Slansky's co-defendants, calling him "my greatest and most bitter enemy," a "creature, whom one cannot call a human being," out "to destroy our ever richer and happier life." Kantorowicz noted: "That is monstrous. It is Streicher's language, Himmler's mindset... the 'morality' of the human-butchers at Dachau and Buchenwald, the gassers at Auschwitz and Majdanek... the triumph of bestiality." For him, comparisons between Nazism and Stalinism were becoming a compelling lens through which to make sense of postwar political experience.[41]

By and large, engaged democrats – like most GDR citizens – were not swept up in the persecutions. The agencies of ideological disciplining were, however, a material factor in their lives. The Kulturbund took its place in the party-state apparatus as a fully-fledged mass organization, its "bourgeois" character reformed: it focused no longer on the self-organization of the intelligentsia but on the organization of cultural recreation, and leisure for the population at large.[42] And cultural production itself was policed directly. The GDR built on the Soviet zone's

---

to the FRG in 1955, where he joined the SPD and became an adviser to Willy Brandt; Peter Brandt and Jörg Schumacher, *Karrieren eines Außenseiters: Leo Bauer zwischen Kommunismus und Sozialdemokratie* (Berlin: Dietz, 1983), 167–290.

[41] Ingrid Langer, Ulrike Ley, and Susanne Sander, *Alibi-Frauen? Hessische Politikerinnen*, vol. I, *In den Vorparlamenten 1946 bis 1950* (Frankfurt a.M.: Helmer, 1994), 205–7; Mayer, *Ein Deutscher*, I:318–19, II:43–8, quote 48; Kantorowicz, *Deutsches Tagebuch* (Munich: Kindler, 1961), II:16–17, 333–5, 339–41, quote 334–5. Kantorowicz's diaries were published in the FRG, after his break with the party and while he sought recognition as a political refugee; it has been surmised that they were reworked. The question cannot be resolved until the original diaries, preserved with his papers, are opened to researchers. See esp. Michael Rohrwasser, *Der Stalinismus und die Renegaten: Die Literatur der Exkommunisten* (Stuttgart: Metzler, 1991), 113–19.

[42] Heider, *Kulturbund*, 94–116; Gerd Dietrich, *Politik und Kultur in der Sowjetischen Besatzungszone Deutschlands 1945–1949* (Bern: Lang, 1993), 179–81; also Esther von Richthofen, *Bringing Culture to the Masses: Control, Compromise, and Participation in the GDR* (New York: Berghahn, 2009).

censorship infrastructure, which was absorbed by the Ministry of Education and soon devolved onto new agencies, an Office of Literature and Publishing, a State Arts Commission, and a State Film Committee. These continued de facto licensing of all print matter and corresponding control over visual art, music, film, museums, and theater.[43] Their mission was what party directives called the struggle against "formalism" and for "socialist realism." This 1930s aesthetic doctrine was revived for the USSR by Andrei Zhdanov in 1946, gained traction in Eastern Germany from 1948, and was enshrined as policy in 1951/52. It vilified modernist formal experimentation as "decadent" – the contentless, abstract effluvia of a dying bourgeois civilization. Celebrated was art that was "close to the people," realistic and accessible to ordinary tastes, addressing "typical" experiences in an "optimistic" way – the concrete, grounded expressions of healthy, proletarian society.[44] (A fixation on rootedness linked political campaigns against "cosmopolitanism" to aesthetic ones against "formalism.") Such constraints – along with other ones about what political and historical topics could be represented and how – asserted a monopoly for socialist realism in culture that complemented the SED's monopoly on political power.

The cumulative effect on engaged democrats was two-sided. Repression and disregard encouraged them to seek spaces of limited autonomy for a bare minimum of thinking, writing, and teaching. At the same time, their basic commitment to the project of a socialist Germany encouraged them to embrace what contributions they could make. These ambivalent spaces within the dictatorship raise much-debated questions about the relationship of GDR state and society. They exemplify how political rule was constituted in and through wider social practices – including stubborn (or fearful) efforts to push back against the regime's imperatives – in a two-way process that involved citizens in their own domination while simultaneously setting limits to domination's scope.[45] In engaged democrats' own immediate experience, these spaces were

---

[43] Heider, *Kulturbund*, 129–33; Simone Barck, Martina Langermann, and Siegfried Lokatis, *"Jedes Buch ein Abenteuer": Zensur-System und literarische Öffentlichkeiten in der DDR bis Ende der sechziger Jahre* (Berlin: Akademie, 1997), 19–36.

[44] Dietrich, *Politik und Kultur*, 161–8; Heider, *Kulturbund*, 117–20; Hartmann and Eggeling, *Sowjetische Präsenz*, 217–23. These obtuse dogmas should not obscure the debates in Marxist aesthetics that addressed similar questions in far more nuanced ways. See, e.g., Eugene Lunn, *Marxism and Modernism: An Historical Study of Lukács, Brecht, Benjamin, and Adorno* (Berkeley: University of California Press, 1982).

[45] See Thomas Lindenberger, introduction to *Herrschaft und Eigen-Sinn in der Diktatur: Studien zur Gesellschaftsgeschichte der DDR*, ed. Lindenberger (Cologne: Böhlau, 1999), 13–44. Lindenberger's understanding of "domination" and "society" as co-constitutive – beyond binaries of "repression" and "resistance" – draws on Alf Lüdtke's notion of *Eigen-Sinn*; Alf Lüdtke, ed. *The History of Everyday Life: Reconstructing Historical Experiences*

understood above all as relative havens from the regime, a perspective effectively grasped in the later image of the GDR as a privatized "niche society," even where the niches in question were found within official institutions.[46] It was not until the successive upheavals of the mid 1950s that engaged democrats emerged from these isolated pockets to overtly challenge the East German order.

Intellectual and political sociability was thus confined to insular circles. Such an incipient social milieu in Berlin is recorded in Kantorowicz's diary as early as his fiftieth birthday party in August 1949. The celebration initially attracted some guests who stood closer to the emerging regime, from Erich Wendt of Aufbau press, Bodo Uhse of *Aufbau*, and Peter Huchel, editor of the new journal *Sinn und Form*, to Jürgen Kuczynski, Anna Seghers, and Friedrich Wolf. Kantorowicz then expressed a measure of relief when he and his friends were later "left to ourselves in our close circle." This group included Ernst and Karola Bloch, visiting from Leipzig, Bertolt Brecht and Helene Weigel, and Gerhart and Hanns Eisler – all recently returned from exile in the USA – as well as Wolfgang Harich and Max Schroeder. These friendships were cultivated in subsequent years, though the circle also changed, with the key addition of Rudolf Leonhard (back from Paris as of May 1950), frequent presence of Maximilian Scheer, and notable absence of the Eislers. Gerhart Eisler became an insider to power in the new GDR, while Kantorowicz saw himself and his circle as outsiders: "Yesterday's politicians have the reins firmly in hand again... Statesmen, thinkers, poets, spiritually creative people in general are left 'outside, before the door.'"[47]

Similar inward-looking islands of sociability emerged in Leipzig. On arrival, Mayer was grateful to his friend Krauss, who had already "distinguished precisely between those with whom one should associate and the others." Among the former, Mayer valued the economists Fritz Behrens and Henryk Grossmann, and he welcomed the wave of re-émigrés from the USA, including Hermann Budzislawski, who founded the journalism institute, and Wieland Herzfelde, who taught modern literature. But his close confidantes were Krauss and Bloch, who arrived on the same Polish liner as his friend Herzfelde.[48] For all Bloch's excitement at his new

---

and *Ways of Life*, trans. William Templer (Princeton, N.J.: Princeton University Press, 1995), 3–40, 313–14.

[46] The notion of a "niche society" was coined by Günter Gaus, *Wo Deutschland liegt: Eine Ortsbestimmung* (Hamburg: Hoffmann & Campe, 1983), 156–233.

[47] Kantorowicz, *Deutsches Tagebuch*, I:638–9, 659–60, II:53, 350, 372–8, 438, 535, 557–9, 660, quotes I:638–9, 647. The reference is to Wolfgang Borchert's well-known drama, *Draußen vor der Tür*, about a returning POW alienated from postwar Germany.

[48] Mayer, *Ein Deutscher*, II:26–7; *Literarische Welt: Dokumente zum Leben und Werk von Hans Mayer* (Cologne: Historisches Archiv der Stadt Köln, 1985), 79. On Behrens and

philosophy institute and at the project of the GDR, he shared Mayer's impression of a vibrant yet small community in a potentially hostile setting. Beyond its confines, Bloch wrote, "the servility all around feels unpleasant." Soon, a group of talented students gathered around him, including Gerhard Zwerenz, who linked their milieu to a wider circle of critically minded young intellectuals, including Erich Loest. By 1951, an astute West German observer – Alfred Andersch, writing in the *Frankfurter Hefte* – lauded Leipzig's "Marxists in hedgehog position" for maintaining one of the few preserves of true *Kultur* in the GDR (alongside Brecht and Weigel's new Berliner Ensemble).[49] Krauss, Mayer, and Bloch were often in Berlin, which remained the hub of East Germany's highly centralized intellectual and political life. Bloch, however, did most – interacting with his old friend Kantorowicz and new comrade Harich – to cultivate connections between the two locales.

In the GDR's first years, engaged democrats embraced the realm of culture, narrowly construed. This was the field of their own potential fulfillment and contribution; it was also where, as writers and scholars committed to the self-forming freedom of *Geist*, they chafed against repression. Leonhard's fears of exclusion and obscurity were confirmed on arrival in the GDR. In just a few months, censors rejected two volumes of poetry and four afterwords to collections. By late 1953, his disillusionment had progressed enough that he requested permission to emigrate; his death obviated the issue.[50] Kantorowicz's experience was more mixed. By his own account, he considered emigrating after *Ost und West* folded, but his friends counseled patience, and the regime offered palliatives. He accepted a professorship in contemporary German literature at the Humboldt University and became the de facto executor of Heinrich Mann's intellectual estate in the GDR. Hero of the popular front campaigns – and Kantorowicz's honored friend – Mann died in California in 1950, just before his planned return as president of East Berlin's new Academy of Arts. Kantorowicz was pleased to curate his papers at the Academy and edit his works at Aufbau. It was the Humboldt

---

Budzislawski, see Peter C. Caldwell, *Dictatorship, State Planning, and Social Theory in the German Democratic Republic* (Cambridge: Cambridge University Press, 2003), 14–56; Fair-Schulz, *Loyal Subversion*, 275–334.

[49] Bloch quoted in Peter Zudeick, *Der Hintern des Teufels: Ernst Bloch, Leben und Werk* (Bühl-Moos: Elster, 1985), 186; Alfred Andersch, "Marxisten in der Igelstellung," *Frankfurter Hefte* 6, no. 3 (1951): 208; Ingrid Zwerenz and Gerhard Zwerenz, *Sklavensprache und Revolte: Der Bloch-Kreis und seine Feinde in Ost und West* (Hamburg: Schwartzkopff, 2004).

[50] Leonhard to Kantorowicz, 11 February 1952, SUBH NL Kantorowicz NK: BI: L22; Kantorowicz, *Deutsches Tagebuch*, II:441–2; Jentzsch, *Leonhard*, 59–60.

University's literature institute, however, that became his refuge of choice. He later recalled wanting "to come to rest, in any case to shield myself for a time... behind the university's thick walls."[51]

Yet party and state remained an ominous outside presence, threatening to encroach on all preserves. The first postwar commemoration of the Nazi book-burnings on 10 May 1947 had been a success, in Kantorowicz's estimation, largely because he and other "independent writers and humanists" had retained control, against "party and government functionaries." The latter gained ground, however, in 1948, and that year, Kantorowicz's address closed on a cautionary note: mere ceremonies were easily lost "in the desk drawers of overburdened Education Ministries or Cultural Secretariats." He called for active vigilance against both bureaucratic neglect and official censorship of culture in the present. To illustrate, he railed against the persecution of "un-American" artists in the USA but avoided publicly expressing his real concern – that these same dangers were at hand in the GDR. Nonetheless, he was excluded from the "May 10th Committee" formed to plan future homages to "the free spirit." And no further commemorations were held.[52] Kantorowicz captured his frustration in a sardonic, unpublished poem entitled "Obituary for a Beautiful Thought." It told the saga of the "Day of the Free Book," which – arisen "like a phoenix from the ashes" and supported by the world's greatest "poets and thinkers" – survived the trials of exile only to die a slow death at the hands of "administrations and authorities" on returning home to Germany:

> Kulturbund secretaries
> carried it home with them
> and made of it, per routine,
> a memo for their files.
>
> That which once had been born
> snatched from embers and flame

---

[51] Kantorowicz, *Deutsches Tagebuch*, I:659, II:17–18, 25–8, 107, quote II:10; Wolfgang Gruner, "Alfred Kantorowicz – Wanderer zwischen Ost und West," in *Zwischen den Stühlen? Remigranten und Remigration in der deutschen Medienöffentlichkeit der Nachkriegszeit*, ed. Claus-Dieter Krohn and Axel Schildt (Hamburg: Christians, 2002), 307–10; also Matthias Braun, *Kulturinsel und Machtinstrument: Die Akademie der Künste, die Partei und die Staatssicherheit* (Göttingen: Vandenhoeck & Ruprecht, 2007), 25–34.

[52] Kantorowicz, *Deutsches Tagebuch*, I:327–8, 462–4; Kantorowicz, "Der Ehrentag der freien Literatur," in *Vom moralischen Gewinn der Niederlage: Artikel und Ansprachen* (Berlin: Aufbau, 1949), 154–6; Kantorowicz, *Deutsches Tagebuch*, I:462–4; II:264–5, 358, 549.

lost its life among the files,
suffocated by dust.[53]

Kantorowicz's central theme of German cultural unity was now subordinated to an opposition between creative spirit and deadening bureaucracy. The latter established itself as a central motif in his correspondence and unpublished writings of the 1950s.[54]

Kantorowicz also suffered censorship and was especially aggrieved by the suppression of two of his works. The first was his play *The Allies*. Set in France toward the end of the war, the piece thematized the plural and supranational character of the antifascist Resistance as well as American power's role in elevating prewar elites above revolutionary partisans after Liberation. It met with official displeasure, on contradictory grounds: it was at once too "sectarian" and (in ominously denunciatory rhetoric) too beholden to an "internationality that was actually just cosmopolitanism with inverted signs." The play was stricken from the Deutsches Theater schedule before the 1951/2 season started, despite a successful press premiere and some support from Pieck.[55] A similar fate befell Kantorowicz's *Spanish Diary*, published by Aufbau in 1948 and slated for republication in the Library of Progressive German Writers in 1951, a mass-produced, inexpensive series designed for wide circulation. Despite the editors' endorsement, a veto came from Franz Dahlem, Politburo member and veteran of the Spanish Civil War. His verdict: it was "not the book on Spain that we need... unmistakably written from the intellectual's perspective" and thus – evidently by definition – lacking "the party standpoint."[56] This was a damning critique, issued by a top official, veteran Communist, and switchman's son (albeit a relative moderate and Ulbricht rival about to encounter his own troubles); its recipient

---

[53] Kantorowicz, "Nachruf an einen schönen Gedanken, gehalten am 10. Mai 1949," n.d., SUBH NL Kantorowicz NK: A: 520. According to Kantorowicz, he mailed his poem to the "May 10th Committee" but received no response; Kantorowicz, *Deutsches Tagebuch*, I:464–5.

[54] Here, I disagree with McLellan, who proposes, along Rohrwasser's lines, that Kantorowicz worked his critique of "functionaries" into his published diaries after emigrating, to distance himself from his own "functionary" past; Josie McLellan, "The Politics of Communist Biography: Alfred Kantorowicz and the Spanish Civil War," *German History* 22, no. 4 (2004): 536–62.

[55] Kantorowicz to Ihering, 2 January 1951, SUBH NL Kantorowicz NK: Ostberlin: 62; Kantorowicz, *Deutsches Tagebuch*, II:180–219, quote 189. Kantorowicz had published the first act anonymously: "Befreiung: Eine Tragi-Komödie," *Ost und West* 3, no. 5 (1949): 32–53.

[56] "Protokoll über die heutige Sitzung des Redaktionskollegiums im Hause des Aufbau-Verlages," 5 December 1951, Bundesarchiv (hereafter BArch) DY 27/170; Kantorowicz, *Deutsches Tagebuch*, II:249–59, quote 254; Carsten Wurm, *Der frühe Aufbau-Verlag 1945–1961: Konzepte und Kontroversen* (Wiesbaden: Harrassowitz, 1996), 169–78.

was a bourgeois literature professor already on insecure footing in a party he had just (re-)joined.[57]

Kantorowicz countered these setbacks with unflagging resolve yet without success. After seeking help from various authorities and prominent acquaintances, he sent long memoranda on each "case" directly to the entire SED leadership. While Kantorowicz clearly felt his misfortune as a personal and professional rejection, he also insisted on its symptomatic character.[58] And he did so in terms that aligned creative freedom with democracy, opposing both to bureaucracy. His play's fate was "not an individual but a typical case." Suppression of works by "administrative measures... executed with truncheon-methods" and in the absence of any dialogue with authors and artists had produced "general... discouragement," reducing even Brecht and Seghers, Wolf and Arnold Zweig to "paralyzed silence."[59] With reference to his other case, he insisted that "not only for the sake of our literature [but also] for the sake of... our struggle for true democracy, it is necessary to discuss and revise... this formally bureaucratic and substantively questionable summary rejection of the Diary." Other than an unspecifically supportive reply from Pieck, his pleas met with silence.[60] In a last letter to the play's director, Kantorowicz lamented a "nearly Kafkaesque atmosphere":

Decisions are made regarding you, about which you learn nothing; discussions are held about you, but you are unfamiliar with the discussants; somewhere there are probably dossiers, but you know not what they contain... you go groping in the dark, [and] in the "Council of the Gods," decrees are perhaps (or perhaps not) being prepared that can strike you suddenly like a lightning bolt.[61]

For the rest of his years in the GDR, he did not venture far beyond the university. He did seed his lectures with well-placed and portentously delivered citations from Brecht or Thomas Mann on Nazism's "terror of

---

[57] Kantorowicz's self-consciousness about his class background is suggested in his autobiographical novel *The Burgher's Son*, serialized in *Ost und West*; Baerns, *Ost und West*, 93. On Dahlem, see Catherine Epstein, *The Last Revolutionaries: German Communists and Their Century* (Cambridge, Mass.: Harvard University Press, 2003).

[58] That is, to present personal and career disappointment as the root cause of his political dissidence and eventual flight flattens a multidimensional dynamic; cf. Gruner, "Kantorowicz," 311–12, 315.

[59] "Der Fall des Schauspiels 'Die Verbündeten,'" February 1952, SUBH NL Kantorowicz NK: Ostberlin: 62. He names other allegedly afflicted writers only in his diary: Kantorowicz, *Deutsches Tagebuch*, II:180. On the celebrated case of Brecht's *Trial of Lucullus*, see Mark W. Clark, *Beyond Catastrophe: German Intellectuals and Cultural Renewal after World War II, 1945–1955* (Lanham, Md.: Lexington, 2006), 143–6.

[60] "Der Fall 'Spanisches Tagebuch,'" February 1952, Wilhelm Pieck to Kantorowicz, 16 April 1952, SUBH NL Kantorowicz NK: Ostberlin: 62.

[61] Kantorowicz to Wolfgang Langhoff, 16 April 1952, SUBH NL Kantorowicz NK: Ostberlin: 62; see also Kantorowicz, *Deutsches Tagebuch*, II:213, 218.

convictions." Kantorowicz was convinced that students would see these for what they were: veiled barbs against the SED regime.[62]

As the experiences of his friend and colleague Harich attest, however, one intellectual's niche could be another's prison. Harich graduated in the first cohort of a new program for social science faculty in 1948 and began a dissertation on Herder in 1950; upon finishing in 1951, he was offered a professorship in the history of philosophy at the Humboldt University (he was twenty-eight). There, his deep engagement with Hegel became a flashpoint. He was entirely in step with Bloch and Georg Lukács, who were each at that time revisiting Hegel's relationship to Marxism. And both influenced Harich, Bloch as a personal friend and Lukács initially through his writings. While their affirmations of Hegel diverged, all three were sharply at odds with postwar pronouncements by Stalin and Zhdanov. This was a luxury young Harich could ill afford, and disciplinary proceedings were initiated. In a quasi-public exchange and a closed-door session in spring 1952, he was subjected to inquisitorial attacks by the keepers of orthodoxy, the philosophy institute's SED party organization.[63] Discussion was predicated on Harich's self-criticism. He was expected to concede that Hegel and German idealism represented an "aristocratic reaction against French materialism and the French bourgeois revolution," per the official line. Harich refused, insisting – in Marx's name – on a more nuanced view of the relationship between materialism and idealism. He dismissed the meeting as not a dialogue but a campaign to silence and defame, led by dogmatists who appeared to have "no concrete knowledge of the history of philosophy." Unsurprisingly, this drew reprimands for his "arrogant" manner toward "Soviet scholarship" and his own colleagues. Although Harich asked various officials including his friend Becher to intervene, the authorities proved less interested in debating Hegel than Harich had hoped.[64]

---

[62] Kantorowicz, *Deutsches Tagebuch*, II:27–8.

[63] Siegfried Prokop, *Ich bin zu früh geboren: Auf den Spuren Wolfgang Harichs* (Berlin: Dietz, 1997), 56–69; Georg Lukács, *Der junge Hegel: Über die Beziehungen von Dialektik und Ökonomie* (Berlin: Aufbau, 1948); Bloch, *Subjekt-Objekt: Erläuterungen zu Hegel* (Berlin: Aufbau, 1951). See, e.g., Camilla Warnke, "'Das Problem Hegel ist längst gelöst': Eine Debatte in der DDR-Philosophie der fünfziger Jahre," in *Anfänge der DDR-Philosophie: Ansprüche, Ohnmacht, Scheitern*, ed. Volker Gerhardt and Hans-Christoph Rauh (Berlin: Links, 2001), 194–221.

[64] Wolfgang Harich, "Bericht über die Hegel-Diskussion (Mittwoch, d. 9. April 1952)," n.d., Internationaal Instituut voor Sociale Geschiedenis (Amsterdam, hereafter IISG) NL Harich 161; Harich, "Protokoll der Sitzung des Philosophischen Instituts (Mittwoch, den 16.4.52)," n.d., IISG NL Harich 23; Harich to Johannes R. Becher 6 April 1952, 25 April 1952, AdK Becher-Archiv 4262–3 (including copies of letters to Fred Oelßner at the Central Committee and several essays on Hegel, progress, and reaction in classical German thought).

Into East Germany: intelligentsia and the Apparat    261

In the wake of these confrontations, Harich's position at the university rapidly deteriorated. One of his main antagonists, Klaus Schrickel, was appointed to monitor his lectures, the popularity of which had not escaped his colleagues' notice. When his overseer demanded that Harich finally tender his lecture notes for pre-approval, Harich's reaction was telling: "You asshole! You are not my censor! . . . at a European university? Such a thing was abolished in the eighteenth century!" Invoking the struggles of Enlightenment scholars against absolutist censors, Harich reflexively framed the conflict as one of autonomous *Geist* versus bureaucratic authority. A severe rebuke followed, and Harich scaled back his teaching.[65] He devoted his energies instead to his position at Aufbau press, which he would recall as "an Elysium of intellectual breadth, measured thoughtfulness, [and] fruitful tolerance" by comparison. Harich had started there in 1950, focusing on canonical literature and philosophy as well as some newer works, including those of Bloch and Lukács, and he became deputy lead editor to Schroeder in 1954, responsible for the "classical heritage and philosophy" department. His other main activity was as editor in chief of the *Deutsche Zeitschrift für Philosophie*, which he co-founded in 1953 with Bloch, legal theorist Arthur Baumgarten, and logician Karl Schröter. While Schrickel initially served as managing editor (and party supervisor), he was soon replaced by Harich's colleague Manfred Hertwig.[66]

Engaged democrats' dissatisfactions in the early GDR were aired largely in private and focused on the cultural realm. The first of these aspects changed – and the second almost did – during the regime's first crisis. In 1952 (later than in other satellites), the leadership announced that East Germany's transition had ended and the "building of socialism" begun, which meant ratcheting up industrial production, expropriating smaller firms, and collectivizing agriculture. After Stalin's March 1953 death, however, new leaders in Moscow encouraged a "new course" across the bloc. This was announced in the GDR in early June, and reforms rolled back some of the previous year's more onerous effects; at the same time, cross-border travel was liberalized. This staved off dissatisfaction among the embattled middle classes. Among working men

---

[65] Marginalia on Klaus Schrickel to Harich, 4 May 1953, IISG NL Harich 45; Prokop, *Geboren*, 63–4. His lectures remained well attended; Warnke, "Der junge Wolfgang Harich: Seine Vorlesungen zur Geschichte der Philosophie 1951–1954," in *Anfänge*, ed. Gerhardt and Rauh, 469–91.

[66] Harich, *Keine Schwierigkeiten mit der Wahrheit: Zur nationalkommunistischen Opposition 1956 in der DDR* (Berlin: Dietz, 1993), quote 15; Prokop, *Geboren*, 62, 69; Wurm, *Aufbau-Verlag*, 104–7; Rauh, "Hommage: Die Anfangsjahre der Deutschen Zeitschrift für Philosophie (1953 bis 1958)," in *Zwischen "Mosaik" und "Einheit": Zeitschriften in der DDR*, ed. Barck, Langermann, and Lokatis (Berlin: Links, 1999), 434–45.

and women, the retention of increased production norms and ongoing consumer shortages sparked serious discontent. Around 17 June, a wave of strikes and protests swept across the GDR, bringing over one million citizens – at least half of whom were industrial workers – into the streets of over 700 cities and towns. Their demands soon expanded from lower norms and prices to civil liberties, free elections, and the government's dissolution. Amid serious challenges from intra-SED reformers and leadership uncertainty in Moscow, the crisis threatened both East Germany and the Eastern bloc. The uprising was crushed by Soviet tanks and blamed on "fascist provocateurs" from the West. Then, Ulbricht reckoned with his party rivals by alleging a conspiratorial plot and purging Rudolf Herrnstadt, Wilhelm Zaisser, Elli Schmidt, and several others from their positions.[67]

The purge was standard Stalinist fare. What haunted officials and other observers was the vision of regular, working citizens rising up against the socialist state. The intelligentsia's responses, in comparison, have long been considered conformist, and not without reason. Most famously, a public statement by Writers' Union secretary Kurt Barthel, called KuBa, expressed disappointment in the people for violating the regime's trust. Such reflexive authoritarianism and blindness to the people's will and welfare provoked Brecht's wry reply:

> ... Would it not be easier
> In that case for the government
> To dissolve the people
> And elect another?

"The Solution" was never published in his lifetime. During the uprising itself – just prior to its suppression – he had written to Ulbricht and Grotewohl, expressing solidarity with the party (of which he was not a member) but urging a serious discussion with "the masses" about their concerns.[68]

The poem's biting irony was one private manifestation of a broader mobilization among GDR intellectuals in summer 1953, one rooted in longer-standing dissatisfactions that soon exacted significant concessions

---

[67] See, e.g., Kleßmann and Bernd Stöver, eds. *1953 – Krisenjahr des Kalten Krieges in Europa* (Cologne: Böhlau, 1999); Katherine Pence, "'You as a Woman Will Understand': Consumption, Gender, and the Relationship between State and Citizenry in the GDR's Crisis of 17 June 1953," *German History* 19, no. 2 (2001): 218–52; Gareth Dale, *Popular Protest in East Germany, 1945–1989* (London: Routledge, 2005), 9–36; Epstein, *Revolutionaries*, 158–63.

[68] Bertolt Brecht, "The Solution," in *Poems, 1913–1956*, ed. John Willett and Ralph Manheim, 2nd edn. (London: Methuen, 1979), 440; Clark, *Beyond Catastrophe*, 149–52, quote 150.

from the regime.[69] East Germany's engaged democrats were provoked to action, and the crisis opened a space for a partial yet public recovery of some of their original vision's thrust. On 17 June, both Kantorowicz and Harich happened to be convalescing in Berlin's Charité hospital, the former from complications after a lung infection and the latter from gastric issues attributed to stress. Kantorowicz spoke with Leonhard, Scheer, and Schroeder, among others, who all aired their dismay at the regime's armed "victory" over the GDR's own citizens, the workers and farmers of the "people's state."[70] Harich welcomed various friends and colleagues too, who found him energetically advocating a "Titoist" resolution. One year earlier, over dinner at Ernst Rowohlt's home in Hamburg, Harich had been locked in debate with an independent-minded Marxist named Fritz Sternberg, an important *Weltbühne* author and SAPD theorist (and influence on Brecht) in the 1920s. That night, over Harich's initial resistance, Sternberg sparked his interest in the Yugoslav model of worker self-management, as a means to remedy the GDR's glaring democratic deficit. In the 1953 uprising, Harich sensed a great opportunity to push such a restructuring of both polity and economy. Walter Janka, the new head of Aufbau press, seemed receptive to such notions. Brecht, on a separate visit, counseled caution. He suggested a campaign against the cultural bureaucracy instead, whose overreach had only grown amid the anti-formalism hysteria. That seemed the more feasible and effective (not to say less dangerous) course.[71]

In the wake of the popular uprising, then, Brecht and Harich played leading roles in an initiative to reform the cultural apparatus. The ground was prepared by two organizations presided over by their ally Becher (and monitored for the MfS by Alexander Abusch). On 30 June, the Academy of Arts issued a series of recommendations centered on eliminating censorship and thereby returning control over cultural and intellectual production to the producers. On 3 July, the Kulturbund's presiding council passed an expanded set of demands, asserting that "administrative interference of state agencies in creative questions of art and literature must end" and grounding that demand in the "legal security" guaranteed by "the inviolable constitution of our Republic." This was a rejection of

---

[69] This is the revisionist argument of Prokop, *Intellektuelle im Krisenjahr 1953: Enquete über die Lage der Intelligenz der DDR: Analyse und Dokumentation* (Schkeuditz: Schkeuditzer Buchverlag, 2003). By contrast, see, e.g., Arnulf Baring, *Der 17. Juni 1953* (Stuttgart: Deutsche Verlags-Anstalt, 1983), 69, 85–6.

[70] Kantorowicz, *Deutsches Tagebuch*, II:363–78.

[71] Harich, *Keine Schwierigkeiten*, 24–6; Harich, *Ahnenpass: Versuch einer Autobiographie*, ed. Thomas Grimm (Berlin: Schwarzkopf & Schwarzkopf, 1999), 219–23; Prokop, *Geboren*, 73. On Sternberg, see Helga Grebing, ed. *Fritz Sternberg (1895–1963): Für die Zukunft des Sozialismus* (Cologne: Bund, 1981).

centralized, arbitrary control in one sphere, with larger implications that were not lost on the regime. Still, both proposals were widely distributed and discussed, published – after some stalling by the censors – in *Neues Deutschland* and reprinted in *Sonntag* and elsewhere.[72] Amid the tumult, Brecht and Harich launched a coordinated attack in the *Berliner Zeitung*. Brecht's poems "Unidentifiable Errors of the Arts Commission" and "The Office for Literature," subjected these institutions to withering critique. Harich's article focused on the blunt and undialectical dogma they enforced, whose "flat and un-Marxist" formulae confused the "faithful reproduction of details" with realism and the "banal smile of a toothpaste advertisement" with optimism.[73] Ultimately, the intellectuals' campaign encouraged the dissolution of the Arts Commission and Film Committee, the reform of the Literature Office, and the establishment of a Culture Ministry with Becher at the helm in 1954. In 1956, the Literature Office was dissolved into the new ministry. For a time, East German artists and intellectuals enjoyed freer rein.[74]

### Breaking open: culture and politics circa 1956

The years after 1953 brought a "thaw" to the Eastern bloc, one that reoriented economic priorities, rolled back state security, and liberalized cultural policy. These trends accelerated dramatically in 1956. That February, the 20th Party Congress of the Communist Party of the Soviet Union and Nikita Khrushchev's climactic "secret speech" put destalinization more explicitly on the agenda, shaking the Eastern bloc to its foundations. In Poland, worker strikes led to riots and unrest in the summer while loosened censorship unleashed critical public debates. In October, the "national Communist" reformer Władysław Gomułka

---

[72] Becher privileged the Kulturbund proposals, which were circulated as a flyer, then published on July 8 in *Neues Deutschland*. The Academy's proposals appeared there on July 12, when both also appeared in *Sonntag*. Each was reprinted in the next issue of *Aufbau* and *Sinn und Form*. "Vorschläge des Kulturbundes zur demokratischen Erneuerung Deutschlands für die Entwicklung unseres Kulturlebens," BArch DY 27/1182, 221; Heider and Kerstin Thöns, eds. *SED und Intellektuelle in der DDR der fünfziger Jahre: Kulturbund-Protokolle* (Cologne: Wissenschaft und Politik, 1990), 7–59; Heider, *Kulturbund*, 174–6; Braun, *Kulturinsel*, 75–8.
[73] Brecht, "Nicht feststellbare Fehler der Kunstkommission," *Berliner Zeitung*, 11 July 1953; Brecht, "Das Amt für Literatur," *Berliner Zeitung*, 15 July 1953; Harich, "Es geht um den Realismus: Die bildenden Künstler und die Kunstkommission," *Berliner Zeitung*, 14 July 1953. See Prokop, *Geboren*, 73–4; Prokop, *Intellektuelle*, 126–7; Clark, *Beyond Catastrophe*, 153–5.
[74] Heider, *Kulturbund*, 180–3; Barck, Langermann, and Lokatis, *"Jedes Buch"*, 37–60; Jens-Fietje Dwars, *Abgrund des Widerspruchs: Das Leben des Johannes R. Becher* (Berlin: Aufbau, 1998), 703–5.

rode this wave of discontent peacefully to power. In Hungary, a similar combination of social unrest and intellectual ferment set off a series of regime shifts that culminated in a multiparty government under the reformer Imre Nagy, Hungary's withdrawal from the Warsaw Pact, and mass street protests in Budapest. These more destabilizing developments were ultimately crushed by Soviet military intervention in early November. In the GDR, some strikes and demonstrations broke out as well. Yet there, memories of 1953 dovetailed with leaders' sheer unwillingness to show weakness to largely keep the people off the streets.[75]

East Germany's critical intelligentsia, meanwhile, was spurred to new action, first by the Polish example and then by Hungary, where the Petőfi Circle – a student-led intellectual forum in which Lukács was involved – and spontaneously organized people's councils played prominent roles.[76] The ongoing effects of the 20th Party Congress itself, moreover, are difficult to overestimate. If the "revelations" about Stalin's crimes and the critique of the cult of personality generated interest and anxiety among the party faithful, it was the official sanction of "peaceful coexistence" between East and West and the return of "national roads" to socialism that most inspired engaged democrats.[77] The apparent opportunity for a thoroughgoing transformation ignited the GDR's most fruitful period of discussion yet. It was the turbulence of 1956 that provoked East Germany's engaged democrats to articulate publicly the critique of Stalinism that had been implicit in their vision from the outset. Three exemplary moments illustrate this development, which the authorities perceived – not incorrectly – as a united front of "revisionism."

First, Bloch and Harich organized a conference on "The Problem of Freedom in Light of Scientific Socialism" that convened at East Berlin's Academy of Sciences in March 1956. Just weeks after the 20th Party Congress, it partook of the post-Stalinist climate, albeit at a point when the full content of Khrushchev's "secret speech" was still closely guarded

---

[75] See, e.g., Jan Foitzik, ed. *Entstalinisierungskrise in Ostmitteleuropa 1953–1956: Vom 17. Juni bis zum ungarischen Volksaufstand* (Paderborn: Schöningh, 2001).
[76] Dieter Schiller, *Der verweigerte Dialog: Zum Verhältnis von Parteiführung der SED und Schriftstellern in den Krisenjahren 1956/57* (Berlin: Dietz, 2003); Guntolf Herzberg, *Anpassung und Aufbegehren: Die Intelligenz der DDR in den Krisenjahren 1956/58* (Berlin: Links, 2006); Siegfried Prokop, *1956 – DDR am Scheideweg: Opposition und neue Konzepte der Intelligenz* (Berlin: Homilius, 2006). In a longer-term context, see John Connelly, "Ulbricht and the Intellectuals," *Contemporary European History* 6, no. 3 (1997): 329–59.
[77] See, e.g., Harich, *Keine Schwierigkeiten*, 40–1; Bloch, "Über die Bedeutung des 20. Parteitags," in *Viele Kammern im Welthaus: Eine Auswahl aus dem Werk*, ed. Friedrich Dieckmann and Jürgen Teller (Frankfurt a.M.: Suhrkamp, 1994), 494–505; Wolfgang Leonhard, "Die bedeutsamste Rede des Kommunismus," *Aus Politik und Zeitgeschichte* B17/18 (2006): 3–5.

by the top SED leadership. Visitors hailed from the GDR, all across Eastern Europe, and the USSR as well as the FRG and other countries in the West. From Budapest, Lukács was unable to attend, but prominent speakers included Leszek Kołakowski from Warsaw and Henri Lefebvre from Paris. From West Germany came Hans Heinz Holz, a Bloch student based in Frankfurt, and Rudolf Schottlaender, a Heidelberg-trained philosopher from West Berlin. The GDR delegation ranged from Steiniger and Hermann Duncker, a venerable socialist theorist active already before 1914, to Schrickel and Kurt Hager, a Central Committee member, top cultural functionary, and leading SED ideologue.[78]

Bloch's keynote reflected the ambiguities of his own politics as well as the unsettledness of the moment. He began by interlacing reasoned reflections on the formal "elbow-freedom" of classical liberalism with reflexive invective against contemporary, US-led "Atlantic freedom." The latter had perverted even liberalism's once revolutionary moments by "eliminat[ing] free competition" in the economy and practicing "enslavement" and "aggression" in politics, at home and in the colonized world. Conversely, a "true will to freedom" could critique but never oppose the USSR, which championed the cause of "human liberation itself." For good measure, he defended the "dictatorship of the proletariat," which suspended some bourgeois freedoms as a temporary necessity, en route to freedom in higher form. Such comments exposed the continuing accommodation of his future-oriented utopia to actual unfreedom, and they signaled obstacles on the road to peaceable understanding between East and West. At the same time, Bloch sought to recover potentials embedded in the bourgeois heritage that he refused to reduce to a merely ideological function. "A luster envelops *liberté, egalité, fraternité* that is different from the aroma of free competition," he argued; the crucial task was to realize the "ideal image of the *citoyen*" as a social and economic as well as political being. Conceiving this process in its historical development entailed distinguishing "layers" of freedom: freedom of will, choice, decision, and finally action, that is, truly "political freedom." Characteristically, Bloch's stress was on humanity's willful, world-shaping, de-alienating activity, which gave freedom its "subjectivist-intensive" character and conditioned its relationship to "predominantly objectivist categories" such as possibility and necessity. He explained:

---

[78] On the conference, see Caldwell, *Dictatorship, State Planning*, 127–9; Herzberg, *Anpassung*, 413–23; Prokop, *1956*, 116–17. The proceedings were published but quickly recalled, and authorities recovered most of the copies sold; *Das Problem der Freiheit im Lichte des wissenschaftlichen Sozialismus: Konferenz der Sektion Philosophie der Deutschen Akademie der Wissenschaften zu Berlin* (Berlin: Akademie, 1956).

Although – indeed because – freedom is above all a social category, it is originally... an anthropological one, of human will and ultimately of human-intensive substance, [though] never in the sense... of subject without object. On the contrary, when conditions are formed humanely, so that they no longer appear foreign, that is, as constraints, then they do not stop being object but become for the subject the freedom of its objective-adequate surroundings, order and home. They are finished only as *alienated* objects, while the subject as *liberated* enters into an unalienated environment.[79]

Evocatively, Bloch underscored his distance from Engels' bluntly objectivistic definition of freedom as insight into necessity and affirmed his commitment to a subject-centered Marxism. Reprising his earlier thought figures, Bloch defined fully-realized freedom instead as the creative subject's self-recognition in a social order of its own active making.

Complementing Bloch, Harich explored the anthropology of free subjectivity in a Kantian frame, addressing the "freedom of the will." Justifying his theme, he dismissed as dogmatism the notion that all questions could be resolved simply with reference to Engels' definition of free will as "*nothing but* the capacity to decide with objective knowledge" of social or natural laws. Rather, Harich returned to Kant's ethics, which associated freedom with acting according to self-imposed norms, conditioned by neither external constraint nor animal instinct. What Kant had grasped was the human capacity to interpolate conscious will between needs or desires and their satisfaction, a process that escaped "mechanical causation." And Harich made this insight useful for a "Marxist philosophical anthropology," one that could address the concerns of moral philosophy without reverting from scientific to utopian socialism. He affirmed that "socialist revolution" followed "from the contradictions of the bourgeois social order and not from the abstraction 'human nature.'" However, only socialism established a "human, dignified" relationship between the species and "its own social development" – a relationship of creative "labor," as the "foundation and 'model'" of all "specifically human conduct." If socialist freedom entailed the "knowledgeable mastery of the objectively necessary," then that meant the extension of the subject's conscious control not only over the external world's dynamics but also over internal instincts and drives. This condition, as an "inner-spiritual result," was clearly registered yet "idealistically misunderstood" in Kant's notion of free will.[80] Harich identified Kant's self-legislating moral freedom with socialism as its fullest realization and correlated

---

[79] Bloch, "Freiheit, ihre Schichtung und ihr Verhältnis zur Wahrheit," in *Problem der Freiheit*, 17–19, 21–2, 30.

[80] Harich, "Das Rationelle in Kants Konzeption der Freiheit," in *Problem der Freiheit*, 70–1, 74–5.

both to the creative subject of a Marxian humanism. He formulated – as Bloch had – engaged democrats' common, pre-theoretical sense of spontaneous, world- and self-shaping subjectivity in philosophical terms, explicating its relationship to classical German thought.

These positions on freedom remained abstract and speculative, and Bloch exercised some self-critique on this point in closing. Collectively, the conference had missed the "creative medium between the actual and the conceptual," the mediation of theory and practice that might unfreeze too-fixed categories, also for a consideration of state socialist social and political order. Doing so would entail re-examining their relationship to "bourgeois freedoms, formal though they may have become" and confronting "the limits to freedom in our own house," rooted in "bureaucracy" and "schematism." But they found themselves in a "transitional condition," and they had made a start, he asserted.[81] The difficulty of moving forward, however, was underscored by a position paper from eight GDR philosophers, which dutifully reaffirmed, in Engels' name, the subordination of freedom to necessity.[82]

The second exemplary field of engaged democrats' "revisionism" was literature and literary criticism, where Mayer played a central role. The "thaw" climate of more vigorous discussion was promoted, in part, by Becher's new ministry. In summer 1955, Becher held a Critics' Conference, with Brecht and Mayer on the podium. Although no momentous breakthroughs ensued, it was Mayer's estimation that a high-profile event had been called to uphold the "freedom of opinion" against stifling dogma, and that was itself a crucial step. In January 1956 came the Fourth German Writers' Congress. There, Stefan Heym – who had fled McCarthyism and settled in the GDR in 1952 – raised concerns over the numbing effects of self-censorship on socialist writers, provoking an exchange with Ulbricht himself. Again, it was the fact of the exchange itself that struck observers, which seemed to herald real dialogue between the party and intellectuals.[83] The trend continued at a two-day summer workshop convened by the Culture Ministry. In his keynote, Mayer picked up where Heym left off, taking Ulbricht to task for invoking Stalin's definition of writers as "engineers of the human soul." This

---

[81] Bloch, "Schlußwort," in *Problem der Freiheit*, 344–5. Herzberg's charges that Bloch despised bourgeois liberties and that conference-goers missed the chance for a nondogmatic re-evaluation of freedom thus seem rather one-sided; Herzberg, *Anpassung*, 413, 415, 417.

[82] Erhard Albrecht et al., "Gedanken zum Problem der Freiheit im Lichte des wissenschaftlichen Sozialismus," in *Problem der Freiheit*, 353–62.

[83] Mayer, *Ein Deutscher*, II:124–8; Schiller, *Der verweigerte Dialog*, 11–17; Peter Hutchinson, *Stefan Heym: The Perpetual Dissident* (Cambridge: Cambridge University Press, 1992), 66–7.

metaphor led to the blunt instrumentalization of culture, "a confusion of art and propaganda," Mayer asserted. It also rested on a mistaken analogy between technology and art. The latter involved a "qualitatively different mode of scientific appropriation of reality," unlike science's "mechanical representation" of immediate or direct experience.[84] While others in the GDR were questioning the dogmas of socialist realism, Mayer indicted its literary fruits and offered a controversial antidote: re-engagement with classical modernism. He made both points at the workshop and developed them in a lecture entitled "On the Present Condition of our Literature," recorded for Radio Berlin but blocked from broadcast. The editors at *Sonntag* then published it instead, in early December, when the regime's crackdown on dissenting voices had already begun.[85]

Mayer's point of departure was the empirical observation that the postwar decade had generated little literature of note. Across the globe, this was related to changing conditions of production and reception in media and the arts; in the Eastern bloc, it had also to do with the stultifying effects of socialist realism. "A construction poem with many exclamation marks... and sun in its heart," he insisted, was no more definitively "optimism" than "a sober observation of conditions that concludes the situation... is not good" was necessarily "pessimistic." True pessimism, he asserted, "disputes that bad situations can be changed by human power and praxis" (echoing his earlier critiques of writers from Camus to Jünger). Conversely, true optimism recognized "that human circumstances can be changed and improved... by collective human action." Rendering the "transformable" in art demanded "new forms and methods" of knowing and representing the world. And these were glaringly absent from GDR literature, which was no less "schematic" for all its "rambling on about scientific socialism and working people." Official conventions had, in fact, produced a flood of irrelevant works, aesthetic equivalents of "red-painted gazebos." As a counterpoint, Mayer held up the "literary opulence" of the 1920s, in its sheer variety of new styles and formal experimentation.[86] In one fell swoop, Mayer discounted most

---

[84] "Konferenz am 8. Juni 1956 im Klubhaus Jägerstraße," typed transcript, n.d., 22, 24, 32, Historisches Archiv der Stadt Köln NL Mayer 1333 Box 1. The first quote was not reported in the press; Georg Pilz, "Die Fenster sind aufgestoßen," *Sonntag*, 17 June 1956. See Schiller, *Der verweigerte Dialog*, 35–49; Alfred Klein, *Unästhetische Feldzüge: Der siebenjährige Krieg gegen Hans Mayer 1956–1963* (Leipzig: Faber & Faber, 1997), 28–31; Mayer, *Ein Deutscher*, II:132–6.

[85] Ingrid Pietrzynski, "Ein 'Offener Brief' als Schadensbegrenzung: Hans Mayer und der DDR-Rundfunk 1956," *Rundfunk und Geschichte* 28, no. 3/4 (2002): 129–38.

[86] Mayer, "Zur Gegenwartslage unserer Literatur: Ein Rundfunkvortrag," *Sonntag*, 2 December 1956.

GDR authors' works and affirmed the modernism not only of Hemingway and Brecht but also of Joyce and Kafka, reviled by Eastern bloc orthodoxy. These positions reprised his postwar discussions of literature as well as notions of transformability that were central to engaged democrats' commitments. In the months after the essay's publication, *Sonntag* hosted a "discussion" of Mayer's theses – a forceful reassertion of orthodoxy led by Ulbricht's literary lieutenant (and Mayer's Leipzig colleague) Alfred Kurella.[87] This was only one element in a coordinated counteroffensive against the perceived threat of an intellectual opposition.

In "revisionism's" most explicit challenge, engaged democrats formulated the first comprehensive program for East Germany's destalinizing, democratic transformation. It emerged from conversations within the party organization at Aufbau press. There, as elsewhere, ferment was fueled by the circulation of Khrushchev's speech and by frustration at the regime's evident refusal to openly address its implications. They were further inspired by reports from Poland and (initially) from Hungary and dismayed at the distortion of these events in the GDR media. At Aufbau, Schroeder took part in the discussions (while Uhse, *Aufbau*'s editor, did not), but most intensively involved were Harich, Janka, *Sonntag* editors Gustav Just and Heinz Zöger, and local party secretary Günter Schubert; eventually, they were joined by Hertwig and economist Bernhard Steinberger (while Schubert kept the MfS apprised). The "circle of the like-minded" they formed was only one among dozens of similar conversation nodes.[88] In those heady months, they cultivated ties far and wide – extensively to Bloch and younger Leipzig figures such as Zwerenz and Loest; occasionally to Lukács and his students or to Polish visitors; and, later, to a "Thursday Circle" convened by the young Berlin publisher Fritz J. Raddatz. In the last moments, they planned to contact Kantorowicz, whom they suspected of similar activities.[89]

As they conferred, Harich began to put their thoughts into writing. He presented drafts to Soviet contacts in the summer and to the ambassador in October, expecting them to be less Stalinist than the Germans. Not only was the ambassador unreceptive, but he may also have reported the details to Ulbricht, who summoned Harich to him and warned against

---

[87] Klein, *Unästhetische Feldzüge*, 37–54; Schiller, *Der verweigerte Dialog*, 115–18; Mayer, *Ein Deutscher*, II:137–9.
[88] Prokop, *1956*, 58–61; Harich, *Keine Schwierigkeiten*, 47; Gustav Just, *Zeuge in eigener Sache: Die fünfziger Jahre* (Berlin: Der Morgen, 1990), 151. At the end, Richard Wolf of Radio Berlin and Joachim Wenzel, a Leipzig-based *Sonntag* journalist, were also involved.
[89] Here and below, see Prokop, *1956*, 115–207; also Herzberg, *Anpassung*, 237–41, 489–510; Schiller, *Der verweigerte Dialog*, 87–110.

traitorous delusions à la Poland or Hungary. Still, the reformers were not deterred. They went so far as to vet Merker – recently released from prison and contacted by Janka – as Ulbricht's replacement, a "German Gomułka." Finally, Harich reached out to the hated "East Bureau" of the West German SPD, its agency for clandestine work against the GDR. The last was an act of high treason, one that Harich undertook on his own.[90] In this initially open, later conspiratorial fashion, an oppositional grouping coalesced and worked toward a root and branch overhaul of the party-state's institutions.

The "Platform for a Special German Path to Socialism" that Harich ultimately produced resonated with engaged democrats' earlier vision, just as its title invoked the betrayed promise of an independent postwar trajectory.[91] It called for deposing the leadership, abolishing censorship and state security, and a "socialist democratization" of all institutions. The first requirement was rigorous "intra-party democracy," for which Harich invoked a return to "Leninist norms" – that is, to a "democratic centralism" that embraced intra-party discussion and, in particular, input from the grassroots. For too long, a "mistrust of the masses" had fed "arrogance" and "bureaucratism." While the SED would remain working people's "conscious and organized vanguard," it would not decree correct consciousness from above. Rather, constant interchange between elected officials and popular base via local assemblies would ensure that the party "not only teaches the masses, but learns from them." Furthermore, party institutions were to be disentangled from those of state, economy, and society.[92] The state itself would be decentralized, with "as many competencies as possible... devolved downward." The old eastern federal states (effectively dissolved in 1952) would be rebuilt from the bottom up, with parliaments directly elected at each level (still on the basis of unified multiparty lists, but with contested slots). In the economy, looser planning and non-statist forms of collective ownership as well as limited private property would enable greater autonomy for firms.

---

[90] See also Wolfgang Buschfort, *Parteien im Kalten Krieg: Die Ostbüros von SPD, CDU und FDP* (Berlin: Links, 2000), 136–8.

[91] The original manuscript is among Walter Ulbricht's papers, incorrectly dated and ascribed to Karl Schirdewan; "Rede von K. Schirdewan auf der 26. Tagung des ZK der SED," 22 March 1956, BArch NY 4182/893, 67–116. It was first published as Harich, "Plattform für einen besonderen deutschen Weg zum Sozialismus," in *Keine Schwierigkeiten*, 111–60. See also Andreas Heyer, "Wolfgang Harichs Demokratiekonzeption aus dem Jahr 1956: Demokratische Grundrechte, bürgerliche Werte und sozialistische Orientierung," *Zeitschrift für Geschichtswissenschaft* 55, no. 6 (2007): 529–50.

[92] Harich, "Plattform," 113–21, quotes 113, 117–18. Harich's image of Bolshevik "democratic centralism" is idealized even before the ban on factions Lenin instituted in 1921.

Within each firm, production would be controlled by elected workers' councils, while workers' material interests were represented by elected union leaderships; both would send delegates to higher economic assemblies. At each level, they would have the right to propose legislation to the relevant political assembly. And they would reclaim the right – long dismissed as superfluous by the socialist state – to call strikes for both economic and political aims.[93]

Crucially, this reform of governance was embedded in a broader revitalization and re-pluralization of public life, with an eye toward the eventual reconstitution of an all-German public sphere and national reunification under socialist auspices.[94] Mass organizations would no longer be "transmission belts" of party authority (a Leninist conception) but "supraparty, self-standing" bodies in their own right. The same held for cultural institutions such as theaters, publishers, universities, and the press, which would operate free of oversight. They would become vehicles for the unfettered exploration of ideas, whether about art and science or the day's uncensored news. Above all, print and broadcast media – as "organs of public opinion" – had to become a "forum" for all strata of GDR society, "for the free expression of opinion and critique from below," also for "mistaken views" that would be openly debated and refuted by argument, not force. This thriving public culture would clear the ground for cross-border dialogue with the West, especially about the history and prospects of German socialism. Here, the preparatory burden lay squarely on the SED. Only a public reckoning with Stalinist errors and public discussion of future policies could revive ordinary West Germans' sympathy for socialism and make the SED a viable partner for the SPD. Eventually, conditions in the FRG would be favorable for a repeal of the recent KPD ban and the electoral success of the SPD. Cooperation between SPD, KPD, and SED would then "re-establish the unity of the workers' movement" on a "peaceful, parliamentary path to socialism." A duly elected coalition would preserve the best achievements of both sides and withdraw from both alliances, effecting "reunification . . . on the basis of democracy, socialism, and national sovereignty and independence."[95] This image of a reunited Germany reflected a striking, exaggerated faith

---

[93] Harich, "Plattform," 138–43, 146–50, quotes 138, 140.
[94] On the latter aspect, see also Dominik Geppert, "Auf dem Dritten Weg zu einem sozialistischen Gesamtdeutschland: Revisionistische Opposition und nationale Frage in der DDR," in *Neutralität: Chance oder Chimäre? Konzepte des dritten Weges für Deutschland und die Welt 1945–1990*, ed. Geppert and Udo Wengst (Munich: Oldenbourg, 2005), 79–95.
[95] Harich, "Plattform," 120–7, 130–7, 150–8, quotes 120, 151–2, 130–1, 137.

in the openings 1956 had created. It also echoed renewal visions conceived ten years prior, and it prefigured others yet to come.

Ulbricht, aghast at Poland and Hungary, was determined to keep his rule intact. He had reason to worry, since not only intellectuals but also top party leaders hoped to unseat him. Yet they were not powerful or organized enough, and they failed to find one another. Symptomatically, intellectuals made contact not with the main SED rival Karl Schirdewan but with Merker, a weak and broken figure. Moreover, the USSR greatly valued stability on this key Cold War front, and in the end, Ulbricht could count on their support.[96] Still, he felt pressure as well as resolve, and his retaliation was swift. In general, these years saw a drop in arrests and judicial repression, as even the GDR's hardliners tried to take the new, softer line into account. For intellectuals, they marked the apex of repression. First moves against the "counterrevolutionary Harich Group" came in late November, just days after Harich had finished the "Platform" they planned to publish in *Einheit* or distribute to all SED offices (hoping to the last to spark open, public debate). Harich, Hertwig, Steinberger, and Irene Giersch, a student involved with Harich at the time, were arrested. Janka followed in early December, Just and Zöger in March 1957. Scores more were caught in crackdowns that year, including Loest in Leipzig. Thousands fled to the FRG, including Zwerenz, where the cases of Harich and his associates were closely followed (Figure 6.2). For the "state- and party-subversive Harich-Janka Grouping," months of interrogations and dual show trials followed – a split proceeding that enabled the prosecution to call Harich as their star witness in round two. All received prison sentences ranging from two years (for Hertwig) to ten (for Harich).[97] As the GDR's rulers intended, the show trials had two principal effects: they quashed further stirrings of dissent, and they discredited Harich in his peers' eyes. His confession and testimony, coerced though they had been, caused a permanent rift between him and Janka, who subsequently maintained he had known nothing of Harich's plots.[98]

Although the regime was milder with other "revisionists," it waged concerted campaigns against what remained of the intellectual opposition.

---

[96] Epstein, *Revolutionaries*, 163–77; Johanna Granville, "Ulbricht in October 1956: Survival of the Spitzbart during Destalinization," *Journal of Contemporary History* 41, no. 3 (2006): 477–502.

[97] Prokop, *1956*, 207–19; Herzberg, *Anpassung*, 370–409.

[98] Walter Janka, *Schwierigkeiten mit der Wahrheit* (Reinbek b.H.: Rowohlt, 1989). Janka's autobiographical *Troubles with the Truth* reveals the show trials' demoralizing effect on the intelligentsia. Harich's *No Troubles with the Truth* was written in response to what he saw as Janka's slander and betrayal.

Figure 6.2 The Hamburg-based news magazine *Der Spiegel* features Wolfgang Harich on its cover, 19 December 1956. The case of the "Harich-Janka Grouping" quickly became a celebrated one in West Germany. (*Source*: SPIEGEL 51/1956)

In Leipzig, Bloch had grown increasingly cavalier in discussions about shortcomings in the GDR and developments in Poland and Hungary. These attracted official attention, especially as concern grew over the activities of his friends Harich and Lukács, who was arrested in Budapest.[99] Systematic MfS surveillance of Ernst and Karola Bloch, named Operational Case "Wild" after their street of residence, began in 1957, and years of telephone taps, opened mail, apartment bugs, and reports from acquaintances ensued. Open attacks on Bloch unfolded at the same time. He was relieved of his journal editorship and all teaching duties and ejected from the Kulturbund's presiding council. The party organization at Leipzig's philosophy institute called a conference on "Ernst Bloch's Revision of Marxism," launching a defamation campaign led by his nemesis, Rugard Otto Gropp. Isolated from all but his closest students and colleagues, Bloch withdrew into his writing. He nonetheless fought to hold Aufbau press to their publication agreements at the same time as he began publishing and traveling more outside the GDR. At festivities for the publication of *The Principle of Hope* in the FRG – which finally spurred Aufbau to release the third volume – Bloch's old acquaintance Dolf Sternberger gave a moving welcome. When the Berlin Wall went up in August 1961, Bloch was on vacation in the West. Rather than return, he took up a visiting, later permanent professorship at Tübingen.[100]

His friend Mayer held out longer. When the Wall was built, he too had been visiting the West, and he and Bloch met in Bavaria to discuss their options. Mayer knew he would return. Unlike Bloch, he still enjoyed his university post and classroom as relative havens. But he had also been cast as a revisionist of the first rank and placed under observation. He faced ongoing harassment – monitoring and marginalization by officials, colleagues, and security services – punctuated by occasional sharp attacks on his alleged "opulence theory." A nervous breakdown finally won him a sort of truce with the regime, and Mayer continued to teach

[99] Arpad Kadarkay, *Georg Lukács: Life, Thought, and Politics* (Cambridge, Mass.: Blackwell, 1991), 426–38. Bloch's relations with Lukács, cool since the early 1920s, had warmed again, and the two couples saw each other repeatedly in 1955–6; Karola Bloch, *Aus meinem Leben* (Pfullingen: Neske, 1981), 46, 77; Kantorowicz, *Deutsches Tagebuch*, II:554.

[100] Caldwell, *Dictatorship, State Planning*, 130–6; Jürgen Jahn, "Ernst Bloch im Visier der Staatssicherheit: Der Operative Vorgang 'Wild,'" in *Heimat in vernetzten Welten*, ed. Francesca Vidal (Mössingen-Talheim: Talheimer, 2006), 153–206; Dolf Sternberger, "Rede zur Einführung von Ernst Bloch," in *Schriften*, vol. VIII, *Gang zwischen Meistern* (Frankfurt a.M.: Insel, 1987), 235–40. See also the documents in Volker Caysa et al., eds. *"Hoffnung kann enttäuscht werden": Ernst Bloch in Leipzig* (Frankfurt a.M.: Hain, 1992); Michael Franzke, ed. *Die ideologische Offensive: Ernst Bloch, SED und Universität* (Leipzig: Leipziger Universitätsverlag, 1992).

while traveling and publishing more in the West. From 1959, he was a fixture at the Gruppe 47's annual sessions, where he reconnected with his former student Uwe Johnson and met other writers such as Ingeborg Bachmann and Günter Grass, several of whom he invited to Leipzig. In 1962, however, a collection of his literary criticism again aroused official ire, above all by lauding Pasternak's *Doctor Zhivago*, banned in the USSR. Another wave of intimidation followed, the MfS opened a dedicated file (Operational Case "Literat"), and a student was deployed to write a disparaging piece in the university paper. The last incident finally broke Mayer's bond with the GDR, and he remained in the West while on vacation in 1963. It no longer seemed worth subjecting himself to a "painful... everyday" and to the "slave language" by which intellectual subalterns navigated power, now that – as he wrote in a farewell letter to the education authorities – "nearly all the conditions" that had prompted his hopeful move to Leipzig in 1948 had "fallen away." He spent the rest of his career teaching at Hanover Technical College (later University).[101] His home, however, he made in Tübingen, near Bloch (Figure 6.3).

Kantorowicz did not wait as long. He, too, began to air his discontent more openly from the spring of 1956, initially on the field of literary criticism. But he crossed the political rubicon in November, when he refused his signature on an official Writers' Union statement condemning the "counterrevolutionary uprising" in Hungary. From that moment, he felt endangered. Indeed, his transgressions won Kantorowicz a spot alongside Lukács and Mayer as a leading literary revisionist, as Barthel proclaimed to the SED Central Committee's July 1957 Plenum. In August, he became convinced that he was under surveillance, that a search of his house was imminent, and that incriminating material would lead to his arrest. After seeing his last students through their exams, Kantorowicz – with help from his old friend Eggebrecht – fled to West Berlin.[102] In a statement broadcast on the radio and published in *Der Tagesspiegel*, he explained: His "dream" of a new, just, free Germany – the dream that had led him to Communism – also led him to the GDR. The long struggle for "popular rule," however, had ushered in a "functionaries' dictatorship" instead; they had fought "fascism and barbarism," only to have these reappear with the "apparatchiks." After the recent "terror wave,"

[101] Mayer, *Ein Deutscher*, II:240–2, quotes 263–4, 270; *Literarische Welt*, 63–4, 92, 99–100; Klein, *Unästhetische Feldzüge*, 54–143; Schiller, *Der verweigerte Dialog*, 133–42, 166. See also the documents in Mark Lehmstedt, ed. *Der Fall Hans Mayer: Dokumente 1956–1963* (Leipzig: Lehmstedt, 2007).
[102] Kantorowicz, *Deutsches Tagebuch*, II:658–68, 681, 691–4, 703–10, 719–22; Schiller, *Der verweigerte Dialog*, 70–2, 135–6; Kantorowicz to Eggebrecht, 13 December 1957, 12 August 1958, SUBH NL Kantorowicz NK: II: E27, E33.

Figure 6.3 Ernst Bloch and Hans Mayer reflect on their reflections in Bloch's apartment in Tübingen, 6 August 1963. Mayer had just arrived to join his friend in the West, completing their dual break with East Germany. (fotografie: stefan moses)

Kantorowicz had "lost the last illusions that a new, better world could be born from such scum." Those he left behind were happy to return his invective. A public letter signed by seven ex-colleagues, including Seghers, Hermlin, and Uhse, turned his own earlier words about those who went West against him: "The more of that sort we lose, the better for us." Shortly thereafter, a different message reached him by telegram, from an estranged friend of longer standing: "Welcome. Arthur Koestler, London."[103] In the GDR, his case was detailed alongside all the others in the security services' lengthy concluding report on intellectuals' "enemy activities." In the FRG, Kantorowicz began his new life in Munich but

[103] Kantorowicz, "Warum ich mit dem Ulbricht-Regime gebrochen habe," *Der Tagesspiegel*, 23 August 1957; Anna Seghers et al., "Feststellung," *Neues Deutschland*, 25 August 1957; Arthur Koestler, telegram to Kantorowicz, 26 August 1957, SUBH NL Kantorowicz NK: BII: K156.

soon relocated to Hamburg, where Eggebrecht, Weisenborn, and other friends lived. His claims to recognition as a political refugee were denied for years only to be granted, at the lowest level, in 1966.[104]

Imprisonments and departures were a fitting denouement to the story of engaged democrats in the GDR. They manifested the fate of their ideals of participation in the face of authoritarian centralization and publicness in the absence of a conventional public sphere. Their liaison with the new socialist state had begun in a hopeful if uneasy mood, and their critiques initially remained private and narrow in scope. Quite dramatically by 1956, however, small oppositional circles in the interstices of the GDR system found and formed connections to each other. The intellectuals in question increasingly raised their criticisms in public, including criticisms about the absence of publicness itself, in their robust sense. This principle was a cornerstone of their democratic vision in the years after 1945, and it fueled a belated reckoning with Stalinism in 1956. Most explicitly in Harich's program, key aspects of not only Stalinist but also Leninist political and economic arrangements were recast in the mold of a socialism that aspired to realize both unfettered dialogue and popular self-rule. Instead of reforming, the regime retaliated, and its ruthlessness can be taken as an indicator of the degree to which it perceived these principles as a threat. They were correct to do so. The party-state would continue to face such demands and eventually, under different historical circumstances, it would be felled by them.

[104] "Analyse der Feindtätigkeit innerhalb der wissenschaftlichen und künstlerischen Intelligenz," [October 1957], BArch DY 30/3372, 152–253, here 206–10; Mario Keßler, "Zwischen den Parteifronten auf dem 'Dritten Weg'? Leo Kofler, Alfred Kantorowicz, Ossip Flechtheim," in *Rückblickend in die Zukunft: Politische Öffentlichkeit und intellektuelle Positionen in Deutschland um 1950 und um 1930*, ed. Alexander Gallus and Schildt (Göttingen: Wallstein, 2011), 465–6.

# 7 Into West Germany: nonconformists and the restoration

Like their counterparts in the East, engaged democrats greeted the new West Germany with mixed emotions. Erich Kästner's Munich cabaret Die Schaubude had closed its doors shortly after the currency reform, a setback tempered by the success of his 1949 children's novel *Charlotte, Doubled*. A heartwarming tale of family and reconciliation, it struck a chord, worldwide, in the 1950s.[1] Meanwhile, a new cabaret opened its doors in January 1951. The program began with a fresh Kästner number that gave the theater its name, Die kleine Freiheit (The Little Freedom). Its key stanza took stock of their moment:

> The grand freedom did not come to pass.
> The best intentions came up short.
> Dreams and wants are now self-denial.
> Shining stars are now neon lights.
> Fear is now the citizen's first duty.
> The grand freedom did not come to pass;
> the little freedom – maybe![2]

Once again, Kästner condensed engaged democrats' political sentiments. His pithy lines worried about the fate of spirit and vision in an age of technology and narrow horizons, and they bemoaned new political anxieties that encouraged a reversion to old unpolitical habits (playing on the nineteenth-century motto: "Quiet is the citizen's first duty.") Above all, they conveyed a sense of lost opportunity. Still, at the Bonn Republic's foundation in 1949, a hint of hope remained: if full liberation had eluded them, might humbler freedoms still be theirs? By 1956, even this glimmer had gone out. Kästner accused the FRG of becoming just what he and others had predicted: comfortably modern and superficially

---
[1] Sven Hanuschek, *Keiner blickt dir hinter das Gesicht: Das Leben Erich Kästners* (Munich: Hanser, 1999), 345, 354–9, 370–1. *Das doppelte Lottchen* was adapted for film in West Germany, Japan, Britain, and the USA, as Disney's *The Parent Trap*.
[2] Erich Kästner, "Der Titel des Programms," in *Die kleine Freiheit: Chanson und Prosa 1949–1952* (Zurich: Atrium, 1952), 5; Hanuschek, *Keiner blickt*, 370–1.

in motion, yet politically and spiritually empty. Famously, he dubbed it "motorized Biedermeier," reminiscent of the counterrevolutionary post-Napoleonic era in its philistine, repressive climate.[3]

In other words, Germans were witnessing a "restoration" in the FRG. Engaged democrats pioneered this critique, and not accidentally so. They had sought a revolutionary transformation in a non-aligned Germany – popular mobilization, maximal participation, and democratic socialism – grounded in an honest reckoning with the past. To their dismay, it seemed they got the reverse. Certainly, West Germany was highly modern in its economic dynamism and productivity gains, and the resulting "economic miracle" had important local roots. However, it was conspicuously fueled by US economic aid and secured by the Western Allies' High Commission for Germany (HICOG), representing the three core powers of the anti-Soviet North Atlantic Treaty Organization (NATO). Prosperity was purchased, then, by absorption into a dangerous antagonism and separation from eastern Germany. Moreover, reconstruction enthusiasm and Cold War anxiety siphoned vital energies that might have been put to use reflecting on Nazism and repairing public culture. Instead, a widespread turn to the private realm was reflected in the fixation on careers and comforts, and voters elected the anti-Communist, patrician CDU, narrowly in 1949 and with growing margins thereafter. Konrad Adenauer's blend of personalized and parliamentary rule, later known as "chancellor democracy," was summed up by Kästner as *Demokratur*, an amalgam of "democracy" and "dictatorship."[4] For him and his compatriots, this all amounted to a collapse of collective imagination and will: West Germans squandered the opportunity for radical change after 1945. They opted instead for tried-and-true political forms, social patterns, and mentalities, even tried-and-true leaders. Engaged democrats' critique of a "restoration" was thus the inverted, negative image of their earlier plans for "renewal." It was picked up by a vocal minority of other "nonconformists" in the 1950s and spread widely among activists and intellectuals in the 1960s. By the early 1970s, FRG social scientists (following their GDR colleagues) adopted it as an interpretive frame. In the process, they narrowed the scope of engaged democrats' comprehensive critique to the reconstruction of capitalist economic relations and the political structures congenial to them.[5]

---

[3] Kästner, "Heinrich Heine und wir," in *Gesammelte Schriften*, vol. V, *Vermischte Beiträge* (Cologne: Kiepenheuer & Witsch, 1959), 529–30, quote 530. This talk was held in honor of Heinrich Heine, radical republican gadfly of the original Biedermeier era.
[4] Kästner, "Heinrich Heine," quote 530.
[5] For a useful overview, see Helmuth Kiesel, "Die Restauration des Restaurationsbegriffs im Intellektuellendiskurs der frühen Bundesrepublik," in *Herausforderungen der*

Historians have since jettisoned talk of "restoration," taking the intellectuals of the 1950s to task for blind spots arising from their hostility to liberal modernity and consumer society. Not restoration so much as "modernization under conservative auspices" was the signature of the age.[6] While the FRG's early critics had a keen eye for the un- and antidemocratic tendencies of Adenauer's rule, they could appreciate neither the desires for public order and private freedoms it fulfilled nor the broad social constituency it enjoyed. And outside formal politics, "modernizing" trends abounded. Amid economic boom and corporatist compromise, class identities were being reconfigured. Even if material abundance was not yet realized, it was fervently desired, as scarcity gave way to security and then to youth and popular cultures of mass consumption. And despite the conservative climate, a liberalization of attitudes was underway.[7] Crucially for engaged democrats, the FRG's grudging yet constitutionally enshrined respect for civil liberties eventually enabled a robust civil society and a distinctive culture of discussion.[8] On some level, they knew this well enough; it attracted them to the West over the East. Yet they were perhaps insufficiently aware of its relevance: had the repressive mechanisms of their own time effectively replicated those of the earlier, post-1815 restoration, their incisive critiques would not have received public airing.

Still, overarching continuities with a problematic past left the new West German state and its institutions facing a basic legitimacy deficit.[9] Some engaged democrats with stronger anti-Communist leanings aligned more forcefully with the West, especially in the overheated atmosphere of the

---

*Begriffsgeschichte*, ed. Carsten Dutt (Heidelberg: Winter, 2003), 173–93. In the scholarly literature, see Rolf Badstübner, *Restauration in Westdeutschland 1945–1949* (Berlin: Dietz, 1965); Eberhard Schmidt, *Die verhinderte Neuordnung 1945–1952* (Frankfurt a.M.: Europäische Verlagsanstalt, 1970); Ernst-Ulrich Huster et al., *Determinanten der westdeutschen Restauration 1945–1949* (Frankfurt a.M.: Suhrkamp, 1972).

[6] Christoph Kleßmann, "Ein stolzes Schiff und krächzende Möwen: Die Geschichte der Bundesrepublik und ihre Kritiker," *Geschichte und Gesellschaft* 11, no. 4 (1985): quote 485, distilling Hans-Peter Schwarz, *Die Ära Adenauer*, 2 vols. (Stuttgart: Deutsche Verlags-Anstalt, 1981–3).

[7] Anselm Doering-Manteuffel, "Strukturmerkmale der Kanzlerdemokratie," *Der Staat* 30 (1991): 1–18; Axel Schildt and Arnold Sywottek, eds. *Modernisierung im Wiederaufbau: Die westdeutsche Gesellschaft der 50er Jahre* (Bonn: Dietz, 1993); Hanna Schissler, ed. *The Miracle Years: A Cultural History of West Germany, 1949–1968* (Princeton, N.J.: Princeton University Press, 2001); Ulrich Herbert, ed. *Wandlungsprozesse in Westdeutschland: Belastung, Integration, Liberalisierung 1945–1980* (Göttingen: Wallstein, 2002).

[8] Christina von Hodenberg, *Konsens und Krise: Eine Geschichte der westdeutschen Medienöffentlichkeit 1945–1973* (Göttingen: Wallstein, 2006); Nina Verheyen, *Diskussionslust: Zur Kulturgeschichte des "besseren Arguments" in Westdeutschland* (Göttingen: Vandenhoeck & Ruprecht, 2010).

[9] A. Dirk Moses, *German Intellectuals and the Nazi Past* (Cambridge: Cambridge University Press, 2007), esp. 38–54.

early Cold War. But even these temporary partisans were troubled by the new state's failure to confront the legacies of Nazism, to avoid replicating the patterns that had made it possible, and to explore alternatives. Their postwar demand for radical renewal is what drove their activism, by which they helped shape vital oppositional currents in an only superficially conformist decade. Of immediate and overriding concern were the FRG's willingness to rebuild a German military and its unwillingness to exclude tainted post- and ex-Nazi elites from power. Within the confines of the "social market economy," engaged democrats allied with the unions to continue to push for codetermination, while consumerism became a new focus of critique. They also played formative roles in the early peace movement, as plans to integrate the FRG into a Western military alliance gave renewed urgency to strategies for forging Germany and Europe into a united, neutral zone outside the antagonistic blocs.[10] Finally, they contributed to key intellectual debates: motivated by earlier commitments, they diagnosed the looming dangers of technocratic rule and helped mount a defense of publicness as an alternative mode of socio-political organization.

## Cultural freedom and the restoration critique

Parallel to those of their eastern colleagues, engaged democrats' initial stances in the western zones reveal a mix of alignment and distancing toward the Cold War. As early as November 1947, this process was heralded by Dolf Sternberger's withdrawal from Alfred Weber and Karl Geiler's "Call to German Unity." He then first expressed his preference for a "West German emergency solution" over a united but Soviet-dominated Germany.[11] The culmination was several engaged democrats' involvement with the Congress for Cultural Freedom (CCF) during the early 1950s. This covertly planned and funded, nominally independent organization became a key element of the US-based "state-private network" that waged the cultural Cold War for the Western side. As the best work on the CCF underscores, the organization's success was due precisely to its ability to put nominal independence and relative ideological pluralism convincingly into practice. It championed a superficially apolitical "cultural freedom" of unbridled expression, in distinction to the overt "politicization" of culture and absence of civil liberties in the

---

[10] See, e.g., Wolfgang Kraushaar, *Die Protest-Chronik 1949–1959: Eine illustrierte Geschichte von Bewegung, Widerstand und Utopie*, 4 vols. (Hamburg: Rogner & Bernhard, 1996).

[11] Dolf Sternberger to Alfred Weber, 21 November 1947, Deutsches Literaturarchiv (Marbach a.N., hereafter DLA) A:Sternberger/ Aktionsgruppe Heidelberg/ 89.10.8112.

Communist world. Under this banner, it brought together a wide array of intellectuals, from staunch conservatives through centrists to all shades of the non-Communist left. First in Europe and the USA, then across the globe, it played the crucial role in consolidating a Cold War liberal consensus among Western bloc elites.[12]

Fittingly enough, the CCF was founded in a newly divided Germany. Challenged by a series of Soviet-sponsored conferences culminating at New York's Waldorf-Astoria Hotel in March 1949, pro-Western writers and officials decided to counter with a conference of their own, on the frontlines in Berlin. This project had three pillars of active support: in organizations of ex- and anti-Communist intellectuals in New York, in similar intellectual circles in West Germany, and in an office of the CIA that coordinated planning and covert funding. Melvin Lasky formed the link between the first two and may or may not have known of the third.[13] From late 1949, the conference idea circulated within the movement for European unity, galvanizing a full roster of prominent international figures, including Carlo Schmid and Eugen Kogon. In Germany, Lasky networked furiously, aided by *Der Monat*'s lengthy contact list as well as his well-connected allies – West Berlin mayor Ernst Reuter, councilor Otto Suhr (both SPD), and Edwin Redslob, now rector of the Free University. Lasky had long been in touch with Karl Jaspers, who published his first article in *Der Monat* in early 1949, and Sternberger, Weber, and Kogon were soon among its authors as well. Other connections ran through Suhr, who knew Sternberger from the old *Frankfurter Zeitung* and Weber from the SPD as well as both of them and Kogon from their efforts to establish the FRG's fledgling political science discipline.[14] Further assistance came from Shepard Stone, a German-American journalist who had served briefly as an intelligence officer after the war and

---

[12] Scott Lucas, *Freedom's War: The American Crusade against the Soviet Union* (New York: New York University Press, 1999); Michael Hochgeschwender, *Freiheit in der Offensive? Der Kongress für kulturelle Freiheit und die Deutschen* (Munich: Oldenbourg, 1998); Giles Scott-Smith, *The Politics of Apolitical Culture: The Congress for Cultural Freedom, the CIA, and Post-War American Hegemony* (London: Routledge, 2002).

[13] Michael Warner, "Origins of the Congress for Cultural Freedom, 1949–50," *Studies in Intelligence* 38, no. 5 (1995): 89–98; Hochgeschwender, *Freiheit*, 204–21, 228n78, 239. Warner, in the redacted version of his study, asserts that Lasky was unaware of CIA connections; Hochgeschwender gives rumors to the contrary some credence.

[14] Hochgeschwender, *Freiheit*, 153–6, 222–4; Arno Mohr, *Politikwissenschaft als Alternative: Stationen einer wissenschaftlichen Disziplin auf dem Wege zu ihrer Selbständigkeit in der Bundesrepublik Deutschland 1945–1965* (Bochum: Brockmeyer, 1988), 97–121; Karl Jaspers to Sternberger, 24 February 1949, Melvin J. Lasky to Sternberger, 31 March 1949, DLA A:Sternberger/ 89.10.5231/16, 89.10.5616; Lasky to Weber, 22 February 1950, Universitätsbibliothek Heidelberg (hereafter UBH) NL Weber, Box 4, Kongress für kulturelle Freiheit.

returned in early 1950 to lead the Office of Public Affairs at HICOG. The latter was responsible for all media and cultural relations, including *Der Monat*'s publication. One of Stone's main tasks was cultivating new and renewed contacts – including Kogon and Sternberger – as potential allies in anti-"totalitarianism" and West-orientation.[15]

Little wonder, then, that these engaged democrats entered the orbit of the CCF, given their anti-Stalinist convictions and the concerted attempts to woo them. In advance of the conference, they joined various largely representational bodies: Jaspers, Kogon, and Weber sat on its international committee alongside Schmid and such intellectual lights as Raymond Aron, Benedetto Croce, Ignazio Silone, John Dewey, Bertrand Russell, and Arthur Koestler. On its German counterpart sat Sternberger and Alexander Mitscherlich as well as Theodor Plievier. When the "Congress for Cultural Freedom" convened, on 26–30 June 1950, 118 participants from 21 countries and as many as 1,800 guests filled West Berlin's massive Titania Palace cinema. Weber spoke at the opening rally, Kogon and Sternberger in later sessions; Jaspers' talk was read *in absentia*, and Mitscherlich sent greetings. Afterward, a standing organization was founded. Kogon joined its international executive and, later, its German section as well.[16] Their active affiliation with the CCF is clear, but not unambiguous. On the one hand, it sealed an alignment with the side of "freedom" over "unity" in Germany's cultural Cold War. On the other hand, they reprised key elements of their earlier positions that contested the consensus the CCF attempted to forge.

Sternberger addressed the session on "Art, Artists, and Freedom," one of two panels on the first day devoted to cultural freedom in the strict sense. The panel opened with German-British journalist Peter de Mendelssohn on the "temptation of the intellectual" to relinquish both freedom and responsibility to the insidious coherence of "totalitarian" thought.[17] Russian-American composer Nicolas Nabokov delivered an exposé of the arbitrary censorship and shifting orthodoxies to

---

[15] Volker R. Berghahn, *America and the Intellectual Cold Wars in Europe: Shepard Stone between Philanthropy, Academy, and Diplomacy* (Princeton, N.J.: Princeton University Press, 2001), 32–6, 45–7, 52–9, 130–1. The three had contact in 1945/6, and Stone worked with Kogon and Sternberger during their 1948 study trip in the USA; "Seminar for German Publishers and Editors: Tentative Daily Program," n.d., Archiv der sozialen Demokratie (Bonn, hereafter AdsD) NL Kogon, Reden (bis 1963), Reden 8.48–4.49.

[16] Hochgeschwender, *Freiheit*, 229–38, 243–4, 265, 270, 322; "Liste der Teilnehmer," *Der Monat* 2, no. 22/23 (1950): 476–8.

[17] Peter de Mendelssohn, "Die Versuchung des Intellektuellen," *Der Monat* 2, no. 22/23 (1950): 384–6; see Marcus M. Payk, *Der Geist der Demokratie: Intellektuelle Orientierungsversuche im Feuilleton der frühen Bundesrepublik: Karl Korn und Peter de Mendelssohn* (Munich: Oldenbourg, 2008), 142–55.

which "the artist in the totalitarian state" was subject.[18] Sternberger, in contrast, spoke on "the ambiguity of culture," explicitly rejecting a narrow understanding of the term. "Culture," he insisted, "means cultivation," an activity that pertained to all spheres of life. Reducing it to cultural goods entailed a "double deformation." First, this mistook a process for some of its products, sequestering them to their own "special object domain." Thereby, it consigned all other spheres – "work and economic life, the state, and politics itself" – to "unculture... to mere technique, to useful routine, or to exploitation," which was "the actual opposite of cultivation." So circumscribed, "culture" relegated most of existence to "barbarism." Second, this view truncated freedom itself. On the one hand, it sacrificed the "freedom of the person" in ostensibly non-cultural realms to the barbarism of raw force; on the other, it projected the "freedom of art and science" onto a hypostatized realm apart. This obscured a unified, encompassing freedom of which specific forms were only partial aspects.[19] Here, Sternberger deployed engaged democrats' activist, expansive notion of culture and its correlated, world-shaping freedom.

Weber's address underscored this aversion to a narrow definition of cultural freedom by tracing its fateful consequences. In the eighteenth century, he reprised, Germany had still participated in a unified European consciousness of freedom. Spiritual and political freedom were considered inseparable, a lesson that Kant and Goethe, Schiller and Humboldt had learned from Rousseau's insight into the "dignity of the common man" and its democratic consequences. As Europe's western lands struggled over more free institutions, however, the German bourgeoisie dismissed the revolutionary masses' demands for popular self-rule. After 1848, it fixated on an allegedly more profound inner "German freedom" instead, which complemented its "authoritarian state metaphysics"; inner freedom thus abetted political and social unfreedom. During the twentieth century's "mass-formation of authoritarianism to totalitarianism," this German peculiarity bore catastrophic fruit in Nazism. Contemporary Germans had to recover the eighteenth century's insights and reconfigure them into a freedom adequate to their "mass age," one that realized "the political self-determination of the whole people, that is,

---

[18] Nicolas Nabokov, "Der Künstler im totalitären Staat," *Der Monat* 2, no. 22/23 (1950): 386–9. Nabokov and Michael Josselson (the CIA contact) would become the CCF's top officials. Friends from OMGUS, they were among the first to discuss holding such a conference in Berlin; Warner, "Origins of the Congress," 93; Hochgeschwender, *Freiheit*, 155, 218.

[19] Sternberger, "Von der Zweideutigkeit der Kultur," *Der Monat* 2, no. 22/23 (1950): 376–9.

popular sovereignty with all its consequences."[20] Such a freedom was not best forged through West-orientation, Weber had argued in *Der Monat* a few months earlier. The world was dividing into two blocs with two "social religions," the "democratic-liberal" and the "Soviet-Communist." Weber urged Germans and their fellow Europeans to realize their own indigenous alternative, a "third social religion, the democratic-socialist."[21]

Kogon tackled similar themes in his reflections on "unmastered mass democracy." He asserted that the Cold War's antagonistic socio-political models each represented incomplete attempts to solve this same thoroughly modern problem (thereby rejecting views of Soviet despotism as backward or otherwise essentially different). The East pursued an ideal of "collective freedom" but betrayed it by the "totalitarian means" it employed. The West used "free, democratic means" to pursue "individual freedom," but did so "at the cost of economic, social, and in part even cultural and political freedom." These parallel shortcomings demanded of intellectuals that they unflinchingly assess actual conditions on both sides of the geopolitical divide before taking a position, that they "destroy" – rather than uncritically propagate – the shibboleths of all "ideologies." This held for "liberalism," which in their own historical moment had "conservative" and even "reactionary" socio-economic outcomes. It likewise held for "socialism," which had taken leave of any true "dialectic... between being and consciousness" in slavish obedience to putatively objective laws. All positions were assailable and should be subjected to "productive critique," Kogon concluded.[22] In the face of polarization, the task was to reject one-sided alignments.

Global events conspired to keep the nuanced, critical positioning engaged democrats advocated from gaining ground among the conferees. On the day before the congress, North Korean forces invaded the South, igniting the Korean War, sparking fears of a similar attack in Europe, and giving anti-neutralist positions a powerful boost. As the most radical anti-Communists realized, this presented an opportunity, and the eloquent, charismatic Koestler moved to exploit it. Koestler opened the congress demanding a clear and decisive "yes" toward the free West and "no" toward the totalitarian East; the unfolding crisis, he

---

[20] Alfred Weber, n.t., *Der Monat* 2, no. 22/23 (1950): 352–4. Hochgeschwender calls Weber's position "entirely along the lines of Dewey [and] Santayana," overlooking these intellectuals' autochthonous critique of the "unpolitical German"; Hochgeschwender, *Freiheit*, 235.

[21] Weber, "Geschichte und Gegenwart," *Der Monat* 2, no. 14 (1949): 145–8.

[22] Eugen Kogon, "Die Bewältigung der Massendemokratie," *Der Monat* 2, no. 22/23 (1950): 420–2.

trumpeted, required taking sides with the "unwavering certainty of a biological reflex." Koestler was also featured at the final rally, held outdoors before an audience of 15,000. He closed the proceedings with what was at once a proclamation and an exhortation: "Friends, freedom has seized the offensive!"[23]

At that juncture, engaged democrats felt compelled to part ways. The militant rhetoric and the actionism it demanded provoked swift responses from both Sternberger and Kogon. Sternberger disavowed the "flagrant attack spirit" of Koestler and his ilk, such as Nabokov and James Burnham. Intent on forging a disciplined cadre of freedom-fighters, they sacrificed the "free flexibility and tolerant readiness to discuss" required for the "spiritual freedom" they purported to defend. This was the hallmark of the "propagandist," not the "intellectual," much less the "artist." Kogon took them to task in similar terms. The unconditional partisanship Koestler demanded conflated the careful, critical position-taking that was intellectuals' stock-in-trade with the unambiguous decisions of "statesmen and generals," whose manner was "as strong and simple as it is dangerous." He disavowed CCF activists' "pure battle mentality": "there is no reason that spirit should now view reality only through crosshairs."[24] These were two of the very few critical responses in the West German press. Unsurprisingly, responses from the GDR were uniformly negative. They included Johannes Becher's vehement denunciation (the wedge that finally split the all-German PEN) and a more reflective open letter by Bertolt Brecht, expressing his wish that conference-goers discuss not only cultural freedom but also its indispensable political and economic conditions. Within the CCF, Kogon retained his positions in the executive until 1952, when he stepped down. Having come under fire for what others called "neutralist tendencies," Kogon took pains to emphasize that he remained dedicated to the CCF's cause – as he understood it.[25] To view engaged democrats' affiliations with the CCF as an affirmation of "the West" would be to adopt a binary optic they continued to reject.

---

[23] Arthur Koestler, n.t., *Der Monat* 2, no. 22/23 (1950): 355–6; "Die Schlußkundgebung," *Der Monat* 2, no. 22/23 (1950): 472; Warner, "Origins of the Congress," 94; Hochgeschwender, *Freiheit*, 236–41, 245–6. After leaving Germany in 1933, the Hungarian exile Koestler lived mostly in France and Britain. In the postwar years, he helped link circles of European and American ex-Communists, becoming a crucial bridge in the CCF's international networks; ibid., 97–8, 112–18, 219.

[24] Sternberger, "Künstler – Intellektuelle – Propagandisten," *Die Gegenwart* 5, no. 15 (1950): 10–11; Kogon, "Die Freiheit, die wir meinen: Anmerkungen zum Ja und Nein von Arthur Koestler," *Frankfurter Hefte* 5, no. 8 (1950): 812, 817.

[25] Hochgeschwender, *Freiheit*, 248–52, 278, 330. For Becher's invective-laden response, see Johannes R. Becher, "Die gleiche Sprache," *Aufbau* 6, no. 8 (1950): 702.

In fact, they saw Cold War polarization as a contributing factor in "restoration" in the FRG and across Western Europe. This term and the concerns it encapsulated had often been heard in the first postwar years. Hans Werner Richter lamented the "restoration" of political parties, while Kogon cautioned against "restoration" in the economy; by early 1948, Alfred Kantorowicz alleged a full-bore "restoration" underway in the Western zones.[26] Walter Dirks first used the term in an aesthetic context. In 1947, he opposed the Frankfurt Goethe House's reconstruction as indicative of deeper desires to reclaim a usable past, for a more sweeping "restoration." This had the tenor of a warning, long before hope was lost. In 1949, he glossed plans for the site of a destroyed monument to the German Reich's founding Emperor Wilhelm I in Koblenz: a park with allegorical bronze statuary of the Rhine and Moselle rivers, which converged there. "The impulse to yawn is irrepressible," Dirks confessed. "Nothing occurs to us beyond what already occurred to our great-grandfathers." In a cautionary yet offhand tone, he observed: "We live in the age of restoration."[27] In 1950, convinced that the whole socio-political order had been rebuilt in such a spirit, he made the same claim, this time as a bitter indictment. For good reason, the "restoration" critique remains most closely associated with Dirks and with the *Frankfurter Hefte*, one of the few postwar journals to survive into the Federal Republic.

But what did they mean by this charge? The "restoration" referred comprehensively to received mentalities, modes of comportment, and horizons of political and social imagination. For engaged democrats in the 1950s, unlike their 1970s heirs, the question of renewal was not reducible to capitalism versus socialism, nor was the thrust of their claim that the Federal Republic was a carbon copy of its 1920s predecessor. Rather, their critique grew out of a deeper disappointment: it sought to grasp an atmosphere in which the anxiety provoked by radical possibilities led to their foreclosure by almost deliberate inaction. In a famous essay of September 1950, Dirks asserted that Germans and other Europeans had already failed in "the task that had been set for them: to build a more human world after the collapse of the old." The upheaval that followed the war had presented the alternative to either effect this sort

---

[26] [Hans Werner Richter], "Parteipolitik und Weltanschauung," *Der Ruf* 1, no. 7 (1946): 1; Kogon, "Der Weg zu einem Sozialismus der Freiheit in Deutschland," *Frankfurter Hefte* 2, no. 9 (1947): 877–8; "Suchende Jugend: Briefwechsel zwischen der Studentin Käte Fuchs und Alfred Kantorowicz," *Ost und West* 2, no. 2 (1948): 89–90.

[27] Walter Dirks, "Mut zum Abschied: Zur Wiederherstellung des Frankfurter Goethehauses," *Frankfurter Hefte* 2, no. 8 (1947): 827; "Beobachtungen und Bemerkungen," *Frankfurter Hefte* 4, no. 1 (1949): 15.

of "revolution" or acquiesce in the "restoration" of established values, familiar social and political patterns, and entrenched interests – never precisely as before, but similar enough to forestall real change. Unlike its sometime ally "reaction," which was an active program, "restoration" fed off a "climate" of passivity and inertia; it represented a "sin of omission" rather than one of commission. In this spirit, Europeans "chose the path of least resistance. It had announced itself already in 1945, in the harmless word 'reconstruction.' Fear, the need for security, and comfort were stronger than courage, truth, and sacrifice, and so we live in an age of restoration."[28] The hour of radical and thoroughgoing renewal had come and gone.

In Germany's case, Dirks asserted, this atmosphere was abetted by the occupiers and cultivated by the occupied. The Allied decision to introduce democracy drop by drop and replicate the familiar party configuration at each new level encouraged Germans to embrace old programs and old rifts unadjusted. This deactivated the powerful renewal potential that had existed, above all in unrealized coalitions of workers and Christians. As administrative services were rebuilt, they brought with them the conservative influence of the professional civil service. In the economy, after the failure of socialization and large-scale codetermination, the culprit was currency reform. It had failed to incorporate redistributive provisions for millions of refugees, and by gutting monetary savings and fixed incomes while leaving real property and other assets untouched, it also privileged the propertied classes, rewarded merchants for hoarding, and set the most disadvantaged citizens of the new state on the least secure footing. Yet the restoration was also evident in the construction of cafes and specialty retailers rather than much-needed apartments and schools, in pop-cultural fascination with the lost empire, even in the revival of university fraternities. The Goethe House was completed "just in time" to give the era its symbol.[29] In all domains of existence, the spirit of restoration had trumped the will for regeneration.

Kogon soon elaborated on Dirks' theme, reframing and embedding it in a broader historical account. Modern democracy, he asserted, had been built by the middle classes on twin pillars: the individual and the nation-state, both declared free and sovereign. This new freedom, however, did not constrain itself, generating economic competition and

---

[28] Dirks, "Der restaurative Charakter der Epoche," *Frankfurter Hefte* 5, no. 9 (1950): 942–6. Tellingly, Dirks also used the term "sin of omission" for his own insufficient resistance under Nazism. The clear lesson to be drawn was to "resist the beginnings," as he urged during the Goethe House debate.

[29] Ibid., 945–52.

exploitation among individuals as well as imperialist rivalry and expansionism among states. From efforts to navigate the resultant welter of conflicting "interests" at both levels, specific bureaucratic "regulation[s]" and "rights" proliferated, but never an "ordering of the new society as a whole." This outcome severed "material" social from "formal" political democracy, privileging the latter. The neglect of the former meant that the political enfranchisement of "mass populations" far outpaced infrastructures for their physical well-being and intellectual development. And in the wake of periodic economic crises, all were left equally free "to sleep under bridges." The ensuing chaos provoked still more radical attempts at "organization," but "organization is truly, as we know all too well from experience today, not identical to order." Recent war-wrought upheavals had opened doors toward a new ordering, disrupting rigid class structures and political ideologies.[30]

Because this moment was not seized, Kogon asserted, bureaucracy had been restored instead of democracy being realized. The latter would have required resolving the split between formal and material democracy by implementing "federalism as a universally effective principle" in both "society and in politics," domestically and internationally. After 1945, the most likely agents of such renewal were the working classes, whose core ethic of "solidarity" – a counter to competitive individualism – had an affinity for federalist forms. In Germany and across Europe, however, Social Democrats remained too fixated on acquiring centralized power to explore decentralization (and Communists were a lost cause in that respect). The end result was a "mass society... 'administered' [by] managers and bureaucrats," in which "bourgeois-democratic formalism" left key aspects of existence in anarchy while extending "an ever more enveloping system of bureaucracy," an "ersatz authority," over the others. Kogon explained the system's resilience in large part by the inability of the people – as the actual "carriers of democratic sovereignty" and legitimate "authority" – to imagine a different reality. Lost in an "anonymous" world, threatened by "no longer recognizable but doubtless present forces," they developed "neurotic" symptoms, seeking refuge in economic success, in hedonism or conservatism, in intoxication or apathy, or in the existentialist doctrines of a Sartre or a Heidegger. These were the social conditions for the triumph of a "politics of a lack of imagination," akin to Dirks' path of least resistance.[31] In

---

[30] Kogon, "Die Aussichten der Restauration: Über die gesellschaftlichen Grundlagen der Zeit," *Frankfurter Hefte* 7, no. 3 (1952): 169–71, 175–6.
[31] Ibid., 166, 171–3 (emphasis in original).

Kogon's view, the "restoration" amounted to people's self-subjugation to external bureaucratic authority, unthinkingly seeking compensatory gratifications for their unfulfilled democratic autonomy.

While restoration in the the FRG reflected a broader European tendency, the new state also showed a willingness to revive troubling aspects of a more specifically German past. One of engaged democrats' central concerns was the threat of German rearmament, and they were among its earliest and most vociferous opponents. In military circles and high-level diplomatic discussions, the possibility of a German military contribution to a Western bloc was floated as early as 1947. And Adenauer saw an opportunity to wrest concessions on West German sovereignty by offering such a contribution pre-emptively, publicly signaling this intention from December 1949. Not until the outbreak of hostilities in Korea, however, was British and American public opinion convinced of the need for West German rearmament; meanwhile, the vast majority of Germans remained opposed, as did the French. Nonetheless, Adenauer made his offer to the Allies. By late 1950, a decision in principle to pursue West German rearmament had been reached among the NATO powers.[32]

Kogon was the first to draw public attention to Allied plans, which clearly contravened demilitarization aims. In November 1948, following a meeting of European federalists in Rome, Kogon announced that the question of a West German military contribution had been extensively discussed, much to the FRG delegates' surprise. "The logic of developments points in that direction," he observed, even if German politicians seemed blissfully unaware. He was further reported to assert that the buildup of paramilitary police forces in the Soviet zone had triggered parallel efforts in the American and British zones, raising concerns that a secret rearmament had already begun. Even amid official denials, Kogon's report caused quite a stir.[33] Given his extensive connections in Western Europe and the USA, he was known to enjoy uncommon access to information. Indeed, though he did not reveal it at the time, Kogon first heard of military plans not in Rome but, confidentially, from

---

[32] David Clay Large, *Germans to the Front: West German Rearmament in the Adenauer Era* (Chapel Hill: University of North Carolina Press, 1996), 31–107. On the paradox of CDU electoral success despite popular aversion to rearmament, see Michael Geyer, "Cold War Angst: The Case of West-German Opposition to Rearmament and Nuclear Weapons," in *Miracle Years*, ed. Schissler, 376–408.

[33] "Kogon über deutsche Aufrüstung," *Die Neue Zeitung*, 25 November 1948; Kogon, "Man braucht Deutschland... Auch deutsche Soldaten?" *Frankfurter Hefte* 4, no. 1 (1949): 24–5; Large, *Germans*, 46; Michael Werner, *Die "Ohne mich"-Bewegung: Die bundesdeutsche Friedensbewegung im deutsch-deutschen Kalten Krieg (1949–1955)* (Münster: Monsenstein & Vannerdat, 2006), 85–9.

a top US Army general during his transatlantic study tour a few weeks earlier.[34]

Germans' strong opposition to rearmament rested on a range of rationales and anxieties. For their part, engaged democrats most feared reawakening the nation's militarist tradition. Kogon demanded that Germans – less their political leaders than the citizens themselves – begin asserting control over any rearmament preparations, lest "police and military cadres rule again in Germany" and tempt a Weimar-style disaster. Hans Mayer wrote to his friend for clarification, expressing deep concern over any "new Nazi spirit" in western Germany that would make possible "a repetition of the adventures and crimes of the Hitler period."[35] Despite the Cold War valences of this exchange – Mayer now wrote from the Soviet zone – it rested on the common ground of their earlier convictions. In response to Adenauer's later politicking, Kogon's warnings intensified: to "twist the years of efforts to destroy National Socialism and militarism into their opposite" – that is, a "remilitarization" – would deal a fatal blow to the young republic, precluding the "deeper reflection" on the national past on which "the success of all our efforts toward renewal" hinged.[36] Similar concerns were voiced by Mitscherlich at the time, while Axel Eggebrecht called on Germany's youth to struggle for peace and against all proclamations, resigned or enthusiastic, of the inevitability of a new war.[37] For these critics, militarism had been central to inculcating the obedience that made Nazism possible; the prospect of Germans under arms again was shocking.

As they feared, the rollback of demilitarization worked in tandem with a rollback of denazification. The latter had been flawed enough – contested, incomplete, and gradually undermined as it ground to a halt under its own bureaucratic weight. Nonetheless, in the western zones, hundreds of thousands had been disqualified from positions in politics, administration, and business, and more paid other material penalties. From the FRG's foundation, its government began to pursue their reintegration through a series of measures to lift exclusions, restore pension rights,

---

[34] Kogon, *Gesammelte Schriften*, vol. VI, *"Dieses merkwürdige, wichtige Leben": Begegnungen*, ed. Michael Kogon and Gottfried Erb (Weinheim: Beltz Quadriga, 1997), 114–17. The source in question was General Albert Wedemeyer.

[35] "Remilitarisierung Westdeutschlands," *Rhein-Neckar-Zeitung*, 26 November 1948; Kogon, "Man braucht Deutschland," 18–33; Hans Mayer to Kogon, 21 December 1948, AdsD NL Kogon, EK privat 1949 H-M/ IIIc.

[36] Kogon, "Das Gespenst der deutschen Remilitarisierung," *Frankfurter Hefte* 5, no. 1 (1950): 2–3.

[37] Alexander Mitscherlich, "Wer steht ante portas?" *Neue Züricher Zeitung*, 4 December 1948; Axel Eggebrecht, "Aktiver Friede," introduction to *Welt ohne Krieg: Ein Lese- und Volksbuch für junge Europäer*, ed. Otto Gollin (Düsseldorf: Komet, 1948), 5–9.

release property, and even free convicted criminals. These culminated in 1951 legislation to implement Article 131 of the Basic Law, which rehabilitated the vast majority of civil servants, and an expanded amnesty law for Nazi-era crimes in 1954 (building on one from 1949). Moreover, this process unfolded with widespread support in public opinion, where those affected by denazification and by occupation-era criminal trials were seen as victims subjected to victors' justice.[38]

Engaged democrats railed against these developments. They had long predicted the victory of what Sternberger in 1949 called a "vital forgetfulness" and the regrowth of a "thick skin... after a brief phase of moral 'thin-skinnedness'"; ironically, denazification's privileging of "purely negative means" over the "inner liberation" they had demanded was partly to blame.[39] Regardless, they took the rehabilitation of former National Socialists not only in business but also in the law, higher civil service, and education as an indicator of the collapse of their initial hopes. By 1954, Kogon lamented the impending final victory of these "131ers" over his circle and other "45ers," the "discontented" who, at the end of the war, "had imagined it otherwise and who do not cease to want it otherwise." Soon, the former would reconstitute an officer corps as well, and then "the members of parliament, the judges, the lawyers, the military men, the general managers... will all toast one another" on the elimination of their opponents. After five years of a putatively new Germany, the partisans of real democratic renewal stood "almost with our backs against the wall." Although hope was not yet fully lost, most people were too caught up in "our federal-republican hustle and bustle" to perceive the gravity of the threat.[40] To engaged democrats, remilitarization and renazification were undoing the basic gains of the occupation period and forestalling future reform. In this collective abdication of responsibility, they saw a profoundly inadequate confrontation with the past and a marker of their own isolation.

These disappointments profoundly shaped their stances toward the new state. Yet their restoration critique remained disillusioned without becoming resigned. On the contrary, both Dirks and Kogon uncovered potential counterforces. For Kogon, "anti-restorative" impulses

---

[38] Norbert Frei, *Adenauer's Germany and the Nazi Past: The Politics of Amnesty and Integration*, trans. Joel Golb (New York: Columbia University Press, 2002).

[39] Sternberger, "Versuch zu einem Fazit," *Die Wandlung* 4, no. 8 (1949): 701–2.

[40] Kogon, "Beinahe mit dem Rücken an der Wand," *Frankfurter Hefte* 9, no. 9 (1954): 641–2, 645. His use of "forty-fivers" to refer to those who lamented the lost hopes of the "zero hour" is echoed in the historiography only by Holger Nehring, "Die nachgeholte Stunde Null: Intellektuelle Debatten um die Atombewaffnung der Bundeswehr 1958–1960," in *Streit um den Staat: Intellektuelle Debatten in der Bundesrepublik 1960–1980*, ed. Dominik Geppert and Jens Hacke (Göttingen: Vandenhoeck & Ruprecht, 2008), 231.

were evident in society, less among organized collectives than individuals and informal groups still committed to "renewal." He held out hope that architects and writers, priests and mothers, employers and workers, teachers and unionists, even civil servants could find ways, building on "solidarity" within their distinct spheres of activity, to forge "new forms" for people's "self-develop[ment]" and thus "give content to the grandiose formula human freedom." Dirks placed great hope in codetermination, which if implemented robustly would make the labor movement a powerful "force for renewal." He also identified a resilient "future-oriented consciousness" among certain writers, philosophers, and theologians; the non-party affiliated, so-called "homeless left"; and supporters of a united Europe. The times called for not a formal umbrella organization but a gathering of "anti-restorative forces." For the moment, these should simply "develop a language in which they can speak with one another," in preparation for future opportunities as well as for public dialogue in the present; in the meantime, they should also study "social reality" and "tell how things are." Efforts by an intellectual "elite," however, could only complement those by other agents of renewal, namely workers and youth. The model was not "negotiations from office to office" but self-mobilizing "work 'in the streets'" through multitudinous connections among "cells of living people."[41] Their postwar ideal of plural groups coming together at the grassroots retained its force under 1950s conditions – perhaps especially then.

## Extraparliamentary politics in Adenauer's Germany

Their message did not go unheard by the powers that were; after reading what is still Dirks' best-known essay, Adenauer himself is reported to have said, "what Mr. Dirks writes, that's all wrong."[42] And the chancellor was not the only one paying attention. The "restoration" notion struck a chord with critical intellectuals of all stripes in the 1950s, circulating widely within those minority milieus and into the SPD.[43] Moreover, Dirks and Kogon's discussions of what might yet be done both recalled their own earlier affinities for popular politics and set an agenda for

---

[41] Kogon, "Aussichten der Restauration," 175–7; Dirks, "Der restaurative Charakter," 951–4.
[42] Peter Glotz, "Kurioser Kopf: Walter Dirks, der katholische Publizist," *Süddeutsche Zeitung*, 10 February 2003.
[43] See also Claudia Fröhlich, "Restauration: Zur (Un-)Tauglichkeit eines Erklärungsansatzes westdeutscher Demokratiegeschichte," in *Erfolgsgeschichte Bundesrepublik? Die Nachkriegsgesellschaft im langen Schatten des Nationalsozialismus*, ed. Stephan Alexander Glienke, Volker Paulmann, and Joachim Perels (Göttingen: Wallstein, 2008), 17–52.

renewed efforts in that vein. Over the course of the decade, the FRG's engaged democrats actively sought coalitions with the most promising anti-restorative forces they had identified: the European movement, the younger generation, and the labor movement. At the intersection of formal and informal politics, they helped activate an incipient extra-parliamentary political sphere in the FRG, a conglomerate of critical counter-publics self-consciously opposed to the mainstream of authoritarian institutions, all-too affirmative media, and apolitical associations.

Not for nothing did Kogon and Dirks single out the movement for supranational European federation, organized but outside conventional institutions, as a reservoir of anti-restorative forces.[44] Since 1945, as we have seen, engaged democrats had advocated a unified Germany within a unified Europe as the key platform for an actively neutral "third force" between East and West. Kogon was an officer in the transnational organizations that made this their goal, serving on the central committee of the European Union of Federalists from 1947 and as president of its branch, the Europa-Union Deutschland (Europe Union Germany, EUD), from 1949.[45] Within the larger movement, he was a prominent advocate of a federal, democratic socialist constitution for Europe. As late as June 1948, in the midst of the Berlin blockade, he argued that a Germany unified along such lines was the key step toward a truly unified European continent. A separate West Germany, by contrast, would soon find itself an "Atlantic-West-European march against the East," a militarized if affluent borderland "stuffed full with goods, but also with soldiers." Dirks concurred, insisting that a Europe unified under a polarizing anti-Communism and oriented solely to the capitalist West would represent "a false Europe," one that betrayed both its democratic promise and its mediating mission.[46]

Even after giving up the hope of an East-West unity, the EUD still worked toward unifying Western Europe as an independent entity that could ameliorate global tensions. As "federalists," they struggled for a constitutionally grounded European polity and against the pragmatic step-by-step approach of "functionalist" integration. The advent of the latter was set in the Schuman Plan of 1950 that produced the European Coal and Steel Community, or ECSC, in 1952; Kogon criticized

[44] Dirks, "Der restaurative Charakter," 954; Kogon, "Aussichten der Restauration," 177.
[45] Walter Lipgens, *A History of European Integration*, vol. I, *1945–1947*, trans. P. S. Falla and A. J. Ryder (Oxford: Clarendon, 1982), 361–431, 569–99, 644–57; Vanessa Conze, *Das Europa der Deutschen: Ideen von Europa in Deutschland zwischen Reichstradition und Westorientierung (1920–1970)* (Munich: Oldenbourg, 2005), 223–32, 291–324.
[46] Kogon, "Der entscheidende Schritt," *Frankfurter Hefte* 3, no. 7 (1948): quote 586; Dirks, "Ein falsches Europa?" *Frankfurter Hefte* 3, no. 8 (1948): 698–711.

this framework for resource pooling and market integration in the coal, iron, and steel industries as merely a "partial solution" or "pre-form" of supranational unity.[47] For Europe to realize its full potential, such sector-specific cooperation had to be embedded in an overarching political federation. Given the failure of parties and politicians to effect such a change, the EUD set its hopes on more popular mobilization. For these purposes, its organizational structures seemed an asset: a pyramid of delegated bodies that built upward from the communal to the state and, finally, the federal level. As Kogon put it, "every revolution must seize an Apparat, but Europe as a whole does not yet have an Apparat. We have to make such an Apparat first." Building the popular movement would have the effect of "developing the Europe-yearning of the German people... to an active Europe-will that parliament and government cannot resist."[48] A broad-based movement remained aspirational, but the Europe Union under Kogon thus kept alive the hope for Europe as an actively neutral "third power" into the early Cold War. It could not do so indefinitely; Kogon resigned the presidency in 1953, amid financial troubles caused in part by a US decision no longer to subsidize the neutralist EUD he led.[49] In its structure, the organization also recalled the bottom-up emphasis and party-skepticism of engaged democrats' earlier positions. It was, however, a special case, working to establish entirely new structures outside and above those of official national politics.

Most of engaged democrats' efforts to roll back restoration remained within a domestic frame. For their part, Dirks and Kogon began by adjusting their core journalistic activity to new conditions. Although the *Frankfurter Hefte* survived currency reform, circulation had fallen to levels hardly adequate to their goals. On a changing media landscape, thick and dense journals seemed increasingly anachronistic, and the editors decided to experiment with a sleeker format, founding the weekly *hier und heute* (*here and today*) as a complementary platform.[50] As they explained

---

[47] Kogon, "Zwischen Atlantik-Pakt und Schuman Plan," *Frankfurter Hefte* 5, no. 6 (1950): 569–71; Otto Blessing, "Protokoll des II. Jahreskongresses der Europa-Union am 9. und 10. Dezember 1950 in Köln/Rhein," 17 January 1951, AdsD Europa-Union Deutschland 1A, 3. See John Gillingham, *Coal, Steel, and the Rebirth of Europe, 1945–1955: The Germans and French from Ruhr Conflict to Economic Community* (Cambridge: Cambridge University Press, 1991), 228–97.

[48] See the statutes in Blessing, "Protokoll des II. Jahreskongresses," 19–23, quotes 7, 31.

[49] Conze, *Europa*, 323–7. American funding had been both overt, through HICOG, and covert, via the CIA-funded American Committee of European Integration. After Kogon, the EUD's leaders came largely from the business community, and private funding was secured.

[50] Michel Grunewald, "Die Frankfurter Hefte: Eine Stimme der europäischen Föderalisten," in *Le discours européen dans les revues allemandes / Der Europadiskurs in den deutschen Zeitschriften (1945–1955)*, ed. Grunewald and Hans Manfred Bock (Bern:

to readers, "We have no illusions about our real influence... The republic has lost some battles against restorative interests, and we with it. But the task we are set here and today gets not less, rather more urgent." The publications would work in tandem. While "the monthly has room for the detailed investigation... the weekly remains on the trail of the day's events." With the latter – "quicker, more topical, [and] more effective" – they aimed to get their "informative and critical word" to a broader audience beyond educated elites, "the awake, concerned, lively heads in all classes and strata, especially in the younger generation, not least among the workers."[51] That is, it would be a key vehicle for dialogue among anti-restorative forces.

Fittingly, the new weekly embodied such a cross-generational collective in its personnel. Not by accident did the editors call the *Frankfurter Hefte* "the parents" of *hier und heute*, which involved figures from the two most important publications that had spoken for the "young generation" in the postwar years: *Der Ruf* and *Ende und Anfang (End and Beginning)*, a left-Catholic biweekly published from 1946 to 1949.[52] A growing number of both circles' members began to publish in the *Frankfurter Hefte* from 1949 on, and they stamped the profile of the new weekly in early 1951.[53] From the Gruppe 47, Alfred Andersch, Hans Werner Richter, and several others contributed, most extensively Erich Kuby. Associates from *Ende und Anfang* included Theo Pirker, who moved to Frankfurt to help with the editorial work, and Burkart Lutz, soon known as radical sociologists of industrial relations. In the pages of *hier und heute*, alongside Dirks and Kogon, they sounded the key themes of the restoration critique, from rearmament, neutralization, and unaddressed legacies of Nazism to worker and union rights and capitalist reconsolidation.[54] The

---

Lang, 2001), 220. On the media, see Schildt, *Moderne Zeiten: Freizeit, Massenmedien und "Zeitgeist" in der Bundesrepublik der 50er Jahre* (Hamburg: Christians, 1995), 205–300; Schildt, "Das Jahrhundert der Massenmedien: Ansichten zu einer künftigen Geschichte der Öffentlichkeit," *Geschichte und Gesellschaft* 27, no. 2 (2001): 177–206.

[51] "An unsere Leser!" *Frankfurter Hefte* 5, no. 12 (1950): 1237; "Die 'Frankfurter Hefte,'" *hier und heute* 1, no. 1 (1950): 24.

[52] On the latter, see Martin Stankowski, *Linkskatholizismus nach 1945: Die Presse oppositioneller Katholiken in der Auseinandersetzung für eine demokratische und sozialistische Gesellschaft* (Cologne: Pahl-Rugenstein, 1976), 27–65.

[53] "Die 'Frankfurter Hefte.'" Initial contact ran through Alfred Andersch and Theo Pirker; Stephan Reinhardt, *Alfred Andersch: Eine Biographie* (Zurich: Diogenes, 1990), 149, 162–3; Wolfgang Schroeder, ed. *Gewerkschaftspolitik zwischen DGB, Katholizismus und CDU 1945 bis 1960: Katholische Arbeiterführer als Zeitzeugen in Interviews* (Cologne: Bund, 1990), 375.

[54] See, e.g., Erich Kuby, "Über die gestrige und die heutige Lage der Nationalsozialisten," *hier und heute* 1, no. 1 (1951): 13–14; Theo Pirker, "Der Schritt nach vorn," *hier und heute* 1, no. 8 (1951): 2–5; Kuby and Pirker, "Unfreiwillige Diskussion über die Mitbestimmung," *hier und heute* 1, no. 2 (1951): 7–9; Alfred Andersch, "Skandal

express goal, as Pirker put it, was "building broad coalitions to intervene politically."[55]

The new project ran for a mere ten issues. In a farewell notice, the editors admitted: "We were clear that *hier und heute* was a risky endeavor," one that seemed justified when "right away we made surprisingly many friends (and new contributors)" who "experienced its foundation as virtually a liberation." Unfortunately, they needed revenue, and they had underestimated the time required to develop their subscriber base. Nor were they adept at marketing, and most newsstand suppliers had not picked up the weekly. "We are drawing the appropriate conclusions in time and cutting the 'battle' short – to continue it in another place and by other means... We do not hold it against our readers that they did not appear in greater numbers. Do not lose *your* courage, and we will not lose ours either."[56] Indeed, Dirks and Kogon did not give up their aspiration to reach a broader audience. Each took positions in mass media, Dirks at Cologne's West German Radio in 1956 and Kogon at one of the earliest television magazines, *Panorama*, in 1961.[57] Yet their main focus remained the *Frankfurter Hefte*, where many of *hier und heute*'s authors now published and whose cast of contributors continued to expand.

The most significant extraparliamentary mobilizations of the 1950s grew out of engaged democrats' alliances with that third anti-restorative constituency: the FRG's working class. In practice, this meant its organized representatives, the SPD – a parliamentary force, albeit an oppositional one – and the trade unions, now united in a German Federation of Unions (DGB). While this collaboration later birthed the peace movement, it began in campaigns for economic democratization. The CDU's narrow electoral victory in 1949 brought with it the construction of their "social market economy" – a liberal program with a minimal state role, by contemporary standards – effectively ending the vibrant postwar socialization debates. But even this de-radicalized framework, oriented toward corporatist capital–labor partnership, left various forms of worker codetermination at the level of individual firms on the table. These became the labor movement's focus in the early FRG. Threatening massive strikes, they managed to secure full intra-firm codetermination – from

---

der deutschen Reklame," *hier und heute* 1, no. 1 (1951): 11–12; Richter, "Vor einem deutschen Buchschaufenster," *hier und heute* 1, no. 3 (1951): 6; Burkart Lutz, "Kein Platz für Kleinbetriebe," *hier und heute* 1, no. 6 (1951): 11–12.

[55] Pirker quoted in Schroeder, ed. *Gewerkschaftspolitik*, 375.

[56] "An die Leser von 'hier und heute'!" *hier und heute* 1, no. 10 (1951): 24; reprinted as "'Frankfurter Hefte' und 'hier und heute'," *Frankfurter Hefte* 6, no. 4 (1951): 300.

[57] Dirks, *Der singende Stotterer: Autobiographische Texte* (Munich: Kösel, 1983), 29; Hodenberg, *Konsens*, 303–4.

the plant to the supervisory board, and with formal union involvement – for the coal, iron, and steel industries in 1951, based on the British zone's model. The DGB hoped to extend this framework to other sectors of the economy, to no avail. Demonstrations and warning strikes proved insufficient to block passage in 1952 of a general Works Constitution Law that restricted codetermination to workplace and personnel issues, gave labor minority representation on supervisory boards, and excluded unions from the entire process. In 1955 the public sector was exempted from mandatory codetermination altogether.[58]

In this struggle, engaged democrats were unions' natural allies, given the parallels both drew between participation in the economy and in formal politics. Dirks was eloquent on this point: codetermination represented a crucial step in humanity's progression away from "heteronomy" and "anarchy" toward "freedom, self-determination, and maturity":

The codetermination movement is closely intertwined with the democratic movement. It had to awaken in the moment that the existential meaning of industrial production was recognized. At that moment, the ballot no longer sufficed, no more than it could suffice for a professor forced to research, teach, and live at a university with... an authoritarian constitution. An industrial firm is no university, but [they share] the same problem: How, in this highly differentiated, labor-divided structure, one can have one's share of rights and duties as a mature person, live and work within it as a free person... bound to the authority that arises from [its] law, but not under an alien power independent of this law.[59]

Aligning codetermination with the freedom of self-legislation, Dirks reprised its affinity for engaged democrats' initial vision of self-developing subjectivity. Seeing codetermination only in economic terms, as a tool for advocating material interests or a ticket to "partnership" in productivity and prosperity, gutted its deeper content. Crucially, codetermination would "de-bureaucratize" and "decentralize" economic processes in which workers were ruled as objects – notably, by unions as well as management – by infusing workers themselves into decision making, where they would learn "co-responsibility" by practice. It was indeed a "step toward socialism," as its opponents alleged; however, it centered not on the state but rather on self-organizing economic actors "freely working

---

[58] Christoph Kleßmann, *Die doppelte Staatsgründung: Deutsche Geschichte 1945–1955*, 5th edn. (Göttingen: Vandenhoek & Ruprecht, 1991), 236–9; Andrei S. Markovits, *The Politics of the West German Trade Unions: Strategies of Class and Interest Representation in Growth and Crisis* (Cambridge: Cambridge University Press, 1986), 72–83; also James C. Van Hook, *Rebuilding Germany: The Creation of the Social Market Economy, 1945–1957* (Cambridge: Cambridge University Press, 2004).

[59] Dirks, "Mitbestimmung: Aktuell und mehr," *Frankfurter Hefte* 10, no. 12 (1955): 846–7, quote 847.

together in reciprocal interdependence."[60] Codetermination was integral to democratic autonomy under modern conditions, replacing passive obedience with active self-rule in the economic sphere.

Intellectuals' alliance with the labor movement extended to other arenas too. One noteworthy venue was the annual Ruhr Festival in the mining town Recklinghausen, convened jointly by the DGB and the city. This multi-week summer gala – itself an artifact of the spontaneous solidarities of the immediate postwar period – featured theater and opera as well as art exhibits, film screenings, music, and dance. In large part, these events replayed the elitist, paternalist forms that bringing "culture" to the "masses" had taken for decades. Yet they also tried to dismantle social barriers, by arranging mine expeditions for actors or facilitating exchanges among performers and audience members above ground. Beginning in 1950, "European Conversations" were a regular program component, for which the DGB would invite one to two dozen intellectuals from across western Europe (and occasionally the USA). In later years, prepared papers were the norm; at first, the format was more informal.[61]

The inaugural theme was "Worker and Culture," reflecting on the broader festival project (Figure 7.1). Kogon moderated a fifteen-person conversation, including Dirks and Weber as well as Plievier, Ernst Rowohlt, and visitors from six countries.[62] The results linked engaged democrats' processual notions of culture and participatory ideas about politics in a counter-elitist vein. All agreed that the issue was not so much workers' "receptivity" to high-cultural goods as their "inner subjective power" to shape their lives and their contributions to society. And workers had a vital contribution to make: in their distinctive ethic of "solidarity" lay the wellspring of a new human type, one that could succeed the aristocratic "gentleman" and the bourgeois "entrepreneur" and build a new kind of social order, resolving "the problem of mass democracy" in a "technological age." Workers' culture in this sense had much to do with the character of workplace activities, at the sites where solidarity was practiced. There, however, "growing technicization and functionalization" –

---

[60] Dirks, "Der Kampf um die Mitbestimmung," *Frankfurter Hefte* 5, no. 7 (1950): 687–9.
[61] Matthias Franck, *Kultur im Revier: Die Geschichte der Ruhrfestspiele Recklinghausen 1946–1956* (Würzburg: Königshausen & Neumann, 1986); Hermann Pölking, ed. *50 Jahre Ruhrfestspiele Recklinghausen* (Bottrop: Pomp, 1996). The festival's roots lie in the bitter winter of 1946–7, when Hamburg actors turned up in Recklinghausen seeking coal to heat their theaters. To thank the miners who supplied them, several companies returned to perform in summer 1947. The Ruhr Festival was held annually from 1948.
[62] The proceedings are summarized in Walther Pahl, "Die Arbeiterschaft und die Kultur der Gegenwart: Ein europäisches Gespräch," *Gewerkschaftliche Monatshefte* 1, no. 7 (1950): 297–302.

Figure 7.1 Eugen Kogon speaks with coal miners in Recklinghausen on 5 July 1950. Evident differences of dress and comportment express some of the tensions underlying the Ruhr Festival and the European Conversation's inaugural theme. (*Source*: AdsD / Friedrich-Ebert-Stiftung)

thus "dehumanization" – put the labor process increasingly beyond workers' conscious control. All the more reason, discussants concluded, for organized labor to emphasize codetermination; as the vital cornerstone of a "new, free labor constitution," it could help enable human "dignity and freedom" in the present.[63] Challenges to this project were compounded by the "managerial" cast of postwar society that Burnham had diagnosed. This became the rubric for the next year's conversation, moderated by Kogon and featuring Dirks and Sternberger.[64]

Notably, these were not mere intellectual exercises; rather, they sought to inform the practice of anti-restorative politics. Dirks conceded that, in

[63] Pahl, "Arbeiterschaft," 298–301. Kogon and Dirks quoted Marx, on whose early critique of alienated labor they drew; their comments resonated also with Lukács' on the proletariat's privileged standpoint for recognizing and overcoming "reification." On Dirks' interest in these issues, see Chapter 2.

[64] Pahl, "Manager – Arbeiter – Kultur: Europäisches Gespräch," *Gewerkschaftliche Monatshefte* 2, no. 8 (1951): 457–62. From this second meeting, the proceedings were also published in full; Ernst von Schenck, ed. *Arbeiter, Manager, Kultur* (Cologne: Bund, 1952).

the DGB as in public life more broadly, a variety of ideological languages existed. But if Christians, Marxists, and liberal humanists meant different things by "freedom," "democracy," or even "the human," their shared interest in a new future made it possible to forge common purpose and eventually a "common language."[65] Germany's federated unions were not merely an element in the anti-restorative coalition he envisioned; they were a venue for its realization in microcosm.

Concrete questions of economic democracy and its institutions came to the fore at the 1952 meeting. The theme was "Unions in the State," and the context was intensive public debate on organized labor's societal and political role prompted by the conflict around the Works Constitution Law. In his opening remarks, DGB head Christian Fette stressed the unions' basic position: they were defending the very "rights that animate a social democracy," which the FRG claimed to be. Yet this was to be no propaganda event; rather, they sought an open exchange of different viewpoints, to enrich both their internal debate and the larger public one. Weber chaired the event, in which Kogon and Sternberger also took part.[66] In his talk, Sternberger framed a legitimate but limited political role for unions, as one instance of the right of all subgroups or "minorities" to organize and exert non-electoral pressure for their "particular interest." Kogon countered this by arguing that unions' broad social basis and "solidarity" spirit put them in a unique position to develop an "idea of order" with "general" validity.[67] Weber concurred, embedding this point in a broader theorization of the state. The FRG's liberal jurists, he asserted, had trouble grasping the legitimacy of "extraparliamentary" politics, of political spaces and actors beyond those enumerated in the constitution. Commensurately, they saw the state as a thing central and static. In fact, the state was a "process" and only one among many institutional "integration factors" in society. Unions were another, distinctive insofar as they shared the republican state's goal of "democratic integration"; their mission, a universal one, was to advance the frontier of democracy and human dignity. And when the state failed to defend their

---

[65] Dirks, "Die Gewerkschaft und die Sprachen der Gewerkschafter," *Gewerkschaftliche Monatshefte* 2, no. 12 (1951): 668–72. This essay develops thoughts from 1950, which Pahl encouraged Dirks to put in writing; Pahl to Dirks, 19 July 1950, 11 August 1951, AdsD NL Dirks 50A, 61.
[66] Christian Fette, "Das Europäische Gespräch 1952," *Gewerkschaftliche Monatshefte* 3, no. 8 (1952): 449; Wolfgang Hirsch-Weber, ed. *Gewerkschaften im Staat* (Cologne: Bund, 1955), 38. Dirks' presence is noted in the planned program but not in publications; "Die Teilnehmer des Gesprächs," n.d., AdsD NL Dirks 72A.
[67] Sternberger, "Parlamentarismus, Parteien, Verbände," *Gewerkschaftliche Monatshefte* 3, no. 8 (1952): 475–6; Kogon, "Die Gewerkschaften in der gegenwärtigen gesellschaftlichen Entwicklung," *Gewerkschaftliche Monatshefte* 3, no. 8 (1952): 487.

gains – for instance, by attempting to roll back codetermination rights validated by the highest authority, namely "public opinion" – then it was the unions' duty to take extraordinary measures, up to and including the general strike. These were justified by the "right to resist" illegitimate authority enshrined in post-Nazi constitutional discourse. Weber's arguments, in particular, were widely and warmly received within the DGB.[68] Under the heading "Unions and Parliament," a discussion of these themes was carried forth at the next European Conversation, where Kogon, Sternberger, and Weber were again involved.[69]

While the mobilizations for codetermination were prodigious, it was the peace movement that launched large-scale, broad-based extraparliamentary opposition in the 1950s. As global developments pointed ever more relentlessly toward the FRG's integration into a Western military bloc, engaged democrats joined many others in attempting to shape that outcome. Their various stances on this, the crucial foreign policy issue of the day, shared two common threads: all sought to constitute Germany – and, by extension, Europe – as an actively neutral force, and all were motivated by domestic concerns over "remilitarization" and "renazification." Depending on the circumstances, they sought to reconcile the prospect of rearmed West Germans with these larger goals, or attempted to block it entirely.

For some, rearmament within a federated European context offered a palatable way out. Kogon and the EUD acknowledged that the issue would be significantly recast if German soldiers were integrated into a supranational European force; this ameliorated the risk of reviving German nationalism and militarism as well as consolidating a US-led Atlantic bloc. They insisted, however, that a common western European defense could evolve only on the basis of robust political integration.[70] When the European Defense Community (EDC) was proposed, it represented just the opposite: another framework for functional cooperation without political federation, a military complement to the ECSC. Moreover, though the EDC was put forth by the French in 1950 – to block the reconstruction of an independent (West) German military within a NATO framework – it was ultimately rejected by France's own National

---

[68] Weber, "Staat und gewerkschaftliche Aktion," *Gewerkschaftliche Monatshefte* 3, no. 8 (1952): 478–82; also Weber, *Staat und gewerkschaftliche Aktion* (Cologne: Bund, [1954]). For their appreciation of Weber, see the DGB's obituary: Helmut Wickel, "Alfred Weber," *Gewerkschaftliche Monatshefte* 9, no. 7 (1958): 392–4.
[69] Richard Becker, "Gewerkschaften und Parlament: Das 4. Europäische Gespräch im Rahmen der Ruhrfestspiele 1955," *Gewerkschaftliche Monatshefte* 6, no. 8 (1955): 465–9; Franz Deus, ed. *Gewerkschaften und Parlament* (Cologne: Bund, 1956).
[70] Kogon, "Man braucht Deutschland," 33; Kogon, "Die Verteidigung Europas," *Frankfurter Hefte* 5, no. 12 (1950): 1261–76.

Assembly in 1954, after Adenauer's diplomacy had succeeded in removing many of its controls on German power. Nonetheless, the initiatives of 1950 prompted several years of public debate over the desirability and the details of a military contribution by the Federal Republic. This, in turn, provoked a series of Eastern counterproposals – most prominently from the USSR in spring 1952 – that advocated a unified, "neutralized" Germany.[71] Together, these developments seemed to signal an opening for alternatives.

In this context, Alfred Weber circulated a strategic proposal. The direct impetus was the first conference of foreign ministers in over four years, scheduled for January 1954 in Berlin. Weber saw an opportunity to reframe the problem of European security in terms of how to secure a reunified Germany without posing a threat to either East or West. His so-called Germany Initiative offered a simple solution: unify and rearm Germany but bar it from military alliances and limit it to strictly defensive forces. This would not "neutralize" Germany – like others thinking along similar lines, he was at pains to avoid the language of the Soviet proposals – but establish a "buffer state" that would help mediate superpower tensions by committing both sides to significant concessions. The West would allow a rearmed Germany to remain outside its alliance, while the Soviets would agree to free, all-German elections.[72] Weber thought this would satisfy Western security concerns about potential Soviet aggression and sidestep Soviet opposition to German fighting power in a Western alliance. He was not alone in his optimism; the proposal was discussed extensively in the pages of the weekly *Deutsche Kommentare*, where it was published. And though it received little amplification in mainstream West German media, it enjoyed an enthusiastic reception in the GDR.[73]

It was the prospect of West German accession to NATO, however, that truly galvanized opinion against rearmament. This option had been quietly negotiated in parallel with the ill-fated EDC, and it became the

---

[71] On the EDC, see Large, *Germans*, 111–201. Assessing the "Stalin notes'" intentions remains controversial. For an overview, see Jürgen Zarusky, ed. *Die Stalinnote vom 10. März 1952: Neue Quellen und Analysen* (Munich: Oldenbourg, 2002).

[72] "Professor Alfred Webers Deutschland-Initiative," *Deutsche Kommentare*, 16 January 1954; Weber, "Praktisches zur Deutschland-Initiative," *Deutsche Kommentare*, 13 February 1954. See also Eberhard Demm, *Von der Weimarer Republik zur Bundesrepublik: Der politische Weg Alfred Webers 1920–1958* (Düsseldorf: Droste, 1999), 409–13.

[73] "Ein Wort an die Russen," *Deutsche Kommentare*, 16 January 1954; Karl Mukrosch, "Bravo, Herr Professor!" *Deutsche Kommentare*, 23 January 1954; Bruno Winkler, "Alfred Webers Deutschland-Initiative," *Deutsche Kommentare*, 30 January 1954; H. G. Müller-Payer, "Neutralität oder Integration," *Deutsche Kommentare*, 6 February 1954; Karl Silex, "Deutscher Protest," *Deutsche Kommentare*, 20 February 1954; Demm, *Weimarer Republik*, 411–12.

centerpiece of the Paris Treaties that coupled the FRG's military activation to near-complete sovereignty. All recognized that such a move would render national division irrevocable, and the USSR again made overtures toward neutralization. Weber took up contact with SPD party leaders during the Paris meetings and encouraged them to mold their already quite compatible foreign policy position further along his lines.[74] The most significant outcome was Weber's prominent role in a rally at the Frankfurt Paulskirche in January 1955, planned by the SPD and DGB together with the smaller All-German People's Party (GVP). Although the rally's title was "Save Unity, Freedom, Peace! Against Communism and Nationalism," it had little to do with the latter two issues – such language hoped to deflect critics who decried "neutralists" as either crypto-nationalists or Soviet agents. Rather, it had everything to do with making the case against the Paris Treaties to the German people.[75]

This rally was a watershed for the peace movement, as some 1,000 people from diverse constituencies mobilized against remilitarization. Weber gave the opening address. He reiterated his initiative and its rationale, now in terms of Germany's military "bracketing" out of both Cold War alliances (another circumlocution around "neutralization"). Asserting that the Soviets had effectively conceded all Western demands, he saw the possibility of a bloc-free Germany at hand, with its independence and security guaranteed by its own defensive forces and UN oversight. Once "bracketed," Germany – a potential bridge as well as bone of contention between the superpowers – would help defuse global tensions. Other speakers included Erich Ollenhauer (SPD), Georg Reuter (DGB), Gustav Heinemann (GVP), and Helmut Gollwitzer, a left-Protestant pastor. The "German Manifesto" passed at the conference spoke in the name of "our people's will to unity," presented the Paris Treaties as insurmountable barriers, and called for the people's "concerted resistance" to their ratification. While politicians and union leaders were overrepresented among the signatories, they were joined by intellectuals including Dirks, Günther Weisenborn, and Wolfgang Abendroth.[76] Moreover, the rally initiated the first broad-based extraparliamentary mobilization of the

---

[74] Large, *Germans*, 205–33; Demm, *Weimarer Republik*, 413–15.
[75] For the speeches and manifesto, see *Rettet Einheit, Freiheit, Frieden! Gegen Kommunismus und Nationalismus!* (Frankfurt a.M., 1955). On the conference, see Werner, *"Ohne mich"*, 477–510.
[76] *Rettet Einheit, Freiheit, Frieden*, 2–3, 13–14; "Auszug aus der 2. Liste der Zustimmungserklärungen zum 'Deutschen Manifest,'" n.d., Universitätsbibliothek Heidelberg (hereafter UBH) NL Weber, Box 3, Paulskirche 29.I.55. On Heinemann, see Alexander Gallus, *Die Neutralisten: Verfechter eines vereinten Deutschlands zwischen Ost und West 1945–1990* (Düsseldorf: Droste, 2001), 76–85.

Bonn Republic. A series of marches and demonstrations in cities all across the land, the largest of which drew 25,000 protesters in Munich, turned the rally into a "Paulskirche Movement."[77] These events succeeded at providing release for popular anti-rearmament and pro-unity sentiment but did nothing to dissuade the CDU government. In 1955, the Bundestag ratified the Paris Treaties over the voices of the SPD, and the FRG was released from HICOG oversight and admitted to NATO.

Engaged democrats were also involved in the "Fight Atomic Death" (Kampf dem Atomtod, KdA) campaign.[78] This first wave of antinuclear activism sought to deny the freshly-minted Bundeswehr tactical nuclear weapons, a NATO proposal first revealed by Adenauer and his new Defense Minister Franz Josef Strauß in spring 1957. This immediately incited a declaration against atomic weapons by eighteen top West German nuclear physicists. Their appeal resonated broadly, moving labor and religious groups, students, and intellectuals to action; Kogon publicized it vigorously. In September, twenty writers including Eggebrecht and Wolfgang Weyrauch issued a public statement, followed in December by a telegram to the chancellor from eleven Heidelberg scholars, including Hans von Eckardt, Wilhelm Kütemeyer, Mitscherlich, and Weber. Such disparate initiatives were soon consolidated under the auspices of the SPD-led KdA, resembling an expanded Paulskirche coalition. Initial signatories of their March 1958 manifesto included Dirks, Eggebrecht, Kästner, Kogon, Weber, and Heinrich Böll, a rising star in Gruppe 47, as well as Ollenhauer, Schmid, Reuter, Gollwitzer, Heinemann, and Helene Wessel (formerly GVP, now SPD, like Heinemann). Kogon spoke at the campaign's inaugural rally, in Frankfurt. Independently, Richter convened a "Committee against Atomic Armament" based in Munich, with Kästner, Kolbenhoff, Weisenborn, Weyrauch, and other literati (Figure 7.2).[79] Over the coming months, local and regional offshoots of these organizations formed, and public demonstrations across Germany demanded a popular referendum on the issue. The largest, in

---

[77] Large, *Germans*, 227–32; Werner, *"Ohne mich"*, 491–4.
[78] See Hans Karl Rupp, *Außerparlamentarische Opposition in der Ära Adenauer: Der Kampf gegen die Atombewaffnung in den fünfziger Jahren* (Cologne: Pahl-Rugenstein, 1970); Holger Nehring, *Politics of Security: British and West German Protest Movements and the Early Cold War, 1945–1970* (Oxford: Oxford University Press, 2013).
[79] Kogon, "Im heraufziehenden Schatten des Atomtodes," *Frankfurter Hefte* 12, no. 5 (1957): 301–6; Rupp, *Außerparlamentarische Opposition*, 95–7, 130–5, 153–5, 163–4, 174–5, 185–7; Geppert, "'Kreuzwegqual zwischen Politik und Literatur': Der Umbruch Ende der 1950er Jahre als Zäsur in der Geschichte der Gruppe 47," in *Sonde 1957: Ein Jahr als symbolische Zäsur für Wandlungsprozesse im geteilten Deutschland*, ed. Gallus and Werner Müller (Berlin: Duncker & Humblot, 2010), 351–5.

Figure 7.2 Erich Kästner takes part in a multi-day student-led vigil against nuclear weapons outside the University of Munich. This protest followed a mass rally on 24 June 1958 and was coordinated by the Committee against Atomic Armament. (*Source*: bpk Berlin / Art Resource, NY / Felicitas Timpe)

Hamburg, drew 150,000 participants. Although a referendum did not come to pass, neither did the nuclear armament of the Bundeswehr, despite the Bundestag's vote in support.

The shift of focus to atomic danger fundamentally recast the terms of the anti-rearmament debate. In general, the critique of a specifically German militarist tradition washed out in a "metaphysics of antinuclearism," with its universalizing ruminations on annihilation by unbound, promethean technology.[80] Nonetheless, engaged democrats continued to participate, since this effort also redeployed in yet another context the basic mental geography of their vision: like the Europe Union, the initial anti-rearmament interventions, and the Paulskirche movement, the KdA campaign imagined a European space of active neutrality between West and East. Its manifesto demanded that politicians withdraw the FRG from the superpowers' arms race and commit "to support all efforts toward an atomic weapon-free zone in Europe as a contribution to détente."[81] Kogon published a detailed exposé of the specific plan to which the manifesto referred: the proposal by Polish foreign minister Adam Rapacki, presented to the UN in fall 1957, to create a nuclear weapon-free central European zone that would incorporate Poland, Czechoslovakia, and both German states together. In the Cold War context, of course, this plan was roundly dismissed by Western politicians and instrumentalized in the East.[82]

If their unfulfilled vision from the immediate postwar years oriented engaged democrats in the 1950s, the policies of Adenauer's government galvanized them. Many felt their affinities for the parliamentary opposition solidify as they allied with them in the extraparliamentary realm. This held still more for their friends in the Gruppe 47. Under Richter's leadership, a large faction embraced the SPD – seen as the "lesser evil" in party politics – cautiously at first, but blossoming into active electoral campaigning from the mid 1960s.[83] In its initial phase, this consisted of election-year essay collections entitled *The Alternative; or, Do We Need a New Government?* (1961) and *Plea for a New Government; or, No Alternative* (1965). These were suffused with the restoration critique that engaged democrats had given definitive shape, and

---

[80] Geyer, "Cold War Angst," quote 396; Andrew Oppenheimer, "West German Pacifism and the Ambivalence of Human Solidarity, 1945–1968," *Peace & Change* 29, no. 3–4 (2004): 353–89.

[81] "Aufruf des Arbeitsausschusses 'Kampf dem Atomtod,'" in *Blaubuch 1958: Kampf dem Atomtod – Dokumente und Aufrufe*, ed. Peter Brollik and Klaus Mannhardt (Essen: Klartext, 1988), 11–12.

[82] Kogon, "Atomwaffenfreie Zone in Mitteleuropa," *Frankfurter Hefte* 13, no. 3 (1958): 157–9. See Michael Gehler, "Neutralität und Neutralisierungspläne für Mitteleuropa? Osterreich, Ungarn, Tschechoslowakei und Polen," in *Neutralität: Chance oder Chimäre? Konzepte des dritten Weges für Deutschland und die Welt 1945–1990*, ed. Geppert and Udo Wengst (Munich: Oldenbourg, 2005), 105–31.

[83] Daniela Münkel, "Intellektuelle für die SPD: Die sozialdemokratische Wählerinitiative," in *Kritik und Mandat: Intellektuelle in der deutschen Politik*, ed. Gangolf Hübinger and Thomas Hertfelder (Stuttgart: Deutsche Verlags-Anstalt, 2000), 222–38; Geppert, "Von der Staatsskepsis zum parteipolitischen Engagement: Hans Werner Richter, die Gruppe 47 und die deutsche Politik," in *Streit um den Staat*, ed. Geppert and Hacke, 46–68.

Eggebrecht contributed to both.[84] In the first volume, not short on polemical titles, Eggebrecht's stood out: "Is the Era of Hypocrisy to Continue?" He indicted the young FRG for its "soft unfreedom" of manipulated desires and conformist views, its friend-versus-foe suspicion of dissent, its counterfeit professions of piety, and its cowardly refusals to experiment. All of these underwrote policy outcomes most citizens actually rejected, from suicidal rearmament to unregenerate capitalism. Worse, the era dissembled massively, touting "ringing slogans" in its self-descriptions, like "democratic consciousness," "tolerance," "freedom," and "unity" (notably, *Einigkeit* not *Einheit*, the term favored by the other side). Eggebrecht's verdict: "Twelve years of [CDU] dominance have made us a people of hypocrites."[85] Juxtaposing noble aspirations to bleak realities, his words captured engaged democrats' mood at the turn to the 1960s, just as his old friend Kästner had a decade previously. The indictment was now sharper in tone, the disaffection more energized.

These bookends chart the path taken by most of these intellectuals toward an oppositional stance within the new Federal Republic. The key exception is Sternberger, who became a critically supportive analyst of West German civic culture and parliamentary democracy. And with a flourishing career in political science and journalism (at *Die Gegenwart* from 1950 and the *Frankfurter Allgemeine Zeitung* from 1959), he had an influential voice.[86] His case demonstrates the malleability of engaged democrats' discourse under altered conditions. In this era, the functional side of Sternberger's interest in majority voting – concerned with stable governing majorities and effective parliamentary outcomes – came to overshadow the humanist side – animated by the intrinsic value of participatory process and an aversion to mediating institutions.[87] His analysis of the 1953 Bundestag elections is telling. Much critical commentary registered dismay at the near-absolute majority won by the CDU, which had waged its campaign above all on the promise of security – from material want as well as from Communism, with which it damned the SPD by association. The returns seemed to deliver a mandate for Adenauer's authoritarian "chancellor democracy" and plans for

---

[84] Martin Walser, ed. *Die Alternative oder Brauchen wir eine neue Regierung?* (Reinbek b.H.: Rowohlt, 1961); Richter, ed. *Plädoyer für eine neue Regierung oder Keine Alternative* (Reinbek b.H.: Rowohlt, 1965). A related stock-taking volume to which Mitscherlich contributed was Richter, *Bestandsaufnahme: Eine deutsche Bilanz 1962* (Munich: Desch, 1962).

[85] Eggebrecht, "Soll die Ära der Heuchelei andauern?" in *Alternative*, ed. Walser, quote 25.

[86] Claudia Kinkela, *Die Rehabilitierung des Bürgerlichen im Werk Dolf Sternbergers* (Würzburg: Königshausen & Neumann, 2001), 114, 125.

[87] Kinkela assimilates the latter aspect to the former; ibid., 206–16. See Chapters 2 and 4.

military West-integration.[88] Sternberger and his Wählergesellschaft, in contrast, hailed the outcome as a "German electoral miracle" because it laid the groundwork for a stable interplay of government and opposition despite a basically proportional electoral system. Sternberger's narrowing focus on the institutional over the participatory moment of democracy was entirely compatible with the postwar system's basic terms. Writing to Dirks at the end of the decade, he denied that any tenable distinction existed between "'formal' and 'substantive' democracy," an indicator of how much had changed since the immediate postwar years, when he framed his positions in those very terms.[89]

## The threat of technocracy and the promise of publicness

As these intellectuals helped shape politics in the 1950s, they also elaborated on the conceptual commitments that informed their activities, ideas that would infuse later intellectual debates and activism. At the core of their immediate postwar hopes had stood an image of spontaneous subjectivity inspired by idealist philosophy and literature, one that fed their vision of self-educating citizens forming a self-governing polity. In their view, that vision had not come to pass. In part, engaged democrats laid the blame for this at the door of a favorite bogey of the era: technology.[90] The attempt to mold the social world by "science," functionalizing knowledge and instrumentalizing reason, driven by large-scale institutions beyond popular control and legitimation – this was the very counter-image of their program. Rule by technicians and experts, whether installed by governments or corporations, represented not democracy but technocracy. While engaged democrats used this term only sporadically, it was well established in the early 1960s.[91] Whatever they named the threat, they promoted publicness as an antidote and alternative.

In fact, a critique of technocracy *avant la lettre* was integral to their thought from the start. As we have seen, the historical development

---

[88] Doering-Manteuffel, "Kanzlerdemokratie," 13–14; Thomas Mergel, *Propaganda nach Hitler: Eine Kulturgeschichte des Wahlkampfs in der Bundesrepublik 1949–1990* (Göttingen: Wallstein, 2010), 242, 270–6.

[89] Sternberger, "Das deutsche Wahlwunder," in *Das deutsche Wahlwunder*, ed. Christian-Claus Baer and Erwin Faul (Frankfurt a.M.: Bollwerk, 1953), 13–20; Sternberger to Dirks, 6 September 1960, DLA A:Sternberger/ 89.10.1355/3.

[90] See, e.g., Schildt, *Moderne Zeiten*, 324–50. Schildt tends to identify all cultural critiques of modernity – the wide spectrum of concerns voiced over "technology," "massification," and "alienation" – with anti-modern cultural pessimism. Similarly, see Monika Boll, *Nachtprogramm: Intellektuelle Gründungsdebatten in der frühen Bundesrepublik* (Münster: LIT, 2004).

[91] See, e.g., Claus Koch and Dieter Senghaas, eds. *Texte zur Technokratiediskussion* (Frankfurt a.M.: Europäische Verlagsanstalt, 1970).

and implications of bureaucratic modes of control – as a German specialty as well as a modern condition – were an abiding concern. This issue only gained in prominence into the 1950s. Weber exemplified this development, expanding his reflections on a "fourth human type" at monograph length. The focus of his analytic frame shifted somewhat, from its manifestations in Nazism to those of Stalinism, from the amoral "split personality" that enabled diligent human cogs' "inhumane acts" to the "robot of a bureaucratic-autocratic terror machine." He was quick to add, however, that the era of the spiritually fragmented, too-specialized "functionary" had come in the West as well, rooted in the "organizational concentration" of both capitalism and the state and in the "technicization" and "mechanization" of all work, from manual laborers to clerks to managers. These were all of a piece, based in the "technocratic total apparatification (*Gesamtverapparatung*)" that defined the "modern form of existence." Despite the bleak diagnosis, he still saw transformative potential: a "free, democratic socialism" or even a "transformed democratic liberalism" might yet enable a sweeping "rehumanization" through maximal participation "in life, at work, above all in the public sphere (*Öffentlichkeit*)."[92] It was not too late for people to recognize and reclaim their capacity for history-making freedom. Interest in such themes was keen; his 1953 book reached a wide audience, by which time earlier versions of his arguments had already sparked debate.[93]

Concerns about a specialized, disintegrated human existence also had implications for the human sciences and the sorts of scholarship these academics pursued. Here, a comparison of Weber and Sternberger is revealing. The former teacher took up his old post, but his brand of "cultural sociology" – militantly anti-empirical and given to anthro-historical speculation – was a waning paradigm, even at the institute renamed in his honor.[94] Meanwhile, the former student's profile only rose: he founded a "Research Group Sternberger" within the Alfred Weber Institute in

---

[92] Weber, "Der vierte Mensch oder der Zusammenbruch der geschichtlichen Kultur," *Die Wandlung* 3, no. 4 (1948): 284; Weber, *Der dritte oder der vierte Mensch: Vom Sinn des geschichtlichen Daseins* (Munich: Piper, 1953), 16, 46, 53, 85, 201–2. See also Demm, *Weimarer Republik*, 291–5.

[93] Schildt, *Moderne Zeiten*, 328; Wilhelm Röpke et al., *Kommt der vierte Mensch?* (Zurich: Europa, 1952). Weber added the 1948 essay as a new final chapter to his revised magnum opus in 1950 and sketched its argument in the press as well; Weber, *Kulturgeschichte als Kultursoziologie*, 2nd edn. (Munich: Piper, 1950), 446–98; Weber, "Kommt der 'vierte Mensch'?" *Die Neue Zeitung*, 6 June 1951.

[94] Demm, *Weimarer Republik*, 339–50; Volker Kruse, "Warum scheiterte Alfred Webers Kultursoziologie? Ein Interpretationsversuch," in *Soziologie, Politik und Kultur: Von Alfred Weber zur Frankfurter Schule*, ed. Demm (Frankfurt a.M.: Lang, 2003), 207–33.

1950, and he was made honorary professor at the new Institute for Political Science in 1955.[95] Weber followed his friend's success with mentorly good will. In 1956, Sternberger sent him a copy of *Living Constitution*, a fruit of the group's research on institutional dynamics of representative government – elections, parties, coalitions, and the like. Weber detected in it a whiff of the civilizational climate that worried him. Certainly, Sternberger was no blinkered empiricist, and Weber praised his "overall idea" of reading the tensions between political life and its normative foundations off the "actual course" of intra-parliamentary politics. Weber objected, however, to what he called "the strictly positivist form of your presentation, working with *petits faits*," which left the reader "disappointed when the working-out in thorough scholarly fashion" of the central theme "unravels itself in little pieces." Unsurprisingly, the author cordially disagreed with this assessment.[96] For Weber, however, Sternberger's work now shared in the fragmentation of intellectual labor and scholarly imagination under the reign of the "fourth human type."

In this vein, Weber's orientation has certain affinities for that of the social theorists and interdisciplinary researchers known as the "Frankfurt School."[97] Just as Weber remained a "cultural sociologist" on a specializing disciplinary landscape, so Max Horkheimer and Theodor W. Adorno were "social philosophers" (as their student Jürgen Habermas would be). Amid the positivist disaggregation of the postwar social sciences, it was these compound approaches that preserved the commitment to analyze society as a multifaceted, many-layered whole. Of course, deep differences of theory and method separated Weber's approach from that of Critical Theory. For one, Horkheimer, Adorno, and Friedrich Pollock returned from exile committed to integrating sustained theoretical reflection and empirical social research, a project that built on their own Weimar-era foundations as well as their encounter with American social science.[98] Also, their views on modernity were based not in a sweeping, trans-epochal philosophy of history built on vitalist foundations but

---

[95] Kinkela, *Rehabilitierung*, 115–26; Mohr, *Politikwissenschaft*, 151.
[96] Sternberger, *Lebende Verfassung: Studien über Koalition und Opposition* (Meisenheim a.G.: Hain, 1956); Weber to Sternberger, 8 August 1955, 5 March 1956, Sternberger to Weber, 14 March 1956, DLA A:Sternberger/ 89.10.3131/2, 89.10.7478/9–10.
[97] Weber's biographer has highlighted these: Demm, *Weimarer Republik*, 254, 258–9, 264; Demm, introduction to *Soziologie*, ed. Demm, 10.
[98] Rolf Wiggershaus, *The Frankfurt School: Its History, Theories, and Political Significance*, trans. Michael Robertson (Cambridge, Mass.: MIT Press, 1994), 381–466; Thomas Wheatland, *The Frankfurt School in Exile* (Minneapolis: University of Minnesota Press, 2009).

in historically specific analyses of their social present inspired by Marx, Freud, and Max Weber.[99]

Certainly, the Horkheimer circle shared Alfred Weber's grave concern over technology, articulated in their case via a "critique of instrumental reason."[100] Taking stock of the troubling 1930s and 40s, they reached the pessimistic conclusion that overt class conflict had been superseded in advanced industrial societies, leading not to liberation but to a thoroughly organized unfreedom. Whether in post-liberal capitalism, fascist "state capitalism," or Soviet-type "integral statism," ordinary people were subjected to overt terror or more refined psychological manipulation by bureaucratic regimes. The majority received security in return for submission, while the recalcitrant were assimilated or eliminated. Moreover, authoritarian states, science and technology, mass politics and mass culture were all outgrowths of reason's drive to control the world of nature and humans' own internal nature, which had led inexorably into the present catastrophe. If a glimmer of hope remained, it lay in an obscure possibility: the capacity of reason to recover non-instrumental dimensions of itself, from which it might reflect critically on the disaster it had wrought – a reeducation of reason by reason. This was the argument advanced by Horkheimer and Adorno in their *Dialectic of Enlightenment* in the mid 1940s.[101] Affiliates of Frankfurt's Institute for Social Research – refounded in late 1951, with Horkheimer elected the first Jewish rector of a German university – were occupied not only with theoretical elaboration but also with empirical investigations of West German society. Engaged democrats joined them in both.

In rebuilding an institutional presence, the returning exiles drew on old contacts and built new networks in media, publishing, and the academy.[102] On Horkheimer's first scouting expedition to Germany in

---

[99] On the parallel distinction to Martin Heidegger, see John P. McCormick, "A Critical versus Genealogical 'Questioning' of Technology: Notes on How Not to Read Adorno and Horkheimer," in *Confronting Mass Democracy and Industrial Technology: Political and Social Theory from Nietzsche to Habermas*, ed. McCormick (Durham, N.C.: Duke University Press, 2002), 267–94.

[100] Seyla Benhabib, *Critique, Norm, and Utopia: A Study of the Foundations of Critical Theory* (New York: Columbia University Press, 1986), 147–85; Moishe Postone, "Critique, State, and Economy," in *The Cambridge Companion to Critical Theory*, ed. Fred Rush (Cambridge: Cambridge University Press, 2004), 165–93.

[101] Friedrich Pollock, "State Capitalism: Its Possibilities and Limitations," *Studies in Philosophy and Social Science* 9, no. 2 (1941): 200–25; Max Horkheimer and Theodor W. Adorno, *Dialektik der Aufklärung: Philosophische Fragmente* (Amsterdam: Querido, 1947). Horkheimer's important contribution "Autoritärer Staat" appeared only in mimeograph in 1942; Wiggershaus, *Frankfurt School*, 280–4, 325–44.

[102] Clemens Albrecht et al., *Die intellektuelle Gründung der Bundesrepublik: Eine Wirkungsgeschichte der Frankfurter Schule* (Frankfurt a.M.: Campus, 1999).

the spring of 1948, the institute's 1930s affiliate Hans Mayer hosted a dinner in Frankfurt, where Horkheimer met Adorno's old acquaintance Dirks, along with Kogon. In 1949–50, as Horkheimer and Adorno made their tentative return, the *Frankfurter Hefte* were an important publishing venue.[103] Radio too was central in cultivating the re-émigrés profile. Horkheimer's first broadcast at Radio Frankfurt, during his 1948 visit, was a discussion with Kogon and Mayer. After the institute's return, the station now called Radio Hesse became their main mass media platform, as Andersch facilitated a steady flow of appearances by its members, including several discussions with Kogon.[104] When plans to restart a house journal were shelved, the institute focused on a book series co-edited by Adorno and Dirks. To the inaugural collection *Sociologica* in 1955, Dirks contributed an essay on "Consequences of Denazification," in which he tried his hand at the qualitative analysis of interview data. Another volume reported on a large-scale study of attitudes toward work and industrial relations at a Ruhr steel concern, in which Dirks was also involved. Although he relocated to Cologne in 1956, Dirks continued to co-edit the book series with Adorno, and he made West German Radio second only to Radio Hesse in opening the FRG's airwaves to Critical Theory.[105] Finally, Mitscherlich began a long-term relationship with the Institute in 1949. For the Freud centennial of 1956, he organized a joint lecture series with Horkheimer in Heidelberg and Frankfurt, and ties strengthened further after 1960, as Mitscherlich commuted between his home clinic and Frankfurt's new Sigmund Freud Institute for psychoanalysis, where he was founding director.[106]

[103] Mayer, *Ein Deutscher auf Widerruf: Erinnerungen* (Frankfurt a.M.: Suhrkamp, 1982), I:401–2; Horkheimer, "Philosophie und Studium," *Frankfurter Hefte* 4, no. 8 (1949): 656–66; Theodor W. Adorno, "Auferstehung der Kultur in Deutschland?" *Frankfurter Hefte* 5, no. 5 (1950): 469–77; Wiggershaus, *Frankfurt School*, 398–9, 406–7. *Umschau* (Mainz) had reprinted a few essays and excerpts in 1948; Albrecht et al., *Die intellektuelle Gründung*, 250–2.

[104] Wiggershaus, *Frankfurt School*, 406; Albrecht et al., *Die intellektuelle Gründung*, 225–35; Boll, *Nachtprogramm*, 33–4, 134. The ironies of mass-cultural critique in the mass media are not lost on these commentators.

[105] Dirks, "Folgen der Entnazifizierung: Ihre Konsequenzen in kleinen und mittleren Gemeinden der drei westlichen Zonen," in *Sociologica: Aufsätze, Max Horkheimer zum sechzigsten Geburtstag gewidmet* (Frankfurt a.M.: Europäische Verlagsanstalt, 1955), 445–70; *Betriebsklima: Eine industriesoziologische Untersuchung aus dem Ruhrgebiet* (Frankfurt a.M.: Europäische Verlagsanstalt, 1955); Wiggershaus, *Frankfurt School*, 468–71, 479–88; Albrecht et al., *Die intellektuelle Gründung*, 260–3; Boll, *Nachtprogramm*, 176. The Europäische Verlagsanstalt was the *Frankfurter Hefte*'s second publishing house.

[106] Tobias Freimüller, *Alexander Mitscherlich: Gesellschaftsdiagnosen und Psychoanalyse nach Hitler* (Göttingen: Wallstein, 2007), 202–32. In the 1950s, fruitless discussions about

Shared intellectual concerns motivated these connections. The crucial common ground was staked out in a 1950 radio discussion among Adorno, Horkheimer, and Kogon, entitled "The Administered World" – a notion central to postwar Critical Theory. Typically, Adorno gave the problem its incisive formulation: "The vast majority of all people have long since been demoted to mere functionaries within the monstrous social machinery in which we are all embedded." They were witnessing "the transition of the whole world, the whole of life, into a system of administration, into a definite kind of control from above." Horkheimer largely concurred. While Kogon was receptive, he wondered how one might still act "as if" this were *not* the case, whether it was possible "to take such a stance" in concrete social contexts – in the family, at work, in everyday life – "and make from there a new reality." Over Adorno's objections, Kogon insisted that this was no "purely ethical" position, juxtaposing an abstract normative image to given social reality; rather, "it proceeds from ethics... but leads into this sorry reality and transforms it step by step." Besides, he pointed out, if "the element of the good" were not "present" and "effective" at some deep level, then "I wouldn't know why we should raise the whole situation to consciousness." These intellectuals shared concerns, but they did not speak the same language. For Adorno's taste, Kogon's thought was insufficiently immanent; Adorno resisted any hope that could not be grounded in societal contradiction, even if this meant confronting the absence of both. In response, the Catholic socialist seemed to point the neo-Marxist dialectician toward a different inconsistency: if the system were all-encompassing and hermetically closed, how could he account for his own critical insights?[107]

For their part, engaged democrats continued to invest great hope in "publicness," a notion that both invoked their immediate postwar ideas and stood as a counterforce to restoration in the present. In their journalistic practice, as we have seen, they conceived themselves less as educators of the masses and more as participants in a dialogue. Thereby, they anticipated views that younger reformers would later propagate. Overall, the 1950s were still dominated by elitist perspectives and consensus-oriented journalism, but they bore the seeds of a more

a full-time post at the institute and a professorship at Frankfurt University led to some frictions.
[107] Adorno, Horkheimer, and Kogon, "Die verwaltete Welt oder: Die Krisis des Individuums," in Horkheimer, *Gesammelte Schriften*, vol. XIII, *Nachgelassene Schriften 1949–1972* (Frankfurt a.M.: Fischer, 1989), 121–42, quotes 122–3, 142 (first aired on Radio Hesse, 4 September 1950).

contentious and egalitarian media public. Accordingly, this period saw shifting self-conceptions among reporters and publicists regarding their societal roles.[108] At the same time, new spaces for face-to-face, non-mediated yet open dialogue developed. The "Cologne Wednesday Conversations" were one such venue, mass discussions on literary and political themes that drew hundreds to the train station's main hall every week from 1951 through 1956. Weisenborn, Adorno, Böll, Rowohlt, and Schmid were among the many speakers; Dirks was on the upcoming schedule when the series unexpectedly ended. More conventional in form were the "Darmstadt Conversations," an annual panel discussion and art exhibition. An unabashedly elite, higher-profile counterpart to the DGB's European Conversations, they also began in 1950 and attracted a partly overlapping, politically broader cast of characters. Topics included "The Image of Humanity in Our Time" or "Individual and Organization." Among the participants were Mitscherlich, Weber, Sternberger, Kogon, Dirks, Eckardt, and Marie Baum, alongside Adorno, Horkheimer, Kuby, Schmid, and Otto Bartning as well as conservative icons such as Martin Heidegger and José Ortega y Gasset. Engaged democrats gave vital impulses to this mounting "passion for discussion." It was in the valorization of public dialogue as integral to democratic culture that aspects of their postwar vision found the most mainstream resonance in West German society.[109]

Another indicator of burgeoning self-reflection on such themes was a quickening of scholarly debate around the notion of "publicness" itself. The full spectrum of the FRG's intellectual heavyweights weighed in on this question, from Adorno and other left-tending re-émigrés such as sociologist Helmuth Plessner and political scientist Ernst Fraenkel; to more centrist non-émigrés such as jurists Rudolf Smend and Wilhelm Hennis; to moderate conservatives such as historian Reinhart Koselleck or more strident ones such as sociologist Hans Freyer and jurist Ernst Forsthoff; to liberals such as sociologist Ralf Dahrendorf. In these discussions, anxieties regarding the irrational manipulability of "the masses" – especially by powerful new broadcast media – were widely aired, though affirmations of "the public" as a rational interlocutor and legitimate

---

[108] Hodenberg, *Konsens*, 195–205, 274–82; Payk, *Geist*, 194–217.
[109] *Freier Eintritt – Freie Fragen – Freie Antworten: Die Kölner Mittwochgespräche 1950–1956* (Cologne: Historisches Archiv der Stadt Köln, 1991); Sabais, ed. *Die Herausforderung: Darmstädter Gespräche* (Munich: List, 1963); Verheyen, *Diskussionslust*, 151–224. In this spirit, Kießling rightly calls Dirks and Kogon "discussion democrats"; Friedrich Kießling, *Die undeutschen Deutschen: Eine ideengeschichtliche Archäologie der alten Bundesrepublik 1945–1972* (Paderborn: Schöningh, 2012), 304–12.

political subject could also be heard.[110] Of course, even those who embraced rather than feared "the public" construed its relationship to authority in varied ways. Many focused on its controlling function toward established authority, while some considered it as a locus of self-authorizing authority. This was true, for instance, of Hannah Arendt. Inspired by the Hungarian uprising, she came to regard the councils it spawned – spontaneously self-constituting, self-governing deliberative bodies – as her exemplary model of political action. This kind of "public space" she called the "lost treasure" of council democracy's "revolutionary tradition."[111] But Arendt wrote from an ocean's remove, primarily for the American audience of her exile home.

Doubtless the most prominent West German artifact of these debates is the habilitation thesis by Jürgen Habermas (b.1929). Titled *The Structural Transformation of the Public Sphere*, it was begun in the late 1950s under Horkheimer and Adorno but accepted by Abendroth and published in 1962.[112] Revisiting it in light of engaged democrats' postwar debates historicizes a tension in Habermas' account of "publicness." Most interpretations frame this work in liberal-democratic terms, which is no accident, since Habermas grounded his normative political model in a history of "bourgeois society."[113] With new sites of sociability, associational life, and an explosion of print media in eighteenth-century Europe, a new institutional space emerged, the "political public sphere." There, debate over matters of general interest constituted a new kind of political agency, "public opinion," that then staked its claims against the state, seeking to submit power to rational legitimation. In Habermas' schema, the political public sphere was *of* the private arena, standing opposed to

---

[110] See Hodenberg, *Konsens*, 31–66; Peter Uwe Hohendahl et al., *Öffentlichkeit: Geschichte eines kritischen Begriffs* (Stuttgart: Metzler, 2000), 88–98. Along Schildt's lines, Hodenberg tends to associate cultural critique with anti-modernism, leaving her picture of 1950s debates rather monochrome.

[111] Hannah Arendt, *The Origins of Totalitarianism*, 2nd edn. (Cleveland: World, 1958), 480–510; Arendt, *On Revolution* (New York: Viking, 1963), 217–85. See also Margaret Canovan, *Hannah Arendt: A Reinterpretation of Her Political Thought* (Cambridge: Cambridge University Press, 1992), 144–5, 232–8; Benhabib, "Models of Public Space: Hannah Arendt, the Liberal Tradition, and Jürgen Habermas," in *Habermas and the Public Sphere*, ed. Craig Calhoun (Cambridge, Mass.: MIT Press, 1992), 73–98.

[112] Jürgen Habermas, *Strukturwandel der Öffentlichkeit: Untersuchungen zu einer Kategorie der bürgerlichen Gesellschaft* (Neuwied: Luchterhand, 1962). On Habermas' early career, see Moses, *German Intellectuals*, 105–30; Matthew G. Specter, *Habermas: An Intellectual Biography* (Cambridge: Cambridge University Press, 2010), 27–85.

[113] See, e.g., Calhoun, ed. *Habermas*. Most contributors critically engage with historical and theoretical tensions in the liberal model of the public sphere that Habermas idealizes.

the sphere of "public authority."[114] And although it mediated between state and society, upholding the distinction between them was crucial to its operation; the mutual interpenetration of these spheres under the aegis of the welfare state undermined the public sphere's critical function from the late nineteenth century onward. Even as he exposed its ideological underpinnings and recounted its historical decline, Habermas discerned a transhistorically valid, emancipatory moment in the coming together of private people in the "public use of reason." He called the latter a novel principle of coercion-free control, a "claim to power" that "renounces" any "claim to domination."[115] This idealized principle of communicatively self-generating authority, however, was not logically bound to the historical account of liberalism's emergence as a check or a corrective against established state authority – even if, with no independent historical role to play, it remained obscured from view.[116] The promise accorded publicness as a self-sufficient mode of power expressed a second, more participatory-democratic than liberal, side to Habermas' thinking.[117]

The resonance of engaged democrats' early invocations of publicness with Habermas' later, more systematic formulations is striking. Out of step though they were with the Adenauer era's political climate, such ideas circulated in milieus and media to which Habermas had access, before and after 1949. This was less a question of direct influence and scholarly citation – neither engaged democrats' journalistic nor academic texts are central reference points in Habermas' early work. However, Habermas later recalled the importance of their postwar journals, of the critical impulses preserved into the 1950s by figures such as Jaspers and Kogon, and of the way these were deployed from an "outsider position" against the Adenauer-era "restoration."[118] Their writings and interventions shared with Habermas' emerging theories a common emphasis on the public itself as self-constituting sovereign, rather than on the controlling function of public opinion vis-à-vis the sovereign state. In advance of Habermas' *Structural Transformation*, this nexus of publicness

---

[114] Habermas, *Strukturwandel*, 26–93, here 43.  [115] Ibid., 158–242, quote 41.
[116] Habermas did locate the pre-political roots of the audience-oriented subjectivity of rational-critical public debate in the bourgeois family and its "self-understanding as a sphere of intimately self-generating humanity." He called this self-conception ideological, but "not mere ideology." Ibid., 62.
[117] The distinction drawn here parallels a constitutive tension between liberal legality and democratic legitimacy in Habermas' entire oeuvre; Specter, *Habermas*.
[118] Habermas, *Autonomy and Solidarity: Interviews with Jürgen Habermas*, ed. Peter Dews, rev. edn. (London: Verso, 1992), 229–30. Notably, Mitscherlich and Bloch were among Habermas' influences in this period, as were Jaspers and Sternberger later; ibid., 45, 148; Jan-Werner Müller, *Another Country: German Intellectuals, Unification, and National Identity* (New Haven, Conn.: Yale University Press, 2000), 27–9, 47–8, 93–8.

and democracy infused his 1958 essay on "political participation," which saw participation's potential for the people's democratic self-education being undercut by the mediation of mass parties under elite control.[119] And it was this strand that developed over the 1960s into Habermas' initial formulation of his ideal of consensus rule founded on coercion-free, intersubjective communication unfreighted by the instrumental agendas of money and power.[120] The affinities with immediate postwar affirmations of grassroots, dialogical, extra-institutional political forms are conspicuous. Habermas systematized and formalized pre-theoretical notions that had long been current in engaged democrats' discussions.

These were minority concerns in the new West Germany, ones that engaged democrats championed on the intellectual-political field of the 1950s. Doubtless the most resonant of their positions was the "restoration" diagnosis, the sense that the Bonn Republic's foundation retrod familiar paths under new exigencies and ultimately succeeded in evading the challenge of a sweeping transformation. Although the critique was overdrawn, their disillusionment stimulated productive discontent. Engaged democrats called for a more consequential confrontation with the National Socialist past, supported organized labor's efforts to reform industrial governance and claim political rights, and articulated widespread popular discontent at rearmament and the specter of nuclear destruction. In the process, they helped galvanize fledgling extraparliamentary political initiatives – a version of the cross-class, grassroots coalitions on which they had hoped to build postwar German politics from the start. Both the general diagnosis and the specific critiques and interventions to which it led, however, must be seen in the context of violated immediate postwar hopes. The commitment to "renewal" always accompanied the critique of "restoration," even in its new nightmare configuration of a totally administered world.

Paradoxically, in helping to institutionalize and justify a culture of democratic dissent, of robust public discussion, of reflection on and contrition for Nazism's crimes, and of pro-European idealism, these early critics of the FRG contributed to the gradual, halting establishment of

---

[119] Habermas, "Reflexionen über den Begriff der politischen Beteiligung," in Habermas, et al., *Student und Politik: Eine soziologische Untersuchung zum politischen Bewußtsein Frankfurter Studenten* (Neuwied: Luchterhand, 1961), esp. 15–16, 29–32. See also Moses, *German Intellectuals*, 128–30; Moritz Scheibe, "Auf der Suche nach der demokratischen Gesellschaft," in *Wandlungsprozesse*, ed. Herbert, 254–5.

[120] Habermas, *Technik und Wissenschaft als "Ideologie"* (Frankfurt a.M.: Suhrkamp, 1968), esp. 48–103. This, in turn, planted the seeds of his later discourse ethics and political theory; see also Specter, *Habermas*, 87–132.

its liberal political culture. Yet they also cultivated and sustained a horizon of democratic imagination that exceeded the bounds of postwar Western Europe's democratic model. They continued to place their hopes not primarily in constitutional, representative institutions but in emphatically participatory publicness, as a solution to the democratic renewal of post-fascist Germany. Their unrealized vision from the immediate postwar years thus became a platform from which they contested the postwar order as it consolidated. And the hopes it embodied inspired others as well.

## 8  1968, 1989, and the legacies of participation

Germany's engaged democrats emerged – as a network of actors and an object of study – out of the immediate postwar conjuncture. The imperative they felt to grapple with Nazism's roots and implications converged with their desire to shape a redeemed future, just as Germany's total defeat and four-power occupation left questions of legitimate authority unsettled and the postwar order malleable. Under these unusually favorable conditions, the ideologically plural, loosely bounded intellectual network reconstructed here came together. In their journals, organizations, and congresses, these actors discussed, debated, and proposed concrete measures for Germany's independent renewal. They addressed political and economic institutions as well as the relevance of cultural traditions for a future democratic polity. This was no monolithic program; rather, it embraced liberal, social democratic, left-Christian, and communist variants. These diverse manifestations were linked by a fundamentally participatory sense of what "democracy" meant, one that resisted the imposition of order from above and highlighted the construction of order from below as the actual realization of freedom. Key points of orientation were provided by a cluster of tropes drawn from classical German literature and philosophy, in which these intellectuals saw at once an image of the spontaneous, creative subjectivity democracy required and a symptom of the otherworldliness that had helped make Nazism possible. Engaged democrats hoped to recover and redeploy elements of this national cultural heritage to novel political ends.

The elevated goods of German culture had long served the very prosaic purpose of marking the educated bourgeoisie's status and legitimating their superiority over the "masses." That legacy chafed against the democratic convictions these intellectuals espoused, and they wrestled with its elitist implications. They proposed neither to ennoble working people through access to high culture nor to enshrine themselves as educational dictators but rather to realize a possibility hidden within the tradition: the self-education of each and all through participation itself. At their most consistent, engaged democrats attempted to conduct politics in ways that were adequate to this project. In that sense, there was a homology – albeit an incompletely realized one – between the content of the ideas they formulated and the forms of their other activities. Just as esoteric sociability and aristocratic ideals coincided for postwar Germany's rightist intellectuals, who embraced their temporary exclusion from public life as a virtue, so principles of participation and publicness linked the style of engaged democrats' political thinking to the modes of their intervention and activity.

This immediate postwar vision ran aground on the upsurging Cold War, when the unified, independent Germany on which it was predicated disappeared from the horizon. As an East-West schism set in, some engaged democrats rejected one pole strongly enough that it pushed them to align with the other. Yet even such temporary accommodations were cast in terms that preserved the elements and sustained the force of their earlier positions, despite their manifest defeat at the end of the 1940s. These provided a standpoint from which they then mounted powerful challenges to the order that emerged in the 1950s, on both sides of the geopolitical divide. And these oppositional activities, in turn, transmitted their discourse of participatory publicness well into the postwar period, where it provided a kind of leavening for later political struggles too often seen as appearing *ex nihilo*.

Historians have observed that the years around 1968 and 1989 – like 1945 – witnessed a striking intensification of informal political activism across Europe. War's aftermath, generational transition, and the collapse of state socialism energized various constituencies to pursue an array of political projects outside conventional channels. Scholars have begun to note how these otherwise dissimilar contestations formed and registered a deeper trend: the invigoration of demands for popular participation in the face of established authority, across the postwar decades and to either side of a divided continent. Unsurprisingly, this literature focuses on popular and protest politics.[1] The aim of these concluding reflections is to situate the story of Germany's engaged democrats within that larger frame and ask after their relevance to the broader history of postwar democracy.

### Building the spirit of '68

In the FRG, the complex of agendas and activities conventionally associated under the label "1968" holds pride of place. During the 1950s,

---

[1] This trend is well captured in Gerd-Rainer Horn and Padraic Kenney, eds. *Transnational Moments of Change: Europe 1945, 1968, 1989* (Lanham, Md.: Rowman & Littlefield, 2004) and Belinda Davis, "What's Left? Popular Political Participation in Postwar Europe," *American Historical Review* 113, no. 2 (2008): 363–90.

all across Western Europe, sustained growth, rising affluence, expanding higher education, and proliferating consumer cultures developed alongside a generally conservative, illiberal climate; this stark juxtaposition set the stage for the culturally and politically tumultuous 1960s.[2] At the center of the latter stood a sweeping questioning of authority by a self-consciously young generation (born roughly in the 1940s), whose confrontation with their elders and with established mores and institutions climaxed in open rebellion during the years around 1968. This cohort's youthful self-image can also obscure the wider alliances that brought university and high school students as well as non-academic youth together with their teachers, religious figures, pacifists, publicists, and many others in a transnational, cross-generational "sixty-eighter movement" – one that involved unionists, Social Democrats, and some Communists as well, despite the skepticism of this largely "New Left" configuration toward its "Old Left" predecessors.[3]

In West Germany, global galvanizing issues of university reform and the Vietnam War interacted with local concerns over the legacies of Nazism and the narrowing of party politics. The movement was carried by a motley amalgam of groups that joined forces as an explicitly "Extra-parliamentary Opposition" (APO) after the SPD entered into a Grand Coalition with the CDU in 1966.[4] Intended by Social Democrats as a first step toward parliamentary power, this was widely perceived as the final integration of the last nominally leftist party into the political house that Adenauer built. After the KPD had been banned as an enemy of the constitutional order in 1956, the SPD, at its epochal Godesberg congress of 1959, renounced Marxist theory and class politics, remaking itself as a "people's party" to broaden its appeal after the dispiriting elections of the 1950s.[5]

---

[2] See, e.g., Werner Abelshauser, *Die langen fünfziger Jahre: Wirtschaft und Gesellschaft der Bundesrepublik Deutschland 1949–1966* (Düsseldorf: Schwann, 1987); Arthur Marwick, *The Sixties: Cultural Revolution in Britain, France, Italy, and the United States, c.1958–c.1974* (Oxford: Oxford University Press, 1998).

[3] Ingrid Gilcher-Holtey, *Die 68er-Bewegung: Deutschland – Westeuropa – USA* (Munich: Beck, 2001); Horn, *The Spirit of '68: Rebellion in Western Europe and North America, 1956–1976* (Oxford: Oxford University Press, 2007). Briefly in France and more extensively in Italy and Iberia, middle-class protest also interacted with large-scale working-class activism.

[4] Andrei S. Markovits and Philip S. Gorski, *The German Left: Red, Green, and Beyond* (New York: Oxford University Press, 1993), 46–58; Pavel A. Richter, "Die Außerparlamentarische Opposition in der Bundesrepublik Deutschland 1966 bis 1968," in *1968: Vom Ereignis zum Gegenstand der Geschichtswissenschaft*, ed. Gilcher-Holtey (Göttingen: Vandenhoeck & Ruprecht, 1998), 35–55. To highlight shared opposition to the existing order, Markovits and Gorski refer to the APO as a "negative alliance."

[5] Patrick Major, *The Death of the KPD: Communism and Anti-Communism in West Germany, 1945–1956* (Oxford: Oxford University Press, 1997), 257–93; Kurt Klotzbach,

Engaged democrats' relevance to the sixty-eighter movement can be tracked at a number of interlocking levels. Most generally, they were prominent among those "critical intellectuals" who acted as "custodians of democracy" in the young West Germany, a process of transmission in which older actors served as conduits for oppositional thinking through the 1950s and beyond. Gruppe 47 and the Frankfurt School are usually mentioned in this context, and each had connections to key clusters of engaged democrats.[6] As younger cohorts gained ground within the APO and began to radicalize, however, relations with older figures became tense. Gruppe 47 found itself outflanked on the left and even ridiculed as conformist by younger figures whose critical imaginations their work had helped fire. The resultant frictions within the group itself – pitting those who held fast to pro-SPD positions, such as Heinrich Böll and Günter Grass, against those drawn to the New Left, such as Hans Magnus Enzensberger or Fritz J. Raddatz – led to its demise in fall 1967. Similarly, even as Critical Theory remained a central inspiration for the student movement, tensions mounted between Theodor W. Adorno, Max Horkheimer, and Jürgen Habermas on the one side and their increasingly militant protégés on the other, who often looked to the Frankfurt Institute's more radical affiliate Herbert Marcuse.[7] Engaged democrats likewise came to view younger activists with a mix of support and skepticism. Yet they were encouraged that positions they had helped craft now found a vastly expanded following: the critique of an exculpatory memory politics, opposition to the arms race and Cold War, and dissatisfaction with the prevailing conservative consensus. Their activities had transmitted impulses and a vocabulary of dissent to later protest mobilizations, and the terms in which they castigated the early FRG – "remilitarization," "renazification," and of course "restoration" – resonated widely.

More concretely, ideas and sensibilities were transmitted in specific institutional settings. During the 1960s, engaged democrats continued their activism and circulated in the welter of organizational networks that

---

*Der Weg zur Staatspartei: Programmatik, praktische Politik und Organisation der deutschen Sozialdemokratie 1945–1965* (Berlin: Dietz, 1982), 401–54, 506–32, 588–602.

[6] Rob Burns and Wilfried van der Will, *Protest and Democracy in West Germany: Extra-Parliamentary Opposition and the Democratic Agenda* (New York: St. Martin's Press, 1988), 17–52.

[7] Gilcher-Holtey, "Was kann Literatur und wozu schreiben? Das Ende der Gruppe 47," *Berliner Journal für Soziologie* 14, no. 2 (2004): 207–32; Wolfgang Kraushaar, *Frankfurter Schule und Studentenbewegung: Von der Flaschenpost zum Molotowcocktail 1946–1995*, 3 vols. (Hamburg: Rogner & Bernhard, 1998). On the conflicts among forty-fiver intellectuals precipitated by sixty-eighters' radicalization, see A. Dirk Moses, *German Intellectuals and the Nazi Past* (Cambridge: Cambridge University Press, 2007), 160–218.

constituted the APO. From 1960 on, the initial anti-nuclear movement fed into Easter Marches (a protest form borrowed from Britain), and became the largest pillar of the later APO. The peace movement's constituency grew dramatically as its activities grew less placid and more diverse, a politicizing profile registered in its subsequent name changes: to Campaign for Disarmament (KfA) in 1963 and Campaign for Democracy and Disarmament in 1968.[8] By then, its activities had intertwined with anti-Vietnam protest as well as mounting opposition to proposed emergency laws, which became the APO's second component. A legal framework to expand executive powers and curtail civil liberties in government-declared emergencies had long been on the CDU agenda, and efforts toward that end were a lightning rod for 1960s protest. This opposition had local bases among intellectuals, unionists, and SPD dissenters as well as crucial support from the KfA and the Socialist German Student League (SDS).[9] The latter formed the APO's third, leading element. Founded as the postwar SPD's student affiliate, it came to reject their reformist course, and the SPD declared membership in the two organizations incompatible in 1961. Some faculty and older leftists had organized a Socialist Supporters' Society (SFG) in solidarity, and the SPD ejected those who were members (including Wolfgang Abendroth, who led the initiative). Within the SDS, a traditional, "left-socialist" agenda was dominant until mid decade, when an "anti-authoritarian" faction came to prominence, leading the charge into the APO.[10] Engaged democrats took part in all these mobilizations. Above all, however, it was as publicists and professors that they had contact with younger Germans. Some, such as Alexander Mitscherlich in Frankfurt, Eugen Kogon in Darmstadt, or Ernst Bloch and Hans Mayer, now at Tübingen and Hanover, taught the student rebels. Their and others' published texts and public talks also helped shape activists' perspectives.

---

[8] Karl A. Otto, *Vom Ostermarsch zur APO: Geschichte der außerparlamentarischen Opposition in der Bundesrepublik 1960–1970* (Frankfurt a.M.: Campus, 1977); Holger Nehring, *Politics of Security: British and West German Protest Movements and the Early Cold War, 1945–1970* (Oxford: Oxford University Press, 2013).

[9] Michael Schneider, *Demokratie in Gefahr? Der Konflikt um die Notstandsgesetze: Sozialdemokratie, Gewerkschaften und intellektueller Protest (1958–1968)* (Bonn: Neue Gesellschaft, 1986); Boris Spernol, *Notstand der Demokratie: Der Protest gegen die Notstandsgesetze und die Frage der NS-Vergangenheit* (Essen: Klartext, 2008).

[10] Willy Albrecht, *Der Sozialistische Deutsche Studentenbund (SDS): Vom parteikonformen Studentenverband zum Repräsentanten der Neuen Linken* (Bonn: Dietz, 1994); Siegward Lönnendonker, Bernd Rabehl, and Jochen Staadt, *Die antiautoritäre Revolte: Der Sozialistische Deutsche Studentenbund nach der Trennung von der SPD*, vol. I, *1960–1967* (Wiesbaden: Westdeutscher, 2002); Richard Heigl, *Oppositionspolitik: Wolfgang Abendroth und die Entstehung der Neuen Linken (1950–1968)* (Hamburg: Argument, 2008), 153–7.

In this fashion, established voices of postwar dissent contributed to a mounting critical chorus. Journalists highlighted concerns of the present and the lingering past: Kogon's and Axel Eggebrecht's televised commentary on the 1962 *Spiegel* Affair helped expose the illegality of this government offensive against a critical news outlet, and Eggebrecht's reports from the 1963–5 Frankfurt trial of former Auschwitz staff sought to provoke his radio audience to an overdue confrontation with the Holocaust.[11] Erich Kästner helped establish the standing Easter March organization in 1961 and spoke at the Munich branch's events throughout the decade. Mitscherlich also signed its initial declaration.[12] He was a founding member of the SFG, which Bloch and Alfred Kantorowicz joined as well. Mitscherlich had extensive contact with the SDS, where his daughter Monika was a leading figure, as did Bloch, and others also dialogued with the student organization. SDS Frankfurt, for instance, held a round table with Kogon and Erich Kuby on "Dangers and Opportunities for Democracy" that drew an audience of 900 in 1963.[13] It was above all through the opposition to the Emergency Laws, however, that engaged democrats played roles in the APO. Kogon was central to the coalition building among university-, church-, and union-based circles that fueled the movement. Bloch, Kästner, and Mitscherlich were on the standing "State of Emergency for Democracy" committee; at its founding 1966 congress, which drew 20,000 participants to Frankfurt, both Mitscherlich and Bloch spoke. The crest of the conflict in 1968 saw strike threats, teach-ins, sit-ins, demonstrations, and a 50,000-person march in Bonn. At a last rally organized by Frankfurt intellectuals and televised live on 28 May – two days before emergency legislation passed with SPD support – the roster of speakers included the event's co-conveners Mitscherlich, Adorno, and Habermas, as well as Bloch, Böll, Helmut Gollwitzer, Grass, Kästner, Kogon, and Mayer. It was disrupted by some SDS members in attendance, for whom the assembled professors and literati were insufficiently radical.[14]

---

[11] Christina von Hodenberg, *Konsens und Krise: Eine Geschichte der westdeutschen Medienöffentlichkeit 1945–1973* (Göttingen: Wallstein, 2006), 310–15; Inge Marszolek, "Coverage of the Bergen-Belsen Trial and the Auschwitz Trial in the NWDR/NDR: The Reports of Axel Eggebrecht," in *Holocaust and Justice: Representation and Historiography of the Holocaust in Post-War Trials*, ed. David Bankier and Dan Mikhman (New York: Berghahn, 2010), 131–57.

[12] Otto, *Ostermarsch*, 83, 106–9, 209–10; Sven Hanuschek, *Keiner blickt dir hinter das Gesicht: Das Leben Erich Kästners* (Munich: Hanser, 1999), 402–3.

[13] Tobias Freimüller, *Alexander Mitscherlich: Gesellschaftsdiagnosen und Psychoanalyse nach Hitler* (Göttingen: Wallstein, 2007), 357–76; Heigl, *Oppositionspolitik*, 154; Lönnendonker, Rabehl, and Staadt, *Die antiautoritäre Revolte*, 7, 29, 51, 89, 193, 221.

[14] Schneider, *Demokratie*, 128–9, 152, 182–3, 244–5; Spernol, *Notstand*, 37–9, 49–54, 85–6, 108; Freimüller, *Mitscherlich*, 374–5; "Kundgebung Demokratie im Notstand" flyer, 25 May 1968, Historisches Archiv der Stadt Köln NL Mayer 1333 Box 7.

Engaged democrats' more sustained analyses also gained currency. Responding to a number of triggers, Karl Jaspers sounded the alarm about political conditions in the FRG with his widely read 1966 tract *Where is the Federal Republic Headed?* For him, the *Spiegel* Affair, looming emergency legislation, and the incipient Grand Coalition suggested a recrudescent authoritarianism in formal politics, abetted by apolitical disinterest in the population at large. Moreover, debates about extending the statute of limitations for Nazi-era murder revealed the ongoing inadequacies of Germans' self-reflection on crime and complicity. His reflective intervention provoked strong defensive responses but much agreement in oppositional quarters.[15] In 1967, Alexander Mitscherlich and Margarete Mitscherlich-Nielsen made related claims in a psychoanalytic register. In their controversial *The Inability to Mourn*, they elaborated on Alexander's diagnoses – from as early as 1949 – of Germans' widespread, still unresolved identifications with Hitler and with Nazism's national community. In lieu of processing these losses and forming psychic attachments to the new political order, West Germans had engaged in all manner of defenses and evasions, above all a single-minded pursuit of economic success.[16] These works were highly influential in a climate shaped by extraparliamentary mobilization. Notably, both prescribed an invigoration of popular democratic participation as the cure for what ailed the republic.

Transmitted along such pathways, key elements of engaged democrats' critiques and conceptions reappeared in what social movement analysts call the "cognitive constitution" – the mobilizing values, principles, and aims – of West Germany's diverse New Left.[17] Above all, the "spirit of '68" was shot through with an ideal of participation, as both a prescriptive universal good and a means to the democratic self-education of post-fascist Germans. The student movement, of course, gave "participatory democracy" its name – or rather, the American SDS (Students for a Democratic Society) did, while their European counterparts and interlocutors drew on a more local vocabulary of *Selbstverwaltung, autogestion,* or *autogestione*. This was the language of "self-management" as participatory self-government – rooted first and foremost in the labor movement but also, in Germany, in traditions of university and municipal governance. While engaged democrats had made extensive and intensive

---

[15] Karl Jaspers, *Wohin treibt die Bundesrepublik? Tatsachen, Gefahren, Chancen* (Munich: Piper, 1966); see also Jaspers, *Antwort zur Kritik meiner Schrift "Wohin treibt die Bundesrepublik?"* (Munich: Piper, 1967).
[16] Alexander Mitscherlich and Margarete Mitscherlich, *Die Unfähigkeit zu trauern: Grundlagen kollektiven Verhaltens* (Munich: Piper, 1967); see Freimüller, *Mitscherlich*, 303–21.
[17] Gilcher-Holtey, *68er-Bewegung*, 11–24; Kraushaar, "Denkmodelle der 68er-Bewegung," *Aus Politik und Zeitgeschichte* B22/23 (2001): 14–27.

use of it, the sixty-eighter movement experimented with yet more forms for its realization, not only in the university and the factory but also in a broader palette of "counter-institutions," from alternative kindergartens to neighborhood centers to residential communes.[18] The associated embrace of discussion as participation's privileged medium was taken up and extended by younger activists as well, often in ways that violated the conventions of rational, cultivated exchange to which their elder counterparts hewed, challenging the latter to explore more fully their principles' potentials.[19]

Resonances among engaged democrats' and sixty-eighters' histories and agendas condense strikingly in the figure of West German student activist Rudi Dutschke (1940–1979). He spent his youth in the GDR but grew critical of the regime and relocated to West Berlin in 1961, where he studied sociology at the Free University, joined the situationist group Subversive Action, and soon entered the SDS. He rose rapidly to prominence as the iconic leader and, together with his Frankfurt counterpart Hans-Jürgen Krahl, the most prominent theorist of its new "anti-authoritarian" wing. This faction's distinctive revolutionary conception fused Critical Theory's insights into authoritarian socio-political structures and mentalities with situationist strategies of provocative action.[20] When Dutschke turned to working out a concrete political program, however, he did so in a surprising frame: one centered on Germany's reunification. From the perspective of the cosmopolitan, post-national student movement, this all-German orientation seems perplexing; in light of engaged democrats' earlier programs, it appears less anomalous.[21]

The setting was a heady acceleration of protest in the summer of 1967. The shooting death of an unarmed West Berlin student demonstrator named Benno Ohnesorg on 2 June galvanized unprecedented protest

---

[18] Gilcher-Holtey, *68er-Bewegung*, 113–22; Horn, *Spirit*, 190–220; Detlef Siegfried, *Time Is on My Side: Konsum und Politik in der westdeutschen Jugendkultur der 60er Jahre* (Göttingen: Wallstein, 2006), 645–61.

[19] Nina Verheyen, *Diskussionslust: Zur Kulturgeschichte des 'besseren Arguments' in Westdeutschland* (Göttingen: Vandenhoeck & Ruprecht, 2010), 244–98.

[20] Michaela Karl, *Rudi Dutschke: Revolutionär ohne Revolution* (Frankfurt a.M.: Neue Kritik, 2003), 18–40; Kraushaar, "Autoritärer Staat und antiautoritäre Bewegung: Zum Organisationsreferat von Rudi Dutschke und Hans-Jürgen Krahl," in *Frankfurter Schule*, ed. Kraushaar, III:15–33; Gilcher-Holtey, "Kritische Theorie und Neue Linke," in *1968*, ed. Gilcher-Holtey, 168–87; Siegfried, *Time*, 477–83.

[21] See, e.g., Kraushaar, "Rudi Dutschke und die Wiedervereinigung: Zur heimlichen Dialektik von Nationalismus und Internationalismus," in *1968 als Mythos, Chiffre und Zäsur* (Hamburg: Hamburger Edition, 2000), 89–129; Rüdiger Hentschel, "Zwischen Berliner Kommune und Berliner Republik: Deutschlandpolitische Konzepte bei Rudi Dutschke," in *Die Phantasie an die Macht? 1968 – Versuch einer Bilanz*, ed. Richard Faber und Erhard Stölting (Berlin: Philo, 2002), 50–81.

across the FRG, and SDS leaders moved to formulate strategy for a potentially revolutionary situation. In internal conversations and discussions with associated groups (such as West Berlin's Republican Club), Dutschke elaborated a blueprint for the bottom-up, democratic-socialist transformation and reunification of Germany, one that would serve as a model for overcoming the bipolar global system. Its vital core was a local project: "A West Berlin carried from below by direct council democracy... in all arenas of social life... could become a strategic transmission belt for a future reunification of Germany. Here, an exemplary model of decentralized, real-democratic life could be demonstrated to the two partial states, to the whole world." This participatory-democratic revolution would make West Berlin a global beacon, "a society of true freedom and solidarity," while the Allies would be kept from intervening by the danger of turning the "outpost of the freedom of the Western world" into a replay of "Budapest in 1956, with inverted signs."[22] From West Berlin, an infectious appeal would spread outward, transforming both halves of a divided Germany. Dutschke called this a "national liberation" from "Soviet dictatorship" on the one hand and "American hegemony" on the other. In that frame, he presented council democracy as a specifically German principle, distinct from Western parliamentarism and Eastern statism, one that could serve as a model for the world. Furthermore, he spoke explicitly in terms of recovering a set of positive national traditions last unearthed in the 1950s GDR, in events he had witnessed personally. For his model of spontaneous self-organization, he looked to the uprising of 17 June 1953. And he also connected this workers' revolt to dissident intellectual activity, mentioning the 1956 opposition circles around Bloch and Wolfgang Harich as an inspiration.[23] Dutschke's conception combined a commitment to extra-institutional participatory publicness with a plan for the reunification and neutralization of Germany under democratic-socialist auspices. Rooted in more than a practical recovery of Frankfurt School theory, it was also entwined in the longer history of engaged democrats' activism.

By and large, engaged democrats stood in critical solidarity with the sixty-eighters through the eruptions of 1967–9. Taking to the airwaves as confrontations escalated, Walter Dirks reflected on student activism and the APO as symptoms of a crisis of authority in West Germany. He explained their discontent as a legitimate response to an anachronistic

---

[22] Rudi Dutschke, "Zum Verhältnis von Organisation und Emanzipationsbewegung," in *Frankfurter Schule*, ed. Kraushaar, II:257, 260. This essay appeared in the underground weekly *Oberbaumblatt* on 12 July 1967. On the SDS discussions out of which it arose, see Lönnendonker, Rabehl, and Staadt, *Die antiautoritäre Revolte*, 355–71, 472–7.
[23] Lönnendonker, Rabehl, and Staadt, *Die antiautoritäre Revolte*, 472–3.

project: in the age of modern democracy, the FRG since Adenauer had attempted to re-assert state authority on a "transcendent" basis, expecting "reverence" from its subjects much as divine monarchs once did. Ultimately, its legitimacy deficit was grounded in the "zero hour" of 1945, a "missed chance" to found a true "society of solidarity." It could be redeemed only by a radically forward-looking program to realize the "humane democracy" dreamed of by "rebels" and "reformers" alike.[24] Looking back in 1979, Eggebrecht spoke in similar terms on behalf of West Germany's "angry old men." He wrote of the responsibility they as "grandparents" had felt for the "children's" generation during the "silent" decades, under the sign of their parents' avoidance of the past and their political conformism. The youth had taught their elders new categories such as "repressive tolerance" and "consumption terror" through which to grasp key aspects of that era's "new unfreedom." (Eggebrecht's elisions – that the first phrase stemmed from Marcuse and that he himself had referred to a "soft unfreedom" in 1961 – indicate a more complex set of cross-generational transfers.) In return, he pointed out, the elders had urged more caution in applying terms like "fascistoid" to the FRG; having witnessed actual fascism first-hand, they knew the difference. Although the violence to which such perceived echoes of Nazism had led during the 1970s – as a radical fringe of armed militants clashed with an increasingly securitized state – could not be condoned, it could be understood.[25]

Other distinctions obtained as well. For sixty-eighters, the ideal of participation had loosed itself from the high-cultural moorings that helped suggest it to engaged democrats. The latter, products of an older cultural elite, proved unreceptive to mass culture's democratizing aspects, as new youth and popular styles were crafted to contest the exclusive legitimacy of high culture and the conservative hegemony it underwrote.[26] Nor

---

[24] Walter Dirks, "Autorität," in *Politik für Nichtpolitiker: Ein ABC zur aktuellen Diskussion*, ed. Hans Jürgen Schultz (Stuttgart: Kreuz, 1969), I:48, 54–5. Other contributors to this series of South German Radio broadcasts, "Politics for Non-Politicians," included Kogon, Mitscherlich, Abendroth, Adorno, and Horkheimer.

[25] Axel Eggebrecht, introduction to Eggebrecht, ed. *Die zornigen alten Männer: Gedanken über Deutschland seit 1945* (Reinbek b.H.: Rowohlt, 1979), 8–9, 23–4. Among Eggebrecht's contributors were Kogon, Abendroth, and Böll. On this dynamic of escalating violence as well as its anchors in the wider political-cultural field, see Karrin Hanshew, *Terror and Democracy in West Germany* (Cambridge: Cambridge University Press, 2012), esp. 152–235.

[26] Kaspar Maase, "Establishing Cultural Democracy: Youth, 'Americanization,' and the Irresistible Rise of Popular Culture," in *The Miracle Years: A Cultural History of West Germany, 1949–1968*, ed. Hanna Schissler (Princeton, N.J.: Princeton University Press, 2001), 428–50; Siegfried, *Time*.

were they responsive to the innovative political forms of the sixty-eighter avant-garde, whose protest cultures and lifestyle politics sought a transformation of consciousness through the transformation of everyday practices.[27] Ultimately, a politics of direct action appeared no more on engaged democrats' horizon of possible experience than did experiments in communal living. Much was different in the content and forms of dissent between these older elites and their younger counterparts, who felt themselves a potentially revolutionary constituency at the affluent society's margins. Still, for all the tensions, a kind of mutual recognition held between survivors of the antifascist "other Germany" and the student rebels.[28] Here again, Dolf Sternberger was the exception. Certainly, he shared his peers' concerns over press freedom and emergency legislation. But his response to the protesters, like other moderates provoked into defensive postures by post-1967 radicalization, was markedly more hostile. By 1970, he was experimenting with the self-ascription "conservative," quite explicitly in response to what he saw as student activists' dangerous militancy and dogmatism.[29]

## Revisionism and the revolutions of 1989

In the case of the GDR, the links between engaged democrats' agenda and later dynamics of protest and opposition were more attenuated. The "revisionists" of the 1950s were nonetheless East Germany's first dissidents, and their earlier efforts were recognized and referenced by later initiatives. Viewed in long-term perspective, the Cold War Eastern bloc represents the apex of the socialist tradition's statist, centralizing mainstream, which paternalist Social Democracy bequeathed to vanguardist Leninism and of which Stalinism was both an outgrowth and a distortion. Even so, alternative, decentralist currents and the memory of their mutualist, syndicalist, and council-democratic roots were never eliminated. These militated against socialism's statist incarnations, coming to the fore during periods of upheaval – across Europe in 1945, in 1956 in Hungary, in 1968 in Czechoslovakia, in 1981 in Poland, and across the

---

[27] Gilcher-Holtey, *68er-Bewegung*, 49–56; Martin Klimke, *The Other Alliance: Student Protest in West Germany and the United States in the Global Sixties* (Princeton, N.J.: Princeton University Press, 2009), 54–74.
[28] Claus-Dieter Krohn, "Die westdeutsche Studentenbewegung und das 'andere Deutschland'," in *Dynamische Zeiten: Die 60er Jahre in den beiden deutschen Gesellschaften*, ed. Axel Schildt, Siegfried, and Karl Christian Lammers (Hamburg: Christians, 2000), 695–718.
[29] Claudia Kinkela, *Die Rehabilitierung des Bürgerlichen im Werk Dolf Sternbergers* (Würzburg: Königshausen & Neumann, 2001), 112, 285; Moses, *German Intellectuals*, 198–209, here 201–2, 206.

whole bloc in 1989–90.[30] The linkages that are relevant here belong to this overall trajectory, even if the GDR's special visibility on the Cold War front and the lessons its hardline leadership drew from its early destabilizations (especially that of 1953) kept it locked down and out of the limelight.

After the repressions of 1956–7 revoked all promise of a thaw, many of the GDR's engaged democrats were no longer present to play a role. Going West, however, could also bring hardship. A festschrift on Kantorowicz's seventieth birthday recounted his life's multiple displacements and his isolation in the FRG; its contributors pledged him support as he bore witness to the lost battles of the past, "standing guard in no-man's land."[31] Mayer, in contrast, became a prominent figure on the Western literary-political field, through his work as a scholar and teacher as well as his ongoing association with Gruppe 47. Like many of his peers, he experienced the late 1960s ambivalently. On the one hand, he himself dabbled in activism; on the other, he closed the literary colloquium he had opened at Hanover, for fear of disruptions by unruly students.[32] Bloch embraced the sixty-eighters wholeheartedly, an affinity most directly embodied in his ongoing dialogue and close friendship with Dutschke, which blossomed after they met in early 1968. In return, he was seen as a living icon of Marxism's utopian potential. When Bloch died in 1977, Mayer spoke at a smaller ceremony in his hometown Ludwigshafen. In Tübingen, 2,500 people attended his funeral, and he was eulogized by Dutschke, Oskar Negt, and others. To honor his passing, student activists renamed their Tübingen alma mater "Ernst Bloch University" (although their sign was quietly removed from the school's entrance after a few days).[33] Engaged democrats who remained in the East, in contrast, played marginal roles. By the mid 1960s, the imprisoned were released, but they spent the next decades in relative obscurity: Walter Janka worked in film, Gustav Just as a translator, and Wolfgang Harich

---

[30] Geoff Eley, "Reviewing the Socialist Tradition," in *The Crisis of Socialism in Europe*, ed. Christiane Lemke and Gary Marks (Durham, N.C.: Duke University Press, 1992), 21–60.

[31] Heinz-Joachim Heydorn, introduction to *Wache im Niemandsland: Zum 70. Geburtstag von Alfred Kantorowicz*, ed. Heydorn (Cologne: Wissenschaft und Politik, 1969), 7–33.

[32] *Literarische Welt: Dokumente zum Leben und Werk von Hans Mayer* (Cologne: Historisches Archiv der Stadt Köln, 1985), 95–6, 99–101. For his influence as critic and teacher, see Inge Jens, ed. *Über Hans Mayer* (Frankfurt a.M.: Suhrkamp, 1977).

[33] Peter Zudeick, *Der Hintern des Teufels: Ernst Bloch, Leben und Werk* (Bühl-Moos: Elster, 1985), 315–26; Jürgen Miermeister, *Ernst Bloch, Rudi Dutschke* (Hamburg: Europäische Verlagsanstalt, 1996); Karola Bloch and Adelbert Reif, eds. *"Denken heißt überschreiten": In memoriam Ernst Bloch 1885–1977* (Cologne: Europäische Verlagsanstalt, 1978).

in publishing. While Heinz Zöger rebuilt a career in journalism, he did so in the West, where he fled after his release.[34]

Nonetheless, dissent in the GDR did have a history between the crackdowns of 1957 and the stirrings of the 1980s. Distinct yet parallel "modernizing" trends were shaping the 1960s Eastern bloc. There too, industrial growth and expanding education laid the ground on which belated attention to the consumer sector, limited market mechanisms, access to Western goods and media, and a loosening of overt repression built.[35] Across the satellites, self-consciously cosmopolitan youth cultures as well as critically-minded intelligentsia groups arose. In Czechoslovakia, these met with vigorous liberalizing and democratizing initiatives from within the ruling party itself, producing a dramatic reawakening of public life. The project of "socialism with a human face" flourished in 1968, inspiring reformers everywhere but alarming insecure leaders, especially in Poland and East Germany.[36] This "Prague Spring" and the Soviet-led military intervention that shut it down marked a watershed for the GDR's sixty-eighters. Although they had observed their West German, Czech, and Slovak neighbors with keen interest, the more repressive environment kept restiveness to a minimum. Nonetheless, Czechoslovakia's example galvanized hopes for a humanized socialism just as the SED's support for the invasion undermined the GDR's legitimacy. Spontaneous outbursts of protest occurred, involving workers, students, non-academic youth, and older intellectuals. Gustav Just, a native of the Bohemian borderlands and translator of Czech and Slovak writers, called the Prague Spring "the hope of democratic socialists across the world." It powerfully energized him, and he was bitterly disappointment in its aftermath.[37]

In this, he was far from alone, though others were now the public face of discontent. Above all, these were poet and singer Wolf Biermann (b. 1936) and noted chemist Robert Havemann (1910–1982), committed Marxists who were disciplined for open criticism of the regime in the 1960s. Havemann's sons Frank and Florian were among those arrested

---

[34] Siegfried Prokop, *Ich bin zu früh geboren: Auf den Spuren Wolfgang Harichs* (Berlin: Dietz, 1997), 127–44; Gustav Just, *Deutsch, Jahrgang 1921: Ein Lebensbericht* (Potsdam: Verlag für Berlin-Brandenburg, 2001), 187–213; Helmut Müller-Enbergs et al., eds. *Wer war wer in der DDR? Ein Lexikon ostdeutscher Biographien*, 5th edn. (Berlin: Links, 2010), 605, 1480.

[35] On the GDR's "alternate modernity," see Katherine Pence and Paul Betts, eds. *Socialist Modern: East German Everyday Culture and Politics* (Ann Arbor: University of Michigan Press, 2008).

[36] Kieran Williams, *The Prague Spring and its Aftermath: Czechoslovak Politics, 1968–1970* (Cambridge: Cambridge University Press, 1997).

[37] Stefan Wolle, *Der Traum von der Revolte: Die DDR 1968* (Berlin: Links, 2008); Timothy S. Brown, "'1968' East and West: Divided Germany as a Case Study in Transnational History," *American Historical Review* 114, no. 1 (2009): 69–96; Just, *Deutsch*, quote 201.

for protest in 1968. In the harsher climate that followed the Prague Spring, "dropout" lifestyles absorbed some popular political energies.[38] Others flowed into social niches where oppositional groups began to form, including a "cultural opposition" among artists and writers. During an officially sanctioned concert tour in the FRG in 1976, Biermann – already barred from publishing or performing in the GDR but still a thorn in the regime's side – was stripped of his citizenship and refused re-entry. The action loosed waves of protest at home and abroad, not least an open letter from twelve of East Germany's most famous writers, including Stephan Hermlin and Stefan Heym as well as novelist Christa Wolf (1929–2011) and director Heiner Müller (1929–1995). Soon 106 of their peers had signed, and the letter was published in the West German press, a key vehicle for GDR dissidents. Reinforcing the Prague Spring's effects, the Biermann expulsion helped politicize intellectuals and much broader swaths of activists.[39] In the early 1980s, these gathered in new pacifist, feminist, environmental, and human rights groups as well as an independent peace movement that found shelter under the umbrella of the Protestant Church. Emboldened by Soviet Premier Mikhail Gorbachev's new policies of "openness" and "restructuring," a "civic movement" (*Bürgerbewegung*) of interlinked groups emerged from the church's protected counter-public into the official public sphere, and into confrontation with the regime. A reform movement also developed within the SED, though differences of political orientation and experience made its alliances with the civic movement difficult and fragile.[40]

Economic and political crisis felled the USSR and its empire with unanticipated speed. Viewed schematically, the GDR's 1989 revolution began with a civic movement fronted by intellectuals, gained ground as vast numbers of East Germans mobilized behind calls for democratic reform, and culminated with the people leading the way to national

---

[38] John C. Torpey, *Intellectuals, Socialism, and Dissent: The East German Opposition and its Legacy* (Minneapolis: University of Minnesota Press, 1995), 58–61; Ehrhart Neubert, *Geschichte der Opposition in der DDR 1949–1989* (Berlin: Links, 1997), 154–68; Brown, "'1968,'" 84, 91–4.

[39] Torpey, *Intellectuals*, 64–70; Neubert, *Opposition*, 170–244. On the role of FRG media, see also David Bathrick, *The Powers of Speech: The Politics of Culture in the GDR* (Lincoln, Neb.: University of Nebraska Press, 1995).

[40] Neubert, *Opposition*, 335–823. See also Patrik von zur Mühlen, *Aufbruch und Umbruch in der DDR: Bürgerbewegungen, kritische Öffentlichkeit und Niedergang der SED-Herrschaft* (Bonn: Dietz, 2000); Detlef Pollack, *Politischer Protest: Politisch alternative Gruppen in der DDR* (Opladen: Leske + Budrich, 2000); Rainer Land and Ralf Possekel, *Fremde Welten: Die gegensätzliche Deutung der DDR durch SED-Reformer und Bürgerbewegung in den 80er Jahren* (Berlin: Links, 1998).

unity and material prosperity while leaving the intellectuals behind.[41] In the first two phases, groups that had networked throughout the decade became the catalyzing seeds, gaining mass public support for a vague yet compelling platform in the fall of 1989. On the one hand, this civic revolution called for an invigoration of civil society that the movement itself practiced, from grassroots self-organization to peaceful mass protest to egalitarian "round table" dialogues between government and opposition. On the other hand, activists sought the democratic transformation of socialism from within; most envisioned a future "third way" beyond the Cold War, not a switch from one side to the other. They demanded civil liberties in the classical sense, but as part of a program to expand and deepen democratic participation and popular control, in both politics and the economy. It was these very commitments that left movement leaders unable to engage effectively the desires for basic freedoms and well-being that had brought millions of regular East German citizens out into the streets. Soon, a clear path to realizing these goals was on the table, one that involved not internal reform of the GDR but unification with the FRG. It stoked a groundswell of national feeling.[42]

In linking participation and comprehensive democratization, the activists of 1989 echoed earlier postwar moments. These basic impulses showed clear affinities for those of 1968, although opportunities and outcomes of collective action in those two moments were shaped by important changes in structural context. It was one thing to call for democratic socialism from the seemingly firm ground of postwar economic boom, welfare states in East and West, and Cold War confrontation; it was quite another to do so amid the terminal collapse of state socialism and a globalizing neoliberalism.[43] Beyond 1968, the Soviet satellites had a longer-term tradition of anti-Stalinist mobilization to look back on. Blending an assertion of "bourgeois" freedoms against a rigidly authoritarian state with demands for a de-bureaucratized socialism distinct from both Cold War models, the platforms of 1989 also mirrored those of 1956. Most dramatically in Hungary and Poland, but also in the GDR, the contested

---

[41] Konrad H. Jarausch, *Die unverhoffte Einheit: 1989–1990* (Frankfurt a.M.: Suhrkamp, 1995). On the larger contexts, see also Charles S. Maier, *Dissolution: The Crisis of Communism and the End of East Germany* (Princeton, N.J.: Princeton University Press, 1997); Kenney, *A Carnival of Revolution: Central Europe 1989* (Princeton, N.J.: Princeton University Press, 2002).

[42] Torpey, *Intellectuals*, 79–183; Jarausch, "The Double Disappointment: Revolution, Unification, and German Intellectuals," in *The Power of Intellectuals in Contemporary Germany*, ed. Michael Geyer (Chicago: University of Chicago Press, 2001), 276–94; Martin Sabrow, "Der vergessene 'Dritte Weg,'" *Aus Politik und Zeitgeschichte* B11 (2010): 6–13.

[43] Göran Therborn, *European Modernity and Beyond: The Trajectory of European Societies, 1945–2000* (London: Sage, 1995), 306–34.

legacies of 1950s dissidence served as a reservoir of potent, if sometimes discordant, ideas and identities – not least around democratic socialism – in 1989–91.[44]

It was in this capacity that East Germany's engaged democrats reentered the history of the regime's dissolution. On 28 October 1989, at the civic revolution's height, a long-forgotten Janka was catapulted into the limelight. Three weeks prior, his autobiographical account of the reform discussions of 1956 and ensuing crackdown had been published by Rowohlt and quickly followed by an edition from Aufbau. In East Berlin's Deutsches Theater, at an event facilitated by Müller and introduced by Wolf, vivid excerpts from Janka's memoir were read before an overflow audience. This reading, amplified in radio and television interviews as well as re-stagings elsewhere, caused a sensation. Bringing the "revisionist" moment back into public awareness, it recalled a longer history of struggles, both against state repression and for radical reconstruction.[45] One manifestation of this was activists' demands for the official rehabilitation of earlier victims of "political justice," who had been purged from the party or sentenced for treason. Younger intra-SED reformers joined their civic movement counterparts in cheering the vindication of Janka, Just, and Zöger in early 1990. The judgment against Harich was expunged as well, but to less public fanfare. His reputation had never fully recovered from the 1957 trials, and lingering doubts were fueled by Janka's memoir.[46] Nonetheless, the events of 1989 revived Harich's hopes for a democratic, socialist, unified Germany, and he worked to that end with East German Greens and oppositional Communists. By 1992, however, he bitterly decried the results: not a "reunification" building on accomplishments from both sides but an "annexation" to the West.[47]

The career of one of 1989's leading figures, Stefan Heym (1913–2001), casts a distinct yet related light on that moment's relationship

---

[44] Jarausch, "1968 and 1989: Caesuras, Comparisons, and Connections," in *1968: The World Transformed*, ed. Carole Fink, Philipp Gassert, and Detlef Junker (Cambridge: Cambridge University Press, 1998), 461–77; Eley, "Reviewing," 24–5; Leonid Luks, "Osteuropäische Dissidenten- und Protestbewegungen von 1956–1989 als 'Vorboten' der friedlichen Revolution von 1989–1991," *Forum für osteuropäische Ideen- und Zeitgeschichte* 9, no. 1 (2005): 17–42.

[45] Walter Janka, *Spuren eines Lebens* (Reinbek b.H.: Rowohlt, 1991), 10–11; Janka, *Schwierigkeiten mit der Wahrheit* (Reinbek b.H.: Rowohlt, 1989). For the public resonance, see Alfred Eichhorn and Andreas Reinhardt, eds. *Nach langem Schweigen endlich sprechen: Briefe an Walter Janka* (Berlin: Aufbau, 1990).

[46] Jarausch, *Die unverhoffte Einheit*, 102; Janka, *Spuren*, 12; Prokop, *Geboren*, 170, 179, 277–94. The legal struggle and failed reconciliation efforts that ensued between them gave a late victory to the prosecutors who had long ago set out to divide and conquer the intellectual opposition.

[47] Prokop, *Geboren*, 169–72.

to longer dissent traditions. An antifascist German-Jewish exile and re-émigré, Heym's life path paralleled those of many engaged democrats. As a US Army press officer under Hans Habe, he helped establish *Die Neue Zeitung* but was discharged as excessively pro-Communist in fall 1945. He spent Germany's occupation years in the United States, only to flee the McCarthy era's anti-Communism in 1951 with his wife Gertrude (who, unlike her husband, joined the CPUSA). In 1952, they settled in the GDR. Heym, who never joined a party, wrote plenty that pleased the authorities and was fêted with several prizes. But his work also betrayed an underlying commitment to an ideal of democratic socialism that spared no criticism of socialism's actually existing forms. Loyal, warranted critique was the mode of his 1956 exchange with Ulbricht and his thaw-era journalism, in a widely read Sunday column for the *Berliner Zeitung* called "Speaking Openly" (*Offen gesagt*). Uninhibited dialogue, he explained, was sorely needed while the GDR's citizens worked on their unfinished project together: "Slowly and with difficulty, seeking and often erring, we learn what this new socialist democracy that we want is, and what to do with it." His column's title had occurred to him in June 1953, when the need for "speaking very openly also about very unpleasant things" had made itself clear. Indeed, the workers' uprising deeply unsettled Heym, who wrote about it in his novel *A Day Marked X*. Although this was no unvarnished critique, its depictions of regular citizens' legitimate grievances and the party establishment's bureaucratic blindness were nevertheless unwelcome. In 1957, Heym gave up his column rather than submit to additional censorship, and in 1958, officials rejected his novel about 1953.[48] In subsequent years, he was censured along with Biermann and Havemann, and after he co-organized the protest against Biermann's expulsion, his works were no longer published in the GDR.

In this later phase, both the ideals affirmed in Heym's novels and their historical subject matter put him in proximity to the engaged democrats' project. Two novels in particular traced their author's disillusionment by returning to scenes of earlier dissidence. In his 1979 roman-à-clef *Collin*, the title character and his nemesis Urack are sick old men in the same hospital. One a conformist GDR writer, the other a feared MfS chief, they are bound by an entwined past: Collin is plagued by guilt for remaining silent as his friend Havalka – a Janka-Harich figure – stood trial in the wave of brutal purges overseen by Urack. Collin begins

---

[48] Stefan Heym, *Offen gesagt: Neue Schriften zum Tage* (Berlin: Volk und Welt, 1957), here 8; Peter Hutchinson, *Stefan Heym: The Perpetual Dissident* (Cambridge: Cambridge University Press, 1992), 43–7, 66–7, 82–102. Heym's novel was first published in the FRG as *5 Tage im Juni: Roman* (Munich: Bertelsmann, 1974).

writing his memoirs as therapy, to work through his sickness by bringing to light the truth. Characters resembling Paul Merker, Johannes R. Becher, Georg Lukács, and Helene Weigel populate the novel. Collin dies before finishing, but at the novel's close, a friend finds and spirits the manuscript away, preserving the possibility of a future reckoning with this damaged past. The novel clearly spoke to Heym's present, not least in its central theme of how the goal of a just society had been distorted by the unjust means its builders employed. For his setting, however, he reprised the intellectual opposition of 1956.[49] And in *Schwarzenberg*, published in 1984, Heym went back to the source of engaged democrats' hopes: the moment of liberation. The title referred to a mountainous corner of Saxony that remained unoccupied for six weeks in 1945, forming an oasis of German self-rule that lent itself to subsequent myth-making. In actuality, the everyday tasks of rebuilding and survival dominated local committees' concerns, and a hard core of KPD activists soon embraced authoritarian methods. In Heym's novel, however, the Schwarzenberg district is the site of a self-organizing, grassroots-democratic, nascent socialist republic. A project pursued by the central character Wolfram, it is off to an auspicious start until foiled by doctrinaire party-Communists and the belated Soviet occupation. In the epilogue, Wolfram is a resigned professor in Leipzig who merely lectures on utopian social thought, but the novel closes by suggesting that his students might carry his torch into the future.[50] Together, these two novels sketched a counter-history of the GDR in reverse, reclaiming key moments of what might have been against the grain of what transpired.

It appears Heym sought to reactivate those moments for his present. In the 1980s, he embodied a typically late-socialist paradox: excluded from official public life, he became the GDR's most public intellectual. In 1979, in response to the challenge of *Collin*, the regime took the extraordinary measure of arranging Heym's expulsion from the Writers' Union. On the pretext of currency exchange violations – publishing in the West and receiving royalties without official permission – he was fined and called to account before his colleagues. Heym warned them: besides the SED, "someone else watches how you vote today – the public." Even seemingly insignificant moments could loom large in retrospect,

[49] Heym, *Collin: Roman* (Munich: Bertelsmann, 1979); Hutchinson, *Heym*, 174–85.
[50] Heym, *Schwarzenberg: Roman* (Munich: Bertelsmann, 1984); Hutchinson, *Heym*, 206–13. On the actual history, see Jeannette Michelmann, *Aktivisten der ersten Stunde: Die Antifa in der Sowjetischen Besatzungszone* (Cologne: Böhlau, 2002), 245–66; Gareth Pritchard, *Niemandsland: A History of Unoccupied Germany, 1944–1945* (Cambridge: Cambridge University Press, 2012).

and one day the "citizens of the republic" might ask of them: "How did you act, masters of the word, when it came time to be counted?" Heym and several who stood with him were expelled, but by only a four-fifths majority; his speech emboldened some of his peers to object.[51] Although Heym remained in East Germany, he put the Western media to use in carrying his message, most notably in television interviews easily viewed in GDR living rooms. With the arrival of mass protest in 1989, he played a leading role. The largest demonstration, which saw a half-million marchers in Berlin on 4 November, also marked the apex of cooperation between the civic movement and the critical intelligentsia. Alongside Wolf and Müller, Heym addressed the crowds, clearly elated: "It is as though someone threw open the windows after all the years of stagnation... of phrasemongering and bureaucratic arbitrariness, of official blindness and deafness." Citizens had learned "to speak freely" and "to walk upright," which was crucial. Another step remained: "Let us also learn to govern. Power belongs not in the hands of an individual or a few or an Apparat or a party. All must participate... Socialism – not the Stalinist one, the real one – which we finally want to build... is not thinkable without democracy. But democracy, a Greek word, means rule by the people. Friends! Fellow citizens! Take the power."[52]

Heym did not invest his hopes of 1989 with all-German commitments, like Harich. In fact, he was one of the most scathing critics of the masses' desertion of democratic socialist reform in favor of national unity and consumer capitalism.[53] Yet Heym's invocations of publicness, self-education, and participation powerfully echoed engaged democrats' postwar agenda. It was an agenda to which, however indirectly, they helped ensure activists would have access during East Germany's civic revolution.

Therein lies engaged democrats' signal contribution to postwar German political thought: they justified and defended claims to popular, participatory self-rule against elitist views and their authoritarian implications. In the process, they confronted foils from three distinct contexts of modern political experience simultaneously: from the more distant mandarin

---

[51] Heym, "Nur Devisen – oder nicht doch Literatur?" in *Stalin verlässt den Raum: Politische Publizistik*, ed. Heiner Henniger (Leipzig: Reclam, 1990), 175; Hutchinson, *Heym*, 185–7.
[52] Hutchinson, *Heym*, 188–9, 204–6, 215–24; Jarausch, *Die unverhoffte Einheit*, 79–81; Heym, "Rede auf der Berliner Demonstration," in *Stalin verlässt den Raum*, ed. Henniger, 288–9. See also Heym, *Einmischung: Gespräche, Reden, Essays*, ed. Inge Heym and Henniger (Munich: Bertelsmann, 1990).
[53] Torpey, *Intellectuals*, 163–5.

past, from the recent National Socialist past, and from the Cold War present.

The first context explains the intense stake engaged democrats had in the relationship of German culture to German politics. This gave their participatory agenda a distinctive character, one that fell away in its later permutations. Germans' veneration of *Geist*, *Kultur*, and *Bildung* is often – and not without reason – taken to carry a politically conservative charge. Since the mid-nineteenth century, it served classically educated minorities as a strategy of defense and self-assertion vis-à-vis the uneducated majority. Even for well-meaning reformers and not a few committed revolutionaries, this idealist legacy transmitted a basic elitism that, in the final instance, mistrusted the people to be the agents – not merely the beneficiaries – of their own liberation. In the middle decades of the twentieth century, a wide range of *Sonderweg* theorists diagnosed this German preoccupation with culture as a compensatory outlet for free activity that encouraged submission to worldly authority. Grappling with the latter problem helped engaged democrats work themselves out of the former complex as well. Seeking to overcome the legacy of the "unpolitical German," they recast habits of thought and action typical of the educated middle classes, opening a path from ideas about self-developing subjectivity to affirmations of broad-based democracy, in a paradoxically counter-elitist elite discourse. They then did their part to transmit their concern for the intrinsic value of participation into the postwar period in both West and East, where it became a kind of common ground to the movements around 1968 and 1989. By then, emphases on grassroots democracy and civil society were informed by new accretions of experience and new historical situations, no longer mediated by older ideas about *Kultur*.

Engaged democrats' vision also presented itself as the antipode of a second, more recent German tradition, that of the Weimar and Nazi-era "conservative revolution." The latter had modulated more than transformed itself for the post-Nazi period, and even on the defensive, it loomed large after 1945. In its standard-bearers Carl Schmitt, Martin Heidegger, and Ernst Jünger, engaged democrats discerned a "nihilism" fundamentally opposed to the "humanism" they identified and sought to re-appropriate in the national cultural heritage, the progressive bequest of thinkers from Lessing to Marx. This self-conscious distancing – on which figures from Mayer to Kogon and Harich to Alfred Weber were in agreement – underscores the differences between their critiques of modernity and the cultural pessimism of the right, for all the overlap in their concerns with "technology" and the fate of "the masses." Moreover, it illuminates fundamental contrasts in their basic socio-political principles. Engaged democrats identified the cult of the irreducible "decision" as the polar opposite of the discussion they valued, and they rejected the conception of politics in terms of a struggle between "friend and foe" in favor of broad-based consensus building toward the common good. Above all, they rejected both aristocratic disdain and acclamatory leadership of "the masses" as dangerously elitist political modes, ones that led in fascist directions. In contrast, their views consistently stressed the participatory, self-constituting public as the true subject of politics. The fact that they worked out these positions not only in theoretical or academic texts but primarily in journalistic commentary signals a reconception of intellectuals' roles: they saw themselves as exemplary or model citizens who were nonetheless a part of, not above or outside, the larger public discussion.

In the first postwar decades, these views were those of a minority current. Majority views were more consonant with the socio-political orders of the early Cold War, which each took on their own authoritarian cast. The world of the postwar boom in East and West was one in which large-scale institutional actors coordinated social life to an unprecedented extent — what interest groups, parties, and the state negotiated in welfare capitalism, the central plan arrogated to itself in state socialism's "welfare dictatorship."[54] For all the ideological claim laid to democracy by both sides, and for all the obvious differences between the two systems, power and control in the engineered societies of the era of "high modernism" seemed to rest less with the people than with legions of planners, technocrats, managers, and officials.[55]

The mainstreams of social and political thought during the 1950s and 1960s show clear affinities for this basic orientation. The FRG was consolidated under conservative, if not necessarily restorative auspices, a theme that made room for diverse intellectual variations. The "technocratic conservatism" of sociologists Arnold Gehlen and Helmut Schelsky or jurist Ernst Forsthoff, who adapted Schmittian perspectives to a technological world as virtue to necessity, fit under this heading.[56] So too did the anti-populist constitutionalism of political theorist

---

[54] Therborn, *European Modernity and Beyond*, esp. 55–163; Jarausch, "Care and Coercion: The GDR as Welfare Dictatorship," in *Dictatorship as Experience: Towards a Socio-Cultural History of the GDR*, ed. Jarausch (Providence, R.I.: Berghahn, 1999), 47–69.

[55] David Harvey, *The Condition of Postmodernity: An Enquiry into the Origins of Cultural Change* (Oxford: Blackwell, 1989), 35–6; James C. Scott, *Seeing Like a State: How Certain Schemes to Improve the Human Condition Have Failed* (New Haven, Conn.: Yale University Press, 1998), 88–90; Odd Arne Westad, *The Global Cold War: Third World Interventions and the Making of Our Times* (Cambridge: Cambridge University Press, 2005), 397.

[56] Dirk van Laak, "From the Conservative Revolution to Technocratic Conservatism," in *German Ideologies since 1945: Studies in the Political Thought and Culture of the Bonn Republic*, ed. Jan-Werner Müller (New York: Palgrave Macmillan, 2003), 147–60; also Paul Nolte, *Die Ordnung der deutschen Gesellschaft: Selbstentwurf und Selbstbeschreibung im 20.*

Wilhelm Hennis and the liberal-pluralist elitism of sociologist Ralf Dahrendorf.[57] The GDR stayed the centralized course it had set from the start. This remained the case even as the early planning metaphysics that suffused the work of economists such as Robert Naumann, jurists such as Karl Polak, and philosophers such as Rugard Otto Gropp ceded ground to a 1960s flirtation with cybernetics.[58] What these perspectives shared – for all the distinctions, dissimilarities, and tensions among them – was an emphasis on the integrative legitimacy of superordinate institutions, executive authority, or expert rule. These were top-down orientations fully in tune with the tenor of the period. The alternative, bottom-up vision of the polity burst vividly onto the scene during the social and political ferment of the 1960s, to be reprised, under different conditions, in the large-scale unrest of the 1980s. Decades earlier, however, it had been anticipated in a spark of grassroots counter-elitism from a faction of the postwar elites themselves.

The axis of top-down, authoritarian versus bottom-up, participatory perspectives may constitute the crucial fault line of postwar German political theory. And as the story of Germany's engaged democrats has shown, this cleavage was not limited to major treatises by top thinkers but fundamentally configured a wider field of public debate. To focus on their practical political failure in the occupation period thus obscures their longer-term contribution to political thought, and to more besides. For correspondences emerge between the histories of these intellectual discourses and concepts and other histories of concrete projects and struggles, from the immediate postwar years' antifascist committees to extra-institutional protest movements in the 1950s to diverse experiments in self-management circa 1968 to massive civic mobilizations circa 1989. The homologies among these different kinds of phenomena suggest that participatory democracy has a longer, richer, and potentially more surprising postwar genealogy than we are presently aware.

*Jahrhundert* (Munich: Beck, 2000), 235–350. On the adaptation of these themes by influential "liberal conservatives" after 1968, see Jens Hacke, *Philosophie der Bürgerlichkeit: Die liberalkonservative Begründung der Bundesrepublik* (Göttingen: Vandenhoeck & Ruprecht, 2006).

[57] Moses, *German Intellectuals*, 74–104; Stephan Schlak, *Wilhelm Hennis: Szenen einer Ideengeschichte der Bundesrepublik* (Munich: Beck, 2008), 75–116; Morten Reitmayer, *Elite: Sozialgeschichte einer politisch-gesellschaftlichen Idee in der frühen Bundesrepublik* (Munich: Oldenbourg, 2009), 517–60.

[58] Peter C. Caldwell, *Dictatorship, State Planning, and Social Theory in the German Democratic Republic* (Cambridge: Cambridge University Press, 2003).

# Select bibliography

This bibliography references all unpublished and most published primary sources used. Of secondary works cited and consulted, it lists the more important works.

## ARCHIVES

Archiv der sozialen Demokratie, Bonn (AdsD)
 Nachlass Walter Dirks
 Bestand Europa Union Deutschland
 Bestand Frankfurter Hefte
 Nachlass Eugen Kogon
  (At the time of research, this collection was held privately. It has since been deposited at the AdsD and will eventually be available to researchers there. Box and file designations reflect the collection's organization prior to processing by the AdsD.)
 Nachlass Paul Löbe
 Nachlass Carlo Schmid

Bundesarchiv, Berlin (BArch)
 Deutsche Film AG / DEFA (DR 117)
 Kulturbund (DY 27)
 Ministerium für Hoch- und Fachschulwesen (DR 3)
 Nachlass Walter Ulbricht (NY 4182)
 Zentralsekretariat SED (DY 30)

Bundesarchiv, Koblenz (BArch)
 Nachlass Ferdinand von Friedensburg (N 1114)
 Nachlass Rudolf Pechel (N 1160)
 Nachlass Alfred Weber (N 1197)
 Nachlass Peter von Zahn (N 1524)

Deutsches Exilarchiv 1933–1945, Frankfurt a.M.
 Nachlass Karl Wilczynski (EB 87/100)

Deutsches Literaturarchiv, Marbach a.N. (DLA)
 Nachlass Erich Kästner (A: Kästner)

Nachlass Dolf Sternberger (A: Sternberger)
Nachlass Günther Weisenborn (A: Weisenborn)

Hauptstaatsarchiv Stuttgart (HStAS)
Mikrofiche-Sammlung OMGUS (J384)

Historisches Archiv der Stadt Köln, Cologne (HAStK)
Nachlass Hans Mayer (1333)

Internationaal Instituut voor Sociale Geschiedenis, Amsterdam (IISG)
Wolfgang Harich Papers

Landesarchiv Berlin (LAB)
Nachlass Ursula Madrasch-Groschopp (E Rep 200–63)

Staats- und Universitätsbibliothek Hamburg (SUBH)
Nachlass Axel Eggebrecht (NE)
Nachlass Alfred Kantorowicz (NK)

Stiftung Archiv der Akademie der Künste, Berlin (AdK)
Johannes R. Becher-Archiv
Herbert Ihering-Archiv
Rudolf Leonhard-Archiv
Erik Reger-Archiv
Paul Rilla-Archiv
Maximilian Scheer-Archiv
Archiv Schriftstellerverband der DDR
Max Schroeder-Archiv
Günther Weisenborn-Archiv

Universitätsbibliothek Heidelberg (UBH)
Nachlass Alfred Weber (Heid. Hs. 4069)

## NEWSPAPERS AND JOURNALS

*Aufbau*
*Der Autor*
*Berliner Zeitung*
*Deutsche Kommentare*
*Einheit*
*Frankfurter Hefte*
*Frankfurter Rundschau*
*Die Gegenwart*
*Gewerkschaftliche Monatshefte*
*hier und heute*
*Der Kurier*
*Der Monat*

*Die Neue Zeitung*
*Neues Deutschland*
*Nordwestdeutsche Hefte*
*Ost und West*
*Rhein-Neckar-Zeitung*
*Der Ruf*
*Sonntag*
*Das sozialistische Jahrhundert*
*Der Spiegel*
*Der Tagesspiegel*
*Tägliche Rundschau*
*Der Telegraf*
*Ulenspiegel*
*Die Wandlung*
*Die Welt*
*Die Weltbühne*
*Wissen und Tat*

## OTHER PUBLISHED PRIMARY SOURCES

Ackermann, Anton. "Unsere kulturpolitische Sendung." In *Um die Erneuerung der deutschen Kultur: Erste Zentrale Kulturtagung der Kommunistischen Partei Deutschlands*, 35–54. Berlin: Neuer Weg, 1946.

Adorno, Theodor W., Max Horkheimer, and Eugen Kogon. "Die verwaltete Welt oder: Die Krisis des Individuums." In Horkheimer, *Gesammelte Schriften*, vol. XIII, *Nachgelassene Schriften 1949–1972*, 121–42. Frankfurt a.M.: Fischer, 1989.

Alewyn, Richard. "Goethe als Alibi?" *Hamburger Akademische Rundschau* 3, no. 8–10 (1949): 685–7.

Andersch, Alfred. "Der Seesack: Aus einer Autobiographie." In *Das Alfred Andersch Lesebuch*, ed. Gerd Haffmans, 83–101. Zurich: Diogenes, 1979.

Arendt, Hannah. *On Revolution*. New York: Viking, 1963.

*The Origins of Totalitarianism*. New York: Harcourt Brace, 1951.

Becher, Johannes R. *Briefe*. 2 vols., ed. Rolf Harder. Berlin: Aufbau, 1993.

Bechtoldt, Heinrich. *Literatur und Politik: Sieben Vorträge zur heutigen Situation in Deutschland*. Constance: Asmus, 1948.

Becker, Hellmut. "Freiheit, Sozialismus, Psychoanalyse: Anmerkungen zu Begegnungen mit Alexander Mitscherlich von einem Nichtanalysierten." *Merkur* 32 (1978): 923–37.

Berding, Helmut, ed. *Die Entstehung der hessischen Verfassung von 1946: Eine Dokumentation*. Wiesbaden: Historische Kommission für Nassau, 1996.

Beutler, Ernst. *Besinnung: Ansprache zur Feier von Goethes Geburtstag, gehalten im Freien Deutschen Hochstift zu Frankfurt a.M. am 28. August 1945*. Wiesbaden: Dieterich, 1946.

Birkenfeld, Günther. "Flucht aus der Gegenwart." *Horizont* 2, no. 24 (1947): 3.

Bloch, Ernst. *Freiheit und Ordnung: Abriß der Sozial-Utopien*. Berlin: Aufbau, 1947.

*Das Prinzip Hoffnung*. 3 vols. Berlin: Aufbau, 1954–9.
*Subjekt-Objekt: Erläuterungen zu Hegel*. Berlin: Aufbau, 1951.
"Über die Bedeutung des 20. Parteitags." In *Viele Kammern im Welthaus: Eine Auswahl aus dem Werk*, ed. Friedrich Dieckmann and Jürgen Teller, 494–505. Frankfurt a.M.: Suhrkamp, 1994.
Bloch, Karola. *Aus meinem Leben*. Pfullingen: Neske, 1981.
Brecht, Bertolt. *Poems, 1913–1956*. 2nd edn., ed. John Willett and Ralph Manheim. London: Methuen, 1979.
Brollik, Peter, and Klaus Mannhardt, eds. *Blaubuch 1958: Kampf dem Atomtod – Dokumente und Aufrufe*. Essen: Klartext, 1988.
Burgmüller, Herbert, ed. *Zur Klärung der Begriffe: Beiträge zur Neuordnung der Werte*. Munich: Weismann, 1947.
Caysa, Volker, Petra Caysa, K. D. Eichler, and Elke Uhl, eds. *"Hoffnung kann enttäuscht werden": Ernst Bloch in Leipzig*. Frankfurt a.M.: Hain, 1992.
Crossman, R. H. S., ed. *The God That Failed*. New York: Harper, 1949.
Crusius, Reinhard, and Manfred Wilke, eds. *Entstalinisierung: Der XX. Parteitag der KPdSU und seine Folgen*. Frankfurt a.M.: Suhrkamp, 1977.
Dirks, Walter. "Als wir die Ärmel aufkrempelten – zum Beispiel in Frankfurt." *Neue Gesellschaft / Frankfurter Hefte* 32, no. 4 (1985): 316–18.
"Autorität." In *Politik für Nichtpolitiker: Ein ABC zur aktuellen Diskussion*, ed. Hans Jürgen Schultz, I:47–56. Stuttgart: Kreuz, 1969.
"Folgen der Entnazifizierung: Ihre Auswirkungen in kleinen und mittleren Gemeinden der drei westlichen Zonen." In *Sociologica: Aufsätze, Max Horkheimer zum sechzigsten Geburtstag gewidmet*, 445–70. Frankfurt a.M.: Europäische Verlagsanstalt, 1955.
*Der singende Stotterer: Autobiographische Texte*. Munich: Kösel, 1983.
"Vorschlag zu einer Sozialistischen Einheitspartei." In *Christen für den Sozialismus*, vol. II, *Dokumente (1945–1959)*, ed. Dirks, Klaus Schmidt and Martin Stankowski, 42–4. Stuttgart: Kohlhammer, 1975.
"Zwiespältige Erfahrungen." In *Weihnachten 1945: Ein Buch der Erinnerungen*, ed. Claus Hinrich Casdorff, 83–91. Munich: Deutscher Taschenbuch Verlag, 1984.
Drews, Richard, and Alfred Kantorowicz, eds. *Verboten und verbrannt: Deutsche Literatur 12 Jahre unterdrückt*. Berlin: Ullstein-Kindler, 1947.
Dutschke, Rudi. "Zum Verhältnis von Organisation und Emanzipationsbewegung – Zum Besuch Herbert Marcuses." In *Frankfurter Schule und Studentenbewegung: Von der Flaschenpost zum Molotowcocktail 1946–1995*, ed. Wolfgang Kraushaar, II:255–60. Hamburg: Rogner & Bernhard, 1998.
Eggebrecht, Axel. "Aktiver Friede." In *Welt ohne Krieg: Ein Lese- und Volksbuch für junge Europäer*, ed. Otto Gollin, 5–9. Düsseldorf: Komet, 1948.
*Der halbe Weg: Zwischenbilanz einer Epoche*. Reinbek b.H.: Rowohlt, 1975.
"Der Schriftsteller und der Staat." In *Vorträge gehalten anläßlich der Hessischen Hochschulwoche für Staatswissenschaftliche Fortbildung 23. bis 29. April 1967 in Bad Wildungen*, 55–77. Bad Homburg: Gehlen, 1968.
*Was wäre, wenn...: ein Rückblick auf die Zukunft der Welt*. Hamburg: Hammerich & Lesser, 1947.
*Weltliteratur: Ein Überblick*. Hamburg: Springer, 1948.

ed. *Die zornigen alten Männer: Gedanken über Deutschland seit 1945*. Reinbek b.H.: Rowohlt, 1979.

Engels, Friedrich. *Herrn Eugen Dührings Umwälzung der Wissenschaft.* In Karl Marx and Engels, *Werke*, vol. XX, 1–303. Berlin: Dietz, 1962.

"Entschließung zur Kulturpolitik." In *Protokoll der Verhandlungen des Ersten Kulturtages der Sozialistischen Einheitspartei Deutschlands*, 263–70. Berlin: Dietz, 1948.

"Frankfurter Leitsätze." In Joachim Rotberg, *Zwischen Linkskatholizismus und bürgerlicher Sammlung: Die Anfänge der CDU in Frankfurt am Main 1945–1946*, 223–33. Frankfurt a.M.: Knecht, 1999.

Franzke, Michael, ed. *Die ideologische Offensive: Ernst Bloch, SED und Universität*. Leipzig: Leipziger Universitätsverlag, 1992.

*Freiheit dem Kulturbund: Die Kundgebung in den Sälen des Berliner Funkhauses am 26. Nov. 1947*. Berlin: Aufbau, 1947.

Friedensburg, Ferdinand. *Es ging um Deutschlands Einheit: Rückschau eines Berliners auf die Jahre nach 1945*. Berlin: Haude & Spener, 1971.

Geiler, Karl, Gustav Dahrendorf, Gerhard Kroll, Hans Luther, Ehrhart Heldmann, and Dolf Sternberger. *Das Wählen und das Regieren: Das Problem der parlamentarischen Demokratie*. Darmstadt: Deutsche Wählergesellschaft, 1949.

Habermas, Jürgen. *Autonomy and Solidarity: Interviews with Jürgen Habermas*. Rev. edn., ed. Peter Dews. London: Verso, 1992.

"Reflexionen über den Begriff der politischen Beteiligung." In *Student und Politik: Eine soziologische Untersuchung zum politischen Bewußtsein Frankfurter Studenten*, ed. Habermas, Ludwig von Friedeburg, Christoph Oehler, and Friedrich Weltz, 11–55. Neuwied: Luchterhand, 1961.

*Strukturwandel der Öffentlichkeit: Untersuchungen zu einer Kategorie der bürgerlichen Gesellschaft*. Neuwied: Luchterhand, 1962.

*Technik und Wissenschaft als "Ideologie."* Frankfurt a.M.: Suhrkamp, 1968.

Harich, Wolfgang. *Ahnenpass: Versuch einer Autobiographie*, ed. Thomas Grimm. Berlin: Schwarzkopf & Schwarzkopf, 1999.

*Keine Schwierigkeiten mit der Wahrheit: Zur nationalkommunistischen Opposition 1956 in der DDR*. Berlin: Dietz, 1993.

Hay, Gerhard, Hartmut Rambaldo, and Joachim W. Storck, eds. *"Als der Krieg zu Ende war": Literarisch-politische Publizistik 1945–1950*. Stuttgart: Klett, 1973.

Heider, Magdalena, and Kerstin Thöns, eds. *SED und Intellektuelle in der DDR der fünfziger Jahre: Kulturbund-Protokolle*. Cologne: Wissenschaft und Politik, 1990.

Hermand, Jost, and Wigand Lage. *"Wollt ihr Thomas Mann wiederhaben?" Deutschland und die Emigranten*. Hamburg: Europäische Verlags-Anstalt, 1999.

Hermlin, Stephan, and Hans Mayer. *Ansichten über einige neue Schriftsteller und Bücher*. Wiesbaden: Limes, 1947.

Heydorn, Heinz-Joachim, ed. *Wache im Niemandsland: Zum 70. Geburtstag von Alfred Kantorowicz*. Cologne: Wissenschaft und Politik, 1969.

Heym, Stefan. *Collin: Roman*. Munich: Bertelsmann, 1979.

*Offen gesagt: Neue Schriften zum Tage.* Berlin: Volk und Welt, 1957.
*Schwarzenberg: Roman.* Munich: Bertelsmann, 1984.
*Stalin verlässt den Raum: Politische Publizistik*, ed. Heiner Henniger. Leipzig: Reclam, 1990.
Holborn, Hajo. "Der deutsche Idealismus in sozialgeschichtlicher Beleuchtung." *Historische Zeitschrift* 174 (1952): 359–84.
Janka, Walter. *Schwierigkeiten mit der Wahrheit.* Reinbek b.H.: Rowohlt, 1989.
*Spuren eines Lebens.* Reinbek b.H.: Rowohlt, 1991.
Jaspers, Karl. *Die Idee der Universität.* Berlin: Springer, 1946.
*Die Schuldfrage: Ein Beitrag zur deutschen Frage.* Heidelberg: Schneider, 1946.
*Wohin treibt die Bundesrepublik? Tatsachen, Gefahren, Chancen.* Munich: Piper, 1966.
Jünger, Ernst. *Der Friede: Ein Wort an die Jugend Europas und an die Jugend der Welt.* [Amsterdam]: Die Argonauten, n.d.
Just, Gustav. *Deutsch, Jahrgang 1921: Ein Lebensbericht.* Potsdam: Verlag für Berlin-Brandenburg, 2001.
*Zeuge in eigener Sache: Die fünfziger Jahre.* Berlin: Der Morgen, 1990.
Kantorowicz, Alfred. *Deutsches Tagebuch.* 2 vols. Munich: Kindler, 1959–61.
*Spanisches Tagebuch.* Berlin: Aufbau, 1948.
*Der Tag des Freien Buches: Zum Gedenken an die Bücherverbrennungen vom 10. Mai 1933.* Berlin: Deutsche Verwaltung für Volksbildung, 1947.
*Vom moralischen Gewinn der Niederlage: Artikel und Ansprachen.* Berlin: Aufbau, 1949.
Kästner, Erich. *Das blaue Buch: Kriegstagebuch und Roman-Notizen*, ed. Ulrich Bülow and Silke Becker. Marbach a.N.: Deutsche Schillergesellschaft, 2006.
*Gesammelte Schriften.* Vol. V, *Vermischte Beiträge.* Cologne: Kiepenheuer & Witsch, 1959.
*Die kleine Freiheit: Chanson und Prosa 1949–1952.* Zurich: Atrium, 1952.
*Notabene 45: Ein Tagebuch.* Zurich: Atrium, 1961.
*Der tägliche Kram: Chansons und Prosa 1945–1948.* Zurich: Atrium, 1949.
Klemperer, Victor. *LTI: Notizbuch eines Philologen.* Berlin: Aufbau, 1947.
Kogon, Eugen. *Gesammelte Schriften.* Vol. VI, *"Dieses merkwürdige, wichtige Leben": Begegnungen*, ed. Michael Kogon and Gottfried Erb. Weinheim: Beltz Quadriga, 1997.
*Der SS-Staat: Das System der deutschen Konzentrationslager.* Frankfurt a.M.: Verlag der Frankfurter Hefte; Düsseldorf: Schwann; Munich: Alber, 1946.
Krauss, Werner. *Briefe 1922 bis 1976*, ed. Peter Jehle. Frankfurt a.M.: Klostermann, 2002.
*PLN: Die Passionen der halykonischen Seele: Roman.* Frankfurt a.M.: Klostermann, 1946.
*Vor gefallenem Vorhang: Aufzeichnungen eines Kronzeugen des Jahrhunderts*, ed. Manfred Naumann. Frankfurt a.M.: Fischer Taschenbuch Verlag, 1995.
Lehmstedt, Mark, ed. *Der Fall Hans Mayer: Dokumente 1956–1963.* Leipzig: Lehmstedt, 2007.
Leonhard, Rudolf. *Plaidoyer pour la démocratie allemande.* Paris: Raisons d'être, 1947.
*Unsere Republik: Aufsätze und Gedichte.* Berlin: Kongreß, 1951.

Leonhard, Susanne. *Gestohlenes Leben: Schicksal einer politischen Emigrantin in der Sowjetunion.* Frankfurt a.M.: Europäische Verlagsanstalt, 1956.

Leonhard, Wolfgang. "Im Fadenkreuz der SED: Meine Flucht von der Parteihochschule 'Karl Marx' im März 1949 und die Aktivitäten der Zentralen Parteikontroll-Kommission." *Vierteljahrshefte für Zeitgeschichte* 46, no. 2 (1998): 283–310.

*Meine Geschichte der DDR.* Berlin: Rowohlt, 2007.

*Die Revolution entläßt ihre Kinder.* Cologne: Kiepenheuer & Witsch, 1955.

Lukács, Georg. *Essays über Realismus.* Berlin: Aufbau, 1948.

*Geschichte und Klassenbewußtsein: Studien über marxistische Dialektik.* In *Werke*, vol. II, *Frühschriften*, 161–517. Neuwied: Luchterhand, 1968.

*Der junge Hegel: Über die Beziehungen von Dialektik und Ökonomie.* Berlin: Aufbau, 1948.

*Manifest und Ansprachen: Gehalten bei der Gründungskundgebung des Kulturbundes zur demokratischen Erneuerung Deutschlands am 4. Juli 1945.* Berlin: Aufbau, 1945.

Mann, Thomas, Frank Thieß, and Walter von Molo. *Ein Streitgespräch über die äußere und die innere Emigration.* Dortmund: Druckschriften Vertriebsdienst, 1946.

Marcuse, Herbert. "Über den affirmativen Charakter der Kultur." *Zeitschrift für Sozialforschung* 6, no. 1 (1937): 54–94.

Mayer, Hans. *Briefe 1948–1963*, ed. Mark Lehmstedt. Leipzig: Lehmstedt, 2006.

*Ein Deutscher auf Widerruf: Erinnerungen.* 2 vols. Frankfurt a.M.: Suhrkamp, 1982–4.

*Karl Marx und das Elend des Geistes: Studien zur neuen deutschen Ideologie.* Meisenheim a.G.: Hain, 1948.

*Der Turm von Babel: Erinnerung an eine Deutsche Demokratische Republik.* Frankfurt a.M.: Suhrkamp, 1991.

Meinecke, Friedrich. *Die deutsche Katastrophe: Betrachtungen und Erinnerungen.* Wiesbaden: Brockhaus, 1946.

Menne, Ferdinand. "Dirks & Kogon: Eine Momentaufnahme." *Neue Gesellschaft/Frankfurter Hefte* 50 (2003): 76.

Mitscherlich, Alexander. *Endlose Diktatur?* Heidelberg: Schneider, 1947.

*Ein Leben für die Psychoanalyse: Anmerkungen zu meiner Zeit.* Frankfurt a.M.: Suhrkamp, 1980.

Mitscherlich, Alexander, and Fred Mielke. *Das Diktat der Menschenverachtung: Eine Dokumentation.* Heidelberg: Schneider, 1947.

Mitscherlich, Alexander, and Margarete Mitscherlich. *Die Unfähigkeit zu trauern: Grundlagen kollektiven Verhaltens.* Munich: Piper, 1967.

Mitscherlich, Alexander, and Alfred Weber. *Freier Sozialismus.* Heidelberg: Schneider, 1946.

Mugdan, Ernst, ed. *Die Neutralität Deutschlands und der Friede: Beiträge zur Bildung einer öffentlichen Meinung in Deutschland.* Heidelberg: Schneider, 1947.

ed. *Unteilbarkeit des Friedens und Unteilbarkeit Deutschlands: Eine Diskussion.* Heidelberg: Schneider, 1947.

ed. *Zur völkerrechtlichen Lage Deutschlands – Ruhrfrage und Friedenssicherung – Zur künftigen Deutschen Gesamtverfassung.* Heidelberg: Schneider, 1948.

Pechel, Rudolf. "Von Himmler zu Harich." *Deutsche Rundschau* 69, no. 6 (1946): 173–9.
Pikart, Eberhard, and Wolfram Werner, eds. *Der Parlamentarische Rat, 1948–1949: Akten und Protokolle.* Vol. V, *Ausschuss für Grundsatzfragen.* Boppard a.R.: Boldt, 1993.
Plievier, Theodor. *Einige Bemerkungen über die Bedeutung der Freiheit.* Nuremberg: Nest, 1948.
*Das Problem der Freiheit im Lichte des wissenschaftlichen Sozialismus: Konferenz der Sektion Philosophie der Deutschen Akademie der Wissenschaften zu Berlin, 8.–10. März 1956.* Berlin: Akademie, 1956.
"Protocol of the Berlin (Potsdam) Conference, August 1, 1945." In *Documents on Germany, 1944–1959*, 24–35. Washington, D.C.: U.S. Government Printing Office, 1959.
Reinhold, Ursula, Dieter Schlenstedt, and Horst Tanneberger, eds. *Erster deutscher Schriftstellerkongreß 4.–8. Oktober 1947: Protokoll und Dokumente.* Berlin: Aufbau, 1997.
*Rettet Einheit, Freiheit, Frieden! Gegen Kommunismus und Nationalismus.* Frankfurt a.M., 1955.
Richter, Hans Werner, ed. *Bestandsaufnahme: Eine deutsche Bilanz 1962.* Munich: Desch, 1962.
Ringshausen, Gerhard, and Rüdiger von Voss, eds. *Die Ordnung des Staates und die Freiheit des Menschen: Deutschlandpläne im Widerstand und Exil.* Bonn: Bouvier, 2000.
Röpke, Wilhelm. *Die deutsche Frage.* 2nd edn. Erlenbach-Zurich: Rentsch, 1945.
Röpke, Wilhelm, Arthur Fridolin Utz, Friedrich Wolfhard Bürgi, Jean Gebser, Valentin Gitermann, and Jeanne Hersch. *Kommt der vierte Mensch?* Zurich: Europa, 1952.
Rosenbach, Harald, ed. *Der Parlamentarische Rat 1948–1949: Akten und Protokolle.* Vol. VI, *Ausschuss für Wahlrechtsfragen.* Boppard a.R.: Boldt, 1994.
Sandberg, Herbert. *Spiegel eines Lebens: Erinnerungen, Aufsätze, Notizen und Anekdoten.* Berlin: Aufbau, 1988.
Scheer, Maximilian. ed. *Freunde über Rudolf Leonhard.* Berlin: Verlag der Nation, 1958.
*Ein unruhiges Leben: Autobiographie.* Berlin: Verlag der Nationen, 1975.
Schneider, Lambert. *Rechenschaft über vierzig Jahre Verlagsarbeit 1925–1965.* Heidelberg: Schneider, 1965.
Schnog, Karl. *Jedem das Seine: Satirische Gedichte.* Berlin: Ulenspiegel, 1947.
Steiniger, Alfons. *Das Blocksystem: Beitrag zu einer demokratischen Verfassungslehre.* Berlin: Akademie, 1949.
Stern, Fritz. "The Political Consequences of the Unpolitical German." *History* 3 (1960): 104–34.
Sternberger, Dolf. "Das deutsche Wahlwunder." In *Das deutsche Wahlwunder,* ed. Christian-Claus Baer and Erwin Faul, 13–20. Frankfurt a.M.: Bollwerk, 1953.
*Dreizehn politische Radio-Reden 1946.* Heidelberg: Schneider, 1947.
*Figuren der Fabel.* Berlin: Suhrkamp, 1950.
*Die grosse Wahlreform: Zeugnisse einer Bemühung.* Cologne: Westdeutscher, 1964.

Select bibliography 351

*Lebende Verfassung: Studien über Koalition und Opposition*. Meisenheim a.G.: Hain, 1956.
*Schriften*. Vol. VIII, *Gang zwischen Meistern*. Frankfurt a.M.: Insel, 1987.
Sternberger, Dolf, Gerhard Storz, and Wilhelm Emanuel Süskind. *Aus dem Wörterbuch des Unmenschen*. Hamburg: Claasen, 1957.
Teroni, Sandra, and Wolfgang Klein, eds. *Pour la défense de la culture: Les textes du Congrès international des écrivains, Paris, juin 1935*. Dijon: Éditions universitaires de Dijon, 2005.
Trott zu Solz, Werner von. *Der Untergang des Vaterlandes: Dokumente und Aufsätze*. Olten: Walter, 1965.
Walser, Martin, ed. *Die Alternative oder Brauchen wir eine neue Regierung?* Reinbek b.H.: Rowohlt, 1961.
Weber, Alfred. *Abschied von der bisherigen Geschichte: Überwindung des Nihilismus?* Hamburg: Claassen & Goverts, 1946.
*Der dritte oder der vierte Mensch: Vom Sinn des geschichtlichen Daseins*. Munich: Piper, 1953.
*Gesamtausgabe*. Vol. X, *Ausgewählter Briefwechsel*, ed. Eberhard Demm and Hartmut Soell. Marburg: Metropolis, 2003.
*Kulturgeschichte als Kultursoziologie*. 2nd edn. Munich: Piper, 1950.
*Staat und gewerkschaftliche Aktion*. Cologne: Bund, [1954].
Weisenborn, Günther. *Der gespaltene Horizont: Niederschriften eines Außenseiters*. Munich: Desch, 1964.
*Die Illegalen: Drama aus der deutschen Widerstandsbewegung*. Berlin: Aufbau, 1946.
ed. *Der lautlose Aufstand: Bericht über die Widerstandsbewegung des deutschen Volkes 1933–1945*. Hamburg: Rowohlt, 1953.
*Memorial*. Munich: Desch, 1948.
Weismantel, Leo. "Ein deutsches Kulturparlament." In *Leben und Werk: Ein Buch des Dankes zu des Dichters 60. Geburtstag*, 207–27. Berlin: Nauck, 1989.
Wende-Hohenberger, Waltraud, ed. *Der Frankfurter Schriftstellerkongreß im Jahr 1948*. Frankfurt a.M.: Lang, 1989.
Zwerenz, Ingrid, and Gerhard Zwerenz. *Sklavensprache und Revolte: Der Bloch-Kreis und seine Feinde in Ost und West*. Hamburg: Schwartzkopff, 2004.

## SECONDARY SOURCES

Abrams, Bradley F. "The Second World War and the East European Revolution." *East European Politics and Societies* 16, no. 3 (2002): 623–64.
Albrecht, Clemens, Günter C. Behrmann, Michael Bock, Harald Homann, and Friedrich H. Tenbruck. *Die intellektuelle Gründung der Bundesrepublik: Eine Wirkungsgeschichte der Frankfurter Schule*. Frankfurt a.M.: Campus, 1999.
Albrecht, Willy. *Der Sozialistische Deutsche Studentenbund (SDS): Vom parteikonformen Studentenverband zum Repräsentanten der Neuen Linken*. Bonn: Dietz, 1994.
Amos, Heike. *Die Entstehung der Verfassung in der Sowjetischen Besatzungszone/DDR 1946–1949: Darstellung und Dokumentation*. Münster: LIT, 2006.

## 352 Select bibliography

Angster, Julia. *Konsenskapitalismus und Sozialdemokratie: Die Westernisierung von SPD und DGB*. Munich: Oldenbourg, 2003.
Assmann, Aleida. *Arbeit am nationalen Gedächtnis: Eine kurze Geschichte der deutschen Bildungsidee*. Frankfurt a.M.: Campus, 1993.
Augustine, Dolores, Heinrich Best and Axel Salheiser, Rüdiger Stutz, and Georg Wagner-Kyora. "Nazi Continuities in East Germany." *German Studies Review* 29, no. 3 (2006): 579–619.
Baerns, Barbara. *Ost und West: Eine Zeitschrift zwischen den Fronten: Zur politischen Funktion einer literarischen Zeitschrift in der Besatzungszeit 1945–1949*. Münster: Fahle, 1968.
Bald, Detlef, and Wolfram Wette, eds. *Friedensinitiativen in der Frühzeit des Kalten Krieges 1945–1955*. Essen: Klartext, 2010.
Barck, Simone, Martina Langermann, and Siegfried Lokatis. *"Jedes Buch ein Abenteuer": Zensur-System und literarische Öffentlichkeiten in der DDR bis Ende der sechziger Jahre*. Berlin: Akademie, 1997.
  eds. *Zwischen "Mosaik" und "Einheit": Zeitschriften in der DDR*. Berlin: Links, 1999.
Barclay, David E., and Eric D. Weitz, eds. *Between Reform and Revolution: German Socialism and Communism from 1840 to 1990*. New York: Berghahn, 1998.
Bathrick, David. *The Powers of Speech: The Politics of Culture in the GDR*. Lincoln: University of Nebraska Press, 1995.
Bauerkämper, Arnd, Konrad H. Jarausch, and Marcus M. Payk, eds. *Demokratiewunder: Transatlantische Mittler und die kulturelle Öffnung Westdeutschlands 1945–1970*. Göttingen: Vandenhoeck & Ruprecht, 2005.
Bavaj, Riccardo. *Von links gegen Weimar: Linkes antiparlamentarisches Denken in der Weimarer Republik*. Bonn: Dietz, 2005.
Beiser, Frederick C. *Enlightenment, Revolution, and Romanticism: The Genesis of Modern German Political Thought, 1790–1800*. Cambridge, Mass.: Harvard University Press, 1992.
Benda, Julien. *The Treason of the Intellectuals*. Translated by Richard Aldington. New York: Morrow, 1928.
Benz, Wolfgang. *Auftrag Demokratie: Die Gründungsgeschichte der Bundesrepublik und die Entstehung der DDR 1945–1949*. Berlin: Metropol, 2009.
  *Potsdam 1945: Besatzungsherrschaft und Neuaufbau im Vier-Zonen-Deutschland*. 4th edn. Munich: Deutscher Taschenbuch Verlag, 2005.
Berghahn, Volker R. *America and the Intellectual Cold Wars in Europe: Shepard Stone between Philanthropy, Academy, and Diplomacy*. Princeton, N.J.: Princeton University Press, 2001.
Berndt, Thomas. *Nur das Wort kann die Welt verändern: Der politische Journalist Axel Eggebrecht*. Herzberg: Bautz, 1998.
Bessel, Richard. *Germany 1945: From War to Peace*. New York: HarperCollins, 2009.
Biess, Frank. *Homecomings: Returning POWs and the Legacies of Defeat in Postwar Germany*. Princeton, N.J.: Princeton University Press, 2006.
Blackbourn, David, and Geoff Eley. *The Peculiarities of German History: Bourgeois Society and Politics in Nineteenth-Century Germany*. Oxford: Oxford University Press, 1984.

Blaicher, Günther. "Die Deutschen als 'das Volk der Dichter und Denker': Entstehung, Kontexte und Funktionen eines nationalen Stereotyps." *Historische Zeitschrift* 287, no. 2 (2008): 319–40.
Blessing, Benita. *The Antifascist Classroom: Denazification in Soviet-Occupied Germany, 1945–1949*. New York: Palgrave Macmillan, 2006.
Blomert, Reinhard. *Intellektuelle im Aufbruch: Karl Mannheim, Alfred Weber, Norbert Elias und die Heidelberger Sozialwissenschaft der Zwischenkriegszeit*. Munich: Hanser, 1999.
Bloxham, Donald. "The Genocidal Past in Western Germany and the Experience of Occupation, 1945–6." *European History Quarterly* 34, no. 3 (2004): 305–35.
Bodemann, Y. Michal. "Eclipse of Memory: German Representations of Auschwitz in the Early Postwar Period." *New German Critique* 75 (1998): 57–89.
Boehling, Rebecca. *A Question of Priorities: Democratic Reform and Economic Recovery in Postwar Germany: Frankfurt, Munich, and Stuttgart under U.S. Occupation, 1945–1949*. Providence, R.I.: Berghahn, 1996.
Boll, Monika. *Nachtprogramm: Intellektuelle Gründungsdebatten in der frühen Bundesrepublik*. Münster: LIT, 2004.
Bollenbeck, Georg. *Bildung und Kultur: Glanz und Elend eines deutschen Deutungsmusters*. Frankfurt a.M.: Insel, 1994.
Bores, Dorothée. *Das ostdeutsche P.E.N.-Zentrum 1951–1998: Ein Werkzeug der Diktatur?* Berlin: de Gruyter, 2010.
Bösch, Frank. *Die Adenauer-CDU: Gründung, Aufstieg und Krise einer Erfolgspartei 1945–1969*. Stuttgart: Deutsche Verlags-Anstalt, 2001.
Böttiger, Helmut. *Die Gruppe 47: Als die deutsche Literatur Geschichte schrieb*. Munich: Deutsche Verlags-Anstalt, 2012.
Bourdieu, Pierre. "The Corporatism of the Universal: The Role of Intellectuals in the Modern World." *Telos* 81 (1989): 99–110.
  "Intellectual Field and Creative Project." *Social Science Information* 8, no. 2 (1969): 89–119.
  "Le marché des biens symboliques." *L'Année sociologique* 22 (1971): 49–126.
Boyer, Dominic. *Spirit and System: Media, Intellectuals, and the Dialectic in Modern German Culture*. Chicago: University of Chicago Press, 2005.
Brandt, Peter, Jörg Schumacher, Götz Schwarzrock, and Klaus Sühl. *Karrieren eines Außenseiters: Leo Bauer zwischen Kommunismus und Sozialdemokratie 1912 bis 1972*. Berlin: Dietz, 1983.
Braun, Matthias. *Kulturinsel und Machtinstrument: Die Akademie der Künste, die Partei und die Staatssicherheit*. Göttingen: Vandenhoeck & Ruprecht, 2007.
Brenner, Michael. *After the Holocaust: Rebuilding Jewish Lives in Postwar Germany*. Translated by Barbara Harshav. Princeton, N.J.: Princeton University Press, 1997.
Breuer, Stefan. *Anatomie der konservativen Revolution*. Darmstadt: Wissenschaftliche Buchgesellschaft, 1993.
Bröckling, Ulrich. *Katholische Intellektuelle in der Weimarer Republik: Zeitkritik und Gesellschaftstheorie bei Walter Dirks, Romano Guardini, Carl Schmitt, Ernst Michel und Heinrich Mertens*. Munich: Fink, 1993.

354    Select bibliography

Brockmann, Stephen. *German Literary Culture at the Zero Hour*. Rochester, N.Y.: Camden House, 2004.
"Germany as Occident at the Zero Hour." *German Studies Review* 25, no. 3 (2002): 477–96.
Broszat, Martin. "Resistenz und Widerstand: Zwischenbilanz eines Forschungsprojekts." In *Bayern in der NS-Zeit*, vol. IV, *Herrschaft und Gesellschaft im Konflikt*, ed. Broszat, Elke Fröhlich and Anton Grossmann, 691–709. Munich: Oldenbourg, 1981.
Broszat, Martin, Klaus-Dietmar Henke, and Hans Woller, eds. *Von Stalingrad zur Währungsreform: Zur Sozialgeschichte des Umbruchs in Deutschland*. Munich: Oldenbourg, 1988.
Brown, Timothy S. "'1968' East and West: Divided Germany as a Case Study in Transnational History." *American Historical Review* 114, no. 1 (2009): 69–96.
Buchanan, Tom. "Anti-Fascism and Democracy in the 1930s." *European History Quarterly* 32, no. 1 (2002): 39–57.
Buergel-Goodwin, Ulrike. "Die Reorganisation der westdeutschen Schriftstellerverbände 1945–1952." *Archiv für die Geschichte des Buchwesens* 18 (1977): 361–524.
Burns, Rob, and Wilfried van der Will. *Protest and Democracy in West Germany: Extra-Parliamentary Opposition and the Democratic Agenda*. New York: St. Martin's Press, 1988.
Bussiek, Dagmar. *Benno Reifenberg 1892–1970: Eine Biographie*. Göttingen: Wallstein, 2011.
Caldwell, Peter C. *Dictatorship, State Planning, and Social Theory in the German Democratic Republic*. Cambridge: Cambridge University Press, 2003.
Calhoun, Craig, ed. *Habermas and the Public Sphere*. Cambridge, Mass.: MIT Press, 1992.
Canovan, Margaret. *Hannah Arendt: A Reinterpretation of her Political Thought*. Cambridge: Cambridge University Press, 1992.
Caute, David. *The Fellow-Travellers: A Postscript to the Enlightenment*. New York: Macmillan, 1973.
Clark, Mark W. *Beyond Catastrophe: German Intellectuals and Cultural Renewal after World War II, 1945–1955*. Lanham, Md.: Lexington, 2006.
Classen, Christoph. *Faschismus und Antifaschismus: Die nationalsozialistische Vergangenheit im ostdeutschen Hörfunk (1945–1953)*. Cologne: Böhlau, 2004.
Clemens, Gabriele, ed. *Kulturpolitik im besetzten Deutschland 1945–1949*. Stuttgart: Steiner, 1994.
Connelly, John. *Captive University: The Sovietization of East German, Czech, and Polish Higher Education, 1945–1956*. Chapel Hill: University of North Carolina Press, 2000.
"Ulbricht and the Intellectuals." *Contemporary European History* 6, no. 3 (1997): 329–59.
Conway, Martin. "Democracy in Postwar Western Europe: The Triumph of a Political Model." *European History Quarterly* 32, no. 1 (2002): 59–84.
Conway, Martin, and Volker Depkat. "Towards a European History of the Discourse of Democracy: Discussing Democracy in Western Europe 1945–60."

In *Europeanization in the Twentieth Century: Historical Approaches*, ed. Conway and Kiran Klaus Patel, 132–56. Basingstoke: Palgrave Macmillan, 2010.

Conze, Vanessa. *Das Europa der Deutschen: Ideen von Europa in Deutschland zwischen Reichstradition und Westorientierung (1920–1970)*. Munich: Oldenbourg, 2005.

Conze, Werner, Reinhart Koselleck, Hans Maier, Christian Meier, and Hans Leo Reimann. "Demokratie." In *Geschichtliche Grundbegriffe: Historisches Lexikon zur politisch-sozialen Sprache in Deutschland*, ed. Otto Brunner, Conze and Koselleck, I:821–99. Stuttgart: Klett, 1972.

Coppi, Hans, Jürgen Danyel, and Johannes Tuchel, eds. *Die Rote Kapelle im Widerstand gegen Nationalsozialismus*. Berlin: Hentrich, 1994.

Corino, Karl. *Aussen Marmor, innen Gips: Die Legenden des Stephan Hermlin*. Düsseldorf: ECON, 1996.

Cramer, John. *Belsen Trial 1945: Der Lüneburger Prozess gegen Wachpersonal der Konzentrationslager Auschwitz und Bergen-Belsen*. Göttingen: Wallstein, 2012.

Dale, Gareth. *Popular Protest in East Germany, 1945–1989*. London: Routledge, 2005.

Davis, Belinda. "What's Left? Popular Political Participation in Postwar Europe." *American Historical Review* 113, no. 2 (2008): 363–90.

De Rosa, Renato. "Politische Akzente im Leben eines Philosophen: Karl Jaspers in Heidelberg 1901–1946." In Karl Jaspers, *Erneuerung der Universität: Reden und Schriften 1945–46*, 301–423. Heidelberg: Schneider, 1986.

Deák, István. *Weimar Germany's Left-Wing Intellectuals: A Political History of the Weltbühne and its Circle*. Berkeley: University of California Press, 1968.

Deák, István, Jan T. Gross, and Tony Judt, eds. *The Politics of Retribution in Europe: World War II and its Aftermath*. Princeton, N.J.: Princeton University Press, 2000.

Dehli, Martin. *Leben als Konflikt: Zur Biographie Alexander Mitscherlichs*. Göttingen: Wallstein, 2007.

Demm, Eberhard. *Ein Liberaler in Kaiserreich und Republik: Der politische Weg Alfred Webers bis 1920*. Boppard a.R.: Boldt, 1990.

  ed. *Soziologie, Politik und Kultur: Von Alfred Weber zur Frankfurter Schule*. Frankfurt a.M.: Lang, 2003.

*Von der Weimarer Republik zur Bundesrepublik: Der politische Weg Alfred Webers 1920–1958*. Düsseldorf: Droste, 1999.

Demmer, Manfred. *Spurensuche: Der antifaschistische Schriftsteller Günther Weisenborn*. Leverkusen: Kulturvereinigung Leverkusen, 2004.

Diani, Mario. "The Concept of Social Movement." *Sociological Review* 40, no. 1 (1992): 1–25.

Diers, Andreas. *Arbeiterbewegung, Demokratie, Staat: Wolfgang Abendroth, Leben und Werk 1906–1948*. Hamburg: VSA, 2006.

Dietrich, Gerd. *Politik und Kultur in der Sowjetischen Besatzungszone Deutschlands (SBZ) 1945–1949*. Bern: Lang, 1993.

Diner, Dan. "'Rupture in Civilization': On the Genesis and Meaning of a Concept in Understanding." In *On Germans and Jews under the Nazi Regime: Essays by Three Generations of Historians*, ed. Moshe Zimmermann, 33–48. Jerusalem: Hebrew University Press, 2006.

Dodd, William J. *Jedes Wort wandelt die Welt: Dolf Sternbergers politische Sprachkritik*. Göttingen: Wallstein, 2007.
Doderer, Klaus. *Erich Kästner: Lebensphasen, politisches Engagement, literarisches Wirken*. Weinheim: Juventa, 2002.
Doering-Manteuffel, Anselm. "Im Kampf um 'Frieden' und 'Freiheit': Über den Zusammenhang von Ideologie und Sozialstruktur im Ost-West Konflikt." In *Koordinaten deutscher Geschichte in der Epoche des Ost-West-Konflikts*, ed. Hans Günter Hockerts. Munich: Oldenbourg, 2004.
"Strukturmerkmale der Kanzlerdemokratie." *Der Staat* 30 (1991): 1–18.
*Wie westlich sind die Deutschen? Amerikanisierung und Westernisierung im 20. Jahrhundert*. Göttingen: Vandenhoeck & Ruprecht, 1999.
Dupeux, Louis. *"Nationalbolschewismus" in Deutschland 1919–1933: Kommunistische Strategie und konservative Dynamik*. Translated by Richard Kirchhoff. Munich: Beck, 1985.
Durth, Werner, and Niels Gutschow. *Träume in Trümmern: Planung zum Wiederaufbau zerstörter Städte im Westen Deutschlands 1940–1950*. 2 vols. Braunschweig: Vieweg, 1988.
Dutt, Carsten, ed. *Herausforderungen der Begriffsgeschichte*. Heidelberg: Winter, 2003.
Dwars, Jens-Fietje. *Abgrund des Widerspruchs: Das Leben des Johannes R. Becher*. Berlin: Aufbau, 1998.
Eberan, Barbro. *Luther? Friedrich "der Grosse"? Wagner? Nietzsche? Wer war an Hitler schuld? Die Debatte um die Schuldfrage 1945–1949*. 2nd edn. Munich: Minerva, 1985.
Ehrke-Rotermund, Heidrun, and Erwin Rotermund. *Zwischenreiche und Gegenwelten: Texte und Vorstudien zur "Verdeckten Schreibweise" im "Dritten Reich"*. Munich: Fink, 1999.
Ehrlich, Lothar, and Gunther Mai, eds. *Weimarer Klassik in der Ära Ulbricht*. Cologne: Böhlau, 2000.
Eisenberg, Carolyn. *Drawing the Line: The American Decision to Divide Germany, 1944–1949*. Cambridge: Cambridge University Press, 1996.
Eley, Geoff. *Forging Democracy: The History of the Left in Europe, 1850–2000*. New York: Oxford University Press, 2002.
"Reviewing the Socialist Tradition." In *The Crisis of Socialism in Europe*, ed. Christiane Lemke and Gary Marks, 21–60. Durham, N.C.: Duke University Press, 1992.
Engelhardt, Ulrich. *Bildungsbürgertum: Begriffs- und Dogmengeschichte eines Etiketts*. Stuttgart: Klett-Cotta, 1986.
Epstein, Catherine. *The Last Revolutionaries: German Communists and Their Century*. Cambridge, Mass.: Harvard University Press, 2003.
Erler, Peter, and Manfred Wilke. "'Nach Hitler kommen wir': Das Konzept der Moskauer KPD-Führung 1944/45 für Nachkriegsdeutschland." *Exilforschung* 15 (1997): 102–19.
Eßbach, Wolfgang. "Intellektuellengruppen in der bürgerlichen Kultur." In *Kreise – Gruppen – Bünde: Zur Soziologie moderner Intellektuellenassoziation*, ed. Richard Faber and Christine Holste, 23–33. Würzburg: Königshausen & Neumann, 2000.

Estermann, Monika, and Edgar Lersch, eds. *Buch, Buchhandel und Rundfunk 1945–1949*. Wiesbaden: Harrassowitz, 1997.
Ewald, Hans-Gerd. *Die gescheiterte Republik: Idee und Programm einer "Zweiten Republik" in den Frankfurter Heften 1946–1950*. Frankfurt a.M.: Lang, 1988.
Fair-Schulz, Axel. *Loyal Subversion: East Germany and its Bildungsbürgerlich Marxist Intellectuals*. Berlin: Trafo, 2009.
Faulenbach, Bernd. "Der 'deutsche Weg' aus der Sicht des Exils: Zum Urteil emigrierter Historiker." *Exilforschung* 3 (1985): 11–30.
Feldkamp, Michael. *Der Parlamentarische Rat 1948–1949: Die Entstehung des Grundgesetzes*. Göttingen: Vandenhoeck & Ruprecht, 1998.
Fisher, Jaimey. *Disciplining Germany: Youth, Reeducation, and Reconstruction after the Second World War*. Detroit: Wayne State University Press, 2007.
Flanagan, Clare. *A Study of German Political-Cultural Periodicals from the Years of Allied Occupation, 1945–1949*. Lewiston: Mellen, 2000.
Foitzik, Jan, ed. *Entstalinisierungskrise in Ostmitteleuropa 1953–1956: Vom 17. Juni bis zum ungarischen Volksaufstand*. Paderborn: Schöningh, 2001.
Föllmer, Moritz, ed. *Sehnsucht nach Nähe: Interpersonale Kommunikation in Deutschland seit dem 19. Jahrhundert*. Stuttgart: Steiner, 2004.
Forner, Sean A. "'Deutscher Geist' und demokratische Erneuerung: Kulturbünde in Ost und West nach 1945." In *Rückblickend in die Zukunft: Politische Öffentlichkeit und intellektuelle Positionen in Deutschland um 1950 und um 1930*, ed. Alexander Gallus and Axel Schildt, 221–37. Göttingen: Wallstein, 2011.
"Für eine demokratische Erneuerung Deutschlands: Kommunikationsprozesse und Deutungsmuster engagierter Demokraten nach 1945." *Geschichte und Gesellschaft* 33, no. 2 (2007): 228–57.
"The Promise of Publicness: Intellectual Elites and Participatory Politics in Postwar Heidelberg." *Modern Intellectual History* 9, no. 3 (2012): 641–60.
"Reconsidering the 'Unpolitical German': Democratic Renewal and the Politics of Culture in Occupied Germany." *German History* 32, no. 1 (2014): 53–78.
"'Das Sprachrohr keiner Besatzungsmacht oder Partei': Deutsche Publizisten, die Vereinigten Staaten und die demokratische Erneuerung in Westdeutschland 1945–1949." In *Demokratiewunder: Transatlantische Mittler und die kulturelle Öffnung Westdeutschlands 1945–1970*, ed. Arnd Bauerkämper, Konrad H. Jarausch and Marcus M. Payk, 159–89. Göttingen: Vandenhoeck & Ruprecht, 2005.
Foschepoth, Josef. *Im Schatten der Vergangenheit: Die Anfänge der Gesellschaft für Christlich-Jüdische Zusammenarbeit*. Göttingen: Vandenhoeck & Ruprecht, 1993.
Foschepoth, Josef, and Rolf Steininger, eds. *Die britische Deutschland- und Besatzungspolitik 1945–1949*. Paderborn: Schöningh, 1985.
Franck, Matthias. *Kultur im Revier: Die Geschichte der Ruhrfestspiele Recklinghausen 1946–1956*. Würzburg: Königshausen & Neumann, 1986.
Franz, Trantje. "Philosophie als revolutionäre Praxis: Zur Apologie und Kritik des Sowjetsozialismus." In *Ernst Bloch*, ed. Heinz Ludwig Arnold, 239–73. Munich: Text + Kritik, 1985.

Frei, Norbert. *Adenauer's Germany and the Nazi Past: The Politics of Amnesty and Integration*. Translated by Joel Golb. New York: Columbia University Press, 2002.

ed. *Karrieren im Zwielicht: Hitlers Eliten nach 1945*. Frankfurt a.M.: Campus, 2001.

"Von deutscher Erfindungskraft; oder, Die Kollektivschuldthese in der Nachkriegszeit." *Rechtshistorisches Journal* 16 (1997): 621–34.

*Freier Eintritt – Freie Fragen – Freie Antworten: Die Kölner Mittwochgespräche 1950–1956*. Cologne: Historisches Archiv der Stadt Köln, 1991.

Freimüller, Tobias. *Alexander Mitscherlich: Gesellschaftsdiagnosen und Psychoanalyse nach Hitler*. Göttingen: Wallstein, 2007.

Fröhlich, Claudia. "Restauration: Zur (Un-)Tauglichkeit eines Erklärungsansatzes westdeutscher Demokratiegeschichte." In *Erfolgsgeschichte Bundesrepublik? Die Nachkriegsgesellschaft im langen Schatten des Nationalsozialismus*, ed. Stephan Alexander Glienke, Volker Paulmann and Joachim Perels, 17–52. Göttingen: Wallstein, 2008.

Fröhlich, Claudia, and Michael Kohlstruck, eds. *Engagierte Demokraten: Vergangenheitspolitik in kritischer Absicht*. Münster: Westfälisches Dampfboot, 1999.

Fulda, Daniel, Dagmar Herzog, Stefan-Ludwig Hoffmann, and Till van Rahden, eds. *Demokratie im Schatten der Gewalt: Geschichten des Privaten im deutschen Nachkrieg*. Göttingen: Wallstein, 2010.

Gallus, Alexander. *Heimat "Weltbühne": Eine Intellektuellengeschichte im 20. Jahrhundert*. Göttingen: Wallstein, 2012.

*Die Neutralisten: Verfechter eines vereinten Deutschlands zwischen Ost und West 1945–1990*. Düsseldorf: Droste, 2001.

"'Der Ruf' – Stimme für ein neues Deutschland." *Aus Politik und Zeitgeschichte* B25 (2007): 32–8.

Gallus, Alexander, and Axel Schildt, eds. *Rückblickend in die Zukunft: Politische Öffentlichkeit und intellektuelle Positionen in Deutschland um 1950 und um 1930*. Göttingen: Wallstein, 2011.

Geppert, Dominik, and Jens Hacke, eds. *Streit um den Staat: Intellektuelle Debatten in der Bundesrepublik 1960–1980*. Göttingen: Vandenhoeck & Ruprecht, 2008.

Geppert, Dominik, and Udo Wengst, eds. *Neutralität: Chance oder Chimäre? Konzepte des dritten Weges für Deutschland und die Welt 1945–1990*. Munich: Oldenbourg, 2005.

Gerhardt, Volker, and Hans-Christoph Rauh, eds. *Anfänge der DDR-Philosophie: Ansprüche, Ohnmacht, Scheitern*. Berlin: Links, 2001.

Gerstner, Alexandra. *Neuer Adel: Aristokratische Elitekonzeptionen zwischen Jahrhundertwende und Nationalsozialismus*. Darmstadt: Wissenschaftliche Buchgesellschaft, 2008.

Geuss, Raymond. "Kultur, Bildung, Geist." In *Morality, Culture, and History: Essays on German Philosophy*, 29–50. Cambridge: Cambridge University Press, 1999.

Geyer, Michael. "Germany; or, The Twentieth Century as History." *South Atlantic Quarterly* 96, no. 4 (1997): 663–702.

ed. *The Power of Intellectuals in Contemporary Germany*. Chicago: University of Chicago Press, 2001.
"The Stigma of Violence, Nationalism, and War in Twentieth-Century Germany." *German Studies Review* 15 (1992): 75–110.
Geyer, Michael, and John W. Boyer, eds. *Resistance against the Third Reich, 1933–1990*. Chicago: University of Chicago Press, 1994.
Gienow-Hecht, Jessica C. E. *Transmission Impossible: American Journalism as Cultural Diplomacy in Postwar Germany, 1945–1955*. Baton Rouge: Louisiana State University Press, 1999.
Gieseke, Jens. *Mielke-Konzern: Die Geschichte der Stasi 1945–1990*. Stuttgart: Deutsche Verlags-Anstalt, 2001.
Giesen, Bernhard. *Intellectuals and the German Nation: Collective Identity in an Axial Age*. Translated by Nicholas Levis and Amos Weisz. Cambridge: Cambridge University Press, 1998.
Gilcher-Holtey, Ingrid, ed. *1968 – Vom Ereignis zum Gegenstand der Geschichtswissenschaft*. Göttingen: Vandenhoeck & Ruprecht, 1998.
*Die 68er-Bewegung: Deutschland – Westeuropa – USA*. Munich: Beck, 2001.
"'Askese schreiben, schreib: Askese': Zur Rolle der Gruppe 47 in der politischen Kultur der Nachkriegszeit." *Internationales Archiv für Sozialgeschichte der Deutschen Literatur* 25, no. 2 (2000): 134–67.
Gillessen, Günther. *Auf verlorenem Posten: Die "Frankfurter Zeitung" im Dritten Reich*. Berlin: Siedler, 1986.
Gimbel, John. *The American Occupation of Germany: Politics and the Military, 1945–1949*. Stanford, Calif.: Stanford University Press, 1968.
Glaser, Hermann. *Rubble Years: The Cultural Roots of Postwar Germany, 1945–1948*. Translated by Franz Feige and Patricia Gleason. New York: Paragon House, 1986.
Gleason, Abbott. *Totalitarianism: The Inner History of the Cold War*. New York: Oxford University Press, 1995.
Goldstein, Cora Sol. *Capturing the German Eye: American Visual Propaganda in Occupied Germany*. Chicago: University of Chicago Press, 2009.
Goll, Thomas. *Die Deutschen und Thomas Mann: Die Rezeption des Dichters in Abhängigkeit von der politischen Kultur Deutschlands 1898–1955*. Baden-Baden: Nomos, 2000.
Gramsci, Antonio. "The Intellectuals." In *Selections from the Prison Notebooks*, trans. Quintin Hoare and Geoffrey Nowell Smith, 5–23. New York: International, 1971.
Granville, Johanna. "Ulbricht in October 1956: Survival of the Spitzbart during Destalinization." *Journal of Contemporary History* 41, no. 3 (2006): 477–502.
Grebner, Susanne. *Der Telegraf: Entstehung einer SPD-nahen Lizenzzeitung in Berlin 1946–1950*. Münster: LIT, 2002.
Greven, Michael Th. "Betrachtungen über das Bürgerliche: Dolf Sternberger und die Metamorphosen des Bürgers nach 1945." *Vorgänge* 44, no. 2 (2005): 21–32.
*Politisches Denken in Deutschland nach 1945: Erfahrung und Umgang mit der Kontingenz in der unmittelbaren Nachkriegszeit*. Opladen: Budrich, 2007.

Grossmann, Atina. *Jews, Germans, and Allies: Close Encounters in Occupied Germany*. Princeton, N.J.: Princeton University Press, 2007.
Gruner, Wolfgang. *"Ein Schicksal, das ich mit sehr vielen anderen geteilt habe": Alfred Kantorowicz, sein Leben und seine Zeit von 1899 bis 1935*. Kassel: Kassel University Press, 2006.
Grunewald, Michel, and Hans Manfred Bock, eds. *Le discours européen dans les revues allemandes / Der Europadiskurs in den deutschen Zeitschriften (1945–1955)*. Bern: Lang, 2001.
— eds. *Le milieu intellectuel de gauche en Allemagne, sa presse et ses réseaux / Das linke Intellektuellenmilieu, seine Presse und seine Netzwerke (1890–1960)*. Bern: Lang, 2002.
Grunewald, Michel, and Uwe Puschner, eds. *Le milieu intellectuel catholique en Allemagne, sa presse et ses réseaux / Das katholische Intellektuellenmilieu in Deutschland, seine Presse und seine Netzwerke (1871–1963)*. Bern: Lang, 2006.
— eds. *Le milieu intellectuel conservateur en Allemagne, sa presse et ses réseaux / Das konservative Intellektuellenmilieu in Deutschland, seine Presse und seine Netzwerke (1890–1960)*. Bern: Lang, 2003.
Habermas, Jürgen. *The Structural Transformation of the Public Sphere: An Inquiry into a Category of Bourgeois Society*. Translated by Thomas Burger. Cambridge, Mass.: MIT Press, 1989.
Hacke, Jens. *Philosophie Der Bürgerlichkeit: Die liberalkonservative Begründung der Bundesrepublik*. Göttingen: Vandenhoeck & Ruprecht, 2006.
Hahn, Erich J. "U.S. Policy on a West German Constitution, 1947–1949." In *American Policy and the Reconstruction of West Germany, 1945–1955*, ed. Jeffry M. Diefendorf, Axel Frohn and Hermann-Josef Rupieper, 21–44. Cambridge: Cambridge University Press, 1993.
Hanshew, Karrin. *Terror and Democracy in West Germany*. Cambridge: Cambridge University Press, 2012.
Hanuschek, Sven. *Geschichte des bundesdeutschen PEN-Zentrums von 1951–1990*. Tübingen: Niemeyer, 2004.
— *Keiner blickt dir hinter das Gesicht: Das Leben Erich Kästners*. Munich: Hanser, 1999.
Hanuschek, Sven, Therese Hörnigk, and Christine Malende, eds. *Schriftsteller als Intellektuelle: Politik und Literatur im Kalten Krieg*. Tübingen: Niemeyer, 2000.
Hardtwig, Wolfgang, ed. *Politische Kulturgeschichte der Zwischenkriegszeit 1918–1939*. Göttingen: Vandenhoeck & Ruprecht, 2005.
Hartmann, Anne, and Wolfram Eggeling. *Sowjetische Präsenz im kulturellen Leben der SBZ und frühen DDR 1945–1953*. Berlin: Akademie, 1998.
Hausmann, Katharina. *"Die Chance, Bürger zu werden": Deutsche Politik unter amerikanischer Besatzung: Die "Heidelberger Aktionsgruppe" 1946–47*. Heidelberg: regionalkultur, 2006.
Heider, Magdalena. *Politik – Kultur – Kulturbund: Zur Gründungs- und Frühgeschichte des Kulturbundes zur demokratischen Erneuerung Deutschlands 1945–1954 in der SBZ/DDR*. Cologne: Wissenschaft und Politik, 1993.
Heigl, Richard. *Oppositionspolitik: Wolfgang Abendroth und die Entstehung der Neuen Linken (1950–1968)*. Hamburg: Argument, 2008.

Heil, Peter. "Föderalismus als Weltanschauung: Zur Geschichte eines gesellschaftlichen Ordnungsmodells zwischen Weimar und Bonn." *Geschichte im Westen* 9, no. 2 (1994): 165–82.
Heineman, Elizabeth. "The Hour of the Woman: Memories of Germany's 'Crisis Years' and West German National Identity." *American Historical Review* 101, no. 2 (1996): 354–95.
Herbert, Ulrich. "Drei politische Generationen im 20. Jahrhundert." In *Generationalität und Lebensgeschichte im 20. Jahrhundert*, ed. Jürgen Reulecke, 95–115. Munich: Oldenbourg, 2003.
 "Good Times, Bad Times: Memories of the Third Reich." *In Life in the Third Reich*, ed. Richard Bessel, 97–110. Oxford: Oxford University Press, 1986.
 ed. *Wandlungsprozesse in Westdeutschland: Belastung, Integration, Liberalisierung 1945–1980*. Göttingen: Wallstein, 2002.
Herbst-Meßlinger, Karin. "Der Kritiker als Intellektueller." In *Herbert Ihering: Filmkritiker*, 13–71. Munich: Text + Kritik, 2011.
Herf, Jeffrey. *Divided Memory: The Nazi Past in the Two Germanys*. Cambridge, Mass.: Harvard University Press, 1997.
 *Reactionary Modernism: Technology, Culture, and Politics in Weimar and the Third Reich*. Cambridge: Cambridge University Press, 1984.
Hermand, Jost. *Die deutschen Dichterbünde: Von den Meistersingern bis zum PEN-Club*. Cologne: Böhlau, 1998.
Herzberg, Guntolf. *Anpassung und Aufbegehren: Die Intelligenz der DDR in den Krisenjahren 1956/58*. Berlin: Links, 2006.
Heß, Jürgen C., Hartmut Lehmann, and Volker Sellin, eds. *Heidelberg 1945*. Stuttgart: Steiner, 1996.
Hettling, Manfred, and Bernd Ulrich, eds. *Bürgertum nach 1945*. Hamburg: Hamburger Edition, 2005.
Heukenkamp, Ursula, ed. *Unterm Notdach: Nachkriegsliteratur in Berlin 1945–1949*. Berlin: Schmidt, 1996.
Heyer, Andreas. "Wolfgang Harichs Demokratiekonzeption aus dem Jahr 1956: Demokratische Grundrechte, bürgerliche Werte und sozialistische Orientierung." *Zeitschrift für Geschichtswissenschaft* 55, no. 6 (2007): 529–50.
Hochgeschwender, Michael. *Freiheit in der Offensive? Der Kongress für kulturelle Freiheit und die Deutschen*. Munich: Oldenbourg, 1998.
Hodenberg, Christina von. *Konsens und Krise: Eine Geschichte der westdeutschen Medienöffentlichkeit 1945–1973*. Göttingen: Wallstein, 2006.
Hoenicke Moore, Michaela. *Know Your Enemy: The American Debate on Nazism, 1933–1945*. Cambridge: Cambridge University Press, 2010.
Hohendahl, Peter Uwe, Russell A. Berman, Karen Kenkel, and Arthur Strum. *Öffentlichkeit: Geschichte eines kritischen Begriffs*. Stuttgart: Metzler, 2000.
Horn, Gerd-Rainer. *The Spirit of '68: Rebellion in Western Europe and North America, 1956–1976*. New York: Oxford University Press, 2007.
 *Western European Liberation Theology: The First Wave, 1924–1959*. Oxford: Oxford University Press, 2008.
Horn, Gerd-Rainer, and Padraic Kenney, eds. *Transnational Moments of Change: Europe 1945, 1968, 1989*. Lanham, Md.: Rowman & Littlefield, 2004.

Hübinger, Gangolf, and Thomas Hertfelder, eds. *Kritik und Mandat: Intellektuelle in der deutschen Politik*. Stuttgart: Deutsche Verlags-Anstalt, 2000.

Hurwitz, Harold. *Die Stunde Null der deutschen Presse: Die amerikanische Pressepolitik in Deutschland 1945–1949*. Cologne: Wissenschaft und Politik, 1972.

Hutchinson, Peter. *Stefan Heym: The Perpetual Dissident*. Cambridge: Cambridge University Press, 1992.

Jahn, Jürgen. "Ernst Bloch im Visier der Staatssicherheit: Der Operative Vorgang 'Wild'." In *Heimat in vernetzten Welten*, ed. Francesca Vidal, 153–206. Mössingen-Talheim: Talheimer, 2006.

Jarausch, Konrad H. "1968 and 1989: Caesuras, Comparisons, and Connections." In *1968: The World Transformed*, ed. Carole Fink, Philipp Gassert and Detlef Junker, 461–77. Cambridge: Cambridge University Press, 1998.

*After Hitler: Recivilizing Germans, 1945–1995*. Translated by Brandon Hunziker. Oxford: Oxford University Press, 2006.

ed. *Dictatorship as Experience: Towards a Socio-Cultural History of the GDR*. Providence, R.I.: Berghahn, 1999.

"'Die Teile als Ganzes erkennen': Zur Integration der beiden deutschen Nachkriegsgeschichten." *Zeithistorische Forschungen* 1, no. 1 (2004): 10–30.

*Die unverhoffte Einheit: 1989–1990*. Frankfurt a.M.: Suhrkamp, 1995.

Jarausch, Konrad H., and Hannes Siegrist, eds. *Amerikanisierung und Sowjetisierung in Deutschland 1945–1970*. Frankfurt a.M.: Campus, 1997.

Jay, Martin. *Marxism and Totality: The Adventures of a Concept from Lukács to Habermas*. Berkeley: University of California Press, 1984.

Jentzsch, Bernd. *Rudolf Leonhard, "Gedichteträumer"*. Munich: Hanser, 1984.

Jessen, Ralph. *Akademische Elite und kommunistische Diktatur: Die ostdeutsche Hochschullehrerschaft in der Ulbricht-Ära*. Göttingen: Vandenhoeck & Ruprecht, 1999.

Judt, Tony. *Past Imperfect: French Intellectuals, 1944–1956*. Berkeley: University of California Press, 1992.

Junker, Detlef, ed. *The United States and Germany in the Era of the Cold War, 1945–1990: A Handbook*. 2 vols. Cambridge: Cambridge University Press, 2004.

Kadarkay, Arpad. *Georg Lukács: Life, Thought, and Politics*. Cambridge, Mass.: Blackwell, 1991.

Karl, Michaela. *Rudi Dutschke: Revolutionär ohne Revolution*. Frankfurt a.M.: Neue Kritik, 2003.

Katz, Barry M. *Foreign Intelligence: Research and Analysis in the Office of Strategic Services, 1942–1945*. Cambridge, Mass.: Harvard University Press, 1989.

Keiderling, Gerhard. *Um Deutschlands Einheit: Ferdinand Friedensburg und der Kalte Krieg in Berlin 1945–1952*. Cologne: Böhlau, 2009.

Kersting, Franz-Werner, Jürgen Reulecke, and Hans-Ulrich Thamer, eds. *Die zweite Gründung der Bundesrepublik: Generationswechsel und intellektuelle Wortergreifungen 1955–1975*. Stuttgart: Steiner, 2010.

Kettler, David. "'Erste Briefe' nach Deutschland: Zwischen Exil und Rückkehr." *Zeitschrift für Ideengeschichte* 2, no. 2 (2008): 80–108.

Kießling, Friedrich. *Die undeutschen Deutschen: Eine ideengeschichtliche Archäologie der alten Bundesrepublik 1945–1972*. Paderborn: Schöningh, 2012.

Kinkela, Claudia. *Die Rehabilitierung des Bürgerlichen im Werk Dolf Sternbergers.* Würzburg: Königshausen & Neumann, 2001.
Kirkbright, Suzanne. *Karl Jaspers: A Biography: Navigations in Truth.* New Haven, Conn.: Yale University Press, 2004.
Klein, Alfred. *Unästhetische Feldzüge: Der siebenjährige Krieg gegen Hans Mayer 1956–1963.* Leipzig: Faber & Faber, 1997.
Klein, Thomas. *"Für die Einheit und Reinheit der Partei": Die innerparteilichen Kontrollorgane der SED in der Ära Ulbricht.* Cologne: Böhlau, 2002.
Kleßmann, Christoph. *Die doppelte Staatsgründung: Deutsche Geschichte, 1945–1955.* 5th edn. Göttingen: Vandenhoek & Ruprecht, 1991.
"Verflechtung und Abgrenzung: Aspekte der geteilten und zusammengehörenden Nachkriegsgeschichte." *Aus Politik und Zeitgeschichte* B29/30 (1993): 30–41.
Klimke, Martin. *The Other Alliance: Student Protest in West Germany and the United States in the Global Sixties.* Princeton, N.J.: Princeton University Press, 2009.
Klotzbach, Kurt. *Der Weg zur Staatspartei: Programmatik, praktische Politik und Organisation der deutschen Sozialdemokratie 1945–1965.* Berlin: Dietz, 1982.
Koebner, Thomas, ed. *Weimars Ende: Prognosen und Diagnosen in der deutschen Literatur und politischen Publizistik 1930–1933.* Frankfurt a.M.: Suhrkamp, 1982.
Koebner, Thomas, Gert Sautermeister, and Sigrid Schneider, eds. *Deutschland nach Hitler: Zukunftspläne im Exil und aus der Besatzungszeit 1939–1949.* Opladen: Westdeutscher, 1987.
Koselleck, Reinhart, ed. *Bildungsbürgertum im 19. Jahrhundert, Teil 2: Bildungsgüter und Bildungswissen.* Stuttgart: Klett-Cotta, 1990.
"On the Anthropological and Semantic Structure of Bildung." In *The Practice of Conceptual History: Timing History, Spacing Concepts.* Translated by Todd Samuel Presner, 170–207. Stanford, Calif.: Stanford University Press, 2002.
Koszyk, Kurt. *Pressepolitik für Deutsche, 1945–1949.* Berlin: Colloquium, 1986.
Kraushaar, Wolfgang. *1968 als Mythos, Chiffre und Zäsur.* Hamburg: Hamburger Edition, 2000.
*Frankfurter Schule und Studentenbewegung: Von der Flaschenpost zum Molotowcocktail 1946–1995.* 3 vols. Hamburg: Rogner & Bernhard, 1998.
*Die Protest-Chronik 1949–1959: Eine illustrierte Geschichte von Bewegung, Widerstand und Utopie.* 4 vols. *Hamburg*: Rogner & Bernhard, 1996.
Krauss, Marita. *Heimkehr in ein fremdes Land: Geschichte der Remigration nach 1945.* Munich: Beck, 2001.
Krohn, Claus-Dieter. "Die westdeutsche Studentenbewegung und das 'andere Deutschland.'" In *Dynamische Zeiten: Die 60er Jahre in den beiden deutschen Gesellschaften*, ed. Axel Schildt, Detlef Siegfried and Karl Christian Lammers, 695–718. Hamburg: Christians, 2000.
Krohn, Claus-Dieter, and Patrik von zur Mühlen, eds. *Rückkehr und Aufbau nach 1945: Deutsche Remigranten im öffentlichen Leben Nachkriegsdeutschlands.* Marburg: Metropolis, 1997.
Krohn, Claus-Dieter, and Axel Schildt, eds. *Zwischen den Stühlen? Remigranten und Remigration in der deutschen Medienöffentlichkeit der Nachkriegszeit.* Hamburg: Christians, 2002.

Laak, Dirk van. *Gespräche in der Sicherheit des Schweigens: Carl Schmitt in der politischen Geistesgeschichte der frühen Bundesrepublik.* Berlin: Akademie, 1993.

Lange, Erhard H. M. *Wahlrecht und Innenpolitik: Entstehungsgeschichte und Analyse der Wahlgesetzgebung und Wahlrechtsdiskussion im westlichen Nachkriegsdeutschland 1945–1956.* Miesenheim a.G.: Hain, 1975.

Langer, Ingrid, Ulrike Ley, and Susanne Sander. *Alibi-Frauen? Hessische Politikerinnen.* Vol. I, *In den Vorparlamenten 1946 bis 1950.* Frankfurt a.M.: Helmer, 1994.

Langkau-Alex, Ursula. *Deutsche Volksfront 1932–1939: Zwischen Berlin, Paris, Prag und Moskau.* 3 vols. Berlin: Akademie, 2004.

Large, David Clay. *Germans to the Front: West German Rearmament in the Adenauer Era.* Chapel Hill: University of North Carolina Press, 1996.

Laurien, Ingrid. *Politisch-kulturelle Zeitschriften in den Westzonen 1945–1949: Ein Beitrag zur politischen Kultur der Nachkriegszeit.* Frankfurt a.M.: Lang, 1991.

"Zeitschriftenlandschaft Nachkriegszeit: Zu Struktur und Funktion politisch-kultureller Zeitschriften 1945–1949." *Publizistik* 47, no. 1 (2002): 57–82.

Leffler, Melvyn P., and Odd Arne Westad, eds. *The Cambridge History of the Cold War.* Vol. I, *Origins.* Cambridge: Cambridge University Press, 2010.

Lepenies, Wolf. *The Seduction of Culture in German History.* Princeton, N.J.: Princeton University Press, 2006.

Lienkamp, Andreas. "Socialism Out of Christian Responsibility: The German Experiment of Left Catholicism, 1945–1949." In *Left Catholicism 1943–1955: Catholics and Society in Western Europe at the Point of Liberation*, ed. Gerd-Rainer Horn and Emmanuel Gerard, 196–227. Leuven: Leuven University Press, 2001.

Lindenberger, Thomas. Introduction to *Herrschaft und Eigen-Sinn in der Diktatur: Studien zur Gesellschaftsgeschichte der DDR*, ed. Lindenberger, 13–44. Cologne: Böhlau, 1999.

Lipgens, Walter. *A History of European Integration.* Vol. I, *1945–1947.* Translated by P. S. Falla and A. J. Ryder. Oxford: Clarendon, 1982.

*Literarische Welt: Dokumente zum Leben und Werk von Hans Mayer.* Cologne: Historisches Archiv der Stadt Köln, 1985.

Lönnendonker, Siegward, Bernd Rabehl, and Jochen Staadt. *Die antiautoritäre Revolte: Der Sozialistische Deutsche Studentenbund nach der Trennung von der SPD.* Vol. I, *1960–1967.* Wiesbaden: Westdeutscher, 2002.

Loth, Wilfried. *The Division of the World, 1941–1955.* New York: St. Martin's, 1988.

Luks, Leonid. "Osteuropäische Dissidenten- und Protestbewegungen von 1956–1989 als 'Vorboten' der friedlichen Revolution von 1989–1991." *Forum für osteuropäische Ideen- und Zeitgeschichte* 9, no. 1 (2005): 17–42.

Lunn, Eugene. *Marxism and Modernism: An Historical Study of Lukács, Brecht, Benjamin, and Adorno.* Berkeley: University of California Press, 1982.

Madrasch-Groschopp, Ursula. *Die Weltbühne: Porträt einer Zeitschrift.* Berlin: Der Morgen, 1983.

Major, Patrick. *The Death of the KPD: Communism and Anti-Communism in West Germany, 1945–1956.* Oxford: Oxford University Press, 1997.

Malende, Christiane. "Die 'Wiedererrichtung' und Trennung des P.E.N.-Zentrums Deutschland 1946/48 bis 1951/53." *Zeitschrift für Germanistik* 5 n.s., no. 1 (1995): 82–95.
Malycha, Andreas. *Die SED: Geschichte ihrer Stalinisierung 1946–1953*. Paderborn: Schöningh, 2000.
Mandelkow, Karl Robert. *Goethe in Deutschland: Rezeptionsgeschichte eines Klassikers*. Vol. II, *1919–1982*. Munich: Beck, 1989.
Mannheim, Karl. "The Problem of Generations." In *From Karl Mannheim*, ed. Kurt H. Wolff, 351–98. 2nd edn. New Brunswick, N.J.: Transaction, 1993.
Markovits, Andrei S. *The Politics of the West German Trade Unions: Strategies of Class and Interest Representation in Growth and Crisis*. Cambridge: Cambridge University Press, 1986.
Markovits, Andrei S., and Philip S. Gorski. *The German Left: Red, Green, and Beyond*. New York: Oxford University Press, 1993.
Marszolek, Inge. "Coverage of the Bergen-Belsen Trial and the Auschwitz Trial in the NWDR/NDR: The Reports of Axel Eggebrecht." In *Holocaust and Justice: Representation and Historiography of the Holocaust in Post-War Trials*, ed. David Bankier and Dan Mikhman, 131–57. New York: Berghahn, 2010.
McCormick, John P., ed. *Confronting Mass Democracy and Industrial Technology: Political and Social Theory from Nietzsche to Habermas*. Durham, N.C.: Duke University Press, 2002.
McLellan, Josie. "The Politics of Communist Biography: Alfred Kantorowicz and the Spanish Civil War." *German History* 22, no. 4 (2004): 536–62.
Meier, Bettina. *Goethe in Trümmern: Zur Rezeption eines Klassikers in der Nachkriegszeit*. Wiesbaden: Deutscher Universitäts-Verlag, 1989.
Mergel, Thomas. "Dictatorship and Democracy, 1918–1939." In *The Oxford Handbook of Modern German History*, ed. Helmut Walser Smith, 423–52. Oxford: Oxford University Press, 2011.
Mittenzwei, Werner. *Exil in der Schweiz*. 2nd edn. Frankfurt a.M.: Röderberg, 1981.
*Die Intellektuellen: Literatur und Politik in Ostdeutschland von 1945 bis 2000*. Leipzig: Faber & Faber, 2001.
Moeller, Robert G. *War Stories: The Search for a Usable Past in the Federal Republic of Germany*. Berkeley: University of California Press, 2001.
Mohr, Arno. *Politikwissenschaft als Alternative: Stationen einer wissenschaftlichen Disziplin auf dem Wege zu ihrer Selbständigkeit in der Bundesrepublik Deutschland 1945–1965*. Bochum: Brockmeyer, 1988.
Mommsen, Hans. *Alternatives to Hitler: German Resistance under the Third Reich*. Translated by Angus McGeoch. Princeton, N.J.: Princeton University Press, 2003.
Mooser, Josef. "Liberalismus und Gesellschaft nach 1945: Soziale Marktwirtschaft und Neoliberalismus am Beispiel von Wilhelm Röpke." In *Bürgertum nach 1945*, ed. Manfred Hettling and Bernd Ulrich, 134–63. Hamburg: Hamburger Edition, 2005.
Morat, Daniel. *Von der Tat zur Gelassenheit: Konservatives Denken bei Martin Heidegger, Ernst Jünger und Friedrich Georg Jünger 1920–1960*. Göttingen: Wallstein, 2007.

Moses, A. Dirk. "The Forty-Fivers: A Generation between Fascism and Democracy." *German Politics and Society* 17, no. 1 (1999): 94–126.

"Forum: Intellectual History in and of the Federal Republic of Germany." *Modern Intellectual History* 9, no. 3 (2012): 625–39.

*German Intellectuals and the Nazi Past.* Cambridge: Cambridge University Press, 2007.

Mühlen, Patrik von zur. *Aufbruch und Umbruch in der DDR: Bürgerbewegungen, kritische Öffentlichkeit und Niedergang der SED-Herrschaft.* Bonn: Dietz, 2000.

Mühlhausen, Walter. *Hessen 1945–1950: Zur politischen Geschichte eines Landes in der Besatzungszeit.* Frankfurt a.M.: Insel, 1985.

Müller, Jan-Werner, ed. *Contesting Democracy: Political Ideas in Twentieth-Century Europe.* New Haven, Conn.: Yale University Press, 2011.

"European Intellectual History as Contemporary History." *Journal of Contemporary History* 46, no. 3 (2011): 574–90.

*German Ideologies since 1945: Studies in the Political Thought and Culture of the Bonn Republic.* New York: Palgrave, 2003.

Müller, Tim B. *Krieger und Gelehrte: Herbert Marcuse und die Denksysteme im Kalten Krieg.* Hamburg: Hamburger Edition, 2010.

Musiolek, Berndt. "Peter Alfons Steiniger: Zwischen Illusion und Wirklichkeit." In *Rechtsgeschichtswissenschaft in Deutschland 1945 bis 1952*, ed. Horst Schröder and Dieter Simon, 253–73. Frankfurt a.M.: Klostermann, 2001.

Naimark, Norman M. *The Russians in Germany: A History of the Soviet Zone of Occupation, 1945–1949.* Cambridge, Mass.: Harvard University Press, 1995.

Naimark, Norman M., and Leonid Gibianskii, eds. *The Establishment of Communist Regimes in Eastern Europe, 1944–1949.* Boulder, Colo.: Westview, 1997.

Neaman, Elliot Y. *A Dubious Past: Ernst Jünger and the Politics of Literature after Nazism.* Berkeley: University of California Press, 1999.

Nehring, Holger. *Politics of Security: British and West German Protest Movements and the Early Cold War, 1945–1970.* Oxford: Oxford University Press, 2013.

Neubert, Ehrhart. *Geschichte der Opposition in der DDR 1949–1989.* Berlin: Links, 1997.

Niethammer, Lutz, Ulrich Borsdorf, and Peter Brandt, eds. *Arbeiterinitiative 1945: Antifaschistische Ausschüsse und Reorganisation der Arbeiterbewegung in Deutschland.* Wuppertal: Hammer, 1976.

Nipp-Stolzenburg, Luitgard. "Eine 'Freie Lehrstätte für die geistig Aufgeschlossenen': 50 Jahre Volkshochschule Heidelberg." In *"Volksbildung nötiger denn je..."*: *50 Jahre Volkshochschule Heidelberg*, 69–176. Heidelberg: Winter, 1996.

Nolte, Paul. *Die Ordnung der deutschen Gesellschaft: Selbstentwurf und Selbstbeschreibung im 20. Jahrhundert.* Munich: Beck, 2000.

Oels, David. *Rowohlts Rotationsroutine: Markterfolge und Modernisierung eines Buchverlags vom Ende der Weimarer Republik bis in die fünfziger Jahre.* Essen: Klartext, 2013.

Olick, Jeffrey K. *In the House of the Hangman: The Agonies of German Defeat, 1943–1949.* Chicago: University of Chicago Press, 2005.

Oppenheimer, Andrew. "West German Pacifism and the Ambivalence of Human Solidarity, 1945–1968." *Peace & Change* 29, no. 3–4 (2004): 353–89.

Oswalt, Stefanie, ed. *Die Weltbühne: Zur Tradition und Kontinuität demokratischer Publizistik.* St. Ingbert: Röhrig Universitätsverlag, 2003.
Otto, Karl A. *Vom Ostermarsch zur APO: Geschichte der außerparlamentarischen Opposition in der Bundesrepublik 1960–1970.* Frankfurt a.M.: Campus, 1977.
Palmier, Jean-Michel. *Weimar in Exile: The Antifascist Emigration in Europe and America.* Translated by David Fernbach. London: Verso, 2006.
Pape, Birgit. *Kultureller Neubeginn in Heidelberg und Mannheim 1945–1949.* Heidelberg: Winter, 2000.
Payk, Marcus M. *Der Geist der Demokratie: Intellektuelle Orientierungsversuche im Feuilleton der frühen Bundesrepublik: Karl Korn und Peter de Mendelssohn.* Munich: Oldenbourg, 2008.
Peitsch, Helmut. "Ein Brennpunkt der Nachkriegsliteratur: Der deutsche Schriftstellerkongreß in Frankfurt am Main 1948." In *Heiss und kalt: Die Jahre 1945–69,* 177–83. Berlin: Elefanten, 1986.
Pence, Katherine, and Paul Betts, eds. *Socialist Modern: East German Everyday Culture and Politics.* Ann Arbor: University of Michigan Press, 2008.
Pendas, Devin O. "Retroactive Law and Proactive Justice: Debating Crimes against Humanity in Germany, 1945–1950." *Central European History* 43, no. 3 (2010): 428–63.
Pietrzynski, Ingrid. "Ein 'Offener Brief' als Schadensbegrenzung: Hans Mayer und der DDR-Rundfunk 1956." *Rundfunk und Geschichte* 28, no. 3/4 (2002): 129–38.
Pike, David. *The Politics of Culture in Soviet-Occupied Germany, 1945–1949.* Stanford, Calif.: Stanford University Press, 1992.
Pinkard, Terry. *German Philosophy 1760–1860: The Legacy of Idealism.* Cambridge: Cambridge University Press, 2002.
Pollack, Detlef. "Die konstitutive Widersprüchlichkeit der DDR oder War die DDR-Gesellschaft homogen?" *Geschichte und Gesellschaft* 24, no. 1 (1998): 110–31.
Postone, Moishe. "Lukács and the Dialectical Critique of Capitalism." In *New Dialectics and Political Economy,* ed. Robert Albritton and John Simoulidis, 78–100. Basingstoke: Palgrave, 2003.
Priestland, David. "Soviet Democracy, 1917–91." *European History Quarterly* 32, no. 1 (2002): 111–30.
Pritchard, Gareth. *Niemandsland: A History of Unoccupied Germany, 1944–1945.* Cambridge: Cambridge University Press, 2012.
Prokop, Siegfried. *1956 – DDR am Scheideweg: Opposition und neue Konzepte der Intelligenz.* Berlin: Homilius, 2006.
*Ich bin zu früh geboren: Auf den Spuren Wolfgang Harichs.* Berlin: Dietz, 1997.
*Intellektuelle im Krisenjahr 1953: Enquete über die Lage der Intelligenz der DDR: Analyse und Dokumentation.* Schkeuditz: Schkeuditzer Buchverlag, 2003.
Prowe, Diethelm. "Demokratisierung in Deutschland nach 1945: Die Ansätze des Schlüsseljahres 1947." In *Deutsche Umbrüche im 20. Jahrhundert,* ed. Dietrich Papenfuß and Wolfgang Schieder, 447–57. Cologne: Böhlau, 2000.
"Economic Democracy in Post-World War II Germany: Corporatist Crisis Response, 1945–1948." *Journal of Modern History* 57, no. 3 (1985): 451–82.

"Socialism as Crisis Response: Socialization and the Escape from Poverty and Power in Post-World War II Germany." *German Studies Review* 15, no. 1 (1992): 65–85.
Prümm, Karl. *Walter Dirks und Eugen Kogon als katholische Publizisten der Weimarer Republik.* Heidelberg: Winter, 1984.
Puaca, Brian M. *Learning Democracy: Education Reform in West Germany, 1945–1965.* New York: Berghahn, 2009.
Rabinbach, Anson. *Begriffe aus dem Kalten Krieg: Totalitarismus, Antifaschismus, Genozid.* Göttingen: Wallstein, 2009.
*In the Shadow of Catastrophe: German Intellectuals between Apocalypse and Enlightenment.* Berkeley: University of California Press, 1997.
"Paris, Capital of Anti-Fascism." In *The Modernist Imagination: Intellectual History and Critical Theory: Essays in Honor of Martin Jay*, ed. Warren Breckman, Peter E. Gordon, A. Dirk Moses, Samuel Moyn and Elliot Neaman, 183–209. New York: Berghahn, 2009.
Rahden, Till van. "Clumsy Democrats: Moral Passions in the Federal Republic." *German History* 29, no. 3 (2011): 485–504.
"Fatherhood, Rechristianization, and the Quest for Democracy in Postwar West Germany." In *Raising Citizens in the "Century of the Child": The United States and German Central Europe in Comparative Perspective*, ed. Dirk Schumann, 141–64. New York: Berghahn, 2010.
Raphael, Lutz. "Radikales Ordnungsdenken und die Organisation totalitärer Herrschaft: Humanwissenschaftler und Experten im NS-Regime." *Geschichte und Gesellschaft* 27, no. 1 (2001): 5–40.
Reinhardt, Stephan. *Alfred Andersch: Eine Biographie.* Zurich: Diogenes, 1990.
Reinhold, Ursula, and Dieter Schlenstedt. "Vorgeschichte, Umfeld, Nachgeschichte des Ersten Deutschen Schriftstellerkongresses." In *Erster deutscher Schriftstellerkongreß 4.–8. Oktober 1947: Protokoll und Dokumente*, ed. Reinhold, Schlenstedt, and Horst Tanneberger, 13–76. Berlin: Aufbau, 1997.
Reitmayer, Morten. *Elite: Sozialgeschichte einer politisch-gesellschaftlichen Idee in der frühen Bundesrepublik.* Munich: Oldenbourg, 2009.
Remy, Steven P. *The Heidelberg Myth: The Nazification and Denazification of a German University.* Cambridge, Mass.: Harvard University Press, 2002.
Requate, Jörg. "Öffentlichkeit und Medien als Gegenstände historischer Analyse." *Geschichte und Gesellschaft* 25, no. 1 (1999): 5–32.
Reutter, Friederike. *Heidelberg 1945–1949: Zur politischen Geschichte einer Stadt in der Nachkriegszeit.* Heidelberg: Guderjahn, 1994.
Richards, Robert J. *The Romantic Conception of Life: Science and Philosophy in the Age of Goethe.* Chicago: University of Chicago Press, 2002.
Ringer, Fritz K. *The Decline of the German Mandarins: The German Academic Community, 1890–1933.* Cambridge, Mass.: Harvard University Press, 1969.
Rohrwasser, Michael. *Der Stalinismus und die Renegaten: Die Literatur der Exkommunisten.* Stuttgart: Metzler, 1991.
Rotberg, Joachim. *Zwischen Linkskatholizismus und bürgerlicher Sammlung: Die Anfänge der CDU in Frankfurt am Main 1945–1946.* Frankfurt a.M.: Knecht, 1999.

Roth, Guenther. *Max Webers deutsch-englische Familiengeschichte 1800–1950*. Tübingen: Mohr Siebeck, 2001.
Rüden, Peter von, and Hans-Ulrich Wagner, eds. *Die Geschichte des Nordwestdeutschen Rundfunks*. Hamburg: Hoffmann & Campe, 2005.
Ruge, Undine. "Regionen als organische Gemeinschaften: Der integralföderalistische Diskurs in Deutschland nach 1945." In *Das Erbe der Provinz: Heimatkultur und Geschichtspolitik nach 1945*, ed. Habbo Knoch, 73–96. Göttingen: Wallstein, 2001.
Rupp, Hans Karl. *Außerparlamentarische Opposition in der Ära Adenauer: Der Kampf gegen die Atombewaffnung in den fünfziger Jahren*. Cologne: Pahl-Rugenstein, 1970.
Sabrow, Martin. "Der vergessene 'Dritte Weg'." *Aus Politik und Zeitgeschichte* B11 (2010): 6–13.
Saner, Hans. *Karl Jaspers in Selbstzeugnissen und Bilddokumenten*. Reinbek b.H.: Rowohlt, 1970.
Sartori, Andrew. "The Resonance of 'Culture': Framing a Problem in Global Concept-History." *Comparative Studies in Society & History* 47, no. 4 (2005): 676–99.
Saunders, Frances Stonor. *The Cultural Cold War: The CIA and the World of Arts and Letters*. New York: New Press, 2000.
Scheibe, Siegfried. *Aufbau: Berlin 1945–1958: Bibliographie einer Zeitschrift*. Berlin: Aufbau, 1978.
Schildt, Axel. "Das Jahrhundert der Massenmedien: Ansichten zu einer künftigen Geschichte der Öffentlichkeit." *Geschichte und Gesellschaft* 27, no. 2 (2001): 177–206.
*Moderne Zeiten: Freizeit, Massenmedien und "Zeitgeist" in der Bundesrepublik der 50er Jahre*. Hamburg: Christians, 1995.
*Zwischen Abendland und Amerika: Studien zur westdeutschen Ideenlandschaft der 50er Jahre*. Munich: Oldenbourg, 1999.
Schildt, Axel, and Arnold Sywottek, eds. *Modernisierung im Wiederaufbau: Die westdeutsche Gesellschaft der 50er Jahre*. Bonn: Dietz, 1993.
Schiller, Dieter. *Der Traum von Hitlers Sturz: Studien zur deutschen Exilliteratur 1933–1945*. Frankfurt a.M.: Lang, 2010.
*Der verweigerte Dialog: Zum Verhältnis von Parteiführung der SED und Schriftstellern im Krisenjahr 1956*. Berlin: Dietz, 2001.
Schissler, Hanna, ed. *The Miracle Years: A Cultural History of West Germany, 1949–1968*. Princeton, N.J.: Princeton University Press, 2001.
Schivelbusch, Wolfgang. *In a Cold Crater: Cultural and Intellectual Life in Berlin, 1945–1948*. Translated by Kelly Barry. Berkeley: University of California Press, 1998.
Schlak, Stephan. *Wilhelm Hennis: Szenen einer Ideengeschichte der Bundesrepublik*. Munich: Beck, 2008.
Schneider, Michael. *Demokratie in Gefahr? Der Konflikt um die Notstandsgesetze: Sozialdemokratie, Gewerkschaften und intellektueller Protest (1958–1968)*. Bonn: Neue Gesellschaft, 1986.
Schulz, Eberhart. *Zwischen Identifikation und Opposition: Künstler und Wissenschaftler der DDR und ihre Organisationen von 1949 bis 1962*. Cologne: PapyRossa, 1995.

Schuster, Armin. *Die Entnazifizierung in Hessen 1945–1954: Vergangenheitspolitik in der Nachkriegszeit.* Wiesbaden: Historische Kommission für Nassau, 1999.

Schwab, Hans-Rüdiger, ed. *Eigensinn und Bindung: Katholische deutsche Intellektuelle im 20. Jahrhundert.* Kevelaer: Butzon & Bercker, 2009.

Schwarz, Hans-Peter. *Vom Reich zur Bundesrepublik: Deutschland im Widerstreit der außenpolitischen Konzeptionen in den Jahren der Besatzungsherrschaft 1945–1949.* 2nd edn. Stuttgart: Klett-Cotta, 1980.

Schwiedrzik, Wolfgang. *Träume der ersten Stunde: Die Gesellschaft Imshausen.* Berlin: Siedler, 1991.

Scott, John, ed. *Social Networks: Critical Concepts in Sociology.* 4 vols. London: Routledge, 2002.

Scott-Smith, Giles. *The Politics of Apolitical Culture: The Congress for Cultural Freedom, the CIA, and Post-War American Hegemony.* London: Routledge, 2001.

"'A Radical Democratic Political Offensive': Melvin J. Lasky, Der Monat, and the Congress for Cultural Freedom." *Journal of Contemporary History* 35, no. 2 (2000): 263–80.

Seng, Joachim. *Goethe-Enthusiasmus und Bürgersinn: Das Freie Deutsche Hochstift – Frankfurter Goethe-Museum 1881–1960.* Göttingen: Wallstein, 2009.

Sewell, William H., Jr. *Logics of History: Social Theory and Social Transformation.* Chicago: University of Chicago Press, 2005.

Siegfried, Detlef. *Time Is on My Side: Konsum und Politik in der westdeutschen Jugendkultur der 60er Jahre.* Göttingen: Wallstein, 2006.

Solchany, Jean. *Comprendre le nazisme dans l'Allemagne des années zéro 1945–1949.* Paris: Presses universitaires de France, 1997.

Söllner, Alfons. "'Political culturalism?': Adorno's 'Entrance' in the Cultural Concert of West-German Postwar History." In *Exile, Science, and Bildung: The Contested Legacies of German Emigre Intellectuals,* ed. David Kettler and Gerhard Lauer, 185–200. New York: Palgrave Macmillan, 2005.

Sontheimer, Kurt. *Antidemokratisches Denken in der Weimarer Republik: Die politischen Ideen des deutschen Nationalismus zwischen 1918 und 1933.* Munich: Nymphenburger Verlagshandlung, 1962.

Später, Jörg. *Vansittart: Britische Debatten über Deutsche und Nazis 1902–1945.* Göttingen: Wallstein, 2003.

Specter, Matthew G. *Habermas: An Intellectual Biography.* Cambridge: Cambridge University Press, 2010.

Spernol, Boris. *Notstand der Demokratie: Der Protest gegen die Notstandsgesetze und die Frage der NS-Vergangenheit.* Essen: Klartext, 2008.

Spies, Carola. "Der Kulturbund zur Demokratischen Erneuerung Deutschlands: Seine Anfänge in Westdeutschland aufgezeigt anhand der Entwicklung in Düsseldorf." In *Öffentlichkeit der Moderne, die Moderne in der Öffentlichkeit: Das Rheinland 1945–1955,* ed. Dieter Breuer and Gertrude Cepl-Kaufmann, 69–84. Essen: Klartext, 2000.

Springorum, Ulrich. *Entstehung und Aufbau der Verwaltung in Rheinland-Pfalz nach dem Zweiten Weltkrieg (1945–1947).* Berlin: Duncker & Humblot, 1982.

Stankowski, Martin. *Linkskatholizismus nach 1945: Die Presse oppositioneller Katholiken in der Auseinandersetzung für eine demokratische und sozialistische Gesellschaft.* Cologne: Pahl-Rugenstein, 1976.

Stargardt, Nicholas. *The German Idea of Militarism: Radical and Socialist Critics, 1866–1914*. Cambridge: Cambridge University Press, 1994.
Steege, Paul. *Black Market, Cold War: Everyday Life in Berlin, 1946–1949*. Cambridge: Cambridge University Press, 2007.
Steinmetz, George. "German Exceptionalism and the Origins of Nazism: The Career of a Concept." In *Stalinism and Nazism: Dictatorships in Comparison*, ed. Ian Kershaw and Moshe Lewin, 251–84. Cambridge: Cambridge University Press, 1997.
Stephan, Gerd-Rüdiger, Andreas Herbst, Christine Krauss, Daniel Küchenmeister, and Detlef Nakath, eds. *Die Parteien und Organisationen der DDR: Ein Handbuch*. Berlin: Dietz, 2002.
Stolleis, Michael. "Besatzungsherrschaft und Wiederaufbau deutscher Staatlichkeit 1945–1949." In *Handbuch des Staatsrechts der Bundesrepublik Deutschland*. Vol. I, *Historische Grundlagen*, ed. Josef Isensee and Paul Kirchhof, 269–313. Heidelberg: Müller Juristischer Verlag, 2003.
Stöver, Bernd. *Der Kalte Krieg 1947–1991: Geschichte eines radikalen Zeitalters*. Munich: Beck, 2007.
Strunk, Peter. *Zensur und Zensoren: Medienkontrolle und Propagandapolitik unter sowjetischer Besatzungsherrschaft in Deutschland*. Berlin: Akademie, 1996.
Struve, Walter. *Elites against Democracy: Leadership Ideals in Bourgeois Political Thought in Germany, 1890–1933*. Princeton, N.J.: Princeton University Press, 1973.
Swartz, David. *Culture and Power: The Sociology of Pierre Bourdieu*. Chicago: University of Chicago Press, 1997.
Talata, Danièle. "Die Wandlung: Pour un renouveau de l'Allemagne, revue politique et littéraire 1945–1949." *Allemagne d'aujourd'hui* 164 (2003): 145–60.
Tent, James F. *The Free University of Berlin: A Political History*. Bloomington: Indiana University Press, 1988.
  *Mission on the Rhine: Reeducation and Denazification in American-Occupied Germany*. Chicago: University of Chicago Press, 1982.
Therborn, Göran. *European Modernity and Beyond: The Trajectory of European Societies, 1945–2000*. London: Sage, 1995.
Torpey, John C. *Intellectuals, Socialism, and Dissent: The East German Opposition and its Legacy*. Minneapolis: University of Minnesota Press, 1995.
Treiber, Hubert, and Karol Sauerland, eds. *Heidelberg im Schnittpunkt intellektueller Kreise: Zur Topographie der geistigen Geselligkeit eines Weltdorfes 1850–1950*. Opladen: Westdeutscher, 1995.
Treß, Werner. *Wider den undeutschen Geist: Bücherverbrennung 1933*. Berlin: Parthas, 2003.
Ullrich, Sebastian. *Der Weimar-Komplex: Das Scheitern der ersten deutschen Demokratie und die politische Kultur der frühen Bundesrepublik 1945–1959*. Göttingen: Wallstein, 2009.
Vaillant, Jérôme. *Der Ruf: Unabhängige Blätter der jungen Generation (1945–1949): Eine Zeitschrift zwischen Illusion und Anpassung*. Munich: Saur, 1978.
Van Hook, James C. *Rebuilding Germany: The Creation of the Social Market Economy, 1945–1957*. Cambridge: Cambridge University Press, 2004.

Verheyen, Nina. *Diskussionslust: Zur Kulturgeschichte des 'besseren Arguments' in Westdeutschland.* Göttingen: Vandenhoeck & Ruprecht, 2010.
Vogt, Stefan. *Nationaler Sozialismus und Soziale Demokratie: Die sozialdemokratische Junge Rechte 1918–1945.* Bonn: Dietz, 2006.
Vogt, Timothy R. *Denazification in Soviet-Occupied Germany: Brandenburg, 1945–1948.* Cambridge, Mass.: Harvard University Press, 2000.
Vollnhals, Clemens, ed. *Entnazifizierung: Politische Säuberung und Rehabilitierung in den vier Besatzungszonen 1945–1949.* Munich: Deutscher Taschenbuch Verlag, 1991.
Wagner, Hans-Ulrich. *"Der gute Wille, etwas Neues zu schaffen": Das Hörspielprogramm in Deutschland von 1945 bis 1949.* Potsdam: Verlag für Berlin-Brandenburg, 1997.
Waldmüller, Monika. *Die Wandlung: Eine Monatsschrift.* Marbach a.N.: Deutsche Schillergesellschaft, 1988.
Warner, Michael. "Origins of the Congress for Cultural Freedom, 1949–50." *Studies in Intelligence* 38, no. 5 (1995): 89–98.
Weber, Max. "The Profession and Vocation of Politics." In *Political Writings*, ed. Peter Lassman and Roland Speirs, 309–69. Cambridge: Cambridge University Press, 1994.
Weber, Petra. *Carlo Schmid 1896–1979: Eine Biographie.* Munich: Beck, 1996.
Wehner, Jens. *Kulturpolitik und Volksfront: Ein Beitrag zur Geschichte der Sowjetischen Besatzungszone Deutschlands 1945–1949.* 2 vols. Frankfurt a.M.: Lang, 1992.
Weitz, Eric D. *Creating German Communism, 1890–1990: From Popular Protests to Socialist State.* Princeton, N.J.: Princeton University Press, 1997.
Welzer, Harald, Sabine Moller, and Karoline Tschuggnall. *Opa war kein Nazi: Nationalsozialismus und Holocaust im Familiengedächtnis.* Frankfurt a.M.: Fischer, 2002.
Wende-Hohenberger, Waltraud. Preface to *Der Frankfurter Schriftstellerkongreß im Jahr 1948*, ed. Wende-Hohenberger. Frankfurt a.M.: Lang, 1989.
Werner, Michael. *Die "Ohne mich"-Bewegung: Die bundesdeutsche Friedensbewegung im deutsch-deutschen Kalten Krieg (1949–1955).* Münster: Monsenstein & Vannerdat, 2006.
Westad, Odd Arne. *The Global Cold War: Third World Interventions and the Making of Our Times.* Cambridge: Cambridge University Press, 2005.
Wette, Wolfram, ed. *Schule der Gewalt: Militarismus in Deutschland 1871–1945.* Berlin: Aufbau, 2005.
Wickberg, Daniel. "Intellectual History vs. the Social History of Intellectuals." *Rethinking History* 5, no. 3 (2001): 383–95.
Wiggershaus, Rolf. *The Frankfurt School: Its History, Theories, and Political Significance.* Translated by Michael Robertson. Cambridge, Mass.: MIT Press, 1994.
Wildt, Michael. *An Uncompromising Generation: The Nazi Leadership of the Reich Security Main Office.* Translated by Tom Lampert. Madison: University of Wisconsin Press, 2009.
Wilkinson, James D. *The Intellectual Resistance in Europe.* Cambridge, Mass.: Harvard University Press, 1981.

Williams, Raymond. "Democracy." In *Keywords: A Vocabulary of Culture and Society*, 93–98. New York: Oxford University Press, 1985.
Williams, Rhys W., Stephen Parker, and Colin Riordan, eds. *German Writers and the Cold War, 1945–1961*. Manchester: Manchester University Press, 1992.
Wippermann, Wolfgang. *Faschismustheorien: die Entwicklung der Diskussion von den Anfängen bis heute*. 7th edn. Darmstadt: Wissenschaftliche Buchgesellschaft, 1997.
Wolbring, Barbara. "Nationales Stigma und persönliche Schuld: Die Debatte über Kollektivschuld in der Nachkriegszeit." *Historische Zeitschrift* 289, no. 2 (2009): 325–64.
Wolfrum, Edgar, Peter Fässler, and Reinhard Grohnert. *Krisenjahre und Aufbruchszeit: Alltag und Politik im französisch besetzten Baden 1945–1949*. Munich: Oldenbourg, 1996.
Wolle, Stefan. *Der Traum von der Revolte: Die DDR 1968*. Berlin: Links, 2008.
Wuermeling, Henric L. *Die weiße Liste: Umbruch der politischen Kultur in Deutschland 1945*. Berlin: Ullstein, 1981.
Wurm, Carsten. *Der frühe Aufbau-Verlag 1945–1961: Konzepte und Kontroversen*. Wiesbaden: Harrassowitz, 1996.
Zarusky, Jürgen, ed. *Die Stalinnote vom 10. März 1952: Neue Quellen und Analysen*. Munich: Oldenbourg Wissenschaftsverlag, 2002.
Zipes, Jack. "The Critical Embracement of Germany: Hans Mayer and Marcel Reich-Ranicki." In *Unlikely History: The Changing German-Jewish Symbiosis, 1945–2000*, ed. Leslie Morris and Zipes, 183–201. New York: Palgrave, 2002.
Zudeick, Peter. *Der Hintern des Teufels: Ernst Bloch, Leben und Werk*. Bühl-Moos: Elster, 1985.

# Index

Abendland. *See* Christianity: Occident
Abendroth, Wolfgang, 28, 149n2, 242–3, 305, 317, 325, 330n25
Abusch, Alexander, 31, 47, 65, 198, 263
Ackermann, Anton, 48, 65, 196n8, 197, 225
Adenauer, Konrad, 280, 291, 294, 304, 306, 308, 309
Adorno, Theodor W., 81, 236, 312, 313–15, 316, 324, 326
Aktionsgruppe Heidelberg, 27, 106n115, 162–74, 180–2, 184n125, 184–6
  Call to German Unity, 178–80
  and SPD, 172–3
Alewyn, Richard, 145
Andersch, Alfred, 64, 65, 121, 121n19, 188, 222, 256, 297, 314
*Antifa* committees, 12, 100
antifascism, 9, 11, 21, 40, 207–9, 239
  "other Germany," 59–60, 211, 331
antinuclear movement, 306–8, 325
anti-Semitism. *See under* Jews, persecution of
Arendt, Hannah, 24, 132, 134, 252, 317
*Aufbau* (journal), 31–2, 32n42, 46, 174, 198, 201, 270
Aufbau (publisher), 31, 40, 261, 270
Auschwitz Trial, Frankfurt, 326
Austria, 22, 34
authoritarianism, 117–18, 125–7, 129–30, 133, 166
  "lifeless obedience" (*Kadavergehorsam*), 89, 125, 126

Baden-Baden, 48, 68
Barthel, Kurt, 262, 276
Bartning, Otto, 143–4, 316
Bauer, Arnold, 32, 42, 108n124, 218, 229
Bauer, Leo, 202–3, 252, 252n40
Baum, Marie, 163, 170, 175, 316
Becher, Johannes R., 31, 38, 65, 178, 260, 338
  as Culture Minister, 264, 268
  and Kulturbund, 196–7, 199, 201, 223
  and popular front, 208–9
  and writers' congresses, 211, 212, 215, 228
  and writers' organizations, 210, 235–6
Beckmann, Eberhard, 202–3, 210
Behrens, Fritz, 91n61, 255
Benda, Julien, 15n55, 150n4, 206, 209
Bergen-Belsen Trial, 134
Berlin, 28–34, 40, 178–9, 181, 196–7, 223, 245–6
  Artists' Colony, 37–8, 38n59
  East, 255, 256, 336, 339
  West, 104n109, 276, 283, 284, 328–9
*Berliner Zeitung*, 45, 221, 234, 264, 337
Beutler, Ernst, 140–1, 144, 202
Biermann, Wolf, 333–4
*Bildung* (self-formation, -cultivation, -education). *See* cultural heritage; culturalism
Birkenfeld, Günther, 67, 198, 223, 224, 233, 235
  and writers' activities, 210, 211, 215, 218
Bloch, Ernst, 13, 38, 42, 83, 83n31, 235, 239, 255, 260, 265, 270, 277, 318n118
  on freedom, 84–6, 266–7
  and FRG, 275, 326
  and GDR/SED, 255–6, 268, 275
  and popular front, 84, 209
  and sixty-eighters, 332
  and Soviet Union, 83–4, 109, 266
  on universities, 109
Bloch, Karola, 38, 38n59, 42, 255, 275
Böll, Heinrich, 121, 306, 316, 324, 326, 330n25
Bonn, 182, 326
Bourdieu, Pierre, 15, 15n52, 150n4
Boyer, Dominic, 78
Brandt, Günter, 32, 33

# Index

Brecht, Bertolt, 28, 32, 38n59, 209, 235, 255, 262, 263–4, 287
Bremen, 40
Brentano, Heinrich von, 175, 184, 186
Brill, Hermann, 52, 164
Britain, Great, 19, 28, 98
Buchenwald, 22, 28, 29, 52, 133, 145
Budzislawski, Hermann, 32, 38–9, 40, 255
Burnham, James, 232, 287, 301

capitalism, 19, 59, 87
Carlebach, Emil, 52, 222
Catholicism and Catholics. *See* Christianity
CDU (Christian Democratic Union), 153, 179, 183, 280, 298, 306, 309, 323, 325
 Frankfurt/Hesse, 23, 156–7
censorship. *See* information policy
Chamber of Art Makers, 30, 197, 210
Christianity, 23, 52, 68, 69, 81, 82–3, 83n30, 127, 297, 305
 churches, 20, 95, 334
 Occident, 68–9
codetermination, 90, 97, 98, 99, 298–9
Cold War, 7–8, 9, 177, 221, 223, 242
 cultural, 194, 216–17, 221, 223–5, 236, 282
"collective guilt." *See under* guilt and resentment
Cologne, 153, 298, 316
Communism, 4, 66–7, 85, 153, 331
 and coalition building, 48, 66, 103
 Comintern, 38, 198, 208, 209, 216
 "democratic centralism," 153, 271
 socialist realism, 254
 *See also* KPD; SED; Soviet Union
Congress for Cultural Freedom, 67, 282–4, 287
 1950 conference, 284–7
conservatism, 4. *See also* CDU; culturalism; Christianity: Occident; right-intellectuals
conservative revolution. *See under* right-intellectuals
Constance, Lake, 186, 201, 246
cultural heritage, 77–8, 114, 122–5, 213–14
 engaged democrats on, 10–11, 77, 144–6
Cultural Leagues. *See* Kulturbund organizations
culturalism, 115–16, 119–20, 140–1, 193, 236–7. *See also* elitism; "unpolitical German"
 engaged democrats on, 127

Curtius, E. R., 116, 139
Czechoslovakia, 32, 252, 253, 308
 Prague Spring, 333

Dahrendorf, Gustav, 197
Dahrendorf, Ralf, 316, 342
Darmstadt, 316, 325
democracy, 2, 74–5, 111–13
 council, 97–8, 100, 176
 liberal, 5, 12, 74, 97
 "people's democracy," 5, 48, 102–3, 242
 *See also* participation; publicness; self-education
denazification, 19, 30, 62–3, 103, 110n128
 engaged democrats on, 110
*Deutsche Zeitschrift für Philosophie*, 261
Dewey, John, 117, 284
DGB (German Federation of Unions), 298–9, 300, 302, 303
 and peace movement, 305–6
Dilschneider, Otto, 197, 200
Dirks, Walter, 23, 26, 57–8, 80–1, 128, 134–5, 189n138, 202, 239, 295, 305, 306, 316
 on Christianity, 69, 82, 94
 on coalitions, 94, 187, 301–2
 on codetermination, 97, 299–300
 on cultural heritage, 124, 142–3
 on education, 105, 127–8
 and elitism, 156, 157, 190
 on federalism, 96
 and Frankfurt School, 314
 on freedom, 81–2, 225–6
 and Imshausen Society, 188–90
 on journalism, 50, 161
 and National Socialism, 55, 94
 on "restoration," 143, 288–9, 294, 329–30
 Second Republic program, 94–5
 and unions, 300–1
 on "zero hour," 1–2, 138
Döblin, Alfred, 48, 212, 235
Drews, Richard, 29, 33, 42, 60
Dutschke, Rudi, 328–9, 332

Eckardt, Hans von, 163, 166–7, 169, 170, 306, 316
Edschmid, Kasimir, 229, 230–7
educated bourgeoisie, 114, 118, 119, 146, 193
education, formal, 103–4
 engaged democrats on, 104–5
 *See also* universities

Eggebrecht, Axel, 33–5, 37, 40, 42, 54, 63, 76, 136, 159, 201, 239, 276
  on camp trials, 134, 326
  on cultural heritage, 123, 147–8
  and FRG, 292, 306, 309, 330
  on occupation, 49
  on right-intellectuals, 71
  on socialism, 98, 158
  and *Die Weltbühne*, 57, 58, 155, 223
  and writers' activities, 210, 220, 235
  on "zero hour," 1
*Einheit*, 66, 174, 273
electoral systems, 92, 93, 163–4, 183–4
elitism, 4, 11, 150, 194–5
Emergency Laws, opposition to, 325, 326
émigrés, 44, 48, 49, 59, 61
  in Britain, 58, 117
  in France, 36, 38–9
  in Latin America, 66
  in Soviet Union, 66, 196
  in Switzerland, 36, 203
  in United States, 37, 39–40, 117–18
"émigrés, inner," 1, 24, 53–7
  vs. exiles, 20, 59–61, 216
émigrés, returning, 35, 37, 40, 44, 337
Enderle, Luiselotte, 34
engaged democrats, Germany's, 3, 75, 193–4, 321–2, 339–40
  and occupiers, 4–5, 20, 43, 49
  on right-intellectuals, 71–2, 340–1
  social network among, 13–14, 20, 63–4, 72
Engels, Friedrich, 85–6, 267, 268
Erpenbeck, Fritz, 196, 196n8
Europe Union Germany, 295–6, 303
European integration, 172, 173, 295, 303–4
exiles. *See* émigrés
existentialism, French, 64–5, 230
extraparliamentary opposition, 323, 324–5, 326

family, 80, 95, 111–12, 157, 318n116
Federal Republic of Germany, 238, 280, 281, 298–9, 319–20
  constitution, 98, 182
  engaged democrats and, 280, 281–2
  intellectual foundation of, 12–13
  Parliamentary Council, 182–3, 185–6
  rearmament, 291, 303–5, 306
  reintegration of ex-Nazis, 293
  *See also* public sphere: in FRG
Feuchtwanger, Lion, 208, 209
Fichte, J. G., 122, 123, 124

Fight Atomic Death campaign. *See* antinuclear movement
Forsthoff, Ernst, 316, 341
forty-fivers. *See under* generations
France, 19, 192, 266, 303–4
  revolution of 1789, 124, 126, 266
  *See also* Paris
Frankfurt am Main, 23, 36–7, 139–44, 156, 202–3, 226, 305, 326
Frankfurt School, 117, 312–13, 315, 324, 328
  Institute for Social Research, 36, 81, 313–14
*Frankfurter Hefte*, 23, 23n16, 37, 46, 65, 68, 161–2, 174, 296–8, 314
  and Oberursel Circle, 177
  and personalism, 94
*Frankfurter Rundschau*, 45, 222
*Frankfurter Zeitung*, 23, 25, 54–6, 141, 156
Freiburg im Breisgau, 56, 201
Freud, Sigmund, 313, 314
Friedensburg, Ferdinand, 32, 173–4, 178, 179, 180n105, 180–1, 197, 200
Fröhlich, Claudia, 3n10

*Gegenwart, Die*, 42, 56, 61, 174, 309
Geiler, Karl, 27, 163, 175, 178, 179
*Geist* (spirit). *See* cultural heritage; culturalism
generations, 13, 21–2, 22n10, 64n144, 121, 297, 324
  forty-fivers, 64, 147
  sixty-eighters, 323, 327–8, 330–1, 333;
    engaged democrats and, 329–31
German Democratic Republic, 238, 240–1, 332, 333
  constitution of 1949, 99, 242
  crises of 1953/1956, 261–3, 265, 273, 337, 338
  cultural repression in, 253–4, 258–9, 263–4, 337, 338–9
  engaged democrats and, 239–40, 241
  Ministry of State Security, 251, 263, 270, 275, 276, 337
  political repression in, 251–3, 273
  *See also* public sphere: in GDR
German Voters' Society. *See* Wählergesellschaft, Deutsche
Gesellschaft Imshausen. *See* Imshausen Society
Geyer, Michael, 72
Gide, André, 208, 209
Gilbert, Felix, 117, 120
Goethe, J. W. von, 120, 123, 124, 138–9, 219, 232

# Index

Goethe House, Frankfurt, 139–44, 288, 289
Gollwitzer, Helmut, 305, 306, 326
Gramsci, Antonio, 150n5
Grass, Günter, 121, 121n19, 276, 324, 326
Gropp, Rugard Otto, 275, 342
Grotewohl, Otto, 225
Gruppe 47, 121, 276, 306, 308, 324
guilt and resentment, 18, 61, 171–2
  "collective guilt," 9, 61, 65, 135, 139
  engaged democrats on, 133–8
GVP (All-German People's Party), 305, 306
Gysi, Klaus, 31, 197, 201, 204

Habe, Hans, 44, 337
Habermas, Jürgen, 3n9, 312, 317–19, 324, 326
Hagelstange, Rudolf, 229, 230, 231, 232n125, 235
Hallstein, Walter, 203
Hamburg, 34–5, 40, 201–2, 246, 278, 307
Hanover, 158, 276, 325, 332
Harich, Wolfgang, 13, 30–1, 44, 64, 78, 128, 246, 255, 256, 265, 274, 332, 336, 337
  and centralism, 99–100
  on freedom, 267–8
  GDR reform platform, 271–2
  and GDR/SED, 260–1, 263–4, 270–1, 273
  and KPD/SED, 66, 101, 153–4
  and Kulturbund, 197, 200
  on right-intellectuals, 71
  and Soviet Union, 246–7
  on "totalitarianism," 68
  and *Die Weltbühne*, 33, 154–6
  and writers' activities, 42, 216, 219
Harnack/Schulze-Boysen group. *See under* resistance
Hartlaub, Gustav, 204, 205
Hartmann, Gustav von, 175, 183, 184
Havemann, Robert, 197, 333–4
Hegel, G. W. F., 85–6, 122, 123, 124, 127, 260
Heidegger, Martin, 25, 69–70, 71, 79, 186, 313n99, 316, 340
Heidelberg, 24–7, 53–4, 162–5, 204, 306
Heidelberg Action Group for Democracy and Free Socialism. *See* Aktionsgruppe Heidelberg
Heine, Heinrich, 117, 125, 127, 280n3
Heinemann, Gustav, 305, 306
Henk, Emil, 25–6, 53–4

Hennis, Wilhelm, 316, 342
Herder, J. G., 123, 260
Herf, Jeffrey, 6
Hermlin, Stephan, 36, 36n53, 42, 202–3, 210, 222, 244–5, 246, 277, 334
Hertwig, Manfred, 261, 270, 273
Herzfelde, Wieland, 33, 42, 255
Hesse, 27, 110, 173, 173n81, 175, 177
Heuss, Theodor, 56, 56n118, 144, 201
Heym, Stefan, 44, 268, 334, 336–9
*hier und heute*, 296–8
Hiller, Kurt, 58, 195
Hilpert, Werner, 22, 27, 52, 156, 157, 177, 202
Holborn, Hajo, 117–18, 118n13, 120
Holocaust. *See* Jews, persecution of
Horkheimer, Max, 134, 312, 313–15, 316, 324
Huch, Ricarda, 51, 215–16
Huchel, Peter, 38, 255
Humboldt, Wilhelm von, 107, 123, 124, 127
Hungary, 252, 265, 266, 270, 275, 276, 317, 329, 335

idealism, German, 118, 122, 125. *See also* cultural heritage
Ihering, Herbert, 31, 42, 77, 136, 197, 200, 203, 245
Imshausen Society, 42, 188–90
information policy, 45, 46, 47, 159, 161, 221
  American, 26, 28, 34, 40, 44–5, 46, 55–6, 185n126, 221, 222, 223, 248
  British, 32, 34, 36, 44, 45, 46, 47, 223
  French, 30, 44, 45, 46, 47, 48, 56
  and press freedom, 159–60, 184–5
  Soviet, 31, 32, 40, 44, 46, 47, 197, 221, 222, 223
  *See also* Psychological Warfare Division; Red Army, Political Administration
inner émigrés. *See* "émigrés, inner"
Institute for Social Research. *See under* Frankfurt School
intellectuals, 15n55, 15–16, 16n56, 150n5, 192–3
  self-conceptions, 150–1
International Military Tribunal. *See* Nuremberg Trials

Jacobsohn, Siegfried, 32, 57
Jaffé-von Richthofen, Else, 24, 26n23
Jänecke, Walther, 184–5
Janka, Walter, 263, 270, 271, 273, 332, 336, 337

Jarausch, Konrad, 5
Jaspers, Gertrud, 53, 54
Jaspers, Karl, 24, 53, 69, 116, 206, 318
  and CCF, 283, 284
  on communication, 49, 79
  on cultural heritage, 121–2, 139, 144n77
  and FRG, 327
  on guilt, 61–2
  on occupation, 49
  and universities, 26, 107–8
Jellinek, Walter, 165, 182, 183
Jews, 10, 18, 35, 52–3, 57
  mixed marriages, 53, 75
Jews, persecution of, 32, 53, 54, 55, 136–7, 171
  anti-Semitism, 57, 131, 136
  Kristallnacht pogrom, 142
  in Soviet bloc, 252
  Warsaw ghetto uprising, 137, 171–2
journals, cultural-political, 21, 50, 114–15, 224. *See also specific titles*
July 20, 1944 plot. *See under* resistance
Jünger, Ernst, 25, 69–71, 186–7, 188, 211, 232, 340
Jünger, Friedrich Georg, 69–70, 186, 188
Just, Gustav, 270, 273, 332, 333, 336

Kafka, Franz, 89n50, 232, 259, 270
Kaiser, Jakob, 178, 180–1, 181n109
Kant, Immanuel, 105, 122, 123, 125, 127, 214, 267
Kantorowicz, Alfred, 13, 37–42, 69, 128, 134, 207, 238, 255, 256, 288, 326
  on book burnings, 60, 208, 211–12, 257–8
  and FRG, 277–8, 332
  and GDR/SED, 245, 247–9, 250, 253, 256–7, 258–60, 263, 270, 276–7
  and Imshausen Society, 188, 189
  on journalism, 159, 161
  and Kulturbund, 198, 200
  on occupation, 49
  on "other Germany," 52, 60, 61
  and popular front, 208, 209
  and Soviet Union, 249–50
  and writers' activities, 210, 211, 212, 215, 216, 219, 220, 229, 235
Kantorowicz, Frieda, 37, 38, 40
Karsch, Walther, 58, 67, 210, 224
Kaschnitz, Marie Luise, 37n57, 210
Kästner, Erich, 30, 33–4, 35, 54, 61, 64, 202, 212
  cabarets, 34, 279
  and FRG, 279–80, 306, 307, 326
  on guilt and resentment, 61, 134
  on National Socialism, 130
  and *Die Neue Zeitung*, 36, 39, 222
  and *Die Weltbühne*, 223
  and writers' activities, 159, 210, 235
Kellermann, Bernhard, 197, 199, 210, 235, 246
Kelsen, Hans, 36, 102, 149n2
Klemperer, Victor, 32, 75–6, 198, 200
Knappstein, Karl Heinrich, 23, 55, 97, 156, 170–1, 171n76, 185, 188
  and denazification, 27, 110, 170
Koch, Harald, 172–3
Koestler, Arthur, 38, 67, 209, 232, 243, 277, 284, 286–7, 287n23
Kogon, Eugen, 13, 22–3, 26, 36–7, 64, 78, 97, 123, 156, 189n138, 316, 318, 330n25
  and CCF, 283, 284, 286, 287
  on culturalism, 127, 128
  on denazification, 109, 110
  and Europe/EUD, 228, 295–6
  on federalism, 95–6, 290
  and Frankfurt School, 314, 315
  on freedom, 82, 289–90
  and FRG, 291–2, 293, 306, 308, 326
  on guilt and resentment, 63, 135
  and Imshausen Society, 188, 189–90
  on journalism, 50, 159, 160, 161, 185
  on National Socialism, 131–2, 133–4
  on occupation, 49–50, 63, 135–6, 160
  and resistance, 51–2
  on right-intellectuals, 71
  on socialism, 59, 96
  and unions, 300–1, 302
  and writers' activities, 235, 235n135
  on "restoration," 288, 290–1, 293–4
  on "zero hour," 138
Kohlstruck, Michael, 3n10
Kolb, Walter, 144, 187
Kolbenhoff, Walter, 42, 65, 231
Korn, Karl, 71n165, 155
KPD (Communist Party of Germany), 26, 29, 31, 33, 65–6, 152, 201, 203, 209, 323. *See also* Communism; SED
Krauss, Werner, 26, 37, 42, 65n147, 188, 255
  and GDR/SED, 244
  and resistance, 28, 51
  and *Die Wandlung*, 37, 46, 164
Kreisau Circle, *See under* resistance
Kuby, Erich, 188, 222n96, 297, 316, 326
Kuczynski, Jürgen, 32, 246, 255
*Kultur* (culture). *See* cultural heritage; culturalism

## Index

Kulturbund organizations, 35, 194, 195–6, 200–2
  Berlin, 31, 40, 196–200, 203, 204, 212, 223
  Frankfurt Kulturgesellschaft, 36, 202–3
  GDR, 253, 263–4, 275
  Heidelberg, 201, 203–5
Kurella, Alfred, 208, 270
*Kurier, Der*, 30, 46
Kütemeyer, Wilhelm, 188, 190, 306

Langgässer, Elisabeth, 211, 216, 229, 235
Lasky, Melvin, 217–18, 224, 283
Leipzig, 40, 244, 255–6
Leonard, Hans, 32–3, 154–5
Leonhard, Rudolf, 38, 200, 255
  and GDR/SED, 249, 251, 256
  and popular front, 208, 209
  and resistance, 39, 51
  and socialist unity, 59, 66
  and Soviet Union, 243–4, 250
  and writers' activities, 210, 211, 226, 235
Leonhard, Susanne, 29, 38, 243
Leonhard, Wolfgang, 29–30, 38, 100–1, 243–4
Lepenies, Wolf, 118–19
Lessing, G. E., 65, 122, 136
liberalism, 4, 24, 74, 119
licensing. *See* information policy
Löbe, Paul, 178, 179, 180–1, 181n109
Loest, Erich, 256, 270, 273
Lommer, Horst, 31, 33, 42, 44, 56, 76, 130, 197, 210
Luckau, 28
Luft, Friedrich, 30, 210, 211
Lukács, Georg, 32, 38, 81, 82n29, 124, 128, 206, 214n70, 235, 260, 301n63, 338
  and Bloch, 83, 83n33, 275n99
  and Hungary, 265, 270, 275
  on National Socialism, 124
Luther, Martin, 127

Mann, Golo, 48
Mann, Heinrich, 32, 38, 194–5, 208–9, 256
Mann, Thomas, 61, 117, 235
Mannheim, Karl, 22n10, 105, 105n112
Marcuse, Herbert, 117, 119n15, 324
Marek, Kurt, 232–3, 232n125
Marx, Karl, 81, 83, 84–5, 91, 124–5, 260, 267–8, 301n63, 313
Mayer, Hans, 35–7, 52–3, 57, 86, 124–5, 159, 188, 222, 238, 255, 277

  and Frankfurt School, 314
  and FRG, 276, 292, 326, 332
  and GDR/SED, 244–5, 253, 275–6
  and Kulturgesellschaft, 202–3
  on right-intellectuals, 71, 232–3
  on socialist realism, 268–70
  and writers' activities, 42, 210, 214, 219–20, 229, 230, 232–3, 235, 268
  on "zero hour," 1, 6
media policy. *See* information policy
Meinecke, Friedrich, 120
memory, 8–9, 114, 133, 146. *See also* guilt and resentment
Mendelssohn, Peter de, 34, 34n47, 284
Merker, Paul, 252, 271, 273, 338
*Merkur*, 68
Mihaly, Jo, 36, 38, 202–3, 210, 244, 253
militarism, 19, 33, 45, 126, 292, 307–8
military governments. *See* occupiers, zones, and policies
Mitscherlich, Alexander, 25, 25n20, 26, 26n25, 54, 87–8, 134, 135, 204, 316, 318n118
  and Aktionsgruppe, 163, 170, 172
  and CCF, 284
  on denazification, 111
  and elitism, 89, 186–7
  and extraparliamentary opposition, 326
  and Frankfurt School, 314
  free socialism program, 89–91, 157–8
  and FRG, 306, 327
  on National Socialism, 88
  and right-intellectuals, 25, 186–7
  on technology, 88
  on "zero hour," 138
Mitscherlich-Nielsen, Margarete, 327
Mommsen, Konrad, 163, 170, 172, 173, 175, 183
*Monat, Der*, 67, 224, 283, 284
Moses, A. Dirk, 13, 146–7
Müller, Heiner, 334, 336, 339
Munich, 34, 201, 202, 277, 279, 306
Münster, Clemens, 23, 105
Münzenberg, Willi, 33, 208, 209

Nabokov, Nicolas, 284, 287
Nardi, Pauline, 33, 63, 136–7, 252
National Socialism, 4, 19, 56–7, 62, 152
  book burnings, 60
  as democracy, 70, 112, 131
  engaged democrats on, 133, 214
  and language, 75–6, 129–30
nationalism, 33, 45, 192–3, 215–16
NATO (North Atlantic Treaty Organization), 280, 291, 304–5, 306

*Neue Weltbühne, Die*, 32, 38
*Neue Zeitung, Die*, 34, 44–5, 221
*Neues Deutschland*, 66, 221, 264
Neumann, Franz, 117, 119n15
neutralism, 4–5, 169, 308. *See also* "unity," German
New Left, 323, 327–8
  SDS (Socialist German Student League), 325, 326, 328–9
  Socialist Supporters' Society, 325
  *See also* extraparliamentary opposition
Niekisch, Ernst, 25, 25n20, 32, 71n165, 187, 188, 189
*Nordwestdeutsche Hefte*, 34, 34n48, 37
Nuremberg Trials, 23n12, 62, 134

occupation authorities, joint
  Allied Control Council, 20, 45, 178
  Allied High Commission for Germany, 280, 284, 296n49, 306
  Council of Foreign Ministers, 20, 168, 178
  and German sovereignty, 149–50, 169n72
occupiers, zones, and policies, 4, 18–19, 20, 35, 43, 45, 48, 104, 168
  American, 45, 98, 163–4, 167, 178, 188
  British, 98
  French, 98, 179
  Soviet, 45, 99, 104, 196, 212, 217
  *See also* denazification; information policy; reeducation
Ollenhauer, Erich, 305, 306
Ortega y Gasset, José, 232, 316
Ossietzky, Carl von, 32, 38, 57, 207
Ossietzky, Maud von, 32
*Ost und West*, 40, 40n67, 41, 47, 86, 238
  and SED, 247–9
"other Germany." *See under* antifascism

Paris, 32, 38, 208–9, 249
participation, 4, 11–12, 75, 318–19, 322
  and New Left, 327–8
Paulskirche, Frankfurt, 183, 226, 305
peace movement, 303, 305–6, 325
Pechel, Rudolf, 31, 67, 198, 210, 218, 233, 234, 235–6
Pieck, Wilhelm, 196, 196n8, 243, 248, 258
Pirker, Theo, 297n53, 297–8
Plessner, Helmuth, 117, 316
Plievier, Theodor, 32, 38n59, 196n8, 198, 229–30, 235, 284, 300
Polak, Karl, 242, 342
Poland, 171, 264–5, 266, 270, 308, 335
political culture, 14–15
Pollatschek, Walter, 202, 210, 226, 229

popular front, 38, 198, 208–9
Potsdam Conference, 19
Potsdam consensus, 19–20, 43, 49n90
press freedom. *See under* information policy
Protestantism and Protestants. *See* Christianity
Prussia, 95, 125, 126, 133, 156
Psychological Warfare Division, 22–3, 44
  "white list," 48
public sphere, 317–18
  in FRG, 281, 315–16
  in GDR, 240, 334
  occupation-era, 20–1, 45–6
publicness (*Öffentlichkeit*), 151, 190–1, 316–19

Raddatz, Fritz J., 270, 324
Radio Berlin, 197, 245, 269
Radio Frankfurt/Radio Hesse, 36, 48, 222, 314
Radio Hamburg/Northwest German Radio, 34, 222
Radio, West German (Cologne), 298, 314
Red Army, Political Administration, 44
"Red Block." *See* Berlin: Artists' Colony
"Red Orchestra." *See* resistance: Harnack/Schulze-Boysen group
Redslob, Edwin, 67, 197, 198, 210, 211, 224, 283
reeducation, 23, 28, 43–4, 64, 103, 196
re-émigrés. *See* émigrés, returning
Reger, Erik, 30, 67, 153, 169, 210, 211
Regler, Gustav, 38n59, 208–9
Reifenberg, Benno, 42, 56, 144, 188
resistance, 38, 39, 42, 55n115, 72–3, 143
  Gruppe Ernst, 30, 30n35
  Harnack/Schulze-Boysen group, 26, 26n26, 28, 32, 188
  July 20, 1944 plot, 42, 51
  Kreisau Circle, 54, 188
  as right or duty, 90, 177, 303
"restoration," 17, 280, 288, 294, 318
Reuter, Ernst, 67, 283
Reuter, Georg, 305, 306
revolution of 1848, 126, 127, 129, 159, 214, 226
revolution of 1918/19, 24, 97, 194
revolution of 1989, 334–6, 339
  civic movement, 334
  engaged democrats and, 336
*Rhein-Neckar-Zeitung*, 45, 56
Richter, Hans Werner, 64, 121, 222, 229, 288, 297, 306, 308
right-intellectuals, 70–1, 186
  conservative revolution, 69–70
Ringer, Franz, 204, 205

# Index

Roosevelt, Franklin Delano, 7, 19
Röpke, Wilhelm, 67n155, 67–8, 153
Rousseau, Jean-Jacques, 92, 93n67, 285
Rowohlt, Ernst, 35, 42, 56–7, 201, 232n125, 263, 300, 316
*Ruf, Der*, 42, 64–5, 65n145, 120, 165, 222, 297
Ruhr district, 23, 98, 172, 314
Ruhr Festival, Recklinghausen, 300–3

Salomon, Ernst von, 57
Sandberg, Herbert, 28–9, 197, 222
SAPD (Socialist Workers' Party of Germany), 36, 263
Sartre, Jean-Paul, 65, 230, 232
Schacht, Roland, 105, 210, 211
Scheer, Maximilian, 38–9, 42, 50, 159, 208, 255
Schelling, Friedrich, 122
Schendell, Werner, 210, 211
Schiller, Friedrich, 122–3, 127
Schmid, Carlo, 163n45, 173, 186, 188, 201, 283, 284, 306, 316
Schmidt, Karl Ludwig, 228, 228n115
Schmitt, Carl, 69–70, 71, 102, 186, 340
Schneider, Lambert, 26, 163, 169, 171, 175, 204
Schnog, Karl, 29, 33, 42, 52, 135
Schrickel, Klaus, 261, 266
Schröder, Rudolf Alexander, 229, 230
Schroeder, Max, 38–9, 40, 208, 211, 255, 261, 270
Schwarzenberg, 338
SDA (Protective Association of German Authors). *See under* writers' organizations
SDS (Protective Association of German Writers). *See under* writers' organizations
SDS (Socialist German Student League). *See under* New Left
SED (Socialist Unity Party of Germany), 32, 65–6, 99, 101, 103, 153, 224–5, 251, 334
  cultural interventions by, 223, 229, 247–9, 276
  factions within, 262, 273
  People's Congress, 177, 179, 234
  *See also* Communism; KPD; unity, socialist
Seghers, Anna, 32, 208, 212, 235, 246, 255, 277
self-education, 87, 93, 97
self-management, 90, 101, 106, 107, 108, 173, 244, 263, 327–8
Shirer, William L., 39, 39n64

sixty-eighters. *See under* generations
social networks, 14, 21
social science, 311–12
socialism, 4, 74, 97, 331–2
  Social Democracy, 4, 85, 157, 331
  *See also* Communism
socialization, 87, 97, 98, 99, 172–3, 173n81
*Sonderweg* thesis, 116, 117–18, 129, 129n37
*Sonntag*, 32, 264, 269, 270
Soviet Union, 7–8, 19, 100, 246, 266, 273
  CPSU 20th Party Congress, 264, 265, 270
  cultural repression in, 247
  and neutralization of Germany, 7, 304, 305
  political repression in, 29, 209, 217
  "two camps" doctrine, 216–17
Sovietization/East-orientation, 6, 99, 217, 225, 251
*sozialistische Jahrhundert, Das*, 56, 174
Spanish Civil War, 39, 209, 258
SPD (Social Democratic Party of Germany), 25, 46, 157–8, 179, 183, 271, 298, 308, 309
  in Berlin, 67, 181n109, 283
  Godesberg Program, 323
  and peace movement, 305–6
  and SDS, 325
Sperber, Manès, 38n59, 67, 243
*Spiegel* Affair, 326, 327
*Spiegel, Der*, 36n54, 274
Stalin, Joseph, 7, 19, 249–50, 260, 261, 268
Steckel, Leonard, 36, 38
Steinberger, Bernhard, 270, 273
Steiniger, Peter Alfons, 32, 42, 53, 149n2, 243, 266
  bloc system, 101–3, 164, 242
Stern, Fritz, 118
Sternberger, Dolf, 13, 24, 26, 36, 53, 55, 61, 69, 79, 157, 275, 316, 318n118
  and Aktionsgruppe, 163, 166, 170, 174
  on burgher-ness (*Bürgerlichkeit*), 59, 80, 174
  and CCF, 283, 284, 285, 287
  as conservative, 331
  on cultural heritage, 123, 141–2
  on electoral systems, 92–3, 311–12
  on freedom, 79–80, 225
  and FRG, 282, 293, 309–10
  on guilt and resentment, 137–8, 171
  on journalism, 56, 159, 160, 184, 185
  and Kulturbund, 204–6
  on language, 76

Sternberger, Dolf (*cont.*)
  and National Socialism, 24–5, 54–5, 93, 129–30
  on right-intellectuals, 25, 71
  and unions, 301, 302
  and Wählergesellschaft, 175
  and writers' activities, 235, 235n135
Sternberger, Ilse, 53
Stone, Shepard, 27, 283–4
Stroux, Johannes, 199, 203
Suhr, Otto, 56, 67, 181n109, 283
Süskind, Wilhelm, 76, 215, 219, 231
Switzerland, 25, 36, 244

*Tagesspiegel, Der*, 30, 30n37, 46, 58, 67, 165, 169, 174, 221, 276
*Tägliche Rundschau*, 44, 221
technocracy, 310
*Telegraf, Der*, 46, 58, 181n109, 221
Thieß, Frank, 60, 120
"totalitarianism," 9, 131–2, 252, 252n38
Trott, Heinrich von, 188, 190
Trott, Werner von, 38n59, 42, 187–9, 190
Truman, Harry S., 7, 19
Tübingen, 276, 277, 325, 332
Tucholsky, Kurt, 33, 38n59, 57

Uhse, Bodo, 255, 270, 277
Ulbricht, Walter, 29, 66, 100, 196, 196n8, 262, 268, 270, 273
*Ulenspiegel*, 28–9, 29n31, 155, 222
Union of Persecutees of the Nazi Regime, 36, 52
unions, 46, 97, 99, 167n63, 211. *See also* DGB
united front. *See* unity, socialist
United States, 7–8, 19, 169–70
  anti-Communism in, 218, 337
  intelligence agencies, 117, 283, 296n49
  Truman Doctrine, 217
"unity," German, 169–70, 177–80, 206–7, 218–20, 224–6, 328–9. *See also* neutralism
unity, socialist, 35–6, 152–3
universities, 104, 106, 325
  Frankfurt, 313, 315n106, 325
  Free University of Berlin, 109, 224, 283, 328
  Heidelberg, 24, 25–6, 79, 106–7, 165, 311–12
  Humboldt University, 109, 199, 224, 256, 261
  Leipzig, 37, 42, 109, 245, 275, 276
  Marburg, 26, 244
  Tübingen, 275, 332

"unpolitical German," 11, 115, 117–19, 123. *See also* culturalism

Vishnevsky, Vsevolod, 216–17
VVN. *See* Union of Persecutees of the Nazi Regime

Wählergesellschaft, Deutsche, 27, 162, 174–6, 182–4, 310
Walk, Emil, 175, 183
Wallenberg, Hans, 44, 222
Walz, Ernst, 163, 185, 204
*Wandlung, Die*, 26, 26n25, 27, 37n57, 46, 102, 132, 161, 165, 238
Weber, Alfred, 13, 24, 26, 53n107, 64, 87–8, 107, 175, 204, 316
  and Aktionsgruppe, 163, 165, 167, 169, 170, 172, 174, 178, 179, 180–1
  on bureaucracy, 88–9, 311–12
  and CCF, 283, 284, 285–6
  on cultural heritage, 125
  on education, 106, 108
  and elitism, 24, 89, 90, 90n56, 91n64
  free socialism program, 89–91, 157–8
  on guilt and resentment, 171
  on National Socialism, 89, 130–1
  and peace movement, 304–5, 306
  and resistance, 53
  on right-intellectuals, 71
  and unions, 167, 300–1, 302–3
  on "zero hour," 1
Weber, Marianne, 24, 26, 162, 163, 171
Weber, Max, 16n56, 24, 88, 108, 150n4, 162, 313
Wegener, Paul, 30, 197
Weigel, Helene, 255, 338
Weimar, 22, 123, 133, 145
Weimar Republic, 93, 94, 115–16, 152
Weinert, Erich, 38n59, 47, 65, 155, 196n8
Weisenborn, Günther, 28–9, 31, 35, 233, 245–6, 305, 306, 316
  and Kulturbund, 197, 200
  on language, 76–7
  and resistance, 51
  on right-intellectuals, 71, 211
  and Soviet Union, 246–7
  and *Ulenspiegel*, 28, 222
  and writers' congresses, 42–3, 211, 213, 219, 229
  and writers' organizations, 210, 235
Weisenborn, Joy, 28
Weismantel, Leo, 230–1, 235
*Weltbühne, Die* (1918–33), 32, 33, 38, 57–8

# Index

*Weltbühne, Die* (1946–), 32–3, 33n44, 47, 57–8, 154–5, 222–3
Werkbund, German, 143–4
Westernization/West-orientation, 6, 67–8, 98, 169, 170, 280
Weyrauch, Wolfgang, 29, 42n69, 44, 211, 229, 306
Wiechert, Ernst, 32, 64
Willmann, Heinz, 31, 196, 196n8, 197, 204
Wolf, Christa, 334, 336, 339
Wolf, Friedrich, 38n59, 196n8, 210, 211, 235, 255
writers' congresses, 206, 268
  Congress for the Defense of Culture (Paris 1935), 209
  First German Writers' Congress (Berlin 1947), 42–3, 43n73, 211–20, 228, 231, 235
  German Writers' Congress (Frankfurt 1948), 228–33
writers' organizations, 195, 210–11, 211n60, 226
PEN, 223, 235–6
SDA (Protective Association of German Authors), 210, 228, 233, 234–5
SDS (Protective Association of German Writers), 195, 207–8, 209–10

Yugoslavia, 101, 244, 263

Zahn, Peter von, 34n48, 232n125
Zehrer, Hans, 195, 232
"zero hour," 8–10, 18, 21, 338
Zhdanov, Andrei, 216, 254, 260
Zöger, Heinz, 270, 273, 333, 336
Zwerenz, Gerhard, 256, 270, 273